PRACTICAL POLICE PSYCHOLOGY

ABOUT THE AUTHOR

Laurence Miller, PH.D. is a psychologist in Boca Raton, Florida, specializing in clinical psychology, neuropsychology, forensic psychology, and business psychology. Dr. Miller is the Police Psychologist for the West Palm Beach Police Department, a Forensic Psychological Examiner for the Palm Beach County Court, and a Consulting Psychologist with several regional and national law enforcement agencies.

Dr. Miller is a Certified Trainer by the International Critical Incident Stress Foundation, a Diplomate in Rehabilitation Psychology by the American Board of Disability Analysts, and is Board Certified in Forensic Thaumatology by the American Academy of Experts in Traumatic Stress. He is a member of the Psychology Services Section of the International Association of Chiefs of Police, the International Law Enforcement Educators and Trainers Association, the Society for Police and Criminal Psychology, the National Crime Victims Bar Association, and the Florida Network of Victim Witness Services.

Dr. Miller is an Instructor at the Police Academy-Criminal Justice Institute of Palm Beach County, is on the Adjunct Psychology Faculty at Florida Atlantic University, and conducts continuing educational programs and training seminars across the U.S. and Canada.

Dr. Miller is a frequent commentator on radio and TV, and the author of numerous professional and popular print and online publications pertaining to the brain, behavior, health, law, criminal justice, and business management psychology, including *Shocks to the System: Psychotherapy of Traumatic Disability Syndromes* (Norton).

Dr. Miller can be contacted at (561) 392-8881 or on line at docmilphd@aol.com.

PRACTICAL POLICE PSYCHOLOGY

Stress Management and Crisis Intervention for Law Enforcement

By

LAURENCE MILLER, Ph.D.

CHARLES C THOMAS • PUBLISHER, LTD.
Springfield • Illinois • U.S.A.

Published and Distributed Throughout the World by

CHARLES C THOMAS • PUBLISHER, LTD.
2600 South First Street
Springfield, Illinois 62704

© 2006 by CHARLES C THOMAS • PUBLISHER, LTD.

ISBN 0-398-07636-7 (hard)
ISBN 0-398-07637-5 (paper)

Library of Congress Catalog Card Number: 2005052929

With THOMAS BOOKS *careful attention is given to all details of manufacturing
and design. It is the Publisher's desire to present books that are satisfactory as to their
physical qualities and artistic possibilities and appropriate for their particular use.*
THOMAS BOOKS *will be true to those laws of quality that assure a good name
and good will.*

*Printed in the United States of America
UB-R-3*

Library of Congress Cataloging-in-Publication Data

Miller, Laurence 1951-
    Practical police psychology: stress management and crisis intervention
for law enforcement / by Laurence Miller.
        p. cm.
    Includes bibliographical references and index.
    ISBN 0-398-07636-7 -- ISBN 0-398-07637-5 (pbk.)
    1. Police psychology. 2. Police--Job stress. 3. Police--Mental health ser-
vices. 4. Stress management. I. Title.

HV7936.P75M55 2006
363.201'9--dc22
                                                                    2005052929

FOREWORD

Over the past 50 years, the concept of an applied discipline of *police psychology* as an effective complement for professional law enforcement services has emerged. Through the efforts of early pioneers such as Martin Reiser, Morton Bard, Martin Symonds, and others, and particularly because of the successes and professional acceptance of the FBI's Behavioral Science Unit, law enforcement executives have recognized the value of such a discipline to their agencies.

Early in its development, police officers looked to psychologists and psychiatrists to help better understand, and better yet solve, the increasing number of unexplained crimes of violence, and, ultimately, the concept of "behavioral profiling" has become a common tool of investigators. Later in the evolution of this discipline, in an application of psychology to "in progress" crimes, police administrators began to ask for psychological assistance in more effectively handling hostage negotiations, keeping the hostages alive and taking hostage takers into custody. Even more recently, we've seen its use as we've tried to understand and control crowd and gang behavior and respond to incidents that evolved into "suicide by cop."

But *police psychology* is not just about understanding the bad guys and their actions; it's also about understanding the good guys. In 1973, the Task Force on Police of the National Advisory Commission on Criminal Justice Standards and Goals recommended that "every police agency, by 1975, should retain the services of a qualified psychiatrist or psychologist to conduct psychological testing of police applicants in order to screen out those who have mental disorders or are emotionally unfit for police work." And, as we've learned more about the emotional consequences of policework, we've turned to the discipline of *police psychology* to allow us to better respond to the needs of the men and women in our profession, more effectively and compassionately assuring the safety and well-being of those personnel, our agencies, and our communities.

Yet, as with all applied sciences, *police psychology* brings with it its own unique realities, myths, and misconceptions. That, then, becomes the raison d'etre for a book such as this. Dr. Miller writes as a practicing police psychologist, one who has "walked the walk" and can now, with greater credibility, understanding, and feeling, explain his profession, its strengths, its limitations, and its intricacies to other members of the psychological community and, I believe, to a broad spectrum of our law enforcement community: its executives, its practitioners, and its educators. His tone and his descriptions bespeak one who carries with him the understanding of the academic and psychological worlds, but speaks with the clear language of one who has been at the frontline.

My academic mentor, Dr. Harold J. Vetter, himself a psychologist turned criminologist, always taught me that the most effective teacher is one who is able to educate, communicate, and entertain, all at the same time! In this book, Dr. Miller does exactly that: he educates us about an issue critical to the success of our law enforcement agencies; he communicates in an extremely clear, concise, open, and honest manner; and he entertains us with his war stories and his frank language. Dr. Miller's book is a much needed, much awaited, practical guide to the discipline of police psychology and one which will have an impact on those who practice it, those who use it, and those who need it!

James D. Sewell, PhD
Assistant Commissioner (Retired)
Florida Department of Law Enforcement

PREFACE

Every time we dial 911, we expect that our emergency will be taken seriously and handled competently. The police will race to our burgled office, the firefighters will speedily douse our burning home, the ambulance crew will stabilize our injured loved one and whisk him or her to the nearest hospital. We take these expectations for granted because of the skill and dedication of the workers who serve the needs of law enforcement, emergency services, and public safety.

For police officers, this task is doubly challenging because they are the only public safety professionals whom the law and society grant the authority—indeed, the obligation—to use coercive physical force to influence the behavior of citizens. Further, their decision to use such force is based largely on their own judgment as to what is appropriate in each particular situation. For some citizens, police officers are the only resource they have to depend on in times of crisis and, for many of these, the police are the sole entry point into the broader social services sector. Not surprising, then, that the news media, entertainment industry, and the general public have infused law enforcement with a near-mythic status, both for good and for ill. We rely on the police to protect us, and are quick to condemn them if we feel they have violated our trust.

Practical Police Psychology: Stress Management and Crisis Intervention for Law Enforcement addresses the psychologically complex world of modern policing. This book analyzes both the dramatic crises and everyday challenges faced by all law enforcement personnel, from the street cop to the departmental brass. But analysis is only a first, albeit crucial, step. My aim is to offer usable, down-to-earth, and immediately applicable—that is, *practical*—psychological guidelines and recommendations for improving the quality of policing on a daily basis.

Two major themes inform this book. The first is the concept of *community policing*, which is becoming the model of local law enforcement in a growing number of jurisdictions. It is hard to think of another area of law enforcement where understanding human nature is more important. To be effective in community policing, the best patrol officers are already practical psychologists. They know how to wield influence and authority without resorting to force; to deescalate curbside squabbles from becoming civil disturbances; to calm suicidal, intoxicated, traumatized, and mentally disturbed citizens; to enlist cooperation rather than resistance when investigating crimes; to encourage the communities they patrol to see police officers as resources they can count on, rather than as hostile invaders they must fear.

The second theme is *professionalism*. What most of this book's broad approaches and specific recommendations have in common is the concept of the law enforcement officer as a true professional, charged with the same technical and ethical responsibilities as doctors, attorneys, psychologists, and other professionals, and therefore entitled to commensurate respect. One feature of the job description shared by these professionals is their role as competent *decision makers*. That is, practitioners of all these disciplines follow certain standardized protocols of training and experience, yet each is empowered to use a certain degree of judgment and discretion to deal with individual circumstances in their daily work. Indeed, these professionals couldn't be truly effective without some ideal mix of standardization and flexibility. As the demands of law enforcement become increasingly more complex, citizens will come to expect that those who serve and protect them will meet the highest standards of education, training, and psychological fitness.

These two themes translate into two broad domains of policing where psychological knowledge and expertise can make important contributions. One is the role of law enforcement behavioral science in *operational assistance* of police activities. These include hostage negotiation, suicide-by-cop intervention, criminal investigation, undercover operations, riot and crowd control, dealing with crime victims, and special assignments. It also includes less dramatic, more everyday activities such as citizen-citizen dispute mediation, quieting angry or distraught civilians, dealing with traumatized crime victims, handling mentally disturbed citizens, responding to natural and technological disasters, and interacting smoothly and cooperatively with other public agencies and private businesses.

The second domain has to do with cops taking care of themselves and dealing with problems within their own departments—often subsumed under the broad heading of *psychological services*. This domain includes critical incident stress, postshooting trauma, specialized psychotherapy for law enforcement officers, alcohol and substance abuse problems, police family stresses and family therapy, and departmental stress management and health maintenance programs. It also includes standards and practices to enhance police performance and the overall improvement of law enforcement quality within communities by addressing selection and screening of officers, training and discipline, supervision and leadership, and police departmental organization and management psychology.

The target audience for *Practical Police Psychology* is a dual one. First, law enforcement administrators, line supervisors, and working cops who are committed to quality performance within their departments will learn how to provide the best possible clinical and operational psychological services to the men and women under their command and to the citizens they serve. Second, for psychologists and other mental health clinicians who are involved in, or may be considering law enforcement consultation, this book will provide a comprehensive guide to the unique challenges and rewards of working with police personnel and their departments. The tone of the text reflects this: sometimes, I'll be speaking shrinktalk to my fellow mental health clinicians; other times, I move into cop idiom; often, I'll drift in an out and combine the styles. Only you, the readers, can judge if this is an effective—and practical—mode of transmitting complex interpersonal information through the printed page. Basically, I write the way I teach: I respect my audience and try to communicate at a level that both accommodates and expands their individual perspectives and, at the same time, encourages questions and constructive feedback. So feel free to feed back.

The content of this book reflects a careful survey of the literature on police psychology and law enforcement behavioral science, combined with my own clinical and practical experience. I originally began with the idea of writing a book on police psychology that would cover the entire breadth and scope of the field and, at first, I was concerned that there might not be enough material to address all these areas adequately. Ha. As the research expanded and the piles of notes climbed, I came to realize that there exists a vast and largely untapped storehouse of literature bearing directly or indirectly on the psychology of law enforcement, and soon the task became how to winnow through this silo of data to cultivate a book that would be both authoritative and useful.

The first stage of modification involved a process of binary fission; that is, the material I reviewed seemed to fall into two broad areas where psychology and behavioral science were relevant to police work: stress management and crisis intervention on the one hand, and criminal investigation, interview and interrogation on the other. Rather than attempt to cram everything into an oversized book (yeah, right, you're thinking—like this one is a pamphlet), I decided to deal with the first subject area here; the second area will have to await a forthcoming volume of its own. My prioritization was guided largely by my own daily work and experience in the area of police psychology and by the interest elicited in my police academy courses.

Even within the subjects of law enforcement stress management and crisis intervention, some selectivity was necessary, and no doubt many a reader will be dismayed at his or her pet topic being given short shrift. Another problem was how to organize the chapters as well as the material within the chapters. This book's organization went through numerous revisions, as many of the chapter topics overlap and shade into one another. But of course, this is how it should be, because one of this book's themes is the interrelatedness of crisis intervention and stress management: each necessitates utilizing skills and techniques that are universal in helping human beings in distress. Thus, while each chapter can stand independently on its own merits, I've endeavored to weave this common theme of universality throughout the narrative.

Laurence Miller

ACKNOWLEDGMENTS

A book like this has many influences, and a number of people encouraged and supported this project and/or the work that led to its inception and completion. Many of these people took the time to read pre-publication drafts of many of the book's chapters and to offer useful critiques and suggestions that have improved this volume immeasurably.

Florida Department of Law Enforcement (FDLE) Assistant Commissioner James D. Sewell, Ph.D. has been a long-time supporter of my writings in the police psychology field. He generously critiqued many of the raw chapters of this book and I will never again use an excess comma without wincing at the thought of his blue-inked, fountain-penned redactions. He has been an invaluable source of information on certain technical aspects of law enforcement work that I could not have otherwise known. Jim is also an accomplished author in his own right, with numerous publications to his credit and I look forward to many future collaborations with him.

Over the years, I've had the pleasure of working with Captain James Cummings, M.S.W. of the Boynton Beach Police Department and Palm Beach County School District on a variety of tasks and projects, ranging from emergency call-outs during critical incidents to co-teaching classes and seminars at the police academy. Jim generously took the time to review some of the material for this book in the middle of his own preparation for advanced credentialing in the mental health field to complement his law enforcement experience. This, of course, exemplifies the present book's philosophy of continuing professional growth as the basis for superior law enforcement work. I look forward to continuing our informal "lunchtime seminars" and other work together.

And another Jim. Many of the ideas in this book were honed and developed through courses I teach at the Police Academy-Criminal Justice Institute of Palm Beach Community College. Institute Director Dr. James Marinelli, a former beat cop himself, continues to be a source of insight on how to handle the practical aspects of instructing and motivating law enforcement officers in a classroom setting. This Jim always finds time for our discussions and is always there with words of encouragement, which I appreciate greatly.

It was at the Police Academy–CJI that I met fellow instructor Colonel Jack Maxwell, a law enforcement consultant and hostage negotiator with over 100 successful negotiations under his belt—a "resume of life" if ever there was one. Jack scrutinized the chapter on hostage crises and made a number of critical emendations and suggestions that reflect his practical experience in this dangerous but vital aspect of police work. This chapter also benefitted from the input of Dr. Arthur Slatkin, psychological consultant for the Louisville, Kentucky Police Department and author of *Communications in Crisis and Hostage Negotiations*, a book that exemplifies the "practical" in practical psychology applications to law enforcement.

My affiliation with the West Palm Beach Police Department continues to be instructive and rewarding. Former Chief Ric Bradshaw (now Palm Beach County Sheriff) recognized the importance of psychological services to the health and well-being of his officers and was supportive of my efforts. Current Chief Delsa Bush came up through the ranks and continues the tradition of taking a firm-but-concerned, hands-on approach to the health and well-being of her officers, as well as being dedicated to needs of the community her department serves. She also reviewed the chapter on police officer misconduct and discipline, and was able to inject insightful doses of management savvy and street cred into the narrative. Police Chaplin and EAP Coordinator Carl Cooper and I have co-counseled a number of officers, and I never fail to be impressed by the breadth and depth of his commitment to his colleagues' welfare: If you're a cop in a jam, he's the guy you'd want to go to first. I've also had the pleasure of working with a number of WPBPD assistant chiefs, captains, lieutenants, and sergeants over the years—you know who you are, guys.

Historically, my involvement with the WPBPD came by way of my earlier role as Clinical Director of the Palm Beach County Critical Incident Stress Debriefing (CISD) Team. It was there that I became intimately acquainted with the kinds of work and the kinds of challenges faced by law enforcement, firefighter-paramedic, and other emergency services personnel in their daily jobs. The men and women volunteers of that CISD team continue their dedication to the health and well-being of their colleagues in distress. Such teams throughout the country and the world deserve our respect and admiration, as does their sponsoring agency, the International Critical Incident Stress Foundation (ICISF).

A number of other people have graciously offered their time and expertise to discuss ideas and/or review material relevant to the present book. Police Psychologist Dr. Cary Rostow provided valuable information on conducting law enforcement fitness-for-duty evaluations, and his book, *A Handbook for Psychological Fitness-for-Duty Evaluations in Law Enforcement* (with co-author Robert Davis), is required reading for all police psychologists. Another author, FDLE Special Agent and novelist Jim Born (is that four Jims, now?) took time from his busy writing and book tour schedule to review and offer his comments on some of the present book's material. His novels include *Walking Money* and *Shock Wave*.

Even the feds got into the act. Thanks to Special Agent and Training Director Brian Jerome of the Federal Bureau of Investigation (FBI) Miami Field Office for his helpful comments on some of this book's contents. I look forward to working with Brian in the future. Special Agent Hugh Galyean of the FBI San Francisco Field Office was one of the earliest supporters of this project; he has my enduring gratitude and I still have pictures of his baby on my computer.

I've only just recently met Dr. John Sullivan, Director of the International Center for Leadership and Development (ICLAD) in Boca Raton, Florida, but I'm looking forward to working with him and his organization, as it embodies this book's core philosophy of law enforcement officers as true professionals who are committed to continuing education and career development.

To all the cops in all the departments in all the locations where I've worked, taught, lectured, or consulted: One of the advantages of my being a civilian, and not a sworn officer, is that, while you may take what you do every day for granted, we don't. I know it sounds like a cliché, but I've learned a lot from working with you all and one of the things I hope this book accomplishes is to give people an idea of how difficult and complex a job it is to be a force for peace and stability in an increasingly violent and chaotic society. Thanks, guys, and no, I'm not gonna get all juicy on your asses.

Finally, again thanks to my family for putting up with the schedule-wrecking uncertainties of doing this kind of work and for your general support of my professional efforts. I know I don't say it often, but not a day goes by that I don't appreciate your love and support.

My thanks to Charles C Thomas Editor Michael Thomas for his patience awaiting the completion of this manuscript and for his expertise in helping to shape it into a valuable volume. Aside from being a pleasure to work with, the technical expertise of Michael and his staff are responsible for the appealing style, feel, and layout of the volume you hold in your hands. I look forward to future projects with Charles C Thomas Publishers.

CONTENTS

Page

Foreword–James D. Sewell v
Preface vii

Chapter

  1. Introduction: Practical Psychology, Stress Management, and
     Crisis Intervention in Law Enforcement. 3

PART I. PATROL AND COMMUNITY POLICING

  2. On Patrol: Street Psychology 101 15

  3. Crisis Intervention Strategies for Violence on Patrol 30

  4. Dealing With the Mentally Ill 47

PART II. CRITICAL INCIDENTS AND TRAUMATIC STRESS

  5. Extreme Stress Management for Law Enforcement
     Emergencies 69

  6. Law Enforcement Critical Incident Stress 88

  7. Officer-Involved Shooting 116

  8. Line-of-Duty Death 133

PART III. OPERATIONAL STRESS AND CRISIS MANAGEMENT

  9. Hostage Crises 143

 10. Suicide by Cop 174

 11. Police Officer Suicide 183

 12. Special Units: Undercover and Sex Crimes Investigation 198

PART IV. POLICE ADMINISTRATION AND FAMILY LIFE

13. Good Cop–Bad Cop: Practical Management of Problem
Officers 221

14. In Command: Law Enforcement Administration and
Leadership 244

15. Significant Others: Family Stresses and Family Solutions 262

Bibliography 275
Index 299

PRACTICAL POLICE PSYCHOLOGY

Chapter 1

INTRODUCTION: PRACTICAL PSYCHOLOGY, STRESS MANAGEMENT, AND CRISIS INTERVENTION IN LAW ENFORCEMENT

THE STRESSES AND CHALLENGES OF POLICING

The world of policing at the beginning of the twenty-first century is in some respects unique, in other ways linked to the past (Peak, 2003; Toch & Grant, 2005). The traditional role of the law enforcement officer has always been fighting crime, but today's urban and rural police are confronted with a host of unique challenges, only a minority of which involve the actual apprehension of criminals. On any given day, these may include resolving a dispute between merchants; helping a homeless person get to a shelter; finding a lost child; settling a family or neighbor squabble; taking a mentally disturbed citizen into protective custody; dispersing an unruly crowd of teens; making several traffic stops; applying first aid to an accident victim; or referring an ill, indigent, or elderly person to social services.

Note that all of these tasks require some combination of technical expertise and interpersonal skill, and any of them could devolve into a dangerous crisis situation if handled clumsily or ineffectively.

Indeed, it is a principle of this book's approach and organization that stress management cannot be separated from crisis intervention, as each comprises an essential component of the other. Stress provokes and exacerbates crises; crises elevate stress. Effective crisis intervention reduces stress, which in turn makes crisis management easier. Officers who know how to manage their own stress are less likely to be goaded into escalating a citizen confrontation into a crisis, and will be better able to use clear thinking and effective action if a crisis unavoidably occurs.

POLICE AS PRACTICAL PSYCHOLOGISTS

If law enforcement and mental health professionals share one thing in common, it is that we both spend virtually all of our time dealing with the outer reaches of human nature. That's why I usually begin my police academy classes by telling the officers that "we both do the same kind of work, but I have the easy job." That is, we both deal with extremes of human emotion and behavior, but I get to do it in the relatively secure confines of an office or hospital, while you have to do it on the street. My customers are frequently challenging, sometimes annoying, occasionally threatening, but rarely overtly dangerous; your customers may kill you. I often have to make tricky diagnostic determinations and decide on an appropriate course of action, and so do you. But I typically have the luxury of hours or days to pore over records and interview my patient in a quiet room; you have to make a snap decision in a few seconds under noisy, confusing, or hazardous conditions. If I'm wrong, I can usually go back and try something else; if you're wrong, people may be injured or killed.

Thus, knowledge of practical psychology is essential to police officers, both for their daily effectiveness and personal safety. A large proportion of officer injuries or fatalities occur in the course of routine police activities, such as traffic stops, mediating citizen disputes, or domestic calls. Mastery of interpersonal stress management, conflict resolution, and crisis intervention skills can thus be thought of as a kind of *psychological body armor* that protects cops from unnecessary risk as they carry out their sworn duties to protect and serve. One of the functions of this book is to guide officers in refining, expanding, and solidifying the interpersonal skills many of them already use intuitively to manage stress and crises on the job.

WHY DO MEN AND WOMEN BECOME COPS?

For all the show biz glamour, the real world of policing is far more prosaic, and understanding the details of the job can sometimes make one wonder why men and women choose to become cops. The working conditions can be brutal, especially in inclement climates, assignments can be miserable, especially at the beginning of one's career, and in many cases, promotion and advancement are extremely slow. In fact, about 80 percent of police officers spend their entire career as line officers on patrol, or as plainclothes detectives; 15 percent become supervisors; and only five percent rise to executive rank (Blau, 1994).

It is therefore interesting to examine what police officers do and don't like about their jobs, based on a general consensus from the literature (Anderson et al., 1995; Blau, 1994; Toch, 2002) and my own experience in speaking to officers.

What Police Officers Like About Their Jobs

Many officers are attracted to the power and respect that come with the image of a police officer. Being a member of an elite and honorable warrior culture holds the same fascination as does a career in the military; indeed, for many ex-soldiers, policing is a civilian extension of that role. Associated with this is the gratification of the societal protector role: many officers take justifiable pride in being part of the "thin blue line" that separates civilization from the barbarians. For officers whose beats include the neighborhoods where they grew up, there is the added satisfaction of protecting their home turf, and garnering the respect and admiration of local family members and neighbors—some of whom may well have had their past doubts as to what the officer would ever amount to.

The police role may be close to home in another way, as well. A fair number of police officers choose their profession to uphold a family tradition of law enforcement, and may have been inspired by a parent's or relative's career in this field, or in a related one like the military. The family background of many officers includes one or more relatives who have espoused strong moral and/or religious values, and policing is an eminently concrete way of reinforcing those values on a daily basis. A number of officers speak of their career in policing as a way of "giving back" something to the families and neighborhoods that once nurtured them. The downside, of course, is the potential for disillusionment and cynicism that occurs when the officers are exposed to, or tempted by, opportunities for corruption and misconduct—often made all the more easy by their familiarity with the local culture.

Many officers genuinely enjoy the support and camaraderie of their new "police family," which has become an extension of the extended tribal family group in which they grew up. But I've observed the opposite pattern as well. That is, many officers describe an unpleasant, hostile, and downright abusive early family environment, often characterized by an angry, moralistic, and physically punishing father, for whom the son or daughter "could never do anything right." Not infrequently, this parent was also an alcoholic. Yet, the officer will typically idealize this parent's strict disciplinarianism in one breath ("Dad didn't take no crap—we kids toed the line, or else"), while decrying his gratuitous cruelty in another ("He was a mean sonofabitch, especially when he was drinking—he'd whip our asses for no good reason").

This mental split often results in the officer internalizing the rigid but inconsistent moralistic code expressed by the parent, while externalizing and projecting the meanness and lack of self-control onto the bad elements of society with which the officer is now charged with dealing. Such officers may be especially effective at their jobs, but are at risk for both overaggressiveness and burnout when their moral codes become threatened (see Chapter 13).

Interestingly, however, only a minority of officers cite a desire to "help people" as their first reason for joining the police force. This helping motivation seems to be something that develops over time, as they become more and more comfortable with the responsibility that policing places in their hands. For many, the initial attraction lies more in the perceived action and excitement that policing offers, as well as the autonomy and discretionary decision-making power that officers are typically granted. Indeed, some officers speak with pride of their "people skills," and ability to use "verbal judo" to resolve most of the everyday spats and squabbles that occur on their patrols (Chapter 2). Detectives and members of special units, such as undercover or SWAT, also enjoy the combination of physical activity and mental stimulation that their jobs afford, and many of these officers are quite explicit about the fact that they "wouldn't last a day in some desk job."

More prosaically, many candidates are attracted to policing by the relative job security, pension, benefits, and medical coverage that this kind of public service job affords—especially in the present work environment where such comprehensive job security is becoming a veritable corporate fossil in the private sector. And, yes, a few bad apples actually go into policing with the intention of exploiting their power for their own gain, although the vast majority of abusive and corrupt officers don't start off as crooks with a badge, but transmogrify over time due to a variety of internal pressures and external circumstances (Chapter 13).

What Police Officers Dislike About Their Jobs

Many of the negatives about police work cited by officers represent the flip side of the positives. The relative autonomy and discretionary power of policing also leaves room for ambiguity and second-guessing. Indeed, officers describe their frustration with being told to adhere to a set a rigid rules and protocols, yet at the same time being expected to apply these rules flexibly and creatively to everyday situations, and to get it right every time.

Officers who are into the helping role may become disillusioned by the perceived lack of appreciation, respect, or even common courtesy afforded to them by the citizens they put their lives on the line to protect. Of course, a lot has to do with the demographics of a particular patrol area, but some officers may be more sensitive to this violation of expectations than others.

Death is an inevitable feature of law enforcement work, and many officers describe the exposure to murder and violence as a necessary but aversive aspect of their jobs. Some officers take the counterphobic measure of immersing themselves in what they and society fear and loathe the most, becoming homicide and sex crimes investigators, undercover narcotics operatives, or crime scene investigators (Chapter 12). And of course, there is the ever-present danger of being killed on the job or having to kill others, which gives police work a unique status among civilian public safety roles (Chapters 7 and 8).

But by far, the worst stressors cited by officers come from their own departments. Actually, this should not be surprising, recalling how police departments, and most work organizations, represent an extended family tribal culture. And like any dysfunctional family, sometimes these stresses can lead to internal crises that can undo an officer's career or have severe repercussions for the department as a whole. That's why it is very important that these problems be identified and dealt with constructively as early as possible (Chapters 13 and 14).

TYPES OF CRISIS

Different types and sources of crisis can affect both the personal lives of police officers and the work they do with citizens (Anderson et al., 1995; Toch, 2002). These can be differentiated into several categories, although, as with most naturalistic classifications, several types may blend together.

Personal crises involve family, friends, and significant others. Examples include relationship problems, separation and divorce, parent-child conflict, financial strains, alcohol and substance problems, and stresses within the extended family. At the extremes, these may come to police attention in the form of child abuse, domestic violence, stalking, and harassment, many of these fueled by alcohol or drug abuse.

Professional crises involve stresses related to work. Examples include management-employee conflicts, harassment by coworkers, filing of grievances, and stresses related to discipline, termination, or downsizing. Extreme cases may escalate to sexual harassment and workplace violence.

Situational crises refer to specific, short-term crises that may vary in severity, but are time-limited in nature, even though they may have long-term effects. There are numerous examples of these in almost everybody's life, including bereavement of family members, traumatic termination of a relationship or job, accidental injury, or natural disaster. Law enforcement may become involved when the crisis involves crime victimization or, alternatively, carrying-out of criminal activity in response to overwhelming stress.

Ongoing crises are, by definition, longer in duration and may have an abrupt onset, such as an injury that produces long-term disability or an arrest or lawsuit that is followed by years of legal and financial stress. Or the crisis may evolve more gradually, such as a progressive physical or mental illness, or an escalating series of financial losses.

Again, the boundaries between categories are fluid. A situational crisis of job loss may become an ongoing financial crisis if equivalent alternative employment can't be found in a sagging economy. An ongoing problematic relationship can escalate to violence when prodded by the lack of money and family budget squabbles resulting from the job loss. Violence can lead to arrest, incurring further financial losses and heightening family stress, and so on. How individuals cope with these types of crises depends on the nature and intensity of the crisis itself, the coping resources of the persons involved, and the practical and psychosocial support systems available.

TYPES OF PREVENTION:
THE PSYCHOEPIDEMIOLOGY OF CRISIS MANAGEMENT

Epidemiology is the clinical science that studies the spread of illnesses and their effects within populations. Most familiar in the area of infectious disease, the epidemiological model has also been applied to a range of somatic and psychological disorders, ranging from the mortality from cancer in neighborhoods exposed to toxic pollutants, to posttraumatic stress disorder in populations affected by natural or man-made disasters. Epidemiologists distinguish three main stages of prevention, which are termed primary, secondary, and tertiary. These can also be applied to psychological casualties and disabilities within a population, as well as to individual cases of crisis intervention work (Gilliland & James, 1993; Miller, 1998c).

The goal of *primary prevention* is to prevent as many new cases of the crisis as possible from arising in the first place. In the case of an impending flu epidemic, this might involve vaccinations for vulnerable members of the community, educational programs targeting cleanliness and hygiene for preventing infection, and improved public sanitation and school nutrition programs to bolster physical health and resistance. For impending mental health crises—for example, dealing with potential workplace violence—this might involve public information about practical prevention measures for home, family, and business; education about the nature of workplace bullying and harassment, and the stress syndromes they entail; diversity training, stress management, and conflict resolution skills; and training in how to recognize the warning signs of impending violence.

Secondary prevention assumes that there has already been an initial outbreak of the crisis within the population. The goal is now to prevent it from spreading further and to minimize its effects. In our flu epidemic example, some individuals may have already been infected. Some of the secondary prevention measures involve continuing the same things we did in primary prevention, such as making doubly sure others are fully immunized, and if necessary, even taking such drastic measures as quarantining contagious persons. For a brewing workplace violence crisis, we might recognize that an employee or customer is becoming increasingly agitated and has already threatened one or more persons and perhaps destroyed some property. At this stage, we would try to deescalate the conflict, contain and isolate the subject, call police or security, and begin evacuating nearby employees or students from the area.

In *tertiary prevention*, the crisis has hit its peak or run its course, and what we are actually "preventing" at this stage is the development or worsening of aftereffects that might occur in the aftermath. For the flu, this may involve treating secondary bacterial infections in flu survivors whose immune systems have been weakened, arranging care for children of dead or disabled parents, and maintaining electricity, food, and sanitation in affected areas. For the workplace violence crisis, this means arranging mental health follow-up to limit the development of posttraumatic stress reactions among affected employees and customers, as well as dealing with the media and general public to restore the organization's reputation and image so that the company's viability is not undone by the episode.

The overall concept is that most crises are fluid, organic entities that evolve over a time course—which can range from minutes to years—and that, at each stage, there must be an established set of measures to counteract the traumatic effects of the crisis. Hence, preparation, planning, and training are crucial.

THE BASIC CRISIS INTERVENTION MODEL

Although individual systems differ, a broad consensus on a standard protocol for basic crisis intervention has emerged (Dattilio & Freeman, 2000; Gilliland & James, 1993; Kleespies, 1998). Much of this format has evolved from suicide hotlines and other clinically-oriented crisis intervention services, but can be productively adapted for law enforcement crises and represents the basic model of crisis intervention used throughout this book. A basic outline of the model is presented here, with specific examples appearing in subsequent chapters.

Define the Problem

Some personal crises relate to a specific incident, such as a spouse who suddenly learns of an sudden affair or separation, or a person who has just been the victim of a crime. Often, however, a crisis state will evolve as the cumulative result of a number of overlapping stressors. In such cases, the affected person may be unclear as to what exactly led to the crisis. Furthermore, this confusion typically adds to anxiety and a sense of being overwhelmed, which escalates to panic and despondency in a spiraling vicious cycle.

Thus, the first task is to help the subject clarify in his or her own mind what exactly has led to the crisis state. This often involves a set of focusing and clarifying questions. What is the subject experiencing? What led up to the crisis? What aspects of the situation feel most out of control? Most in control?

Ensure Safety

The goal of crisis intervention is stabilization for later treatment. You want to ensure that the subject stays alive and/or keeps from harming others long enough for him or her to obtain whatever follow-up services are necessary. Assume that if the subject contacted you at all, or is even willing to talk to you at any point, then he or she has not made the irrevocable decision to use violence against self or others. Your job is to use this interval to encourage the subject to put even a few short steps between the thought of a harmful action and its execution. If the subject has a gun, ask him to unload it or at least holster it or decock it. If it's a bottle of pills, ask her to keep the cover on for now. If he's standing on a roof ledge, ask him to take just two steps back in the meantime. The key is to let the subject retain enough control so that he doesn't panic, but keep things as safe as possible while you continue to negotiate a safe resolution to the crisis.

Provide Support

Support means "being there" with the subject, showing that you're trying to understand. As we'll see in subsequent chapters, you don't necessarily have to agree with a distressed subject's reasoning or point of view—and in many cases, it may be counterproductive to disingenuously pretend that you do—but a little empathy and commiseration can go a long way in establishing trust and encouraging a nonviolent resolution to the crisis. It may also elicit some insight into issues that underlie the present crisis or that may have led up to it. But remember, the goal of crisis intervention is not psychotherapy. You don't want to disregard a subject's important feelings and thoughts about his or her situation, but be careful to keep the conversation reasonably focused on resolving the present crisis, perhaps gently suggesting that the larger issues can be dealt with later—which implies that the subject will indeed be around later.

Examine Alternatives

Often, subjects in crisis are so fixated on their pain and hopelessness that their cognitive tunnel vision prevents them from seeing any way out. Your job is to gently expand the range of nonviolent options for resolving the crisis situation. Typically, this takes one of two forms: accessing practical supports and utilizing coping mechanisms.

Practical Supports. Are there any persons, institutions, or agencies that are immediately available to help the subject through the crisis until he or she can obtain follow-up care? Of course, you want to be reasonably sure that these support people will calm, not inflame, the situation until professional help is obtained. Support systems or persons can consist of trusted relatives, friends, clergy, a local mental health clinician, and so on. One caution here is that one or more of these individuals may have had contentious dealings with the subject in the past, and might even have been part of the reason the crisis got out of control in the first place. So try to get a little background information if possible and use your judgment.

Coping Mechanisms. These can consist of cognitive strategies, religious faith, distracting activities, pleasant family images and so on—anything that helps the subject inject an element of comfort and control into an otherwise painful and chaotic situation. You can appeal to both present and past coping mechanisms. For subjects who are feeling hopeless, it is often useful to recall past crises that were resolved—however incompletely—without violence. This shows that it's at least *possible* to get through the present crisis, and possibly come up with an even better solution this time that will prevent things from ever getting this bad again. Success may then build on success. However, the caution here is that the subject may think that this present crisis is a whole lot worse than anything that's happened in the past—and sometimes this may in fact be true—in which case, comparison with past, smaller crises may only serve to highlight the hopelessness of the present "big one." Then, the intervener will have to use his or her judgment and be creative in dealing with this kind of comparison paradox.

Make a Plan

Work out a plan that will ensure the subject's safety, terminate the crisis for now, and provide for follow-up. Make the plan as explicit as possible, giving the subject as much input and buy-in as he or she is able and willing to contribute. Make sure the plan is understood completely by everyone concerned. The plan should contain both short-term elements (Where will you stay tonight? Which clinic will you call in the morning? If you need to go to the ER, how will you get there and who will pick you up and take you home?), and long-term elements (Who will you be seeing for follow-up therapy? How will you contact Legal Aid to get your case handled? Who will let your job know you're taking some sick time?).

Obtain Commitment

Again, the more buy-in the subject has to the initial plan, the more likely he or she is likely to commit to it and follow it through. Obviously, there is no way to contractually enforce an agreement between yourself and the subject, so his or her commitment to the plan will stand and fall based on the level of trust you've built up during the encounter. But often, just promising something out loud to a trusted other can cement a person's commitment to following it through, so get as solid a verbal commitment as possible from the subject, essentially stating that he or she will actually do what the two of you have worked out.

GUIDING PRINCIPLES OF STRESS MANAGEMENT AND CRISIS INTERVENTION

The following principles have evolved out of my own work in police psychology, and grows out of my broader experience in stress management and crisis intervention in a wide variety of setting, including law enforcement and emergency service agencies, schools and workplaces, and medical and mental health facilities (Miller, 1994, 1998a, 1998b, 1998c, 1999a, 1999b, 1999c, 2000a, 2000b, 2002, 2003a, 2003b, 2005). Many of these are commonsensical and relate to the practical psychology that many officers already employ.

The Best Form of Crisis Intervention Is Crisis Prevention

Recalling the principles of primary, secondary, and tertiary prevention, it is clear that the best way to resolve a crisis is to prevent it from occurring in the first place. Hardly a day goes by in the work of law enforcement officers that opportunities for staving off crises do not occur. In fact, police officers may actually have a unique advantage over other emergency service professionals in this regard. Firefighters and paramedics are, by definition, responders to emergencies that have already begun or worsened—a fire in a toxic chemical plant, or an auto accident with injuries, for example. These professionals can react, but they usually can't predict, anticipate, or prevent.

The patrol function of police officers, however, places them in a unique position to see trouble coming and to take action before it boils over to a critical level of harm or an arrestable offense. Of course, not every law enforcement crisis can be anticipated or averted, but those officers who are uniquely successful in their jobs seem to have a talent for keeping problems under control, yet being able to take assertive action when necessary. How these talents can be trained and applied to various enforcement crises is the topic of many of this book's chapters.

All Successful Crisis Intervention Involves Crisis Prevention

This is the corollary to the above principle. Again, the principles of primary, secondary, and tertiary prevention imply that it is virtually never too late to intervene successfully in a crisis and prevent further harm, disability, or trauma from occurring. Further, in the real world, the three kinds of prevention are fluid and overlapping concepts. For example, talking two intoxicated citizens out of a brawl primarily prevents them from incurring physical injuries or legal charges. Quickly breaking up the fight once they have grabbed each other and tussled on the ground secondarily prevents them from racking up more serious arrestable charges and from incurring more than scrapes and bruises but may still primarily prevent bystanders from becoming involved and being arrested or injured themselves.

If one combatant stabs the other or bashes him in the head with a bottle, restraining and arresting the assailant and calling for paramedic and additional police backup secondarily prevents the victim from being killed by another blow or stab wound, while primarily preventing injury to the officer from a now clearly violent subject. Finally, how the arrest was handled, in addition to one or more officers remaining on-scene after the melee is over and reassuring frightened or angry citizens that the officers' actions were justifiable and in the interest of public safety, represents tertiary prevention of a potential civil disturbance or simply smoldering community animosity arising from the original brawl and the police action to break it up.

Stress Management and Crisis Intervention Are Interrelated

It is axiomatic that crises are most likely to arise under conditions of stress, and that stress is almost always further exacerbated by the very crises they provoke. It's all about vicious cycles. Therefore, effective stress management *is* an important crisis intervention skill, a form of primary prevention, as discussed above. Whether the stresses involve citizens in a officer's patrol area or stresses in the officer's own life, learning to deal constructively with life's challenges constitutes a primary layer of the "psychological body armor" noted earlier for deflecting the worst consequences of a stressful critical incident or life circumstance.

Stress Management and Crisis Intervention Principles Are Universal

If readers notice a certain redundancy among chapters dealing with, say, police officer suicide, crime scene victim stabilization, and hostage negotiation, that's because the basic principles of crisis intervention—communication, connection, support, active listening, problem-solving, exploring options, and instilling hope—are broad-purpose skills that can be applied to a wide range of crisis situations. This does not mean that one size fits all: training and experience are still required to be effective in one's particular domain of crisis intervention, since each domain contains distinct features—and indeed, each individual crisis will contain unique elements.

But just as emergency medical care for diverse injuries and illnesses (gunshot wound, heart attack, epileptic seizure) follows certain universal principles (assess vital signs, establish heart rhythm and airway, scan for internal injuries), so it is with emergency crisis intervention. This is all the more true inasmuch as one kind of crisis can easily become another: a domestic squabble turns into a hostage-barricade situation; a citizen dispute becomes a civil disturbance; a burglary investigation jumps into an assault-of-officer or suicide-by-cop episode. Mastering the stress management and crisis intervention skills in this book will enable officers to handle a broad range of situations.

20/20 Hindsight = 20/20 Insight = 20/20 Foresight

20/20 hindsight has gotten a bum rap. Often equated with second-guessing, Monday-morning quarterbacking, or useless self-flagellation, in reality, looking back on an unsuccessful action and analyzing it is an absolutely essential process for developing any skill—*if* the hindsight analysis leads to a certain degree of insight into what went wrong and how it happened. This insight into what happened last time can then be used to create a new set of options and action plans for next time. What we're talking about here is the whole concept of learning from experience.

In fact, this 20/20 principle is used all the time in law enforcement, emergency services, and the military, under the heading of *operational debriefing*. Within law enforcement, it is an essential component of hostage negotiation team training and undercover operations, as later chapters of this book will illustrate. Consistent with this book's theme, all true professionals engage in an ongoing process of continuing education and self-improvement—the *culture of knowledge* noted in Chapter 14—and the present volume is intended to contribute to that process.

Learning Never Stops, or "It's the Training, Stupid"

Consistent with the 20/20 principle, all the natural skill and talent in the world won't make you an expert in anything unless you develop and train that talent to the fullest it can be. Consider the professional athlete, artist, or musician. Certainly, without a natural gift for his or her sport or skill, training alone won't take the individual past the mediocre range. But raw talent alone is insufficient: the athlete or artisan has to work at developing that skill to its ultimate level in order to attain excellence and stay in the upper one-percent zone, to continue to push the envelope. Indeed, *the best form of stress management is proper training and knowledge* because the more automatic, flexible, and generalized a particular area of skill and expertise, the less surprised and overwhelmed you'll be in any situation.

In fact, research shows that those individuals at the top of their fields never coast; if anything, they actually put in many times more effort than those with less innate talent. That is, they take what's great and make it greater (Briggs, 1988; Simonton, 1994). That's why one of this book's guiding principles—indeed, the main reason it was written—is that, for true professionals in any field, learning, training, and teaching never stop. In the culture of knowledge, we keep growing and, as we do so, we contribute to the growth of our colleagues and our organization.

CONCLUSIONS

Intimately involved on a daily basis with the vagaries of human nature and behavior, successful police officers have always been skilled practical psychologists. Stress management and crisis intervention are cyclical, recursive processes, because stress precipitates crises and crises contribute to heightened stress. Both with the citizens they serve and in their own lives and work, law enforcement professionals must master these human relations and communications skills for optimum success and satisfaction on the job. This book will serve as a guide to police officers and the mental health clinicians who assist them in promoting excellence and professionalism in the practical psychology of police work.

PART I

PATROL AND COMMUNITY POLICING

Chapter 2

ON PATROL: STREET PSYCHOLOGY 101

THE ROLE OF PATROL IN POLICING

When most people think of police officers, they think of the beat cop, and indeed, the police patrol function continues to be the backbone of community law enforcement (Peak, 2003). This seemingly simple police activity is really composed of a variety of complex daily decisions and activities. These include the discretionary use of authority and prevention of criminal activity by an assertive police presence. It also involves maintaining good relations with citizens in the community because, like it or not, cops may at times have to depend on those citizens to help them do their jobs effectively; for example, obtaining useful information in trying to solve a crime, or helping to maintain order and calm neighbors' anger to forestall a potential civil disturbance. If nothing else, officers know they will encounter the same people—"repeat customers"—on a regular basis, and so maintaining good relations works in everybody's favor.

While the actual effect of foot patrol officers on crime statistics is still being debated, surveys clearly show that citizens feel safer and more confident in their local police department when the officers are a living, breathing presence in their daily lives. Ironically, however, it is the foot patrols that are often the first to undergo budget cuts in favor of more flashy special tactics and investigative units (Thibault et al., 2004).

For patrol cops to do their jobs effectively, they must adopt a constructive territoriality about their patrol areas, sometimes known as *owning the beat* (Peak, 2003). By becoming increasingly familiar with the geography, economy, personality, and sociology of their beats, patrol cops come to know intuitively what's normal or what's out of place for their respective neighborhoods. Additionally, by adopting the optimal blend of professional detachment and emotional involvement in their neighborhoods, patrol officers develop what the business world calls *buy-in*, a personal stake in the welfare of their patrol community, a situation in which it is important to them to keep the peace and provide the highest quality of service: "This is my 'hood,' and I'm going to do everything I can to make sure that it stays safe."

Relatedly, officers who feel they are an integral part of their communities are less likely to resort to physical force to resolve crisis situations that could be verbally de-escalated. In return, citizens come to trust and respect those officers they perceive as consistently trying to keep order without excessive harshness, and who truly try to understand the community's concerns (Toch & Grant, 2005; Wadman & Ziman, 1993). Thus, this is truly one aspect of policing that exemplifies the principle that the best form of crisis intervention is crisis prevention.

ELEMENTS OF EFFECTIVE PATROL POLICING

Survey research (Baehr et al., 1968, cited in Peak, 2003) has identified a number of tasks and responsibilities that patrol officers must carry out in order to successfully perform their patrol duties. Although TV cop shows often portray police work as nonstop action, in real life the patrol officer's job is more like that of a firefighter, paramedic, or air traffic controller: long periods of monotony punctuated by brief episodes of intense, life-and-death activity. Officers have to be able to react quickly and go from "0 to 60" at a moment's notice. They have to be able to respond courageously and aggressively in critical situations, yet possess sufficient presence of mind not to overreact and risk inflaming the situation further. In between, they must deal with various and sundry crises, ranging from citizen disputes to traffic violations.

To be effective, officers have to gain intimate knowledge of their patrol areas: the geography, economy, demographics, crime statistics, local culture, and quirky characters of their beats. Only in this way will they hone their instincts as to what's normal and what's suspicious in their patrol areas. This practical expertise further enables officers to quickly size up situations and make prompt, effective decisions with regard to what specific actions to take, such as a crime in progress, family crisis, or citizen dispute—the kind of *recognition-primed decision making* (RPDM) discussed further in Chapter 14.

While not all officers can be Olympic athletes, they are expected to maintain some basic standards of physical conditioning and psychomotor skill with respect to strength and endurance, manual dexterity, facility with firearms and equipment, driving skill, and so on. In the same way, while not all officers can be paragons of psychological health and virtue, all

cops are expected to have the basic mental skills of mature judgment, problem-solving, and independent thinking. Indeed, even more so than other emergency responders, police officers are given wide latitude in how to handle many types of routine and complex policing situations, ranging from the decision to write a traffic ticket, to whether to use their taser or firearm in a dangerous criminal confrontation. In this regard, police officers need to be able to work under varying levels of supervision; from tight micromanagement of their every move to almost no supervision at all, leaving important decisions to the officer's discretion.

Important psychological skills extend to the interpersonal domain as well. Patrol officers, especially in larger metropolitan areas, will have to deal with a wide range of citizen ages, ethnicities, cultures, economic strata, and personalities. Officers must sometimes endure impolite or verbally abusive behavior, while maintaining a professional presence at all times and carefully treading the line between authori*tative* and authori*tarian* police presence. Effective officers must be able to utilize appropriate conflict-resolution skills to prevent situations from escalating, while maintaining objectivity, balance, and the perception of fairness. They must be able to cope with different kinds and varying levels of stress, and yet at all times maintain a high level of personal integrity and ethical conduct. This is not just a nice, politically correct idea; it is essential to maintaining authority and credibility on patrol.

RESPONSES OF DISRESPECTED CITIZENS

As noted above, one of the practical benefits of a friendly, or at least nonadversarial, relationship between police and citizenry is the ability to solicit their cooperation when necessary. Overall, congenial relations between police and public make the officer's job easier and help citizens feel safer. Conversely, there are a number of different reactions that citizens typically show in response to their perception of being ignored, abused, or disrespected by the police (Wadman & Ziman, 1993):

Apathy-antagonism. "Why should I report crimes to the police? They don't care." This reflects citizen dissatisfaction with police response to their concerns. If citizens feel that their good-faith efforts in being the

eyes and ears of law enforcement are rewarded by halfhearted or neglectful follow-up, they will naturally be reluctant to report such activity in the future. If they feel really ignored or abused, this may manifest itself as pointed noncooperation: "Get your own information—I'm not telling you anything." A vicious cycle may then develop where police take this as a sign of deliberate community apathy or scorn, and thereby restrict their patrolling activities still further, or become even more impatient and irritable with citizens.

Formal complaints. "That's it, I'm filing a complaint." Disrespected citizens may channel their frustrations into written complaints against officers. As in any relationship, unwelcome or mildly irksome behavior may be tolerated if it occurs in the context of basic trust and common purpose. But in the presence of an already existing tense and adversarial relationship, even seemingly inconsequential annoyances may be interpreted as signs of malign abuse, and some departments may be flooded with verbal and written complaints, sometimes against the same officer, over and over again (see Chapter 13). On the one hand, this uses up personnel resources that might be productively allocated elsewhere. On the other hand, a complaint that is registered is at least one that can be addressed; far more ominous are the numerous unrecorded slights and hostilities that are left to fester within a community.

Verbal confrontation. "Get out of my face—you can't talk to me that way." Discourteous officer conduct may lead to verbal confrontations between officers and citizens. Often, this represents the outburst of a cumulative build-up of frustration from past unpleasant interactions on the part of both officer and citizen. At the very least, repeated hostile interactions like these are grating to the morale of officers and citizens alike; at worst, they lead to physical confrontations necessitating frequent arrests that further inflame community hostility.

Physical confrontation. If matters have escalated to this point, verbal conflict-resolution strategies can be assumed to have failed, if they have been tried at all. Even more so than with verbal confrontation, repeated citizen experiences of being roughed up by the police—even if the arrest started with an assault by the angry citizen—are corrosive to the morale of patrolling officers and only highlight to citizens the image of the police force as a hostile army of occupation.

COMMUNITY-ORIENTED POLICING

While the beat cop was a stable fixture of most urban areas from the beginning to the middle of the twentieth century, the decades of the 1960s, 70s, and early 80s saw American police forces become more insular and reactive, as a wave of crime and social disorder seemed to sweep over the country. Officers were rarely seen on the street; rather, they cruised their patrol areas in cars, or appeared only in response to emergency 911 calls. Naturally, many citizens felt alienated from their local police forces, and the feeling was mutual.

The latter part of the 20th century and beginning of the 21st has seen movements within policing to enhance relations within the community and to enlist the community as a partner in combating crime and improving overall quality of life (Goldstein, 1987; Peak, 2003; Peak & Glensor, 2002; Thibault et al., 2004), although in the very recent political climate, this movement may be threatened by unfavorable fiscal policies at the local, state, and federal levels.

Community-oriented policing, or COP, developed in the past two decades as an alternative to the reactive "911 mentality" of policing. COP is more than a police-community relations program; it attempts to address crime control through a working partnership with the community. In essence, it is a systematized return to the old-fashioned beat-cop model of policing, with the added feature of endeavoring to proactively address the needs of the community. In fact, much of what has just been described as the ideal role of the patrol officer encompasses the substance of community-oriented policing.

For traditional departments, COP represents a long-term process that involves fundamental institutional change. This concept redefines the role of the officer on the street, from that of crime fighter to that of problem solver and neighborhood ombudsman. This philosophy asks officers to break away from the incident-driven model of policing and to seek proactive and creative resolution to the problems of crime and disorder in their communities. Not all officers or all departments are comfortable with this.

PROBLEM-ORIENTED POLICING

One extension of COP is *problem-oriented policing,* or POP, which begins with the recognition that much criminal activity can be prevented by establishing and maintaining a working partnership between police and community. Instead of viewing police officers as after-the-fact reactors to crimes, this model takes a more involved and proactive approach, preferring to place officers in the role of problem-solvers in their patrol neighborhoods (Goldstein, 1990; Peak & Glensor, 2002; Toch & Grant, 2005).

POP has the added benefit of generally increasing positive contact among citizens and police officers. Traditionally, the only time that many citizens see officers is when something bad happens, or when they themselves are the brunt of a police action. Having officers proactively seek out solutions to community problems within their purview places policing on a whole different level. One model of POP uses a four-stage problem solving process, abbreviated as SARA, for *Scanning, Analysis, Response*, and *Assessment*. In many ways, this process resembles the diagnostic and treatment process that clinicians are familiar with.

Scanning is the initial step and involves identifying the problems on the officers' beats, especially looking for patterns in repeat incidents. This scrutiny may range from known or suspected crack houses in the neighborhood to busy intersections that seem to have more than the usual number of traffic accidents. As noted above, problem identification usually requires officers to become sufficiently familiar with their territories to be able to spot patterns and anomalies.

Analysis is the heart of problem solving, and involves officers generating working hypotheses as to the causes of each of the problems they've identified. Then, specific strategies are developed to address each of the problems. For example, the accident-prone intersection may have traffic light intervals too short or too long, so motorists are tempted to run yellow lights to make the crossing. Or a suspected crack house may continue to operate because local residents are bribed or intimidated

into silence when it comes to making complaints or being witnesses. Then, the challenge is to convince the citizens of the benefits of having the crack den out of there, such as fewer assaults, robberies, and burglaries. The more detailed the plans, and the more they are based on an accurate, citizen-guided analysis of the problem, the more effective they are likely to be.

Response involves putting the plan into action. If it has been well thought out, if it has been based on reliable information, and if there are no major unforeseen glitches, things should work more or less according to plan. Any snafus that do arise are dealt with in the fourth phase, which is:

Assessment. How well is the plan working? There are usually a range of possible outcomes to a given response plan, with the middle of this range of possibilities more likely to occur than the extremes. That is, if the plan was well-founded to begin with, it is unlikely to be a complete and utter failure. This kind of total crash usually only occurs if something important was missing from the planning stage, in which case it may be "back to the drawing board." Equally unlikely is for the plan to go flawlessly smooth, without a hitch. Typically, things will work out generally according to plan, but certain details will require fine-tuning based on additional information that comes in as the plan is implemented.

In fact, in any well-run program of problem-solving, the four stages blend and interact with one another. Initial scanning yields data points on which to analyze the problem and develop a plan. Assessment of plan implementation yields further information that is then incorporated into revisions of the plan, and so on. While this may seem complicated, as with many concepts described in this book, it basically involves the familiar concept of "learning from experience."

COMMUNITY-ORIENTED POLICING AND PROBLEM-SOLVING

Incorporating the COP and POP concepts yields yet another acronym, COPPS for *community-oriented policing* and *problem solving* (Goldstein, 1987, 1990; Herbert, 2001; Peak & Glensor, 2002; Toch &

Geller, 2005). Readers who are tiring of this law enforcement alphabet soup may set their spoons down for a moment, as long as they recall that the basic concept of this model is to view the patrol officer as an autonomous, thinking professional who is given a great deal of discretion and decision making ability and is trusted with a wide array of responsibilities. In this model, patrol officers continue to handle routine calls, but they are also much more involved in their community as law enforcement and community safety professionals.

Importantly, in this model patrol duty is not regarded as a low-status activity to be passed through as quickly as possible. Serving the community should not be seen as a demotion or punishment, as in: "McGillicuddy, if you screw up again, I'm busting you down to flatfoot!" Of course, inculcating line officers into this new way of thinking will require a good deal of education, as well as a change in orientation from the top brass. It involves conceptualizing officers not just as arrest-makers or even exclusively as crime-fighters, but more broadly as public safety professionals. (Indeed, in a few jurisdictions, this is literally true: police officers, firefighters, and paramedics are all cross-trained and rotate roles and responsibilities.)

Similar to POP, the COPPS model is a proactive philosophy of crime-fighting and community safety enhancement. For your departmental COPPS model to succeed, the following measures must be employed (Peak, 2003; Peak & Glensor, 2002):

First, *conduct an accurate community needs assessment* to determine whether your department's and your community's priorities are on the same page.

Next, *mobilize appropriate personnel to brainstorm strategies.* These may be your fellow officers, members of special units, or consultants called in from outside the department who have special expertise in the particular problem area.

An often-neglected step is *determining the appropriate resource allocation* in terms of both budget and personnel. It's all well and good to come up with a grand crime-fighting and community safety plan, but who's going to staff it and pay for it?

As in the SARA model, eventually you must *develop and implement the relevant plans and programs* you've worked so hard on.

Finally, *evaluate* the success of your program and *modify* it where needed, again invoking the interactive cycle of learning-by-doing and the 20/20 hindsight-insight-foresight rule (Chapter 1).

IMPORTANCE OF COMMUNICATION SKILLS IN POLICING

I've had cops tell me, "I catch criminals; I'm not paid to talk." But verbal communication skills are crucial for success in community policing efforts. Unless an officer intends to either ignore or arrest any citizen he or she comes in contact with on patrol, communication skills are vital for both solving mundane problems and defusing potentially explosive situations. Bradstreet (1986) has further delineated some of the reasons underlying the importance of training police officers in communication skills.

First, the majority of patrol time is spent in routine citizen contact that does not involve serious criminal law enforcement action. Traffic stops, accident investigations, mediating neighbor quarrels, calming angry or intoxicated citizens, and handling complaints all require good verbal skills to handle the situation without allowing it to escalate.

Second, successfully resolving a minor crisis, such as a family dispute or neighbor quarrel, might obviate the need for later call-backs to the same scene for a major crisis, such as domestic battery or destruction of property. It thus makes an officer's job easier.

Third, those crisis situations that begin as hot calls can be more effectively de-escalated by officers who possess good verbal skills, potentially eliminating the need for physical force, restraint, and arrest. Again, less risk of injury and less paperwork.

BASIC COMMUNICATION SKILLS FOR POLICE OFFICERS

In line with the idea of cross-training and generalizable skills (Chapter 1), many of the important communication skills patrol officers can use to defuse tension and increase cooperation in the face of everyday crises are also applicable to more serious emergencies, such as hostage and barricade situations (Chapter 9). So practicing these skills on daily patrol will enhance your application of them to a wide range of crisis situations. Basic street-level communications skills include the following (Bradstreet, 1986).

To begin with, angry citizens may just want to vent. To a certain extent, allow this venting to occur, as long as it does not escalate to rageful spewing or cross over into physical violence. Venting uses up adrenalin and sometimes allows the venter to gain some insight into his own thoughts and feelings. Listen patiently at first, without trying to dissuade or argue. Show interest in what the person is saying through eye contact and attentive body posture. Even if a disturbed or intoxicated citizen is acting crazy or goofy, avoid patronizing him. If your partner is present, avoid the temptation to give each other snickering glances, which is a sure sign of disrespect to a citizen who thinks what he's saying is important. If the subject curses or insults you, try to respond calmly without being baited into retaliating with anger or sarcasm. Of course, if a subject threatens or attacks you, and this is an arrestable offense, do your job. But remember that many situations are far from clear-cut and that officers have great discretion in how they choose to respond to a wide range of obstreperous citizen behavior.

Certain tactics are useful for calming angry citizens and reducing the potential for violence. Start with your voice. For some officers, voice control is a natural talent, but for most, this skill can be trained and improved with daily practice. Learn to respond calmly to insults and challenges, without resorting to sarcasm or harshness of tone. If you feel yourself getting agitated, make a conscious effort to modulate the pace of your speech and tone of your voice. Modulating your breathing helps keep you voice cadence under control. As part of your self-training, practice different speech styles: sympathetic, commanding, reassuring, business-like, logical, and so on. The goal is not to act like a trained parrot, but rather to become familiar and comfortable with different communication styles in order to increase your repertoire of flexible skills in handling interpersonal encounters. This gives officers tremendous power to handle virtually any kind of crisis.

Sometimes, just changing the subject to a more neutral topic can ratchet the tension level down a few notches. In general, be careful not to abruptly shift to a whole new topic, which may be interpreted as rude or manipulative by the citizen. Rather, try to segue into a topic that is related to the one now under discussion, but is less emotionally charged. For example:

Citizen: "I know she took those garden tools from my shed, because I could hear my dogs barking in the yard, and the next thing I saw was her going into her house."
Officer: "What kind of dogs do you have?"
C: "Two rotweilers. What the hell difference does it make what kind of dogs they are?" [C annoyed at perhaps too sharp a shift in topic].
O: "I mean, do you find that dogs are a good way of knowing who's coming and going on your property?"
C: "Yeah, they scared off some robbers a few months ago. Nobody wants to mess with rotweilers."
O: "So somebody would have to be pretty crazy to steal something from your yard if they knew you had these dogs there."
C: "I guess so."

Perhaps more subtle, but equally potent, are a range of nonverbal behaviors that powerfully influence human interaction. Depending on the nature of the interaction, officers may want to manipulate their own *authority image* (Bradstreet, 1986). For example, when interviewing suspects, unruly citizens, or general "hard cases," projecting a firm position, standing in a commanding manner, decreasing personal space, moving slowly and confidently, and making steady but not challenging eye contact all serve to increase the controlled intimidation factor that may mollify otherwise overly attitudinal or uncooperative subjects.

Conversely, some meeker, more skittish law-abiding citizens may be *so* intimidated by the police presence that they are almost paralyzed with fear and are unable to get their story out. In such cases, it is better to stand back a few paces, relax your stance or even sit down, focus some attention on note-taking and other non-eye contact activity, and speak in a reassuring tone of voice—similar to the approach you would take with children or the mentally disabled (Chapter 4). Remember, the goal of almost any citizen interview is to increase the flow of communication and gain cooperation.

Note-taking, by the way, serves another important function when trying to maximize information-flow from citizens. Seeing an officer write down what the subject says gives that subject the impression that his or her input is important, which may mean a great deal to citizens who are accustomed to having their comments sloughed off by seemingly uncaring officers. But be careful about using this device with citizens who may be suspicious that you're "making a record" of what they're saying.

Finally, it may be necessary to physically separate two sparring citizens to keep a verbal fight from escalating to blows, thereby necessitating an arrest. As will be discussed in Chapter 3, this is a common way of handling domestic violence calls.

INTERPERSONAL COMMUNICATION PROCESSES

The majority of police-citizen contacts occur face-to-face, either one-on-one or in small groups. Accordingly, certain types of interpersonal communication processes are applicable to daily police work on the street. As noted above, a good deal of this communication occurs nonverbally (Pritchett, 1993; Shea & Harpool, 1988).

If language refers to the verbal content of our speech, then *paralanguage* is the message we send by our tone of voice, pitch, inflection, and phrasing. Neuropsychologists refer to this as the *prosodic* features of spoken language, which is mediated by the brain's right hemisphere, as opposed to the vocabulary and grammar of language, which is a left-hemisphere function. Everybody knows that the same literal sentence, e.g., "I'm feeling just fine," can be expressed and interpreted as a statement or a question, as serious or sarcastic, by the style of vocal inflection used. Other paralinguistic features that may be useful include pauses, stutters, lowering or raising of voice pitch or volume, interjected phrases ("uh," "y'know"), and so on.

Active listening denotes putting conscious effort into a dialogue, which is different from casual conversation. Giving a subject your full attention and focus, and indicating your involvement and concern for what he or she is telling you, will almost always serve to increase communication, trust, and cooperation. This can be vitally important in resolving acute crises such as suicide and hostage incidents (Chapters 9, 10 and 11).

Kinesics describes nonverbal, body-language aspects of communication, such as facial expression, gestures, posture, and other physical movements that transmit messages that either reinforce or contradict the spoken message. This aspect of communication is of interest to law enforcement investigators and poker players alike. In fact, paralanguage and kinesics are included in training in interview and interrogation strategies (Zulawski & Wicklander, 1993); however, beware of overinterpreting the signals as sure-fire "lie detectors," because there are wide individual differences in how people communicate under stress (Kassin, 2005; Kassin & McNall, 1991).

Yet another dimension of communication is *proxemics*, or the science of personal and social space. In many street interactions, officers intuitively judge the comfort level of their own and the citizen's personal space and adjust their stance accordingly, so as to tread a happy medium between standing too distant, which may signal unconcern and disrespect, and being too "in your face," which is typically taken as confrontational or aggressive. Proxemics can further be differentiated (Pritchett, 1993) into several categories:

Intimate space extends from actual physical contact outward, from about six to eighteen inches. This is usually the province into which we comfortably allow friends or close associates.

Personal space continues out from eighteen inches to about four feet. This is the comfort zone of most business and personal acquaintances.

Social space extends the perimeter to about four to twelve feet. This is about the range that most strangers feel comfortable interacting within, and which will contain most nonconfrontational police encounters on patrol. If officers find themselves moving closer during an encounter, it usually signals some trouble on the psychological radar.

Public space includes everything at 12 feet and beyond. Of course, in crowded urban areas, it is not uncommon to see individuals physically jammed together, yet maintaining psychological distance by focusing on their own activities–just think of a crowded bus, subway, elevator, or supermarket check-out line.

As with all of these skills, patrol officers who adeptly manipulate interpersonal space will experience the greatest success in dealing with citizens on their beats. Many officers do this instinctively, but it is a skill that can be learned and refined with practice.

WORKING THE STREET:
MEDIATION AND ARBITRATION FOR PATROL OFFICERS

It's one thing to tell police officers to go out there and be community problem-solvers, to employ sound judgment and street-corner diplomacy, and to gain the respect and cooperation of the citizens on their beats. It's quite another thing to show these cops how to do it, to train them in the practical skills and techniques that they can use in their daily patrol interactions.

That's why the excellent mediation and arbitration protocol set out by Cooper (1999) forms the foundation of the present section, supplemented by my own experiences and observations in training officers. Indeed, most of the approaches and strategies outlined here apply to more than just the world of patrol policing, and can, for example, be productively adapted for the business world, political negotiation, or family counseling (Slaiku, 1996).

Situations where these mediation and arbitration techniques can be used in policing include public and community-based disputes, domestic situations not involving violence, bystander/onlooker conflicts, traffic disputes, "assist with property/clothing" calls, parent-child conflicts, neighbor disputes, and others.

Purposes of Conflict Resolution

In daily patrol work, conflict resolution between citizens typically serves one of two basic functions. The first in to settle the issue right then and there: "Okay, so you'll pay her the 20 dollars for the dog grooming, even if it wasn't exactly how you wanted it, and she'll throw in a free cut and wash for next time."

The second function of patrol conflict resolution is to serve as a stopgap measure until further legal or other action can be taken: "You've filed a complaint, so this is going to have to go before a judge in small claims court. In the meantime, he's not going to go on your property until this is settled. I

want you to stay away from him, because if you threaten him again, I'm going to have to arrest you, and that's not going to help your case, is it?"

Contextual Factors in Conflict Resolution

Although some interpersonal conflicts encountered on patrol deal with single, one-time beefs between strangers, such as traffic disputes or customer complaints, other conflicts reflect long-standing issues between the disputants; most commonly, these involve family and neighbor disputes. Here, officers need to be aware that what the parties are actually arguing about at the moment ("You took those apples off the tree in my yard") may only be the proverbial tip of the iceberg of a larger, ongoing area of conflict ("She's been stealing stuff off my property ever since she moved next door–and besides, she keeps her yard like a pigsty and it brings down the whole neighborhood").

While not completely ignoring or discounting the context in which the dispute occurs, the challenge for the officer in such cases is to keep the discussion focused on the present disagreement. Sometimes, showing disputants that they can successfully resolve the present problem may have a positive ripple effect in encouraging them to productively tackle the broader issues.

Mediation vs. Arbitration

In essence, the basic difference between these two conflict resolution strategies is whether or not the officer actually imposes a decision (arbitration) or assists disputants in arriving at their own agreement (mediation). In both types of interventions, the solution ultimately arrived at may not be the best solution or a perfect solution, but should at least be a mutually acceptable decision that both disputants can live with, or at least accept provisionally until further action can be taken.

In the present context, *mediation* is defined as the process whereby a neutral third party, in this case a police officer, assists two or more citizens in resolving a conflict or dispute. The main role of the mediating officer in is not to impose the actual decision, but to serve as what Cooper (1999) terms an *active-assertive facilitator*, to assist the two sides in arriving at a mutually agreeable resolution of their dispute.

The primary roles of the officer in mediation include: (1) listening to the disputants to make sure their positions have been clearly expressed; (2) helping each side frame their issues and communicate them to the opposite party; and (3) keeping the discussion goal-oriented and on track, to prevent the conflict from escalating into an emotional fracas or being diverted to tangents and side-issues. In general, people tend to adhere to agreements to which they have had the most participation in formulating, what the business negotiation world calls buy-in.

Arbitration involves much of the same intervention style and substance as mediation, but here the officer is the one who makes the final decision. The officer listens carefully to both sides of the dispute, analyzes the facts and issues, and imposes a decision. Arbitration may be used when both parties agree at the outset that they want a neutral third party or authority figure to "settle this." Sometimes people find it easier to accept a less-than-perfect solution that has been externally imposed because it relieves some of their responsibility for it: "Hey, don't bitch at me—the cop told us you gotta pay back half that money."

In other cases, the intervention may begin as mediation but evolve into arbitration when it becomes clear that the disputants cannot resolve this on their own. Here, the disputants may agree to let the officer "take over the case," or the officer may have to make a command decision when it becomes obvious that the negotiations are going nowhere. More rarely, arbitration may soften to mediation when the very process of negotiating a dispute rather than battling over it convinces the disputants that they can independently resolve their differences in a civilized way.

THE PATROL POLICE MEDIATION PROCESS

The mediation process consists of several steps or phases (Cooper, 1999).

Step 1. Suggestion of Mediation and Opening Statement

Typically, an officer will arrive at a scene where a conflict is already in progress. If the situation seems amenable to mediation, the officer first introduces himself and then suggests that he may be of service in mediating the dispute. Sometimes, the officer may state this overtly; at other times, he may subtly ease in the suggestion during the course of conversation. If the parties agree, the officer then explains the process of mediation, i.e., that it is the officer's job to help the disputants reach a decision; that once the decision is agreed to, it is binding on both parties; and that if the parties are unable to reach a resolution on their own, the officer may then have to impose one (arbitration).

If the disputants agree thus far, the officer then states the basic ground rules for mediation. These include: no shouting or profanity; no hitting, threatening, or intimidating; no interruptions: one person speaks at a time; keep the discussion focused on the dispute in question; confidentiality: as long as no laws are broken, the officer will keep this matter to himself, and the parties are expected to respect each other's privacy and not blab about the dispute to others.

The officer then explains one primary mechanism used in mediation, known as *caucusing* (Slaiku, 1996). In this procedure, the disputants are separated and the officer moves back and forth between them, gathering information and presenting each party's offers and counteroffers—a kind of street-level "shuttle diplomacy." Caucusing is used in situations where the disputants just can't seem to negotiate face to face without getting agitated, or when one party feels intimidated by the other. Sometimes, one or both parties will suggest such a caucusing approach; in other cases, it is up to the alert officer to perceive the need for such an approach. For example:

Officer: "Okay folks, I can see you're having difficulty working this out, so maybe I can help here. We're going try something called mediation. I'm going to hear each of you out, get each of your sides of the story, and then I'll help you come to a decision. Hopefully, I'm not going to have to make the decision for you because if you come to some agreement, I want it to be *your* agreement. But my role is to help clarify the situation and help each of you understand where the other one is coming from. Hopefully, you can then work it out between you. Remember, this is voluntary, but if you agree to try to settle things this way, the decision will be binding, all right? If it seems clear that we're getting nowhere, or if you just don't want to do things this way, then I'll have to make a command decision so this doesn't blow out of control. But my first choice is that you guys work it out for yourselves.

"Okay, a couple of ground rules. The basic word here is 'respect,' otherwise this is not going to work. So no shouting, cursing, or threatening. You know if anyone gets physical, that's an arrestable offense, so keep it peaceful, all right? I want to make sure everybody gets heard, so when one person is speaking, no interruptions from the other side; the next speaker gets the same courtesy. Also, this is between us. As long as I don't have to make an arrest or disclose something reportable, this conversation stays with me. So I urge you to keep things confidential between yourselves so this doesn't become the latest gossip of the neighborhood. If you're having trouble dealing with this face to face, I may have to separate you and shuttle back and forth to help you hammer out an agreement. And if we're still getting nowhere, I'll have to play Judge Wapner and make the final decision myself. But hopefully, I can help you guys work it out for yourselves."

Step 2. Each Side Conveys Their Version

Who speaks first might be agreed on by the parties, or it may literally come down to a coin toss, but whoever is speaking gets the full attention of all present. The officer listens and perhaps takes notes (if this is not objectionable or too distracting to the parties). The officer does not interject at this time, except to correct any violation of the ground rules. Usually, the most common example of inadvertent rule violation at this stage involves the tendency of subjects to go

off on tangents when describing their side of the story. Subjects may try to incorporate all past injustices by the opposing party or by society in general, or describe personal problems that have little or nothing to do with the dispute in question. In such cases, the officer may have to verbally intervene to keep the discussion focused and on track, mainly by the use of subtle verbal "nudges" in the right direction.

Citizen: "And she's always stealing my stuff. Not just the tools this time, but wood slats and a bunch of lawn ornaments were missing last month, and I saw her out there then, too. This whole neighborhood seems to be filled with crooks these days."

Officer: "And this time you think she took the tools. Tell me more about that."

When each of the disputants has finished his or her respective versions, the officer then asks each one if they have anything to add, again controlling for rambling or extraneous material. When each party feels that their side has been reasonably expressed, it's time to move on to the next step.

Step 3. Officer's Reiteration of Key Issues

In any mediation process, whether between competing corporations, warring countries, or sparring neighbors, clarity is crucial. So in Step 3 of the mediation process, the officer ascertains that everybody is on the same page by asking probing questions that help to clear up any confusions or misunderstandings. Sometimes, the officer gets the clue as to what to ask from picking up the confused or mixed messages that one or both of the disputants are sending; at other times, it's what is *not* said by either party that prompts a query.

After questioning, the officer then restates each side's position, and solicits verification from each of the parties that these are indeed their views on the subject. If there is any discrepancy, the party is asked to clarify. Sometimes the parties will start to argue, in which case the officer points out that the purpose of the discussion at this stage is just to clarify positions, and that both parties will soon have an opportunity to negotiate their agreement. The officer then summarizes the key negotiable issues in the dispute, as well as what needs to be left out or deferred to later.

Officer: "Okay, Sue says that Jane borrowed the tools and didn't give them all back, so she believes Jane stole some of the tools and she wants Jane to pay for them. Jane says she did return all the tools and that Sue probably lost them and now wants to blame Jane and make her pay for them. Sue says that she's warned Jane in the past about borrowing things and not returning them, but we've agreed that we're just going to deal with the tool issue now, and not worry about the past stuff, so we can make some progress here. Am I missing anything, or is that about it?"

Step 4. Brainstorming Possible Solutions

Believe it or not, this is the easier part. Professional negotiators know that the toughest aspect of most dispute mediations is getting the parties to agree on the causes of the problem (Slaiku, 1996). Once such an agreement has been reached, it is often surprisingly simple to arrive at a mutually satisfactory solution, because the resolution often arises naturally out of an understanding of the problem, once the core issues have been narrowed down and each side believes it will be treated fairly.

In this next phase, each party is asked to generate their version of a *best-case solution* to the dispute. The actual nature of the interaction between the parties will determine the level of officer involvement at this point. At one end of the involvement spectrum, the officer stands back and lets the parties bandy ideas about until a solution is reached all by themselves. At the other end, the officer may have to caucus back and forth between separated parties, presenting each offer and counteroffer, helping the parties identify areas of potential agreement, and suggesting possible refinements on the ideas generated by the disputants. In reality, the officer's role will probably be somewhere between these two extremes, but the emphasis should always be on helping the parties reach their own solution.

Cooper (1999) identifies two possible pitfalls of the brainstorming phase. The first is *irrational conceding*, where one party—out of frustration, spite, or intimidation—makes a patently unfair or one-sided concession: "Let her have my damn tools, and while she's at it, she can keep all the wood and my lawn ornaments, and she can pick all the oranges off my tree for all I care." If this attitude persists beyond a momentary spasm of emotion, the officer may have

to conclude that mediation is not best forum to resolve a dispute under these circumstances and may have to move to an arbitrated decision.

The second pitfall may be related to the first and results from *power imbalances* between the disputants. If one party is physically, financially, socially, or emotionally more dominant than the other, the weaker party may feel that "the deck is already stacked against me," and may have limited motivation to participate in a mediated solution. The opposite problem occurs where one party feels superior or entitled to have the upper hand by virtue of some personal characteristic or connection: "I've lived in this neighborhood twenty years; she just moved in six months ago;" or, "You know, my brother's a cop." In such cases, the officer should try to effect a more equitable balance of power by assuring both parties that he will act as fairly and objectively as possible. But if this cannot credibly be accomplished, the officer may have to make the call to arbitrate the dispute.

Step 5. Agreement

The most important thing to remember at this stage is that the agreement arrived at is not necessarily the best of all possible agreements, but merely one that will enable the parties to put aside their dispute, either permanently or at least until a more formal process can be put into place, such as a civil lawsuit or complaint to a regulatory agency (Slaiku, 1996).

When the parties feel they have reached an agreement, the officer listens carefully to the plan, and then restates it in his own words, to make sure everyone is clear about the terms of the agreement. Any last minute fine-tuning by the officer at this stage will usually involve helping the disputants to develop a practical strategy for implementing their plan. The final step is to put it in writing because any kind of document, even a hand-written one, conveys authority upon the decision.

Officer: "Okay, Jane is going to look through her house and see if she may have accidentally misplaced any of the tools. If they're found, they'll be returned to Sue, no questions asked. Meanwhile, Sue will check her place to see if she may have accidentally lost any of them. If the tools stay missing, Jane will offer to help Sue on some yard work as a good faith measure, and Sue will drop the matter and move on. For the future, to prevent further mis-understanding, nobody will lend anybody any-thing. Also, each of you will notify the other if you need to go on each other's property, even for a minute. Any questions or additions? No? Okay, let's write it up."

POLICE PATROL ARBITRATION

If mediation is the method of choice for bring-ing citizens together to solve their own disputes, then why use arbitration, where the officer essen-tially makes the judgment for the disputants?

First, there are a number of situations where mediation is either inappropriate to the dispute in question or is just unworkable. As noted above, any kind of significant power imbalance between the parties may intimidate one member from speaking up and presenting his case. In such cir-cumstances, it may feel safer for the weaker party to have the decision made for him rather than pre-sent it as his own idea. This is often the case for people who will continue to have contact with one another, such as family members, coworkers, or neighbors.

Sometimes the case is so clear-cut that there is really nothing to mediate: blame might be squarely ap-portioned 50–50, or alternatively, one party may be clearly at fault. In such cases, the officer essentially tells the disputants what to do. In other cases, the situation may be more ambiguous, but the scene is so chaotic or dangerous that the officer has to make at least a pro-visional decision until such time as more reasoned negotiation can take place; this is often true of traffic accident scenes or customer-merchant disputes. Some-times, one or both parties may be intoxicated or just unavailable, precluding useful mediation. Or the situa-tion may have escalated to the point where a crime has been committed and arrest action is called for. Finally, mediation may have already been tried and failed, so an arbitrated decision must be made by the officer.

THE ARBITRATION PROCESS

The basic steps or stages of arbitration are simi-lar to those of mediation, except that the final deci-sion is made by the officer, not arrived at by the disputants (Cooper, 1999).

Fact-Finding Stage

Initially, the officer does his or her best to gather all the relevant information. In some cases, this can occur within seconds where the nature and causes of the dispute are obvious. In other cases, a great deal of time and care may be needed to sift through the different versions of the story and to winnow out the important information from the associated historical and emotional context. The officer may even utilize caucusing, but its purpose in this case is not to solicit disputants' offers of their own solutions, but simply to check facts and perceptions against one another ("Jane says the two of you frequently borrow tools and things from each other and she never ques-tioned you about returning stuff before this. Is that your recollection?"). The goal of this stage is to glean as much relevant information as possible in order to make an informed judgment about the case at hand.

Analysis Stage

Here, the officer puts it all together in his or her mind and formulates some tentative hypotheses as to the causes of the dispute and possible solutions. As noted above, in some cases, this may be imme-diately obvious, while in others, the officer may have to invoke Solomonic wisdom to make a fair decision. In some circumstances, a sort of hybrid between mediation and arbitration emerges when the officer presents a finite range of options for the disputants to choose among. If they can work out a solution from among these choices, fine. If not, the officer makes the call, period.

Decision Stage

At this stage, the officer actually determines what the resolution will be. In most cases, the decision should be rendered in the same meeting as the arbitration takes place. Sometimes the decision has to be deferred to give the officer time to gather outside information relevant to the dispute, to interview third parties, or just because the officer gets another call which takes priority. Remember, the goal is to resolve the issue as quickly and expeditiously as possible—but not at the expense of fairness.

Explanation Stage

The officer now carefully lays out his resolution to the disputants. It is vitally important that the officer be crystal clear about his or her decision, as people naturally tend to interpret any ambiguity in the direction of their own biases and agendas. The officer must be as detailed and specific as possible, so as to leave the least possible room for doubt. It's a good idea to have each disputant repeat the officer's decision in the officer's words and then in their own words. Finally, put it in writing, in language understandable by all, and have the disputants read it out loud to be sure they understand it. If possible, give each disputant a copy.

One or both disputants may request an explanation as to how the officer reached his decision. While you are not required to defend or justify your conclusions, you may, as a matter of respect and common courtesy, allow the disputants some insight into the basis for your decision; remember, the more understanding and buy-in shown by the two parties, the better chance of them abiding by the decision. But make it clear that the decision is binding, whether the disputants agree with your reasoning or not—making such a command decision is, after all, the primary function of arbitration.

The only exception to finality would be if some startlingly new piece of information emerges during the explanation stage, necessitating a return to fact-finding in order to ensure as much accuracy and fairness as possible. Typically, this should not take too much additional time to resolve, but remember, *fairness* is key, or the whole officer intervention concept loses its meaning. An officer can lawfully and authoritatively order citizens to do any number of things in the interests of maintaining order, but this is not necessarily conflict resolution, just a way of keeping the peace—for now. The processes of mediation and arbitration, in their ideal conflict-resolution roles, cannot be forced on unwilling disputants without their being seen as just another form of police authoritarianism. So if you decide to mediate or arbitrate, be prepared to do some mental and verbal heavy lifting that may require an investment of time and make good use of your people skills.

CONFLICT-RESOLUTION SKILLS FOR PATROL OFFICERS

In carrying out the kinds of mediation and arbitration processes described above, certain intervention skills are valuable for ensuring the success of the interaction (Cooper, 1999). As with all operational and behavioral skills, from firearms proficiency to hostage negotiation, some individuals will naturally be more talented than others, but virtually all officers can achieve adequate proficiency in these skills with proper training and practice. For patrol mediation and arbitration, the following general guidelines apply:

Utilize active listening skills. Active listening lets the speaker know that you are truly interested in understanding what he has to say, that it is important to you that he or she be heard. Active listening techniques include emotion labeling, paraphrasing, reflecting/mirroring, minimal encouragers, silence and pauses, I messages, and open- and closed-ended questions. Active listening is essential to managing conflicts ranging from minor neighborhood spats to life-and-death confrontations (Chapter 9-11).

Spot the issues. Skilled mediators are able to sift through a lot of complex and confusing information in order to zero-in on the key issues relevant to resolving the current dispute.

Transform raw data into manageable form. Once the core issues have been identified, the officer needs to be able to clarify them in his or her own mind. Only then can he or she begin to communicate these issues to each of the disputants. Try to be as clear about the issues in your own mind as possible before expressing them to the disputants. But also be aware that sometimes you may have to bounce the ideas off the disputants and get their feedback in order to further clarify your own thinking.

Articulate the issues. Here, the officer must be able to express the substance of the dispute clearly and concisely to the disputants. This is especially important during the caucusing phase, when it is vital that each side clearly understand the other's point of view. This can only happen if the mediating officer is able to express both sides clearly and fairly. Note that it is equally important to articulate areas of agreement as areas of conflict in order to create a foundation for productive problem solving.

Don't show favoritism. This may seem obvious in a situation where the officer is trying his best to mediate or arbitrate a fair decision; however, most of this type of bias is not deliberate, but may "leak out" subtly in words and body language because of similarities in age, sex, race, language, social class, and so on, between the officer and one of the disputants. Subconsciously, the officer may speak a little more calmly to one party, stand a little closer, make a little more eye contact, smile a little more at that person, allow that party a little more time to speak, and so on. Just as the commission of these interpersonal inequities may be subliminal, so may one of the parties' perception of it, which may result in the mediation going sour without anyone consciously realizing what happened. The only cure is for the officer to be as conscious as possible of any imbalances of this nature and to make a deliberate, conscious effort not to favor one party over the other.

Show cultural sensitivity. Bear in mind that persons from different cultures may have different attitudes and behaviors when it comes to voice volume, body proximity, gesturing, and beliefs regarding fairness and loss of face. Be aware of general cultural issues of the citizens in your patrol area and try to strike a balance in your communication style.

Don't take it personally. This is general advice when handling disputes on the street. As long as no crime or serious threat occurs, allow a certain amount of venting to blow off steam and expend adrenalin—even if the indignities are hurled at you. Remain professional and absorb the verbal blows. Maintain your poise and dignity, and usually the citizens will soon calm down and follow your example.

FURTHER COMMUNICATION SKILLS FOR PATROL OFFICERS

To round out the comprehensive list of verbal conflict resolution strategies that patrol officers can draw on, the following communication skills (Shea & Harpool, 1988) may added to the officer's psychological toolkit.

Attending skills include eye contact, attentive body language, and sensitivity to individual "cultural hints."

Expressive skills include deflective techniques, empathic responses, reflective techniques, and paraphrasing.

Questioning skills include open-ended questions for engagement, and closed-ended questions for specifics.

Process skills include the timing and pacing of communication and the appropriate use of questioning to ensure that the officer and other person are working together.

Summarizing skills include providing perspective and clarification, giving the officer the opportunity to feed back the overall content, message, or plan that has been heard or formulated.

CONCLUSIONS

Like any skill in police work, dealing assertively and nonviolently with citizens on patrol takes training and practice. Officers who are able to use these skills productively typically find that their respect in the community goes up. The citizens understand that the officer will not shrink from using force if he has to but that, all things being equal, he or she prefers to work things out nonaggressively and fairly. This then puts the ball in the citizen's court: "You make me take you down, I take you down, and you're gone. But first I'd like to try to pretend that we all have brains here, and see if we can settle this like adults. Your call."

As an added benefit, the more adept officers are at using verbal de-escalation techniques and conflict resolution skills, the fewer citizen complaints of excessive force or other uncivil behavior will plague the department (Chapter 13). Officers who are "good talkers" tend to pride themselves on their ability to handle virtually any kind of situation without putting themselves or others in physical danger. They feel more confident, not less, than the officer whose automatic response to every confrontation is to reach for the handcuffs, pepper spray, taser, or baton. Law enforcement agencies that are serious about community policing should make verbal skills training a standard part of their academy and continuing education curricula.

Chapter 3

CRISIS INTERVENTION STRATEGIES FOR
VIOLENCE ON PATROL

POTENTIALLY VIOLENT SUBJECTS: A REALITY OF POLICE PATROL

One theme of this book is that the best form of crisis intervention is crisis prevention. Preventing a violent episode from occurring forestalls the need for forceful arrest and minimizes the safety risk for the subject, the officer, and other citizens. If nothing else, think of all the paperwork you won't have to do. The following intervention techniques apply to any subject whose behavior appears at risk of escalating to violence.

Causes of Citizen-Officer Violence

Every officer has his or her own theory as to what causes a citizen-officer encounter to turn violent, but there have been only a few systematic studies of these factors to date (Binder & Scharf, 1980; Horstman, 1973; Reese, 1988; Russell & Beigel, 1990; Toch, 1977). To summarize, there appear to be two major kinds of circumstance in which officers are assaulted.

The first involves the citizen's perception of the initial verbal encounter as unnecessarily demeaning, as when the officer uses derogatory or disrespectful language or tone of voice ("He talked to me like I was a dog"); is physically intimidating ("He just got right up in my face"); does not want to consider the subject's side of the story ("He didn't ask me anything, he just assumed I did something wrong"); prematurely orders or physically moves the subject around ("He could've just asked me to step to the curb; he didn't have to shout at me and push me"); or humiliates the subject in public ("If

he wanted to search me, why couldn't he do it up on my porch instead of out on the sidewalk for all the neighbors to watch?").

The second situation in which officers are assaulted involves a compatriot of the citizen jumping in to "help" his friend in what he perceives to be unjust manhandling by the police officer. Although there will always be a small cadre of violence-prone citizens who react with hair-trigger aggression to even the most minimal provocation, clearly, a large number of violent episodes between police officers and citizens could be averted by the use of verbal de-escalation techniques, applied in the context of basic courtesy and good common sense.

Handling a Potentially Violent Episode

Unless there is an emergency, approach the subject slowly and cautiously. Try to size up the situation and analyze the scene as you get closer. Begin the encounter with tact, patience, and respect, but don't "play games" with a clearly defiant subject if he clearly has no intention of cooperating. Allow a few minutes for the subject to calm down. If the subject vents, listen to both the content and emotional tone of what's being said. Remember, nonviolent verbal venting uses up energy and adrenalin and also establishes a rudimentary form of communicative bond. But also remember that venting should not escalate to ranting, because the latter can inflame the subject's own emotional agitation and lead to physical violence.

30

Keep your tone and demeanor professional—don't take the bait with personal insults hurled at you, but calmly deflect these and return to the matter of calming down. You don't have to be a robocop; you can show a little human emotion and personality, and even a little humor, but be careful about overusing jokes, because disturbed subjects tend to be very literal and concrete, and your well-intended kidding around to lighten up the moment might be interpreted as mocking the subject. Again, use your perception and judgment of the situation to guide your behavior.

Avoid making any threats that you aren't prepared to back up. Use force as a last resort, but if it comes to that, use it swiftly, decisively, and as non-injuriously as possible. But first, always try to leave the subject a face-saving way out of his predicament: this will make his voluntary cooperation more likely. Also, remember about repeat customers: the next time you encounter this individual or his family and friends, do you want the first thing they recall about you to be how you shamed and humiliated the subject the last time you and he danced?

Some officers advocate applying a version of the old standby "Mutt & Jeff" interrogation room technique to the setting of the street interview. In this scenario, there are two officers, one who acts as the angry, hot-headed Officer Mutt, ready to bust the subject at a moment's notice, while the other plays the calm, cool and collected good-guy, Officer Jeff, who really wants to keep Mutt off the subject's back, if only the subject would cooperate. The problem is that, in such situations, it is all too easy for Mutt to take things too far, triggering a violent response in the subject. Again, use your training, judgment, and common sense.

JUVENILE SUBJECTS

From the switchblade-wielding "JD's" of the 1950s, to the 9mm-packing "boyz" of today, police have always had a special relationship with youthful offenders (Russell & Beigel, 1990; Schmallenger, 2002). Their young age makes these individuals especially brash and impulsive, while at the same time limiting the range of penalties available to the criminal justice system for deterring their behavior. Juveniles get much of their personal identity and self-esteem through their peers and may feel compelled to put on a tough attitude, to "not let those cops push me around." Also, for juveniles who have been mistreated by family members, school authorities, neighborhood merchants, and other adults, the police may become the symbolic surrogate authoritarian focal point for all their rage and resentment. Unfortunately, many of these youths may have had very unpleasant interactions with officers in the past, which only serves to further poison their attitude toward the next police encounter.

As with all citizens encountered on patrol, your interaction with juvenile subjects will have repercussions and ramifications for future officers who deal with these youths. This is all the more so for juveniles because their ideas, conceptions, and opinions of police may still be forming, and your interaction may have a much more powerful effect in influencing the youths' lifelong perception of the law and its representatives.

Dealing with Potentially Dangerous Juvenile Behavior

As with all citizens, your attitude should convey a combination of courtesy, respect, and firm, no-nonsense commitment to enforcing the law. Especially because juveniles are quick to size up adult insecurities, it is important to remember the difference between *authoritativeness* and *authoritarianism*—think of the contrasting styles of TV's Sheriff Andy Taylor and Deputy Barney Fife: calm, commanding presence vs. blustery, defensive posturing.

Part of respect is giving your full attention. No matter how young he is, actively listen to what the juvenile subject is saying. If he appears to be making lame excuses, take them seriously and explain why you do or do not accept his reasons. If more than one officer is present, avoid talking about the juvenile as if he's not there. Also, kids may be even more concrete and sensitive to disrespect than adults, so be careful about making even innocent, well-meaning jokes, which may be taken as an insult by the young subject.

In terms of actual enforcement, use your discretion. Strictness or leniency may depend on the subject or the situation. No one can tell you not to enforce the law, but there may be times that you feel that by overlooking a minor infraction, you may accrue a tremendous amount of goodwill that can lead to greater cooperation and less trouble in the future. On the other hand, you always have to be careful not to be played for a chump, thereby eroding your authority and encouraging future escalating lawlessness by showing the juvenile that he can get away with his misbehavior. As in most discretionary situations, use your training, your judgment, and your experience with the neighborhood culture of your patrol area.

Controlling Teenage Crowds

A common scenario that illustrates the role of crisis prevention involves groups of male teens who may be congregated in a particular area, as yet not necessarily engaged in any illegal activity, but comprising a volatile mix of adolescent hormones, boredom, immaturity, and impulsivity, perhaps fueled by alcohol or drug use. To complicate matters, there may be a rival group or gang in the neighborhood and the present crowd might be waiting for them to show up for a bop n' rumble. The size of such youthful crowds may range from a handful to dozens. Officers may receive a call based on a citizen complaint or they may come upon the scene in the course of their patrol. The officers' task is now to disperse this crowd before trouble escalates. Typically, dispersing and leaving are the last things these youths want to do.

The available literature (Broadfoot & Jones, 2005; Golden, 2004; Russell & Beigel, 1990; Schmallenger, 2002) allows the development of a composite model intervention protocol for dealing with potential juvenile aggression and youthful crowds, which should be flexibly adapted to the needs of each situation. To begin with, if nothing explosive has yet occurred, a little planning and preparation can make a big difference. When getting the call or coming upon the scene, decide how much backup will be needed and whether medical services might be required. Crowd control is almost never something a single officer should try to handle alone, although there may be exceptions in small communities where citizens and police are well known to one another. Too little backup risks the responding officers

being intimidated and overwhelmed. Too much of a show of force may give the impression of an invading armada, sparking anger and retaliation.

For a typical small or medium-sized crowd, have one or more officers slowly approach about eight to ten feet from the crowd's edge, while a few more officers hang back to observe the scene. Address the youths directly; don't talk about individuals in the third person as if they're not present. Opinions diverge on how best to deal with apparent ringleaders or big talkers in the crowd, who may be instigating trouble or advising the crowd to "stand up to these cops." Russell and Beigel (1990) advocate ignoring the leaders and engaging two or three peripheral group members in conversation to distract and deflect the crowd's attention from the leader. In my police academy training classes, most of the officers presented with this scenario tend to disagree. Their experience is that, essentially, "the best way to kill the beast is to chop off its head," that is, go directly for the leader and "talk him down or take him down." Still, whether dealing with the leader or peripheral group members, there is a better and worse way of doing this.

The worse way is to make an unnecessarily flashy show of force, humiliating the leader and virtually forcing him to resist you in order to save face in front of his minions. Remember, your agenda may be to neutralize him as quickly as possible, but at that moment he doesn't care about being arrested, physically restrained, or going to jail. All he's thinking about right now is: how's this gonna look in front of my people? And so he will fight to the bitter end, and the more force you need to subdue him, the more the crowd will become agitated and hostile, risking a full-scale riot.

If for no other reason than to avoid a slow burn becoming a conflagration and risking your own and others' safety, the better way of handling the situation is to confront either the leader or a peripheral member in a way that allows him to save face by contributing to the de-escalation of the situation–in a sense, making a treaty.

Your style of interaction should be firm but not grim, neither Officer Friendly nor Officer Hardass. If you have been called in response to a citizen complaint, there is no need to mention this fact, which will only give the crowd members something more to argue about. In general, explain but don't justify—that is, tell the crowd what you want them to do, but don't get into disputes about the rightness or wrongness of your request. If crowd members want to express their opinion in a reasonably civilized way, use a little reflective listening, if only to encourage the idea that dialogue is a viable alternative to force; however, be careful to observe the line between venting and ranting, and don't allow inflammatory speech to further incite the crowd.

If the youths are violating a specific law or ordinance, such as public safety, inform them of this and don't argue about it. If any further explanation is necessary, frame your actions in terms of ensuring everyone's safety. Don't lecture, sermonize, or admonish them; that's not your job here. Don't take it or make it personal. Make fact-based descriptive statements, and emphasize I-statements rather than you-statements: "Guys, this crowd is too big to be hanging out on this corner; it's not safe and it's violating Ordinance XYZ with regard to public safety. I need you to move away so people and cars can get by." *Not:* "This little party's getting out of hand. You guys better move or else."

Initially, state your instructions without consequences. Rather than rely on threats up front (which will probably have minimal effect anyway), convey the message that it is your authority as a police officer that is the primary justification for your directives. If crowd members continue to ignore or resist, then state the consequences clearly, and make sure you're prepared to back it up: "Guys, I told you what I need you to do. If you leave the area now, our business is done. But if you don't start moving out, we're going to make arrests. So what's it gonna be, guys, we gonna have an easy night here or not?" As in most situations, don't lie—remember the rule about repeat customers: you'll probably be dealing with these kids again.

DOMESTIC DISPUTES

The "community" of community policing includes not just the streets and public places of civic life, but sometimes the intimate inner lives and territories of home and family. There is an instinctive reluctance to intrude into the physical and psychological private spaces of a person's homestead, but for police officers to uphold the law and to protect victims, this sometimes becomes necessary.

Police Response to Domestic Calls: Facts and Stats

There must be reasons why most cops loathe and dread intervening in family disputes more than almost any other kind of police work (Blau, 1994; Russell & Beigel, 1990). Part of the reason no doubt inheres in the interpersonally demanding aspects of such calls. The response to a domestic call does not always require an arrest, unless violence has been committed. Thus, sorting out and calming down a domestic dispute—essentially performing crisis intervention, mediation, and arbitration, all in the midst of a chaotic scene that may involve adults, children, intoxicated subjects, and potentially hidden weapons—stretches an officer's communication and diplomacy skills to the limit. If an officer is not already somewhat experienced and comfortable in using these skills, this will prove to be a painfully challenging call. In self-defense, many officers consider domestic calls not to be "real" police work; or more prosaically, to be "bullshit calls."

Additionally, intervening in domestic disputes resonates with the personal experiences of many officers, whose own family lives may have been and/or continue to be far from idyllic (Chapter 15). Thus, the personal identification factor is especially strong for this kind of police work: "Jeez, this crazy family sounds like the fighting that goes on in my house." Not surprisingly, then, the group role-plays in my police academy training classes that involve simulated domestic dispute intervention typically elicit the greatest amount of nervous joking among the participants; indeed, it is virtually impossible to get through one of these enactments without the group defensively cracking up numerous times—because it's all too close.

Not all concerns are unfounded, however. Domestic disturbance calls remain among the most dangerous police interventions from the perspective of potential officer injury, and about a third of these calls involve a violent crime. People are typically in an extreme emotional state, often intoxicated, rarely rational, and therefore most prone to suspend judgment and caution and to assault an officer. The paradox is that, because many officers regard these as candyass calls, they may be even less likely to take appropriate precautions than they would in responding to a robbery in progress or even a suspicious traffic stop. Recall, too, that domestic disturbance calls can easily escalate to assault, murder, or hostage and barricade situations, thereby posing further danger to officers and civilians.

Overall, the most frequent type of response to domestic disturbance calls is no action taken, probably (hopefully!) because the responding officers have been able to resolve the situation before physical violence and an arrestable offense take place. Alternatively, the situation has spontaneously cooled, or one party has left the scene, by the time the officers arrive. Of course, when domestic assault has occurred, officers are mandated to make an arrest. Domestic battery tends to be a repeat crime, and as much as a psychologically-oriented book like this one would like to say that talking and counseling will resolve such situations and influence a batterer to give up his evil ways, the fact is that arrest of the perpetrator is what usually has the strongest deterrent effect on recidivism. The time for talking is before violence has occurred; once the attacker has made his move—committed his crime—officers must use the necessary force and restraint to take the offender into custody.

Unfortunately, those batterers most likely to "learn their lesson" from such an arrest action are those least likely to be repeat offenders. That is, they are ordinarily nonviolent, law-abiding, well-educated, and gainfully employed citizens who have something substantial to lose from being arrested and prosecuted for a crime. Typically, the domestic assault was a one-time overreaction by a distraught person, not a recurring pattern of behavior. For the chronic repeat offender, however, even multiple arrests are not likely to be an effective deterrent, nor will the abuse be stopped by restraining orders or any other measures, short of incarceration of the offender or the spouse extricating herself from the relationship and getting as far away as possible.

As noted above, once a domestic assault has occurred, officers are mandated to take the necessary arrest action. But like all of the police response scenarios discussed in this book, having an interpersonal skill-set to use in family dispute and domestic violence calls can greatly decrease the potential for escalation and the necessity for making arrests or using physical force in a subject's home. As always, the best form of crisis intervention is crisis prevention. In addition, the tact and sensitivity—or lack of it—with which officers handle domestic dispute calls will resonate with the household and the community and will influence citizens' subsequent interactions with the police. Therefore, it is useful to have some perspective on how citizens perceive local law enforcement responses to their domestic conflict calls.

Citizen Dissatisfaction with Police Domestic Violence Response

Just such constructive criticism was solicited in a study by Kennedy and Homant (1984), who surveyed the reactions of a group of citizens who had called police to respond to a domestic crisis. They found that citizen dissatisfaction with officer response to domestic violence calls could be sorted into several categories:

Minimizing the situation. Citizens were distressed when responding officers seemed to play down the seriousness of the assault or severity of the injuries: "That just looks like a scratch; it's not even hardly bleeding much." "He only hit you once with the plate? Was it a ceramic or a plastic plate?"

Disbelieving the victim. Citizens felt that officers treated them as if they were lying or at least exaggerating: "You sure that bruise is new? It looks like something you might've bumped into a few days ago. Sometimes you can bang your arm and not even realize it." "Well, if you say he's been beating on you all afternoon, how come you waited till now to call us?"

Uncaring attitude. Victims felt like the officers were "just going through the motions" of taking the report, giving the impression that they had any number of better things to do than to waste their time on this domestic call. This attitude was conveyed by distracted attention, disinterested or skeptical tone of voice, minimal eye contact, and often cross-talk, knowing glances, and joking with other officers or civilians on the scene, sometimes even including the accused perpetrator.

Macho cop. Officers sometimes (defensively?) adopted a tough, no-nonsense, "just-the-facts-ma'am" attitude, without showing a trace of concern or consideration for the distraught emotional state of the victim. In fact, these officers seemed to get annoyed when victims broke down with emotion or failed to give an orderly narrative of events that the officer could record.

Little or no practical information provided. Citizens were dismayed that many officers failed to offer practical information or guidance about victims' shelters, legal and financial support services, the procedures for filing complaints, obtaining restraining orders, and so on. Often, when victims asked these questions directly, they received disdainful shrugs or don't-know responses, or officers who were persuaded to yield this information gave the impression that this was one more imposition on their time.

The common thread in these officer reactions seems to be a mixture of distaste for the domestic call itself and contemptuous disregard for the victims. As noted earlier, one reason for this may be the defensively macho orientation of many cops who regard victims as "losers," no matter where the fault lies, and are thus fearful of their own unconscious identification with the victim. Therefore, they distance themselves psychologically by downplaying the seriousness of the harm and/or denigrating the victim's motives and reactions.

However, the Kennedy and Homant (1984) study did find that some citizens expressed satisfaction at responding officers' actions when these actions could be characterized as *small human acts of caring and consideration.* These included an engaged, interested interpersonal style; waiting for the victim to tell her whole story; questioning the victim to make sure the officer understood what she was saying; providing follow-up information and referrals; offering to call social services for the victim; and even making a follow-up call a few days later to check how the victim was doing. Citizens who got this, unfortunately much rarer, form of police response reported overwhelmingly more positive views of their local law enforcement agency. The general lesson for community policing is obvious: treating citizens with respect applies both to public and private venues, and includes both suspects and victims. More specific lessons for practical crisis intervention in domestic disturbance calls are as follows.

Domestic Crisis Intervention: Assessment and Approach

Based on the experiences of law enforcement officers and behavioral science practitioners, a number of recommendations have evolved (Garner, 2005; Russell & Beigel, 1990; Sanders, 1997).

The response to a domestic disturbance call–indeed any call–typically begins with the dispatcher's communication to available officers. Officers should try to obtain as much information about the disputants as possible, as this will partly determine the nature of their response. Have there been previous calls to this residence? What happened? Are there likely to be weapons in the home? Are drugs and alcohol likely to be involved? Are there children or other vulnerable family members or residents in the home? In general, the more information, the better, so that officers can plan their response.

And plan they should. No matter how "routine" the call seems, and no matter how often the officers have been through this scenario before, they should always have some sort of front-end and back-up plan for the response. At least it should be determined how many officers will respond. For a very simple call, only two responders may be necessary. Where the potential for violence exists, several vehicles and officers may respond. Also, be prepared to call for medical assistance in case of injury. Be aware that a domestic disturbance carries a high potential for escalation, and never treat it as a bullshit call.

When you arrive at the residence, first assess the scene from your vehicle. Unless this is an emergency requiring immediate entry, take a minute to drive by to check out the surrounding neighborhood. Park a little away from the house, if possible, so the intervention doesn't seem like a sudden blitz. Approach the residence with full caution. Try to look through the windows to get a sense of what's going on inside. If the disputants are outside the house or in the street, try to move them inside, or onto the property. At the very least, segregate them from any onlookers or neighbors. When you announce your presence, don't stand directly in front of the door. Introduce yourselves, using your full name and police title. Make it clear who you are and what you're there for.

Domestic Crisis Intervention: Interpersonal Strategies

Once inside, position yourself between the conflicting parties. If possible, have one officer interview one disputant, and the second officer interview the other party, with one or more additional officers maintaining vigilance on the scene, watching out for kids, and so on. If possible, separate the disputants so that they're out of vision and earshot from each other. If this is not possible, at least insist that one person speak at a time: recall the ground rules for mediation and arbitration discussed in Chapter 2. Exclude third parties from the discussion, unless it is clear that the third party is indispensable to figuring out the dispute and/or coming up with a solution. Even then, try to interview the third party separately.

Always maintain the highest vigilance and awareness; always be making a safety assessment. Scan the environment for weapons or ordinary objects (scissors, lamp, rope) that could be used as weapons. If possible, interview the disputants in relatively safe and "soft" rooms like bedrooms or living rooms, rather than more dangerous and "hard" rooms like kitchens or garages that are likely to contain hard surfaces, sharp instruments, or heavy tools. Vigilance also applies to your own weapon and utilities. Never let your attention wander from the disputants' hands. Also watch their body language. Always inquire as to who else may be in the house and always maintain awareness of others entering or leaving the scene.

By your own body language, tone of voice, and content of your speech, try to create a calm, nonconfrontational atmosphere, and emphasize that you are there to help solve the problem. Your initial position should be fair but firm: "Look, I understand you're both upset, and we're here to help, but if either of you gets violent or commits a crime, we *will* arrest you, okay? So let's see if we can settle this without more trouble." Ask the disputants to sit down, and then sit down yourself, again always remembering to maintain vigilance for possible signs of danger. Show appropriate courtesy and respect by giving the parties your undivided attention and

taking their comments seriously, making written notes, if possible, and using other effective interpersonal interview skills.

Try to ascertain the facts, i.e., who made the call, are there restraining orders in force, has a crime been committed, etc. If no mandatory arrestable crime has yet been committed, try to get the parties to resolve their dispute, or agree to separate for the rest of the day, or until the next morning, till they cool off. Often, one disputant or the other will try to get the officers on their side; sometimes the man if it's another male officer ("You know how these women get, man—what choice did I have?"), or the woman, if she made the original call ("I called you here to help me—what are you going to do about this?"). Make every effort to allow both parties to save face, so one side doesn't feel defeated by the other, which will only lead to retaliatory trouble later on.

If the parties have trouble calming down, ask diversionary reality questions to tone down the hostility and anger, e.g., "How old are your kids? Where do they go to school? They doing okay? What's your son want to be when he grows up?" But as always, don't make it obvious that you are trying to change the subject, which may make the speaker feel disrespected. Use your judgment.

Domestic Crisis Intervention: Medication and Arbitration

Like many of the dispute resolution scenarios in this chapter and in this book, domestic conflicts can often be addressed using the mediation and arbitration strategies described earlier (Cooper, 1999; Goldstein, 1977). Recall from Chapter 2 that the goal of the *mediation* process is to help disputants solve their own problem rather than trying to solve it for them. In the cases of domestic disputes, mediation would involve the following steps:

Step 1. The officer makes the offer to mediate the domestic dispute, informing the disputants that they must solve the problem themselves, but that the officer will help them clarify the issues so that a fair settlement can be reached.

Step 2. Each side conveys their version of events. Officers may have to actively solicit suggestions from the disputants as to how to best resolve the crisis.

Step 3. The officer restates the key points conveyed by each side, so that everybody is on the same page, understanding-wise, even if there is not yet complete agreement.

Step 4. Possible solutions to the domestic dispute are brainstormed and discussed, the officer utilizing shuttle diplomacy, probably in combination with other officers at the scene of the domestic dispute.

Step 5. Some agreement is reached, and the officer encourages follow-through to the agreed-upon solution.

If mediation has proven ineffective, or if it clear from the outset that either or both of the disputants are too angry, agitated, fearful, irrational, or inebriated to productively participate in a mediation, *arbitration* may then be the strategy of choice. As noted previously, this generally involves four stages:

Fact-Finding Stage. The officer tries to ascertain as much as possible about the situation that led up to the domestic dispute, emphasizing recent triggers rather than long-term relationship factors, unless the latter are pertinent to directly dealing with the present conflict.

Analysis Stage. The officer attempts to come to as clear an understanding as possible as to what set off the present conflict and what measures will be most effective for resolving it for now. In the context of a domestic crisis, much of this brainstorming may take place with the collaboration of other officers who are interviewing family members and other parties to the dispute.

Decision Stage. The brainstorming officers come up with the fairest and safest decision that will resolve the crisis for now.

Explanation Stage. The officer or officers convey their decision to the two parties, emphasizing that this decision is binding, as originally agreed upon by the disputants. In many cases, the alternative to accepting the officers' decision may be more drastic measures, such as arrest of one or both parties, protective removal of children from the home, and so on. It is also important to make recommendations for follow-up services to minimize the chances of a recurring crisis.

CRIME VICTIMS

As first responders, it might seem obvious that police officers are in a unique position to help crime victims deal with the impact of their ordeal, to help restore a sense of safety and control to an otherwise fearful and overwhelming situation. Officers can also make a big difference in how a subsequent criminal investigation is handled and in the confidence—or lack of it—that victims, their families, and the larger community have in their police department's ability to protect them.

Police officers themselves may not even be aware of the tremendous impact they have on crime victims, but those victims often report that the treatment they received in the immediate aftermath of a crime greatly influenced their future perceptions of, and interactions with, law enforcement, as well as their ability to move on with their lives. Victims who receive the support they need—starting with law enforcement's first responders—not only recover more quickly, but will be more inclined to fully cooperate with the subsequent investigation and prosecution of the crime. They are also more likely to work with the police officers in their neighborhoods in other, more general, aspects of crime control and community policing. In short, properly supported victims become more effective and more willing participants in the criminal justice system (Herman, 2002).

Yet many officers feel somewhat uncomfortable dealing with crime victims on-scene, partly as a result of individual factors and partly due to lack of training. With regard to the latter, this section will offer some practical guidelines.

The Psychology of Crime Victimization

Each year, more than 25 million people in the US are victimized by crime (Herman, 2002). Russell and Beigel (1990) conceive of crime victimization as comprising several layers in relation to a person's core self. For example, a property crime like a burglary generally hurts victims only at the outermost self-layer, i.e., their belongings, although the theft of certain meaning-laden family heirlooms can have a much greater emotional impact. An armed robbery, which involves personal contact with the criminal and threat to the physical self of the victim, invades a deeper psychological layer. Assault and battery penetrates still deeper, injuring the victim both physically and psychologically. A crime like rape goes to the very core of the self, harming far more than the body and affecting the victim's basic beliefs, values, emotions, and sense of safety in the world.

Society's response to crime also plays a role in how supported or helpless victims feel (Russell & Beigel, 1990). For example, when a child comes home from school and tells his parents that the teacher was mean and made him sit in the corner, a common parental response is to inquire, "What did you do to make the teacher punish you?" From experiences such as this, many people grow up thinking that if something bad happens, they deserved it. Also, taking the blame for something, even if you logically know it's not your own fault, is often a more existentially reassuring stance than having to believe that something this terrible can just happen for no reason—because, if there's nothing you did to contribute to it, then there's nothing you can do that will prevent it from happening again, or from something even worse happening, any time, anywhere (Miller, 1998a, 1998b, 2001).

Society often regards victimization as contagious. In modern American culture, with its emphasis on fierce competition for limitless success and "having it all," victims are often equated with losers. Most of us want to believe that crime victimization is something that happens to somebody else. The victim must have done something to bring it on

him or herself, otherwise, I'm just as vulnerable too, and who wants to believe that? We may thus be reluctant to associate with the victims for fear that their bad luck will "rub off." All of these beliefs and reactions further contribute to the feelings of blame and shame that many crime victims experience (Miller, 1998a, 1998b, 2001).

Effects of Crime on Victims and Survivors

First responders, such as police officers, may face a confusing scenario when arriving at a crime scene (Herman, 2002; Miller, 1998a). Traumatized victims may be in a state of shock and disorientation during the initial stage of the crisis reaction. Crime victims have experienced a situation totally beyond their control, and most will feel helpless, vulnerable, and frightened. Other victims may be in a state of flight-or-fight panic, and some will actually try to flee the scene of the crime. Some victims may be combative with arriving police officers, adding to the confusion as to who is the victim and who is the offender. In some instances, physical and emotional paralysis occur, rendering the victim unable to make rational decisions, speak coherently, or even move purposefully, much less seek medical attention or report an incident to the police.

Long-term psychological effects of crime victimization include persisting anxiety, depression, phobic avoidance, physical symptoms, substance abuse, PTSD, shattered sense of safety and security, "mean world syndrome," cynicism, and distrust. Victims may be unable to function normally at their jobs or family life (Miller, 1998a, 1998b, 2001). Indeed, much of the lasting impact of crime victimization depends on the actions of first responders in the immediate postimpact minutes, hours, and days. That's why law enforcement's proper handling of crime scenes and victims is so important.

ON-SCENE LAW ENFORCEMENT CRISIS INTERVENTION WITH VICTIMS OF CRIME

What Crime Victims Say They Need from Police

Police officers sometimes complain that when they try to help crime victims at the scene, their efforts

are often misinterpreted or unappreciated. So it might be useful to go "right to the source(s)" and find out what crime victims themselves would find helpful from a police response to a crime. In a study of crime victims' feelings, perceptions, and wishes with regard to police interactions at the scene, Herman (2002) found that these victims are often very clear about what they feel they most need from the initial police contact at the crime scene. The responses tend to cluster in three categories.

First, crime victims need to *regain a sense of safety and control*. They want the responding officer to interview them in a safe, quiet location, preferably away from the site of the trauma. They want to be reassured of their safety, that the immediate crisis is over and that the perpetrator can't harm them again. They would like the officer to speak in a calm, reassuring voice, not pepper them with questions in a brusque, staccato tone. They especially don't want officers stating or implying judgments about what the victim could or should have done before, during, or after the crime; victims feel bad enough without these recriminations.

Second, victims need some time to vent, to *talk about their experience*. For most victims, this is the most horrible things that has ever happened to them, and they need the opportunity to describe the event at their own pace and in their own way. This may prove frustrating to investigators who are eager to get "the facts" as quickly as possible. Although some gentle prodding and guiding may be appropriate to keep the narrative on track, officers should hold their questions or comments until the victims have finished telling their story. The presentation may be emotional and rambling, as it often is with individuals under extreme stress, but ultimately, officers will get a more complete picture if they let the victim tell it her way. What officers can and should do is reassure, normalize, and validate the victim's experiences and reactions so that she does not feel even more stigmatized by thinking she's acting crazy or being a crybaby for expressing her feelings.

Third, victims need to know how to *access additional support*. Officers should describe the upcoming steps in the criminal investigation and legal proceedings. Without further frightening the victim, they should inform her of the possibility that emotional "delayed reactions" may occur over the next few days and, importantly, new memories of the crime may emerge, in which case you want her to feel confident enough in you that she'll be willing to call you with such additional information. Indeed, victims themselves say they'd like officers to make the first move in encouraging further contact

with law enforcement, since victims often feel embarrassed or intimidated to call on their own; some don't want to be seen as a "pest."

Finally, victims are frightened, confused, and in pain, and most of them understand that there's a limit to what the responding officer can do in his law enforcement role. So victims want to be referred to community services and other agencies that are set up for crime victim assistance. Taking the time to ensure that the victim knows what comes next and what to do about it is a big plus in police-victim and police-community relationships.

On-Scene Crisis Intervention

The first point of contact between responding officers and crime victims is often at the crime scene itself, although this contact may take place in an ambulance or emergency room if the victim is already receiving medical care. Here, the officer is confronted with a victim whose emotional behavior may run the gamut from numbed unresponsiveness to raw panic. Aside from providing medical and psychological first aid, a frequent practical task of the first responder is to obtain as much information as possible from the victim about the crime itself in order to maximize the possibility of apprehending the perpetrator(s), preventing further violence, and planning for aid to other potential victims. Balancing concern for victim welfare and the need to obtain detailed information is thus a delicate dance and requires some degree of interpersonal skill on the part of the investigator. The following are some practical recommendations for officers who have to deal with crime victims on-scene (Clark, 1988; Frederick, 1986; Miller, 1998a; Silbert, 1976).

First, *introduce yourself by name and full title* to the victim and bystanders. Even if you are in uniform, have a picture ID tag, or clearly "look like a cop," the victim may be too distraught to understand who you are. You may need to repeat the introduction several times. Remember that victims who are still in shock may respond to you as if you are the criminal, especially if you arrived quickly on the scene. Children traumatized by adults may respond with fear to any new adult in their environment.

The first priority is to make sure any *physical injuries get treated*. In fact, with serious injuries, any further law enforcement interaction may have to be deferred to the hospital after the victim's medical condition has been stabilized. Yet a substantial number of mugging, robbery, and even sexual assault victims may have few or no significant physical injuries, at least not ones that are immediately detectable. If the direct victim is the child or other family member of the interviewee, the parent or relative may be physically untouched, but emotionally in shock at the attack against their loved one.

Sometimes you may have to *apply first aid* until further medical help arrives. If this is the case, calmly explain what you're doing, especially when you are touching the victim or doing an otherwise intimate procedure, such as applying a breathing mask, or removing clothing. If possible, let the victim help you treat her if she wants. This may be as simple as having her hold a bandage on her arm or letting her undo her own clothing, but it can offer a much-needed quick restoration of a sense of control in a situation where the victim is otherwise reeling in a state of helpless disorientation. In particular, many children respond well to this "helping" maneuver. Other victims may be so paralyzed with fear that they "forget" how to do simple things like untying shoelaces or unbuttoning a shirt.

Also related to restoration of control is *respect for the victim's wishes* whenever reasonable. If, for example, the victim wants a family member or friend to remain with her during treatment or questioning, let that person stay. Don't take offense if the victim refuses to let you touch, treat, or even talk to her: you may look, act, speak, smell, or have the same name as the perpetrator. Youthful victims are often unable to express their fears and may just flail or shout for you to "get away from me!" Perhaps another member of the law enforcement or emergency response team can interview the victim more comfortably.

After ascertaining that the victim is physically intact and in sufficient emotional shape to even have a conversation, *briefly verify the crime:* "Please tell me what happened to you. Did it happen here or in another location?" Do whatever you can to secure the crime scene while calling for appropriate backup. If possible, remove the victim from the scene to a safer or more neutral location. Be sensitive and tactful with onlookers and media, and cooperate with paramedics and other vital responders.

Avoid even unintentional accusatory or incriminatory statements such as "What were you doing in that building so late at night?" These not only needlessly upset and retraumatize the victim, but also erode trust, making further interview and treatment attempts extremely difficult. Try not to overuse platitudes such as "It's okay" or "Everything will be all right," which will doubtless sound hollow and insincere to a victim whose world has just been shattered. More helpful are *simple, supportive, concrete statements* such as "It's okay now. We're going to go to a safe place so you can tell us what happened."

Avoid statements or implications indicating to an adolescent or young adult victim that you think he or she should "act your age." Most people don't behave normally when they've been victimized, and many crime victims may regress to childlike behavior immediately after the incident. In such cases, *simple, nonjudgmental statements* such as "I can understand why you're upset" or "What can I do to help?" can ease the victim's distress. Always try to validate the traumatic ordeal the victim has been through and reinforce, as realistically as possible, his or her resilience and coping efforts thus far: "I can see this must have been a horrible experience for you. Most people would be feeling pretty much like you are under these circumstances. But I'm glad to see you're handling it as well as you are." Build on the victim's own resources to *increase his or her feelings of self-efficacy and control.*

Related to the issue of restoring control is having some kind of *clear plan* to provide further structure and control to an otherwise overwhelming situation. You don't have to feel bound to follow the plan to the letter if contingencies change, but some structure is almost always better than none. It's also useful to back up this plan with concrete suggestions for action: "We're going to move to a safe areas, have the medics take care of this laceration, then I'm going to ask you a couple of questions, if that's all right. After I'm done, I'm going to explain what happens next in the police process and legal area, then I'll give you a card with some phone numbers of victims' assistance agencies you can contact. I'm also going to give you my card, and you can contact me at any time for any reason. Do you have any questions?"

Even the most hardboiled investigator should understand that a *sympathetic, supportive, and non-judgmental approach* can do much to restore the crime victim's trust and confidence and thereby facilitate all aspects of the case. So listen to the victim if she wants to talk, even if she digresses, rambles, or strays off topic. Let her express emotion if she has to "get it all out." At the other extreme, tolerate silence without feeling compelled to jump in with a question or comment. At this stage, don't press for more detail than necessary for purposes of immediate treatment or case investigation—crime victims will be forced to tell their stories again and again as the investigation proceeds.

On-scene, use a *combination of open-ended and closed-ended questioning*: "Can you remember what your attacker looked like? Tell me. About what age was he? What race do you think he was? Was he taller than me? Was he thin or stocky? What else can you remember? That's all right—take your time." Always *provide assurances of safety*, and repeat as often as necessary. Also utilize active listening techniques, such as reflective, clarifying, and summarizing statements to let the victim know you understand her and to assure that her information is understood correctly by you.

If the victim seems to be getting more and more agitated, disoriented, or frightened during her narrative, employ *diversionary reality questions*. These serve to defocus the victim's attention from the most horrifying aspects of the event, while keeping the topic related to the subject in question, for example:

Victim: The guy who jumped me on the shop floor was a new hire. I never saw it coming. He just started beating me. They never check the background of these new guys. We're all going to be killed here. We're all dead sooner or later. . . .

Officer: How many people work here?

Employ humor judiciously. A well-placed witticism may put some perspective on the crisis and ease an otherwise tense situation, but many victims are very literal and concrete under stress, and well-meaning humor may be mistaken for mocking or lack of serious concern. As with all such recommendations, use your judgment.

Never overlook the interpersonal power of a *reassuring presence, both verbally and nonverbally*. Pro-

vide a model of composure for the victim to emulate. Eye contact should be in the manner of a concerned, connected gaze; neither a detached glance nor a fixed stare-down. Stand close enough to the victim to provide proxemic contact comfort, but don't crowd or intimidate by invading the victim's personal space. Use physical touch carefully. Sometimes a brief tap on the shoulder or comforting grasp of the hand can be very reassuring, but it may frighten a victim who has just been physically assaulted. Take your cue from the victim.

One technique I've found useful for both direct victims and distressed responders during critical incidents is what I call the *therapeutic hand-clasp*, which can be adapted to a regular handshake for both men and women, or a more supportive handhold, usually for female victims or responders. For a subject who feels they're losing control, ask them to squeeze your hand and sort of mentally transfer the overwhelming emotions to the physical activity:

Intervener: Okay, just squeeze my hand, put the fear into my hand, just hold on and let it drain into my hand like an electric current, like you're discharging a battery. Feel yourself relax as the fear drains away. That's it, all the excess fear and tension is flowing out of you: you can handle this, you're getting stronger, you'll make it, you'll be okay. All right, take a deep breath, and let go slowly when you're ready.

At subsequent intervals during the critical incident, this technique can be repeated silently and unobtrusively when necessary, appearing like a normal handshake. With practice, it can be internalized so all the subject has to do is think about it, or clench his or her own fist to re-evoke the positive feeling. The technique is simple to use and relies on the basic therapeutic principles of psychological suggestion, human physical contact, and interpersonal support.

Other kinds of body activity can be therapeutic. To break the sense of physical and mental paralysis that often accompanies posttraumatic numbing, have the victim take a little walk with you, let her get a drink of water, give her some simple but useful task to perform. Just being able to move one's body around in a productive way can sometimes restore a feeling of efficacy and control: "See, my legs work, I can move my hands, I'm not a complete basket case." Even where there has been a limiting physical injury, there is almost always some activity or body function that the victim can perform. Anything that will show the victim that there's some shred of normality left, that something still "works," contributes to a sense of safety and hope.

With extremely distraught or disoriented victims, you may have to provide a *breakthrough stimulus* to capture the person's attention. This may involve shouting, making a loud noise, or gently shaking the severely traumatized victim to "break the spell" of dissociation that he or she is in (Everstine & Everstine, 1993). This technique should be reserved for situations where it is an emergency matter to get the subject's attention and cooperation, such as getting out of a dangerous area quickly. Otherwise, you may risk further traumatizing an already overfrightened victim. P.S. Forget about slapping: that's for the movies and almost never works in real life; besides, you could risk a lawsuit. No cold water in the face, either; but giving the victim a sip of a cold drink often helps.

Sometimes you may have to physically restrain a traumatized victim or others at the scene for their own protection. Here, however, you should think more in terms of *containment* than restraint per se. Sometimes people who are out of control will derive a primitive sense of safety and peace by being enveloped in a cocoon of benevolent external containment. Use the minimum force and restraint necessary, for example, wrapping in a blanket as opposed to handcuffs. Again, remember that if the subject is not actually being arrested, physical restraint should be used as a last resort, and only in the interest of the subject's own safety.

Another technique that often works with severely traumatized victims can be referred to as *augmented behavioral mirroring*. For example, if a victim is sitting on a curb or on a hospital cot, rocking rhythmically back and forth, humming to herself, gradually imitate and replicate her movements, until both of you are in a comfortable rhythm, and then augment with the repeated phrase, "It's all right, you're safe. It's all right, you're safe" (Everstine & Everstine, 1993). Once again, these types of specialized techniques should be reserved for extreme situations.

Death Notification

A frequently neglected topic in the criminal justice and mental health treatment process is the nature of proper notification of family members that a loved one has been killed or that the body of a missing relative has been located and identified. Though not a routine police patrol function, officers in the homicide investigation division of their departments may be called upon to make such notifications as part of their duties. In other jurisdictions, special crisis outreach workers make the call, or it is something undertaken by supervisors or administrative staff. Most officers dread this kind of assignment for good reason: it is unpleasant, stressful, and emotionally draining. However, like all of the law enforcement activities in this book, the task of death notification can be made more effective and tolerable by understanding a few basic principles and implementing a few key strategies. For the present discussion, a thoughtful and practical death notification protocol is adapted from several sources (Dewey-Kollen, 2005; Hendricks, 1984; Spungen, 1998).

To begin with, always *go in person.* Unless there is absolutely no other choice, death notification should never be made over the phone. *Go in pairs,* and decide who will be the lead person, the one who's job it will be to actually say the words and give the bad news. The other team member provides backup support, monitors the survivors for adverse reactions, and provides temporary supervision of young children during the notification, if needed. If no one is home when you get there, wait a reasonable amount of time. If you are queried by a neighbor, ask about the family's whereabouts, but don't reveal the purpose of your visit to anyone but the immediate family. If the family still doesn't show up, leave a card with a note and a number to call. When the call comes, return to the family's home to make the notification.

Needless to say, make sure you have the correct family and residence. This may seem obvious, but under circumstances of stress and confusion, or where the name is unfamiliar or too familiar (Smith, Jones, etc.), it may be easy to confuse the victim's residence with someone else's. When you do arrive, ask for permission to enter. Suggest that family members sit down face-to-face with you. *Get to the point quickly and state the information simply and directly.* If the facts are clear, don't leave room for doubt or false hope. You needn't be brutally blunt or insensitive, but try to use straight language and avoid euphemisms. Use the deceased's name or his or her relationship to the family member being informed, for example, "We're sorry to have to bring you this terrible news, Mrs. Jones. Your daughter, Mary, was killed in a convenience store robbery by suspects who we're actively trying to apprehend. Mary and her personal effects are at Municipal hospital."

Allow time for the news to sink in. It may be necessary to *repeat the message* several times in increasingly clear and explicit terms. Tolerate silence and be prepared for the calm to be broken by sudden explosions of grief and rage. *Intense reactions* should be physically restrained only if there is some danger to self or others. Other family members may embrace you and literally cry on your shoulder. Be prepared to tastefully and respectfully offer this physical solace, if necessary.

In the face of outright denial, be as gentle as possible but make it clear that the death has in fact occurred. *Answer all questions tactfully and truthfully,* but don't reveal more information than is necessary at that time. Repeat the answers to questions as many times as necessary. Try to be as calm and supportive, as comforting and empathic as possible. Let the tone and cadence of your voice register the appropriate amount of respect and dignity, but don't become overly maudlin or lose control yourself. Death notifications are not rush calls: be prepared to spend as much time as necessary with the family.

Offer to make phone calls to family, friends, neighbors, employers, clergy, doctors, and so on. Ask family members if they want you to get someone to stay with them. Respect the family's privacy, but don't leave a family member alone unless you're sure he or she is safe. High emotionality can impair memory, so *give pertinent information and instructions in writing.* Provide family members with the names and telephone numbers of a victim advocate, prosecutor, medical examiner, social service agency, and hospital; try to consolidate all the information onto one sheet. Many departments have printed information cards for this purpose.

Explain to family members what will happen next, e.g., body identification, police investigation,

and criminal justice procedures. If this is a high-profile case, brief them on how to handle the media. Give family members as much information as they ask for, without overwhelming them. Repeat the information as many times as needed.

Determine if the family members require some *means of traveling* to the medical examiner's office, hospital, or police station. Offer to drive them or arrange for a ride if they have no transportation. Be sure to provide for a ride back home, and try to assist them with babysitting arrangements and other needs. If the notifying team is made up of police personnel and a victim advocate, the advocate may remain with the family members after the police leave.

Body Identification

The finality of identifying the deceased's body can have a paradoxically dual effect. On the one hand, there is the confrontation with the victim's remains and the final shattering of any hope that he or she may still be alive. On the other hand, the actual sight of the deceased often provides a strange sort of reassuring confirmation that the victim's death agonies may actually have fallen short of the survivor's imagined horrors, and even if not, that the physical presence of the body at least means that the victim's suffering is finally over (Dewey-Kollen, 2005; Rynearson, 1988, 1994, 1996; Rynearson & McCreery, 1993). Outcome studies of relatives after a death from natural causes report shorter periods of denial and higher total recall of the deceased in mourners who were able to view the body prior to burial (Sprang & McNeil, 1995); whether this applies to cases of traumatic bereavement such as murder has not been systematically studied.

Like death notification, body identification is not usually a routine patrol officer function, but all law enforcement personnel who assist in this activity should be guided by a few basic principles. Dewey-Kollen (2005) and Spungen (1998) provide useful guidelines for helping survivors through the process of body identification.

Unless there is a legal requirement or restriction, *let survivors make* the choice as to whether they want to view their loved one's remains. Some family members may be anxious or intimidated about making or declining such a request or articulating their wishes, so ask them directly. In cases where it is forensically essential to involve the family in the identification process, as when the victim has been missing for a long time, be sure to provide the appropriate support.

Family members may want to *touch the deceased*. For some, it may be a way of beginning to accept the reality of the death, a way of finally saying goodbye. If the victim's body is mutilated, dismembered, burned, decomposed, or disintegrated, identification may have to be made through dental records, personal effects, or other artifacts. Explain to the family members why this is necessary and give them the choice of whether or not to view the remains. Again, provide the appropriate support.

Where *no body has been recovered*, state this plainly. If there is hope that remains may yet be found, state this, but try to be as realistic as possible about the odds. There is, in fact, some past and recent precedent for this. Ships sunk at sea or planes immolated in crashes rarely produce remains—not to mention the victims pulverized in the ruins of the collapsed twin towers on September 11. In cases like these, notify the family of whatever identification procedures may be occurring, such as DNA-matching, and direct them to the proper authorities. Also, if artifacts from the victim are found at the scene, such as a pair of glasses, a piece of jewelry, or a child's toy, these might be in police custody for use as evidence in later prosecution. Let the family know this, and explain to them the procedures for reclaiming these hierlooms, should they wish to do so.

Crisis Intervention and Victim Advocacy

In the aftermath of a criminal assault or homicide, the direct police role with regard to victims or families will gradually be taken over by existing victim service agencies. In the United States, an estimated 10,000 such victim service agencies are providing direct help to millions of crime victims and families. A small but growing number of victim service programs operate within law enforcement agencies, prosecutors' offices, juvenile justice departments, probation and parole offices, and correctional institutions. *Crime victim advocates* also are located in community-based settings, such as rape crisis centers and domestic violence shelters (Herman, 2002).

These professional groups provide a wide range of services, including supportive counseling, crisis intervention, safety planning, emergency financial assistance, witness assistance, and court escorts. Victim service providers also assist victims and families in accessing victim compensation, and advocate on behalf of victims when they are not able to receive the services they are entitled to.

Nevertheless, most victims of crime are not being referred to the resources they need. According to a recent survey of crime victims in Washington, D.C., some of this is due to the responding officers' failure to provide victims with information about available resources (Herman, 2002). As emphasized throughout this book, simple, authoritative information delivered by a credible source can often provide a much needed sense of safety and control in a crisis situation. The type and timeliness of support services provided to victims and families in the immediate criminal aftermath can have a profound effect on long-term psychological functioning.

Postincident crisis intervention may include support services at the crime scene, hospital, medical examiner's office, survivor's home, police station, or court setting. Interventions at this stage may include nonjudgmental listening, provision of practical information, and referrals to additional services. This information should be provided verbally and in writing, in language the recipient can understand. Ideally, phone numbers should be provided where the victim or family member can get information 24/7 (Spungen, 1998; Young, 1988, 1994).

Many court jurisdictions assign a *victim advocate* to direct victims of violent crime, and some jurisdictions may provide this service to homicide family covictims as well. The advocate's accompaniment of the survivors to court can provide them with the needed strength and support to deal with the painful and intimidating court proceedings. Unfortunately, victim advocates themselves may sometimes feel frustrated because they seem to be primarily serving the criminal justice system, especially the prosecutor's office and the police, and only secondarily the victims or survivors (Spungen, 1998).

Accident Victims

Patrol officers will probably have to deal with accidents far more frequently than with serious crime victimization. Most commonly, these will involve traffic accidents and medical emergencies. In the latter, such as an elderly citizen's having a heart attack in a public place, or a worker falling off a ladder, the officer's first responder role will typically be limited to providing emergency first aid while summoning paramedics. Motor vehicle accidents add another element, because here a misdemeanor or felony traffic violation may have occurred.

In general, much of the same on-scene crisis intervention techniques that are useful with crime victims also can be applied to accident victims (Russel & Beigel, 1990). These include the following recommendations:

Encourage relaxation. "Take a deep breath, we're going to help you relax and get through this."

Provide realistic reassurance. "It's over, you're safe now. The paramedics are on their way, and they're going to check you out and make sure you're okay."

Emphasize the practical. Even in the presence of victims who appear unconscious, avoid potentially alarming or upsetting statements like, "Oh-oh, this looks like a broken neck;" or even, "It's not a good idea to move him." If you need to communicate with fellow officers or other first responders on the scene, stick to concrete, task-specific statements: "Let's keep his head and body still until the paramedics get here with the backboard."

The Citizen-Observer Victim

We should remember that the ordinary citizen who observes a crime, accident, or other crisis situation may also suffer traumatization, especially if the scene was especially grisly or violent. Especially where officers must quickly gather on-scene information about a crime or accident that has just occurred, they may first have to calm down an emotional citizen-observer before they will be able to carry out other necessary police duties. Several techniques are useful in calming observers in a state of emotional crisis (Goldstein et al., 1977; Russell & Beigel, 1990); these are similar to the techniques used for direct crime or accident victims:

Show understanding. By tone of voice, facial expression, and gestures, become an ally the respondent

can trust: "It's pretty frightening when something like this happens. I know you're feeling very upset."

Model composure. If officers respond calmly to the crisis, their appearance of control serves as a model and support for the involved citizen.

Reassure by authority and experience. "We've handled lots of calls like this; we've got the situation under control."

Encourage talking. Although sometimes you have to get the subject to calm down before they can speak coherently, paradoxically, it can work the other way, too. That is, encouraging the subject to talk can be an effective means of easing his or her distress because it is difficult for somebody to yell, scream, cry, fight, or hyperventilate if, at the same time, he or she is trying to answer questions posed slowly and calmly. Sometimes police officers may encourage the person to talk about the crisis itself. This can be a form of ventilation. However, if talking about the crisis gets the citizen more agitated, officers may calm the situation by continuing to ask questions themselves and taking notes at a slow and steady pace. At first, don't be too concerned with the cohesiveness of the narrative, just let the person talk, rephrase questions as necessary, and eventually the respondent will ease into a more articulate form of communication.

Use distraction. As noted above, distraction is useful for defocusing from traumatic perceptions or feelings, although its effect may be temporary. Distraction may be accomplished by asking the subject to perform a task ("May I have a glass of water?") or asking a question that is not directly related to the crisis situation ("How long have you worked here").

Use humor. Humor can help keep the crisis in perspective and cool tempers in a very tense situation. However, as noted in several places, humor must be used cautiously. At no time must the subject feel they are being dismissed or made fun of.

Temporarily ignore, if there is a more pressing need. Sometimes officers can calm the emotional citizen by temporarily ignoring him or her while handling someone in more acute distress, such as a bleeding accident victim. This reminder of reality may help calm the emotional citizen, but again, don't give the impression that you are deliberately snubbing the victim.

CONCLUSIONS

Handling crises on patrol places the police officer in the tremendously important position of potentially changing lives forever, based on what he or she says and does within the space of a few minutes. More broadly, the more skillful and effective officers become in authoritatively de-escalating potentially violent situations and providing useful and supportive assistance to victims of crime and accidents, the greater will be the overall respect and credibility of the police force within the community it serves.

Chapter 4

DEALING WITH THE MENTALLY ILL

Like it or not, in almost every community there are citizens with one or more kinds of mental disorder, many of them homeless, and most of them not receiving any effective treatment. Dealing with these individuals is a necessary part of police patrol work. Many officers actually feel less comfortable handling mentally ill citizens than they do criminal suspects because the latter, ironically, are often more predictable and more clearly in control of their behavior than the former. There also remains the socially stigmatized, general "creepiness factor" of the mentally ill which most people, including most cops, share.

Nevertheless, most officers perceive a need for special training in dealing with the mentally ill (Borum et al., 1998; Hill et al., 2004; Vermette et al., 2005). Accordingly, this chapter provides some insight into the variety of mentally ill citizens that officers are likely to encounter in their patrol work. It also offers some practical strategies for dealing with mentally ill citizens in a way that preserves the balance between respect for individual rights and dignity, and enforcing the law and maintaining social order within the community.

LAW ENFORCEMENT RESPONSE TO THE MENTALLY ILL

It is important to understand some of the facts and statistics regarding mental illness and the police response to mentally ill citizens (Borum et al., 1998; Carter, 1993; Cordner, 2000; Dupont & Cochran, 2000; Finn & Stalans, 2002; Reuland & Margolis, 2003).

Approximately 5 percent of the American population has some form of serious mental illness. In jail or prison populations, this proportion rises to 16 percent. Almost three-quarters of these mentally ill inmates have a coexisting substance abuse problem. Most mentally ill persons are not violent, but there seems to be a somewhat higher ratio of violence among the seriously mentally ill than in the general population. The factors most often associated with violence are paranoid schizophrenia with associated command hallucinations. However, the mentally ill are far more often the victims of crime than the perpetrators and are three times as likely

to be crime victims than ordinary citizens. When mentally ill persons do commit a violent crime, the victim is familiar to them in more than half the cases; indeed, most perpetrators of violence have some personal connection with their victims.

Across the United States, mental health calls account for 5 to 10 percent of calls for police service, ranking on a par with robbery calls. A significant number of these mental health calls relate to aggressive behavior, making them at least as dangerous as robbery calls. A large number of mental health calls overlap with domestic dispute calls, which are themselves potentially dangerous situations for responding officers (Chapter 3). Arrest rates for mentally ill suspects are about the same as for domestic violence suspects, and both are higher than rates for the general population. Displayed disrespect for officers—*contempt of cop*, or COC—is equally likely to increase arrest rates for all suspects, with or without mental illness.

Officers tend to view mentally ill subjects as more dangerous and less in control of their actions than other citizens. While the mere presence of a psychiatric disorder does not necessarily increase a citizen's risk of violence, the risk is highest for psychotic subjects experiencing paranoid delusions and persecutory command hallucinations. Substance abuse multiplies the violence risk among the mentally ill, and dual diagnosis (substance abuse plus mental illness) subjects are more likely to be taken into custody, either because of their greater violence risk or because they are more

likely to be accepted by hospital receiving facilities (Bonta et al., 1998; Eccleston et al., 2005; Monahan, 1996). Officers are more likely to use civil commitment as an alternative to arrest and jail detention if they believe that the mental health system will accept potentially violent cases. Until recently, there have been few formal training programs for police officers on how to deal with the mentally ill, although such collaborative types of programs are beginning have success in some municipalities (Borum et al., 1998; Hill et al., 2004; Vermette et al., 2005; Wiley, 2005).

SIGNS AND SYMPTOMS OF ABNORMAL BEHAVIOR

In medicine, a *sign* is an objective observation or finding on a clinical examination. Examples include a limp while walking, high blood pressure on a cuff reading, or disorganized speech during conversation. A *symptom* is a subjective experience that is reported by the patient, such as pain in the knee, throbbing headaches on exertion, or voices in his head telling him to fight off the evil forces threatening him.

A *syndrome* is a standard cluster of signs and symptoms that occur in a regular pattern, and are typically associated with a particular etiology, and/or occur in a particular subset of the population. Examples include degenerative arthritis of the knee in an ex-athlete, hypertensive headaches in an overweight woman with a high-salt diet, and paranoid schizophrenia in a homeless young man who abuses amphetamines and alcohol. A syndrome becomes a *disorder* when it interferes with important life functions of the patient, such as shortening life; decreasing the quality of health and well-being; or interfering with job, family, or social functioning.

Although different syndromes have different symptom clusters, there are some general signs of mental disorder that police officers should recognize (Pinizzotto & Deshazar, 1997; Russell & Beigel, 1990; Will & Peters, 2004).

General inappropriateness of behavior may be a sign of mental illness, although it may also be due to intoxication or even just youthful exuberance. Individuals with mental disorders tend to have their cognitive and behavioral gyroscopes set to extremes, characterized by either inflexibility and rigidity, or impulsivity and lability. Emotions may range from

elated to depressed, calm to panicked, and there may be an unnatural changeability of mood that is inconsistent with the circumstances. Attention, concentration, and memory may be impaired, either due to an organic brain syndrome or heightened distractibility from the anxiety of an internal dialogue. Severely disturbed subjects may be *disoriented* for *time* ("What day is this? Is it morning or afternoon?"), *place* ("Do you know where you are now? Where do you live?"), or *person* ("What's your name? How old are you?").

Speech may be *tangential*, flitting from topic to topic without a clear connection between them, or it may be *circumstantial*, remaining on or returning to the same topic, even after the conversation has moved on. *Perseveration* refers to abnormal persistence or repetition of speech or behavior. *Pressured speech* occurs in a rapid, staccato, jumbled form, as if the person is rushing to spill it all out as fast as possible; conversely, speech output may seem *abnormally slow*, as if the subject is weighing and measuring every word.

Aphasia refers to a group of organic language disorders characterized by various disturbances in comprehension and expression. Most commonly seen in elderly persons with dementia, subjects with *receptive aphasia* fail to comprehend normal speech, and may appear to be ignoring or defying the officer's commands. The speech output of subjects with *expressive aphasia* may seem garbled and confused, and in severe cases may be limited to one- or two-word answers that are off the mark. *Aprosodia* refers to an abnormally flat and unexpressive tone and cadence of speech, even where the vocabulary and grammar are essentially intact. Some subjects may remain completely *mute*, either due to organic language disturbance or psychotic fear of saying anything. Remember, too, that perfectly healthy subjects may clam up to avoid incriminating themselves or just to be obstinate.

What someone is thinking (a symptom) can usually only be inferred from what they are saying and doing (signs). *Flight of ideas* refers to a rapid jumping around of thought processes that often occurs in manic states or as part of the routine of certain "gonzo" stand-up comics. *Paranoia* refers to the belief or feeling that one is being plotted against or harmed (assuming these feelings don't have a basis in fact). *Grandiose ideas* relate to one's inflated view of his or her own self-importance, and *ideas of reference* cause the person to regard otherwise neutral events as pertaining to him or her.

These four cognitive symptoms often occur together in several types of bipolar manic or schizophrenic syndromes, e.g., "They must be out to destroy me [paranoia] because they know I've discovered the secret to world peace [grandiose idea], and the proof is that TV show about the Vatican where I could tell they were talking about me [idea of reference], and maybe I should go on TV myself, or maybe I should get a lawyer and sue the net-works, or maybe I should network with other people who believe in world peace, because Jesus caught the fishes with a net, he worked with a net [flight of ideas]."

Delusions are false beliefs that are clung to in spite of what would appear to be objective evidence to the contrary. *Hallucinations* are abnormal sensory experiences that are most often auditory in mania and schizophrenia states, visual or tactile in organic brain syndromes, or more rarely, affect the other senses as well. Many patients have *somatic delusions,* in which they believe their bodies are infected, decaying, or changing in size and shape. Hallucinations and delusions may occur together, as in a paranoid subject who hears voices telling him he is targeted for termination, consistent with his belief in a government plot to destroy him, or they may occur separately.

The personal and social behavior of seriously mentally ill persons is usually observably abnormal. Social interactions may be suspicious and guarded, or confrontational and combative. Subjects may be uncooperative or overly compliant. They may appear confused or disoriented. In some cases, they may show a hair-trigger response to the smallest provocation, becoming terrified or aggressive or both, and requiring restraint for their own safety and/or that of others.

RESPONDING TO MENTALLY DISTURBED SUBJECTS: BASIC STRATEGIES FOR PATROL OFFICERS

Many of the basic techniques described for interacting with ordinary citizens in Chapter 2 may also be used with mentally ill subjects. But, given that these subjects may not respond in the normal manner to normal interventions, some special considerations apply to dealing with mentally ill citizens (Borum et al., 1997, 1998; Fyfe, 2000; Janik, 1992; Russell & Beigel, 1990).

Proper response to the mentally ill begins with the call. Sometimes, officers will just come upon a situation involving a mentally disordered subject, but in many cases, such calls come over the radio, usually in the form of someone "acting crazy" on a street or in a store. Such calls should be answered by more than one officer, preferably in uniform, so there is no doubt in the subject's mind as to the identity of the officers. One officer should try to engage the subject in conversation, while others control any crowds that might contribute to a spectator circus.

The first priority is ascertaining the physical health and safety of the subject and others who may be at the scene. When first approaching the subject, keep your distance and move slowly. One officer should be the talker and the rest keep silent, to avoid simultaneous conversation, which will likely be confusing and irritating to an already disturbed subject. Employ the technique of a *calm show of force:* by a combination of strength of numbers and easygoing demeanor, make it clear to the subject that you would prefer him to comply willingly and will respect his decision to do so, but you are prepared to use physical restraint if he leaves you no other choice.

For many disturbed subjects, this approach accomplishes the dual purpose of imposing some external control over an otherwise overwhelming experience, and at the same time, leaving an otherwise resistant subject a face-saving way out of appearing weak by giving in—after all, he's facing six cops. Also, many mentally ill subjects are so disturbed that an otherwise intimidating show of force by a single officer may be completely missed or ignored. For example, a drawn baton or firearm may have little meaning to an already frightened, hallucinating subject.

In line with this, provide reasonable assurance that you're there to make things better, not worse. With angry and agitated subjects, avoid unnecessary threats and try to meet hostility with deflection and de-escalation, but be cautious about letting down your guard. Remember, mentally disordered persons are unpredictable, so never underestimate a subject's size or appearance—it's amazing what a oversupply of adrenalin can enable a terrified or enraged person to do. Even though the subject appears disturbed, try to keep your conversation geared to that of a normal, reasonable person. As much as possible, don't lie, deceive, unnecessarily manipulate, or treat the subject like a baby—remember the adage, "just because they're crazy doesn't mean they're stupid."

If the subject expresses delusional thinking, neither dispute nor agree with the content. Arguing against someone's perception ("there's no plot to kill you, pal—it's all in your head") is likely to be irritating and alienating, while too-quickly agreeing with the delusion ("yeah, they're tying to get you,

but we'll take care of it") or hallucination ("sure, sure, we see the guys with the trenchcoats, too") may be taken for the phony camaraderie that it is, further inflaming the subject by convincing him that he can trust no one and is being manipulated by everyone. A better strategy is to present yourself as an honest broker who frankly can't pretend to see or believe what the subject does, but is prepared to keep an open mind in the service of helping the subject: "Sir, I really don't know if they're after you or not, but if you think they are, let's figure out how to keep you safe for now, okay?"

It's a good idea to record the gist of the subject's delusional content because this may prove valuable to both the criminal justice and mental health follow-ups, especially if this involves overtly paranoid, aggressive, or suicidal ideation. Note any threats made, especially if directed against specific persons or agencies. If no arrestable offense has been committed and the subject is basically cooperating, exercise caution, but utilize the same tact and respect as you would with any citizen. Even if things seem to calm down, stay with the subject until help arrives. Sometimes it may be your role to transport the subject to the appropriate facility, so know which facilities exist in your community. Usually, any such transport will be made by the paramedics you've contacted, and if the subject declines to be treated or transported, they will make the call as to whether or not to involuntarily commit the person. In the simplest cases, you may have no option other than to let the subject go peaceably on his way.

DEALING WITH DIFFERENT MENTAL DISORDERS: ABNORMAL PSYCHOLOGY FOR POLICE OFFICERS

To supplement the basic general recommendations above, this section offers more specific advice for handling subjects with specific kinds of mental disorder. This is not a comprehensive course in psychopathology and psychotherapy but is more focused toward the kind of street-level crisis intervention

that virtually all officers inevitably have to deal with in their patrol activities. In addition, officers may be charged with the responsibility of locating appropriate services for these individuals (APA, 1994; Garner, 1995; Mohandie & Duffy, 1999; Russell & Beigel, 1990).

ANXIETY AND MOOD DISORDERS

For most people, their normal mood is neither especially happy or sad, angry or loving, agitated

or calm, but just a steady sense of what I call *provisional well-being:* the overall feeling that life has its difficulties but everything is basically okay and we hope for better days. It's like the feeling between meals when we are neither hungry nor full, when, in fact, we're too preoccupied with what we're presently doing to pay conscious attention to our gastronomical—or emotional—states at all. All healthy people show a range of moods, getting periodically happier, sadder, angrier, calmer, and so on in response to various life circumstances, and some otherwise normal people seem to be dispositionally predisposed to either the cheerier or more dour side of the mood spectrum. Like any trait or syndrome, it is the *extremes* of mood that characterize a disorder, especially when these mood disturbances impair healthy life functioning or produce unreasonable conflict with others.

Clinical Features

Mood disorders generally fall into the two broad categories of anxiety disorders and depressive disorders, although the symptoms often overlap.

Anxiety disorders are characterized by heightened worry, fear, and arousal. *Generalized anxiety disorder* (GAD) involves a pervasive feeling of anxiety that is not necessarily tied to any specific event or circumstance, sometimes referred to as "free-floating anxiety." These individuals are always anxious about something, although the level of anxiety may wax and wane in response to different situations. Others may perceive these individuals as never being able to relax or be at peace.

Some individuals, with or without GAD, may suffer from *panic disorder*, which involves brief episodes of extremely elevated physiological arousal and fear. The individual may experience a racing, pounding heart, profuse sweating, rapid, shallow breathing, numbness and tingling in the face and extremities, and faintness or lightheadedness—all the hallmarks of sheer terror. Many subjects fear they will pass out during an attack, although this is actually extremely rare. The attacks may occur in response to certain events, or they may happen randomly "out of the blue." Panic attacks are also likely to occur in the context of depression, often in response to perceived abandonment or loss of support.

If the anxiety and panic are associated with particular places or situations, the individual may develop one or more *phobias*, which are irrational extreme fears of particular persons, places, or things. Note that these are not delusions, because the person recognizes that the fear is not rational, yet he or she feels powerless to control it and must avoid the feared situation to forestall panic. Thus, sufferers often feel demoralized and out of control at not being able to will themselves out of these irrational fears. Phobias may be generalized, involving fears of a wide variety of people, places, or things that are usually related or have some elements in common, or they may be quite specific, e.g., to a particular room, class of objects, or type of animal.

Posttraumatic stress disorder is a severe anxiety disorder that arises in reaction to a specific traumatic event, and is characterized by a standard set of symptoms. This syndrome is discussed comprehensively in Chapters 3 and 6 in connection with crime victim trauma and critical incident stress.

Mood disorders are generally classified into unipolar and bipolar types, depending on whether the extreme changes in mood are in one direction (down-depressed) or both directions (down-depressed and up-elated or up-angry). *Major depressive disorder* is characterized by episodes of depressed mood that may last for days, weeks, or months at a time. In severe cases, the individual may be virtually immobilized. More characteristically, subjects feel dejected, demoralized, helpless, and hopeless. Sleep and appetite may be impaired; alternatively, some individuals become hypersomnic (sleep virtually all the time) or may binge-eat. Concentration and memory may be affected to the point where individuals feel they are becoming demented. Gone is any motivation or enthusiasm for work, play, or family activities. Accompanying emotions may include anxiety, panic, irritability, or anger. The disorder usually occurs in cycles over the lifespan, and, in most cases, is very responsive to treatment.

Dysthymic disorder is a more persistent, but less severe, mood disorder. Such individuals mentally limp through their daily activities, able to perform sufficiently to get by at work or at home, but experiencing little pleasure or excitement from life—the "walking wounded," leading a drab, joyless life. Many of these individuals will deny being depressed, per se, but report that they've never known what it's like to feel happy. Some individuals with major depression will recover from their severe episodes, but only to a bland baseline state of dysthymia, rarely experiencing anything that could be called a happy or even normal mood.

Bipolar disorder, also known as *manic-depressive illness* is characterized by extreme shifts in mood, from elation to depression, usually with an absence of normal mood in between: for such individuals, there are only highs and lows. The manic phase typically begins with the individual feeling energized and overconfident–"pumped." He becomes hyperactive and grandiose, spinning all kinds of half-baked unrealistic plans, but being increasingly impulsive and distractible. Thinking and speech become rapid and forced. Need for sleep decreases and the individual may be hypersexual; all appetites are on sensory overdrive. The overall impression is of someone on stimulant drugs, and indeed, such individuals may abuse amphetamines, cocaine, or alcohol to enhance the natural high and try to keep it going.

At the beginning of the manic phase, the individual may appear quite engaging and entertaining in a kind of gonzo-comic kind of way, but as the manic phase progresses, he becomes increasingly short-tempered, irritable, anxious, and paranoid. Inevitably, the crash comes as the individual cycles into the depressed phase. At this point, he may increase his use of stimulants to try to prolong the high, but eventually even this isn't enough to stave off the depressive avalanche. Suicide is a distinct risk at this stage. In other bipolar patients, the manic episodes do not involve much elation at all, but are characterized mainly by irritability, anger, and paranoia, and may be misdiagnosed as schizophrenia.

Law Enforcement Response

The most frequent law enforcement crisis intervention context for an anxious or depressed subject is potential *suicide*, although depressed subjects are frequently seen in correctional and other institutional settings, as well as on daily street patrol.

The first priority is safety. Assess for suicidality and emphasize the subject's well-being, especially since the police response is often associated with a confrontation: "I'm officer Smith and this is officer Jones. We're here to make sure you're okay and to get you any help you need right now."

Violence against others is rare in unipolar depression, although it may occur as part of a "suicide pact" with another person, usually an elderly couple with a serious illness or disability. Violence is a more likely risk for bipolar manic individuals who may be angry and delusional. Move slowly and take your time, avoiding any unnecessary intimidation. Use verbal nonverbal calming techniques, and employ cautious physical restraint where necessary. Subjects in a manic state may not initially intend to attack you, but may be subject to explosions of anger upon hair-trigger provocation. And if they do get physical, you'll be dealing with a huge adrenalin factor and it's going to take a lot of force to keep this person under control, so injuries on all sides are a distinct risk. Especially in these cases, *then*, your judicious use of verbal and nonverbal de-escalation techniques can make the difference between a subject who gets talked-down and treated and one who gets restrained and arrested for assaulting an officer. Assuming no arrest is called for, if the subject requires further disposition, transport him or her to an appropriate receiving facility.

PSYCHOSES: SCHIZOPHRENIA AND OTHER DELUSIONAL DISORDERS

Psychotic disorders comprise a group of syndromes, the main common feature of which is a significant break with reality, characterized by severe disturbances of mood, thought, and goal-directed action. The most common form of psychotic disorder is *schizophrenia*, which is a progressive syndrome, usually first presenting in adolescence or early adulthood (although childhood forms occur), and characterized by delusional thinking and the presence

of hallucinations, which are typically auditory (hearing voices), and more rarely, visual (seeing things). Untreated schizophrenics may suffer episodic bouts of delusional and hallucinatory psychosis, between which they may appear simply odd or weird, unable to maintain any consistent work or other activity.

Many of these individuals swell the ranks of the "street people" comprising a proportion of an officer's patrol area in any major metropolitan jurisdiction. Although diagnostic overlap is common, schizophrenia may be primarily of the *paranoid* type, characterized mainly by delusions of persecution and accusatory hallucinations; the *disorganized* type, characterized by general aimlessness and lack of contact with reality; the *catatonic* type, which is more commonly seen in institutional settings because of their near-immobility; or the *undifferentiated* type, which may comprise features of the other three classifications or show additional symptoms.

Delusional disorders are distinguished clinically from schizophrenia by the fact that the affected individuals may function adequately in most life areas, despite the presence of isolated, fixed ideas, which themselves are sufficiently out of sync with reality to qualify as delusions. Thus, a movie fan convinced that a starlet is in love with him would have an *erotomanic* type of delusional disorder. A *grandiose* type of delusion would involve the belief that one has the true secret for world peace, if only he could get before the UN General Assembly and tell everyone. *Persecutory* delusional disorder would characterize the individual who believes that "they" (whoever they are) are after him (often for the purpose of stealing or silencing his grandiose idea). The *jealous* type of delusion would apply the husband who is absolutely convinced that his wife is having an affair, despite no shred of hard evidence. Someone convinced that his body is decaying from within, shrinking or expanding, or that radio waves are changing his skin color or brain patterns might be suffering from the *somatic* type of delusional disorder.

Psychotic Disorders: Risk Factors for Violence

Although not intended to needlessly stigmatize the mentally ill, the clinical evidence to date does suggest that subjects with schizophrenic disorders do have a higher risk of violence than the population at large. The rate of schizophrenia is three times higher in prisons than in the general population, although this may reflect differential rates of arrest or access to competent legal representation, as untreated mental illness is typically associated with poverty and lower social status. When asked to describe their own behavior, the prevalence of self-reported violence is five times higher among schizophrenic subjects than among the general population.

Paranoid schizophrenic subjects may be an especially dangerous group. Shore et al. (1985, 1988) investigated the arrest records of paranoid schizophrenic former psychiatric patients who attempted to gain access to the U.S. President or other high government officials. It was found that one in seven had been arrested for murder or aggravated assault during the nine to twelve years following their discharge from mental hospitals where they had been committed.

Certain factors serve to increase the risk of violence among psychotic subjects. Some of these are associated with generic violence risk factors, such as access to weapons and coexisting substance abuse. More syndrome-specific risk factors include the presence of persecutory delusions which may impel psychotic subjects to lash out as a way of protecting themselves—a "preemptive strike." Also, command hallucinations that order the subject to use offensive or defensive aggression are an important risk factor.

Psychotic Disorders: Police Response

Officers who encounter a psychotic individual should observe a few basic rules of engagement (Mohandie & Duffy, 1999). First, if possible, assess the nature of the subject's psychotic state and overall behavior before approaching. This is to prevent either a lapse of precaution on the one hand, or an unnecessarily aggressive response on the other. Approach the subject as slowly and as nonthreateningly as possible. If more than one officer is present, keep the sensory overload to a minimum by having only one officer speak at a time. Try to determine if the subject can be verbally engaged. Always speak and act slowly, firmly, and deliberatively—remember the difference between authoritative and authoritarian.

If the subject is willing to talk, encourage venting, but not ranting. If the subject expresses delusional ideas and beliefs, neither argue nor agree with the delusions. Through their painful life experiences, most schizophrenics have learned that other people don't believe their delusional ideas, so pretending to do so may only serve to alienate or enrage a disturbed psychotic subject further. Conversely, it is highly unlikely that trying to "talk sense" into a delusional subject is going to make him suddenly see things more rationally. Instead, acknowledge the content of the delusion and try to ally yourself with the subject's perspective and perception of the situation, while keeping the focus on present reality: "Let me try to understand this. The terrorists have been sending you messages through your radio and cell phone, telling you of their plots to kill people, and you're trying to fight them off. Do I have that right? That must be pretty frightening." Utilize active listening skills with the goal of calming the situation as much as possible.

If physical restraint or arrest is required, utilize appropriate backup and safe takedown procedures. Remember that psychotic subjects can be very unpredictable—sitting and mumbling distractedly one moment, thrashing and kicking violently the next. If an arrest is not made, transport the subject to an appropriate medical or psychiatric receiving facility. Unfortunately, many mentally ill subjects who would best be served by a medical-psychiatric facility are nevertheless turned away from such facilities due to lack of funding or the facility's refusal to accept intoxicated or potentially violent patients. In such cases, officers often have no choice but to arrest the subject on a misdemeanor charge in order to transport him to jail for his own and others' safety.

Paranoid Disorders: Police Response

Paranoid schizophrenia presents a special challenge to nonviolent law enforcement intervention because the subject is already predisposed to mistrust everything you do or say. It is here that the concepts of de-escalation and preventive intervention are crucially important to keep the situation from escalating to violence.

Paranoid subjects are hypervigilant and suspicious. They are on high alert for the slightest hint of attack or treachery and tend to interpret every statement or action in a malevolent light. With such subjects, adopt an attitude of friendly and detached neutrality, of understanding without condescention. That is, commiserate with the distress the subject is obviously feeling, but don't dismiss or talk down to him. This may sometimes be a challenge due to the natural tendency most people have to treat a "crazy person" like a child, which will only further infuriate a paranoid subject.

Wrong: "C'mon now, nobody's after you, it's just your imagination. Why don't you be a good boy and come with us."

Better: "I'm not sure I understand the whole situation, but I can see this is really upsetting you. Anything we can do to help?"

As with psychotic subjects in general, neither argue nor agree with the subject's delusional content, but empathize with the distress the subject is expressing, and show open-mindedness to the validity of the subject's complaints. Remember that many paranoid delusions may accrete around a kernel of reality, e.g., a worker may have truly been unfairly fired—not because of any secret government plot to silence him, but because the small company was downsizing, and they had to lay off somebody, so they picked the weird guy, betting that he wouldn't have the mental wherewithal to pursue an antidiscrimination or unfair labor practices claim.

One thing to be especially alert for in the content of a paranoid subject's verbalization is any risk of suicidality or violence, particularly if expressed toward specific targets ("Those commies can't do this to me—I'm gonna teach that Red boss a lesson!"). Again, it is probably futile to try to correct the subject's misinterpretations of reality, so keep your statements simple, concrete, and focused on the subject's safety and well-being.

To this end, utilize appropriate proxemics (personal space) and body language, as well as verbal and nonverbal calming techniques (Chapters 2 and 9). Remember that paranoid subjects are particularly skittish about physical boundaries and proximity—they're always on the alert for an attack. Unless and until physical restraint becomes necessary, keep a reasonable distance and inform the subject of what you are about to do: "Sir, I'm going to reach into my pocket to take out a pen and a pad, so I can write down some notes, okay? It's just a pen and pad." Then move slowly. Always use caution, however, because the subject may become panicked and turn violent in a flash.

When the decision to take down the subject has been made, do so quickly and purposefully. If the paranoid subject needs to be taken into custody, try to allow for some degree of self-respect to be preserved. Barking orders or playing rough as a "show of force" to cow the subject into submission is less likely to be effective with paranoid subjects and may only serve to further crank up the adrenalin spigot, heightening the risk of injury to all parties.

PERSONALITY: TRAITS, TYPES AND DISORDERS

We all have different personality traits, which contribute to our psychological uniqueness as human beings. But when these personal quirks begin to grate harmfully on others or significantly derail our own success, psychologists speak of an individual having a *personality disorder*, which is defined as "an enduring pattern of inner experience and behavior that deviates markedly from the expectations of the individual's culture, is pervasive and inflexible, has an onset in adolescence or early adulthood, is stable over time, and leads to distress or impairment" (APA, 1994).

Personality-disordered individuals typically show little insight into their own behavior and have a poor understanding of the adverse impact they have on themselves and others. They characteristically justify their self-defeating or offensive behavior as being due to uncontrollable fate or someone else's fault. It is the *extremes* of their self-perception and conduct toward others that distinguish personality disordered individuals from those with more moderate personality traits and styles (Millon & Davis, 2000; Sperry, 1995). This may have implications for police officer interaction with these citizens while on patrol, as well as in other law enforcement contexts (Miller, 2003, 2004).

Histrionic Personality

Histrionic personality is a pattern of excessive emotionality, attention-seeking, need for excitement, flamboyant theatricality in speech and behavior, an impressionistic and impulsive cognitive style, and use of exaggeration to maintain largely superficial relationships for the purpose of getting emotional needs met by being admired and cared for by others.

These will be the overemotional citizens that police encounter, for whom every rebuff and inconvenience is a major tragedy. These are also the subjects who may try to ingratiate themselves with local officers by virtue of their wit and charm. They crave attention, and officers who are able to project an attitude of empathic concern will probably find these subjects more than willing to cooperate. One problem is that, in their desire to please, they may often change their story to suit what they believe you want to hear. This is usually not deliberate deception, but a virtually unconscious attempt to do anything to put themselves in the best possible light and get you to like them. Careful, gentle probing of inconsistencies may be necessary to get at the facts of a given case.

Borderline Personality

Borderline personality is a pattern of instability in interpersonal relationships, fragile self-image, and wild emotional swings. In this pattern, individuals may exhibit a pattern of erratic and intense relationships, alternating between overidealization and devaluation of others. They may show self-damaging impulsiveness in the form of risky activities, substance abuse, and emotional explosions. Signs of emotional instability include inappropriately intense anger and/or depressive mood swings and possible suicidality. Persistent identity disruption may manifest itself as disturbances in self image, blurred interpersonal boundaries and relationships, confused goals and values, and a chronic feeling of emptiness that may propel the quest for stimulation via substance abuse or provocation of incidents.

Officers most commonly encounter these individuals on domestic calls or in workplace disputes, since their most intense conflicts involve those with whom they've had some kind of previous relationship. Extremely sensitive to rejection or betrayal, they may respond with intense anger, which may escalate to violence. In such cases, be sure to separate the disputing parties and use calming techniques and active listening to convey a sense of sincere concern, backed by no-nonsense resoluteness that violence won't be tolerated. Stay away from discussing issues, which may only further inflame the borderline subject, and focus concretely on what you want the subject to do.

Narcissistic Personality

Narcissistic personality is a pattern of grandiosity, sense of entitlement, arrogance, need for admiration, and lack of empathy for others' feelings or opinions. Citizens with this pattern typically get in trouble because they believe rules are for other people and that they are allowed to bend the law because of their special entitlement and powers of perception, insight, and judgment. They expect others to appreciate, admire, and defer to them, and will become irritated or rageful when they don't get the respect they feel they naturally deserve.

Expect two kinds of reactions from narcissistic subjects. One is an overfamiliar, back-slapping camaraderie that implies that he and you are really of equal status or have a common bond: "It's okay, officer, I understand what you're trying to do." "Hey, my uncle's a cop in Atlanta." You can use this to your advantage by allowing the subject to "take your side" and emphasize how what you're asking him to do is of mutual benefit: "I'm glad you have an understanding of law enforcement protocol, sir. That's why I know you'll appreciate the need to move your vehicle to make it easier for us to do our job here."

The other reaction (sometimes after the first reaction fails to get the anticipated response) is outrage at not being respected as a special case: "I'm an important man in this community–you can't treat me like a common criminal!" In these situations, verbally disarm the subject by being somewhat deferential, but at the same time, maintaining the need for your actions: "We understand, sir, but it's necessary for the thoroughness of our investigation that we ask these questions of anyone. We do appreciate your patience and cooperation."

Avoidant and Dependent Personalities

Avoidant personality is a pattern of social inhibition, feelings of inadequacy, and hypersensitivity to criticism. Even relatively neutral interpersonal interactions or confrontations are approached with trepidation. These are the citizens who may inexplicably go all to pieces at a simple traffic stop.

Their extreme nervousness may convince the officer that they've got "something to hide," thus prompting more a more extensive search and questioning, further agitating the subject. In some cases, the otherwise innocent subject may become so fearful, he may attempt to flee or forcefully resist commands, and the ensuing pursuit and/or restraint will then lead to even further decompensation, producing a vicious cycle. These are also the subjects that are most likely to just break down and cry during an encounter.

If you need to question these subjects, a collaborative and supportive interview style, rather than a cold and confrontational interrogation, will be the most productive approach. Such individuals may seem to be holding back, but not because of lack of cooperation per se. Rather, their extreme shyness makes it excruciatingly difficult for them to give a coherent narrative in the presence of another human being. In such cases, you may want to emphasize a more gently directive, structured, question-and-answer format of the interview protocol, which may actually make it easier for avoidant types to reveal what they know in piecemeal fashion.

Dependent personality is a pattern of submissive and clinging behavior stemming from an excessive need for care and nurturance. Whereas avoidant subjects fear people and prefer to be away from them, dependent personalities cling to people for guidance and support, and fear only their rejection and abandonment. Even more so than with avoidant personalities, dependent types will respond well to a supportive, collaborative approach to questioning. The danger is that, in their eagerness to please, they may be apt to tell you what they think you want to hear, not necessarily what is actually the case, so follow up your open-ended questions with a few close-ended queries to nail down the details. Be careful, however, not to give the impression that you don't trust the subject, which he or she will take as a mortal wound, and which may therefore close off any further productive communication.

Schizoid and Schizotypal Personalities

The central characteristics of both schizoid and schizotypal personalities include avoidance of others, severe deficiencies in social skills, generalized withdrawal from life, and sometimes impairment in perceptual and cognitive capacities. *Schizoid personality* is a pattern of aloof detachment from social interaction, with a restricted range of emotional expression. These are people who don't need people and are perfectly happy being left to themselves. *Schizotypal personality* involves more serious disturbances of thinking, more bizarre behavior, and possibly delusions. It is thought that these two personality disorders really represent points on a continuum from schizoid to schizotypal to outright schizophrenia, the latter characterized by severe distortions of thought, perception, and action, including delusions and hallucinations (see above). In fact, schizoid and schizotypal personality disorders may episodically deteriorate into psychotic states, especially under conditions of stress.

The main interactive feature of interest to patrol officers is that these subjects may seem detached and disinterested during an encounter, not because they're ignoring or disrespecting you, but because they may be internally preoccupied or because human interaction is of little interest to them to begin with. In most cases, their blank, far-away facial expression and attitude will be quite noticeable. Even where they do communicate, the sometimes bizarre and delusional nature of the information they provide may compromise its validity and usefulness. Encouraging a free narrative will likely yield either an incoherently rambling stream-of-consciousness oration, or a rigidly obsessive reiteration of key ideas or phrases. Instead, it will be more effective to use a firm and directive approach to focus the schizoid subject's attention on simple, precise questions. These queries should be designed to yield specific, tangible bits of information that can then be painstakingly fitted together to create a coherent narrative of useful information.

Antisocial Personality Disorder

Subjects with *antisocial personality disorder* are frequently encountered in law enforcement settings because this is as close as one gets to a quintessential "criminal personality." These *psychopaths*, the older term for these subjects, are characterized by a completely self-centered worldview, lack of empathy for others, and a craving for immediate gratification, with little or no frustration tolerance. They have an excessive need for stimulation and excitement, and

their behavior is impulsive, erratic, and characterized by difficulty in sustaining any long-term, goal-directed behavior. More so than other offenders, punishment seems to have little effect on them, a feature that has both been noted behaviorally and documented neurophysiologically (Raine, 1990). Commonly, there is a long history of substance abuse and criminal activity, dating from childhood, at which ages the syndrome is known as *conduct disorder* (APA, 1994).

In their youth, antisocial personalities typically have done poorly in academics, especially verbal subjects, although they may possess contrastingly high mechanical skill and athletic prowess. They were probably bullies since grade school. When older, they tend to be unreliable workers. They usually perform poorly on IQ tests, again especially in the verbal areas, yet they typically possess a very keen social intelligence that they use to "psych out" others in order to exploit them for their own ends. They can be glibly persuasive, seductive, or threatening with facile ease, often in the same conversation. They are the classic con artists who can turn on the charm or flare into fury if that's what it takes to get what they want from others. Human beings, in their minds, are just objects to use and throw away, and there is no true sense of loyalty or friendship. People who value such human traits as love, honesty, commitment, or honor are seen by antisocial personalities as fools and suckers who deserve to be exploited.

Probably, the first guideline for law enforcement interaction with these individuals relates to the old adage of not trying to outbullshit a bullshitter. Any intervention that is perceived or misinterpreted as a ploy—and many psychopaths show paranoid traits as well—will be manipulated and exploited by the subject. It's not all nastiness, either. Officers should be alert to the cunning-conning dimension of the antisocial personality: many of those who deal with these characters, whether law enforcement officers or mental health clinicians, often find themselves "liking this guy too much." Lubit (2003) speaks of the "intense, emotionless gaze" that many antisocial personalities fix on their interlocutors, their attention seeming to be riveted on you in a kind of sham active listening posture, but their facial expression revealing no particular genuine feeling state because there isn't any—they're just searching for an angle to exploit. Often, in dealing with these characters, their overpolite, deferential and friendly demeanor may give you the distinct impression that you're being greased, or they may be so smooth that you can't even tell. Don't fall for it.

The best approach is the most direct. If an arrestable offense has not yet occurred, clearly and firmly explain to the subject what he has to gain from cooperating with you and what he has to lose if he doesn't. Don't get into a discussion about reasons and explanations; antisocial personalites are experts at using vague or confusing language to manipulate the situation. Here is one situation where you *don't* want to engage the subject in lengthy dialogue. Your attitude should be authoritative: not abrasive, which may impel him to try to save face by becoming confrontational, but not too "officer friendly," either, which will invariably be seized upon as a weakness to exploit. Remember, the one thing antisocial personalities do respect is power,

and if you provide him a face-saving means of ensuring compliance with your request, and firmly present yourself as a reasonable, but no-nonsense officer, the subject may eventually, grudgingly comply—often with a big, shit-eating grin, like the solution was all *his* idea:

Officer: Look, you may have your reasons for waiting here, but I need you to move off this street corner right now. If you leave now, our business is done. If you continue to give me a hard time, I *will* arrest you for loitering and take you in. Please make your decision so we can get on with our day.

Subject: [after a tense moment, seeming to be deciding what to do, lets out a big laugh] Sure, officer, whatever you say—always want to be a good citizen who helps out the police any way I can. Catch you later, brother. [Saunters away, laughing.]

ALCOHOL AND DRUG INTOXICATION

Aside from schizophrenic subjects, alcohol- and drug-intoxication disturbances comprise the bulk of mental disorder-related police patrol interactions (Garner, 1995; Russell & Beigel, 1990). In fact, the two diagnoses frequently overlap, as many mentally disturbed individuals are also abusing substances at any given time.

Intoxication and Withdrawal: Signs, Symptoms, and Syndromes

Signs of *alcohol intoxication* are familiar to any officer who has ever pulled over a drunk driver: slurred speech, unbalanced posture, impaired coordination, and so on, although it is possible for many drinkers who are legally intoxicated to act relatively normally, especially when trying to impress the officer with their intactness. Alcohol has varying effects, depending on the particular user, with some inebriated drinkers becoming more mellow and tractable, others becoming more angry and agitated. In general, alcohol and most other drugs lower inhibitions and self-control, so any intoxicated person has to be approached with caution.

Less common, but potentially more serious, are signs and symptoms of *alcohol withdrawal* in subjects who are physiologically addicted to alcohol. This

usually presents as an agitated state with tremors ("the shakes"). In severe cases, this can be accompanied by hallucinations and/or seizures. An acute state of agitated delirium, characterized by intense fear and tactile and visual hallucinations of vermin crawling on the skin, is called *delirium tremens* ("the DT's"). Typically, such individuals will be so clearly impaired that the need for transport to a medical facility is obvious. Years of long-term heavy abuse of alcohol can also lead to *alcoholic dementia*, but these patients are likely to be confined to institutions and not typically encountered during regular patrol.

A rare, but more dangerous syndrome is *pathological intoxication*, where even small amounts of alcohol trigger violent rages in susceptible individuals, which is thought to be due to an electrophysiological disturbance in sensitive limbic areas of the brain. Witnesses will describe an explosion of rage in which the subject appears to be "on automatic" or "like a runaway train," fueled by adrenalin and capable of inflicting severe damage to anyone who gets in his way. These episodes typically last only a few seconds to minutes, and there is usually at least some recall of the incident by the subject, who may also subsequently express regret at losing control (also see below). During these brief episodes, it is useless to try to talk the subject out of his aggressive action.

The only effective strategy is to use appropriate physical restraint to keep him from harming others.

Other substances of abuse have different effects on behavior, depending on their biochemical action within the nervous system. *Stimulants* ("uppers"), such as cocaine and amphetamine, produce a "racing" kind of high, with rapid thought and speech, erratic and impulsive behavior, and a suped-up energy level. Such individuals may occasionally become violent, but more commonly, they will present as simply annoying and raucous, quite similar to the manic state described earlier; in fact, many manic subjects deliberately use stimulants to enhance and extend their natural high. Danger may arise when their overconfidence and impulsivity lead to temper flare-ups provoked by confrontations with police.

Central nervous system *depressants* ("downers"), such as barbiturates (e.g., Quaaludes) or benzodiazepines (e.g., Valium), have effects similar to alcohol, which include a calming effect, but accompanied by a loosening of inhibitions, which may lead to impulsive and illegal actions. Most calls for service for these users tend to be due to their passing out unconscious in a public place, but they may become combative if they are still confused and disoriented when police or paramedics arrive.

The effects of *hallucinogens*, such as marijuana, LSD, or angel dust, may range from mellow loopiness to violent delirium. *Organic hydrocarbons*, such as the glue and paint thinner enjoyed by sniffers or "huffers," tend to produce a toxic delirious state; these latter substances are also extremely injurious to brain tissue and can produce long-term cognitive impairment.

Dealing with Intoxicated Subjects

Because a behaviorally deteriorated state can be caused by a variety of factors, it is first important to distinguish drug or alcohol intoxication from other medical or psychiatric conditions. Remember, several syndromes may go together; for example, the delusions of a paranoid schizophrenic may be exacerbated by using cocaine, so he smokes some pot to calm down and begins hallucinating, so then he drinks some beer to quiet the voices, and this interacts with the postconcussive effects of a recent head injury he sustained in a fight. Now you're faced with a fearful, angry, and confused person who's behavior is erratic and unpredictable.

In most cases of alcohol use, the subject's breath will give him away. Otherwise, you may have to rely on your knowledge and experience (observational and personal) of intoxicated states. Always approach an intoxicated person with caution. Try to gather as much information as possible about how that person has gotten to where he or she is and whether there is a need for medical attention. Check for weapons and generally assess for danger to self or others. Use tact, patience, and verbal intervention skills—but only to a point. Remember, you're dealing with a person whose powers of perception, comprehension, reasoning, and self-control have all been impaired by the substance they've ingested.

If necessary, call for backup and be prepared to use defensive and/or control techniques, such as spray, impact, taser, or restraint, if necessary. If the subject has not yet committed an arrestable offense but cannot be safely left on his own, arrange for transport to a receiving facility; better to call the paramedics and let them handle the medical aspects if the subject is refusing treatment or transport. Use your authority appropriately, but always try to treat subjects with reasonable respect—remember, these are often the repeat customers whom you will have to deal with in the future.

MENTALLY RETARDED SUBJECTS

Characteristics of Mental Retardation

The formal definition of *mental retardation* is a measured IQ of below 70. However, there are probably millions of people leading productive, satisfying lives with IQs at, or even lower than, that number. More functionally, if a person's intellectual deficiency interferes with his or her ability to fulfill the normal adult roles and responsibilities of daily life, he or she may be classified as mentally retarded, even without a formal IQ score. Although mental retardation is not a mental illness per se, it may be associated with other kinds of mental disorder, so it is possible to see mood disorders, anxiety disorders, or psychotic disorders coexisting with intellectual deficiency.

Mentally retarded subjects may become involved in the criminal justice system in a number of ways. Their often childlike impulsivity may make them prone to misdemeanor crimes, such as shoplifting or public nuisance. When confused or frightened, they may easily become silent and withdrawn or defensively violent. They are also hardly immune to alcohol and drug abuse, and this may make their behavior even more unpredictable. Ordinarily, they tend to be quite compliant and trusting, and thereby make perfect patsies for other criminals to use as drug couriers or stashers of stolen goods. In criminal trials, mental retardation may be raised as a competency issue or as an exculpatory or mitigating factor; nevertheless, mentally retarded offenders comprise about 5 to 10 percent of the convicted prison population (Bowker, 1994).

Identifying and Dealing with Mentally Retarded Subjects

Most of the mentally retarded citizens that officers encounter on their street patrols will not be found in the course of committing a crime, but are more likely to be lost and confused. In most cases, a brief interaction will be sufficient to determine that something is not right about this person. Pay attention to missing, excessive, or disheveled clothing or other unusual style of dress. There may be peculiarities in the subject's gait and movement, as many mentally retarded individuals also have mild-moderate disturbances in motor coordination. The subject's speech may have a simplistic, childlike quality; it may be characterized by various speech disorders, such as lisps, stutters, or variations of volume and pitch; or it may sound relatively normal. When confronted by authorities, such as the police, these subjects are likely to become afraid or confused, or to be overcompliant and dependent.

If it is unclear as to whether the subject is mentally retarded or suffering from some other form of disorder, Bowker (1994) recommends a few curbside tests of cognitive and intellectual functioning. Can the subject identify their name and residence?

Can they give coherent directions to where they live or where they're going? Can they repeat a question in their own words? Can they write their names clearly? Can they recognize coins and make change? Tell time? Use a telephone?

When questioning subjects suspected to be mentally retarded, keep it simple. Begin with open-ended questions, rather than yes-or-no questions because mentally retarded subjects tend to be overcompliant; they will often answer a question based on what they believe will please the questioner, especially an authority figure like a police officer. However, questions that are not understood are likely to be repeated back to you. In such cases, if necessary, reduce questions to a yes or no. For example:

Officer: Where do you live?"
Subject: Where do I live? Where do I live? In the home.
O: Where's the home?
S: The home? The home? I dunno, I live in the home. By the school.
O: Is the school in the same building as the home?
S: No, across the street.
O: Do you know which street?"
S: No.

This may sound frustrating; however, you're already getting some information that may enable you to track down where this subject resides. For example, how many group homes across the street from a special school can there be in your municipality? Also, don't overlook the obvious, such as asking for ID or seeing if the subject has some identifying information on his or her person.

If you come across the scene of a crime or other disturbance involving a mentally retarded subject and other people, it may not be immediately clear who is the suspect, victim, witnesses, or bystanders. The mentally retarded subject may be intimidated and be silent while the others do the talking and make their own cases. Be careful to question everyone present very carefully and document these interviews. If you must arrest the mentally retarded subject, ensure that Miranda rights are understood; for example, ask the suspect to rephrase them in his own words. This might not always be possible. If a mentally retarded suspect has to be criminally detained, all care should be taken not to house him with the general population, where he may be abused. Of course, this will depend on the realities of the situation and available facilities.

ATTENTION DEFICIT HYPERACTIVITY DISORDER

ADHD: Clinical Characteristics

A lifelong difficulty in focusing and sustaining attention on tasks and goals, a tendency toward impulsive action, poor tolerance of frustration, heightened emotional reactivity, a desire for immediate gratification, and poor planning, judgment, and anticipation of consequences are traits that characterize children, adolescents, and adults with *attention deficit hyperactivity disorder,* or ADHD. To complicate matters, ADHD is typically comorbid with other syndromes, such as conduct disorder, antisocial personality disorder, mood disorders, learning disabilities, and substance abuse, which makes overall adjustment to school and work extremely problematic for these individuals. It is not surprising, then, that many of them become involved in the criminal justice system; in fact, approximately half of ADHD subjects evaluated in clinics are later identified by law enforcement as delinquents (Goldstein, 1997).

Involvement in the criminal justice system may occur in two ways. ADHD subjects may commit crimes such as shoplifting, theft, robbery, assault, drug-related offenses, and traffic violations due to their impulsivity and heightened emotional reactivity. Alternatively, their desire to be liked and accepted, and often poor judgment of social cues, may make them easy chumps for set-ups by other criminals. Indeed, far more ADHD subjects are probably victims of crime than its perpetrators. It is generally believed that for a true criminal career path to develop, ADHD must be combined with conduct disorder that progresses to antisocial personality disorder in adulthood (Riccio et al., 2005; Wilens & Dodson, 2004).

Dealing with the ADHD Subject

ADHD subjects may irritate officers who are trying to question them because they seem to be internally preoccupied and to be disregarding what the officer is saying. This is probably an expression of their difficulty focusing on what's being said; after all, the hallmark of this syndrome is impaired ability to pay attention. Keep your questions and statements clear, simple, and direct, and repeat as often as necessary. Use calming techniques for the subject's agitation and emotional outbursts. ADHD subjects may have difficulty with verbal expression, so make use of clear questioning and paraphrasing. They also tend to have poor memories, so what seems to be evasiveness to your questions may actually represent a true problem with remembering what you said or recalling what actually happened. Their sense of direction may also be impaired, so they may have trouble accounting for their whereabouts.

Emotionally, ADHD subjects may have difficulties in two areas. Their need for stimulation may cause them to get bored very easily, in which case they may start to "yes-yes" you just to get the interview over with. At the same time, their poor frustration tolerance may cause them to fly off the handle if they perceive something you do or say as annoying or threatening. All of these problems are exacerbated by increasing fatigue. If your goal is to get as much cooperation and useful information as possible, schedule sufficient breaks in the interview to allow the subject to "recharge his batteries." Also be alert for coexisting intoxication.

DEMENTIA

Dementia: Symptoms and Syndromes

The term *dementia* refers to an organic brain syndrome that impairs perception, thinking, language, memory, and behavior. As the American population continues to age, police officers can expect to have to deal with an increasing number of such individuals in their daily patrols. The main causes of dementia in the elderly are Alzheimer's disease, Parkinson's disease, and stroke. In younger subjects, dementia may occur as the result of AIDS, toxic-metabolic and medical syndromes such as kidney or liver disease, or from heavy drug use or overdose.

The difficulty an officer will have in dealing with a organically demented subject is largely determined by how severe the disorder is. Mildly impaired subjects may seem only a bit befuddled and absentminded, while more severely demented subjects will be unable to communicate or understand you, and will be virtually oblivious to their surroundings, aimlessly wandering, and becoming fearful and combative if restrained.

Symptoms of dementia include *disorientation to time* ("What day is this? What year are we in?"), place ("What street are we on? Do you know what city we're in? Where do you live?"), and person ("What's your name?"). *Aphasia* is a disturbance of language and can involve the comprehension of speech, the production of speech, or both (Will & Peters, 2004). *Aprosodia* is a flattening of the emotional expressiveness of speech. *Agnosia* is impaired perceptual recognition, and *apraxia* is a disturbance of complex movement. Other signs and symptoms of dementia include general agitation and *sundowing*, which is a tendency to become more active and agitated at night. This makes it more likely that these individuals will wander out of their homes at night, especially since the rest of the family may be asleep.

Typically, the behavior of subjects with dementia will be relatively peaceful, albeit confused; however, they may become defensively aggressive if they feel threatened. Most cases of law enforcement contact with these individuals will involve trespassing,

where they simply wander onto private property; theft or shoplifting, where they pick up a store item because they think it's theirs or just because it's there; assault related to defensively lashing out when they feel threatened, such as when confronted by an irate shopkeeper; or more rarely, sexual offenses based on inappropriate comments or physical contact with others.

Handling Citizens with Dementia

Don't overlook the obvious—check for ID. Most nursing home residents have wrist bands. Assess if there is any medical need. Even if not ill or injured, many such subjects may be malnourished or dehydrated because they literally forget to eat or drink. In your interactions with the subject, assess for specific signs or symptoms such as perceptual disturbances, difficulty completing sequences of actions, or language difficulties. If the subject is confused, frightened, and agitated, use very basic calming techniques, such as slow, even pace of voice, easy body language, and short, simple, reassuring phrases ("It's okay, we're going to take you home"). Most of these subjects will be reassured more by the demeanor and tone of what you say than by the content.

Be gently directive—tell and show the subject what you want him to do; most cognitively impaired subjects will display an easy, childlike compliance as they don't feel threatened. If you can identify where the subject resides, call the facility and offer to transport him or her back there. If not, or if there appears to be any injury or other medical problem, call for paramedic backup or transport to a hospital.

EPILEPSY

Like dementia, epilepsy is actually a medical-neurological disorder, not a psychiatric disorder per se, and most seizures are fairly unmistakable while they are occurring. However, there are a number of seizure types that produce disturbances primarily in thought, consciousness, and complex behavior; these may not be readily identifiable as manifestation of a medical disorder. In addition, epilepsy may be comorbid with a variety of other medical and mental disorders, including substance abuse, which can exacerbate it.

Epilepsy: Seizure Syndrome Types

Epileptic seizures are classified into several main subtypes. *Grand mal seizures* conform to most people's conceptualization of a seizure: an abrupt whole-body spasm that causes the subject to lose consciousness and fall to the ground, followed by several seconds of whole-body muscular contractions that gradually abate and leave the subject mentally confused and physically exhausted when he regains consciousness. *Focal seizures* involve only a portion of the body or one side of the body, usually the arm or leg, and are characterized by a few seconds of rapid, involuntary, stereotyped contractions, for which the subject typically remains conscious. In *petit mal seizures,* more common in children, there is a very brief loss of consciousness for perhaps a few seconds, but no significant disturbance of posture or muscle tone: the individual may be observed to "blink out" for a brief spell. The subject may experience anywhere from a few to several hundred such spells in the course of the day, which can disrupt the continuity of perception, learning, and memory.

Temporal Lobe Epilepsy

The type of epilepsy most often associated with behavioral disturbances leading to trouble with the law is *psychomotor epilepsy,* also known as *temporal lobe epilepsy,* or TLE, because the electrophysiological disturbance most commonly originates from the brain's temporal lobes, a region associated with emotion, motivation, and memory. During a temporal lobe seizure, awareness of the person's surroundings may be severely disturbed, and his behavior may or may not appear to be under his control. The seizure has an abrupt onset and gradual recovery, and can last for several minutes.

Subjects describe all manner of sensory, perceptual, cognitive, and emotional alterations heralding the onset of a TLE seizure, ranging from shapes and colors; strange sounds; religious visions and voices; sudden fear, sadness, or elation; sudden memories from the past; feelings of great profundity and mystical clarity; stomach flutters and other physical sensations. A common TLE experience is *deja vu,* or false familiarity, the feeling that "I've been here before." A dreamy, partial-consciousness state of disorientation often prevails during the seizure, during which the subject may be nonresponsive or only minimally responsive to others' questioning or commands. After the seizure passes, the subject may have spotty recall or no memory at all for the event.

The TLE symptoms most likely to get the subject in trouble are collectivedly known as *automatisms,* which are stereotyped, repetitive actions that, in themselves, are normal in the proper contexts, but occur during the seizure in an inappropriate form or circumstances. These include wandering around;

dressing and undressing; sexual and bathroom behavior; picking up and carrying off objects; and approaching others with short, repeated vocalizations. One of my patients had several arrests for indecent exposure for taking off his clothes and walking around a supermarket and up and down the street. Another patient was arrested for gathering up objects in a barbershop while waiting for a haircut.

In between seizures, many TLE patients display what clinicians call the *interictal TLE personality,* with a characteristic set of symptoms, including emotional intensity; interpersonal clinginess (*viscosity*); obsessive-compulsive preoccupations and behavior; excessive writing and note-taking (*hypergraphia*); and sometimes bizarre sexual interests (*fetishisms*). It is thought that this personality style develops from the frequent and repeated abnormal excitation of the brain's temporal lobe limbic system by frequent TLE seizures in childhood and adolescence.

Finally, patients with TLE and other forms of epilepsy are likely to be treated with *antiseizure medications,* many of which have strong sedating, disinhibiting, and cognitively confusing effects of their own. Unsupervised patients can miss doses or take overdoses because of memory problems, or may simply choose to misuse their medication if these are not controlled by a third party.

Epilepsy and Violence

There has been a longstanding debate about the relationship of epilepsy in general, and TLE in particular, to violent behavior (Elliott, 1982, 1984, 1992; Mark & Ervin, 1970; Miller, 1994a, 1994b; Monroe, 1982; Pincus & Tucker, 1978; Williams, 1969; Wood, 1987). It is now generally agreed that, like organic conditions generally, most aggressive activity in TLE is related to defensiveness out of a feeling of fear or to combativeness upon being restrained while in a state of confusion.

In a rare condition called *episodic dyscontrol syndrome* (EDS), or *intermittent explosive disorder* (IED), more severe aggressive behavior can appear as a sudden, often unprovoked, "storm-like" outburst, primitive and poorly organized–flailing, spitting, scratching, punching, throwing–and usually directed at the nearest available person or object. The act itself can be quite destructive to furniture, pets, or people who happen to get in the way, but serious injury to bystanders is usually the result of misguided efforts by observers to subdue the patient during an episode. In such cases, the wild thrashing that inflicts the injurious blows probably represents a desperate attempt to escape restraint, rather than a directed assault against a particular individual—although sudden, directed, but usually unsustained, attacks may occur.

More complex, better-organized outbursts are typically short-lived and may be followed by feelings of regret and remorse when the individual becomes aware of what he has done. Murder carried out in such states may be characterized by "overkill," such as an assailant beating or stabbing his victim dozens or hundreds of times, often in what witnesses describe as a "frenzy." Such uncontrolled violence is likely to be further fueled by alcohol or drugs. Indeed, EDS can often be triggered by even small amounts of these substances, producing the syndrome of *pathological intoxication*, which is characterized by uncontrolled violence following seemingly trivial drug or alcohol ingestion (also see above). Although these violent behavioral states have been shown to be associated with distinct electrophysiological brain changes, it is still unclear whether they represent true seizures per se.

Planned, purposeful homicide is almost never a seizure phenomenon, because it requires complex preparation and action sequences that are beyond the mental capability and time frame of a TLE seizure. Even in the case of sudden, impulsive violence,

remember that many people simply fly into a rage and commit murder without any particular brain syndrome being the cause. Indeed, the medicolegal status of these syndromes is still being debated, and having any type of medical or mental disorder is not necessarily exculpatory to the commission of a crime; however, this topic is beyond the scope of the present book (see Miller, 1998, 2000).

Handling Subjects with TLE Seizures

As always, safety first—and this applies both to the officer and the citizen. Check for a medical ID bracelet or other identification. Also check for medication containers that may yield clues to what illness is being treated. If this is a true TLE seizure, it will pass in a few minutes. In the meantime, use the minimum amount of restraint necessary to control the situation. Don't waste time trying to talk the subject down; it's unlikely he will comprehend complex verbal interventions—if he hears you at all. Instead, try the "*herding*" *technique*: simply stand a few feet in front of, or off to the side of, the subject and gently direct him in the direction you want to go, using slow, easy body language and gestures. Simple, direct instructions may work with some subjects: "This way, it's okay." Try not rush or crowd the subject; remember cases of violence during TLE episodes almost always occur when the subject feels confined or threatened. When the seizure passes, determine if medical treatment is necessary. When in doubt, call for paramedic backup.

OTHER BRAIN SYNDROMES

Although much rarer, a number of other neurobehavioral syndromes may be encountered during patrol.

Narcolepsy

Narcolepsy is an organic sleep disorder characterized by poor nighttime sleep and excessive daytime sleepiness. The subject typically experiences vivid, dream-like hallucinations that occur just when he is falling asleep (*hypnogogic hallucinations*) or waking up (*hypnopompic hallucinations*), and are associated with *sleep paralysis*, the transient inability

to move while experiencing these "waking dreams." During the day, the subject may experience *sleep attacks*, causing him or her to abruptly fall asleep in the middle of whatever he or she is currently doing. These attacks may be associated with *cataplexy*, which is a sudden loss of muscle tone that causes the subject to abruptly collapse and fall. These episodes can be triggered either by boredom or, conversely, by sudden strong emotion.

A likely scenario for patrol policing involves a driver who becomes excessively drowsy at the wheel and acts like he's intoxicated, weaving all over the road. When apprehended by police, he becomes frightened and promptly passes out. Of course, true intoxication and many kinds of medical conditions, from a stroke to a diabetic coma, can cause a person to pass out, but in narcolepsy the person will usually awaken after a few minutes with little or no residual symptoms. The most important thing an officer can do in such circumstances is to assure the subject's safety and call for medical attention.

Tourette Syndrome

Beginning in childhood, *Tourette syndrome* (TS) is characterized by the progressive development of multiple *tics*, which are rapid, involuntary, coordinated spasms of small muscle groups. Most TS tics are of the motor variety, in which case the subject may appear characteristically "twitchy." A number of TS patients have *vocal tics*, which usually consist of throat-clearing, grunts, single syllables, or other simple vocalizations. A smaller proportion of TS patients suffer from *coprolalia*, in which they utter various kinds of foul language, typically involving sexual or racial epithets, probably because most of these words contain hard consonants emitted with explosive breath—the vocal equivalent of a motor tic. Not surprisingly, these subjects may get into big trouble if they are heard to be uttering "fuck," "spic," or "cunt" in a public place.

Of course, people curse each other out for any number of reasons, and most don't have a brain syndrome. Although an officer needn't make a formal diagnosis, note if the subject seems to be in control of his utterances, and whether the verbal curses occur in the context of overall twitchy, agitated behavior. Usually, in addition to coprolalia, TS subjects will manifest a number of other vocal and motor tics. If this seems to be the case, and no real harm has been done, escort the subject to a location where his involuntarily obnoxious verbiage is less likely to get him into trouble.

Traumatic Brain Injury

Individuals who have suffered a blow to the head may suffer temporary or permanent brain damage producing a *postconcussion syndrome* (Miller, 1993; Parker, 2001). Physical symptoms include headache, dizziness, disturbance of equilibrium and hypersensitivity to light and sound. Cognitive symptoms include attention and concentration, poor short-term memory, and, in severe cases, general disorientation and confusion. Emotional-behavioral symptoms include increased irritability and anger, poor frustration tolerance, lack of good judgment, and impulsivity.

The most likely setting for a police officer's interaction with a brain-injured subject is at the scene of an assault or accident, immediately following the injury. The subject may have difficulty answering the officer's questions and giving a coherent account of what happened. If the subject was unconscious for any length of time, he will have trouble remembering events following his regaining of consciousness (*anterograde amnesia*), as well as for several seconds, minutes, or hours prior to the actual impact, as those memories had not had sufficient time to be consolidated to long-term storage prior to the injurious blow (*retrograde amnesia*). Some subjects even show a *lucid interval*, where they will appear relatively normal right after the accident or assault, even give a reasonably coherent account of events, then seem to slip into unconsciousness, from which they emerge with no recollection at all of the preceding interaction with the officer.

Occasionally, officers may encounter subjects with past head injuries who are still showing residual postconcussion effects. These individuals may seem confused and disoriented and may be mistaken for being intoxicated. Or they may well *be* intoxicated in addition to having a brain injury, which is hardly a great combination. In fact, demographically, the likelihood of a head injury, or any injury, is higher in individuals with an already impulsive, sensation-seeking lifestyle, which often includes the use of drugs and alcohol. These individuals are far more likely to drive unsafely, get into fights, and otherwise expose themselves to risk. Thus, a vicious cycle ensues: those most prone to sustaining a traumatic brain injury are even more likely to suffer its disinhibiting effects on behavior, further exposing them to risk of repeat injury, and so on (Miller, 1994b, 1998).

In practical terms, treat these subjects as you would any cognitively-impaired citizen: utilize safety precautions, assess for medical need, apply verbal de-escalation strategies, and take appropriate action if necessary.

CONCLUSIONS

As noted in Chapter 1, I like to tell the officers in my classes that they are already the best "practical psychologists," because they understand and utilize, on an intuitive basis, much of the information that I've discussed in this chapter in my more clinical and classificatory psych lingo. But hopefully, gaining a little more formal diagnostic insight should help put many of these behavioral syndromes in a clearer context, so that an officer's actions on the street can become even more effective in maintaining order, enforcing the law, and enhancing the community's overall quality of life.

PART II

CRITICAL INCIDENTS AND TRAUMATIC STRESS

Chapter 5

EXTREME STRESS MANAGEMENT
FOR LAW ENFORCEMENT EMERGENCIES

Most people would describe their jobs as stressful to one degree or another. Yet, in only a few professions—police, emergency services, disaster management, the military—does this stress literally involve making critical decisions in life-and-death situations.

Most "stress management" programs thus focus almost exclusively on mental and physical calming and other low arousal techniques for preparing for, or dealing with, the aftermath of a stressful experience. Far less attention has been paid to training emergency responders to manage stress *during* a critical life-and-death encounter. Yet stress management in critical situations has been applied to a number of high-demand performance areas, from emergency services to athletics and show business—professions where maintaining peak efficiency under conditions of extreme stress is crucial. Furthermore, being able to display such grace under pressure is a key ingredient in the area of *performance enhancement*, which enables soldiers, police officers, emergency responders, soldiers, professional athletes, and entertainment performers to exert their personal best under conditions of extreme stress and competition (Hays & Brown, 2004; Thelwell & Maynard, 2003; Scanff & Taugis, 2002; Thelwell & Greenless, 2001, 2003).

LIFE AND DEATH OF OFFICERS ON THE JOB

In few professions, other than policing and the military, is the risk of violent death an inherent part of the job description (Henry, 2004; Honig & Sultan, 2004; Violanti, 1999). Certain factors appear to contribute to some officers being more likely to be killed on the job than others. These variables fall into two broad categories (Blum, 2000), but, as I'll discuss below, these have a certain characteristic in common.

The first category can be described as *too cocky*. This officer tends to be overconfident during traffic stops or questioning of citizens, to the point of carelessness and complacency. His overconfidence in his ability to "handle anything" may lead him to prematurely let down his guard and to discount signs of danger. He may position himself poorly, making him vulnerable to a sudden lunge by a suspect. During searches, he may scrimp on proper technique, and find himself flipped over or, worse, with his gun in the suspect's hand. In a threatening confrontation, he may make poor use of cover, further exposing himself to danger. During an arrest, he may improperly use handcuffs or other restraints. To compensate for his poor technique or lack of communication skills, this officer may use an overly aggressive form of policing to demean and intimidate suspects, thereby generating even greater hostility and risk of violence. Such officers are advised to remember the law enforcement adage that there are only two types of stops: "high risk" and "unknown risk" (Van Blaricum, 2005).

The second category of officer is *too nice*. This officer is the typical "officer friendly" who wants to be liked. He is a hard-working, service-oriented officer with an easygoing style, who may believe that he can intuitively read a situation and therefore drop his guard. He may use less force than necessary with certain suspects, believing that by cutting them some slack, his benevolent gesture will be reciprocated, only to find himself exploited by the suspect or manipulated into a position where he can be attacked and overpowered. In his effort to peacefully resolve an encounter, he may wait too long to call for backup, until the situation has escalated beyond his control and turned deadly.

Paradoxically, both kinds of officers share an important feature in common: both fail to acknowledge the unpredictability and potential dangerousness of citizen encounters because both want to believe they are always in control—the too-cocky officer because he's a take-no-shit ass-kicker who knows how to deal with these scumbags; and the too-nice officer because he wants to live in a world where people are basically good and words are mightier than force.

In other research (Band & Vasquez, 1999), officers themselves have identified several factors that they perceive to be most critical to their survival:

Self-confidence, in this usage, does not refer to the inflated overconfidence of the too-cocky officer described above, but represents a realistic belief that the officer can perform a critical task with a high probability of success. This realistic self-confidence is based on a number of other factors noted below.

Training provides the skills and knowledge necessary to build realistic self-confidence. Knowing that you can handle a wide range of situations because you have been thoroughly trained and tested enables you to enter a situation with faith in your own abilities, which, consequently, increases your survivability in those circumstances.

Effectiveness in combat is the mindset in which the officer can visualize victory in a life-and-death confrontation. Specific techniques for doing just that will be described later in this chapter.

Decisiveness refers to the officer's ability to make rapid and accurate decisions and take appropriate action in a critical situation. Again, this is based on the realistic self-confidence that comes from training and experience.

Perseverence under stress means that the officer is able to continue to perform critical mental and physical tasks under complex, confusing, and stressful conditions, even when injured.

PEAK PERFORMANCE UNDER PRESSURE: THE "FLOW" EXPERIENCE

Although many authors have discussed the so-called *flow* experience as it pertains to athletics, the arts, business, communication, and personal relationships (Csikszentmihalyi, 1990; Privette & Bundrick, 1991; Williams & Krane, 1997), this concept has been specifically applied to the world of law enforcement and emergency services by Asken (1993), who believes it has been sorely underutilized. Whether called "flow," being in "the zone," or having a "peak experience," this experience of almost transcendentally heightened performance has certain characteristics, familiar to anyone who has ever experienced it:

Merging of action and awareness. There is a loss of self-consciousness as knowing flows into doing in one seamless process. The athlete's legs seem to run by themselves; the musician's piece seems to effortlessly issue forth from the instrument. The performer is "at one" with the experience.

Centering of attention on a limited field. The performer is fully focused on the activity of importance and is able to tune out any extraneous distractions. Depending on the task, this beam of attention may vary from broad to narrow, and later in this chapter, I'll discuss techniques for learning to control attention.

Sense of control. There is a sublime self-confidence, a consummate sense of control over the situation and one's own actions. This is by no means a reckless disregard for danger or impulsive overconfidence, but a smooth, calm, and total faith in one's ability to handle the challenge at hand.

Clear purpose and direction for action. There is no doubt or hesitation, and decisions seem easy.

Intrinsic motivation. While one may embark on a law enforcement, military, athletic, or performance arts career for any number of purposes, such as money, prestige, and so on, during the critical activity itself, the only reason for doing it is that it *has* to be done; we *can't not* do it; we climb the mountain because "it's there." The joy is in the doing, and nobody has to persuade or force us to do what we love.

It bears repeating that the flow experience is predicated on lots and lots of practice, training, and experience, and occurs when physical and mental skills have been blended and rehearsed. The reason peak performances appear so effortless and to be operating "on instinct" is because they are not instinctual at all: they are so well-trained and practiced that the person has become a supreme exponent of that skill. That is what we will try to inculcate in this chapter, and we will return to this theme in Chapter 14 when we discuss the concept of *expertise* in command leadership.

PSYCHOLOGICAL SKILLS FOR PEAK PERFORMANCE IN LAW ENFORCEMENT

In the more narrow domain of law enforcement and emergency services, Asken (1993) and others (Scanff & Taugis, 2002; Thelwell & Greenless, 2001, 2003; Thelwell & Maynard, 2003) have described a set of skills that seem to correlate with the ability of a police officer or emergency service worker to exert peak performance in critical situations:

Commitment refers to the officer's dedication to and positive involvement in his law enforcement work. The officer receives great satisfaction from doing a job well done, but without becoming unhealthily enmeshed to the point of overdependence on the police role to unilaterally bolster his or her personal identity.

Confidence is the officer's belief—based on evidence from training, experience, and external performance appraisals—that he or she will have what it takes to handle an emergency situation when it arises.

Arousal control is the skill that allows the officer to tone down the adrenaline rush that can lead to panicky decision-making and poor performance, as well as to pump up the emotional juice when flagging energy or motivation impedes optimum

performance. The key is flexibility of arousal control, as will be discussed below.

Attention control permits the officers to broadly scan the environment or focus attention on a specific feature as a consciously controlled process. Again, flexibility is the key.

Imagery is the ability of the officer to visualize himself performing well, to engage in a "virtual rehearsal" of his actions to instill a sense of mastery.

Self-talk refers to the officer verbally guiding himself through a difficult task. The talk can either be instructional or motivational, but serves as an "inner voice" for direction and encouragement.

Cognitive restructuring allows the officer to reframe negative events as opportunities for positive action. It is not denial of reality, but rather a creative exploration of options to counteract despair and pessimism when things are not going as expected.

The remainder of this chapter will expand on these concepts and applications.

CONTROLLING AROUSAL

The Nature and Purposes of Arousal

Arousal is the state of awareness and readiness for action that characterizes all conscious states. And

like virtually all mental states, arousal must be maintained in the right amount for the right situation in order for a person's activity to be adaptive for a given task. For most active tasks, too little arousal results in flagging motivation and attention and a desultory, inefficient approach to the task, like sitting through a boring classroom lecture and trying to catch what the instructor is droning on about. Too much arousal, on the other hand, sends you into adrenalin overdrive, and you become scattered, panicked, and again unable to complete the task effectively, like suddenly having the final exam thrown on your desk without preparation. Psychologists will recognize this as the famous *Yerkes-Dodson law* or "inverted-U" graph, where too little arousal bogs down task efficiency and too much derails it.

For the present discussion, arousal can be divided into two main types (Asken, 1993). *Primary arousal* flows from the performance demands of the situation and provides the preparatory physical and mental readiness for, and focus on, the challenge at hand. *Secondary arousal* is extraneous and unhelpful; it comes mainly from worrying, doubts, and concerns about how the officer will be evaluated—by superiors, peers, or his own self-scrutiny—and is thus closely connected with the concept of *performance anxiety* (Hays & Brown, 2004).

Actually, these are not two distinct states of arousal, but rather different points on a continuum. Recall the relationship between arousal level and performance (inverted-U curve). The optimum state of arousal in any emergency situation is that which energizes you for proper action but does not distract or impede you from the performance of your duties.

Another important variable influencing arousal level is *task complexity*. High arousal has less of a disruptive effect on simple tasks than on complex ones. Actually, we know from the field of neuropsychology (Miller, 1990) that there are three important variables that affect task performance, which can be remembered by the acronym CNS (as in "Central Nervous System"), in this case standing for Complexity, Novelty, and Speed.

Complexity refers to how many different elements of a task or situation you have to juggle at one time. For example, calming a distraught domestic assault victim is difficult enough, but is far more challenging if there is also a drunk partner who needs to be contained or arrested, and screaming children running around the house.

Novelty refers to how unfamiliar the task is. A skilled hostage negotiator may have handled hundreds of home, workplace, and bank robbery hostage calls, all with certain similarities, but if this particular call involves political terrorists who are making unfamiliar demands, it will require far more concentration, focus, and outside information to handle effectively.

Speed refers to how quickly something must be done. All things being equal, tasks that have to be completed swiftly, such as directing traffic and pedestrians away from a potentially explosive chemical spill, will be more difficult that those in which the officer can take his time and deliberate over his actions, for example, sorting out who did what to cause the tanker truck rollover.

The goal then, is to strive neither for a state of blissful relaxation nor five-alarm hypervigilance, but to be able to induce an *optimum arousal level* (OAL) that is appropriate for a given task or situation. Some situations may require ramping up your arousal level to deal with the threat, while in other situations it may be necessary to calm yourself down so that extraneous arousal does not distract and disrupt your performance. Expert responders and peak performers in all fields seem to be able to control their level of arousal so that they can generate the necessary OAL for specific situations (Flin, 1996; Hanin, 2000; Hays & Brown, 2004; Klein, 1996). Like any ability, some people have more innate talent in doing this than others, but for most of us, it is a skill that can be mastered with practice.

Increasing Arousal

Students in my courses and seminars are often surprised that I introduce the topic of heightened arousal as part of the curriculum of stress management: "Aren't we supposed to be learning to relax?" But as explained above, it is just as important to be able to increase your arousal level when necessary as it is to reduce it: "Do you want to be all mellow and chilled out for your forced entry of a crack house with armed suspects inside?" I ask them. The key, then, is to be able to voluntarily induce, adjust, and maintain the OAL for any particular situation and to flexibly moderate it up or down and circumstances change. Some techniques for increasing arousal level range from the familiar to the unusual, and include the following (Asken, 1993; Hays & Brown, 2004).

Mental and physical arousal typically go together, and getting the blood pumping is a well-known method of psyching oneself up: just watch boxers, football players, and other athletes prior to a match or game. Such *physical warm-ups* can consist of push-ups, jumping jacks, a jog around the track, and so on. This also has the added beneficial effect of limbering up the body for physically demanding tasks to come. Just be careful not to prematurely exhaust yourself.

Another common psycher-upper is *music*. Everybody's got their favorites, but pick a style of music that gets your heart thumping in a positive, enthusiastic way. Combining a rocking beat with physical exercise is a common method for jacking up your motivation and energy level.

If you're gearing up for an important operation, you probably don't want to spend the immediately preceding period hanging out with a roomful of slugs and couch potatoes. *Selective association* refers to spending time with others who are as excited and enthused as you are. It doesn't mean they have to be doing the same activity as you—they don't even need to be in the same room; for example, you can vicariously selectively associate with the players on a TV football or hockey team, if watching the game will give you the physical and mental pump you need.

Cues are prompts you give to yourself to influence your mental state, in this case, in the direction of increased arousal. *Cue words* to increase arousal can be general ("Win!" "Kick ass!") or specific to the person or situation ("First one in owns the room!"). These can be said out loud, muttered under one's breath, or just thought internally. *Cue sounds* ("Hoo-ah!") serve the same function, as do *cue images*, such as visualizing yourself controlling a crowd, apprehending a suspect, and so on (imagery and visualization will be discussed further below).

Arousal can also be increased by using *attentional focus*, which involves bringing to bear all of your awareness and concentration on the task you need to perform and on the skills necessary to get the job done. This will be elaborated below.

Self-efficacy statements involve telling yourself—again, either out loud or to yourself—that you can indeed carry out the task before you ("I can do it." "Piece of cake"). These are often combined with cue words, sounds, or images for maximal effectiveness. In fact, many officers naturally utilize a combination of the above techniques when gearing up for a dangerous or challenging operation.

Anger transformation involves thinking about something that makes you mad and gets your juices going. In essence, it's akin to "method acting" that Hollywood performers often use to psyche themselves into a role, and is also commonly used by athletes before a competition. Again, the guideline is situation-appropriateness. The danger is that anger may get out of control and then become either an emotional distraction from peak performance or lead to inappropriately forceful action that can end up getting the officer in trouble. A similar kind of *mental conditioning* technique will be discussed further below.

Decreasing Arousal

This is usually the substance of most courses and programs in stress management and basically involves learning to control the physiology of arousal—to moderate the adrenalin rush that typically accompanies emergency situations. As noted earlier, most emergency situations cannot be handled very effectively if the officer's mental state is akin to floating on a cloud. Still, there are many benefits to being able to calm one's own body and mind during critical situations (Asken, 1993). Arousal control reduces anxiety and increases confidence during a call. A more relaxed state reduces the likelihood of impulsive action and resultant injury. A relatively relaxed, but assertively motivated, state is conducive to learning new skills and to learning from one's mistakes on the spot: a kind of real-time 20/20 hindsight = 20/20 insight = 20/20 foresight (Chapter 1).

Remember that a state of physical and mental relaxation is not an all-or-none phenomenon. Many cops, whose primary mental state on the job involves being alert and vigilant at all times, only understand relaxation from the perspective of a total letting down of one's guard, as during family vacations or a night at the pub with the guys. To them, "relaxation" may be equated with vulnerability and befuddlement. But one can be both relaxed and alert, in a state of calm determination that seems to characterize those who show stable and effective command leadership under fire (Flin, 1996; see also Chapter 14🍎🍎).

It's kind of like the caffeine boost you get from a strong cup of coffee: alert, focused, and motivated, but not agitated or overly anxious. The more coffee you drink, however, the more the pumped-up feeling turns to jitteriness and crankiness. There's a neurobiological reason for this: All stimulant substances (and the brain doesn't care if they're legal or not) increase the amount of *dopamine* in central nervous system, which is the "hey-I-can-do-it-let's-go" neurotransmitter. But with continued high stimulation over time, more and more of the dopamine becomes metabolized to *norepinephrine*, the "hold-it-I'm-getting-a-bad-feeling-about-this-let's-check-it-out-first" neurotransmitter. Eventually, even norepinephrine is exhausted, and the person just crashes into a state of fatigue or depression (Miller, 1990). That's why it's important to be able to moderate the level of arousal, not just keep it on the highest setting all the time: you don't want to flame out prematurely.

Therefore, a particularly important role for relaxation and arousal control in law enforcement concerns calls in which there exists high personal danger over a relatively prolonged period of time, and where there is little the officer can do but bide his time and wait. These include being trapped in building and hoping for rescue, being a hostage during a prolonged negotiation, being pinned down by hostile fire and waiting for backup, and so on. Getting through such situations requires that the officer be able to go into mental hibernation, or put his mental computer on standby mode, or keep the mental engine in neutral—pick whatever metaphor you like—to avoid expending precious energy, but at the same time being alert and aware enough to seize the initiative should the opportunity to act present itself.

Even if not in actual danger, prolonged law enforcement and emergency service operations are likely to involve long work shifts, alternating with briefer rest periods, such as in hostage negotiations or mass casualty rescue operations. Most people find it difficult to go from high alert to standby at the drop of a hat. With the adrenalin still pumping, but physical, cognitive and emotional energy reserves depleted, the officer may find himself in a state of "agitated exhaustion"—too burned out to function, but too jacked up to rest or sleep. It is in just these situations that the ability to consciously reduce your level of arousal can spell the difference between recharging your batteries or burning out your engine. In this sense, the term *relaxation* denotes a flexible range of low-arousal techniques that can be utilized when the situation warrants.

Relaxation Techniques

For more than half a century, the technique of *progressive muscle relaxation* has been the standard recipe of stress management and is by now so well-known that it will only be summarized here. Essentially, the exercise focuses on one muscle group or body area at a time and guides the subject through an alternate tense-and-relax sequence until all major muscle groups are in a state of relative physiological quiescence. This is typically combined with slow, steady, diaphragmatic breathing (deep stomach breathing as opposed to shallow chest breathing) and one or more mental cuing or imagery techniques (see below) to further induce a state of psychological calm.

Obviously, officers can't carry couches and lounge chairs to emergency calls or take a time-out from a burning building or gun battle to go through a tense-and-relax and breath-control protocol. Indeed, one of the features of effective, practical low-arousal techniques that make them useful in the field is the ability to whip them out and utilize them quickly under all sorts of adverse circumstances. Accordingly, the technique is first practiced in a peaceful, stress-free environment, such as in a psychologist's office, guided by the clinician's soothing words or, alternatively, by use of a commercially prepared or custom-made relaxation tape or CD. Later, with continued practice in a variety of settings and conditions, the goal is for the subject to be able to self-induce the relaxed state on his own, in his natural environment, without external prompting, and without having to necessarily go through the whole tense-and-relax sequence. For example, someone who finds himself tensing up in traffic might be able to induce a more relaxed, yet alert, state while sitting behind the wheel.

Once the progressive relaxation technique has been practiced and mastered, many individuals are able to employ a kind of *instant relaxation*, or *conditioned relaxation*, technique. By voluntarily reducing muscular tension, taking a calming breath, and using a cue word, the subject is able to immediately lower physiological arousal and thereby induce a more calm and focused mental state. Like any highly trained technique, this becomes easier and more automatic with repeated practice.

Other low-arousal techniques utilize some components of the progressive relaxation protocol and add certain others.

Diaphragmatic breathing involves using the deep-breathing technique described above to cue the entire relaxation response. This is often used along with a *cue word or phrase,* which may range from the spiritual ("God is with me;" "Om") to the mundane ("Chill;" "Okay, I'm good"), and is basically any word or phrase you've paired frequently with the full relaxation response and that you can now say to yourself to signal your body to relax. Similarly, a *cue image* is any mental scene you can invoke that has a calming effect, especially by virtue of having been paired with your initial relaxation response practice. Pick the modality or technique that works best for you: the key is to invoke some cue that enables you to quickly and volitionally lower your arousal level to a degree that is appropriate for the situation you're in (Hays & Brown, 2004; Miller, 1994; Olson, 1998).

Centering (Asken, 1993) is a technique derived from Eastern meditation that involves combining diaphragmatic breathing with a centering cue image. Begin by taking a slow, deep diaphragmatic breath. On exhaling, slowly let your eyes close and focus your awareness on some internal or external point, such as your lower abdomen or an imaginary spot on the wall. This technique combines features of arousal control with attentional focusing, discussed further below.

Centering is itself incorporated into a technique called *attention control training* or *attention management* (Hardy et al., 1996; Nideffer & Sharpe, 1978), which begins with inducing the centering response, and then presenting yourself with a task-relevant cue or instruction that focuses your attention on the immediate challenge at hand. This will be discussed further below.

In *mindfulness* training (Kabat-Zinn, 1994, 2003; Marra, 2005), the individual makes no conscious attempt to relax, but simply allows him- or herself to take in the sensations and images in the surrounding environment. This kind of free-floating receptivity underlies many of the attention-focusing strategies to be described later.

Finally, just as *externally-based techniques* can be used to increase arousal, they can also be used to calm it down. These include music (calm instead of raucous) and selective association (spend your off hours at the beach or library instead of a hockey game or race track). Again, the more internal and external arousal control techniques you can use together, the greater will be the overall cumulative effect. Indeed, recent clinical research and practice have been moving away from an overreliance on structured breathing and muscle relaxation techniques in favor of more naturalistic strategies (Huppert & Baker-Morissette, 2003; Marra, 2005; Miller, 1994).

CONTROLLING ATTENTION

The Nature and Purposes of Attention

The ability to concentrate and focus attention is one of the most important mental skills for peak performance–a fact that is most glaringly apparent when things go wrong. To use one example, too narrow an attentional focus is often characterized as *tunnel vision,* which involves "missing the forest for the trees," that is, overfocusing on details, while losing sight of the big picture. Conversely, trying to get a little of everything at once results in a *lack of focus*–here, the beam of attention is too broad, diffuse, and scattered to yield any useful information on how to respond. In emergency situations, one of the first mental faculties to be affected is the ability to control one's attentional focus as required.

Attention is what allows you to focus on a situation or task so that sensory input is processed in a meaningful pattern. *Concentration* is the ability to consciously and purposefully direct and maintain your attention to a particular object or activity over the appropriate span of time. By concentrating, you make a point to avoid distractions that could disrupt your performance. At the same time, it is important to be able to switch attention to another subject when warranted, and even maintain different types, levels, and targets of attention and concentration as needed at any given time.

Effortful concentration, especially if prolonged, takes a great deal of mental energy and is fatiguing. Accordingly, the key is to be able to produce a match between the often-changing demands of a critical situation and the level and direction of attention and concentration needed. For some, this happens relatively automatically and instinctively; for many, it requires training and practice.

In fact, control of attention and concentration is so important that the brain has a whole neural network devoted to it, called the *reticular activating system* or RAS (Miller, 1990). This system consists of a complex pattern of neurons and fibers that connect the basic sensory modalities (vision, hearing, touch, pain, smell, taste, temperature, balance, and others) with the arousal, emotional, motivational, and thinking centers of the brain, so that what we experience through our senses is automatically coordinated with the proper response to that situation. Individuals who have suffered damage to the RAS may have eyes and ears that work fine, but the perceptions they experience have no significance to them; they are essentially unresponsive, even though the primary visual and auditory pathways are intact. Thus, they may appear uninvolved with their surroundings, but they are not sleeping or in a coma—they just don't respond because the sensory information isn't "getting in."

The closest any of us gets to this state in normal life is when we fail to hear someone right next to us talking in our ear because we're so focused on another person's conversation, riveted to a TV show, engrossed in a magazine article, or preoccupied with an internal thought. An observer might say we're "distracted" or that our "attention is focused elsewhere." In fact, it may take an unexpected stimulus, such as a jabbing finger or a loud "Hellooooo. . . ." to refocus our attention to the person trying to capture it. The neuropsychological bottom line is that we have a finite ability to focus attention on more than a few things at a time, on ourselves and in the environment. The key is to train the RAS to do this more efficiently and controllably.

In fact, focus of attention may be one feature of *cognitive style* that varies among individuals and may be associated with certain personality traits (Gardner et al., 1959; Klein, 1954; Miller, 1990; Shapiro, 1965). This explains why some people are noted to be punctilious to the point of obsession,

while others are more scatter-brained to the point of irresponsibility.

But like any human ability, mental or physical, while some people may possess more of an innate talent for it than others, attentional control is a skill that can be learned, indeed, *must* be learned, for effective response in critical situations, because in emergency circumstances, a lapse or misfocus of attention and concentration can lead to costly mistakes. "I wasn't paying attention," "I missed the cue," "I wasn't thinking," "I had tunnel vision," "I dropped the ball," "I was too slow on the uptake," "I was somewhere else," "It got past me," are all phrases officers have used to describe lapses or disruptions of attention during critical calls.

Asken (1993) conceptualizes the faculty of attention along two interrelated dimensions. *Breadth of focus* describes how narrow or wide the beam of attention is. When first encountering an unknown scene, officers typically set the scan relatively wide to take in as much information as possible, so as not to overlook something important, much like using the wide angle lens setting of a surveillance camera. But if something critical is identified, then focus narrows, like looking through a rifle sight to concentrate on the target and eliminate distractions. Here, all of your attention is riveted to the task at hand, at the calculated expense of losing information at the perceptual periphery; in other words, you're deliberately inducing tunnel vision, because that's what is required for the specific task of acquiring a target and hitting it, either with a bullet or a camera click. Many situations require you to flexibly shift concentration from broad to narrow and back again, or even to maintain a kind of divided consciousness, focusing on a subject of interest but keeping part of the attentional beam in a scanning mode so as not to overlook existing or emerging threats.

Another dimension is *direction of focus*, which can be internal or external. External focus is the most obvious, as it is important to be able to focus on the events taking place during the critical situation. But it may be just as important to focus internally on what is taking place mentally and physically within the officer's mind and body during the critical incident. This includes his or her own arousal level, energy reserves, fear and anxiety, presence or threat of injury, or basic requirements like need for air or taking a bathroom break. Again, flexibility is the key, and during a critical incident, attention should monitor back and forth between internal and external, coordinating thought, feeling, and arousal with optimum task performance.

Training Attention

Successful control of attention requires the mastery three dimensions of attention:

Intensity = Can I concentrate *hard* enough?
Duration = Can I concentrate *long* enough?
Flexibility = Can I *shift* my attention when necessary?

Mastering these three dimensions involves practicing what Asken (1993) calls the *attention-fixation-generalization technique*, which I have adapted for use in my police academy training courses. For this technique, think of attention as a kind of flashlight beam with a constant wattage but with a variable aperture. This allows you to broaden the beam to a soft glow that completely but dimly illuminates the whole room, or narrow it down to a single, thin, bright shaft of light that can create a tiny but blazing spot on the wall. Another analogy is to an adjustable garden hose nozzle that allows you to cover a wide swath of lawn with a broad, misty spray or zero-in on a single shrub with a fast, concentrated water jet. Beam or stream—pick whatever metaphor best helps you grasp the concept and master the methodology.

Also bear in mind that you probably won't become a proficient exponent of all the following steps in one or two sessions. Like any other skill, keep practicing these techniques, sequentially and concurrently, until you achieve your desired level of proficiency.

To begin training in this technique, first assume a relatively comfortable position, relatively free of distractions. Eventually, you should be able to evoke and utilize this technique even under conditions of extreme stress and chaos but, at first, practice it in a relatively quiet setting.

Pick an object in the room—a picture, lamp, cup, even a spot on the wall—and visually focus your attention on it as intently and as long as possible. Try to keep all of your attention on the object, tuning out any other stimuli in the room. Hold that focus for as long as possible. Then, voluntarily shift your

attention away from the object to another object in the room. Make that your focus of attention. Try this with a few objects around the room.

Now, try it with sounds. Focus on a lawnmower in a neighbor's yard, a TV mumbling in the next room, or the hum of the fridge. Pick one sound source and hone in on it. Now, switch to another sound, and then another, as you did with the visual objects. Now, try going back and forth between visual and auditory stimuli. To make it interesting, try it with different objects (switch from a visual image of the couch to the sound of the fridge) or within the same object (swing your attention back and forth from the TV picture to the sound). Remember to take your time and not try to rush things.

Now, broaden the beam. Scan the entire room and become aware of as many sources of stimuli as possible: the objects in the room, their shapes, colors, textures, and proximity to one another, the drone of the air conditioner or people talking, any street noise coming in from outside, any smells or temperature changes, the level of illumination in different parts of the room, the pressure of the seat on your legs and tush, the feel of your clothes on your skin.

Pay attention to internal sources of physical and mental stimulation, as well: Are you hot or cold, hungry or thirsty? Are you comfortable in your seat? Do you have to use the bathroom? Tired or rested, calm or nervous, happy or sad?

You may find it overwhelming at first to try to attend to so many features of your internal and external environment at once. As the attentional beam gets stretched more and more broadly, you may find it thinning out to the point that you're not really paying attention to anything in particular—the mental flashlight flickers, the garden hose sputters. This scanning ability will improve with practice, and improves as you learn to also control the *intensity* of the scanning beam. For now, however, pull the beam-width in a little bit to the point where you are able to focus on as many things as possible, while keeping those percepts reasonably within your span of attention.

Next, keep maintaining multiple focuses of attention but start varying the intensity and beam-width of each. Now, you'll actually have several beams of attention branching out, some narrowly and intensely focused on one feature of the environment, such as a person talking to you or a scene played out on the TV, and others more broadly scanning the environment, such as the number of people in the room, the layout of the furniture, points of access and exit, and so on.

Ideally, in a real-life police emergency, your intense, narrow attentional beam might be focused on a criminal making a threatening gesture toward you, with other beams more broadly and less intently scanning important peripheral and internal features of the environment: being alert for sounds of footsteps behind you, avenues of escape around the room, your own heartbeat and respiration rate, the smell of gunpowder or drug residue, and so on. It is in just these kinds of critical situations that the ability to flexibly allocate attention in many directions in response to changing circumstances might save your life.

One practical example concerns officer-involved shootings (Chapter 7), in which officers typically describe a sense of tunnel-vision during the episode. In retrospect, many report that they were so focused on the suspect's gun or their own actions, that they completely tuned out anything else that was going on; as a consequence, they have difficulty remembering what transpired during the event. This is probably because all the environmental stimuli that

were shut out of the brain's perceptual channels by an overfocused RAS during the emergency never got the chance to be recorded accurately by the brain's memory system. I have no hard data on this, but it would be intriguing to do a study that applied the present kind of attentional training to just such types of critical incidents, and gauge the effects.

More practically, in my police academy courses, I ask each officer to recount a personal critical incident from his or her own career and describe the thoughts, feelings, and actions that accompanied it. Then, as a class, we run through some practice sessions of the attention-fixation-generalization technique described above. After that, I ask each officer to recreate his or her own incident in their minds, and imagine how it might have been different if they had used the attentional technique they just learned. Finally, I encourage the officers to practice the technique in their daily patrol activities until it becomes natural and automatic, so they will be ready to employ it in the event of an emergency.

As always, the goal of learning any skill is for it to become so ingrained and natural that you're hardly aware that you're using it. This can only be achieved through practice and application in as wide a variety of settings as possible.

EFFECTIVE IMAGERY

The ability to use imagery to mentally project oneself into a different mindset or state of being is a time-honored psychological technique for improving skills in sports and the performing arts (Hays & Brown, 2004).

This is sometimes referred to as *visualization* training (Olson, 1998), but I agree with Asken (1993) that *imagery* is the preferable term because such training should involve sensory images in all modalities, not just vision. Like any skill, the use of effective imagery requires practice, general at first, but ultimately focused on the type of imagery that most closely replicates the actual situation that the performer will be in.

This presupposes adequate training and experience with the skill itself. You can spend all day imaging yourself playing a killer lead guitar solo or competing in a Nascar race but, if these are not part of your regular experience, if they have no real-world

referent in actual practice, then you might as well image yourself flying like Superman.

Imagery, then, is a technique to enhance performance of a skill, once that skill has been fundamentally learned and mastered in real life. That is, imagery is not the same as fantasy. It does not take the place of hard work in the real world, but may improve it in proportion to how much the real-life skill improves. To be effective, the image must be as accurate as possible.

Uses of Imagery

Asken (1993) cites several uses of effective imagery for enhancing the performance of emergency services personnel.

A basic use of imagery is for *situation simulation*, which is an important component in all uses of imagery. You can't be in every situation every time you want to, but you may be able to conjure up the scenario mentally. Combined with actual practice in real-life and realistic-simulation settings (obstacle track, firing range), mental drilling can integrate with real-life drilling for enhanced performance.

This leads directly to the use of imagery for *skill enhancement*, in which the imagery is used to mentally rehearse a particular physical activity. For example, an officer might image himself conducting a crime scene search or accurately drawing down his weapon on a difficult target.

Another use of imagery is for *error analysis and correction.* Here, the officer engages in a kind of internal operational debriefing, mentally "replaying the tape" of a recent real-life incident, recalling as many details as possible, and utilizing the *20/20 hindsight/insight/foresight* principle to self-correct any errors or misjudgments that were made. This technique can be effectively combined with real-life operational debrief data from outside sources, so that the officer can include this factual information in his mental operational critique. Note than many officers do this spontaneously to some extent after a difficult call. The key is to master the use of this kind of imagery so that accurate details can be recalled during the hindsight review and appropriate corrections can be made during the projective foresight mental rehearsal. This prevents an internal operational review from devolving into an emotionally disruptive self-flagellation session that has little practical benefit.

Imagery can also be used proactively at the front end of an anticipated critical operation, for *response preparation*. In addition to regular mental drills for possible future events, imagery for response preparation can be used on-scene, in the immediate preparatory phase of an operation, such as a narcotics raid or SWAT team tactical assault. For example, officers can imagine themselves moving in, securing the scene, and making arrests. Again, it's important that these internal scenarios be as realistic as possible, not simply wishful-thinking fantasies. Many officers instinctively use these kinds of psyching-up techniques before a complex and difficult operation.

Finally, imagery can be used for *confidence enhancement*. Recalling past successes and utilizing multimodal imagery of the sensory, emotional, and visceral exhilaration of completing a task well done can enhance self-confidence. This can also be used as part of response preparation noted above. And both these techniques interplay with arousal regulation, discussed earlier.

VISUAL-MOTOR BEHAVIOR REHEARSAL

Developed by Suinn and colleagues (1972, 1984, 1985) in the domain of sports psychology and adapted by Asken (1993) to the needs of emergency service workers, this technique combines the relaxation response with multisensory practice imagery to mentally rehearse and enhance skills for peak performance.

To utilize *visual-motor behavior rehearsal* (VMBR), first employ the relaxation response discussed earlier. This will allow you to get into state of emotional calmness and clarity that will enhance your ability to focus and evoke a complete simulation of the imagined scenario. Now, pick a situation that you have trained for and experienced in real life. Mentally walk yourself through the scene in real-time, evoking as many sensory and experiential details as possible.

For an error-correction exercise, mentally replay yourself doing exactly what you recall doing during the actual event. Then, mentally rewind the tape and image yourself performing the way you would now that you have additional data and insight. Rewind to the beginning of the incident and image yourself mentally preparing for the incident. Fast-forward and image yourself feeling competent and confident after successfully completing the task. Then, splice the parts together and mentally play the scenario in real-time sequence as many times as necessary, until it feels natural and unforced.

Despite Asken's (1993) extensive use of this technique with firefighters and emergency service workers, I was able to locate only one study that empirically evaluated the effectiveness of VMBR in the skill enhancement of police recruits. Shipley and Baranski (2002) randomly assigned 54 members of the Ontario Provincial Police Force training program to either a VMBR treatment or a nontreatment group prior to undergoing a highly stressful live-fire exercise. Results showed that members of the VMBR group did not show any differences from the control group in the physical manifestations of anxiety or in overall self-confidence, but they did show lower levels of cognitive anxiety (i.e., their thought processes were clearer, less negative, and less distractible), and–most importantly–they showed better actual performance on the critical event scenario; that is, they achieved significantly higher scores on "assailant hits" during the live-fire exercise.

What is especially intriguing about these findings is that they do not oversell VMBR (and, by implication, other mental training techniques) as a magical solution or miracle cure. Indeed, the VMBR subjects felt just as much somatic anxiety (heart thumping, palms sweating) as the control group, yet they were able to cognitively keep it together more effectively in order to focus on the task at hand.

Additionally, even though the training group did not report feeling more confident than the control group, when it came to real-world performance–number of hits on the live-fire target range–they performed significantly better.

Thus, one of the strengths of mental training techniques is precisely that they are not all-or-nothing: even if you're feeling nervous and unsure, you may still show peak performance by focusing on the job that needs to be done, tuning out distractions, and letting your training click in. That is, while confidence certainly helps, just because you're not strutting around with a cocky "bring-em'-on" attitude before an operation, doesn't mean you won't perform effectively. Remember, this study did not specifically incorporate self-confidence imagery; it would be interesting to see if that variable was affected in a subsequent study replication that incorporated it.

POSITIVE AFFIRMATIONS

Related to the subject of confidence-enhancement is the technique of using *affirmations* (Asken, 1993). Basically, these are positive statements we make to ourselves about ourselves, referencing our own abilities. They are not narcissistic self-inflations or empty boasts; on the contrary, to be effective, what is being affirmed has to be based on genuine, real-life competencies that have been worked for and earned, otherwise, such empty affirmations can quickly approach "Saturday Night Live"-like levels of parody. But sometimes, when we're under stress, or have just been pummeled by a series of downturns, we may forget that we still have positive qualities and competencies we can be proud of. And if no one is there to remind us, we have to be able to remind ourselves, lest our brooding turn into despair and further drag down our performance.

Types of Affirmations

Although these are hardly rigid categories, and frequently overlap, Asken (1993) divides affirmations into three main groups:

Personal affirmations are self-statements that recognize your positive qualities as a human being: "I'm a stand-up guy." "I'm a smart gal." "My family

knows I'd do anything for them." "I'm in great shape; I really take care of my health." "There are people out there who really love me."

Professional affirmations are self-statements that recognize the positive aspects of your work in law enforcement: "The citizens in my patrol area respect me because they know I'm fair but I won't take crap." "I've earned every promotion honestly and I deserve every bit of credit." "I'm the go-to guy in the department when anybody needs advice about weapons and tactics."

Performance affirmations are self-statements that recognize positive aspects of your skills or performance as they relate to a specific incident or operation: "Nobody was able to make sense of that crime scene till I came along." "Those hostages would've been toast if I hadn't talked the bad guy down." "I think fast, I speak well, and that's why that couple didn't end up bashing each other and hurting the kids."

Using Affirmations

It often helps to make up a realistic list of the positive qualities you can feel proud of. Again, you needn't—indeed, shouldn't—go around waving this list in your colleagues' or family's faces, unless you enjoy being the object of scorn and ridicule. No one needs to know about the list, except you. In fact, it can be a strictly mental list, as long as you can recall the items when you need them. The objective is to have a ready set of positive qualities about yourself that you can invoke when you start to feel dejected and demoralized.

Asken (1993) delineates a number of principles to guide the use of positive affirmations. None of these is written in stone, and if you have a more comfortable way of expressing these affirmations, go ahead. That is, think of the following as suggestions, not directives.

Practice affirmations daily. Keep them handy but don't overdo them to the point where they become meaningless, parroted repetitions.

State affirmations in the positive tense. Not: "My record-keeping could be better, but at least I'm no slouch on the range;" *but:* "I'm a damned good marksman, and if I put my mind to it, I can bring my paperwork up to speed."

Use the first person tense—the "I" word. Not: "A lot of people seem to appreciate my investigative skills;" *but:* "I'm the top crime scene analyst in the department."

State affirmations in the present tense. Not: "I've been a great patrol cop," or, "I'll try to improve my people skills;" *but:* "I know how to talk to citizens to keep trouble from escalating on my beat."

Affirmations must be truthful. Basically, a positive self-statement can't help if deep down you know it's bullshit.

Affirmations do not replace skills and training. Actually, none of the stress-management and motivational techniques described in this chapter are intended to substitute for skills and training, but to enhance them.

Affirmations should not create unrealistic expectations. Affirmations are different from self-coaching or motivational self-talk (see below), which are aspirational encouragements for future performance. Affirmations, as discussed here, are positive confidence-bolstering statements that are based on skills and accomplishments that have already been earned and recognized. Consistent with the truth-and-reality guidelines above, if the affirmations aren't real, they won't stick.

THOUGHT STOPPING

This is not as strange or diabolical as it sounds, and in fact is only a systematic application of something we all do when we need to keep unproductive ruminating thoughts from clogging our cognitive channels. During an emergency call, the combination of high internal arousal and high external distraction may propel cycling loops of negative thoughts and images that prevent you from making important judgments and decisions. Think of *thought stopping* as the Ctrl + Alt + Del key of your cognitive keyboard that clears your mental screen when it gets stuck. Thought stopping can also be used before a critical incident to keep negative ruminations from sapping your motivation and determination, or be used following the incident to prevent pointless, unproductive second-guessing or self-criticism that may impair your

performance on the next call (as distinguished from more productive 20/20 hindsight/insight/foresight review).

Thought stopping is not an instant cure-all for negativity in general; you will eventually need to resolve the mind-set and situations that generate the negative thoughts in the first place. But a critical incident is not a time to deal with issues; it's a time for rapid, effective action. If untreated diabetes makes you more prone to cardiovascular injury, you can deal with your blood glucose levels and insulin dosages at the next visit to your endocrinologist; but if you're lying in the street bleeding after a car wreck, the paramedic is only interested in keeping you alive long enough so that you can manage the underlying condition later. For now, the priority is to survive. So it is with mental emergencies: first stay safe and complete the mission; then deal with the background issues when you can.

Utilizing Thought-Stopping

Thought stopping can be combined with imagery to clear the mind and enhance performance (Asken 1993).

The first step is to monitor your consciousness for the presence of negative thoughts. Usually, this will be the least of your problems, since the negative thoughts may be screaming louder than anything else in your head.

To stop the negative thought, forcefully tell yourself "No!" or "Stop!" Or visualize a flashing STOP sign or neon slash-in-circle symbol. Be as creative as you want to be and utilize whatever phrase or image works best for you (many of the examples cited by the officers in my courses are

unprintable). Say them out loud if necessary, of course, being mindful of the sensibilities of others around you, or say them to yourself. If a word or image doesn't do it for you, try some other stimulus: a sharp breath, a pinch on your arm, a riff or lyric from a favorite song–basically, any cue you can give yourself that will jarring enough to abort the negative thought.

But, like nature, the human mind abhors a vacuum, so the best way to keep the negative thought from returning is to put something into your consciousness to take its place, something that is diametrically opposed to, and incompatible with, the negative thought. This would be the place to insert a confidence-building affirmation, positive mental image, or instructional cue (see below). Then, actually perform the activity to the best of your ability so that your real-world success becomes the basis for future positive thoughts.

COGNITIVE RESTRUCTURING

This mechanical-sounding mental technique helps you break out of certain rigid thinking traps that jam your cognitive gears and make flexible decision-making and problem-solving difficult in stressful circumstances. In *cognitive restructuring*, you are once again using your metacognitive, or observing ego, function to make a command decision about what thoughts you will permit to dominate your thinking before, during, and after the critical event. Cognitive restructuring is aimed at unjamming and retuning certain *automatic thoughts* or *cognitive distortions* that we build up out of habit, and that get in the way of clear, adaptive thinking.

There are several types of automatic thoughts that can plague law enforcement and emergency service workers, with various solutions for dealing with them (Asken, 1993).

In *all-or-nothing thinking*, things are either black or white, never shades of gray. The most common expression of this in law enforcement work is the attitude that if I didn't do everything perfectly, the whole operation was a screw-up: "If I'd seen the knife in his hand a second earlier, he wouldn't have had time to stab that kid." "If I hadn't made that comment on the phone, he would've let all the hostages go." "If we don't bust all the dealers in this

ring, the undercover operation will be a failure." Because human nature is normally risk-averse, we tend to pay more attention to the negatives than to the positives, which is okay if the goal is to operationally debrief ourselves so that our performance is better next time (the 20/20 principle). But focusing on negatives as if the positives didn't exist serves only to drain energy and sap motivation. It's counterproductive to future performance.

To counteract all-or-nothing thinking, remind yourself that you are absolutely responsible for what you can control but not what you can't. Another way of putting this is that you are responsible for your *efforts*, not the *outcome*. Now, of course, your efforts contribute to the outcome, and it's your responsibility to ensure you have the proper talent, training, and practical experience for a particular operation. But if you can honestly tell yourself (or have someone else more objectively tell you) that you did everything you realistically could, but some or all aspects of the call turned bad due to circumstances beyond your perception or control, then go ahead and feel bad about what happened, but don't unnecessarily *blame* yourself. Success is never guaranteed, and carrying around excess tons of unwarranted martyrdom can only slow you down the next time.

In *overgeneralization*, we take one example of something and apply it to all future situations. Or we pick one characteristic of a person—our self or others—and make that the sole defining feature of that person, excluding or minimizing everything else (trial lawyers will recognize this as the *fundamental attribution error*). Once we've pegged the person or situation, then we interpret everything about them in terms of this first impression. If that sounds a lot like the definition of *prejudice*, it's because prejudice almost always involves some degree of overgeneralization ("Those people are all . . ."). And it's sometimes too easy to prejudice ourselves against ourselves when we feel we're somehow not measuring up ourselves.

The keywords of overgeneralization are *always* and *never:* "Domestic assault calls always turn out bad." "I never seem to say the right thing when I'm mediating a citizen dispute on my patrol." To counteract overgeneralization, actively seek out exceptions to the supposed rule and focus on them: "Well, there was this domestic call where I was really able to connect with the husband because it turns out we both came from the same small town, and then I was able to talk him down."

A related distortion is *disqualifying the positive:* "Okay, so I was able to talk down the guy from my home town, but how many calls are going to have that kind of lucky coincidence? I'm still lousy at communication." You can counteract this in two main ways. One is to remind yourself that you still had to communicate with the guy; your common geographical origin didn't solve the problem all by itself. So maybe you can learn to generalize these talk skills to the next situation where your background is different from the citizen's. The second strategy is to recall task-relevant information: remember your training, do your best job, and expect a positive outcome. If you're really using your skills correctly, this is not wishful thinking, but a realistic bumping up of the odds.

TASK-RELEVANT INSTRUCTIONAL SELF-TALK

When you first learn a skill during training, it is common to have your instructor talk you through the steps. For example, learning to use the equipment in a patrol car or mastering proper firing patterns on the range typically involve first being shown how to do the task, then doing it with explicit verbal guidance from the trainer, then only with a few cues, then maybe with the instructor just observing and making a few comments afterward, and finally doing it all by yourself.

In times of stress, automaticity of performance of even well-trained skills often breaks down, and the smooth flow of the activity can be disrupted by distraction, confusion, and high emotion. Athletes, musicians, stage actors, and politicians all speak of "choking under pressure." Worse, negative self-statements tend to become increasingly pessimistic and self-deprecatory, ranging from a simple "Oh, shit" to, "This is going bad, we'll never make it through this one. What an idiot—I thought I could do this, but I can't. How do I get myself into these hopeless situations?"

At such times, it can be very useful to invoke an internalized representation of your teacher or mentor mentally talking you through a skill or procedure. As with many of the techniques in this chapter, many officers do this automatically and instinctively during stressful operations. Asken (1993) makes this process explicit in describing what he calls *task-relevant instructional self-talk* (TRIST), which involves using clear, succinct, short phrases by which you instruct yourself to execute your skills. This is not the same as using motivational self-statements, which were discussed above, although they may be especially useful when used in conjunction. In TRIST, you mentally put your instructor on your shoulder—or become your own instructor—to guide you through the nuts and bolts of the skill or activity. Accordingly, in TRIST, your self-talk focuses on the response-enhancing, task-relevant technical instructions on how to carry out the task.

Employing TRIST During a Critical Incident

Although the focus of TRIST is mainly cognitive and instructional, there are some arousal-regulating and emotion-modulating components, gleaned from some of the techniques discussed above, that set the stage for the proficient application of TRIST.

The first step is to relax, or at least lower your arousal sufficiently so you can focus on the self-instruction you're about to give yourself—or, for that matter, focus on anything else that's relevant to the situation at hand.

Next, use positive self-statements and confidence-building affirmations and imagery to encourage yourself: "I'm doing fine; this is just a tough call. I'm going to get my bearings and nail this thing." Pessimism can be contagious, so if realistic and feasible, encourage a positive attitude in others around you as well. As everybody's confidence increases, this will raise the morale and motivation of the whole team, increasing the chances of a successful operation.

Negative thinking almost always involves one or more of the cognitive distortions discussed above.

If these are clogging your thinking, utilize the counteracting techniques described above.

Now, focus on the skill or technique you need to handle the call. For now, try to forget about the outcome and the consequences, and focus on the process and execution of the skill. If it helps, put your instructor on your shoulder and speak through his or her voice. Express the instruction in relatively short, task relevant phrases and as positive statements: "Scan and clear the room; okay, level 1, level 2, level 3—clear." You can try combining the instructional talk with instructional imagery, picturing yourself doing the task correctly, but use this only if it helps, not if it distracts from the task at hand. Remember that the skill-focused TRIST is not the same as using motivational affirmations, but you may want to intersperse the latter with the former to bolster overall confidence during the operation.

MENTAL CONDITIONING AND PSYCHOLOGICAL SURVIVAL TRAINING

Here is where many of the psychological training techniques come together to enhance survival in the most extreme police emergencies, when the officer's life is in immediate mortal danger. In his work with police officers, Blum (2000) has noted repeatedly that, all other things being equal, a crucial factor that makes the difference between whether an officer survives or succumbs to a deadly encounter is something that he calls *positive mental attitude*, which seems to be a simple term for the iron will to survive. Conversely, whether engaged in a life-and-death physical struggle with a suspect, or being pinned down under gunfire, what has often contributed to the officer being killed, rather than surviving, is what Blum (2000) terms a *psychology of defeat*; that is, under tremendous, overwhelming stress, the officer seems to just give up, believing that "this is too much for me."

Thus, to survive a brutal, deadly encounter, an officer must be able to marshal every particle of his willpower and resolve, every ounce of physical and mental strength, to defeat the forces trying to overwhelm him. While operational training—firearms proficiency, martial arts, concealment and cover, etc.—will help prepare the officer for the technical aspects of survival training, mental conditioning for

the will to survive prepares the officer cognitively and emotionally for extreme survival crises. This combination of rational-intuitive decision making, temporary adaptive denial of weakness, and powerful focus of will and effort is sometimes referred to as the "warrior mentality" (Norcross, 2003; Pinizzotto et al., 2004; Shale et al., 2003). In the world of stress management, this is as intense as it gets, because here the stress is literally whether or not you make it out alive.

Blum (2000) has broken down the elements of *psychological survival training* to a series of steps that I use in my police academy training courses, with a few modifications noted here. Remember, like all of the techniques discussed in this chapter, the idea is to initially practice under relatively low-challenging conditions, then gradually apply the skills in more and more stressful situations, until they become automatic and "second nature" even under extreme conditions.

Extreme Imagery I: The "Loved-Ones-in-Danger" Scenario

The first step involves using the attention and arousal control strategies learned earlier to induce a state of optimum level of arousal. Once you've gotten good at this skill, you'll be able to turn it on and off at will. The next skill to be called into play is imagery. In this particular application, image the most important thing in the world to you, something that would not only be worth fighting for, not only be worth dying for, but worth *living for*, worth surviving and continuing to struggle against the odds long after you think your energy is gone and your will drained away.

For most officers, this involves images of their loved ones in danger. Imagine one or more of these people in mortal peril: threatened by criminals, attacked by terrorists, trapped in a burning building. Use all of your well-practiced powers of sensory and cognitive imagery to conjure up the full scene of danger. This may be hard to do at first precisely because it is so unpleasant to imagine your loved ones being threatened in this manner. In fact, the more successful you are in evoking this imagery, the more distasteful it may seem, because it actually feels like *you're* the one hurting them, just by creating the scene. But stick with it. The goal is to be able to create a mental state so ferociously determined that nothing–*nothing*–short of your being cold stone dead, will deter your will to survive and get the job done.

Feel it all: the raging adrenalin, the clenching muscles, the pounding heart, the medicine ball in your stomach. Now image yourself saving your loved ones in danger. Mentally fight off the thugs who have them tied them up; carry them in your arms from the burning plane crash; lift the front end of the car off them; rip through the rubble of the bombed office building to untrap them. Do whatever it takes in your imagination, because that's sure as hell what you'd do in real life.

Now, imagine yourself having successfully saved your loved ones from attack and danger: hugging them, feeling the relief and pride in having overcome impossible odds to do the right thing. Make this part of the mental imagery exercise as vivid as possible. Feel their sweaty embraces and their wet tears of joy; hear their voices rise and fall. Be the hero–you've earned it.

Why use this loved-ones-in-danger scenario for a mental practice module? The reason is simply that, for most people, even most police officers, real-life extreme life-and-death situations are actually quite rare. That's the good news. The bad news from a training standpoint is that there are very few "test cases" on which to hone these psychological survival skills. So the better you can learn to mentally evoke and anticipate the overwhelming and conflicting emotions of sheer terror, boiling rage, and fierce determination, using an example of something that's categorically important to you, the better you will be able to channel these emotions into real-life action if and when an actual law enforcement emergency arises.

Extreme Imagery II: Police Emergency Scenarios

When you've mastered the loved-ones-in-jeopardy scenario in all its emotional vividness, the next step is to create a multisensory image of a work-related police scenario in which you are responding to a call of uncertain danger. Visualize yourself walking or driving to the scene. Use any relevant past experiences in your own career to give the image vividness and credibility. Feel the uncertainty, the combination of fear and exhilaration, as you scan the environment for signs of trouble.

Now, image yourself being ambushed, jumped from behind, or cold-cocked from around a corner or behind a desk. Feel the shock and initial fear with all your senses. Image yourself being thrown to the ground, and feel the suspect trying to pin and overpower you or take your weapon. Feel the initial helplessness, as you at first realize your vulnerability and reel from the unexpected blows, uncertain about what to do next. Vividly image a group of suspects holding you down, pinning you so you can't move, holding a knife at your throat, or pummeling you with a brick, or choking you with an extension cord. Feel that initial sinking feeling of panic and helplessness, as you wonder if you'll ever make it out alive, ever see your loved ones again: "Holy shit, I'm gonna die."

Now explode. Yes, go ballistic–you're dead anyway, what the fuck have you got to lose? Experience yourself filling up with inhuman rage and hatred against the scumbags who would take it all from you. Fight back with everything you've got– it's your goddamn life or theirs. Forget pain, forget fear–if they're truly threatening your life, *kill* the motherfuckers. Visualize yourself fighting back, seizing the advantage, fear turning to confidence as the assailant is deterred, then overpowered, by you. Feel the exhilaration as you turn deadly defeat into victory.

Okay, hold it. I hope you understand that the object of this exercise is *not* to encourage excessive force, or to impel you to rash action when the best course may be to wait and bide your time, as in a hostage situation or armed standoff. Indeed, a guiding theme of this book is that many confrontations can and should be prevented and defused before they turn violent—when possible. So this imagined fight-or-die scenario represents an absolute last resort tactic, an exercise designed to prepare you for those extreme, and hopefully rare, situations, where your life is in imminent danger: you are about to be killed here and now; you have nothing to lose, so fight like hell.

Also note that fighting like hell doesn't mean forgetting your tactical combat training and just flailing around. On the contrary: here's where all those years of real-life martial arts practice finally pay off. Fight hard but fight smart. Even in the most extreme situation, your most effective weapon is still your brain.

Understandably, this exercise generates a great deal of emotion in my police academy classes. Often, the first few tries dissolve into nervous laughter, as the officers' natural defensiveness tries to deflect this unpleasant, albeit imaginary, confrontation with their own mortality. But once they get into it, it gets intense. The cops sweat, they squirm in their seats, and even an occasional chuckle can't break the concentrated spell of this exercise. It's precisely because it may be hard to put yourself completely into this extreme imaginary situation the first few times you try it, that you must keep practicing it. The whole point is to make the imaginary emergency real enough so that should you ever encounter a *real* life-and-death emergency, you won't be overcome by the novelty and intensity of the experience.

CONTROLLING THE SCENE

In this phase of training, we transition from mental exercises to real-life training scenarios. Remember one of the core themes of this book: The best stress management strategy is proper training, experience, and confidence. Once the mental skills of this chapter have been practiced and mastered, it is now time to apply them to the following aspects of controlling a scene (Blum, 2000). In so doing, you combine mental practice with real-life practice, so that your response to an emergency situation may include any of the following.

Initiative control refers to the process of taking control of a subject or command of a situation as soon as possible when coming into a critical scene. It is literally "seizing the initiative" by acting first. An example would be surprising and drawing down on an armed suspect and commanding him to drop his weapon before he has time to react.

Sometimes, however, you may be the one surprised, suddenly finding yourself in a definite OSS ("oh-shit situation"). In such circumstances, when you can't act proactively, it is vital that you bounce back as quickly and as forcefully as you can, that you do everything possible to gain *reactive control* of the situation. For example, if you're jumped by a suspect, you must be able to engage your martial arts and takedown tactics smoothly and instantaneously to regain control. Some situations may call for an explosive response, while others may require you to wait and bide your time, such as in a "Mexican standoff" with an armed subject. But even waiting is a proactive response if you use the time to calculate options and strategies to employ when the opportunity presents itself.

How smoothly you are able to bring your skills into play is determined by your level of *adaptive expertise*, which is the product of ongoing training and practice in as many diverse situations as possible. This involves both direct skill training, and the kind of mental preparation training described in this chapter. Contributors to adaptive expertise include *accurate expectations* about what to expect in most kinds of critical incident settings, *awareness and presence of mind* achieved by utilizing many of the attention and arousal control strategies discussed earlier, and *confidence* in your ability to handle virtually anything they can throw at you because you have trained, practiced, and are mentally and physically prepared for action.

OFFICER SURVIVAL TRAINING

Now, it's time to put it all together, to develop an overall protocol for managing extreme stress in critical situations and emerging victorious. This *Officer Survival Training* protocol (Blum, 2000) includes the following integrated components:

Physical and mental conditioning. This involves keeping your body and mind in peak condition, maintaining your physical and psychological health and fitness.

Training. You must acquire and maintain familiarity and proficiency with tactics, procedures, and equipment relevant to your law enforcement work.

Planning. This means developing and rehearsing tactical plans that can be adapted to as many types of diverse scenarios as possible. Only in this way can officers build the confidence that will enable them to think decisively and act effectively in emergency crisis situations.

Performance. Here, you actually practice the tactics and strategies under as many kinds of real and simulated conditions as possible.

Communication and teamwork. Most successful police operations require tight coordination among many team members, so it is important to establish means of communication under what might be very difficult conditions.

Attitude. As this chapter has hopefully made clear, "attitude" is not some ephemeral, airy-fairy, psychobabble, throwaway concept, but an indispensable ingredient in having the will to survive and prevail in a deadly encounter. At the risk of repetition, a proper confident, assertive attitude is fostered by utilizing many of the mental training exercises in this chapter, but it depends vitally on nuts-and-bolts skills training to provide a realistic basis for that confidence.

CONCLUSIONS

Probably in no other area addressed by this book is psychology so practical for actually saving an officer's life in a critical situation. Being able to use your mind as an adaptive tool and, when necessary, a life-defending weapon adds a whole new dimension to your law enforcement skill set. Even without your gun, your gear, your vehicle, or your backup, you still have your body and your brain, and as long as you know how to use them effectively, then no matter what the danger, you will never be entirely helpless.

Chapter 6

LAW ENFORCEMENT CRITICAL INCIDENT STRESS

"I've seen dead bodies–fresh ones and ripe ones. I've scraped an eyeball off a bedroom wall in a suicide shooting, I've investigated murder scenes you wouldn't believe. But this was different, this was a little kid, this could have been *my* kid. And there was no reason for it, just no reason."

This grim testimonial came from a veteran detective following the shooting death of a young child by his mentally handicapped brother who had been left unsupervised by the children's parents in the same house as an unsecured handgun. It wasn't the worst death the emergency responders had ever seen, it wasn't the grisliest, nor the most touch-and-go in terms of lifesaving attempts–the child had apparently died instantly from a .357 magnum round to the head. The main traumatizing effect of this call was the sheer existential indigestibility of the death circumstances: an innocent victim, even an essentially innocent perpetrator, both set up by stupidly careless adults who should have known better–there was just "no reason."

The men and women of law enforcement are exposed to special kinds of routine and unusual traumatic events and daily pressures that require a certain adaptively defensive toughness of attitude, temperament, and training. Without this resolve, they couldn't do their jobs effectively. Sometimes,

however, the stress is just too much, and the very toughness that facilitates smooth functioning in their daily duties now becomes an impediment to these helpers seeking help for themselves. Indeed, the last chapter has provided explicit guidelines for inculcating and training the kind of tough but resilient mental attitude needed to deal with a variety of mundane-to-catastrophic law enforcement critical incidents. But that doesn't mean that these episodes are without psychological repercussions.

This chapter first describes the types of critical incidents and other stresses experienced by law enforcement officers. Many of these challenges affect all personnel who work in emergency services, public safety, and the helping professions, including police officers, firefighters, paramedics, dispatchers, trauma doctors, emergency room nurses, teachers, and mental health clinicians (Miller, 1995a, 1997a, 1998a, 1998b, 1999a, 1999b, 1999c, 2000a, 2000b, 2002a); however, the focus here will be on the stressors most relevant to law enforcement personnel. Second, this chapter will describe the practical interventions and psychotherapeutic strategies that have been found most useful for helping cops in distress. The general principles outlined in this chapter will also serve as a template for the more in-depth discussions of specific topics to be found Chapters 7, 8 and 11.

STRESS AND COPING IN LAW ENFORCEMENT

We know that police officers can be an insular group, and are often more reluctant to talk to outsiders or to show weakness in front of their own peers than even other emergency service and

public safety workers. Part of this may be because officers typically work alone or with a single partner, as opposed to firefighters or paramedics, who are trained to have more of a team mentality (Blau,

1994; Cummings, 1996; Kirschman, 1997, 2004; Reese, 1987; Solomon, 1995). This presents some special challenges for peers, supervisors, and clinicians attempting to identify and help officers in distress. Many of the topics reviewed in this section are covered more extensively in subsequent chapters.

The Patrol Cop

The essential nature of their jobs regularly requires police officers to deal with the most violent, impulsive, and predatory members of society, to regularly interact with citizens undergoing the most emotional events of their lives, to frequently confront cruelties and horrors that most civilians only view from the sanitized distance of their newspapers and TV screens, and, at any moment, to be expected to put their lives on the line. In addition to the daily grind and unpredictable crises, officers are frequently the target of criticism and complaints by citizens, the media, the judicial system, adversarial attorneys, crusading politicians, "do-gooder" clinicians, social service personnel, and their own administrators and law enforcement agencies (Blau, 1994).

Police officers generally carry out their sworn duties and responsibilities with dedication and competence, but some stresses are too much to take, and every officer has his or her breaking point. For some, it may come in the form of a particular traumatic experience, such as a gruesome accident or homicide, a vicious crime against a child, a close personal brush with death, the death or serious injury of a partner, the shooting of a perpetrator or innocent civilian, or an especially grisly or large-scale crime. As will be discussed below, in some cases the traumatic critical incident can precipitate the development of a full-scale *posttraumatic stress disorder* (PTSD) syndrome. For example, following the massacre at a San Diego McDonald's restaurant in which 21 people were gunned down, half the officers exposed to the aftermath of this mass killing developed full-blown PTSD, twice the rate for the department as a whole (McCafferty et al., 1992).

For other officers, there may be no singular trauma, but the mental breakdown caps the cumulative weight of a number of more mundane stressors over the course of the officer's career. In either case, the officer all too often feels that the department doesn't fully support him and that there is nowhere else to vent his distress. So he bottles up his feelings, acts snappish with coworkers, superiors, civilians, and family members, and becomes hypersensitive to small annoyances on and off the job. As his isolation and feelings of alienation grow, his health and home life begin to deteriorate, work becomes a burden, and he may ultimately feel he is losing his mind, or going "squirrelly."

Several authors (Carlier, 1999; Henry, 2004; McCafferty et al., 1992; Sugimoto & Oltjenbruns, 2001) have commented on the "death-saturated" culture that pervades many forms of police work, likening it to guerilla warfare or antiterrorist combat, right down to the military-style training and weaponry used and the us-against-them mentality that is often instilled in both rookie and veteran officers. Indeed, law enforcement critical incident response has been described as "police combat" (Violanti, 1999) and the types of posttraumatic responses seen in police officers typically resemble those observed in military combat personnel (Corbett, 2004; Creamer & Forbes, 2004; Galovski & Lyons, 2004; Nordland & Gegax, 2004). Such an atmosphere may create a psychological set-up for traumatization when law enforcement critical incidents occur.

Most police officers deal with both the routine and exceptional stresses of their work by a variety of situationally adaptive coping and defense mechanisms, such as repression, displacement, isolation of feelings, humor—often seemingly callous or crass humor—and just generally toughing it out. Officers develop a closed society, an insular "cop culture," centering around what many refer to as *The Job*. Part of this closed-society credo is based on the shared belief that no civilian or outsider could possibly understand what they go through on a day-to-day basis. A smaller number of police officers spend most or all the their time with other cops, watch cop shows, read cop stories, log on to cop websites, and so on. For these few, *The Job* becomes their life, and crowds out other activities and relationships (Blau, 1994).

Apparently, police pressures and the responses to them are remarkably similar in most Western societies where these have been observed. A study of Australian police officers (Evans et al., 1993) found that most prefer problem-focused and direct action methods of coping rather than social support, self-blame, or wishful thinking. A study of Scottish constables (Alexander & Walker, 1994) found their coping methods to consist of displacement onto colleagues or the public, delegating work, taking sick leave, using psychotropic medication, seeking spiritual help, engaging in physical exercise, relaxing, smoking, eating, or using alcohol. A frequently reported coping method was talking things out with colleagues. However, in general, the report found that these constables were generally not very satisfied with the methods they used to counteract work-induced stress.

According to one estimate (Sewell et al., 1988), after a traumatically stressful incident, such as an officer-involved shooting, approximately one-third of officers have minimal or no problems, another third have moderate problems, and a final third have problems severe enough to affect the officer, his family, and the department. Police are admitted to hospitals at significantly higher rates than the general population and rank third among occupations in premature death rates. Seventy percent of officers involved in line-of-duty shootings leave the force within seven years of the incident (Sewell et al., 1988). Up to two-thirds of police officers involved in shootings experience significant emotional reactions, which include a heightened sense of danger, flashbacks, intrusive imagery and thoughts, anger, guilt, sleep disturbances, withdrawal, depression, and other stress symptoms (Solomon, 1995; Solomon & Horn, 1986; alsosee Chapter 7).

But stressful incidents include more than shootings. By focusing too much on these high-profile events, police managers often overlook the cumulative effect of more common critical incident stressors, such as long overtime shifts during disasters, dealing with child victims, attempting resuscitation on a person who eventually dies, or working a fatal accident where the officer personally knows the victim.

Emotional reactions of guilt, irrationally taking responsibility for events that were beyond one's control, and rage at being lucklessly involved in a no-win situation—being "at the wrong place at the wrong time"—are common themes of law enforcement stress. This also includes escaping serious harm where others have been killed or wounded. Failure to resolve these issues often leads to a variety of maladaptive response patterns. Some officers

begin to overreact to perceived or imagined threats, while others ignore clear danger signals. Some cops quit the force prematurely, while others become discipline problems or develop increased absenteeism, burnout, physical symptoms, substance abuse, or a host of other personal problems that can interfere with functioning at home and on the job (Ostrov, 1991; Solomon, 1995; Solomon & Horn, 1986).

The most tragic form of police casualty is suicide (Cummings, 1996; Hays, 1994; McCafferty et al., 1992; Seligman et al., 1994). Twice as many officers, about 300 annually, die by their own hand as are killed in the line of duty. In New York City, the suicide rate for police officers is more than double the rate for the general population. In fact, these totals may actually be even higher, since such deaths are sometimes underreported by fellow cops to avoid stigmatizing the deceased officers and to allow families to collect benefits. Most suicide victims are young patrol officers with no record of misconduct, and most shoot themselves off-duty. Often, problems involving alcohol or personal crises are the catalyst, and easy access to a lethal weapon provides the ready means. Cops under stress are caught in the dilemma of risking confiscation of their guns, transfer to desk duty, promotional setbacks, mandatory fitness-for-duty referrals, or general loss of face if they report distress or request counseling. This topic is covered more extensively in Chapter 11.

Homicide Investigators

Aside from the daily stresses of patrol cops, certain pressures are experienced by specially assigned officers, such as homicide detectives, who are involved in the investigation of particularly brutal crimes, such as multiple murders or serial killings. Stereotypes of the "hardboiled" detective, both from within and outside the law enforcement profession, have contributed to the underrecognition and undertreatment of critical incident stress and posttraumatic stress syndromes in this group. The socially and culturally expected protective role of the police officer becomes accentuated at the same time as their responsibilities as public servants who protect individual rights are compounded by departmental and societal pressure to solve the crime (Sewell, 1994).

A multiple or serial murder investigation forces an officer to confront stressors directly related to his projected image of showing unflagging strength in the face of adversity and frustration, responding competently and dispassionately to crises, and placing the needs and demands of the public above his personal feelings. The sheer magnitude and shock effect of many mass murder scenes and the violence, mutilation, and sadistic brutality associated with many serial killings–especially those involving children–often exceed the defense mechanisms and coping abilities of even the most jaded investigator. Revulsion may be tinged with rage when "innocent" victims or fellow officers have been killed, and the murderer seems to be mocking law enforcement's attempts to capture him (Miller & Schlesinger, 2000; Sewell, 1993, 1994).

As the investigation drags on, the inability to solve the crime and close the case further frustrates and demoralizes the assigned officers and seems to jeeringly proclaim the hollowness of society's notions of fairness and justice. All the more vexsome are situations where the killer is known but the existing evidence is insufficient to support an arrest or conviction, leading the officers to fear that the perpetrator will remain free to kill again. Stress and self-recrimination are further magnified when the failure to apprehend the perpetrator is caused by human error, as when an officer's bungled actions or breach of protocol lead to loss or damage of evidence or suppression of testimony, allowing the killer to "walk" (Sewell, 1993, 1994).

All of these reactions are magnified by a cumulatively spiraling vicious cycle of fatigue and cognitive impairment, as the intense, sustained effort to solve the case results in sloppy errors, deteriorating work quality, and fraying of home and workplace relationships. Fatigue also exacerbates the wearing down of the investigator's normal psychological defenses, rendering him or her even more vulnerable to stress and failure (Sewell, 1993, 1994).

Especially in no-arrest cases, and particularly those involving children, some homicide detectives may become emotionally involved with the victims' families and remain in contact with them for many years. Some detectives become obsessed with a particular case and continue to work on it at every available moment, sometimes to the point of compromising their work on other cases and leading to a deterioration of health and family life (Spungen, 1998).

Undercover Police

Probably the epitome of stressful law enforcement work involves undercover policing, the realities of which rarely resemble glamorous movie or TV portrayals. Undercover work is grueling, often boring, frequently terrifying, and occasionally lethal. Accordingly, individuals successful in such assignments need to have the right mix of narcissistic toughness and adaptive psychological resilience. Still, 16 percent of undercover officers in one study (MacLeod, 1995) suffered major psychological disturbances, including PTSD. These officers are even more likely than most to deny problems and attempt to tough it out until cumulative stress causes them to make careless mistakes, necessitating their reassignment to other duty, which itself can be demoralizing. In the worst cases, complete decompensation or breakdown may occur, with psychotic symptomatology, substance abuse, or violence. This topic is covered more extensively in Chapter 12.

Rescue and Recovery Teams

A plane goes down, a building is bombed, a fire razes a neighborhood, a flood drowns a town. After those who can be rescued have been taken to safety, somebody has to go in and pick up the pieces–sometimes literally. Although firefighters and paramedics are the usual responders involved in rescue and body recovery, in large-scale disasters, where the demand for personnel is great, various groups of responders may be called upon to transport fatally injured survivors or to retrieve human remains; these personnel may include police, firefighters, paramedics, military personnel, and sometimes civilian volunteers.

Rescue workers endure a double stress, the event itself plus their role as help providers, and many experience feelings of fear, anger, and resentment that interfere with effective functioning both during the recovery task and subsequently (Raphael, 1986). In many cases, close peer and administrative support can help ameliorate some of the emotionally disturbing effects of such unpleasant duty (Alexander,

1993; Alexander & Wells, 1991). However, in other circumstances, exposure to such grim visual, auditory, and olfactory images–charred corpses, screaming victims, scattered personal effects–may leave a powerful, enduring traumatic impact.

Recent historical events have given us ample anecdotal examples of the kinds of stress reactions that occur to mass casualty and terror attacks among response personnel and civilians alike. Insight into what may be expected in this grim new world can be gleaned from research on reactions of police officers to previous crises. For example, in 1987, Northwest Airlines flight 255 out of Detroit crashed on takeoff. Bodies and body parts were strewn over a large area and police and other rescue workers were sent in to remove the remains. Many of these officers had previously dealt with assaults, rapes, shootings, and various forms of violent death, but none of these experiences had adequately prepared them for the scope of the carnage they encountered at the crash site. A number of these rescue workers were Vietnam veterans, and one man described the emotional scene as like being on patrol in hostile territory back in the jungle. For some of these vets, the sight of dismembered human remains triggered PTSD flashbacks of decades-old combat experiences, while other workers continued to be plagued for weeks by persistent intrusive images of the crash scene (Davis & Breslau, 1994).

There is something inherently horrifying about encountering a dead human being, especially if we identify with the victim in some way. The handling of human remains, or even the anticipation of having to do so, appears to produce especially high levels of stress among rescue workers (McCarroll et al., 1995; Ursano & McCarroll, 1990). This has been documented among rescuers who responded to the Jonestown mass suicide and the more recent mass suicide of the Heaven's Gate cult in California. It was observed among the rescue and recovery personnel at Oklahoma City, in military personnel assigned to mortuary duty in Operation Desert Storm, and is still being seen among rescue and recovery teams who responded to the World Trade Center's Ground Zero in New York (Henry, 2004). The handling of the bodies of children, or even their personal effects–clothes, toys, etc.–appears to be the most severe stressor for rescue and recovery personnel, particularly for workers who have children

of their own. Additionally, there appears to be an overall "gruesomeness factor" associated with human remains and the overall death scene that strongly affects the level of traumatic stress experienced by body handlers (McCarroll et al., 1993; McCarroll et al., 1995).

Dispatchers and Support Personnel

In addition to line officers and sworn personnel, a vital role in law enforcement is played by the workers who operate "behind the scenes," namely, the dispatchers, 911 operators, complaint clerks, clerical personnel, crime scene investigators, and other sworn and nonsworn personnel (Holt, 1989; Sewell & Crew, 1984). Although they are rarely directly exposed to actual danger (except where on-scene and off-scene personnel rotate shifts), several high-stress features characterize the job descriptions of these workers.

Multiple calls. Much as with air traffic controllers, simultaneous peak traffic on the radio–"a million things going on at once"–is a particularly significant source of stress for dispatchers.

Required decisions. The potential life-threatening nature of many 911 calls and the sense of urgency involved in handling people's emergencies magnify the pressures created by multiple calls and constraints on time.

Low control. Unlike on-scene personnel, who can exert more discretion and control over their responses to requests for service and the actual actions they take, communications personnel are necessarily limited in the flexibility of their responses to demands from superiors, on-scene workers, and the public.

Citizen contact. Intense stress can result from dealing with citizens who are experiencing life-threatening emergencies. The dispatcher must handle a wide range of human emotions with calm professionalism, and attempt to impose some measure of order and control on a confusing and chaotic situation. The reactions are particularly complicated when distraught citizens provide incomplete or inaccurate information to communications personnel.

In general, the combination of high stress, low control, life-and-death decision making in the absence of complete information, having to bear the brunt of citizen outrage, and failure to enjoy the status and camaraderie of on-scene personnel all take their toll on police dispatchers and support workers (Holt, 1989; Sewell & Crew, 1984). After particularly difficult calls, dispatchers may show many of the classic posttraumatic stress reactions and symptoms, including numbed responsiveness, impaired memory for the event alternating with intrusive disturbing images, irritability, hypervigilance, sleep disturbance, and interpersonal hypersensitivity.

In a number of critical incident stress debriefings I've participated in, the dispatchers and clerical staff have seemed genuinely surprised at being included, since they assumed that the on-scene workers would not take their ordeal seriously, inasmuch as they were physically removed from the crisis. Happily, on-scene officers have often shown tremendous empathy and support for these desk and phone personnel. Perhaps some of this relates to the fact that in some departments, personnel rotate desk and field assignments, so everyone gets a taste of both activities. Even when this is not the case, if the department overall is a cohesive one, a sometimes unexpected level of mutual support and validation emerges in dealing with the aftermath of crises and critical incidents. But, unfortunately, not always.

CRITICAL INCIDENTS AND POSTTRAUMATIC STRESS DISORDER

Critical Incident Stress

A *critical incident* is defined as any event that has an unusually powerful, negative impact on personnel. In the present context, it is any event that a police officer may experience that is above and beyond the range of the ordinary stresses and hassles that come with the job. Major classes of critical incidents include: a line-of-duty death (Chapter 8); serious injury to police personnel; a serious multiple-casualty incident such as a multiple school shooting or workplace violence incident; the suicide of a police officer (Chapter 11); the traumatic death of children, especially where irresponsible or frankly malevolent adults were involved; an event with excessive media interest; or a victim who is a family member or otherwise well-known to one or more responding officers (Everly & Mitchell, 1996). Recent times have multiplied exponentially the range and scope of horrific law enforcement critical incidents to include acts of mass terror and destruction, involving multiple deaths of civilians, fellow officers, and other emergency personnel (Henry, 2004; Karlsson & Christianson, 2003; Miller, 2003a, 2003b, 2004, 2005).

Susceptibility to stressful events varies among different persons, and many individuals are able to resolve acute critical incident stress through the use of informal social support and other adaptive activities (Bowman, 1997; Carlier & Gersons, 1995; Carlier et al., 1997; Gentz, 1991). However, critical incident stress that is not resolved adequately or treated appropriately in the first few days or weeks may evolve into a number of disabling psychological traumatic disability syndromes (Miller, 1998b).

Posttraumatic Stress Disorder (PTSD)

The concept of critical incident stress grew out of the larger tradition of trauma psychology. Although persisting and debilitating stress reactions to wartime and civilian traumas have been recorded for centuries (Trimble, 1981; Wilson, 1994), *posttraumatic stress disorder* (PTSD) first achieved status as a codified psychiatric syndrome in 1980 (APA, 1980), and is still only reluctantly coming to be accepted as a legitimate medical casualty in wartime and civilian combat (Clary, 2005; Corbett, 2004; Galovski & Lyons, 2004; Nordland & Gegax, 2004; Paton & Smith, 1999; Tyre, 2004). A number of other kinds of psychological syndromes, such as phobias, anxiety, panic attacks, and depression may follow exposure to traumatic events (Miller, 1994a, 1998b; 1999d), but the quintessential psychological syndrome following psychological traumatization is PTSD (APA, 1994; Meek, 1990; Merskey, 1992; Modlin, 1983, 1990; Weiner, 1992).

Diagnostically, PTSD is a syndrome of emotional and behavioral disturbance following exposure to a traumatic stressor that injures or threatens self or others, and that involves the experience of intense fear, helplessness, or horror. As a result, following a law enforcement critical incident, there may develop a characteristic set of symptoms, which can include any of the following:

Anxiety. The officer experiences a continual state of free-floating anxiety and maintains an intense hypervigilance, scanning the environment for impending threats of danger. Panic attacks may be occasional or frequent.

Physiological arousal. The officer's nervous system is on continual alert, producing increased bodily tension in the form of muscle tightness, tremors, restlessness, heightened startle response, fatigue, heart palpitations, breathing difficulties, dizziness, headaches, or other physical symptoms.

Irritability. There is a pervasive edginess, impatience, loss of humor, and quick anger over seemingly trivial matters. Friends and coworkers may get annoyed and shun the officer, while family members may feel abused and alienated. Interactions with citizens on patrol may grow testy and lead to unwarranted confrontations.

Avoidance/denial. The officer tries to blot out the event from his mind. He avoids thinking or talking about the traumatic event, as well as news items, conversations, TV shows, or even coworkers that remind him of the incident. Part of this is a deliberate, conscious effort to avoid trauma-reminders, while part involves an involuntary psychic numbing that blunts incoming threatening stimuli. On the job, the officer may "lie low," minimizing his contact with the public and his fellow officers, and thereby underperform in his law enforcement duties.

Intrusion. Despite the officer's best efforts to keep the traumatic event out of his mind, the disturbing incident pushes its way into consciousness, typically in the form of intrusive images or flashbacks by day and/or frightening dreams at night.

Repetitive nightmares. Sometimes the officer's nightmares replay the actual traumatic event; more commonly, the dreams echo the general theme of the trauma, but miss the mark in terms of specific

content. The emotional intensity of the original traumatic experience is retained, but the dream may partially disguise the actual event. For example, one officer who was jumped and beaten by a suspect in an unlighted room reported recurring dreams of "tripping over a rock and being bit by a snake."

Impaired concentration and memory. Friends and family may notice that the officer has become a "space cadet," while supervisors report deteriorating work performance because the officer "can't concentrate on doing his job." Social and recreational functioning may be impaired as the officer has difficulty remembering names, loses the train of conversations, or can't keep his mind focused on reading material or games.

Withdrawal/isolation. The officer shuns friends, schoolmates, and family members, having no tolerance for the petty, trivial concerns of everyday life. The hurt feelings this engenders in those rebuffed may spur resentment and counteravoidance, leading to a vicious cycle of mutual rejection and eventual social ostracism of the officer.

Acting-out. More rarely, the traumatized officer may walk off his patrol, wander out of his familiar jurisdiction, or take unaccustomed risks by driving too fast, associating with unsavory elements on his beat (or within his own department), gambling, using substances, being insubordinate, or acting recklessly with suspects and citizens, thereby putting himself or other officers in unnecessary danger (also see Chapter 13).

Overlapping Syndromes and Differential Diagnosis

A wide variety of psychological reactions may occur in the aftermath of a law enforcement critical incident, and PTSD may overlap with a number of other posttraumatic disorders, including, depression, phobias, generalized anxiety disorder, panic disorder, chronic pain, somatization disorder, postconcussion syndrome, and neurotoxic trauma (Miller, 1991, 1993a, 1993b, 1993c, 1995b, 1997b, 1999d, 2002b).

Subsyndromal or partial forms of PTSD may also occur, in which fewer than the usually required number of symptoms exist to make a formal diagnosis, but the effects may be nonetheless psychologically disabling and produce significant impairment in family, vocational, and psychosocial functioning (Stein et al., 1997). It is thus possible to find different degrees of PTSD, with varying levels of distress and disability.

To account for the different types of trauma response that are often observed in clinical practice, an expanded typology of PTSD has been proposed by Alarcon et al. (1997), which I have adapted for police officers as follows:

Depressive subtype. This subtype presents with psychomotor retardation, social withdrawal, inability to deal with everyday matters, loss of interest and motivation, low self-esteem, self-criticism, guilt feelings, and suicidality. An officer with a severe form of this subtype may be completely unable to function on the job, and may take a disability-related leave of absence due to a "nervous breakdown."

Neurotic-like subtype. This is characterized by anxiety, phobic avoidance, restlessness, hypersensitivity, obsessionalism, and panic attacks. Symptoms may be pervasive and generalized, and officers may not be able to identify a specific critical incident that precipitated the anxiety; alternatively, the syndrome may be the culmination of a series of cumulative stressors.

Psychotic-like subtype. The officer displays distortions of consciousness, fantasizing, staring, inattentiveness, impaired motivation and activity, and sometimes paranoia and behavioral regression. This kind of syndrome may be both frightening to the officer himself and extremely disruptive to job performance and family functioning.

Dissociative subtype. This involves a predominance of flashbacks, hallucinatory experiences, *depersonalization,* fugue-like *automatistic* (stereotyped, repetitive) behavior, *depersonalization* (the individual doesn't feel real), *derealization* (the external world doesn't feel real), and, more rarely, symptoms resembling multiple personality disorder. The

bizarre and frightening nature of these symptoms may lead the officer to conclude he is "going crazy."

Somatomorphic subtype. The primary manifestation of this subtype is chronic pain or other physical symptomatology, typically without clear localization or identifiable cause, and usually resulting in disability that seems out of proportion to the initiating injury (Andreski et al., 1998). In some cases, the stress reaction manifests itself in the form of "psychosomatic" physical complaints, such as headaches; chronic pain; or stomach, cardiac, respiratory, or musculoskeletal symptoms. Since physical symptoms are more objectifiable and external to a person's self-image than "mental stress," intractable *physical* pain often represents a more face-saving way for officers to stay removed from the frightening work situation than admitting to *psychological* pain, which is seen as admitting to weakness and vulnerability (Benedikt & Kolb, 1986; Hall, 1986; McFarlane et al., 1994; Miller, 1998b, 1999c; Trimble, 1981).

Organic-like subtype. This presents with impaired attention, concentration, learning, memory, and reasoning abilities, along with confusion and slowness in thought, speech, and behavior. In some cases, there may be a dementia-like presentation which may be confused with postconcussion syndrome due to head trauma (Miller, 1993c; Reed, 1986).

The somatic and organic-type presentations of PTSD are important to recognize because PTSD often arises following an event that has also caused significant physical injuries. The psychological significance of the physical symptom is easy to miss, since the medical clinician is likely to assume that it relates to the bodily injury itself. This can lead to prolonged and exaggerated physical disability as well as underdiagnosis of PTSD. But while somatic expressions of anxiety, depression, and PTSD in emergency personnel may "mask" the emotional distress, just as commonly, the emotional distress is experienced clearly, consciously, and severely. Nevertheless, emotional and psychiatric disturbances may go largely underdiagnosed in law enforcement and emergency personnel, especially if clinical attention is limited to physical injuries (McFarlane et al., 1994). At the same time, it is just as important for mental health clinicians not to make the opposite mistake of overlooking a physical etiology of a supposedly "psychological" symptom, such as misinterpreting postconcussion syndrome caused by a closed head trauma (Miller, 1993c; Parker, 2001; Reed, 1986) as a somatoform disorder or "stress effect."

Delayed, Displaced, or Prolonged Reactions

In some cases, especially if no treatment or other appropriate support has been provided, the aftereffects of a traumatic incident may persist for many months or longer in the form of anger, hostility, irritability, fatigue, inability to concentrate, loss of self-confidence, neglect of health, increased indulgence in food or substances, or problems with authority and discipline. Many of these long-term effects obviously will interfere with work performance and threaten the stability of close personal relationships. Ultimately, they may be responsible for early retirement, burnout, or even suicide (Bohl, 1991, 1995).

In some cases, an officer may appear to emerge from a dangerous situation or series of emergencies emotionally unscathed, only to later break down and develop a full-blown PTSD reaction following a relatively minor incident like a traffic accident (Davis & Breslau, 1994). The fender-bender, certainly far less traumatic than the dramatic scenes encountered in emergency work, seems to have symbolized vividly the personal risk, sense of human fragility, and existential uncertainty that the officer's professional activities entail but that he is unable to face directly if he is to maintain his necessary defenses and get the job done. The stifled emotion may then be projected onto the minor incident because it is a "safer" target to break down or blow up at. Unfortunately, this may instigate a

fear of losing control and going crazy, further propelling the vicious cycle of increased stress but greater reluctance to report it. Here, alert spouses, coworkers, or supervisors may be of help in urging the stricken officer to get the help he or she needs.

Risk and Resiliency Factors for PTSD

As noted previously, not everyone who experiences a traumatic critical incident develops the same degree of psychological disability, and there is significant variability among individual levels of susceptibility and resilience to stressful events (Bowman, 1997).

Risk factors for PTSD or other traumatic disability syndromes in officers may be *biological*, including genetic predisposition and inborn heightened physiological reactivity to stimuli; *historical*, such as prior exposure to trauma or other coexisting adverse life circumstances; *psychological*, including poor coping and problem-solving skills, learned helplessness, and a history of dysfunctional interpersonal relationships; and *environmental/contextual*, such as inadequate departmental or societal support (Carlier, 1999; Paton et al., 2000).

Equally important, but often overlooked, are *resiliency factors* that enable officers to withstand and even prevail in the face of seemingly overwhelming trauma. These include superior training and skill development; a learning attitude toward the profession; good verbal and interpersonal skills; higher intelligence; adequate emotional control; optimism; good problem-solving and adaptive coping skills; and the ability and willingness to seek help and support where necessary (Miller, 1998c; Paton et al., 2000). Proper intervention services for PTSD and other critical incident stress reactions should make good use of these inherent resiliency factors wherever possible.

INTERVENTION SERVICES AND PSYCHOTHERAPEUTIC STRATEGIES

While some police officers are willing and even eager to utilize mental health services to "get things off my chest," other cops would rather swim through boiling oil than sit in a psychologist's office and betray any sign of weakness. Accordingly, to avoid overly "shrinky" connotations, mental health

intervention services with law enforcement personnel are often conceptualized in such terms as *stress management* or *critical incident debriefing* (Anderson et al., 1995; Belles & Norvell, 1990; Mitchell & Bray, 1990; Mitchell & Everly, 1996). In general, one-time, incident-specific interventions will be most appropriate for handling the effects of overwhelming trauma on otherwise normal, well-functioning personnel. Where posttraumatic disturbances persist, or where the psychological problems relate to a longer-term pattern of maladaptive coping, more extensive individual psychotherapeutic approaches are called for.

To have the greatest impact, psychological intervention services should be part of an integrated mental health program within the department, and have full administrative commitment and support (Blau, 1994; Sewell, 1986). However, there is still a long way to go toward achieving this ideal in many departments. Over the last several decades, many police and emergency services administrators, particularly those of the "old school" invested in maintaining their tough guy image, and especially in smaller departments, have actually discouraged the utilization of psychological support services. Even where such utilization is officially sanctioned, the subtle negative attitudes of the departmental commanders inevitably filter down to the line personnel, who then take their cue as to what is acceptable and appropriate versus what is shameful and stigmatizing. Things are changing, albeit slowly.

CRITICAL INCIDENT STRESS DEBRIEFING: MODELS AND METHODS

Critical incident stress debriefing (CISD) is a structured group intervention designed to promote the emotional processing of traumatic events through the ventilation and normalization of reactions, as well as to facilitate preparation for possible future crisis experiences. Although initially designed for use in groups, variations of the CISD approach have also been used with individuals, couples, and families (Miller, 1998b, 1999b; Mitchell & Everly, 1996). CISD is actually one component of an integrated, comprehensive crisis intervention program spanning the critical incident continuum from pre crisis, to crisis, to post-crisis phases, subsumed under the heading of *critical incident stress management* (CISM), which has been adopted and modified for law enforcement and emergency services departments throughout the United States, Britain, and other parts of the world (Dyregrov, 1989; Miller, 1999b, Mitchell & Everly, 1997).

The full CISM program includes individual and organizational *precrisis preparation*; large-scale *demobilization* procedures following mass disasters; on-scene, *one-on-one supportive counseling* for acute, individual crisis reactions; *defusings*, which represent a shorter, compressed stress debriefing protocol for small groups under acute stress; *critical incident stress debriefing*, described more extensively below; *family crisis intervention* and supportive counseling; and referral for *follow-up mental health services* as needed (Mitchell & Everly, 1996, 1997).

Indications for CISD

As noted previously, the major classes of critical incident capable of causing distress for law enforcement and emergency personnel are a line-of-duty death; a serious injury to officers; a multiple-casualty incident; the suicide of an officer; the traumatic death of children; an event with excessive media interest; a victim known to the officer; or bascially any event that has an unusually powerful impact on the personnel.

There are a number of criteria by which peer support or command staff might decide to provide a CISD to law enforcement personnel after a critical incident: many officers within a department or interagency work team appear to be distressed after a call; the signs of stress appear to be quite severe; officers demonstrate significant behavioral changes; officers make significant errors on calls occurring after the critical incident; officers directly request help; or the event is unusual or extraordinary in any other respect (Mitchell & Bray, 1990; Mitchell & Everly, 1996).

Structure of the Debriefings

A CISD debriefing is usually a peer-led, clinician-guided process, although the individual roles of clinicians and peers may vary from setting to setting. The staffing of a debriefing usually consists of a mental health clinician and one or more peer debriefers, i.e., fellow police officers, firefighters, paramedics, or other crisis workers who have been trained in the CISD process and who may have been through critical incidents and debriefings in their own careers.

A typical debriefing takes place within 24 to 72 hours of the critical incident and consists of a single group meeting that lasts two to three hours, although shorter or longer meetings may be dictated by circumstances. Group size may range from a handful to a roomful, the determining factor usually being how many people will have time to fully express themselves in the number of hours allotted for the debriefing. Where large numbers of workers are involved, such as in mass disaster rescues, several debriefings may be held successively over the course of days to accommodate all the personnel involved (Mitchell & Everly, 1996).

The formal CISD process—often referred to as the *Mitchell model*, after its chief originator—consists of seven key phases, designed to assist psychological processing, beginning with more the objective and descriptive levels, progressing to the more personal and emotional, and back to the educative and integrative levels, focusing on both cognitive and emotional mastery of the traumatic event.

Introduction. The introduction phase of a debriefing is the time when the team leader—either a mental health professional or peer debriefer, depending on the composition of the group—gradually introduces the CISD process, encourages participation by the group, and sets the ground rules by which the debriefing will operate. These include confidentiality, attendance for the full session, unforced participation in the discussions, and the establishment of a noncritical atmosphere.

Fact phase. During this phase, the group members are asked to briefly describe their job or role during the critical incident and, from their own perspective, provide some facts about what happened. The basic question is: "What did you do?"

Thought phase. The CISD leader asks the group members to discuss their first and subsequent thoughts during the critical incident: "What was going through your mind?"

Reaction phase. This phase is designed to move the group participants from a predominantly cognitive mode of processing to a more expressive, emotional level: "What was the worst part of the incident for you?" It is usually at this point that the meeting gets intense, as members take their cues from one another and begin to vent their distress. Clinicians and peer-debriefers keep a keen eye out for any adverse or unusual reactions among the personnel.

Symptom phase. This begins the movement back from the predominantly emotional processing level toward the cognitive processing level. Participants are asked to describe cognitive, physical, emotional, and behavioral signs of distress that appeared immediately at the scene or within several hours of the incident, a few days after the incident, and continually, persisting at the time of the debriefing: "What have you been experiencing since the incident?"

Education phase. Continuing the move back toward intellectual processing, didactic information is provided about the nature of the stress response and the expected physiological and psychological reactions to critical incidents. This serves to normalize the stress and coping responses and provides a basis for questions and answers.

Re-entry phase. This is the wrap-up, during which any additional questions or statements are addressed, referral for individual follow-ups are made, and general group bonding is reinforced: "What have you learned?" "Is there anything positive that can come out of this experience that can help you grow personally or professionally?" "How can you help one another in the future?" "Anything we left out?"

This is not to suggest that these phases always follow one another in an unvarying, mechanical sequence. I've often found that once group participants feel comfortable with the debriefing process and start talking, there is a tendency for the fact, thought, and reaction phases to blend together. Indeed, as Mitchell and Everly (1996) recognize, it would seem artificial and forced to abruptly interrupt someone expressing emotion just because "it's not the right phase." As long as the basic rationale and structure of the debriefing are maintained, the therapeutic effect will usually result. Indeed, on a number of occasions, previously silent members have spoken up at literally the last moment, when the group was all but getting up to leave. Clinician team leaders typically have to intervene only when emotional reactions become particularly intense, or where one or more members begin to blame or criticize others.

For a successful debriefing, timing and clinical appropriateness are important. The consensus from the literature and my own clinical experience support the scheduling of debriefings toward the earlier end of the recommended 24–72 hour window (Bordow & Porritt, 1979; Miller, 1999b; Solomon & Benbenishty, 1988). To keep the focus on the event itself and to reduce the potential for singling-out of individuals, some authorities recommend that there be a policy of mandatory referral of all involved personnel to a debriefing or other appropriate mental health intervention (Horn, 1991; McMains, 1991; Mitchell, 1991; Reese, 1991; Solomon, 1988, 1990, 1995). However, in other cases, mandatory or enforced CISD may lead to passive participation and resentment among the conscripted personnel (Bisson & Deahl, 1994; Flannery et al., 1991), and the CISD process may quickly become a boring routine if used indiscriminately after every incident, thereby diluting its effectiveness in those situations where it really could have helped. Departmental supervisors and mental health consultants must use their common sense and knowledge of their own personnel to make these kinds of judgment calls.

SPECIAL APPLICATIONS OF CISD FOR LAW ENFORCEMENT

As noted earlier, police officers tend to be clannish and reluctant to talk to outsiders. At the same time, they may be more resistant to showing vulnerability and weakness in front of their own peers than are other emergency personnel. Cops typically work alone or with a single partner, unlike firefighters and paramedics who are trained to have more of a team mentality (Blau, 1994; Kirschman, 1997; Solomon, 1995). This has led to some special adaptations of the CISD approach for law enforcement.

To encourage participation and reduce fear of stigmatization, the administrative policy should strongly and unequivocally state that debriefings and other postincident mental health and peer-support interventions are *confidential.* The only exceptions to confidentiality are a clear and present danger to self or others or disclosure of a serious crime by the officer. Team members should be instructed to call the department psychologist (if there is one) or the CISD team coordinator when confidentiality cannot be honored (Solomon, 1995). Temporary administrative leave or light duty may be appropriate following high-impact events such as shootings (Solomon, 1990; also see Chapter 7).

In cases where only one officer is involved, or as an individual follow-up to a formal group debriefing, Solomon (1995) recommends that individual debriefings be conducted by a trained mental health professional. In an individual debriefing, the emotional impact of the incident is assessed and explored as thoughts, feelings, and reactions are discussed. An effective format for individual debriefing sessions is to go over the incident *"frame by frame,"* allowing the officer to verbalize the moment-by-moment thoughts, perceptions, sensory details, feelings, and actions that occurred during the critical incident. This format helps the officer become aware of, sort out, and understand what happened.

Getting in touch with the perceptions and state of mind experienced during the critical incident may help the officer understand why certain actions were taken or specific decisions were made. The frame-by-frame approach helps defuse inappropriate self-blaming by encouraging the officer to differentiate what was under his control from what was not, and what was known at the time from what was impossible to know then, but may appear crystal clear in retrospect.

In cases of an officer-involved shooting (Chapter 7), when there is an ongoing or impending investigation, Solomon (1995) recommends that the group debriefing be postponed until the initial investigation has been completed and formal statements have been taken by investigators. Otherwise, debriefing participants may be viewed as witnesses who are subject to questioning about what was said. For particularly sensitive or controversial situations or complicated investigations, it may be advisable not to hold a group debriefing until the investigation has been legally resolved. Individual debriefings can be provided for the involved officer(s) in the meantime, while a group debriefing may proceed with other personnel who, although not directly involved in the incident, have nevertheless been affected by it.

In such sensitive cases, Solomon (1988, 1995) suggests using a mental health professional who is bound by law to certain rules of confidentiality, rather than a peer, but it should be made clear that clinical confidentiality is not as inviolate as attorney-client privilege, and that clinicians and their records may be subpoenaed. As always, a combination of legal protocol, departmental policy, sound clinical judgment, and basic common sense should guide decisions in individual cases. Ideally, these kinds of contingencies will have been planned for in advance when setting up departmental protocols and standard operating procedures (SOPs) for handling critical incidents.

Finally, as a follow-up measure, Solomon (1995) recommends what he terms a *critical incident peer support seminar*, which provides a retreat-like setting for the involved officers to come together for two or three days to revisit their experience several months following the critical incident. The seminar is facilitated by mental health professionals and peer-support officers.

Perhaps the most extensive and comprehensive adaptation of the CISD process for law enforcement comes from the work of Bohl (1995) who explicitly compares and contrasts the phases in her own program with the phases of the Mitchell CISD model.

In Bohl's program, the debriefing takes place as soon after the critical incident as possible. A debriefing may involve a single officer within the first 24 hours, later followed by a second individual debriefing, with a follow-up group debriefing taking place within one week to encourage group cohesion and bonding. This addresses the occupationally lower team orientation of most police officers who may not express feelings easily, even—or especially—in a group of their fellow cops.

The Bohl model makes no real distinction between the cognitive and emotional phases of a debriefing. If an officer begins to express emotion during the fact or cognitive phase, there is little point in telling him or her to stifle it until later. To be fair, the Mitchell model certainly does allow for flexibility and common sense in structuring debriefings, and both formats recognize the importance of responding empathically to the specific needs expressed by the participants, rather than just following a rigid set of rules.

In the emotion phase itself, what is important in the Bohl model is not the mere act of venting, but rather the opportunity to validate feelings. Bohl does not ask what the "worst thing" was, since she finds the typical response to be that "everything about it was the worst thing." However, it often comes as a revelation to these law enforcement tough guys that their peers have had similar feelings.

Still, some emotions may be difficulty to validate. For example, guilt or remorse over actions or inactions may actually have some basis in reality, as when an officer's momentary hesitation or impulsive action resulted in someone getting hurt or killed. In Bohl's model, the question then becomes: "Okay, you feel guilty—what are you going to do with that guilt?" That is, "What can be learned from the experience to prevent something like this from happening again?"—a prime application of this book's 20/20 hindsight/insight/foresight principle.

The Bohl debriefing model includes an additional phase, termed the *unfinished business phase*, which has no formal counterpart in the Mitchell model. Participants are asked, "What in the present situation reminds you of past experiences? Do you want to talk about those other situations?" This phase grew out of Bohl's observation that the incident prompting the current debriefing often acts as a catalyst for recalling past traumatic events. The questions give participants a chance to talk about these prior incidents that may arouse strong, unresolved feelings. Bohl finds that such multilevel debriefings result in a greater sense of relief and closure than might occur by sticking solely to the present incident. This jives with my own experience that, during a current debriefing, feelings and reactions to past critical incidents will sometimes spontaneously come up and this must be dealt with and worked through as it arises, although team leaders must be careful not to lose too much of the structure and focus of the current debriefing.

The education phase in the Bohl model resembles its Mitchell model counterpart, in that participants are schooled about normal and pathological stress reactions, how to deal with coworkers and family members, and what to anticipate in the days and weeks ahead. For example, an officer's child may have heard that his or her parent shot and killed a suspect, and the child may be questioned or teased at school (see Chapter 15). How to deal with children's responses may therefore be an important part of this education phase.

Unlike the Mitchell model, the Bohl model does not ask whether anything positive, hopeful, or growth-promoting has arisen from the incident. Officers who have seen their partners shot or killed or who have had to deal with child abuse or other senseless brutality might be forgiven for failing to perceive anything "positive" about the incident, and expecting them to extract some kind of existential growth experience from such an event may seem like a sick joke. On the other hand, as will be discussed in more detail below, this kind of post-traumatic growth sometimes does occur—spontaneously or with gentle guidance—in the wake of a horrible event (Almedom, 2005; Dunning, 1999; Stuhlmiller & Dunning, 2000; Tedeschi & Calhoun,

1996; Tedeschi et al., 1998; Violanti, 2000). In such cases, it should be nurtured and encouraged, but should never be an expectation that might set struggling trauma survivors up for further disappointment and self-reproach.

A final non-Mitchell phase of the debriefing in the Bohl model is the *round robin* in which each officer is invited to say essentially whatever he or she wants. The statement can be addressed to anyone or to no one in particular, but others cannot respond directly; this is supposed to give participants a feeling of safety. My own concern is that this may provide an opportunity for last-minute gratuitous sniping, which can quickly erode the supportive atmosphere that has been carefully crafted during the debriefing. Additionally, in practice, there doesn't seem to be anything particularly unique about this round robin phase to distinguish it from the standard re-entry phase of the Mitchell model. Finally, adding more and more "phases" to the debriefing process may serve to decrease the forthrightness and spontaneity of its implementation. Again, clinical judgment and common sense should guide the process, but Bohl's (1995) work in law enforcement debriefing is an important contribution to the treatment of critical incidents in policing.

CRITICAL INCIDENT PEER SUPPORT PROGRAMS

One of the attractive features of the CISD model is the demedicalization and destigmatization achieved by the involvement of peer debriefers along with professional clinicians; the latter, however, still play a central role in the Mitchell-model debriefing process. Seeking to enhance the "street cred" of the stress management process further, several *critical incident peer support or peer counselor programs* have emerged that endeavor to keep the role of mental health clinicians as covert as possible, or essentially eliminate them altogether, at least past the training phase. The idea is that cops are more likely to talk to other cops about their experiences than they are to mental health clinicians. Although I have not found this to be the case in my own practice, such a means of dealing with critical incidents should certainly be available as an option for those officers who will unburden themselves only to one of their own. Indeed, some authorities regard peer

support as an indispensable component of critical incident follow-up (Sheehan et al., 2004).

In such critical incident peer support programs, issues that must be dealt with include fitness-for-duty and chain-of-command; confidentiality and privacy when non-clinicians are used; the ease of speaking frankly to officers in your own department who you may have to work with every day; legal liability issues; and the problems of referral for further clinical work in the case of severe reactions (Toch, 2002). Several representative examples of peer support programs from different types of law enforcement agencies are presented below.

California Peace Officer Commission Peer Counselor Training

This peer counselor training program was implemented in 1983 by the State of California

Commission on Peace Officer Standards and Training (Linden & Klein, 1986). The training takes the form of a 24-hour course, paced over three days, with class size limited to 16. Materials include a 100-page training manual, and the course is co-taught by a police sergeant and a psychologist, which provides the students with a blend of perspectives, as well as generally reinforcing the kind of productive relationship that the law enforcement and mental heath fields ought to have. The course emphasizes that it is *not* designed to produce professional mental health clinicians, but to guide officers in constructive ways of helping their peers in distress.

The course curriculum includes a brief introductory session, followed by a section on basic counseling skills, which are explained and demonstrated. The course makes extensive use of role-plays and practice groups to hone and consolidate the classroom-taught skills in as many realistic examples as can be simulated by the students. Next, the students are asked to generate lists of the most common problem areas in their daily work with other officers, to which they might apply these counseling skills, such as relationship crises, substance abuse, depression and suicidality, critical incident stress, burnout, and conflicts with supervisors and coworkers. Each of these problem areas is discussed by the class and instructors (sometimes supplemented by a relevant videotape), and then role-played both in the general class setting and in small practice groups.

Salt Lake City Police Department Traumatic Incident Corps

A 1980 study of the Salt Lake City Police Department found that one of the major sources of stress following critical incidents, such as officer-involved shootings and assaults on officers, was the reaction of fellow officers. At the same time, the study found that involved officers still preferred to speak to their peers about the incident, rather than someone from the mental health field or even the clergy. Thus, involvement of the officers' peers appeared to have tremendous power to help or harm following a critical incident. Accordingly, since 1980, the Salt Lake City Police Department has utilized a *Traumatic Incident Corps* (TIC) for the purpose

of ameliorating the impact of traumatic events such as shootings and assaults on police officers (Nielsen, 1991).

The members of this team are all volunteers selected from among officers who have themselves at one time been involved in a critical incident, who have adequate social skills and ability to empathize with other individuals, and who are generally seen as "okay guys and gals," known and respected within the police department. These officers are trained through the departmental Psychological Services Unit in the recognition and understanding of traumatic incident reactions, general techniques of crisis intervention, strategies for social support and, when necessary, indications for referral to a mental health clinician.

The program emphasizes ongoing skill-enhancement in the form of bimonthly training modules of four hours. Such training typically focuses on reviewing specific case examples that have occurred within the department, with constructive critiquing and recommendations for improved interventions in the future.

FBI Critical Incident Stress Management Program

Since 1986, the Employee Assistance Program of the Federal Bureau of Investigation (FBI) has developed its own CISM program that explicitly utilizes peer support (McNally & Solomon, 1999). Team members are drawn from the Employee Assistance Program (EAP) staff, FBI chaplains, the FBI peer support team, and mental health professionals with expertise in police psychology and law enforcement traumatic stress.

In this program, a standard CISD debriefing may be followed by a one-on-one peer support contact, which consists of an individual meeting with the agents involved in the critical incident. This kind of support from a fellow agent who has "been there" is seen to have enhanced credibility. In addition, the FBI program provides group debriefings and one-on-one support for families of affected agents. Another vital component of the program is support from above, that is, from superiors who validate and show concern for the actions and reactions of their agents. If the affected agent continues to suffer posttraumatic stress reactions, the agency provides referrals to qualified mental health clinicians.

A unique feature of the FBI critical incident program is a four-day *postcritical incident seminar*, which includes 15 to 25 individuals meeting in a safe and supportive retreat-like environment, where they can access clinicians who specialize in law enforcement traumatic stress. This is similar to Solomon's (1995) *critical incident peer support seminar*, described above. Another unusual and controversial feature of the FBI program is its explicit endorsement of a particular therapeutic technique, *Eye Movement Desensitization and Reprocessing* (EMDR). I have critiqued the general overenthusiasm for this technique elsewhere (Miller, 1998b) and, hopefully, experience with a range of therapeutic strategies will expand and diversify the healing armamentarium for dealing with law enforcement traumatic stress beyond the focus on one or more single modalities.

U.S. Secret Service Critical Incident Support Team

The small, but select cadre of men and women charged with protecting the lives of government officials and other dignitaries might be expected to experience their share of stressful critical incidents. At the same time, the elite tough-guy personas of many of these agents, not to mention the secrecy and confidentiality of their security work, often makes these professionals very reluctant to show weakness to outsiders (June, 1999).

In 1988, the United States Secret Service sponsored two critical incident seminars for agents who had been involved in life-threatening incidents at some point in their careers (Britt, 1991). The format was a three-day course taught by a police psychologist with assistance from the FBI Critical Incident Team Project Manager. Seminar participants generally regarded the experience as very helpful in destigmatizing their reactions and facilitating the resolution of personal issues related to their stressful experiences. A further benefit was enhanced communication among the agents and their family members, many of whom had felt equally affected by the traumatic incident, but "shut out" by the agent's reluctance to talk about it. An unexpected bonus was that agents reported greatly enhanced mental preparedness for future critical incidents—

essentially turning 20/20 hindsight into 20/20 foresight—so much so, in fact, that such *stress inoculation* was made an explicit component of subsequent seminars. As with other programs of this type, team members endorsed the need to maintain regular updates on training and honing of skills.

Legal Issues in Peer Support and Other Critical Incident Services

Well-meaning though it may be to involve peers in helping peers, and to destigmatize and depathologize the helping process by keeping professional clinicians in a peripheral, advisory role, certain administrative and legal issues may arise when peers are the primary helpers (Finn & Tomz, 1999).

The main legal issue is privileged communication and confidentiality. Under most state and local laws, patients are entitled to confidentiality when speaking to a doctor or other licensed clinician. This means that an investigative agency cannot have access to my notes, unless my patient authorizes me to release them. However, *doctor-patient confidentiality* does not provide the same level of protection as *attorney-client privilege*. Anything said in private between you and your attorney cannot be compelled to be revealed to any party, except under the rarest and most extreme conditions, such as imminent matters of national security. However, my clinical notes and testimony may be subpoenaed or court-ordered, and then I must either: surrender the records and/or testify; seek legal assistance in quashing the subpoena or staying the court order; or simply refuse to comply and risk being held in contempt of court and possibly fined or jailed or both.

When nonlicensed peer support persons are used instead of clinicians, the protections are even weaker. During critical incident debriefings or one-on-one sessions, officers in emotional distress often make statements about their feelings of guilt, regret, or fear that could later be construed as admissions of wrongdoing in criminal cases or civil suits, e.g., "If only I had . . .," "I should have . . .," "What if I screwed up?" and so on. In such cases, courts and departmental Internal Affairs (IA) investigators may have the legal right to ask what was said during the peer debriefing or one-on-one session. Naturally, the prospect of an officer's words coming back to bite him would immediately stifle participation in any such program.

To my knowledge, there is no generally accepted standard for dealing with this problem, but individual agencies have handled it in different ways. The first is by truth-in-advertising. That is, debriefing or individual counseling participants must be informed of their legal rights and liabilities at the outset of the session. Of course, this implies that program coordinators know these issues after consultation with departmental legal counsel.

Some jurisdictions have dealt with this problem by not having peer support programs at all, while others require that its members obtain sufficient training and credentialing to be licensed in some mental health field, such as social work, marriage and family therapy, or substance abuse counseling. Whether cops-turned-counselors have any greater therapeutic success with law enforcement officers than more traditionally trained clinicians who come to work with police agencies is still an open question, but the mental health field should welcome law enforcement professionals who can bring their unique perspective and experience to counseling officers in distress.

CRITIQUES OF CRITICAL INCIDENT DEBRIEFING

Despite the enthusiasm for the debriefing model of crisis intervention, the CISD approach is not without its critics and detractors, especially when it is viewed as being used indiscriminately or regarded by its proponents as the only necessary and sufficient form of intervention. Bisson & Deahl (1994) have reviewed the literature suggesting some of the limitations, pitfalls, and drawbacks of the CISD approach. They note that even Mitchell (1988) acknowledges that not everyone in every critical incident situation will require or benefit from a debriefing. In some cases, more extensive, individualized interventions may be called for. In most other cases, the individual will recover on his or her own, with minimal, basic social support.

Often, it's a matter of timing. There seems to be a general consensus that, consistent with crisis intervention as a whole, debriefing is most effective if carried out sooner rather than later (Bordow & Porrit, 1979). My own clinical experience suggests holding debriefing sessions toward the earlier end of the recommended 24- to 72-hour window. Working with Israeli soldiers suffering combat stress during the Lebanon war, Solomon and Benbenishty (1988) found that, while early brief intervention did not entirely eliminate posttraumatic stress reactions, it helped to reduce their intensity and duration.

There may be some adverse side-effects of inappropriate CISD. In the well-known Australian brushfire study, McFarlane (1988) found that firefighters who received CISD shortly after the incident were less likely to develop acute posttraumatic stress reactions than nondebriefed workers, but they were more likely to develop delayed PTSD.

McFarlane (1988) expressed concern that overreliance on quick-fix, preventive treatment methods might delay the diagnosis and implementation of effective therapy for workers who suffer more serious psychological sequelae and require more extensive follow-up interventions. This can be avoided by remembering that debriefing is not a substitute for psychotherapy when the latter is necessary (Miller, 1998b, 1999b; Mitchell & Everly, 1996).

Griffiths and Watts (1992) examined relationships between stress debriefing and stress symptoms in 288 emergency personnel involved in rescue efforts at bus crashes. They found that those who attended debriefings had significantly higher levels of PTSD symptoms 12 months later than those who were not debriefed. Furthermore, there was no relationship between the perceived helpfulness of the debriefing and the symptoms. However, rescuers who experienced greater distress at the time of the crash were likely to have attended more debriefing sessions and to have perceived those sessions as more helpful.

Kenardy et al. (1996) studied the effect of stress debriefing on the recovery rate of 195 emergency service personnel and disaster workers following an earthquake in Newcastle, Australia. They found no evidence of an improved recovery rate among those helpers who were debriefed, even when levels of exposure and helping-related stress were taken into account.

Police officers who had responded as rescuers to a civilian plane crash and later debriefed were evaluated and compared to a matched sample of nondebriefed officers at two subsequent points in time by Carlier et al. (1998). Results showed that at eight months, there were no significant differences between the groups, and that at 18 months, the debriefed officers showed significantly more disaster-related hyperarousal symptoms related to their rescue work than nondebriefed officers.

There even appears to be somewhat of a disconnect between the self-perceived helpfulness of debriefing by attendees versus objective measures of longer-term psychological adjustment. Arendt and Elklit (2001) reviewed the debriefing literature and concluded that participants typically evaluate debriefing sessions as very helpful, even though there is little evidence for a longer-term beneficial effect in terms of preventing psychological stress disability. The CISD may inhere in the nonspecific factor of just being able to talk about the experience in a supportive atmosphere and being able to receive validation and practical information about stress reactions and coping strategies. This, of course, does not negate debriefing as a beneficial strategy, but calls for more study as to what exactly are the essential elements that make stress debriefing more or less effective than other modalities, and how the technique can be broadened and made more flexible, without diluting its applicability or credibility.

Mitchell and Everly (1996, 1997) have responded to these critiques by noting that many critical studies of so-called CISD fail to use the true Mitchell model, pointing out that the overuse or misuse of any technique hardly means that it is never effective when used properly, and counter-citing empirical studies that do support the efficacy of Mitchell-model CISD.

For example, Robinson and Mitchell (1993) conducted an exploratory, descriptive study of 172 emergency service, welfare, and hospital personnel who took part in 31 debriefings. Emergency service workers rated the debriefing as having considerable personal value. Most participants who experienced stress at the time of the incident attributed a reduction in stress symptoms, at least in part, to the debriefing. Similarly, Wee (1996) found that CISD significantly reduced stress symptoms in emergency service personnel operating during the 1992 Los Angeles riots.

Everly & Boyle. 1999 carried out a meta-analytic review of the effectiveness of psychological debriefing techniques, and found compelling evidence for the clinical utility of such strategies in mitigating the psychological stress of different types of critical incidents. The therapeutic benefits were revealed despite wide diversity in subject groups, types of traumatic event, and types of outcome measure used, indicating potentially wide generalizability of stress debriefing applications. A non-meta-analytic review focused specifically on Mitchell model CISM (Everly et al., 2000) produced the following set of conclusions: critical incidents with accompanying PTSD are frequent events; the psychological sequelae of critical incidents may be effectively addressed by CISD and other CISM interventions; more empirical research on CISM interventions is needed; and increased organizational and administrative support is needed for the study and prevention of adverse critical incident effects.

Mitchell and Everly (1997) have called for an end to the "study wars" trying to demonstrate that CISD does or doesn't work, but in the spirit of the present review, I think empirical studies should continue to examine what forms of CISD-type interventions work best with which populations and under what circumstances. As is the case with any wholesale application of a promising psychological treatment modality, further research and clinical experience are likely to narrow and refine, as well as extend and expand, CISD's appropriate therapeutic applications and identify certain limitations and even potentially harmful side-effects for certain groups. This has been the case, for example, with cognitive rehabilitation (Hall & Cope, 1995; Miller, 1992), relaxation training (Lazarus & Mayne, 1990), biofeedback and behavioral medicine (Miller, 1994b; Silver & Blanchard, 1978), and eye movement desensitization and reprocessing (Allen & Lewis, 1996).

Excessive and/or inappropriate use of mandatory CISD can lead to passive participation and resentment among workers (Bisson & Deahl, 1994; Flannery et al., 1991) and the CISD process may quickly become a boring routine if used indiscriminately after every incident, no matter how "critical" it may seem. The danger is that the therapeutic impact and credibility of CISD may then become diluted and fragmented, reducing its potential effectiveness in those situations where it really might have helped.

Some particularly vocal detractors have accused CISD of having assumed a cult-like status that is cashing in on what amounts to nothing more than a repackaging of the informal types of peer support that emergency workers have always used. Somewhat more high-toned critiques cite the frequent overuse of CISD, diluting both its effectiveness and its credibility, and asserting that there is no "objective" evidence of its efficacy. It is worth noting that many of these self-styled devotees of clinical scientific rigor have no problem accepting other, less-well empirically validated treatment modalities for PTSD and critical incident stress, such as EEG neurofeedback or EMDR.

One group of commentators (Dunning, 1999; Stuhlmiller & Dunning, 2000; Violanti, 2000) seeks not necessarily to do away with critical incident debriefing entirely but to reframe it in both focus and content. Their main criticism of the formal CISD model is that it pathologizes stress reactions and, at the same time, allows departmental insurance companies to cheaply discharge their obligation to emotionally wounded officers by offering debriefing as a quick-fix, one-size-fits-all package of therapeutic intervention. These authors propose an alternative *salutogenic debriefing* model that views critical incident reactions as opportunities for adaptive coping and personal growth, to foster not the learned helplessness of a traumatized victim mentality, but a sense of competence, confidence, resilience, hardiness, and learned resourcefulness (Almedom, 2005; Antonovsky, 1987; Higgins, 1994; Kobassa et al., 1982; Miller, 1998c; Tedeschi & Calhoun, 1996; Tedeschi et al., 1998).

In fairness, the purpose of all traumatic stress interventions is to reduce hopelessness and helplessness and foster adaptive coping, but going too far in the other direction and adopting a "Clarence the Angel" approach to intervention (Miller, 1998b) may only serve to put too much pressure on traumatized subjects who understandably can't bring themselves to turn a horrific episode into a personal growth experience, and may therefore feel like failures if they don't meet this high bar of recovery. As always, we have to use our professional judgment.

More broadly, most authorities would endorse the idea that CISD, or any other systemized approach to intervention, should supplement and enhance—not replace—each individual's natural coping resources (McNally et al., 2003; Sheehan et al., 2004). In other words, consistent with the guiding philosophy of this book, *all* psychological services for law enforcement should be in the direction of empowering officers to deal with challenges as independently and effectively as possible.

Overall, whether considering the strict Mitchell model or the variants thereof, there now exists substantial clinical, empirical, and anecdotal support to document the efficacy of CISD-type interventions in a wide variety of crisis situations and settings, from law enforcement to emergency rescue, school crises, disaster relief, workplace violence, and civilian crime victimization (Miller, 1998b). While many critical incidents will not require any special intervention, and while the majority of those that do will be well served by a CISD approach, it is the responsibility of departmental administrators, and the mental health professionals who advise them, to ensure that debriefing modalities are used responsibly and that other forms of clinically appropriate psychotherapeutic intervention are available to those who need them. CISD, like all successful treatment modalities, must be a living, evolving organism. Continued research and clinical ingenuity will hopefully further texturize and expand the stress debriefing approach into new and different applications.

LAW ENFORCEMENT PSYCHOTHERAPY

Contact with mental health services for critical incident stress sometimes goes beyond debriefing and involves more extended and individualized interaction with a professional clinician. In other cases, it may not be one particular event that leads to a mental health referral, but rather a cumulative build-up of stressors that the officer him- or herself, or the supervisor, feels would be amenable to psychological treatment. Whether self-referred, mandated by the department, or a little of both, psychotherapy with law enforcement officers requires a few special considerations.

As noted above, police officers have a reputation for shunning mental health services, often perceiving its practitioners as softies and bleeding hearts who love nothing better than to coddle the very criminals the officers risk their lives to apprehend, and then helping them go free with overcomplicated psychobabble excuses. Other cops may fear being "shrunk" by the departmental squirrel, having a notion of the psychotherapy process as akin to brainwashing, a humiliating and emasculating experience in which they are forced to lie on a couch and sob about their inner child. Less dramatically and more commonly, the idea of needing "mental help" implies weakness, cowardice, and lack of ability to do the job. In the environment of many departments, some officers realistically fear censure, stigmatization, ridicule, thwarted career advancement, and alienation from colleagues if they are perceived as the type who "folds under pressure." Still others in the department who may have something to hide may fear a colleague "spilling his guts" to the shrink and thereby blowing the malfeasor's cover (Miller, 1995a, 1998b).

Administrative Issues

There has always been some debate about whether psychological services, especially therapy-type services, should be provided by a psychologist within the department, even a clinician who is also an active or retired officer, or whether such matters are best handled by outside therapists who are less involved in departmental politics and gossip (Blau, 1994; Silva, 1991).

On the one hand, the departmental psychologist is likely to have more knowledge of, and experience with, the direct pressures faced by the personnel he or she serves; this is especially true if the psychologist is also an officer or has had formal law enforcement training or ride-along experience. On the other hand, in addition to providing psychotherapy services, the departmental psychologist is likely to also be involved in performing work status and fitness-for-duty evaluations, as well as other assessments or legal roles which may conflict with that of an ally and helper. An outside clinician may have less direct experience with departmental policy and pressures, but may enjoy more clinical independence and therapeutic freedom of movement.

My own experience has been that officers who sincerely come for help are usually less interested in the therapist's extensive knowledge of *The Job*, and more concerned that he or she demonstrate a basic trust and a willingness to understand the officer's situation—the officer will be more than happy to provide the technical details. These officers expect mental health professionals to "give 110 percent" in the psychotherapy process, just as the officers do in their own jobs; they really don't want the doc to be another cop; they want him or her to be a skilled therapist—that's why they're talking to us in the first place. This is often the case with many individuals in masculine-oriented professions: they respect straightforwardness and competence because they believe in it themselves (Brooks, 1998).

Many cops are actually glad to find a secure haven away from the fishbowl atmosphere of the department, and relieved that the therapeutic sessions provide a respite from shop talk. This is especially true where the referral problem has less to do with direct job-related issues and more with outside pressures, such as family or alcohol problems, that may impinge on job performance. In any case, the therapist, the officer, and the department should be clear at the outset about issues relating to confidentiality and chain of command, and any changes in ground rules should be clarified as needed. Technically, the jurisdictional rules of confidentiality, privilege, and duty-to-protect apply to law enforcement officers just as they do to other psychotherapy patients. Since ground rules and role boundaries are paramount issues with this group, it is important that the officer understand from the beginning the standards and protocols in the therapist's jurisdiction. Mishandling of a psychological referral can have devastating consequences for the officer and the department (Max, 2000), so police administrators should ensure that they are kept up to speed as to the nature and quality of the mental health services provided by their psychologists.

An additional issue for law enforcement personnel is the knowledge and attitude toward their treatment on the part of command staff and coworkers. Therapists should be clear with commanders and supervisors regarding what information is relevant to the patient's job role and work performance and what will remain confidential. In many cases, the therapeutic referral is concluded by a written summary that may subsequently be relevant to a fitness-for-duty or other job rating or qualification (Chapter 13). It is crucial that the therapist phrase any such report in a way that honestly and succinctly presents his or her conclusions as they pertain to the job-fitness question, while not violating trust and confidentiality about the specific content of the sessions (Blau, 1994; Silva, 1991). Admittedly, this is sometimes a delicate dance. However, in my experience, most commanders who refer their cops for psychotherapy—and actually get them to go—are willing to give me wide discretion with regard to confidentiality, as long as the clinical treatment process will help the officers get back to productive work.

Trust and the Therapeutic Relationship

Difficulty with trust appears to be an occupational hazard for law enforcement officers, who typically maintain a strong sense of self-sufficiency and insistence on solving their own problems. Therapists who work with police officers may at first need get past some testing and questioning on the part of their patients: "Why are you doing this?" "What's in it for you?" "Who's going to get this information?" Officers may expose the therapist to mocking cynicism and criticism about the job, baiting the therapist to agree, and thereby hoping to expose the therapist's prejudices about law enforcement culture and practices (Silva, 1991).

The development of trust during the establishment of the therapeutic alliance depends on the therapist's skill in interpreting the officer's statements, thoughts, feelings, reactions, and nonverbal behavior. In the best case, the officer begins to feel at ease with the therapist and finds comfort and a sense of predictability from the psychotherapy process. Silva (1991) articulates several guidelines for establishing therapeutic mutual trust:

Accurate empathy. The therapist conveys his or her understanding of the officer's background and experience (but beware of premature false familiarity and phony "bonding").

Genuineness. The therapist is spontaneous, yet tactful, flexible, and creative, and communicates as directly and nondefensively as possible.

Availability. The therapist is accessible and available (within reason) when needed, and avoids making promises and commitments he or she can't realistically keep.

Respect. This is both gracious and firm, and acknowledges the officer's sense of autonomy, control, responsibility, and self-respect within the therapeutic relationship. Respect is manifested by the therapist's overall attitude, language, and behavior, as well as by certain specific actions. These include signifying regard for rank or job role by initially using formal departmental titles, such as "officer," "detective," or "lieutenant," at least until trust and mutual respect allow an easing of formality. Here it is important for clinicians to avoid the dual traps of overfamiliarity, patronizing, and talking down to the officer on the one hand, and, on the other hand, trying to "play cop" or force bogus camaraderie by assuming the role of a colleague or supervisor.

Concreteness. Therapy should, at least initially, be goal-oriented and have a problem-solving focus. Police officers are into action and results, and to the extent that it is clinically realistic, the therapeutic approach should emphasize active problem-solving approaches before exploring more sensitive and complex psychological issues.

Therapeutic Strategies and Techniques

Since many law enforcement and emergency personnel come under psychotherapeutic care in the context of some form of critical incident posttraumatic stress reaction, clinical experience, as well as the relevant literature, reflect this emphasis (Blau, 1994; Fullerton et al., 1992; Kirschman, 1997, 2004). In general, the effectiveness of any therapeutic technique will be determined by the timeliness, tone, style, and intent of the intervention. Effective psychological interventions with law enforcement officers share in common the elements of briefness, focus on specific symptomatology or conflict issues, and direct operational efforts to resolve the conflict or problem and to reach a satisfactory short-term conclusion, while planning for the future if necessary.

Blau (1994) recommends that the first meeting between the therapist and the officer establish a safe and comfortable working atmosphere by the therapist's articulating a positive endorsement of the officer's decision to seek help, a clear description of the therapist's responsibilities and limitations with respect to confidentiality and privilege, and an invitation to the officer to state his or her concerns.

A straightfoward, goal-directed, problem-solving therapeutic intervention approach includes the following elements: creating a sanctuary; focusing on critical areas of concern; specifying desired outcomes; reviewing assets; developing a general plan; identifying practical initial implementations; encouraging self-efficacy; and setting appointments for review, reassurance, and further implementation (Blau, 1994).

Blau (1994) delineates a number of effective individual intervention strategies for police officers:

Attentive listening. This includes good eye contact, appropriate body language, genuine interest, and interpersonal engagement, without inappropriate comment or interruption. Clinicians will recognize this type of intervention as a form of "active listening."

Being there with empathy. This therapeutic attitude conveys availability, concern, and awareness of the disruptive emotions being experienced by the traumatized or distressed officer. It is also helpful to let the officer know, in a nonalarming manner, what he or she is likely to experience in the days and weeks ahead.

Reassurance. In acute stress situations, this should take the form of realistically reassuring the officer that routine matters will be taken care of, deferred responsibilities will be handled by others, and the officer has administrative and command support. This, of course, should be realistically based.

Supportive counseling. This includes effective listening, restatement of content, clarification of feelings, and validation. It also may include such concrete services as community referral and networking with liaison agencies, if necessary.

Interpretive counseling. This type of intervention should be used when the officer's emotional reaction is significantly greater than the circumstances of the critical incident seem to warrant. In appropriate

cases, this therapeutic strategy can stimulate the officer to explore underlying emotional or psychodynamic issues that intensify a naturally stressful traumatic event. In a few cases, this may lead to continuing, ongoing psychotherapy (Blau, 1994).

Not to be neglected is the use of *humor*, which has its place in many forms of psychotherapy (Fry & Salameh, 1987), but may be especially useful in working with law enforcement and emergency services personnel (Fullerton et al., 1992; Miller, 1995a, 1999c; Silva, 1991). In general, if the therapist and patient can share a laugh, this may lead to the sharing of more intimate feelings. Humor serves to bring a sense of balance, perspective, and clarity to a world that seems to have been warped and polluted by malevolence and horror. "Show me a man who knows what's funny," Mark Twain tells us, "and I'll show you a man who knows what's not."

Humor, even sarcastic, gross, or callous humor, if handled appropriately and used constructively, may allow the venting of anger, frustration, resentment, or sadness, and thereby lead to productive, reintegrative therapeutic work. This is true, however, only insofar as the therapist is able to keep a lid on destructive forms of self-mockery or inappropriate projective hostility in the shape of sleazy, cynical, or meanspirited wisecracking or character assassination.

Also remember that many traumatized persons tend to be quite concrete and suspicious at the outset of therapy, and certain well-intentioned kidding and cajoling may be perceived as insulting to the officer or dismissive of the seriousness of his plight. In such cases, the constructive therapeutic use of humor may have to await the formation of a therapeutic relationship that allows some cognitive and emotional breathing room, as well as the reclaiming of enough of the officer's confidence and self-esteem so that he can take some perspective on the situation and "lighten up." Some extreme events, however, such as the death of a child or partner, may never be funny—period, and this has to be respected.

Phases of Law Enforcement Psychotherapy

Although therapeutic progress typically proceeds in the form of a cyclical flywheel, with alternating starts and stops, forward thrusts and backslides, it may be useful to consider Kirschman's (1997) division of the therapeutic process with law enforcement officers into two phases, which may at times overlap.

The *stabilization phase* allows the officer to gradually turn down the emotional intensity of the traumatic experience in order to create a secure and safe psychological environment for dealing with the effects of the critical incident. Therapeutic strategies and activities at this phase include encouraging the officer to attend a critical incident debriefing with his peers and to obtain as much information and feedback about the event as he is able to assimilate. Time off from work or assignment to light duty might ease the transition back to the officer's prior full-status work assignment. Inasmuch as many officers may be reluctant to ask for such duty for fear of seeming weak, some departments institute a mandatory waiting period until the officer is cleared by the departmental psychologist. Where appropriate, medication for mood stabilization or sleep may be helpful. Also, the officer should be encouraged to obtain as much positive psychological support as possible from friends and family, while steering clear of people who only serve to bring him down.

In the *working through* stage of therapy, the officer begins to find meaning in what happened to him and to integrate the experience into his personality and belief systems. In constructing such a personal narrative, some elements of the experience and his reactions may fit into his existing worldview; in other cases, his core beliefs may have to be expanded or amended to accommodate the traumatic event. It is here that some of the lessons of salutogenic debriefing or therapy, discussed above, might prove beneficial. Officers may have to mourn the parts of themselves that have been lost as a result of the traumatic experience and develop plans for the future that stake out new territory in terms of their roles as officers, family members, citizens, and so on.

Utilizing Cognitive Defenses

In psychology, *defense mechanisms* are mental strategems that the mind uses to protect itself from unpleasant thoughts, feelings, impulses, and memories. While the normal use of such defenses enables the average, nonpathologically affected person to

avoid conflict and ambiguity and maintain some consistency to their personality and belief system, most psychologists would agree that an overuse of defenses to wall off too much painful thought and feeling leads to rigidity and dysfunctional coping with life. Accordingly, much of the ordinary psychotherapeutic process involves carefully helping the patient to relinquish pathological defenses so that he or she can learn to deal with internal conflicts constructively. However, in the face of immediately traumatizing critical incidents, the last thing an affected person needs is to have his or her defenses stripped away. If anything, the proper utilization of psychological defenses can serve as an important "psychological splint" that enables the person to function in the immediate posttraumatic aftermath and eventually be able to productively resolve and integrate the traumatic experience (Janik, 1991).

Law enforcement and public safety personnel usually need little help in applying defense mechanisms on their own. Examples (Durham et al., 1985; Henry, 2004; Taylor et al., 1983) include:

Denial. "Put it out of my mind; focus on other things; avoid situations or people who remind me of it."

Rationalization. "I had no choice; things happens for a reason; it could have been worse; other people have it worse; most people would react this way."

Displacement/projection. "It was Command's fault for issuing such a stupid order; I didn't have the right backup; they're all trying to blame me for everything."

Refocus on positive attributes. "Hey, this was a one-shot deal–I'm usually a great cop. I'm not gonna let this get me down."

Refocus on positive behaviors. "Okay, I'm gonna get more training, increase my knowledge and skill so I'll never be caught with my pants down like this again."

Janik (1991) proposes that, in the short term, therapists actively support and bolster psychological defenses that temporarily enable the officer to continue functioning. Just as a physical crutch is an essential part of orthopedic rehabilitation when an injured patient is learning to walk again, a psychological crutch is perfectly adaptive and productive if it enables the officer to get back on his psychological two feet right after a traumatic critical incident. Only later, when he or she is making the bumpy transition back to normal routine functioning, are the defenses revisited as possible bars to progress. And just as some orthopedic patients may always need some assistive walking device, like a special shoe or a cane, to lead a normal life, some degree of psychological defensiveness may persist in officers, so that they can otherwise productively pursue their work and other interests. Indeed, rare among us is the person who is completely defense-free. It is only when defenses are used inappropriately and for too long, do they constitute a "crutch" in the pejorative sense.

Survival Resource Training

In line with the concept, discussed further in Chapter 5, that management of stress in acute danger situations often requires the marshalling of strength and resistance, Solomon (1988, 1991) has capitalized on the idea that active denial of vulnerability and mortality can be an adaptive response in coping with ongoing critical incidents and their immediate aftermath. Solomon points out that, following critical incidents characterized by fear, danger, injury, or death, officers often dwell on their mistakes and overlook what they *did right* in terms of coping with their emotions and getting the job done. Thus, being realistically reminded by the therapist of their own adaptive coping efforts may prove especially empowering because it draws upon strengths that came from the officer him- or herself. Termed *survival resource training*, this intervention allows officers to utilize their fear response to gain access to a psychological state characterized by controlled strength, increased awareness, confidence, and clarity of mind.

In this technique, the therapist encourages the officer to view the critical incident he was involved in from a detached, objective point of view, "like you were watching a movie of yourself," and to go through the incident "frame-by-frame." At the point where he visualizes himself fully engaging in his activity (negotiating, arresting, taking cover, firing his weapon, etc.), the officer is instructed to "focus on the part of you enabling you to respond." In most cases, this leads to a mental reframe characterized by controlled strength, heightened awareness, confidence, and mental clarity, as the officer mentally zooms in on his capability to respond, instead of focusing on the immobilizing fear, perceptions of weakness, loss of control, or perceptual distortions. Often, this results in an officer's being "reminded" of how he put his fear on hold in order to get the job done. The reframing thus focuses on efficacy instead of vulnerability, strength instead of weakness. As noted in Chapter 5, however, this presupposes that adequate training was in place to handle situations that may occur.

Although originally developed for individual counseling sessions, Solomon (1991) has also incorporated this approach in group debriefings, to expand the thought and reaction phases to include the frame-by-frame analysis of what the officers did, thought, and experienced, and to focus on the survival resources that enabled them to soldier through the ordeal.

In addition to processing past critical incidents, realistic feelings of efficacy and competence can also shade over into future incidents, as officers have reported increased confidence and ability in handling subsequent calls, such as arrests, shooting incidents, domestic disturbances, and traffic chases. In addition, officers have felt more confident in other nonemergency but stressful situations, such as court testimony and personal matters, such as family discussions (Solomon, 1988). It is especially gratifying to clinicians and officers alike when their mutual efforts can turn vicious cycles of demoralization and despair into positive cycles of confidence and optimism. Indeed, this is the hoped-for outcome of all forms of psychotherapy.

ORGANIZATIONAL AND DEPARTMENTAL SUPPORT

Not all interventions involve psychotherapy or formal debriefings. Following a department-wide critical incident, such as a line-of-duty death, serial homicide investigation, or mass casualty rescue and recovery operation–Oklahoma City and September 11th certainly come to mind–the departmental psychologist or consulting mental health professional can advise and guide law enforcement agencies in encouraging and implementing several organizational response measures (Alexander, 1993; Alexander & Walker, 1994; Alexander & Wells, 1991; DeAngelis, 1995; Fullerton et al., 1992; Palmer, 1983). Many of these strategies are proactively applicable as part of training before a critical incident occurs. Some specific measures include the following.

Encourage *mutual support among peers and supervisors*. The former typically happens anyway; the latter may need some explicit reinforcement. Although not typically team workers, police officers frequently work as partners and understand that some degree of shared decision-making and mutual reassurance can enhance effective performance on the job.

Utilize *humor as a coping mechanism* to facilitate emotional insulation and group bonding. The first forestalls excessive identification with victims; the second encourages mutual group support via a shared language. Of course, as noted above, mental health clinicians and departmental supervisors need to carefully monitor the line between adaptive humor that helps healing and gratuitous nastiness that only serves to entrench cynicism and despair.

Make use of *appropriate rituals* to give meaning and dignity to an otherwise existentially disorienting experience. This includes not only religious rites related to mourning, but such respectful protocols as a military-style honor guard to attend bodies before disposition, and the formal acknowledgement of actions above and beyond the call of duty.

Important here is the role of *grief leadership*, i.e., the commanding officer's demonstrating by example that it's okay to express grief and mourn the death of fallen comrades or civilians, and that the dignified expression of one's feelings about the incident will be supported, not denigrated. Indeed, this healthy combination of manful task-orientation and validated expression of legitimate grief has largely characterized the response of rescue and recovery personnel at the New York World Trade Center site (Henry, 2004).

FAMILIES AND CRITICAL INCIDENT STRESS

Officer and Family Reactions to the Stress of a Critical Incident

The concept of *secondary traumatization* states that others not directly exposed to the critical incident stressor may often experience its effects by way of the primary subject. In most law enforcement families, the main brunt-bearer of the officer's critical incident stress is the spouse. Sheehan (1991) has described a variety of reactions to a stressful critical incident that officers may show which may, in turn, have repercussions on the couple's relationship. Most of these reactions reflect the extreme bipolarity of emotional response that traumatized individuals display as their emotional gyroscope wobbles along, trying to reright itself.

Human beings under severe stress become very egocentric and concrete: the world revolves around them and they lose their sense of proportion and perspective, seeing everything in terms of black-and-white. In this almost childlike regression, it may not take much to frustrate and irritate officers who have been traumatized by a critical incident. Another unfortunate, but fundamental, aspect of human nature is that we tend to be on our best behavior in front of strangers, and to take out our frustration and pain on those closest to us because, ironically, we know that they're the ones who'll take it. So it is that officers in distress may project their toxic feelings onto family members, while towing the line with peers, supervisors, and citizens. This may drive family members crazy: "He's all sweetness and light with the Citizen Review Board and his buddies at work, but he comes home and gives me hell for the slightest little thing."

The *embrace-alienate* syndrome (Sheehan, 1991) describes an alternating pattern of seeking intimacy and then abruptly withdrawing. The officer in crisis wants to get closer to his primary support person, but then, fearing that intimacy will turn to vulnerability, he panics at the perceived loss of defensive strength and control, and recoils from the emotional connection. But now he is emotionally alone and interpersonally isolated, and fears as well the desperate pain of abandonment, causing him to rush forward to merge again with his loved one's protective support. Then, he again feels naked and exposed, again panics, again withdraws, and so on, in a vicious cycle. Not surprisingly, the spouse soon comes to feel frustrated and drained by this emotional rollercoaster.

Another bipolarity is the tension between the officer's wariness, suspiciousness, or frank paranoia, and his fear of his own hostile, retaliatory impulses. He may stalk around in a hypervigilant state but avoid people to keep from being "set off." Others, cowed by his smoldering emotional state, may soon come to avoid him as well. He is fearful of attack precisely because he currently feels so weak and vulnerable, and his self-protective emotional stoniness may at intervals be punctuated by defensive outbursts if he feels he's being physically crowded or emotionally threatened. His family, by this time, will be walking on eggshells, always waiting for the next shoe to drop. More maddening still, he may try to initiate family contact, and then react to his loved ones' understandable wariness with increased hostility and resentment: "Where the hell are you people when I need you?" And if that weren't enough, well-intentioned family members may try to warm up to the officer, but he then becomes frightened by the intimacy and again lashes out. No wonder families soon come to feel that "we can't win."

Family Strategies for Dealing with an Officer's Critical Incident Stress

As noted above, the family member who typically bears the brunt of an officer's stress reaction is the spouse, and Kirschman (1997) has provided a useful set of principles to help spouses deal with their officer in crisis. Mates who feel the well-intended impulse to "do something" for their spouse should realize that, often, the best help is quiet and passive. Simply indicating your understanding of your mate's distress, acknowledging what he's going through, and offering to just listen without judgment, to provide reassurance and companionship, and to let him know you're the one person who won't abandon or fold on him, is a powerful form of psychological support.

Letting your spouse know that it's okay for him to take a break from some household responsibilities while he regains his emotional bearings can relieve pressure on him to "keep his end up" while he's recovering from his stressful experience. You may have to fill in for certain roles and tasks, such as paying bills, driving the kids around, and running interference in certain social functions he feels unable to attend. But be sure to let him know that you understand this is only temporary: you're not trying to usurp his family role, only pinch hit till he can resume his rightful place at bat—just as he would help you out (and may have actually done so in the past) if you were temporarily benched by an adverse life event.

At the same time, cutting some slack doesn't mean allowing a wholesale abrogation of family responsibilities. You don't want to reinforce your mate acting like an complete emotional invalid; indeed, it is a sign of respect not to overly coddle a wounded warrior, but to expect that he do those things he is legitimately capable of doing: "I know the doc said to get as much rest as possible, and that's why it's okay for now for you to spend most of your time in your room. But the kids and I really need to see you at the dinner table, just so we know we're a family." If conflicts arise over matters like these, be careful to pick your battles. In the early stages of recovery, it may be all right to err on the side of too much leeway, but if the slack-off persists past the point of reason, you might suspect that there are other issues going on beyond the effects of the critical incident itself. At that point, you may consider getting professional help.

Kirschman (1997) also offers recommendations on how spouses of officers in crisis can help themselves cope with the stresses of secondary traumatization, some of which I elaborate on here, based on my own observations. First, take care of yourself. This refers not just to your physical health, but your basic sanity. As much as you truly want to help your mate, you need not and should not be a full-time caretaker. Take a break. See a movie. Go out to dinner with friends. Take the kids to the carnival. Seek the support of others in your situation, but don't become a support-group junkie. Try to find someone you can safely talk with about your feelings. If the main source of your own distress is related to bottled-up emotions, you may not necessarily need a shrink, just a sympathetic ear. Only when the usual methods of coping don't seem to work is professional help likely to be indicated.

Don't try to be "Ms. Fixit." If you just use your best helping instincts with some the recommendations described above, your mate will gradually recover. It may take some time, so don't try to rush it. Sometimes, a year has to pass to get the anniversary reactions over with, but that doesn't mean that no progress can be made in that time. It's also useful to think about what you and your family mean by "progress" and "recovery." Basic family functioning? Return to full normality? Transcendent coping and a new lease on life? Try to set realistic short-term and long-term goals for the restoration of family stability, and approach these goals successively. And if it seems that nothing is improving over the long term, then you'll know that additional measures are called for, in the form of individual or family therapy.

Departmental Responses to Law Enforcement Families in Distress

Virtually all police agencies have some kind of formal departmental program of services for the families of officers who are killed or seriously injured in the line of duty (Chapter 8). However, far fewer departments have a formal system set up for helping spouses and families of officers in distress following a less dramatic critical incident, and for this reason, Hartsough (1991) has offered some recommendations for police departments to help such family members.

All forms of intervention, whether clinical or administrative, function best when they address themselves to the unique characteristics and requirements of the individual, rather than relying solely on prepackaged, cookie-cutter forms of response. Families should not just be seen as extensions of the distressed officer, but the question should be: "What does the family need from the department, and can the department legitimately meet those needs?" This includes acknowledgement of needs for material help and access to services while the officer is recovering. It also means providing the family with accurate and authoritative information about any legal, disciplinary, or vocational issues that may affect the officer's case. It also includes a standing invitation for the family to remain part of the police community while the officer is recovering, such as being included in departmental ceremonies and events.

Children of Officers Experiencing Critical Incident Stress

Children of families of a critical incident-stressed officer may respond in a variety of ways, depending on their ages (Kirschman, 1997). Younger children will fear family separation and abandonment by the atmosphere of tension and distress within the home. Older children may show regressive behaviors and withdrawal from family and social activities. Children's sleep may be disturbed by nightmares and they may want to sleep in their parents' bed. Anger and tantrums may appear or become more more frequent. Situational anxiety and depression are common and may range from mild to severe.

Kirschman (1997) and Williams (1991) offer some useful recommendations for parents to help their kids deal with an officer-parent in crisis (also see Chapter 15). The first priority is to establish a sense of relative safety and normalcy. Here, actions speak louder than words. Saying, "Everything is all right" when it isn't will only confuse and frighten children. It's much better to set a positive example of calm courage under pressure by your actions. Help children deal with their emotions by modeling appropriate behavior and decorum. Allow them to express their feelings in an age-appropriate way. Be prepared to accept and absorb some of the toxic emotions that may emerge. Where possible, channel feelings into productive activity.

Don't underestimate the power of just being there. Children will be reassured more by your presence than your words, so spend a little extra time with them, even if it's just to watch a neutral TV show together, read a story, or discuss the life and times of a cartoon character. This lets the child know you're there when he or she needs you. Some separations may be unavoidable after critical incidents, such as appearances at trial or travel to arrange medical care or financial matters. The key here is to keep children productively busy: give them projects to do that they can show you with pride when you return. Arrange to have them taken by trusted friends or relatives to enjoyable activities—as a form of relief and diversion, but not denial or "sugar-coating" of the stressful family situation.

Many children, especially older children, will want information about the critical incident and its effect on their parent. To avoid overwhelming the child with grim details, provide age-appropriate information in graded doses. Start with a little; you can always add more.

If children behave in regressed or immature ways, cut them some slack. For example, be tolerant of overly clingy behavior or demands for more attention. Understand that this is a temporary reaction and that they will return to their previous age-appropriate level of functioning when the crisis has resolved. Don't tell them to "grow up" or "act your age," which will only serve to further demoralize them. However, don't be afraid to set reasonable limits, especially if there are safety issues involved. Also, let the school know what's going on, so the child will not be unfairly penalized for latenesses, absences, or missing homework during the stressful time.

Similar to the phenomenon described with critical incident debriefings, some children may show "delayed reactions" or "sleeper effects" of prior traumatic experiences which emerge by virtue of a summation of previous stressful experiences with the current crisis. If this happens, be prepared to discuss whatever is bothering the child and don't dismiss anything with such comments as, "Why are you bringing that up now? That happened a long time ago." Try to be a healing presence for your kids; sometimes this has a recursive effect and turns into a form of self-healing as well.

CONCLUSIONS

Critical incident interventions and psychotherapy with law enforcement officers entail their share of frustrations as well as satisfactions. A certain flexibility is called for in adapting traditional psychotherapeutic models and techniques for use with this group, and clinical work frequently requires both firm professional grounding and seat-of-the-pants maneuverability. Incomplete closures and partial successes are to be expected, but in a few instances, the impact of successful intervention can have profound effects on morale and job effectiveness that may be felt department-wide. In the best cases, the psychologist working alongside the department administrator will have the satisfaction of knowing that they have helped restore the productive careers of one or more highly trained public servants.

Chapter 7

OFFICER-INVOLVED SHOOTING

Among all public safety and emergency service workers, the unique and ultimate symbol of the law enforcement officer is *the gun.* No other nonmilitary occupational group is mandated to carry a lethal firearm as part of their daily equipment, nor charged with the responsibility to use their own discretion and judgment to make split-second decisions as to whether to use deadly force and take a human life in the line of duty. Although watching any typical cop show on TV might convince the viewer that most officers blithely pop off rounds at perps without a second thought, in reality, the firing of one's weapon in the line of duty is a profound event that almost always leaves a psychological trace and, in some cases, may be traumatic enough to end a career in law enforcement.

COP AND GUNS: FACTS AND STATS

Statistics indicate that about six hundred criminals are killed each year by police officers in the United States. Some of these killings are in self-defense, some are accidental, and others are to prevent harm to others. By comparison, about 135 officers are killed in the line of duty each year (Chapter 8). In most cases, taking a life occurs in the context of trying to save a life. The sources of stress attached to an *officer-involved shooting* (OIS) are multiple, and include the officer's own psychological reaction to taking a life; the responses of law enforcement peers and the officer's family; rigorous examination by departmental investigators and administrators; possible criminal and civil court action; attention and sometimes harassment by the media and "crusading reporters"; and possible disciplinary action or change of assignment (Baruth, 1986; Russell & Beigel, 1990).

In most jurisdictions, the legal test for justification of legitimate use of lethal force by police officers requires that any reasonable person with the training and experience of the involved officer would have perceived a lethal threat in the actions taken by the suspect (Blum, 2000). Line-of-duty deadly force actions are most likely to occur in the following situations, in descending order of probability: (1) domestic or other disturbance calls; (2) robbery in progress; (3) burglary in progress; (4) traffic offense; (5) personal dispute and/or accident; and (5) stake-out and drug busts (Blau, 1994; Russell & Biegel, 1990).

Of American police officers who kill a suspect in the line of duty, 70 percent are out of law enforcement within five years (Horn, 1991). According to McMains (1986a; 1991), by the early 1980s, an estimated 95 percent of police officers involved in a line-of-duty shooting had left police work within five years. By the mid-1980s, large departments had cut that rate to 3 percent, while smaller departments were still losing about two-thirds of officers involved in a shooting. The important difference seems to be in the level of administrative and mental health support provided to officers by the larger departments (either because of broader philosophies or broader budgets), giving their officers the clear message that helping them resolve the trauma and maintain their mental health is a departmental priority.

OFFICER-INVOLVED SHOOTING: PERCEPTUAL, COGNITIVE, AND BEHAVIORAL DISTURBANCES

Most officers who have been involved in a deadly force shooting episode have described one or more alterations in perception, thinking, and behavior that occurred during the event (Artwohl, 2002; Honig & Roland, 1998; Honig & Sultan, 2004; Solomon & Horn, 1986; Wittrup, 1986). Most of these can be interpreted as natural adaptive defensive reactions of an organism under extreme emergency stress.

Most common are *distortions in time perception.* In the majority of these cases, officers recall the shooting event as occurring in slow motion, although a smaller percentage report experiencing the event as speeded up.

Sensory distortions are common and most commonly involve *tunnel vision,* in which the officer is sharply focused on one particular aspect of the visual field, typically, the suspect's gun or weapon, while blocking out everything in the periphery. Similarly, *"tunnel hearing"* may occur, in which the officer's auditory attention is focused exclusively on a particular set of sounds, most commonly the suspect's voice, while background sounds are excluded. Sounds may also seem muffled or, in a smaller number of cases, louder than normal. Officers have reported not hearing their own or other officers' gunshots. In a few cases, officers have reported hearing "the bad guy's blood drip" (James Sewell, personal communication). Overall perceptual clarity may increase or diminish.

Some form of *perceptual and/or behavioral dissociation* may occur during the emergency event. In extreme cases, officers may describe feeling as though they were standing outside or hovering above the scene, observing it "like it was happening to someone else." In milder cases, the officer may report that he or she "just went on automatic," performing whatever actions he or she took with a sense of robotic detachment. Some officers report intrusive distracting thoughts during the scene, often involving loved ones or other personal matters, but it is not known if these substantially affected the officers' actions during the event.

A *sense of helplessness* may occur during a shooting episode, but may be underreported due to the potential stigma attached (Honig & Sultan, 2004). A very small proportion of officers report that they "froze" at some point during the event: either this is an uncommon response or officers are understandably reluctant to report it. In a series of interviews, Artwohl (2002) found that most of these cases represented the normal *action-reaction gap* in which officers make the call to shoot only after the suspect has engaged in clearly threatening behavior. In most cases, this brief evaluation interval is a positive precaution, to prevent the premature shooting of a harmless citizen. But in cases where the prudent action led to an tragic outcome, this appropriate hesitation may well be viewed retrospectively as a fault: "If I hadn't waited to see him draw, maybe my partner would still be alive."

Disturbances in memory are commonly reported in shooting cases. About half of these involve impaired recall for at least some of the events during the shooting scene; the other half involve impaired recall for at least part of the officer's own actions—this may be associated with the "going-on-automatic" response. More rarely, some aspects of the scene may be recalled with unusually vivid crystal clarity—a *flashbulb memory.* Over a third of cases involve not so much a loss of recall as a distortion of memory, to the extent that the officer's account of what happened differs markedly from the report of other observers at the scene. For example, it is common for officers not to remember the number of rounds fired, especially from a semiauto handgun.

A few cases I've interviewed could be described as *tunnel memory,* where some part of the scene is recalled especially vividly, while others are fuzzy or distorted. As with research on eyewitness memory in general (Loftus et al., 1989), one's subjective vividness of recall is often uncorrelated with the accuracy of the material recalled. An administrative implication is that discrepant accounts among eyewitnesses to a shooting scene should not be automatically interpreted as one or more persons lying or consciously distorting his report (Artwohl, 2002), but may well represent honest differences of perception and recall.

A general neuropsychological explanation for these constrictions of sensation, perception, and memory is that the brain naturally tries to tone down the hyperarousal that occurs during a critical shooting incident, so that the individual can get through the experience intact using his or her "mental autopilot" responses. In a smaller number of cases, heightened perceptual awareness occurs to those features of the scene that are essential for the officer's survival. And the processing of accurate memories for later use seems to take a neuropsychological back seat to the mechanisms necessary for getting the officer through the situation alive, right here and now (Miller, 1990, 1998). The implication for training is that a greater depth, range, and flexibility of attention and arousal control will allow officers to use such automatic responding adaptively in a wider range of extreme situations, a topic covered in Chapter 5.

REACTIONS OF OFFICERS TO AN OFFICER-INVOLVED SHOOTING

The etiology of many postshooting reactions lies in the emotional disconnect between most officers' expectations about a heroic, armed confrontation and the actual reality of most shooting scenarios, which typically involve petty criminals, mentally disordered suspects, or accidents (Russell & Biegel, 1990).

Reaction Typologies

Although the reaction to an OIS will necessarily be influenced by the individual personality and experience of the officer, certain common factors seem to underlie a few types of reaction.

Several analyses (Anderson et al., 1995; Blau, 1994; Blum, 2000; Nielsen, 1986) have suggested three general typologies of postshooting reaction, which parallels the three types of reaction noted to occur in the wake of traumatically stressful events in general (Bowman, 1997). These, of course, should be thought of as a continuum, not discrete categories. In addition to individual officer characteristics, the severity of a postshooting reaction will be determined by a host of situational factors, such as the nature of the shooting itself; the postincident investigation; reactions of brass, peers, and family; and so on. Each of these reaction types also has its own therapeutic implications for helping officers in distress.

The first type of reaction involves a *transitory period of postincident psychological distress*, which the officer is able to resolve within a few weeks, largely by self-coping efforts, such as talking with colleagues and family, praying and reflecting, and reexamining and renewing life priorities and goals. The psychological distress does not appear to substantially affect the officer's daily functioning. Peer counseling, a CISD debriefing (Chapter 6), and perhaps one or two visits with a mental health professional or clergyperson are usually the extent of any intervention required.

The second type of reaction is somewhat more intense, with *posttraumatic symptoms persisting* for several weeks or months. The officer's daily functioning may be impaired, often with a "good days/bad days" pattern. In addition to peer support and group debriefings, short-term crisis counseling with a psychologist over several weeks may be indicated to help the officer work through the traumatic elements of the shooting, as well as to provide support through any contentious administrative proceedings that may follow the incident.

The third type of reaction is characterized by *severe psychological disability*, what officers often describe as a "mental breakdown." The shooting incident has so traumatized the officer that he is unable to function. In most cases, this kind of severe reaction occurs in the context of some degree of vulnerability in the premorbid personality of the officer, often exacerbated by a particularly adversarial investigation and perceived lack of support from colleagues, the department, family, and/or the community. In essence, this is similar to the so-called *Vietnam syndrome* that characterized many of the returning soldiers who had killed enemy combatants or ambiguously hostile civilians during that war. Treatment will necessarily involve more long-term psychotherapy, perhaps with medication. Although some of these officers will ultimately leave police work, many of these careers may be salvaged by timely and appropriate psychological intervention.

Reaction Phases

Some authorities (Nielsen, 1986; Williams, 1991) have divided the postshooting reaction into several basic phases or stages, starting with an *immediate reaction* or *impact phase*. For officers who have just shot a suspect during a dangerous confrontation, there may be an initial reaction of relief and even exhilaration at having survived the encounter.

Later, feelings of guilt or self-recrimination may surface, especially where the decision to shoot was less clear-cut or where the suspect's actions essentially forced the hand of the officer into using deadly force, such as in botched robberies, domestic disputes, or suicide-by-cop (Chapter 10). Or the officer may simply be faced with the fact that, however justified his response, he has nevertheless taken a human life. During this *recoil* or *remorse phase*, the officer may seem detached and preoccupied, spacily going through the motions of his job duties, and operating on autopilot. He may be sensitive and prickly to even well-meaning questions and attaboys by his peers ("Way to go, Bobby–you got the guy"), and especially to accusatory-like interrogation and second-guessing from official investigators or the press ("Officer Jackson, did you really fear for your life and believe you had no choice but to fire on the suspect?").

As the officer begins to come to terms with the shooting episode, a *resolution* or *acceptance phase* may be seen, wherein he or she comes to grips with the fact that his or her actions were necessary and justified in the battle for survival that often characterizes law enforcement deadly encounters. This process may be complicated by persisting departmental investigations or by impending or ongoing civil litigation. In addition, even under the best of circumstances, resolution may be partial rather than total, and psychological remnants of the experience may continue to haunt the officer periodically, especially during future times of crisis. But overall, he is eventually able to return to work with a reasonable sense of confidence.

In the worst case, sufficient resolution may never occur, and the officer enters into a prolonged *posttraumatic phase*, which may effectively end his or her law enforcement career. In less severe cases, a period of temporary stress disability allows the officer to seek treatment, eventually regain his or her emotional and professional bearings, and ultimately return to the job. Still other officers return to work right away, but continue to perform marginally until their actions are brought to the attention of superiors (Chapter 13).

In my experience, many officers who have been traumatized by their own deadly use of force can be effectively returned to work with the proper psychological intervention and departmental support. Indeed, this very support from above is typically what prompts the referral for mental health counseling in the first place.

Types of Postshooting Symptoms and Reactions

Again, the officer's individual personality and experience will influence the type of postshooting reaction he or she experiences, but certain commonalities of reactions emerge from various reports (Anderson et al., 1995; Blum, 2000; Cohen, 1980; Geller, 1982; Honig & Sultan, 2004; Russell & Beigel, 1990; Williams, 1991). Some of these will represent general posttraumatic reactions familiar from Chapter 6, while others will have a specific line-of-duty shooting focus.

Physical symptoms may include headaches, stomach upset, nausea, weakness and fatigue, muscle tension and twitches, and changes in appetite and sexual functioning. Sleep is typically impaired, with frequent awakenings and possibly nightmares. Typical *posttraumatic reactions* of intrusive imagery and flashbacks may occur, along with premonitions, distorted memories, and feelings of déjà vu. Some degree of anxiety and depression is common, sometimes accompanied by panic attacks. There may be unnatural and disorienting feelings of helplessness, fearfulness, and vulnerability, along with self second-guessing and guilt feelings. Substance abuse is always a risk.

There may be a pervasive irritability and low frustration tolerance, along with anger and resentment toward the suspect, the department, unsupportive peers and family, or civilians in general. Part of this may be a reaction to the conscious or unconscious sense of vulnerability that the officer experiences after a shooting incident. Sometimes, this is projected outward as a smoldering irritability that makes the officer's every interaction a grating source of stress and conflict. All this, combined with an increased hypervigilance and hypersensitivity to threats of all kinds, may result in overaggressive policing, leading to abuse-of-force complaints (Chapter 13).

Ultimately, this may spiral into a vicious cycle of angry and fearful isolation and withdrawal by the officer, spurring further alienation from potential sources of help and support. At the same time, some officers become overly protective of their families, generating an alternating *control-alienation syndrome*, (Sheehan, 1991) which is disturbing and disorienting to the family. All this, combined with cognitive symptoms of impaired concentration and memory, may lead the officer to fear that he or she is "going crazy."

Incident-Specific Factors Influencing the Postshooting Reaction

Apart from the universal reactions and individual personality and experience of the officer, certain factors inherent in the line-of-duty shooting incident itself can influence the severity, persistence, and effects of postshooting symptoms and reactions (Anderson et al., 1995; Blau, 1986).

One obvious factor is the *degree of threat to the officer's life*. This can operate in two ways. First, the officer who feels that he or she was literally about to die may be traumatized by the extreme fear involved, but may feel quite justified and relatively guilt-free in using deadly force on a clearly murderous suspect. But where the danger was more equivocal, there will be less of the fear factor and more second-guessing about what degree of force was actually necessary. Police officers pride themselves in their ability to manage a tense situation and may thus feel overwhelmed by doubt and self-recrimination where the situation abruptly got out of control and turned deadly.

Related factors include the *amount of preparation and warning* prior to the shooting and the *length of time the dangerous incident persisted*, which also may have varying effects. On the one hand, officers caught off guard are unlikely to have even a brief interval to think through their decision to shoot and may later perceive themselves, or be perceived by others, as having reacted out of fear, no matter how justified the shooting is later judged to be. On the other hand, where the shooting follows a prolonged stand-off, with a lot of back-and-forth negotiating and maneuvering, the extended period of time the officer has spent agonizing over the decision to use deadly force may later take a negative psychological toll.

All of the above factors relate to the *amount of control* the officer feels he or she had over the situation and degree of conflict that exists over the necessity to take a human life. Generally, the less control and the more conflict the officer has experienced during the event, the more severe will be the psychological distress.

The officer's reaction to the shooting may also be related to the *characteristics of the suspect*. At one extreme is the armed bank robber who, having been duly warned and ordered to surrender, brazenly draws down on the officer or puts a gun to a hostage. In such a case, there is likely to be universal agreement that the officer had no choice–indeed, was duty-bound–to fire on the perp in order to save innocent lives. At the other extreme is the obnoxiously inebriated, but otherwise harmless, high school punk who is pulled over for a traffic violation, exchanges a few sharp words with the officer, and is shot for refusing to drop an object in his hand that turns out to be a cell phone. A similar example is the schizophrenic homeless person who has heretofore been known only as a noisy neighborhood pest, but now, in the throes of a paranoid psychotic episode, is waving a brick or a kitchen knife, and is shot while lunging at the officer.

A common reaction is *anger at the suspect* himself for forcing the officer to take a life, even the suspects own life. Understanding that anger and guilt are often intertwined, it is not so difficult to see that this anger may actually be greater at a relatively more "innocent" suspect who's stupid behavior resulted in a totally unnecessary shooting–e.g., the psychotic street person or the kid with the big mouth–than at a suspect who more clearly "deserves" to get shot, e.g., the armed robber fleeing a bank who fires at the officer first. Much of this anger may smolder below the surface and emerge as general irritability, problems with authority, and family conflicts (Chapters 13 and 15).

Degree of control and conflict extend into the postshooting phase. The *amount and kind of attention* the officer receives from his administration, peers, the community, and the media will influence his own reaction to the event (Blau, 1994; Henry, 2004; Klein, 1991; Russell & Biegel, 1990; Rynearson, 1988; Rynearson & McCreery, 1993; Sprang & McNeil, 1995). Supervisors are typically concerned about the public relations aspect of a shooting, and although most are generally supportive of their personnel, their effort to appear objective and unbiased may make it seem at times as if they're coming down too hard on the officer.

The *reactions of the officer's peers* may help or harm his attempts to cope with the situation. As noted above, at first he may receive accolades from his fellow officers for "getting the job done." Because of the powerful identification factor, peers may want to hear all about the event because, someday, they may be there too and they want to believe that, in the breach, they will do the right thing. Many of these peers also hope that the officer's guts to pull the trigger will "rub off" on them should they encounter a similar situation. However, if the officer fails to regale them with an uplifting narrative of struggle and triumph, and instead reveals the conflict, doubt, and pain he is going through, the contagion effect may cause his fellow officers to shy away and avoid him.

The implied psychological contract of such postcrisis mutual congratulatory rituals seems to involve a kind of blanket immunity against what Solomon and Horn (1986) call the *mark of Cain* and Henry (2004) describes as the *death taint:* "You have made real for us the life-and-death situation we all fear. You'd better show us how nobly and heroically you're dealing with this, throw us a positive spin, or all you've done is shove our mortality up in our faces, which freaks us out, and then to protect ourselves, we will shun you or degrade you." This probably accounts for the creepily uncomfortable backslapping attaboys that are so commonly inflicted on the officer by his colleagues after a shooting. Unfortunately, these reactions may only serve to heighten the officer's anxiety about what he would really do "next time."

Even if they won't admit it to their departmental brethren, many officers feel genuinely sad at having to take a human life, even if they objectively recognize that they had no choice in the situation and that the perp clearly asked for it. Human nature being what it is, police officers and soldiers, who are trained to kill when necessary, cannot just shed their familial, religious, and cultural upbringing when they don the uniform. An officer may thus become irritated at his colleagues who want him to play the happy warrior, while they have no clue as to the turmoil the officer is going through. But he still needs all the support he can get and, fearing rejection, he may not want to burst his colleagues' bubble. He thus feels compelled to put up a brave front so as not to alienate this well-meaning, if lunkheaded, source of support from his peers. Painful as putting up a false front may be, it's still better than total isolation.

OFFICER-INVOLVED SHOOTING: ON-SCENE RESPONSE

All of the factors noted above have profound implications for productive departmental management and helpful clinical intervention of OISs at every stage of the event. By far, the most common complaint voiced by these officers concerns their treatment by their own departments, from the first postincident moments onward. Even in uncontestedly "righteous" shootings, officers often feel demeaned and treated like guilty suspects, setting up a vicious cycle of recrimination from the get-go.

The prescriptive corollary is that every officer who has risked his life should be treated with respect. Even if there is a suspicion of misconduct, there is nothing to be gained from an adversarial attitude—indeed, an officer who is treated decently will be more inclined to cooperate with investigators. Thus, the proper handling of involved officers begins at the shooting scene itself.

On-Scene Law Enforcement Response

In many departments, an OIS results in the callout of many departmental personnel, including other officers, the involved officer's supervisors, the chief of police in some smaller jurisdictions, paramedics, and typically the department psychologist, if there is one. One composite model protocol for on-scene response to officer-involved shootings (Baruth, 1986; Blau, 1994; IACP, 2004; McMains, 1986a, 1986b, 1991; Williams, 1991) is presented that can be adapted and modified to the needs of the individual police agency. How this protocol is carried out in practice can make a tremendous difference in the later psychological adjustment of the involved officers and the department.

In the policy-and-procedure planning stages, it should have previously been decided which personnel respond to what types of critical incidents, including shootings. Responders may include back-up officers, administrative officials, departmental investigators, peer support staff, mental health professionals, departmental attorney, media spokesperson, and others. At the time of the shooting, all relevant personnel should respond to the scene.

Reassurance to the involved officer should be provided by departmental authorities. "Reassurance" doesn't have to (and at this early stage, probably shouldn't) entail any positive or negative judgment about the officer's actions, but should simply communicate an understanding and appreciation of what the officer has just experienced, and the assurance that the department will support him or her as much as possible throughout the process. As noted above, one of the biggest complaints officers have about the postshooting departmental response is the feeling that they are "treated like a criminal by my own people." Especially at this psychologically sensitive stage, the officer should be given the benefit of the doubt and treated with respect by departmental authorities.

The officer should be provided *on-scene access to legal counsel and a mental health professional.* In many jurisdictions, officers may refrain from making any statements to authorities at the scene until an attorney is present and/or until they have been assessed as mentally fit to make a statement by a qualified mental health professional. On the one hand, this protects the officer's rights and at the same time, assures that any statements made cannot later easily be challenged as having been made under duress.

The *officer's weapon* will almost always be *impounded.* This is a fairly standard on-scene policy, but the way it is carried out will make a big difference in how the officer adjusts to the postshooting aftermath. In the worst case, the officer is unceremoniously stripped of his sidearm in full view of his colleagues, and in some cases even in front of jeering bystanders, and forced to parade around with an empty holster–the epitome of emasculatory humiliation (Ayoob, 1981, 1984). In the best case, the weapon is turned over in private, with an attitude of respect, and in many cases, a *replacement weapon*

is provided or the empty holster removed while the on-scene investigation proceeds.

At some shooting scenes, personnel remain at the site for hours. This may be necessary for purposes of the investigation and to deal with community members and the media, but no one should hang around the scene longer than necessary and everything possible should be done to discourage a carnival atmosphere. In particular, it is recommended that the *officer be removed from the scene as quickly as possible.* Again, this should be done in a private and respectful way, perhaps the officer being driven home or back to the station by two colleagues, to await further action. They should accompany him to his door and leave only when he has assured them he is okay. Of course, the officer should be provided with any necessary *medical care,* either at the scene or at a local hospital. The *officer's family should be notified* of the shooting in person as soon as possible, even if everybody is still on-scene: the last thing you want is for the family to hear of the shooting on the radio or TV, or get a call from neighbor who's seen or heard the story. If the family is out of town, every effort should be made to contact them, preferably through direct contact by another law enforcement agency.

If media arrive at the scene, the officer should be shielded from them and any statements should be made through a departmental spokesperson. Most medium-to-large size departments have a *Public Information Officer* who is part of the critical response team. In general, any statement that could affect the internal investigation or other legal action should be avoided. Agencies should consult with their attorneys about local and state regulations in these areas as part of the process of developing their own policies for OISs.

On-Scene Psychological Intervention

Encouragingly, at least one study has found that 100 percent of large departments and 69 percent of small departments provide professional support for traumatized officers (McMains, 1986a; 1986b). As part of the on-scene response team, the departmental psychologist has a specific but important role to play (McMains, 1991).

First, *determine the nature of the incident.* When you get the call, try to find out as much about the incident and the current scene as possible. This may vary, depending on the timing of the call. Sometimes, you may get called within minutes of the shooting incident, in which case there is not much info to be had, other than the location of the scene. Other times, you may be called almost as an afterthought, hours after the rest of the responders have arrived, only because someone has suggested that the psychologist be called due to unforeseen complications at the scene. This usually represents a problem with the call-out policy at the planning stages or it may occur in a very dangerous or complex scene where other services, such as medical, may take precedence. As a rule, if there is a call-out psychologist, he or she should be summoned to the scene as early as possible.

When you arrive at the scene, *identify the involved officer(s)* and *determine their psychological status.* This may range from the extremes of panic, confusion, and disorientation–rare, in my experience–to unnatural calmness and stoic denial ("I'm okay; no problem")–a far more common response. Frequently, emotions will swing at the scene, the officer blank and icy one moment, then nervous and shaky the next. As discussed below, validating these reactions as normal stress responses is an important part of on-scene intervention.

Try to find a *comfortable place* to conduct your interview with the officer. "On-scene" doesn't necessarily mean standing over the body or pacing back and forth in front of the news cameras. I've conducted on-scene interviews behind bushes, under trees, behind a throng of officers or a row of vehicles, in the back seat of patrol cars, and in a SWAT wagon. As long as the officer stays inside the established perimeter and can be found by authorities when needed, he or she is still technically on-scene.

For the visibly upset officer, you may have to use *calming and distraction techniques* to bring his mental state into a more rational and receptive mode. For the defensive, sealed-over officer, what I often find helpful is a version of the CISD procedure (Chapter 6), condensed into a tripartite, one-on-one model, called a *defusing.*

First, ask the officer to tell you what happened. This will typically elicit a stiff, dry, detail-laden rendition of events, as if the officer were testifying before a review board or in court:

Officer: I saw the guy coming out the dark breezeway, carrying a box or something bulky like that, hugging the wall like he was trying to hide. I identified myself as a police officer and told him to stop, put the box down slowly, and face the wall. He dropped the box and put his hand in his pocket. I drew my weapon and ordered him to freeze. He pulled out something metal, which I took to be a blade or a firearm. I drew down on him in a Weaver stance and ordered him to drop the object. He raised it higher and started coming towards me. In fear for my life, I fired, I think, three or four times. He fell and was quiet, and the object skidded several feet away into the grass. I radioed for backup and attempted to administer aid, but I think he was already dead. I located the object and found that it was a butterfly knife with the blade out.

Listen to the story until you have a good sense of the sequence of events. Next, ask the officer to describe "what was going on in your mind while it was happening." This often elicits clues to the officer's cognitive and emotional state:

Officer: The guy and me kind of surprised each other. I guess neither of us expected the other one to be on the campus that time of night, so we both sort of jumped when we saw each other. I could feel the adrenalin jack up my body. I don't think I really had time to be nervous, I just kind of went on automatic and the whole thing had a kind of unreal aspect to it, you know what I mean?–like it was me doing it, but it wasn't me. After I found the knife and called on the radio, that's when it hit me I could've been killed if I waited a second longer to fire. Then, shit, suddenly I'm shaking like a little girl; it was embarrassing. But I pulled it together before the other guys got there.

Finally, *provide information and support* regarding any disturbing reactions the officer may be having at the scene. Remember that the goal of on-scene psychological intervention is not to perform in-depth psychotherapy–that may or may not come later. Rather, you want to allow the officer to loosen up just enough for you to be able to assess his mental status but be able to use mental strengthening techniques (Chapter 5) to help him "keep it together" until the immediate crisis is resolved:

Psychologist: Hey, man, you're just following the textbook. Any time somebody's in an emergency or crisis mode, human nature puts us on autopilot so we know just enough of what to do so we can live through the experience. It's like the adrenalin acts like mental Novocain to numb you out just enough to survive and let your survival instinct and training kick in. Then, after this "Novocain" wears off, you feel all the emotions as a delayed reaction. So, from what you're telling me, there's nothing unusual about your response. It's not my ultimate judgment call, but from how you described it, it sounds like you did what you had to do.

One reason for an accurate assessment of the officer's mental status at the scene is the determination of *mental fitness to make a statement to authorities,* which may be very important for subsequent legal aspects of the case. Although in my experience this is rare, some officers may be sufficiently confused, disoriented, emotionally vulnerable, and cognitively suggestible to be legally incompetent to understand their legal rights and/or to make a statement to authorities at the scene–a kind of "temporary insanity" caused by extreme traumatic stress. In such cases, the psychologist may recommend that investigators wait until the officer has had a chance to recover some measure of psychological equilibrium, which may require only a few minutes to calm down or some basic reassuring intervention at the scene, or, in the extreme case, may necessitate removal to a safe facility for further evaluation and treatment.

Psychologists who make the recommendation to wait can expect flak from investigators who want to get on with the process, and sometimes from the on-scene departmental attorney, although the latter will typically support any recommendation that will prevent unnecessary self-incrimination of the officer. A related issue is *confidentiality.* Technically, anything said in confidence to a licensed mental health clinician is protected by doctor-patient confidentiality. But, as mentioned in Chapter 6, this is not as strong as attorney-client privilege, and in extremely politically sensitive cases, psychologists' records and/or testimony may be subpoenaed if one side or the other is being particularly aggressive in pressing their case. In such circumstances, it is important to remember that, from a psychological point of view, the exact details of what happened in the incident are less important than the officer's psychological reaction, and that your job as an on-scene mental health professional is not to record all the details of the officer's recollection or judge the merits of his actions, but to determine how the incident is affecting him at the scene.

Following my on-scene evaluation and while still at the site, I usually make a recommendation for at least one follow-up evaluation at my office, scheduled several days postincident. This gives the officer a few days to calm down and loosen up, and allows me to get a better perspective on how he or she is coping psychologically after the initial shock of the incident has worn off. This also serves as an informal *fitness-for-duty evaluation* in a nonconfrontational setting; additionally, such an FFD evaluation may be formally mandated by some departments as a precondition of the officer returning to work (Rostow & Davis, 2004). If I assess the officer to be experiencing no unusual signs or symptoms (some degree of residual distress is normal for a few days or weeks), I will recommend release to full duty. Otherwise, I may make a range of recommendations, such as more time off with subsequent follow-up or continued psychotherapy. Again, police psychologists should always consult with their departments regarding protocols for such incidents–ideally, they should be involved in developing those protocols.

PSYCHOLOGICAL INTERVENTION FOR OFFICER-INVOLVED SHOOTINGS

Principles and Guidelines of Postshooting Intervention

Following the original shooting incident and the follow-up session, some officers may require or request additional sessions with the psychologist "to get my head straight about this." In other cases, there may not have been any on-scene intervention at all, and the follow-up consultation is the first contact between the officer and the psychologist. As with any critical incident, it is important that each department have in place a system for smooth and nonstigmatized referral of officers for mental health counseling when they need it.

McMains (1986a, 1991) and Wittrup (1986) have developed a set of recommendations for implementing psychological services following a shooting, which have been adapted here. The reader will note that most of these are in fact specialized applications of the general principles of law enforcement critical incident intervention discussed in Chapter 6.

The *intervention should begin as soon after the shooting incident as possible*, even, as noted above, on-scene. In some cases, an officer's obvious distress at the scene or shortly thereafter creates the need for an immediate intervention. In other cases, distress may be suppressed or concealed for hours, days, or weeks, so intervention must await the time that the problems in coping become apparent. In such cases, intervention should not be rushed, but should be started as quickly as possible when the need surfaces. In any event, a departmental policy should be developed that gives priority to these referrals, so that at a minimum, an officer can be seen within 24 hours of a request.

McMains (1986a, 1991) believes that the intervention should occur as close to the time of the shooting as possible in order to minimize the sensitization to any possible trauma. This, of course, is the essence of on-scene intervention. However, I believe that clinical judgment should prevail on a case-by-case basis, and that in some cases, as just noted above, the best thing that can be done is to remove the officer from the scene to prevent heightened sensitization and continual retraumatization. This is especially the case where it is apparent that the officer's on-scene distress continues to grow with each passing minute spent at the site.

Nevertheless, to provide for the most efficient and effective use of time and resources, *subsequent intervention* should be undertaken at a location that *the officer finds safe and nonthreatening*, usually an office away from the department. Depending on the officer's shift schedule, a regular time should be established for the sessions.

Intervention should be short-term and focused on supporting officers through the crisis, as well as returning them to active duty as soon as possible. How narrow or broad the range issues to be covered will be determined on a case-by-case basis, depending on how the incident has affected the officer, his family, his colleagues, and others. But the general guideline is that postshooting psychological intervention should be focused on resolving the critical incident in question.

Clinically, the psychologist should remember that his or her role in these treatment settings is as therapist and supportive advocate, not investigator or judge. What the psychologist is advocating for is the officer's mental health and stability, not any particular side of the case. Accordingly, a *realistically positive atmosphere* should prevail during the course of the intervention. Absent clear evidence to the contrary, the assumption should be that the officer acted properly, can successfully manage the current crisis, and will soon return to active status. Indeed, during particularly contentious investigations, the psychologist's office may be the only place the officer does not feel like a suspect.

Administratively, *confidentiality* should be respected and protected by the department, and the only information from psychological counseling available to outside authorities should be the psychologist's written summaries of case status, fitness-for-duty, and other administratively-relevant data. As noted many times throughout this book, to have any credible program of psychological services, officers must feel secure that, except insofar as they relate to a specific departmental referral question, personally sensitive information, thoughts, and feelings, do not leave the psychologist's office.

Even if the department goes the extra mile to respect doctor-patient confidentiality, other individuals or entities may not be so accommodating. For example, relatives of shooting victims who bring civil rights violation charges against the officer or file lawsuits against the department or municipality may try to subpoena psychological records or testimony to pursue their case. Accordingly, Wittrup (1986) recommends that police psychologists receive from the city a formal, written "*statement of referral*," along with a "*save from prosecution and/or civil litigation*" document, so that they are relatively insulated from such assaults on confidentiality. Again, psychologists should be aware of the laws, rules, and regulations of their respective jurisdictions.

Postshooting Psychotherapeutic Strategies

On initial contact with the officer, the psychologist's role may incorporate the basic intervention stages of the CISD model (Chapter 6).

First, *review the facts of the case* with the officer. Similar to the fact phase of a CISD, this allows for a relatively nonemotional narrative of the traumatic event. But in the case of an OIS, it serves a further function. Precisely because of the cognitive and perceptual distortions that commonly occur in these kinds of incidents, what may be particularly disturbing to the officer is the lack of clarity in his own mind as to the actual nature and sequence of events. Just being able to review what is known about the facts of the case in a relatively safe and nonadversarial environment may provide a needed dose of mental clarity and sanity to the situation. If the narrative seems "stuck," employ the frame-by-frame technique, discussed in Chapter 6.

Next, *review the officer's thoughts and feelings* about the shooting incident. This resembles the thought and reaction phases of a CISD but may not be as cut-and-dried as with a typical group debriefing. Remember, an OIS represents a special kind of critical incident and it make take more than one go-round for the officer to productively untangle and reveal what's going on in his mind. Give him extra time or extra sessions to express his thoughts and feelings, and be sure to monitor the reaction so as not to encourage unproductive spewing or loss of control. One of the most important things the

psychologist can do at this stage is to help modulate emotional expression so that it comes as a relief, not as an added burden.

Provide authoritative and factual information about psychological reactions to a shooting incident. The kinds of cognitive and perceptual distortions that take place during an OIS, the posttraumatic symptoms and disturbances, and the sometimes off-putting and distressing reactions of colleagues and family members are likely to be quite alien to the officer's ordinary experience, and might be interpreted by him or her as signs of going soft or crazy. Normalize these responses for the officer, taking a somewhat more personal and individualistic approach than might be found in the typical CISD information/education phase. Often, just this kind of authoritative reassurance from a credible mental health professional can cut an officer's anxiety considerably.

Finally, *provide for follow-up services* which may include additional individual sessions, family therapy, referral to support services, possible medication referral, and so on. As with most cases of critical incident psychological intervention, follow-up psychotherapy for OISs tends to be short-term, although additional services may be sought later for other problems partially related or unrelated to the incident (Chapter 6). Indeed, any kind critical incident may often be the stimulus to explore other troublesome aspects of an officer's life, and the success in resolving the incident with the psychologist may give the officer confidence to pursue these other issues in an atmosphere of trust.

PEER SUPPORT PROGRAMS

As discussed in Chapter 6, to augment or supplement professional mental health services, an increasing number of police departments have instituted *peer support programs* for the psychological aftermath of OISs and other critical incidents. Some general assumptions underlie the use of peers as counselors (McMains, 1991). First, it is assumed that fellow police officers will have more credibility than mental health professionals because the former have "been there" and "know the job." However, while basic familiarity with police work is an obvious prerequisite to being a police psychologist, the argument that one has to live through

a particular experience in order to help someone else through it is belied by the ridiculousness of its logical extension. Can traumatized people be helped only by other traumatized people? Can schizophrenic patients only be treated by schizophrenic psychologists? Can depressed, suicidal hostage takers be talked down only by depressed, suicidal negotiators?

Okay, maybe that's a bit of an exaggeration, and there may well be legitimate situations where an officer may feel more comfortable with a fellow officer. In my experience, this has not been an issue, and I have never had an officer refuse to see me (that I know of), or hold back on self-disclosure, because I'm not a sworn officer. In fact, the opposite seems to be true. Many officers have commented that they are relieved to talk to someone outside the departmental fishbowl and outside of law enforcement generally. They already know, or think they know, the predictable response they're going to get from their brass and colleagues, and they're looking for a fresh perspective. Additionally, talking to a nonofficer removes the "competition factor"–that is, no matter how sympathetic a fellow officer may be, the officer in crisis may still fear appearing weak or ineffectual before one of his own if he reveals too much about his reactions to the critical incident.

I've gotten some feedback from colleagues who are both licensed mental health professionals and sworn active or retired officers, and even they have experienced a reluctance of officers to open up because the officer-therapist "is still a cop at heart." Other officers have commented that officer-therapists sometimes take a presumptive attitude that "because I am/was an officer, I know what you're going through," even before letting the officer in crisis fully express himself. Remember, an officer in crisis after an OIS is often in a prickly hypersensitive state of "no-you-*don't*-friggin-know-what-I'm going-through," and may resent even well-meaning expressions of commiseration by peers. In such cases, a civilian psychologist may actually be a more sympathetic and receptive audience because he or she humbly understands that there is something to learn from the officer's experience.

On the other hand, some officers may simply be too creeped-out by the thought of seeing a "real shrink" to avail themselves of formal psychological services. Or they may have had bad experiences with mental health professionals in the past, either within or outside the context of their law enforcement careers. Many officers just feel more comfortable talking with fellow cops. Some of the old-timers, who began their careers before the modern therapy-culture era, may be more used to the command structure model of discussing problems with their senior officer. And, just because I personally have experienced little difficulty with officers' willingness to see me, I'll never know how many officers silently declined to make the call because they felt that I just wouldn't understand where they're coming from, or were just too put off

by the prospect of seeing a mental health practitioner. Still another consideration concerns the demographics of the law enforcement community I serve, which may be somewhat more receptive to mental health services than police departments in other parts of the country.

For these reasons, I do encourage the development of law enforcement peer support programs, not because professional psychologists are necessarily less effective at helping cops, but because there will be times when another cop is the best resource, or at least the best first point of contact, for an officer in distress. In fact, a fair number of referrals to my office have come from officers who know me and have encouraged other, more skittish, cops to "at least give the guy a shot." One further advantage of using officer peers as counselors relates to basic bullshit-detection. In a few cases, some officers, especially if they are under investigation for a suspicious shooting, may actually prefer talking to a civilian psychologist precisely because they feel they can do a snow job on the unsuspecting clinician. This may be less successful with a peer-counselor who knows the ropes.

Another assumption of peer counseling is that police officers don't usually require extensive mental health services because they are a select sample of professionals, at least somewhat more mentally stable than the general population by virtue of their initial screening and training (McMains, 1991). Critical incident stress responses, including officer-involved shootings, are seen as normal reactions to an abnormal situation by relatively normal people, and the goal of peer counseling is to restore officers' original psychological equilibrium, not make fundamental changes in their personalities. This, of course, is consistent with the whole philosophy of critical incident intervention (Chapter 6).

Peer counseling teams almost always consist of volunteers who have a good performance history with the department, and who have gone through some form of formal training and certification program, which includes a basic understanding of psychological stress syndromes; basic crisis intervention and counseling skills; understanding special problems encountered with officer-involved shootings and other critical incidents; and knowing when and how to refer for professional mental health services when necessary. In this regard, departments that institute peer counseling programs should be sure to make professional psychological backup help available if further treatment is indicated.

Always important is the issue of confidentiality Chapter 6). Especially with counselors who are peers and not licensed professionals, officers may fear unwarranted disclosure. This issue cannot be overemphasized. The success of a peer support programs will stand or fall based on the confidence officers have in the peer counselors' discretion and competence. Again, this fear of the fishbowl and rumor mill is one of the reasons officers may actually prefer to talk to an outside clinician. More practically, what happens if the peer-counseled officer admits that he was intoxicated during the shooting or expresses a clear racist bias that may have contributed to his decision to use deadly force? What does the peer counselor do then? These issues must be carefully worked out in advance for a peer counselor system to work.

The basic elements of peer counseling are not that different from professional intervention in noncomplex cases, and include active listening skills; allowing the officer to ventilate and tell his story in a supportive, nonjudgmental atmosphere; provision of reassurance and accurate information about stress syndromes; recommendation of strategies for handling symptoms and dealing with other people during the recovery process; and referral for professional mental health services, if necessary (Klein, 1991).

MODEL POSTSHOOTING INTERVENTION PROGRAMS

In reviewing several postshooting intervention programs from around the country, I have picked two to describe here because they illustrate and exemplify the main points discussed in this chapter. Please note the points of commonality between the two programs, many of which are already standard procedures in postshooting protocols of many departments. For agencies seeking to develop or modify programs of their own, these two can serve as useful templates on which to adapt the specifics of your own program to the needs of your department.

Dallas Police Department Postshooting Program

Somodevilla (1986) has described a postshooting intervention program at the Dallas Police Department that was empirically designed around the expressed needs of officers, as gleaned from a survey of those officers as to what they felt they needed following an OIS. This information was then developed into a set of formal policies and procedures for the program. The program contains a number of elements, which I have here divided into two categories: general support and practical support.

General support involves attitude, departmental philosophy, and ways of dealing with the officer during and following the critical incident, and includes the following elements:

Compassion. Officers unanimously agreed that, in the swirl of postshooting investigations and inquiries, they would have liked to have one person who would serve as an advocate, support person, and companion, someone with no ax to grind and no motivation other than to provide emotional backup and support for the officer: "someone who just cares about me." This could be a supervisor, colleague, or just a friend who could serve as a nonjudgmental sounding board for the officer and who had the officer's best interests at heart.

Departmental reassurance and validation. "You did the right thing; we're behind you," is the basic message that officers want to hear following a shooting. Not that they expect the department to automatically take the officer's side in every detail, but they want to feel that, until proven otherwise, the officer is given the respectful benefit of the doubt that he or she acted appropriately in the face of danger, and used deadly force only to protect his life or the lives of others. The crucial elements here are timeliness and truthfulness. That is, the supportive message is given as soon as possible, and it is based on a credible analysis of the facts by someone in a position of authority in the department, e.g., "Officer

Sanchez, we still don't have all the facts about this shooting and some of the witnesses' reports are contradictory. And you know we have to follow our procedures for a rigorous investigation. But until we know different, as long as you give us your cooperation, we're going to back you up and not let you be treated unfairly, to the best of our ability."

Information flow. Paradoxically, during a post-shooting investigation, the involved officer is often the "last to know" about proceedings in his case. This is especially likely if he is temporarily off-duty and staying away from the department. In extreme cases, officers may discover information about their own cases, such as the death of the suspect or the filing of a legal charge, by watching the evening news, reading a newspaper article, or getting a call from a reporter—all of which contribute to feelings of disrespect and neglect. All officers in the survey felt the need for a systematic and orderly mechanism of keeping them informed about facts of their case in a timely manner.

Practical support involves putting these attitudes into action through specific steps the department can take, at the shooting scene or later, to assure that the officer and his or her family are supported throughout the process. The elements of this practical support echo some of the recommendations for on-scene response noted earlier and include the following:

Removal from the scene. As discussed earlier, following an OIS, it can often be many hours before all relevant personnel arrive at the scene, do their work, and finally depart. The officers surveyed felt that they would have liked the opportunity to be away from the sights and sounds of the scene, at least for a short period of time. Some departments do set up a kind of mini-command post a block or so away from the scene, so that officers can be interviewed by investigators and by the on-scene psychologist and attorney, in relative privacy. Down here, in the hot, muggy South Florida climate, an air-conditioned room or vehicle is an essential piece of on-scene apparatus; I conducted one such interview in July the back of a mercifully frigid SWAT van.

Replacement firearm. Not surprisingly, officers felt awkward, embarrassed, emasculated, and like they were "being treated like a criminal" when their weapon was impounded at the scene. The officers surveyed would have liked to be able to keep their weapons holstered until they were taken back to the department. At the very least, they would like to be issued a replacement weapon at the scene, so as not to be seen walking around with an empty holster.

Access to an attorney. The officers felt strongly that they should have an attorney present from the very beginning of the postshooting process, including at the scene. Officers were concerned about making statements that could come back to haunt them, and the presence of an attorney was felt to be a re-assuring factor.

Family welfare. "I need to let my family know I'm all right," seems to be a universal concern of surveyed officers. Preferably, they would like to be the ones to make the call, just to reach out and make that personal family contact, but if this is not possible, they would at least like someone from the department to let their families know they're okay. Knowing that one's family is not suffering unnecessarily seems itself to be a tremendous stress-reducer for many officers immediately following a critical incident.

Shooting folder. This is a special file devoted to the shooting incident and subsequent events, kept by a high-ranking official in the officer's department or division. The purpose of this file is to provide an orderly and systematic collation and dissemination of factual information that can minimize rumors and misinformation by providing members of the department with relevant facts, always respecting the twin concerns of officer privacy and departmental confidentiality. By the time the officer returns to duty, most of the major issues that are appropriate for general dissemination will be common knowledge, thus sparing the officer from a barrage of questions by colleagues or others that might re-evoke the traumatic feelings: "Just tell them what they need to know, and leave me out of it."

Handling media. Although it may seem obvious, the officer needs to hear from someone in authority that there is no obligation to respond to the news media, and that indeed, he or she may be prohibited from making any response while the investigation is proceeding. Most departments have a media spokesperson or public information officer to handle such matters, or statements may come from the upper brass, but most officers would appreciate the structure of clear guidelines as to what they can and cannot say while their cases are in flux.

Administrative leave. All officers felt that some time off following a shooting is imperative, and that this should be mandated by the department. The length of time cited varied, but included at least a day off. More time could be taken per the officer's request or per the recommendation of the department psychologist. It is critical that everyone understand that this is an administrative leave, not a suspension or disciplinary action.

Psychological intervention. Most officers felt that consultation with a psychologist should be available, but should not be mandatory, as that would add pressure to an already stressful situation. This group of officers made the somewhat unusual suggestion that it be the psychologist who contacts the officers, perhaps to provide access to this kind of help without the stigma of actively seeking help: "Oh well, the psych called me, so I guess I gotta go." The further common-sense recommendation was made that all information about the psychology sessions be kept confidential, except when there were extreme issues of safety or fitness for duty. Even then, only as much information as is necessary to address the narrow practical issue should be provided.

Somodevilla (1986) reports that since the adoption of these recommendations by the Dallas Police Department, there have been, up to the time of that publication, 81 shootings, following which none of the involved officers had resigned, and only a few officers had requested more than the mandatory one day off. It is possible that part of this very positive effect is related to the feeling by the officers that their department is truly concerned about them, a kind of "psychological placebo effect" (organizational psychologists will recognize this as the famous *Hawthorne effect*). But this certainly can't be all of it. As noted above, many of this program's

policies and procedures are consistent with the general principles of post-OIS intervention described in this chapter, so there appears to be a certain validity of the principles of good postcritical incident intervention in general.

Bureau of Alcohol, Tobacco and Firearms Peer Support Program

In 1988, the Bureau of Alcohol, Tobacco and Firearms (BATF) implemented a critical incident program involving a peer support team, composed of BATF agents who themselves had previously been involved in critical incidents and who had received a three-day course of training (Solomon & Mastin, 1999). As with most peer support teams, there was a back-up psychologist available as well. Nowhere did the effectiveness of this team face a greater challenge than during and following the BATF raid on the Branch Davidian compound in Waco, Texas, in which several agents were killed or injured, and which resulted in the fiery deaths of many compound residents. The support team was deployed immediately following the incident, and the program included a number of components. Again, I have divided these components into two categories: program content and program implementation.

Program content includes the actions and interventions of the peer support team, as well as the supportive attitudes and behaviors of the sponsoring agency, as follows:

Concerned leadership. Support from the top was a critical element in the initial reaction and subsequent recovery of the BATF agents. This reinforces the generally recognized role of concerned, supportive leadership for officers involved in deadly force incidents (Horn, 1991; McMains, 1991; Zeling, 1986). This is especially helpful if the leadership is seen as taking the initiative in arranging services for affected agents and officers. Indeed, there appeared to be a direct relationship between level of perceived support and recovery, with teams reporting the highest level of support showing the lowest level of psychological trauma casualties.

Peer support. In this case, peer support took on two separate meanings. The whole rationale for any peer support program is to provide affected officers with counselors who have "been there," who have experienced similar, though not necessarily identical, law enforcement-related critical incidents. However, although agents reported the formal peer support team to be helpful, what they found even more beneficial was to talk with other BATF agents who were actually at Waco. Probably, participants in this unique kind of critical incident felt themselves to members of a very special "club," and therefore found particular comfort in forming their own special informal support group with their true peers.

Support from the wider law enforcement community and concerned citizens. Adding yet a broader dimension to peer support, fellow law enforcement officers from all over the country, and from all types of agencies, expressed concern and support to the BATF agents, which the latter found extremely helpful, often taking great comfort in speaking to officers whom they had never met, but who had called in from near and far just to offer moral support. More surprising, and particularly heartening, was the deep level of support and appreciation shown by the ordinary citizens of Waco, which was immensely helpful in assuaging some of the bad press that emerged following the raid.

Reinforcement of group cohesion and support. Building on the findings from military psychology and general social psychology (Antonovsky & Bernstein, 1986; Milgram & Hobfoll, 1986) on the importance of unit cohesiveness and morale, a main focus of the BATF support team's efforts was to reinforce group cohesion and support, as well as a sense of personal efficacy among the agents. Accordingly, following their involvement in the critical incident, they were not simply yanked from service and benched, but were given meaningful assignments that reinforced their law enforcement identity, typically remaining on duty until they went home to attend funerals.

Opportunity to mourn. With regard to the last point, being able to attend funerals for deceased agents in units and to mourn together was important in reinforcing group cohesion and in helping to work through the traumatic event.

Opportunity to remember. Agents were encouraged to find meaning in the event by honoring those who did their job and may have been physically or emotionally scarred in the process, and by memorializing those who died in the line of duty. This kind of constructive grieving is important to integrating trauma and moving on with one's life.

Access to factual information. As noted earlier, one of the most frustrating and demoralizing aspects of an officer's involvement in any use-of-force incident is a lack of basic information about his case that makes him feel that everybody's being kept in the loop but him. Within two months of the Waco raid, BATF authorities organized special presentations for involved agents by an administrator, investigators, and one of the raid planners. These forums were intended to explain the facts, outline the reasons behind the decisions and actions taken, and to dispel rumors and answer questions.

Alleviating agents of blame. In such a large, complex, and deadly incident, it was inevitable that formal investigations and analyses, as well as plenty of informal second-guessing, would be commonplace and there was—and still remains—much doubt, anger, and recrimination about the Waco raid and its aftermath. One agent committed suicide in the wake of extreme criticism about the raid. In a few cases, some degree of criticism may have indeed been justified. But the support team made a special effort to prevent or alleviate agents' unwarranted guilt and responsibility for the tragedy that resulted. As discussed in several places in this book, the line between constructive criticism and destructive bashing—by others or oneself—is often not a clear one, and one lesson learned from Waco (and other incidents) is that *how* the criticism is presented is vitally important.

Learning from it. Although it can sometimes seem trite to try and extract a "learning experience" from horrific trauma, most of the BATF agents involved in the raid felt that by learning something from what happened in Waco, they might become more effective agents in the future. Again, this is part of the function of productive meaning-making from a traumatic experience and, more practically, relates to this book's principle of 20/20 hindsight = 20/20 insight = 20/20 foresight.

In addition to program content, *program implementation* includes some specific measures provided by the BATF Peer Support Team, including the following:

Immediate availability of peer support and psychological services. Psychological services and peer support were available within a day of the raid, situated in a secure, private setting, but close enough to the duty stations to be accessible. Peer support personnel were also assigned to local hospitals where wounded BATF agents were being treated. The formal peer team did their job of defusing immediate stress reactions and referring seriously affected agents to further services. Additionally, numerous low-key, informal individual and group support sessions coalesced spontaneously in the week following the raid.

Psychological services upon returning home. In the weeks following the raid, critical incident stress debriefings (CISDs) were conducted shortly after the agents returned home, led by police psychologists and peer debriefers. The general consensus was that these debriefings were helpful in reducing the overall severity of posttraumatic reactions in the involved group of agents.

Availability of specialized psychological services. For agents experiencing especially severe and/or persistent symptoms, specialized mental health resources with expertise in law enforcement trauma were made available.

One lesson learned from the Waco experience is that greater attention should have been given to the needs of family members of affected agents and officers; indeed, this was already a primary component of the Dallas Police Department program described above (Somodevilla, 1986). Otherwise, the two programs share the important common elements of: (1) flexible access to either peer counselors or mental health professionals; (2) maintenance of an attitude of respect for involved officers or agents, backed up by appropriate actions; and (3) unequivocal support and encouragement from the top levels of the department or agency.

CONCLUSIONS

Officer-involved shootings need not be the most traumatic critical incidents in policing, but when they are, the reasons are usually due to a mix of incident characteristics, officer response styles, and departmental handling. By providing immediate administrative, legal, psychological, and peer support services to officers in need, investigators typically find their jobs easier. Even in the unfortunate case of a "rogue cop" being found to have negligently or deliberately used excessive force, how a department deals with its worst will be watched very carefully by officers who want to infer what will happen to the rest among them if they ever have to discharge their weapon to discharge their duty to protect.

Chapter 8

LINE-OF-DUTY DEATH

In the world of law enforcement critical incidents, there are few events more traumatic to officers than the death of a comrade, or *line-of-duty death* (LODD) (Blum, 2000; Henry, 2004). In addition to the normal grief and loss reactions that officers feel at the death of someone they knew and worked with, the death of an officer, even in a different department, even in a different city, reverberates with all officers because of the powerful identification factor: "It could happen to any of us."

LINE-OF-DUTY DEATHS: FACTS AND STATS

When people think of mass casualties of police officers and other emergency service workers, they tend to evoke the September 11, 2001 terrorist attacks on the World Trade Center in New York. This was, indeed, the single deadliest day in the history of U.S. law enforcement, with 72 police officers killed that day. But almost as many law enforcement personnel were slain by ordinary criminals around the country in 2001, which represented a four-year high in murders of police officers. Every year, at least 52 police officers are killed in the line of duty, and 26,000 others are injured in service-related assaults. Overall, since 1960, 2,219 police officers have been killed in the line of duty, and 328,000 more have been injured in assaults. Law enforcement's dirty little secret is that a high proportion of officers (43 percent in one study) are killed or non-fatally shot by their own gun or a fellow officer's weapon. Nevertheless, fewer officers are dying in the line of duty today as there were back in the 1970s, which is largely attributable to better officer training, more cops on the street, better use of protective gear, and improved firepower of officers relative to the criminals they confront.

Police are most likely to be slain with a handgun. Two-thirds of assailants have prior criminal records. Most police homicides occur at night, with Friday being the most dangerous day; Sunday is the least violent. Most officer deaths occur in the course of making an arrest; the next highest category is during workplace or domestic disturbance calls. The South is the most dangerous part of the U.S. for police officers, with more than twice the number of LODDs occurring there than in any other region. A sizable number of officers also die in job-related accidents, which is a line-of-duty death that does not often get the same attention as deaths at the hands of criminals. Most of these involve car and motorcycle accidents (Anderson, 2002; Geller, 1993; Haddix, 1999; U.S. Department of Justice, 2003; Violanti, 1999).

REACTIONS OF FELLOW OFFICERS TO A LINE-OF-DUTY DEATH

As noted above, there are few incidents more traumatic to a police agency as the death of one of their own in the line of duty. Blum (2000) describes several stages of the grief reaction to a fellow officer's

LODD. In my experience, these do not necessarily occur in chronological "stages" per se, but I have observed these reactions in some form or another in most officers following a LODD within a department. Similar reactions have been described by Henry (2004).

Shock and disbelief are often the first reactions to a comrade's LODD. Officers may feel numbed and disoriented and "go through the motions" of their jobs while trying to get their minds around the enormity of what has just happened. Many report that they expect to see the slain officer at his desk or in his patrol car. Some will even reluctantly admit to quasi-hallucinations of the dead compatriot, which under these extreme circumstances is not necessarily a psychopathological reaction, but a form of perceptual-fantasy wish fulfillment.

Telling stories about the deceased is a form of self-prescribed narrative therapy, whereby the officers share reminiscences and experiences involving the deceased officer. Often, this takes place at the local bar and this is not necessarily a bad thing, as long as the alcohol is used moderately and constructively to oil the machine of self-expression in a supportive atmosphere, not self-destructively to drown feelings by getting smashed and/or drinking alone.

Aside from states of intoxication, another place where officers should feel free show tears is at the slain officer's funeral. It is here that the proper example of *grief leadership* by upper management can have a powerful healing effect. These tough guys need to see that normal expressions of grief do not make someone a weak person and that showing one's honest feelings in a dignified way is actually a sign of respect for the deceased.

As time since the funeral passes, many surviving officers continue to experience a feeling of *profound sadness*. Officers may experience a sense of overwhelming fatigue, of feeling "drained" most of the time, of dragging themselves through their shifts. Appetite and sleep may be affected and they may have dreams of the slain officer. It is probably incorrect to label this as depression per se, because this is usually an expectable part of the grief process; however, some officers may actually become clinically depressed if they had a special relationship to the slain officer or if they have had a history of mood disorders in the past.

Sadness may be tinged with *anger*, which may be directed at several shifting targets. Anger at the perpetrator of the officer's death—whether a cold-blooded shooter in a gunshot death or a stupidly careless motorist in a traffic fatality—is common, often fueled by what cops see as the inadequacies of the criminal justice system in redressing this outrage against one of their own. Anger may also be directed against members of the perpetrator's broader group, such as all lawbreakers or all traffic violators; this may lead to overzealous enforcement efforts on the surviving officers' parts. Finally, a general smoldering resentment may adhere to friends, family members, and the general civilian population who "just don't get it" about the dangerous work police officers do, and who are regarded as spoiled, ungrateful recipients of society's protections that these officers risk their necks to provide.

Some of this anger may be stoked by *survivor guilt*, especially where the LODD incident involved a number of officers on the scene: "There but for the grace of God could've gone I." More rarely, grief over the comrade's death may be admixed with anger at the slain officer himself, where it is believed that he somehow contributed to his own death by impulsivity, negligence, or frankly illicit action—especially if his actions also put other cops in danger and/or may now result in more work and stress for the surviving officers: "Dammit, we told Manny to wait for back-up, but he always had to be Mr. First-Fuckin'-In." "What the hell was Jonesy doing in a high-speed chase during a damn thunderstorm? We all could've been killed in that pile-up, and now we're all gonna be investigated." "I didn't want to believe J.D. was involved in that drug deal, but it looks like the bangers greased him, and now we gotta run this down and fix it."

In still other cases, there may be anger at command staff who assigned the patrol or operation, or more generally at the department or city government for cutting manpower and equipment that might have prevented the death, or for hamstringing the cops' ability to adequately control the scene through the imposition of cluelessly soft policies for dealing with suspects.

Although most officers in most departments are able to resolve their grief and get on with their lives and work, a few are unable to let go of the LODD and may experience a permanently altered worldview about policing, society, or life in general. A small percentage of these may leave the police profession, but most hang on, although with a radically changed perspective on their job and their role in society. Still other officers work out their distress by becoming disciplinary problems–although, in my experience, it is rare for this to happen in officers who have never had these problems before. In such cases, it is important to determine if the LODD or other traumatic critical incident is the main contributor to the problem behavior, or if it represents the continuation or accentuation of a previously existing and long-standing problem (Chapter 13). In the best cases, surviving officers continue to do their good work as a way of honoring their fallen comrade.

FAMILY SURVIVORS OF A LINE-OF-DUTY DEATH

The untimely death of a loved one under any circumstances is a wrenching experience, and family members of a slain officer must undergo the further trauma of investigations, court proceedings, and media exposure, during which they will be forced to relive the tragedy again and again.

To add further stress, not all family survivors of slain officers are treated equally, and the difference typically depends on the cause of death, with families of officers slain by criminal assailants tending to receive preferential treatment over those killed in accidents (Haddix, 1999). Perhaps this relates to the warrior-mentality notion that the death of a cop while facing down an evildoer is somehow more noble than that caused by a mere accident. Whatever the case, law enforcement agencies must assure that all families get the care and consideration they deserve.

Common Family Reactions to an Officer's LODD

Family members, especially spouses, of slain officers typically show a number of physical and psychological reactions in the aftermath of their loved one's death (Danto, 1975; Niederhoffer & Niederhoffer, 1978; Rynearson, 1988; Rynearson & McCreery, 1993; Sawyer, 1988; Sheehan, 1991; Sprang & McNeil, 1995; Stillman, 1987; Violanti & Aron, 1994). Many of these are similar to the symptoms of traumatic bereavement experienced by the slain officer's colleagues but are usually more long-lasting. That's because the other officers have their own intact families to provide support, and they can mentally get away from their preoccupation with their comrade's death by immersing themselves in work and family activities. No such respite is afforded family members of the deceased officer who must live with the tragedy 24/7, and will experience the practical and emotional effects of the loss for years to come.

For many family survivors, the first news of the LODD strikes a *mortal blow to the self,* evoking their own *sense of personal loss.* Family members are often preoccupied with the nature of the injuries inflicted on the officer, the brutality of the killing, the types of weapons used, and whether and how much the officer suffered. Families may clamor for information about the identity of the murderer, and the circumstances under which the killing occurred. Unlike accidental death, murder always involves a human perpetrator, and the greater the perceived intentionality and malevolence of the killing, the higher the distress of the survivors (Carson & MacLeod, 1997; MacLeod, 1999). Indeed, the psychological distress of family members bereaved by any kind of homicide can persist undiminished for as long as five years following the murder (Kaltman & Bonanno, 2003).

Family survivors may be seized with an impulse to "do something." A deep and justifiable *anger toward the murderer* alternately smolders and flares as the investigation and trial meander along. Even after sentencing of the perpetrator, the anger may persist for years. A common coping dynamic consists of ruminating on fantasies of revenge. Actual vengeful attacks by family members on perpetrators are extremely rare, probably due in large part to the sheer impracticability of getting at the murderer, who, especially in high-profile cases, is always seen accompanied by a phalanx of bodyguards and protectors during the trial, and also to the basic moral values and common decency of most families, who are not looking to correct one atrocity with another. Some of the anger may be projected onto the department: "You gave him this dangerous assignment, you took him away from me." Most families eventually direct their energies toward efforts to aid in the apprehension and prosecution of the killer, which can be seen as either a help or hinderance by investigators and prosecutors.

Even more common than anger, a pervasive *free-floating anxiety*, or *"fear of everything,"* begins to loom in the survivors' consciousness, beginning with their first news of the slaying and persisting for several years or more. Survivors' heightened sense of their own vulnerability may spur them to change daily routines, install house and car alarms, carry weapons, or refuse to go to out after dark or to visit certain locales. There may be phobic avoidance of anything related to the trauma, including people, places, certain foods, music, and so on. Due to a combination of aversion and anger, family members may shun even well-meaning approaches by departmental representatives, other officers and their families, or anyone associated with law enforcement. They may have an ambivalent relationship with their slain spouse's police artifacts: some spouses may sleep in their deceased loved one's uniform, others may burn it.

Family survivors may experience psychophysiological hyperstartle responses to such ordinarily nonthreatening stimuli as crime shows on TV or news stories of any tragedy, including noncriminal deaths such as traffic fatalities or fatal illnesses. The survivors' usual range of territorial and affiliative activity becomes constricted as the home is turned into a protective fortress by the, strangers are avoided, and unfamiliar surroundings are circumvented. All family members may be outfitted with pagers and cell phones, and may have to submit daily schedules of activity, as there develops a compulsive need for family members to be close at hand or reachable at a moment's notice. Older children and adolescents may resent this "babying" restriction of their autonomy and independence.

While some family members come to develop a feeling of support and kinship with fellow bereaved victims and covictims of tragedy, others come to *feel like lepers or pariahs*—cast out of a pretrauma state of normal existential comfort that the majority of civilians take for granted to assuage their sense of vulnerability, but which no longer is a coping option

for the family survivors of a LODD: "We know better—the world is a cruel and ugly place." Survivors may have frequent *disturbing dreams* of the imagined death of the officer, or wish-fulfillment dreams of protecting or rescuing him. This may be compounded by *guilt* if they somehow feel, however irrationally, that they should have "done more" to keep their loved one safe: "He had the flu that day, but he said 'no big deal,' he needed the overtime to cover the trip he planned for us for our twentieth anniversary and was glad to go in. I should never have let him go to work sick for a goddamn stupid vacation—I'll never take a vacation again!"

Everybody's health suffers. Common *psycho-physiological disorders* include appetite and sleep disturbances, gastrointestinal problems, cardiovascular disorders, decreased resistance to infections, and increased anxiety and depression. A few family members may show classic signs of PTSD.

Aggravating Factors in Family Reactions to a LODD

Certain factors exacerbate the stressful challenges of families trying to cope with an officer's LODD. "Cop-killed-in-the-line-of-duty" stories are second only to "cop-gone-bad" stories in terms of being media favorites. Indeed, where the media can connect these two themes, the prurient interest level of the story rises exponentially. The elevated visibility and scrutiny of such *high-profile cases* virtually assures that family members will be assailed by the media, using every available channel—phone calls, home visits, mobbing on the courthouse steps, and so on. Even if the family could, for a few blessed moments, forget the tragedy they are going through, there will always be the TV, radio, internet chatter, and so on, to remind them. Alternatively, in *low-profile cases*, some families may feel that the plight of their loved one and themselves is being totally ignored: "Doesn't anyone even care what happened?"

LODD-bereaved police family members form a small subfraternity within the larger police extended family system. Other spouses may knowingly or unconsciously avoid them, fearing the reminder of their own loved one's vulnerability. As noted above, families of LODDs involving accidents may not be afforded the same respect and consideration of those slain by criminal assailants. Officer LODD survivors may not even be fully able to bond with other types of bereaved family members whose loved ones died of illness or other "natural" causes. Even families of civilian murder victims may have difficulty understanding the special stresses that families of LODD experience. In some cases, other family survivors of homicide may actually resent the LODD families because of the preferential treatment they believe a slain officer's case gets over those of mere civilians.

Family Coping Strategies in a LODD

Grief work is the term often used for the psychological process that moves the survivor from being preoccupied with thoughts of the murdered victim, through painful recollections of the loss experience, to the final step, where possible, of integrating the experience into one's world-meaning system (Parkes, 1975). Those who appear to adapt best to painful and stressful experiences generally have a range of available coping strategies and resources which permits them greater flexibility in dealing with the particular demands of the traumatic event (Aldwin, 1994; Bowman, 1997; Miller, 1998a; Silver & Wortman, 1980). In fact, psychotherapists may capitalize on the individual's natural coping processes to aid him or her in their grief work and eventual resolution of the trauma.

Following a LODD, police families may employ a range of *coping strategies* to help themselves make it through the aftermath of the death (Sheehan, 1991;

Violanti, 1999). Some try to *mentally distance themselves* from the experience, at least for brief periods of time, by immersing themselves in work or family responsibilities. Even the myriad details surrounding the arrangements for funerals and financial matters in the wake of the death can be helpful if it permits a temporarily defensive intellectualization that protects against being emotionally overwhelmed.

To this end, many families describe feeling drained and beaten by their own emotional storms and make a conscious effort to exert self-control whenever they can, keeping their feelings to themselves, especially in front of outsiders. Paradoxically, this may cause well-meaning others to urge them not to "hold back," to "let it all out," when that's exactly what the family members may have been doing for the past 48 hours, and now crave some composure so they can feel normal even for a brief time.

Many families seek *social support*, and are able to accept sympathy, understanding and advice from friends and family members. On the other hand, some withdraw from people and isolate themselves. Others become irritable and snappish, and eventually alienate potential sources of support. Children may complain that their surviving parent is "taking it all out on us." Many survivors are so cracked and scarred emotionally that they fear any kind of human contact will cause them to "split wide open." Others are still dealing with rage and resentment at how "other people just get to go along with their damn lives because their spouse wasn't a cop."

PSYCHOLOGICAL INTERVENTIONS FOR
FAMILY SURVIVORS OF A LODD

The principles of psychological intervention with family survivors of a LODD represent applications of generally validated principles of grief counseling and bereavement therapy to the special population of law enforcement families (Green, 1993; Kirschman, 1997; Lindy et al., 1981; Rynearson, 1994, 1996; Sprang & McNeil, 1995; Spungen, 1998; Violanti, 1996, 1999).

The basic element of all effective psychotherapy is to *provide support*. In cases of LODD bereavement, this covers emotional, educative, and material

support. In addition to regularly scheduled sessions, psychotherapists should be available by phone or beeper for family members who just need to reach out for a few words during periods of crisis. Mental health clinicians should educate family members on the nature of the grief process and identify and normalize the sometimes baffling and frightening symptoms and reactions that family members may experience. Realistic reassurance should be provided that families can live through this, but stay away from comments that suggest that the experience will be "resolved" or that families will "get over" the loss any time soon. At this early stage of the traumatic bereavement, there is no way families will believe this, and they may resent what they perceive as you trivializing their pain by suggesting it is something that can be "gotten over with."

Trying to help families achieve some measure of control in the midst of such an emotional maelstrom may seem like an impossibly daunting task, but sometimes the place to start is with the physical. Most survivors will be on high physiological alert, experiencing anxiety, panic, dizziness, headaches, stomach distress, sleep disturbances, ruminating thoughts, impaired memory and concentration, and other signs and symptoms. Training family members in relaxation, biofeedback, or meditation exercises that reduce arousal (Chapter 5) can show them that they can at least control *something*—their own bodies. This may give them the confidence to try to gain increasing degrees of control over other chaotic aspects of their now-upside down lives.

Some survivors cope by maintaining a steely reserve, an unnatural calmness of mood, speech, and behavior which may reflect an innate stoicism of character but may also be a typical posttraumatic sign of emotional numbing. In the early stages, this should be accepted, since this rigid emotional splint may literally be the only thing that is holding the person together. As time goes on, therapists should gently guide the explorative process to gradually unbind the emotionally constricted survivor, but always in the context of respecting the individual's ability to handle the emotions, and always with the ultimate goal of increasing, not diminishing, the person's sense of control.

Other survivors may want to vent and, indeed, the therapist's office may be the only place where they feel safe enough to do so. With such individuals, therapists need to remember the difference between *venting* and *spewing.* The former is a cathartic, albeit sometimes painful, expression of suppressed emotions that leads to a feeling of relief and possibly greater insight and control. The latter is an unproductive emotional regurgitation that often heightens distress, clouds understanding, and leaves the person feeling even more out of control. Therapists have to monitor and guide the expressive process so that it heals, not hurts.

Spungen (1998) cites Getzel and Masters' (1984) delineation of the basic tasks of family therapy after bereavement by homicide: helping the family understand and put into perspective the rage and guilt they feel about their loved one's murder; helping survivors examine their grief reactions and other people's availability to them so that they regain their confidence in the social order; helping the family accept the death of their relative as something irrevocable yet bearable; and assisting members of the immediate and extended kinship system in establishing a new family structure that permits individual members to grow in a more healthy and fulfilling manner.

Two especially important issues that are often intertwined are *guilt* and *anger.* As noted above, in an attempt to make some existential sense out of their loved one's death, family members may blame themselves for their officer's fate. As unfair to oneself as some of these self-reproachful rationales may seem to others ("If we didn't have a fight the night before, he wouldn't have left work so early in the morning, and so he wouldn't have been the one to make that fatal traffic stop"), families may cling to these pseudoexplanations to provide at least some kind, any kind, of meaning. Being angry at oneself is at least one way to seize a form of psychological control of the situation, and some of this internalized anger may be projected outward onto the police department, the criminal justice system, or society in general.

Or vice-versa. Sometimes there is a legitimate basis for the family's anger that is partly expressed outward, and partly internalized. Maybe the criminal really was let out of jail too early. Maybe the city really should have authorized funds for body armor for all law enforcement personnel, instead of spending it on a damn stadium. Maybe the media really are acting like slime in calling the house every five minutes and ambushing the family outside their home or business. Maybe those blissfully stupid and uncaring civilians really do have absolutely no clue and don't give a crap about the sacrifices made every day on behalf of their safety by police officers and their families.

Therapeutically, anger must be handled carefully, allowed to come out at a controlled pace in the venting-not-spewing format noted above. The feeling of anger must be acknowledged, even if the therapist doesn't necessarily agree intellectually with its intensity or its targets. Guilt feelings should also be acknowledged, and it is usually a vain exercise to try to talk someone out of the self-reproachful mentality that is temporarily allowing their psyche to stay glued together. Having the individual explore the reasons for his or her feelings can often delicately guide them into a more realistic view of causation and responsibility. Equally important is helping the family–when they are ready–to channel guilt and anger feelings into productive activities that may actually make a difference in how the system works and may serve to memorialize the slain officer.

One way to do this is to help the family members *reconfigure their respective roles* in the absence of the missing loved one. Aside from all the other stresses associated with the traumatic LODD, different family members will have to pick up new and different responsibilities, from paying the bills, to preparing meals, to helping with homework, to participating in social functions. The stresses associated with these role shifts should be expressed and acknowledged, and the therapist should support and assist family members in making these transitions.

Related to this are *grief and closure exercises* that enable the family to master and integrate the traumatic bereavement, partly through memorialization activities that allow planning for the future while honoring the past. For example, pictures and other mementos of the deceased officer can serve as comforting images. In reviewing family picture albums together, the therapist and survivors can try to summon nurturant, positive imagery that may counterbalance the grotesque recollections of the homicide. Similar memorializing activities include writing about the deceased or creating a scrapbook. Again, none of this should become an unending, unhealthy, consuming preoccupation, although in the early stages, some leeway should be afforded to allow the memorializers to "get it out of their systems." If possible, family members should collaborate in these personalized memorial rituals and projects as a way of forging a renewed sense of meaning and commitment within the family structure.

Finally, although some families have actually described eventually creating a posttraumatic growth experience out of the LODD of their loved one (Bear & Barnes, 2005), psychotherapists should be cautious not to turn this into an expectation, which can risk further demoralizing an already-reeling family by giving them one more thing to feel bad about. However, when family members indicate an ability and willingness to take this existential step, therapists must be willing an able to guide them gingerly along this path (Miller, 1998b).

CHILDREN AND LODD

The death of a parent or other close relative from any cause has a special impact on children, and this applies poignantly to children of officers killed in the line of duty (Williams, 1999). As with all untimely deaths, children must cope with the loss of the parent and the disruptions in family routines, living standards, and family roles that this entails. At too early an age, children are faced with the existential reality of life's fragility and impermanence and the fact that bad things can happen to good people at any no-good time. Unlike the anticipated, albeit tragic, death of a loved one from illness, death that is sudden and unexpected leaves no chance to say goodbye or to take care of unfinished business. Death that additionally is violent and traumatic can leave bereaved children with mixed feelings of shame and horror.

The palpable distress of the surviving parent, as well as his or her distraction by numerous activities and responsibilities following the officer's death, may cause children to fear that they will be abandoned, either because the parent has "better things to do," or because their last remaining caretaker will die too. Compounding the distress, the high media attention afforded a law enforcement LODD virtually assures that families, including children, will be subjected to endless replays and retellings of the event that keep the traumatic memories fresh in everyone's mind long after bereaved families of more "ordinary" deaths have had a chance to apply the balm of time and regain their bearings.

Williams (1994a, 1994b, 1999) has outlined a set of psychological principles for dealing with children of LODD officers that are similar to those I have found effective more generally in treating traumatically bereaved children and families (Miller, 1999a, 1999b, 2003). First, *accurate information,* at a level and in a tone that is appropriate for the child in question, should be provided. Contrary to popular belief, children are hardly ever reassured by dismissive "there-there; it's nothing for you to bother about; everything will be alright"–type answers to their questions about the most jarringly traumatic event in their lives (Yalom, 1980). On the contrary, such ambiguity only adds to their anxieties and amplifies their fearful fantasies about what may have happened to the deceased parent.

As much as possible, the surviving parent and other family members should strive to create as much of a *semblance of normalcy* as possible, so that the child does not feel that his or her whole world has been completely tossed on its head. At the same time, as noted above, adults should not go too far in the opposite direction of pretending that "nothing's wrong," because, clearly, the child will be aware of the overall atmosphere of grief and stress hanging over the family. Such mixed messages can only further confuse and frighten children. A much better response is to *model mature strength under pressure:* adults should strive to let their children know that it is okay to grieve and that the adults are hurting too, but that they will not break under the pressure and that, above all, they will be there to protect and take care of their children as needed. This is, in fact, the family version of *grief leadership* shown by supervisors in law enforcement agencies where a fellow officer has been slain.

As discussed earlier, children can participate productively in *memorialization activities* by helping with funeral and other memorial arrangements–at an age-appropriate level, and *only* if the child wants to–as well as writing stories, drawing pictures, making a photo scrapbook, and other activities to remember the slain parent.

Finally, the help of the *child's school* should be enlisted by informing teachers and school officials about the bereavement, providing classmates with age-appropriate information, helping the other kids know how to make the returning child feel safe and welcomed, and by trying to make the classroom an oasis of stability and normalcy, a haven apart from the turmoil that may be going on at home in the first few months and years after the traumatic bereavement.

ADMINISTRATIVE POLICIES AND ACTIONS IN LODD

Police agencies have been criticized for abandoning the bereaved spouse and family after a line-of-duty death by failing to provide follow-up support services (Sawyer, 1988; Stillman, 1987). Surviving officers and their wives may dislike interacting with the widow of a slain officer because it reminds them of their own, and their loved one's, vulnerability and mortality. Both police administrators and mental health clinicians can encourage the sharing of grief responses with others who have walked in the same shoes, as an adjunct to more formal psychotherapeutic grief work (Sprang & McNeil, 1995). Recently, a number of law enforcement family self-help support groups, such as *Concerns of Police Survivors (COPS)* and others, have begun to respond to the challenge; survivors should be urged to consult local directories and websites (see Kirschman, 1997). A cop's life encloses all around him in police family and home family alike. Each deserves proper consideration, support, and respect.

CONCLUSIONS

A line-of-duty death slams home the risk and vulnerability of all law enforcement officers and so may be reacted to by a paradoxical combination of morbid fascination and numbed avoidance by members of the immediate and extended police family. Police psychologists and mental health clinicians can be of tremendous service to surviving officers and their families by applying the principles of trauma therapy and grief counseling to the special needs of the law enforcement community.

PART III

OPERATIONAL STRESS AND CRISIS MANAGEMENT

Chapter 9

HOSTAGE CRISES

As with a number of other topics in this book, hostage negotiation has achieved iconic status in the world of popular drama. And, as with other glamorized aspects of police work, such as undercover operations and homicide investigation (Chapter 12), this chapter will attempt to sort the fact from the fiction and present the practical psychological dimensions of this crucial area of police work. Probably in no other area of law enforcement response does the negotiating officer bring to bear the full range and depth of crisis intervention psychology as in his or her efforts to resolve hostage crises, and in probably no other kind law enforcement response are the stakes so high in terms of immediate threat to human life. Correspondingly, mastery of the full armamentarium of crisis intervention skills necessary for negotiating hostage crises successfully can be generalized to virtually all the kinds of crises described in this book.

HOSTAGE CRISES: FACTS AND STATS

Some basic background information will provide an appropriate context for discussing the collaboration of psychology and law enforcement in successful hostage negotiation (Borum & Strentz, 1992; Greenstone, 2005; Hammer & Rogan, 1997; Hare, 1997; McMains & Mullins, 1996; Rogan, 1997; Slatkin, 2005).

Popular TV and movie portrayals aside, only a small percentage of law enforcement critical incidents deal with actual hostage taking. Nevertheless, the prospect of innocent civilians being deliberately and callously placed in mortal danger for criminal purposes heightens the sense of importance and urgency of these crises, and strikes an emotional chord among professional rescuers and the general public alike.

There are *three especially dangerous periods during a hostage crisis.* The first is the *initial 15 to 45 minutes* when confusion and panic are likely to be at their peak. The second is *during the surrender of the hostage-takers (HTs),* when hair-trigger emotions, ambivalence, and lack of coordination among negotiators, tactical team members, HTs, and hostages can cause an otherwise successful resolution to go bad.

Finally, *tactical assault by the SWAT* team carries the highest casualty rate, probably for two interrelated reasons. First, the very fact that tactical intervention has become necessary indicates that all reasonable attempts to resolve the crisis by negotiation have failed and that violence has already taken place or is imminently about to occur. HTs already predisposed to harm hostages during the siege will probably have no qualms about "finishing the job" when they feel they are being threatened by tactical assault. Second, if a firefight ensues, the resulting panic and confusion may result in hostages being inadvertently injured by running, not staying down, and being confused with perpetrators by the rescue team.

To put some perspective on the contrast between tactical and negotiated resolution of hostage crises, tactical assault results in a 78 percent injury or death rate to hostages and/or HTs. Sniper fire results in a

100 percent death rate to the target. On the other hand, containment and negotiation strategies yield a 95 percent success rate in terms of resolving a hostage crisis without loss of life. If the goal is to minimize casualties, it is clear that negotiation is the preferred strategy in a hostage crisis.

In general, crisis teams that include a *mental health consultant* are rated as more effective than those that don't. Again, there may be a number of reasons for this. Hopefully, a mental health consultant can provide valuable services in both training and on-scene support that can enhance the overall effectiveness of the team. Another important difference, however, may relate to departmental attitude. A law enforcement agency that is willing to allocate resources for a mental health consultant is also probably more likely to have a greater investment and commitment to performance excellence in general, and so may take special care in the training and provisioning of *all* units, including mental health, weapons and tactics, communications, and so on. In this regard, police department crisis team members generally rate communications training as the most valuable skills utilized by negotiators. It is here that psychologists can make some of their most valuable contributions.

TYPES OF HOSTAGE CRISES

Every situation is different, but there appear to be some general categories of hostage crisis (Bolz et al., 1996; McMains & Mullins, 1996; Rogan, 1997), although the types may overlap.

In one relatively rare scenario, *planned criminal hostage taking*, perpetrators actually plan to use hostages as part of a robbery attempt. Inasmuch as the presence of hostages, or of any other unwanted third parties, usually complicates a criminal heist, robbers will consider this drastic plan only when the stakes are comparatively high and when escape is deemed to be virtually impossible without the insurance of hostages. Usually, these are one-time, big-score robberies by ruthless perpetrators who plan to disappear forever with the loot. These types of crimes sometimes overlap with political motives.

Much more common is the ordinary *robbery gone sour*. In this scenario, the crooks plan for a quick in-and-out of the bank or jewelry store, but law enforcement may appear on the scene more quickly than they bargained for, and now the robbers are trapped in the building with unwitting employees and customers who have just become de facto hostages. Seeking to exploit the situation, the robbers may then attempt to use the hostages as bargaining chips to effect their escape.

Another common scenario that may create inadvertent hostages is a *domestic crisis* that spins out of control. Here, what begins as a fight between the couple escalates to the point where one of the combatants, usually the male, effectively barricades his mate inside the dwelling and refuses to let her leave. When law enforcement arrives, the perpetrator then makes demands for her release and for that of any other family members present, as well as for his own escape. In another version of this scenario, an estranged spouse or lover shows up at the worksite of the mate, often prepared for a confrontation, and sometimes armed (Miller, 1997, 1999, 2001a, 2001b, 2001c, 2002, 2005). This then becomes a de facto workplace violence/hostage situation when the subject refuses to let the other employees leave, threatens their safety, and makes demands for their release. In many cases, this category overlaps with a suicidal crisis in which the main purpose of the staged hostage-taking is to provide a pretext for suicide-by-cop (see Chapter 10).

Overlapping with the above category is the *mentally disordered HT* who stages an action involving hostages in order to press demands related to his delusional ideas. He may be frankly psychotic and his demands way out of bounds with reality ("Release all the political prisoners of the great capitalist conspiracy"), or there may be a plausible-sounding, tightly paranoid delusional agenda that drives his actions ("Let my brother out of prison before the guards poison him"). The delusional type of HT often overlaps with the religious or political extremist type (see below). The sheer unpredictability of mentally disordered behavior makes this type of hostage situation one of the most dangerous with respect to hostage safety. It is here that the crisis team psychologist can make an important contribution in determining the diagnostic category and practical psychodynamics of the perpetrator that will yield the most productive negotiating strategy.

The *politically or religiously motivated HT* typically has an ideological agenda for his actions, although it may include petty robbery to finance his cause. This may overlap with the classic definition of a terrorist (Bolz et al., 1996; Miller, in press-b). This is probably one of the most dangerous hostage situations, because many of these perpetrators are quite willing to die for their cause and to kill others with impunity.

Prisoners planning an escape may deliberately include hostages in the their plans, since they know that there is virtually no other leverage they have for getting out. These situations may be especially dangerous for hostages (usually guards or other prison personnel but also sometimes fellow inmates) because such would-be escapees feel they have nothing to lose and because they may already harbor deep grudges against their captives. In other situations, the prison uprising may involve demands for better conditions or other concessions—or a thwarted escape may develop into such a situation by default—in which case the hostages still provide some leverage but are apt to be treated more humanely in order to generate maximum sympathy for the inmates' cause.

CRISIS RESPONSE TEAM STRUCTURE

Consistent with the evolving conceptualization of law enforcement crisis teams as mutidimensional response units, hostage negotiators need to see themselves as part of the larger context of crisis management that includes suicide, robbery, hostage, barricade, bomb threat, terrorist attack, and other emergencies (Fuselier & Noeser, 1990; Hare, 1997; Terestre, 2004). This approach is also consistent with this book's emphasis on the generalizable skill model of psychological crisis intervention principles for diverse applications. Different departments may have different team structures, depending on their individual needs, but some basic, universal components of team structure include the following (Fusilier, 1986; Greenstone, 1995, 2005; Hammer et al., 1994; McMains & Mullins, 1996; Noeser, 1999; Regini, 2002, 2004; Rogan et al., 1994).

The *team leader* is a senior officer who is instrumental in organizing the crisis response team, selecting its members, planning and overseeing training, and making deployment decisions in emergencies. His role may or may not overlap with that of the *on-scene commander*, who is the person in charge of the actual hostage crisis. This individual is responsible for everything that goes on at the crisis scene, from establishing perimeters and traffic control, to directing the activity of negotiators, to deploying the tactical team, to liaising with emergency medical and community services. Naturally, a tremendous degree of pressure is involved and the team leader must rely on the coordinated expertise of the other team members, but the ultimate responsibility for the outcome of the crisis typically falls on the on-scene commander.

Of course, the essence of a hostage crisis response team is the *negotiator*. Depending on the size of the team and the nature of the emergency, there may be one or several negotiators. The preferred model is to have one *primary negotiator* and one or more *secondary* or *backup negotiators*. The backups take over if the primary is unable to establish sufficient communication with the hostage takers, if there are language or cultural barriers involved, if the primary negotiator begins to fatigue after many hours of talking, or for any other reason in which it is felt that greater success can be achieved by the secondary taking over. It is important to emphasize the team nature of any negotiation, so that the primary doesn't feel that he has "failed" if the secondary steps in.

The *intelligence officer's* job is to gather information about the hostage-taker and hostages, including family members, past criminal and/or mental heath treatment history, demographics, identity of the hostages and their relation to the HT, and any other intelligence that will be useful in planning and carrying out the negotiation. It is important to emphasize that, for hostage crises as well as any other type of rapidly unfolding critical emergency scenario, too much raw information can be as confusing as too little. The goal is not merely to throw as many undigested facts as possible at the negotiating team, but to try to organize the material so as to paint a coherent picture of the individual and the situation that the crisis team is dealing with (Blythe, 2002).

The role of the *communications officer* is to keep in contact with all of the individuals and agencies that are important in successfully managing the crisis. These can include firefighting and emergency medical services, local electrical power and phone companies, public transportation agencies, local businesses, and the media. The communications officer is responsible for getting outside information in to the crisis negotiation team and for getting accurate information from the team, usually by way of the on-scene commander, out to other agencies, the news media, and the community. Many departments have a special *community affairs* or *public information officer* who is charged with the specific duty of dealing with the media and the general public, so that timely, accurate, and rumor-free information is appropriately disseminated, without compromising the operation.

The *tactical team* typically consists of a Special Weapons and Tactics (SWAT) unit, specialized marksmen, and other professionals whose sole job is to make a forced entry if and when it is determined by the on-scene commander that negotiations have failed and that hostages are in imminent danger. Considering that the highest fatality rate in hostage crises occurs during tactical incursion, the decision to order such an action is an excruciatingly difficult one. In some cases, no actual forced entry may occur, but other tactical measures may be utilized, e.g., sniping the HTs or sending in gas to immobilize the HTs or flush them out. Again, these measures are best used with extreme caution and only as a last resort, under special circumstances.

The team *psychologist* generally has two primary roles: (1) participation in team development and training of team personnel, and (2) operational assistance during the crisis itself. These will be considered further below.

ROLE OF THE POLICE PSYCHOLOGIST IN CRISIS RESPONSE TEAMS

Different authorities emphasize different roles for the police psychologist in hostage team training and operational assistance in negotiations (Baruth, 1988; Bohl, 1997; Fuselier, 1988; Hatcher et al., 1998; Greenstone, 1995, 2005; McMains, 1988a, 1988b; McMains & Mullins, 1996; Slatkin, 2005; Van Hasselt & Romano, 2004), so this section attempts to synthesize these views and present a practical consensus.

Team Development and Training

While it may seem obvious, it is important to emphasize that the primary role of the crisis team psychologist—indeed of the police psychologist in general—is that of an expert in human behavior, not an expert in law enforcement. Naturally, as I note throughout this book, the more "practical psychology" police officers employ, the more effective will be their daily work. Similarly, the more about law enforcement organization, culture, and technology the police psychologist understands, the more effective he or she will be in serving the needs of these professionals. Nevertheless, it is important for the boundaries not to be blurred. With this in mind,

psychologists must coordinate and cooperate with many other team members in all phases of the hostage team's operation.

One important role of the psychologist in team formation is in the *selection of team personnel*, including negotiators. Characteristics of effective negotiators will be considered below. Selection procedures may be by way of clinical interview, record review, standardized psychological tests, or a combination of all three. But in many cases, the psychologist will come on board after the crisis team has already existed for some time in the department, with the criteria for membership consisting of some form of negotiations training course and practical experience.

Where training exists, either within the department or as part of police academy curriculum or continuing education, psychologists can offer *training modules* related to psychological aspects of crisis management and hostage negotiation. These include basic communication techniques for effective negotiation, different categories of mentally disordered subjects and the effects of such psychopathology on crisis management, and other psychologically relevant topics.

Psychologists may also assist in *organizational development and team-building*, enhancing crisis team cooperation and morale, and advising supervisors and police administrators on the art and science of personnel management. In this role, the psychologist will probably be acting within the larger role of consultant in organizational psychology within the department (see Chapter 14).

Other practical contributions include *consulting with departmental legal counsel* regarding any liability issues that may arise from perceived lack of screening, training, and preparation of personnel or from allegedly mishandled crisis situations that eventuate in death or injury. Additionally, the overall image of departments may be enhanced by the presence of a psychologist on the crisis team, which contributes an element of professionalism.

Operational Assistance

During an actual hostage crisis, the on-scene psychologist can *monitor the progress of negotiations*, usually through a *dead phone* (earpiece but no voice piece), and make recommendations based on the perceived mental status of the HTs and the negotiation strategies used. The psychologist may make actual recommendations to the negotiator, either verbally or in written notes, or may simply provide mental status updates on how the HT appears to be responding, letting the negotiator use his or her own skill and judgment to manage the negotiation.

Part of the psychologist's job may involve *HT profiling*, based on a combination of on-scene monitoring and background information provided by the intelligence officer. Relevant information may range from broad diagnostic categories to moment-by-moment mental state (intoxicated, exhausted, delusional, etc.). All this may be relevant to the negotiation process and the strategies employed.

An important aspect of HT profiling and negotiation monitoring is the *assessment of risk and danger level*. Psychologists may have crucial input as to when threat levels are escalating to the point where the decision to go tactical is necessary. It will rarely be the psychologist himself who makes this call; rather his or her assessments and recommendations are conveyed to the on-scene commander, who integrates this input with all the other relevant data and makes the ultimate decision.

Even more rarely, the psychologist may do the actual *negotiating*. Virtually all authorities agree that psychologists should not be negotiators: some of the reasons for this I consider to be valid, others I think reflect outdated conceptualizations of the mental health profession. To begin with, it is true that psychological training doesn't automatically guarantee negotiation skill, and no one who has not been specifically trained and/or has had practical experience in hostage and crisis management should undertake this life-and-death task, no matter what their academic credentials. Additionally, many HTs may be offended at talking to a shrink; perpetrators typically resent the implication of being crazy and many of these individuals have dealt with mental health professionals only in the aversive context of enforced examinations in the criminal justice system or mandatory counseling for substance abuse, domestic violence, and so on. In such cases, it makes perfect sense for the team psychologist to play a behind-the-scenes supporting role in the negotiation process.

However, in some very rare circumstances, especially where a mentally disturbed HT is involved, some authorities (e.g., Russell & Beigel, 1990) believe that it may be appropriate for the psychologist to take over the primary negotiation task, as it is only in this manner that he or she can both monitor the moment-to-moment fragile mental state of the HT and respond in real-time with the appropriate negotiation strategy, without having to first communicate this to another negotiator. Also, if for whatever reason, the psychologist is the person on scene who can establish the best rapport with the HT, he or she may be in the best position to handle the negotiation. Remember, while standards and protocol are important, the ultimate goal is to do whatever is necessary and practical to resolve the crisis safely. Clearly, psychologists who do any kind of crisis work must have at least some training and experience in dealing with disturbed, distraught individuals, and must be able to use their generalizable skills to manage a hostage negotiation, at least until someone more suitable can take over.

One reason sometimes cited for leaving psychologists out of the negotiation process, or even for excluding them from the on-scene team entirely, is that their do-gooder nature and warm-fuzzy mental health acculturation will make them too likely to overempathize with the disturbed HT and therefore be "too soft" to recognize when a situation is turning dangerous, in turn making them reluctant to recommend a forceful tactical response even when it is crucial to saving lives. There are a number of practical ways to deal with this concern.

To begin with, selection and training of team personnel also includes the team psychologist. The team leader should pointedly evaluate whether the candidate psychologist would be willing to recommend a life-and-death decision that would involve the death of HTs and possible casualty to hostages if a tactical response became necessary. Hatcher et al. (1998) and McMains and Mullins (1996) point out that a hostage team psychologist will typically be known previously to the department through his activities in other areas, such as officer counseling, critical incident debriefing, and on-scene officer-involved-shooting responses, so in some sense he will be a "known quantity." Still, as noted above, training and preparation are important for *all* team members, including the psychologist.

In sum, while I agree that the team psychologist should never be the first choice as an on-scene negotiator, every psychologist who works on a crisis team should receive the necessary training to be able to take over a negotiation if there is indeed no other choice.

Another important operational role for the psychologist involves his or her on-scene interactions with the hostage team members themselves. Hostage negotiation is among the most cognitively and emotionally demanding aspects of law enforcement work, both in terms of the responsibility for human life and the sheer grueling length of some episodes which can extend into hours or days. In such situations, the psychologist can monitor the stress levels of the team members themselves. If the primary negotiator appears to be succumbing to fatigue or otherwise losing his edge, it may be time for the secondary to take over. The best negotiators recognize their own limitations and act accordingly for the overall good of the operation, but sometimes it is wrenchingly difficult for a negotiator to give up on a process he has worked on for hour after hour and which he may feel is on the verge of a successful resolution. In such cases, a decision by the on-scene commander, based in part on the psychologist's recommendation, may be needed to replace the negotiator with a backup. Disappointment, guilt, and resentment will then have to be dealt with, both on-scene and later, by the team psychologist or other mental health services. In other cases, the HT will literally refuse to speak with anyone other than the primary negotiator with whom he has established some rapport. In such cases, the psychologist must do what he or she can to shore up the exhausted negotiator until the crisis is resolved or an acceptable substitute is found.

Finally, after the crisis is over, the psychologist may participate in both *operational and stress debriefings,* the former to review and critique the incident and learn from it (the 20/20 principle), the second to deal with the emotional repercussions of the incident on the part of the team members, especially where the event has gone bad.

Special Considerations and Problems

Mental health clinicians, particularly psychologists, are used to functioning as autonomous clinical decision-makers, and many of us have a tough time accepting that we're not the boss at a crisis-intervention scene. It is essential for psychologists to *respect the command structure* of any crisis operation, especially one that so crucially involves the lives of other people. Two opposite problems that psychologists sometimes have with their role are under- versus overparticipation. In the first instance, the psychologist hangs back, offering little and participating minimally, even when his input is needed and requested. In most cases, this is due to lack of experience and, through continued training and practical experience with the team, the psychologist learns where his input is appropriate. The opposite problem involves the psychologist who makes a grand entrance onto a crisis scene and promptly attempts to take over and run the show. Here, the psychologist needs to learn his place within the command structure. Again, training and experience are usually good correctives to well-meaning over-enthusiasm of this kind.

A similar problem involves not the misjudged self-perceptions and misapplied actions of the psychologist, but the misguided *expectations of the other crisis team members.* At one extreme, the law enforcement professionals may discount or even resent the contribution of a mental health clinicians, because, as noted above, they harbor a notion of such professionals as exponents of a squishy ambivalence ill-suited for tough-minded crisis work. At the other extreme, the team may imbue the psychologist with almost mystical powers of perception and prediction, expecting a point-for-point instructional playbook for dealing with "this type" of HT. Once again, education and training are key. Psychologists have the responsibility to convey to their team the strengths and limitations of the behavioral sciences in contributing to crisis resolution of all types. Crisis team training should include this orientation as an essential curriculum module.

More practically, the role of the psychologist on-scene will necessarily vary from crisis to crisis, depending on a host of parameters including the nature of the HT and the tactical considerations involved. In some crisis situations, the psychologist's main role may consist of standing around, drinking coffee, and offering the occasional gesture of encouragement to team members. In other situations, the psychologist will hit the ground running, performing most or all of the activities mentioned above in a virtual frenzy of activity. Commonly, long stretches of boredom will be punctuated by episodes of frantic action. The key is for the team to operate in a smooth, coordinated manner. Similar to a sports team or a musical band that plays together frequently, repeated training allows crisis teams to get "tight," so that their actions at each performance are smooth, coordinated, and effective.

PSYCHOLOGICAL TRAITS AND CHARACTERISTICS OF SUCCESSFUL HOSTAGE NEGOTIATORS

As noted above, one of the functions of the team psychologist is in selection and training of hostage negotiators. While there is probably no single ideal hostage negotiator profile, there does seem to exist a rough consensus on which qualities contribute to a successful negotiator (Allen et al., 1991; Bolz, 1996; Fuselier, 1986; Getty & Elam, 1988; McMains & Mullins, 1996; Misino, 2002; Russell & Beigel, 1990; Slatkin, 2005). As with any attempt at categorizing psychological traits, some overlap between categories is natural.

Determination and success-orientation. Successful negotiators like to win and see their role as carrying out a single-minded mission to successfully resolve hostage crises. Most professional negotiators will describe the pump they get from the process of negotiation, and the rush that follows a successful resolution. The downside is the exhaustion and dejection that may follow a hostage crisis that goes bad despite the team's best efforts. Nevertheless, without that relentless drive to succeed, it is doubtful that most negotiators could maintain the psychological momentum and energy level needed to stay sharp and negotiate for hours on end.

Self-confidence and self-reliance. While it is emphasized that hostage crisis resolution is a team effort, negotiators must have some comfort level with occasionally going out on a limb and making a judgment call to take a calculated risk. After all, sometimes after hours of negotiation, with hordes of personnel all over the scene, it all comes down to you and the HT. That's a tremendous responsibility with lives hanging in the balance. Without a basic sense of self confidence and self-reliance, such a task would be impossible to carry out. We're not talking about inflated narcissism, but rather a firm and realistic belief in one's own ability to handle situations one is trained and mentally prepared for.

Assertiveness and decisiveness. While rash, impulsive action is always discouraged, in most hostage crises there is little room for vacillation and indecisiveness. Negotiators must make quick decisions in real-time, and if they are based on skill, knowledge, training, and experience, these decisions are usually the right ones (Flin, 1996; also see Chapter 14).

Ambiguity tolerance. Obviously, there are some standard ways of doing things that remain consistent across situations, otherwise learning the concepts and techniques in this or any book would be pointless. However, events rarely follow a set formula and the negotiator must be prepared to switch gears, change expectations, and settle for partial solutions as the circumstances require. In both thought and action, *flexibility* is the key.

Frustration tolerance, persistence, and self-control. During a prolonged hostage crisis, there are bound to be many occasions where negotiators are ignored, taunted, baited, cursed at, or otherwise abused by the HT. The negotiator's actions must always be informed by his best judgment as to what is appropriate to that situation at that point in time. Here's where the balance between reckless self-assurance and prudent self-restraint is crucial. Particularly vexing is when, after hours of grueling negotiation, the HT appears ready to come out or to release hostages, only to change his mind at the last moment, either because of his own internal mental state or, perhaps most galling of all, because of some careless move by other members of the crisis team or the media. At times like these, negotiators must always keep in mind that their job is to focus on the process, not worry about the outcome.

General intelligence. While a genius-level IQ is not required to be a successful negotiator, general intelligence seems to be a broad index of the ability to handle complex situations effectively. At the very least, a negotiator must have the brainpower to absorb the required training, to learn and develop from experience, to think quickly and clearly, and to communicate skillfully and effectively.

Practical "street-wise" intelligence. The negotiator should have some knowledge and understanding of the culture and language of the HT, both to establish rapport and to deflect and manage any subtle manipulations the HT may attempt to palm off on the negotiator and the team.

Insightfulness. This is the ability to size up a situation quickly and to "think on one's feet" in terms of coming up with practical strategies in real-time during a crisis.

Logical and abstract thinking. This doesn't imply a rigid, Mr. Spock-like style of problem solving. Indeed, as will be seen in Chapter 14, most experts use an effective form of intuitive, knowledge-based style of decision making in crisis situations (Flin, 1996; Klein, 1998). But logic and abstraction allow

one to see many sides to a problem simultaneously, and this is usually helpful in generating multiple alternative strategies for crisis resolution.

Imaginative and creative problem solving. This is the flip side of logical thinking, the right hemisphere as opposed to the left hemisphere brain style of cognition. Based on a solid rational understanding of the problem, the crisis worker is then able to go an intuitive step further and "think out of the box." In practice, the two styles work together; that is, solid grounding in skill and knowledge—*expertise* in the true sense of the word—allows a certain degree of improvisation to adapt to a particular person or circumstance. The overall effect often looks like a seamless process of analysis, synthesis, and solution generation by a master of his or her craft (Flin, 1996; Klein, 1998; see Chapter 14).

Verbal fluency. The bottom line for any type of crisis negotiation is the ability to communicate effectively, and unless someone is comfortable in the world of spoken language, he or she will not make an effective negotiator. Such skill involves the ability to clearly articulate one's thoughts and intentions to the HT in terms that both parties are comfortable with, and to modulate the content, tone, and timing of one's speech to the requirements of the audience. Verbal fluency also means being a good listener, and negotiators have to know when to shut up and open their ears; according to expert negotiator and instructor Jack Maxwell, the modus operandi of the hostage negotiatior is "Talk to me." While many of the necessary crisis communication skills can be taught and practiced, there probably has to exist a baseline ability and comfort level with two-way interpersonal communication in general. Words have to be the negotiator's friend and ally.

Interpersonal perceptiveness and intuitiveness. A well-honed ability to "read" others is an invaluable negotiating skill. Often, any cues to a HT's emotional state must be gleaned by voice only, since phone contact is the most common negotiation medium. Sensitivity to speech content, inflection, rate, tone, and other features is thus important.

Use of "constructive manipulation." Here, the negotiator attempts to influence the HT's mental state and behavior by the careful timing, phrasing, and choice of content of his communications. The manipulation is constructive because the overall goal is not to exploit the HT, but to verbally nudge him toward a view of the situation in which release of hostages and surrender are the best possible options. The goal is less to trick than to persuade.

Truthfulness. In this context, constructive manipulation and truthfulness are perfectly compatible. This goes beyond the standard protocol of not lying to HTs out of fear of compromising future credibility, but also involves a certain honesty of purpose: "I'm gonna do what I'm gonna do, but my goal is ever and always to get everybody out of this crisis alive and safe." After a well-negotiated hostage crisis resolution, it is not uncommon for a HT to relate that the main reason they decided to end the crisis peacefully was because they really felt the negotiator's sincere concern for *everybody's* safety. That's something that's hard to fake, especially over hours and hours of prolonged negotiation.

Total commitment to the negotiating approach. Again, being a good talker doesn't mean being a bullshitter. Successful negotiators will tell you that you can't do this job right if you don't truly believe on some level that words are more powerful than weapons when it comes to resolving life-and-death hostage crises with minimal or no casualties. Surely, a certain amount of manipulation is involved in talking a distraught HT out of harming innocent hostages and/or himself, but a commitment to the power of negotiation is not something you can fake. Indeed, the overwhelming success of the negotiation approach in resolving hostage crises around the world is the best argument for its effectiveness when used by skilled professionals.

HIGH-RISK FACTORS IN HOSTAGE CRISES

Certain factors make some hostage crises more dangerous than others (Fuselier et al., 1991; Greenstone, 1995, 2005; Slatkin, 2005). Some of these factors are related to the general context in which the crisis unfolds and the demographics and life circumstances of the HT. Other high-risk factors relate to the specific moment-to-situation of the particular crisis.

One especially dangerous risk factor is whether the *hostage is known to and/or deliberately selected* by the HT. This is consistent with the general finding that most interpersonal violence is perpetrated on people known to the aggressor. Unlike the accidental bank robbery HT, a HT who purposefully selects his victim is usually on a mission to make a statement or "teach them a lesson." Common examples include romantic quarrels and workplace beefs. The goal often involves at least frightening or intimidating the intended hostages, if not actually injuring or killing them. Particularly dangerous is a situation where the HT intends to commit a murder-suicide (Hillbrand, 2001). In fact, such situations often inadvertently become hostage crises when police arrive and surround the area.

In many such cases, there has been a history of problems between HT and victim that have required a police response in the past, most commonly domestic disturbance calls, and the couple may be well-known to local police. This time, however, the incident has escalated to a hostage and barricade situation, and the stakes are higher. There is often an associated past *history of generally impulsive and aggressive acts* on the part of the HT. As the best predictor of future behavior is past behavior, someone who has a track record of using threats or force to get his way will be especially likely to do so in a high-tension hostage situation, and he may correspondingly be more dangerous and unstable during that crisis. A diagnosed *major mental disorder* is another general risk factor for violence.

Although, by itself, stress rarely makes an otherwise peaceful person turn violent, the *cumulative build-up of multiple stressors* over time is a general risk factor for violent acting-out, especially in persons already predisposed to impulsivity and low frustration tolerance. This is commonly associated with a *lack of family grounding or social support*, itself a general risk factor for dysfunctional behavior. A sense of isolation can fuel paranoid thinking, leading to an impulse to "do something about it." Correspondingly, obnoxious and intimidating people tend to alienate those around them, often leading to self-fulfilling prophecies of mutual recrimination, mistrust, and animosity, setting the stage for violence.

Certain cultures condemn any *show of weakness* or loss of face. The crossover point between a common domestic dispute or convenience store holdup and escalation to a full-blown hostage-barricade crisis often comes when police arrive and order the surrender of the suspect, who then feels compelled not to back down at any cost. This may bode ill for negotiations if the HT feels that making concessions, releasing hostages, or settling for anything less than his full demands is "punking out."

Conversely, expressions of *hopelessness and helplessness* are a sign of clinical depression and may be a risk factor for suicide. Anything that indicates that the HT has already decided not to live through the crisis is a bad sign, inasmuch as a person with no hope or regard for his own life will typically have little regard for the lives of others. Of course, some HTs will explicitly declare that they are going to die by their own hand, and some will deliberately provoke suicide-by-cop confrontations (see Chapter 10). A fair number of suicides during a hostage crisis actually spare the hostages–perhaps the HT's last noble gesture–but this certainly cannot be counted on, and such situations must be treated as extremely dangerous.

Making a *verbal will*, or "setting affairs in order" is a somewhat less direct but nevertheless ominous way of indicating that the end is near. Often, this is done precisely for dramatic effect in front of the hostages, especially in a domestic situation, to show them how badly the HT has been hurt by the family members. In some cases, this may actually be a good sign, as the intent of the suicidal HT is to have the family live on and suffer with the memory of "what they drove me to." Again, however, always err on the side of caution. Also, where there are *no substantive demands for escape*, this usually indicates that the HT knows he's not coming out alive.

Sometimes, HTs will make *direct threats to hostages*. This may just be a desperate ploy to manipulate authorities into granting demands but it may also represent a clear and present danger to the hostages by a HT who is growing increasingly desperate. As with suicidal threats, saying they're going to do it is, more often than not, a signal that they *are* going to do it.

In between the first few confusing minutes of the hostage crisis and the end-point surrender or tactical entry, most HTs do not deliberately and gratuitously abuse their captives during the prolonged negotiation phase. The HTs are usually more focused on their demands for escape or validation, and realize that unnecessary harm to hostages will only further antagonize the authorities. *HTs who abuse their charges* are usually mentally disturbed, have a past history of abusive or contentious interactions with the hostages, such as in family quarrels or workplace vendettas, may be religious or political terrorists who single out certain hostages to make a point, or a HT may simply be a sadistic psychopath on a power trip.

Test-firing or threat-firing of a weapon, or other deliberately provocative action, may be a sign of impulsivity, poor judgment, or a tendency toward especially violent behavior. Such *display behavior* only serves to heighten the unpredictability and dangerousness of the situation as a whole. It may also represent a suicide-by-cop gesture.

HOSTAGE CRISIS RESPONSE: BASIC PROTOCOL

Expertise and innovation are best played out on the framework of a basic procedural structure for managing hostage episodes. While most life-and-death crises rarely go by the numbers, there does appear to be a certain regularity that guides the evolution of the crisis and the measures used to contain it, although not always in same order. The following should be thought of as an overall outline protocol for the psychological principles and practices of hostage and crisis negotiation (Fuselier, 1981a, 1981b; Greenstone, 1995, 2005; Lanceley, 1999; McMains & Mullins, 1996; Miller, in press-a; Russell & Beigel, 1990; Slatkin, 2005; Wind, 1995).

The first priority is to *isolate and contain the HT* and to *secure the perimeter*. You don't want an armed HT roaming throughout a busy office building, or fleeing onto a bank or grocery store parking lot, where they have access to vehicles and other civilians. As a general rule, the perimeter should be large enough to allow freedom of movement of the tactical and negotiating teams, and small enough to be kept under observation and control by the authorities. More than one perimeter, e.g., inner and outer, may be necessary.

You need to provide for *scene control.* The world hasn't stopped just because you're trying to manage a crisis situation. You now have the dual task of working around the realities of the surrounding community, and where possible, getting the surrounding community to work around your needs. This includes marshalling medical services, controlling local traffic, dealing with the media, and keeping the surrounding community sufficiently informed to protect their safety. An ironic experience in my local South Florida area has been that many community residents will be far more tolerant of a temporary shut-down of routes and services to accommodate the filming of a movie than they will

be of an equivalent disruption for a police action that might save lives.

Obviously, some form of *communication needs to be established with the HT* because the function of the negotiating team is to negotiate. As a rule, the sooner you begin a dialogue with the HT, the less time he has to stew and consider drastic options.

While face-to-face contact between the negotiator and the HT is usually discouraged because of the potential danger involved, any safe means of communication—line phone, cell phone, bullhorn, or even digital pager or e-mail—should be established as soon as possible. Although less relied upon in this age of ubiquitous cell phones, a *throw phone* (as in thrown through the window) is a telephone specifically designed for the HT to plug into a jack in order to establish a direct, dedicated line to the negotiating team. During prolonged negotiations, this apparatus may become necessary if the HT's cell battery dies or if structural impediments interfere with the cell signal.

GENERAL COMMUNICATION STRATEGIES IN HOSTAGE NEGOTIATIONS

While always striving to customize your communications approach to your best understanding of the HT's motives and personality, there are a number of general recommendations for dealing with crisis situations that can be applied to hostage negotiations (Call, 2003; Greenstone, 1995, 2005; Lanceley, 1999; McMains & Mullins, 1996; Misino, 2002; Noeser, 1999; Noeser & Dolan, 1992; Slatkin, 2005).

Although law enforcement agencies always strive for prompt response times by their crisis teams, sometimes reality dictates that the first officer on the scene must begin communication with the HT—a kind of "psychological CPR"—until the full crisis team can be mobilized and take over. In such cases, the first responder's job is to keep basic lines of communication open until the crisis team negotiator can assume the primary communication task. Whether involving the first-responding officer or the official departmental negotiator, there are several important principles to keep in mind when *beginning negotiations.*

As much as is within your control, *minimize background distractions.* This applies both to yourself and

the HT. Distractions include more than one person speaking at a time, background radio chatter, road noise, etc. If there is noise at the HT's end, ask him if he can go to a quieter part of the room, speak up a little, or otherwise enhance the clarity of the communication channel.

Open your dialog with an *introduction and statement of purpose.* "This is Sgt. Bruce McGill of the Metropolitan Police Department Crisis Unit. I'm here to listen to you and to try to make sure everybody stays safe." Keep the introduction as simple as possible, and always strive for honesty and credibility. Keep your voice firm but calm, and convey your confidence that this is a temporary crisis that will be resolved safely. Everybody at the scene—including the HT—knows that the negotiator's and hostage team's first and foremost priority is to ensure the hostages' safety. At the same time, it is still possible to evince a sincere concern for *everybody's* well-being, including the HT's by communicating with respect, directness, lack of deception, and integrity. From a practical standpoint, if the HT feels he's being duped, patronized, or manipulated from the get-go, he's not going to want to cooperate with you, which only serves to put everybody in greater danger.

To build rapport, *ask what the HT likes to be called.* When in doubt, address him respectfully. As much as possible, you want to address the HT by a name that is familiar to him. At the same time, you want to avoid phony camaraderie, so try to find out what he likes to be called. If not sure, don't automatically assume that William will respond favorably to "Bill" or "Willy." If no first name is available, use respectful titles, like "Mr. Smith." If the name is unknown, use "sir," rather than "pal" or "buddy."

Speak slowly and calmly. People's speech patterns often mirror the tone of the dominant conversation, so provide a model of slow, calm, clear communication from the outset. This doesn't mean speaking in a mechanical, droning monotone, but avoid letting your pitch rise or your speech rate quicken excessively in response to frustration, irritation, or provocation. Set the standard of mature, adult conversation from the beginning of the communication. If the HT wants to talk, listen. One general rule of thumb of negotiations is to *listen* approximately twice as much as you talk (Jack Maxwell, personal communication), but adapt your communication style to the needs of the situation.

Adapt your conversation to HT's vocabulary level. You want to avoid either talking over the head of the HT, which most people find irritating, or patronizing him by talking down to him or trying to mimic his pattern or level of speech too closely. A few minutes of conversation should allow you to adapt your own speech to his style and rhythm. Of course, if the HT's native language is not English, a negotiator fluent in his language would be ideal, but if this is not possible, at least a skilled interpreter should be available.

Even with foul-mouthed HT's, *avoid unnecessary profanity.* Negotiators sometimes confuse the active listening technique of mirroring (see below) with matching the HT, epithet-for-epithet. People under stress are more likely to use profanity. If you response in kind–even in a well-meaning attempt to "speak the guy's language"–you may end up only with an unproductive back and forth stream of "shit-this/fuck-that" invective. Remember, you're trying to model mature, adult speech and behavior in order to calm the situation. So just as you modulate your voice tone in the direction of greater control

and rationality, so with your speech content, which should always be less inflammatory than the HT's. This doesn't mean you have to orate like a schoolteacher or church pastor, just use a bit of verbal decorum, which, incidentally, is also a sign of respect.

Your communication may be met with anything from stony silence, to explosive cursing, to psychotic ranting, to confused rambling, to intoxicated mumbling. *Allow productive venting but deflect dangerous escalation of speech tone and content.* In many instances, the whole rationale for the hostage situation is for the HT to "make a point" or "tell his story." Good. If that's what he wants, allow him to freely express his frustrations and disappointments, but don't let venting become ranting, which can lead to further loss of control. The goal of emotional expression should always be to blow off steam, not to further stoke the boiler. When the HT's ventings seem to be bubbling over, use appropriate de-escalation techniques, as described below.

If you're not sure what the HT is saying, *ask for clarification.* Clarity is a general principle of negotiation and all forms of crisis intervention. Don't respond to or act on a HT's statement unless you're reasonably sure you know what he means. Remember the principle of listening twice as much as you talk. Don't be afraid to directly ask for clarification: asking someone to help you understand what they're saying is a sign of interest, concern, and respect.

Focus your conversation on the HT, not the hostages. In most circumstances, the less the HT thinks about the hostages, the better. This is especially true where the hostages are not neutral, i.e., family members or coworkers who have been targeted to make a statement. Remember that hostages represent power and control to the hostage taker, so try not to do anything that will remind him of this point.

Inquire about the welfare of all parties, but focus on the HT first, and then weave in concern for the other people: "Are you okay? Are you injured? Does anyone in there need medical attention? Is everybody safe for now?" This is an exception to the general rule of not soliciting demands, because you want to firmly establish your concern for *everyone's* welfare, including the HT's, from the outset. Also, if someone really does require emergency medical attention, you don't want to overlook the opportunity to provide it early on.

Be supportive and encouraging about the outcome. Downplay the HT's actions so far: "Right now, it's only an attempted robbery, nobody's been hurt [or if there has already been an injury or fatality] ". . . nobody else has been hurt." Remember, the goal is to prevent the further escalation of violence *from this point on.* If there is a chance of saving lives, then spin the situation any credible way you can. If shots have been fired, point out that no one has yet been hurt. If injuries have occurred, emphasize the lack of fatalities so far. If a hostage has died, focus on saving the rest. The emphasis should always be on what the HT can *still do* to save his own life and create a favorable impression that will score him points later on. The basic message is that whatever the HT has done so far, the situation is still salvageable and the HT can still earn credit for doing the right thing:

> "William, I want you to know that, even though the guy got shot *[passive tense: it wasn't completely your fault]* in the leg *[not a critical wound]* at the beginning of this thing *[everybody was confused]*, all kinds of unexpected stuff can happen in a panic situation. But you've done a good job of keeping things cool from that point on *[you're still in control, but in a positive way]*, and no one else has been hurt *[you're now part of the solution, not the problem]*. That counts for a lot, and everybody here knows it *[there's still hope of avoiding dire consequences]*. Let's see if we can keep on keeping the peace for now so we can all come out of this safely, okay? *[we want you to be safe, too, not just the hostages]*."

In line with the above, compliment the HT for any positive actions he's taken. If the HT does something constructive, reinforce it. This applies whether the action is a major event, like release of one or more hostages, or a seemingly minor thing like allowing the hostages to eat or go to the bathroom, or keeping the phone line open. The aim here is to establish a pattern of constructive actions that allows the HT to reap repeated positive reinforcement, leading ultimately to the "big score" of surrender with no further injuries to anyone.

Throughout the communication process, you should be attempting to *gather information* about the HT's background, criminal history, mental health and/or substance abuse history, family structure, employment status, and so on. Psychologists can aid the crisis team by providing practical guidance as to the nature of any diagnoses or personality patterns observed, and their implications for approaches to negotiation strategy. It may also be important to know something about the hostages as well, as this may have implications for their response to the crisis and their safety. Such intelligence-gathering also includes basic tactical items such as the physical layout of the hostage scene, surrounding community, and access to support services.

VERBAL COMMUNICATION TACTICS IN HOSTAGE NEGOTIATION

Aside from general communication strategies, certain specific verbal communication tactics may prove useful in hostage crises (McMains & Mullins, 1996; Noeser, 1999; Noeser & Webster, 1997; Slatkin, 2005). Think of these as a repertoire of roles to play during a crisis–not "roles" in a deceptive, theatrical sense, but in the manner of being what Lazarus (1993) calls an *authentic chameleon*, that is, coloring your style of communication and interaction to best fit the subject, but with the overarching goal being a sincere and honest commitment to everyone's welfare. In that regard, always read your subjects as accurately as possible and customize your negotiating approach using one or more combinations of the following communication tactics and roles.

Reasonable problem-solver. "I know we both want this to be over with nobody getting hurt. A lot of confusing stuff's gone down so far and I'm not sure we all understand each other. But let's put our heads together and figure out how to solve this."

Buddy-fellow traveler. "I hear you, man. I had my beefs with lousy bosses in my time, too. They can fry your brain and make you want to blow. But you proved your point, man. No one's gonna forget this lesson. So let's keep it that way. End it now and he's the one they're gonna blame. If you hurt someone, they're all gonna be distracted from the main point of what he did, and then it may all fall on you. What do you say?"

Dumb-but-trying–"Detective Columbo." This tactic may be used to buy time or deflect attention from unreasonable demands. "Let me see if I have this straight. You want food and a 12-pack of Bud placed outside the building door, right? Is that the hall door or the outside door? Because I think you gotta unlock one to get to the other; I don't know that building too well." Don't overdramatize this role, however, or the subject may quickly suspect you're playing him and become angry.

Firm, accepting–directing. "Look, we all want to come out of this alive. You're in there and I'm out here, so I can't make you do anything. But if you want to live through this safely, let me suggest a few things that can help us all get this mess behind us." This presumes that the HT is not suicidal or psychotic and has a personal stake in surviving the crisis.

Nonjudgmental and helpful. "Hey, you can't help how you feel, right? But let's see if we can keep things as safe a possible here, okay?"

Compassionate but competent. "I understand that what your boss did to you was way out of line. That kind of unfairness can drive someone up a wall. Before you know it, things get out of control. That's why I'm trying to help us all take things down a notch and get through this all right."

Reinforce appropriate behavior. This applies not only to big concessions, like releasing a hostage, but to even small steps in the right direction. "I'm glad you called back when you said you would. That shows me I'm dealing with a straight-up guy."

"Authentic chameleon"–flexibility. This requires being familiar enough and comfortable enough with a range of conversational idioms and interpersonal styles, in order to gear your speech style to that of the subject. This only works if it sounds natural, so don't force it. If you're not fluent in "street language," for example,

just use your own style. Remember, the more real you are, the less anxious you'll be, and the more honest and confident you'll sound, thereby increasing the chances for a productive communication.

Verbal Strategies to Avoid

These may seem obvious, but in the heat of the moment, it is easy to slide back into casual styles of interpersonal banter which may be okay with your poker buddies, but can dangerously derail a hostage negotiation. These include the following.

Arguments. You need not be overly ingratiating, but don't outright argue with the HT, especially with regard to the content of his complaint: "Well, what did you expect your boss to do–you were caught stealing, weren't you?"

Power plays. Any statement along the lines of "Do what I say because I'm in charge here." Guess what–you're not.

Moralizing. This can be blatant: "What kind of person does something like this?" Or subtle: "C'mon, what are your kids going to think if this turns out bad?" Remember, many HTs may already be depressed and/or enraged, and the last thing you want to do is further inflame or demoralize them and give them an excuse to get violent. So avoid being judgmental, and remind yourself that your only priority is to resolve the situation safely for everyone.

Diagnosing. For most people, any suggestion of a "mental problem" amounts to an insult. Again, this can be overt, as in, "Look, it's obvious you're laboring under some kind of delusion" (alternatively, try: "I'm not sure I get it yet, but I'm trying to understand where you're coming from"); or subtle, as in "Hey, buddy, you sound a little depressed" (instead, try: "You seem down about something; want to tell me about it?").

ACTIVE LISTENING SKILLS

Active listening techniques comprise the fundamental skills set for any kind of crisis intervention. They are multipurpose communication tools that

can be effectively applied to hostage negotiations (Call, 2003; Lanceley, 1999; McMains, 2002; McMains & Mullins, 1996; Noeser, 1999; Noeser &

Webster, 1997; Rogan & Hammer, 1995; Rogan et al., 1990; Slatkin, 1996, 2005).

Emotion Labeling

Emotion labeling helps the subject clarify what he's feeling. It contributes to a state of calmness by reducing internal confusion. Sometimes, just giving an intense feeling a name shows that the emotion is understood and that the subject is less out of control than he might think. Also, by focusing on the HT's emotions, you allow a break from discussing demands and issues, and at the same time let the HT know you're interested in how he feels about things, not just in what he's currently complaining about or what he and you may want from each other.

Indeed, with disturbed or incoherent subjects, it may not be immediately apparent what the HT wants—in fact, he may hardly be clear about this himself. In such cases, the initial step may be to clarify what he's thinking and feeling. In general, respond first to emotion, not content. That is, address your responses to the HT's emotional state, while sidestepping any demands or arguments. But be careful not to convey the impression that you're ignoring or discounting his issues if that's what he really wants to discuss. The important thing is to demonstrate to the HT that you are tuned in, that he has your undivided attention, either by an "um-hmm"-type interjection or by encouraging him to go on. Utilize *emotion labeling phrases*, such as: "You sound . . .," "You seem . . .," "I hear . . .," and so on.

HT: "I'm getting really pissed off at everyone trying to screw me over. My boss messes with me, then my old lady gives me a hard time, and my kids do nothing but complain. I'm at the end of my rope, man."
Negotiator: "You sound like you're feeling really angry and beaten down about things."

Paraphrasing

Paraphrasing is basically rephrasing the subject's statement in your own words. This accomplishes several things. First, it reinforces empathy and rapport, i.e., if I can restate your meaning in my own words, I must have some understanding of what you're experiencing, which conveys to the HT that

"I'm really hearing you." Second, effective paraphrasing actually clarifies what the HT is saying: it is the clarification-of-content counterpoint to the clarification-of-feelings that occurs with emotion labeling. Third, it encourages the subject to slow down and listen, and may deflect any hostile action against hostages. It also promotes a verbal give-and-take that does not automatically put the subject on the defensive. Finally, just hearing one's own thoughts spoken out loud by someone else can provide clarification and a new perspective.

When paraphrasing, summarize in your own words what the subject has just told you.

HT: "I'm getting really pissed off at everyone trying to screw me over. My boss tries to mess with me, then my old lady gives me a hard time, and my kids do nothing but complain. I'm at the end of my rope, man."
Negotiator: "Seems like you're tired of people taking advantage of you."

The negotiator should be careful not to add or embellish, as in: "They just keep pushing and pushing you, don't they? They never give you any peace, do they?" This is not an effective response because it may serve to further inflame. Remember, the overall goal of every negotiation is to calm things down, not stir them up.

Structure paraphrases in a way that solicits confirmation of the subject's thoughts and feelings. This can be explicit, like adding "—right?" at the end of your paraphrase. Or it can be more subtle, such as leaving your paraphrase dangling by the intonation of your voice, or following your restatement with silence, creating a verbal vacuum for the subject to fill. Paraphrasing wordings can include: "Are you telling me . . .?" "What I hear you saying is . . .," "Let me see if I have this right . . .," "So . . .," and similar phrases.

As always, if you are not sure what the HT just said or meant, ask him to repeat it: "I don't know if I got all that, William. Could you say it again, please. I want to make sure I understand exactly what you're telling me."

Reflecting/Mirroring

Here, the negotiator repeats the last word or phrase, or the main word or phrase, of the subject's statement in the form of a question, thereby soliciting more input without actually asking for it. It also allows the negotiator to buy time if he cannot immediately think of an appropriate emotional label or paraphrase, while still encouraging the HT to think about what he's just said. Early in the negotiation, it allows information to be gleaned in a non-confrontational way, and is a generally good initial rapport-builder.

HT: I'm getting really pissed off at everyone trying to screw me over.
Negotiator: You're pissed off?
HT: Yeah, my boss, my wife, my kids. They bug me and bug me, and won't get the hell off my back.
Negotiator: They're bugging you, huh?

Minimal Encouragers

Minimal encouragers are nothing more than the little conversational speech fillers we all use to indicate that we're paying attention to someone during a conversation. In the hostage negotiation context, these consist of short utterances and questions that let the HT know that the negotiator is listening, but don't interfere with the HT's narrative flow. Indeed, the purpose is to encourage the HT to keep talking. Examples include: "Oh?" "I see." "Yeah." "Uh-huh." "When?" "And?" "Really?" "You do?" " She did?"

Silence and Pauses

Aside from just buying time, silence can be used strategically. For one thing, in a relatively active conversation, your silence encourages the subject to fill it the gaps, which keeps him talking. Following a statement by silence is also a way of emphasizing a point you've just made.

Negotiator: "I know this looks like it's gotten out of control, but not everything that starts bad, ends bad. It doesn't have to end bad" [pause].

You can also use silence to frame the HT's point or to encourage elaboration.

HT: "I'm trying to think my way out of this, but what am I supposed to do, just give up?" [negotiator stays silent].

HT: "Is there a way to end this without me being taken out?"

Like all active listening techniques, silence and pauses are best used in combination with other techniques, and may be particularly effective when used in conjunction with minimal encouragers. Be careful about too much silence, however, because you don't want the HT to think he's being ignored or was forgotten about. Generally, subjects will indicate this by "are you still there?" statements. Again, know your subject as well as possible, and fine-tune your approach.

"I" Statements

People under extreme stress often become suspicious and defensive, and any statements that are too directive may sound like an insult or attack. In such circumstances, "Maybe you ought to . . ." will be interpreted as "You better or else . . ." To keep potentially accusatory-sounding "you's" out of the conversation, I-statements clue the subject in on what effect he's having on the negotiator's perception, while at the same time allowing for some subjectivity and personalization of the negotiator. The basic model is "I feel . . . when you . . . because . . ."

This technique may help defuse intense emotions, and may help refocus the HT during verbal attacks.

HT: You don't give a shit about me—all you want is to get these people out of here so you can blow me away. You're a goddam liar like the rest of them.
Negotiator: When you're yelling at me like that, it's hard for me to focus on what we're talking about.

I-statements can also be used to deflect the HT's demands and manipulations, especially when used with paraphrasing and the dumb-but-trying ("Detective Columbo") approach.

HT: You don't have that car here in 10 minutes, the bodies start piling up—you got that?
Negotiator: Give me a second to get all this, okay, 'cause when you're talking fast like that, it's hard for me to concentrate, and I want to make sure I

understand you completely. You're talking about getting transportation, is that it?

Open-Ended Questions

This technique has wide applicability in law enforcement work, from crisis negotiation to interview and interrogation. Here, the negotiator asks questions that cannot be answered with a simple yes-or-no. This encourages the subject to say more without the negotiator actually directing the conversation. This technique may be used in combination with other active listening techniques, such as minimal encouragers, reflecting/mirroring, and silence. As with interview techniques, open-ended questions can be followed or combined with closed-ended queries.

HT: Nothing ever works out for me. My whole damn life, it's been one screw-up after another.
Negotiator: Like what?
HT: What do you mean, "like what?" Everything, man, everything. It's all screwed up.
Negotiator: I really want to understand this. Can you give me an example?

DEMANDS AND DEADLINES

One of the defining characteristics of most hostage crises is the presence of some form of demand, which may range from the concrete and immediately practical (food, transportation) to the more grandiose and expansive (release of political prisoners, access to media) to the abstract, bizarre, or psychotic (freedom from CIA persecution; emancipation of downtrodden classes). Most demands will be of the first type, and most experts would agree with the following principles regarding such demands in hostage crises (Bolz, 1996; Lanceley, 1999; McMains & Mullins, 1996; Greenstone, 1995, 2005).

Demands: Negotiating Strategies

A fundamental guiding principle of hostage negotiations is to make the HT work for everything he gets by extracting a *concession in return*, no matter how small, for each demand satisfied. In essence, this is the basis for all types of negotiating, whether a business contract or a crisis resolution: get your counterpart used to saying yes and making concessions. Of course, if your business associate doesn't like the bid you put on the table, he's not likely to fly into a rage and kill innocent people. The challenge in hostage crises, then, is to maintain your bargaining position without unduly agitating the HT and triggering a violent confrontation. Also, you can use demands as a profiling and intelligence gathering tool: beyond basic physical needs, what a HT asks for in a crisis can yield clues to his personality and priorities.

Other guidelines include: don't ask the HT if there are any demands ("What do you want?"), don't offer anything not explicitly asked for, and don't deliver more than absolutely necessary to fulfill the request. The conventional wisdom is to never say "no" to a demand, but not saying no is not the same as saying yes. That is, deflect, postpone, and modify: "Okay, you want a helicopter out of here, right? I'll see what I can do about transportation. Meanwhile, tell me. . . ."

Don't give anything without getting something in return: "The electricity turned on? I'll work on that, but I'll need you do something for me, okay? Can you keep the phone line open so we can stay in contact while they're hooking up the cable?"

When negotiating for release of multiple hostages, start with the most vulnerable or least desirable, from the HT's standpoint. Where the hostages are strangers to the HT, as in the case of robberies, and where the HT has specific, utilitarian demands (food, escape), many HTs will relinquish hostages that they perceive as being "too much trouble" to keep around, such as sick or injured victims, children, or overly hysterical hostages, while holding on to the more healthy and manageable ones. As in any bargaining maneuver, let the HT make the first offer, that is, how many hostages he's willing to release. If only a few, you can try upping the ante, but only to a point—remember, better to get one or two people out safely now, rather than risk having the HT change his mind because he feels you're "pushing" him.

Where there is only one or a few hostages, and where the hostages are known to the HT, as in family hostage-barricade or workplace revenge scenarios, the situation is more precarious because the hostages have a particular personal or symbolic value to the HT. Additionally, in such cases, there is a greater chance that the HT is laboring under some kind of delusional disorder and may be suicidal. He may not care about negotiating for demands because he's already resolved to kill everyone in the room, including himself. In such cases, conventional hostage negotiating strategies may overlap with suicide intervention and other crisis intervention strategies.

Negotiable and Nonnegotiable Demands

In the broadest sense, *all* demands are negotiable, but whether the authorities will agree with certain demands varies widely depending on their safety and feasibility, what is at stake if the demands are not met, and what there is to gain by meeting the demands. While there may be exceptions in individual circumstances, the following principles are generally accepted by hostage negotiation professionals.

Negotiable demands include food, drinks, cigarettes, blankets, and environmental controls, such as heat, air conditioning, electricity, plumbing, and so on.

Nonnegotiable demands include illegal drugs, weapons, release of friends or relatives in prison, or exchange of hostages.

"Gray area" demands that may depend on the special circumstances and judgment of the negotiating team include alcohol, money, media access, transportation, or freedom.

Demands, Deadlines, and Time

A common feature of HT *demands* is that they often come with a *deadline*: "I want that car here by 12 noon, or someone's gonna get it." To begin with, although deadline demands are relatively common, very few deaths have actually occurred as the direct result of a deadline not being met, especially in more common robbery or domestic dispute hostage crises. Always assess each individual situation for risk.

Although this may seem obvious, don't set deadlines yourself. If the HT makes a deadline, log it, but don't mention it again to the HT if he doesn't bring it up. The goal is to ignore the deadline and let it pass by keeping the subject engaged in conversation. If there has been no conversation with the HT for a while, initiate contact prior to the deadline and keep him engaged, but don't bring up the deadline itself. Use the passage of time to expend adrenalin and let fatigue set it, but beware of total exhaustion which may lead to heightened irritability and impulsive action.

Problem-Solving Structure of Dealing with Hostage Taker's Demands

As always, the goal is not to provide a cookbook approach to negotiation, but as with all complex, team-based activities, most authorities believe that the negotiation process runs most smoothly if there is some kind of guiding framework or structure upon which the team members can then improvise as needed (Greenstone, 2005; Lanceley, 1999; McMains & Mullins, 1996). This is, in fact, the basic model of all crisis intervention in mental health and emergency services (Dattilio & Freeman, 2000; Flin, 1996; Gilliland & James, 1993; Greenstone & Leviton, 2001; Kleepsies, 1998; Miller, 1998). Basic elements of crisis intervention for dealing with demands in hostage scenarios include the following.

Define the problem. Question: What do we want to do here? Answer: Get everybody out safely.

Brainstorm solutions. What are some of the ways that we can achieve the goal of resolving this crisis without injury? Allow the HT to make suggestions and amend and supplement them with your own. Give the HT as much input into the problem-solving process as he is willing to provide, since people are more likely to stick with plans they've had a hand in crafting, otherwise known as "buy-in."

Eliminate unacceptable solutions. Some of the HT's suggestions and demands may be reasonable ("If I put down my weapon and let these people go, I don't want the shit beat out of me when I come out"), others may be clearly out of the question ("I need drugs and ammo"), and still others may be negotiable

("Give me some food and turn on the AC, and maybe we'll talk").

Choose the best possible solution. Try to narrow it down to one or two points that can be agreed upon for the present. "Okay, we're going to send in some McDonald's, and then you're going to let the women and the guy with the chest pain go, then you'll keep the phone line open, we'll turn the AC on, and we'll talk further, is that agreed?"

Plan the implementation. Whatever the choice of alternatives, make sure everybody understands exactly who's going to do what and when. Under states of extreme emotional tension, it only takes one small glitch to foul everything up: "So let's make sure we're all on the same page. Someone is going to put the food in the metal can by the stairs, then go back to our line. You're going to check the food, and if everything's okay, you're going to send the people out like we said. The chest pain guy is going to come out first, then the two women, one at a time. Then you'll get back on the phone and we'll turn the AC on. If you want to eat while we're talking, that's fine. By the way, is it okay if we send in a couple of extra burgers and Cokes for the other people?"

This last request can serve several purposes. Most obviously, it allows the hostages to be fed. But it also may reassure a suspicious HT who suspects that his food might be drugged or poisoned, because he can always switch the meals around with the hostages and he will usually assume that the authorities are not going to risk poisoning innocent civilians. Of course, overtly paranoid HTs will be reassured by nothing—but then, they are not likely to ask for potentially contaminated food in the first place.

Importantly, too, sharing a meal is a very intimate form of human interaction, and may encourage the development of the *Stockholm syndrome* (Fuselier, 1999; McMains & Mullins, 1996), in which initially adversarial captors and hostages, bound together through crisis under extreme emotional circumstances, come to develop a feeling for, and allegiance to, one another. In its original definition, the Stockholm syndrome describes the circumstance of hostages who develop sympathy for their captors and may go so far as to try to protect them and justify their actions. Reciprocally, the HTs grow to develop a grudging admiration and affection for their unwilling charges on the basis of sharing a prolonged, intense experience (mental health clinicians should think of the concepts of *transference* and *countertransference* in psychotherapy).

Usually, this kind of reaction is uncommon in hostage crises that last only a brief time, and almost always involves prolonged sieges lasting days or weeks, where captives and captors have the opportunity to share more and more intimate communication. For the more common hostage scenarios, negotiators can never count on such a connection taking place, but virtually all authorities agree that any positive communication or interaction, such as eating together or the HTs making provisions for the hostages' comfort and safety, will serve to humanize the hostages to the HTs and will lessen the chance of their being injured or killed (Giebels et al., 2005). As noted elsewhere, however, this may backfire with certain types of mentally disturbed HTs or HTs who purposefully select their victims, so always use caution and judgment.

Implement the plan. If possible, walk the HT through the steps that have been laid out in your mutual planning by keeping phone communication open at all times: "Good, I see the guy coming out. There's the first woman. Okay, there's number two, good. All right, you've kept your word, we've got your AC back on, and you've had something to eat. Now let's talk about you and everybody else coming out of this safely."

Assess the outcome. Whatever the action and its outcome, big or small—release of a hostage, delivery of food, opening of a phone line—assess and log how smoothly the deal went down, as this will provide a pretty good indicator of how subsequent negotiations will play out. If problems are identified, modify the approach accordingly.

Repeat and modify as necessary. Always be flexible. If the approach needs to be modified in light of new circumstances, do so.

Generally, the more time that has passed without injury, the more likely is a successful outcome to the crisis. The downside of time passage concerns the greater mental and physical exhaustion of the HT and the corresponding increased risk of impaired judgment or impulsive action. Exhaustion on the negotiator's part is usually dealt with by having several negotiators rotate during a prolonged crisis, although sometimes this is not an option.

SIGNS OF PROGRESS IN NEGOTIATION

No seasoned negotiator will categorically swear by any given index sign of negotiation progress, but most experts agree on some generally reliable prognosticators of how things are going (Greenstone, 1995; Lanceley, 1999; McMains & Mullins, 1996; Noeser, 1999).

Positive signs of negotiation progress include positive changes in the quality and content of the HT's communication. As the negotiation proceeds, the HT may seem to get more used to speaking with the negotiator. He will make more frequent verbal contact with the negotiator and sustain it for longer periods of time. There will be generally less violent and threatening content to the HT's speech, and he may begin to talk more about personal issues.

There may be signs of increased identification with, or sympathy for, the hostages ("Hell, I didn't want these people in here; it's not their fault these damn cops showed up"). Threats against hostages may decrease or cease, and deadlines may pass without incident. In some cases, this is because the HT is distracted from the passage of time by the negotiator's conversation, but in other cases, the HT may deliberately choose to let the deadline pass and use "forgetting" as a face-saving excuse.

Another positive sign is the HT asking about the procedures for, and consequences of, surrendering ("I'm not making any promises, but what would I have to do to get out of here without you guys killing me?"). Generally, the longer the passage of time without injury to hostages, the better the outlook. Of course, one important sign of progress is the release of hostages, but this may sometimes be a bad sign for the HT himself if it is a prelude to his own suicide.

Negative signs of negotiation progress include refusal of the HT to talk and/or lack of rapport between the HT and negotiator; indeed, if a basic communication fails to take place for any length of time, consideration should be given to using an alternate negotiator. An overtly suicidal HT is usually a bad sign because a HT who makes deadlines for his own death may very well be planning to take hostages with him. Suicidal HTs may make final plans or verbal wills, apologize to loved ones for the harm and shame they've caused, or call for clergy to come to the scene for confessions. Alternatively, a clearly depressed HT who denies suicidality and swears everything is "fine" may be at risk for impulsive suicide and hostage killing.

HTs who insist on face-to-face negotiations may be planning to go out with an audience. Similarly, a HT who insists that particular persons be brought to the scene may be planning a similarly dramatic finale. A notable absence of substantive demands or demands that are clearly outrageous may signal that the HT really doesn't intend to leave the scene alive.

Nonsuicidal HTs may also show a poor prognosis. Use of alcohol or drugs is usually a bad sign because of generally heightened excitability and lowered impulse control. HTs who repeatedly become angry and emotional during negotiations may also be at risk for impulsive violence. A weapon tied to a hostage or, in the case of more sophisticated HTs, wiring the surroundings with explosives, may signal a low regard for innocent human life on the part of the HTs. The latter cases typically involve well-planned hostage-taking activities, such as those carried out by professional criminals or organized extremist groups (Miller, in press-b).

HOSTAGE NEGOTIATION WITH MENTALLY DISORDERED SUBJECTS

Except for political terrorism or the Hollywood-style "grand heist," most HTs that local police departments will have to contend with will either be of the common-criminal-caught-in-a-robbery type or will have some kind of diagnosable mental disorder, the latter being more common in domestic and workplace hostage situations. Thus, to be truly effective, negotiators need to wed the art and science of crisis management to the insights on personality and psychopathology offered by mental health professionals (alsosee Chapter 4). It is in this aspect of hostage and crisis negotiation that the police psychologist can make an especially important contribution (Borum, 1988; Borum & Strenz, 1992; Corcoran & Cawood, 2003; Lanceley, 1999; McMains, 1988a, 1988b; McMains & Mullins, 1996; Miller, in press-a; Rodriguez & Franklin, 1986; Rogan, 1997; Russell & Beigel, 1990; Slatkin, 2003, 2005).

Schizophrenic Hostage Takers

Schizophrenia is a major mental disorder characterized by disruption and disorganization in thinking and behavior, impaired emotional experience and expression, and the presence of delusions and hallucinations. Most schizophrenic hallucinations are auditory *persecutory hallucinations* that involve hearing voices that degrade and demean the subject. These subjects are usually in a state of extreme fear and agitation in response to these hallucinations. The second most common type of hallucination is the *command hallucination*, which orders the subject to do something.

Frequently, persecutory and command hallucinations occur together, along with corresponding delusions. For example, voices may tell the subject that he is vile and wicked, and the only way to atone for his sins is to "save" his ex-wife and children from her new boyfriend. Or the subject may interpret a TV newscast about airport security as warning him about his former boss's attempts to plant a monitoring device in his body. If the subject is already predisposed to aggressive behavior, the response to these delusions and hallucinations may take the form of violence, from impulsive attacks on the street to well-planned, Rambo-like tactical campaigns involving weapons and hostages.

In negotiating with a schizophrenic HT, remember that the predominant underlying emotion is likely to be some combination of fear and anger, so the use of calming techniques may seem like the obvious choice. However, schizophrenic subjects tend to be less responsive to normal emotional cues, so don't expect a close correspondence between your active listening interventions and the subject's response. Often the basis for rapport in these situations comes from the subject's need to explain himself and his motives, so by all means let him talk, interjecting only when his speech tone and content reflect an extreme escalation that might lead to violence.

In dealing with the schizophrenic HT's delusions, a kind of constructive ambivalence may prove the most effective intervention. That is, neither agree nor disagree with the delusional ideas or motives. On the one hand, attempting to falsely buy in to the subject's delusional system may come off as phony and insincere and thus erode rapport—remember, even psychotic subjects are not necessarily stupid, and they may know if you're playing them. On the other hand, trying to "talk some sense" into the subject will be equally ineffective, and may quickly brand you as just another treacherous enemy. A better strategy is to acknowledge the content of the delusion and try to ally yourself with the subject's perspective and perception of the situation, while keeping the focus on present reality. This is actually an application of more general rapport-building active listening skills to the specific case of a delusional subject.

Negotiator: Let me understand this. The people with you in that Workers Compensation office have been monitoring your home computer and your car and telling you to commit sex crimes so they can blackmail you and discredit your disability claim. Is that right?

HT: No, that's not it. You just don't get it. Why is it so hard for everybody to understand?

Negotiator: Okay, sorry, please explain it to me again slowly, because I want to make sure I understand what you're telling me.

HT: [Explains the conspiracy again and asks for confirmation] "Okay, now do you see what I'm up against?

Negotiator: Well to be honest with you, I don't have the electronics expertise to know how they can set up these things, but if that's what you think they're doing, it must make you feel pretty mad and scared. I wonder if there's a way to get more information on this before anyone gets hurt.

In negotiating with schizophrenic subjects, some authorities recommend avoiding the use of, or reference to, family members, as they may be part of the HT's delusional system. Again, use your judgment, based on your knowledge of the subject and the situation. Also be aware that such subjects may have had unpleasant experiences in the past with mental health professionals and the general health care system, so this is one area where the team psychologist may want to take a backseat role. In addition, schizophrenic subjects may be especially sensitive to having their belief systems–which are very real to them–dismissed as delusions by mental health "experts." In either case, be careful about offering the schizophrenic HT any kind of psychological interpretation or "therapy," which may only serve to further alienate and infuriate the subject.

As with family members, if the HT requests to speak to a particular mental health clinician, try to ascertain the subject's agenda to avoid giving the subject a forum for violently acting out. In some cases, however, a trusted therapist–or clergyperson or other confidante–may be the only person who can connect with the disturbed HT sufficiently to nudge a stalled negotiation process in a productive direction.

Paranoid Hostage Takers

This diagnostic category will often overlap with the above one in the form of paranoid schizophrenia, characterized by paranoid delusions and persecutory hallucinations (Chapter 4). However, all levels of paranoia can be seen in psychological practice, and even subjects who are not overtly psychotic may harbor self-referential beliefs that only boil to the surface under stress. Many of these individuals are able to hold a job and maintain a semblance of a normal lifestyle, all the while possessed of an unshakable conviction about religious, political, or familial conspiracies that they must be ever vigilant and on guard about. If confronted with an overwhelming crisis, paranoid individuals may feel compelled to take drastic action in their own defense, which may include violence and hostage taking.

In negotiating with a paranoid HT, forget about changing his mind or reasoning him out of his belief. One of the characteristics of paranoid beliefs is their imperviousness to disputation. Paranoid subjects are also exquisitely sensitive to attempts to fool or manipulate them and are often quite perceptive in this regard, so stay away from tricks and strategems as much as possible. Straightforwardness and calmness are the keys to a successful negotiation with this subject.

Open negotiations in a logical, factual, respectful, and unemotional manner: "Mr. Jones, this is Sgt. Bruce McGill, a negotiator for the Municipal Police Department. I want to hear your side of this so we can keep everyone safe." Keep your voice calm and even, but not at such a monotone that it sounds contrived and artificial. Ask for the subject's view of the situation and request clarification if necessary. If the subject gets angry, keep your cool and request further clarification of the subject's complaint. Allow productive ventilation, but beware of the subject self-escalating himself into a rage. If this starts to happen, utilize distraction techniques, again, without being too obvious about it. As with schizophrenic subjects, if frankly delusional material comes up, try to sidestep it, but without making the subject think you're dismissing or disrespecting him.

A particularly sensitive issue with paranoid HTs regards the use of rapport. For the most part, any attempt to "get close" to a paranoid subject is likely to be interpreted as an attempt to attack or manipulate him, so negotiators need to tread a thin line between being too cold and standoffish versus trying to be too inclusive and engaging. Keep things clear and direct and focus the negotiation on solving concrete problems.

HT: They're all trying to destroy me, my company, my ex-wife, and now you damn cops. What do I have to do to convince you I mean business!

Negotiator: The police are here, the paramedics are here, and I'm here to see that nobody gets hurt. I don't know about those others, but once everybody's safe, I'd bet people would be more likely to listen to your point.

Depressed Hostage Takers

Depression in HTs presents a different kind of problem for negotiators. Initially, at least, most HTs have either escape or some intrumental goal on their minds. In most cases, they want to survive. This leaves some negotiating room because the HTs and negotiators have something to offer each other.

On the other hand, depressed subjects may be despondent and suicidal and therefore especially dangerous precisely because they have nothing to lose by taking hostages to the grave with them. If one or more of the hostages has a bad past history with the HT, such as a hated boss or estranged family member, there may be no substantive demands aside from an audience for their act of desperate revenge. Other depressed hostages may not be overtly suicidal but may still be relatively unresponsive to a negotiated settlement due to simple emotional and behavioral inertia, sometimes associated with older age and a feeling of "nothing left to live for."

Without overpatronizing, the stance of a nurturant parental model or supportive authority figure may appeal to a depressed subject because it provides a framework of structure and control. Don't verbally "rush" the subject; rather, begin the conversation at a slow pace and gradually pick up the tempo as you go along. Begin with open-ended questions and allow for long pauses before the answers come. If this goes nowhere, ask simple, direct, closed-ended questions. Use reflection of feelings as necessary. If the subject begins to dwell on a painful, unjust past or a bleak, purposeless future, try to keep the time perspective grounded in the present. Avoid deep religious or philosophical issues, if possible, but if the subject seems intent on discussing these, let him speak, and use gentle verbal direction to keep things focused on the here-and-now.

If the subject brings up suicide, address it forthrightly. If he doesn't explicitly mention it, but nevertheless seems suicidal, gently inquire. Ask what he's thinking of doing. Usually, attempts to "talk him out of it" are of little avail, but find out what's important to him, and try to give him a glimpse of a better future. Avoid admonishments along the lines of, "Think how your kids will feel if you kill yourself." Remember, a suicidally depressed subject already feels worthless and hopeless—you don't want to add to that.

A better strategy is to "postpone" the suicide, rather than attempt to dissuade: "Look, William, I know you think this is the only way out now, but give me an hour, okay? I know I can't talk you out of what you're gonna do, but let me understand why this is happening, okay? I really want to understand

this." If there seems to be an opening, offer the promise of immediate help, i.e., if the subject works with you to end this crisis without harm, you'll see that he gets taken to someplace safe to talk to someone right away. Be sure to be able to back up this promise.

Finally, be careful of the depressed, suicidal subject who suddenly seems to get better, and whose mood improves without any substantive reason. He may have made his peace with death and is planning to check out imminently, perhaps taking hostages with him. This may be a good time to inquire about any unstated intentions on the HT's part and deal with them accordingly. It is in situations like these that the incident commander's decision to go tactical may be especially difficult, because the depressed HT's quiet resignation may seem less overtly threatening than the loud, overtly violent paranoid or psychopathic HT, even though all three may be equally lethal.

Avoidant-Dependent Hostage Takers

Avoidant personality is a pattern of social inhibition, feelings of inadequacy, and hypersensitivity to negative evaluation or criticism. Dependent personality is a pattern of submissive and clinging behavior stemming from an excessive need for care and guidance. Often, these two personality types are combined, with the subject generally being shy and socially anxious, but latching onto one person, who becomes the psychological lifeline to the subject's sense of identity and purpose in life. If he or she then experiences rejection or separation from that person, it will feel like the end of the world, and the subject will do *anything* to restore that connection, including pleading, threatening, stalking, and perhaps hostage-taking to convince the rejecting person to "take me back—or else." Many domestic violence perpetrators fit this profile, as do the more rare female HT.

In negotiating with an avoidant-dependent HT, try to provide a firm, supportive presence, in essence becoming the new, if temporary, parental figure. It is very important for the negotiator to help the insecure avoidant-dependent HT find a resolution to the crisis that doesn't leave him feeling like he's failed again, which may impel him to do something even more desperate "to show them I mean business." Let the initial ideas for peaceful resolution come from the HT, expand and refine them with your own good suggestions and, as much as possible, make it seem like everything positive that happens is the subject's idea, adding your own mentor-like praise and support. It's also a good idea to keep friends and relatives away from the scene so that the subject is not tempted to prove himself by "going out like a man."

Antisocial/Psychopathic Hostage Takers

Antisocial personality is a pattern of consistent disregard for, and violation of, the rights of others, associated with impulsivity, criminal behavior, sexual promiscuity, substance abuse, and an exploitive parasitic, and/or predatory lifestyle. Even more than other types of criminals, the antisocial personality is distinguished by an utter lack of conscience that allows him to regard other people simply as sources of his own gratification. Antisocial personalities, sometimes referred to as *psychopaths*, are ruthless and remorseless, but can also be quite shrewd in a cunning-conning type of way, and are often geniuses at manipulating and intimidating those around them.

Forget the Stockholm syndrome. Their complete self-centeredness and paucity of any real human attachment makes it probable that hostages will represent nothing more than human bargaining chips to antisocial HTs, to enable them to achieve some utilitarian purpose, for example in robberies, police pursuits, or prison escapes. The antisocial HT won't give a damn about your concerns for his or the hostages' safety, and will at best be amused by your attempts to commiserate with his existential angst, because he doesn't have any. If the hostage-taking wasn't cold-bloodedly planned in advance as a means of escape, then it is likely to be a crime of impulse—but not passion. The hostages are objects, pure and simple, and he could care less whether they live or die, as long as he gets what he wants.

What he wants, of course, is to escape—or at least to avoid serious consequences of his actions. Paradoxically, the antisocial HT's very coldbloodedness can actually facilitate negotiations if you can convince him that sparing lives is the easiest way for him to at least partially achieve his objective. Forget touchy-feely empathy; in this type of negotiation,

you are literally *negotiating*. Appeal to his self-interest: releasing at least some of the hostages leaves you with less baggage to deal with; a goodwill gesture may result in a lighter penalty; don't give the SWAT guys an excuse to move in and take you out; and so on.

Even more so that for other HTs, a key element in negotiation with antisocial subjects is the tried-and-true adage: don't try to outbullshit a bullshitter. Antisocial personalities live by their wits and their strength, and their greatest thrill comes from conning and intimidating other people. At the same time, much like the paranoid, they are exquisitely sensitive to being fooled themselves, and may react with rage if they think you're trying to play them. Promise only what you can deliver.

Tone-wise, a reasonable, problem-solving approach probably works best—involved, but unemotional. You want to keep things somewhat bland because psychopaths are power-trippers and thrill-seekers, and the last thing you want to do is egg him on; at the same time, you don't want things to get too draggy, or the subject may feel the need to do something exciting to pump up the adrenalin quotient. Also remember that while antisocial HTs typically have utilitarian aims, occasionally revenge is the primary motive, as these individuals are notorious for holding grudges and valuing payback. To keep the HT's mind off the hostages, keep him busy with you, the negotiator. Be as straightforward as possible, and realize that virtually nothing he says can be taken at face value.

Again, keep in mind this stark paradox: The antisocial HT is most likely to spare hostages if this achieves his goals because he's the least likely to be emotionally involved with them, but this very human disconnection makes him the most likely to slaughter a hostage in the blink of an eye if he thinks that's what it takes to convince you of his determination and power. Negotiate cautiously and straightforwardly.

Borderline Hostage-Takers

Borderline personality is a pattern of instability in interpersonal relationships, fragile self-image, wild emotional swings, vengeful anger, and self-damaging impulsiveness. Such individuals may exhibit a lifelong pattern of erratic and intense relationships, alternating between overidealization and devaluation of friends, family members, and coworkers. Signs of emotional instability include inappropriately intense anger and/or depressive mood swings and possible suicidality. Persistent identity disruption may manifest itself in disturbances in self-image, blurred interpersonal boundaries and relationships, confused professional and personal goals and values, and a chronic feeling of emptiness that may impel the quest for stimulation via substance abuse or provocation of hostile incidents. Many borderlines function well–even superbly–in the eyes of casual observers, only decompensating into minipsychotic episodes under external or self-induced stress.

The borderline hostage situation is most likely to be relationship-based, as in the case of an estranged family member or fired worker coming back to home or jobsite to even the score of a real or imagined betrayal. White-hot righteous anger is often the key motivating emotion, as borderlines' scorched-earth policies toward those who have spurned them blot out any glint of reason or empathy. In hostage situations, such subjects may make no demands at all–they just want their victim to suffer. Or they may make unreasonable demands, such as oaths of unending loyalty from the erstwhile mate, or access to unlimited material possessions of the hated party, or a media-broadcast apology by all the heads of the company that mistreated them.

With borderline HTs, use the relationship factor to your advantage. Careful application of active listening techniques will help build rapport and diffuse toxic emotions. Try to show the subject that you're on his or her side by providing soothing reassurance, empathy, support, and structure. Interestingly, many borderlines are so starved for nurturant human connection that they may be unusually susceptible to such rapport-building approaches. The downside is that their feelings can turn on a dime: when they feel you've connected with them, they completely love and trust you, but once they believe you've crossed them or let them down, they want you worse than dead.

For similar reasons, be wary of the Stockholm syndrome. Especially in domestic or workplace crises, borderline HTs are likely to *already* have superheated emotional relationships with their hostages, probably not good ones, and here you want to keep the focus off these relationship and on the current interaction with you in safely resolving the situation. So carefully take your cue from the subject. Commiserate and try to understand. Be alert for signs of suicide or violence. Try to preclude impulsive action by gently guiding the subject to alternatives or switching the focus to the reasons for their pain and outrage. As with other types of HTs, encourage talking, but be cautious not to let blowing off steam escalate into volcanic loss of control. Be especially careful about involving family members or other third parties, who may inflame the situation.

COMING OUT: THE SURRENDER RITUAL

Nobody likes to surrender, to give up, to capitulate, to lose. Yet, by definition, the successful resolution of a hostage crisis entails the safe release of the hostages and surrender of the HT to authorities. Thus, anything the negotiating team can do to make this action easier for the HT will work in favor of saving lives. On the strength of practical experience from many sources, a basic protocol, or *surrender ritual*, has evolved to guide negotiators in their efforts to safely resolve a crisis (Greenstone, 1995, 2005; Lanceley, 1999; McMains & Mullins, 1996). As with all such guidelines, each negotiator must adapt this system to his or her particular situation and type of HT.

To begin with, understand that a HT usually has only four possible options: (1) surrender, (2) escape, (3) suicide, or (4) killing of hostages. Only the first option is preferred by law enforcement, although a HT's nonviolent escape (option 2) at least spares hostages and may enable authorities to track the suspect down later. Trying to manipulate or browbeat a HT into capitulation may have the opposite effect because few people want to give up as a sign of weakness. Rather, a successful resolution will usually involve allowing the HT to come out on his own with as much dignity preserved as possible.

Aside from release of hostages, the subject's surrender is the most critical aspect of the negotiation, so great care and preparation should be taken for this event. Certainly, everyone on the negotiating and tactical teams needs to be on the same page, and any plan must be understood, agreed to, and followed by all. To be clear with the HT, the crisis team must be clear within itself. Work out how the HT will come out, how the arrest will be made, and what will happen next. Remember, the team's initial version of the plan is not the last word; the plan may go back and forth between the negotiator and the HT until a mutually agreeable sequence is established. At this early phase, you need to establish with the team what are the limits of acceptable and unacceptable terms, and what are the practical constraints of the situation.

Having said this, there may be occasions where the HT just spontaneously offers to give up and come out. If this happens, great. Work out a safe deal as quickly as possible and let him come out. But these situations are likely to be the exceptions; in most cases, getting the HT to surrender will be a long, delicate process.

Watch your language. When dealing with the HT, avoid the use of words like "surrender," "give up," or other terms that connote weakness and loss of face. Use whatever euphemisms seem appropriate: *"coming out"* is a preferred term because it implies a proactive decision by the subject himself to resolve the crisis. Even amongst team members, get in the habit of using these positive terms, making it less likely that "surrender" slips out during conversations with the HT—remember, everyone is stressed and exhausted.

To begin the discussion of coming out, emphasize to the HT what he has to gain by this action at the present time. Be realistic but optimistic. Minimize any damage done so far. This is relatively easy where no one has yet been seriously harmed, but in cases where hostages have already been injured or even killed, you may have to be creative in your reassurances. The basic strategy is to emphasize what bad things have *not* happened and the subject's role in preventing further harm: "We understand you felt you had no choice but to shoot that guard when he went for his gun—it was a split-second decision, right? But I want to thank you for keeping rest of those people in the bank safe while we talked this out. That's going to count for a lot if we can end this now without anyone else getting hurt."

Find out what assurances are needed by the HT and if the team can accommodate them. Be sensitive to personal and cultural issues involving pride and respect. Discuss various coming-out scenarios and identify a mutually acceptable plan. Here's where the real "negotiating" aspect comes in, which may involve some good old-fashioned horse-trading, as you go back and forth, discussing scenarios and conditions. As in any kind of negotiation, the more buy-in the subject has, the more he feels the plan is his own as well as yours, the more likely he is to comply. In planning for a successful resolution, let the subject set the pace; if he is agreeing to come out at all, this is not the time to rush things.

Once the final plan is put together, the task now becomes making sure everybody understands what they're supposed to do. This is superhigh-adrenalin territory; a misunderstanding or misstep could blow the whole deal and cost lives. First, clarify the plan with the negotiating and tactical teams. Then, carefully explain to the HT what will happen and what to expect. Be as explicit as possible—explain what the subject will see and hear and what he should do. When you've completed your account, ask the subject to repeat it back to you. Make it clear to him that this rehearsal is not because you distrust him or think he's stupid, but for his own safety and to make sure everybody follows the agreement he and you have worked out. For example:

Negotiator: Okay, here's what we agreed on. You're going to take off your jacket so everyone can see you in the tee-shirt, see that you're not hiding anything. Don't carry anything out or have anything in your hands or pockets. Open the front door slowly with your left hand and keep your right hand on your head. When you step out onto the front porch, slowly put your right hand on your head, too. Then drop slowly to your knees and keep your hands on your head. I know it's raining, so if you start to slip, just ease yourself to the ground and make sure we can always see your hands. Remember, the word is slow, slow, slow—no sudden moves. When you're on the ground, you'll see the SWAT guys approach you. They'll probably have their weapons drawn, and one of them will have a large black shield, so don't move; it's just their normal procedure. If they order you to lie down and put your hands behind your back, do it.

Do whatever they tell you. They're going to cuff you. They may seem a little rough, but they're not trying to hurt you, they've just got to restrain you, that's their procedure. After they're sure you're secure, they'll either walk you or carry you to the holding area, and one of our team will meet you there. We want to make sure this goes smoothly like we planned, so tell it back to me like I just explained it."

In some instances, a confused, delusional, ambivalent, or suicidal subject may emerge with an actual weapon in his hand and offer to surrender it to authorities. In other cases, he may have the weapon inside the structure and offer to give it to you prior to his coming out or in lieu of surrendering, as a kind of goodwill gesture. In such cases, apply the protocols and recommendations for disarming suspects. Never offer to take a loaded weapon from a subject's hands. If he offers the weapon, ask him to unload it and to throw the weapon out the window. Alternatively, ask him to leave it unloaded in a safe place inside the dwelling and come out empty-handed as planned. Sometimes, surrendering HTs want to come out with a cell phone, prized keepsake, or other seemingly harmless object. Make it clear to him that *anything* in his hand or on his person may be mistaken for a weapon and will put him in danger of being shot: "Let's not leave anything to chance, okay? Just come out with *nothing*. Whatever's important in there we can always go back and get later, but it's not worth getting yourself killed."

While following standard procedures for control and restraint, the tactical team should avoid any unnecessary verbal or physical roughness during the arrest. In keeping with the strict division of negotiating and tactical roles, the negotiator should not be the arresting offer. During and after the arrest, the negotiator should maintain engagement, rapport, and communication with the HT. If possible, and after any necessary on-scene first aid has been applied and the subject has been read his Miranda rights, a brief informational debriefing with the HT should occur in a secure place close to the scene. This is to gather any information that might be forgotten or discarded later on and also gives the negotiator the opportunity to praise the subject for his contribution to successfully resolving this crisis. Why?

Remember the point about "repeat customers" in the criminal justice system. Although a certain degree of verbal suasion and manipulation is integral to a successful resolution of a hostage crisis, you really don't want the subject to think that the whole negotiation was some kind of trick to get him to give up, because this may have dire repercussions for future communications and interactions with the same or different subjects, whether they involve hostage-taking or not. In a very real sense, the negotiation is never really over, even during the arrest and informational debriefing, and throughout the trial and incarceration process. You want your team and your department to maintain the reputation of being tough but fair and honorable throughout all your interactions with the community. Always be looking ahead to the next incident.

HOSTAGE REACTIONS

So far, very little has been said about the hostages themselves. Good community-oriented law enforcement would dictate that these most special of crime victims be given the care and treatment they deserve.

Positive and Negative Survival Predictors

Posttraumatic stress reactions of crime victims are described in Chapter 3. Although each crisis has its own unique characteristics and circumstances, re-

search has shown that certain types of hostage traits and behaviors seem to predict who will survive a crisis and who will succumb (McMains & Mullins, 1996). In this sense, "survival" has a dual meaning: first, literally surviving by living through the hostage crisis, and second, surviving and recovering emotionally in the aftermath versus succumbing to PTSD or other posttraumatic psychological disorders.

In general, *survivors* of a hostage crisis avoid standing out as a target and are able to blend in with the other hostages, not trying to be spokespersons or leaders. They contain outward emotional expressions of fear or anger, keep a low profile, stay away from debates or confrontations, and obey reasonable orders from the HTs. They are able to project an overall attitude of calmness and confidence, but not cockiness or disrespect. They are able to accept and adjust to the currently helpless situation, yet retain faith in rescue and a positive outcome, utilizing constructive humor and imagery. They rely on positive fantasy and daydreaming about loved ones and other personally important things. If possible, they form affiliations with other hostages to help each other "get through this." During prolonged hostage sieges, they try to get some rest, if possible.

Succumbers, by contrast, make themselves dangerously conspicuous by showing hostility, acting defiantly, and trying to take charge in a leadership role. Alternatively, they may act overanxious and panicky, be overcompliant, subservient, and accommodating to the HTs, and may plead and beg. This serves both to raise the overall anxiety level of the other hostages and to irritate the HTs, who may view such behavior as a sign of sniveling weakness or just too much damn trouble—all of which emotionally destabilizes the situation and increases the risk of violence. Succumbers also show poor coping skills, focusing on their abandonment and hopelessness of the situation, and despairing of rescue. They tend to isolate themselves from the other hostages, and indeed, the others may reject such "downers." They also allow themselves to become fatigued and exhausted, further destabilizing the situation.

Recommendations for Hostages During a Crisis

Research in the area of hostage reactions has led to some specific recommendations for those who find themselves taken hostage. Obviously, this is the kind of information that is most useful prior to such a situation, and may have limited benefit in a postincident debriefing, but many organizations are including such recommendations for possible hostages-to-be in their crisis-management training. Indeed, this is becoming standard practice for training modules in political and corporate crisis prevention and management (Corcoran & Cawood,

2003; June, 1999, 2000; Katz & Caspi, 2003; McMains & Mullins, 1996).

First, remember that the first 15 to 45 minutes of a hostage situation are the most dangerous. If you're caught in a hostage crisis, stay as calm as possible until the situation has at least stabilized. Also understand that time is usually on your side: the longer you and the HT are together, the less likelihood of harm. During the initial stages, and afterward, follow any reasonable instructions by the HT that don't endanger your life. When things seem to have calmed down, you may inform the HT of any injuries or other medical needs, but be careful of overwhelming or irritating him. Otherwise, speak only when spoken to and answer questions concisely, without blathering.

In general, be cooperative and don't argue. Body language is also important. Don't stare at the HT but don't turn your back on him either, unless he tells you to. Resist the temptation to ingratiate yourself with the HT by offering suggestions or help; if he asks a specific question, give him a specific answer to that question.

HT: Is there a back door to this place?
Hostage: Behind the bathroom.
HT: Where the fuck is the bathroom?
Hostage: [points] At the end of that wall, just around the corner. First door is the bathroom, next door is the back exit.

Advice to stay calm in a life-threatening situation may seem like a contradiction in terms, but try to be patient, have faith, and get some rest. Unlike the quick wrap-ups seen on TV, many real-life hostage crises can last many hours or even days; don't exhaust yourself. Remember, a resting or even a sleeping hostage is a less threatening target for the HT. If permitted by the HT, maintain affiliation and positive communication with the other hostages. To pass the time constructively and to avoid emotionally corrosive rumination, utilize fantasy and daydreaming about loved ones and positive plans for the future. Another time-passer is observing the surrounding environment and events for later debriefing by law enforcement, but don't be too obvious about this. If the HT lets you speak to authorities on the phone, use yes-and-no answers; the authorities will probably ask you to do this anyway.

A difficult decision sometimes involves efforts to escape, and there is no generally agreed-upon rule for this. A consensus seems to be that if you are in no immediate danger, attempts at escape may only inflame the HT and lead to retaliation, or at least to more restrictive and confining conditions for you and the other hostages. However, if you are being ordered to do something clearly dangerous, and/or the situation appears to be deteriorating into a potential for real violence, you may have to do whatever you can to save yourself. This will probably be the toughest decision you'll ever make, but remember that the overwhelming majority of hostage crises are resolved without casualties. So trying to escape on your own should always be a last resort in circumstances of immediate danger. Also recall that the second most dangerous time in a hostage crisis is during a tactical rescue attempt, so if such an action does occur, stay down and obey the instructions of the incoming tactical team.

On-Scene Debriefing of Hostages

Sometimes, the only opportunity law enforcement authorities will get to interview hostages is immediately following the crisis, either on-scene or close to it. Many of the basic recommendations for interviewing crime victims in general (Chapter 3) can be adapted to the special case of hostage crisis survivors (Bolz et al., 1996; McMains & Mullins, 1996).

First, realize that you will be dealing with people whose reaction to their recent ordeal may range from numbed disorientation to wild panic. Obviously, arrange for any medical or mental health first aid that can be applied on the scene. Interview victims in as safe and comfortable environment as possible, and as a further empowering tool, allow victims to choose the site ("I don't want to sit in that cramped truck, can't we just walk around while we talk?"). Allow the victim to ventilate; don't rush questions. Even though finally rescued, former hostages may resent that "it took so long," or that the rescuers were unnecessarily rough with everybody till they sorted out who's who. Therefore, explain why authorities acted as they did and answer any reasonable questions. In general, while gratitude is often shown by rescued hostages, authorities should understand that "sometimes the price that law enforcement pays for a living hostage is an angry hostage" (Jack Maxwell, personal communication).

Another common postcrisis emotion of hostages is guilt or self-doubt about something they did, or failed to do, or should have done during the crisis. Accordingly, reassure the ex-hostages that they acted properly and did whatever they could under the circumstances. To further empower them, ask hostages what advice they may have for negotiators in future crises ("We want to learn from your experience"). Also, keep the hostages' families in the loop, and refer the hostages and their families for further medical, mental health, or social services, if needed.

In many cases, some of the hostages may be released while others are still held captive. In these situations, good intelligence based on careful and sensitive interview of the just-released hostages may be essential for resolving the crisis without further violence.

HOSTAGE-TAKING-BY-COP

It is rare, but not unknown, for a current or former law enforcement officer to become a criminal perpetrator involving hostage-taking as either a planned or inadvertent part of the criminal act. Most frequently, this takes place in the context of a domestic dispute. The FBI reports 22 incidents of a barricaded or suicidal officer between 1995 and 2002. The actual number may be higher than that, since fellow officers may attempt to protect one of their own from embarrassment by attempting to resolve the incident quietly and privately. Whether or not the producers were aware of it, the protagonist in the movie, *The Negotiator*, actually has a precedent in at least one case of a former hostage negotiator himself becoming the principal subject in a hostage crisis. Nevertheless, such cases of what could well be called *hostage-taking-by-cop* (HTBC) actually respond fairly well to the usual negotiation format, but this particular HT's knowledge of negotiating strategies, as well as the reactions of his

172 Practical Police Psychology: Stress Management and Crisis Intervention for Law Enforcement

fellow officers to the crisis, will require some special considerations (Russell & Zuniga, 1986; Terhune-Bickler, 2004).

HTBC: Officer Profile

Since this special type of crisis is rare, there is not much of a database on such individuals. But extrapolating from the few existing cases that have been reported, the profile of a HTBC perpetrator turns out to be not that different from other officers in crisis, such as potentially suicidal officers (Chapter 11). The typical HTBC officer is in his late twenties to early thirties with at least five years of service. A major source of stress is often family or relationship problems, and he may have just experienced, or be on the verge of, a painful divorce or separation. He is known as being a "cop's cop," very dedicated and invested in his job and identity as a law enforcement officer. He is no stranger to crisis and may have had several incidents of overzealous police work result in citizen complaints of excessive force or other improprieties (Chapter 13). There may also be a history of domestic violence or other violence, with several police calls to his home.

The hostage crisis usually involves family members and may begin when cumulatively mounting stresses of severed relationships and threatened loss of his job exceed his coping skills and drive him over the edge, to the point where he sees no way out. Such cases may be particularly dangerous when they are associated with substance abuse and suicidality. As one such subject in a recent Florida case put it, "If I can't live like a cop, I'll die like a cop" (Jack Maxwell, personal communication).

HTBC: Effects on Other Officers

Policing is a stressful profession, and a number of the officers I've worked with have wondered out loud about what it would take for them to "snap"— far more have probably wondered the same thing to themselves. So when one of their colleagues does go off the deep end in any way, it's extremely traumatic for fellow officers because of the strong identification factor. This often expresses itself through the twin reactions of fear and anger. The anger may be focused on the fact that the offending officer

should "know better" than to force his brother officers to put their lives on the line, because he well understands how dangerous these situations can get and what a strain they are on all personnel involved.

Even though angry, however, the loyalty factor to a brother officer can compromise the tactical response. Snipers and SWAT team members may question whether, if it came down to it, they could take out one of their own. In situations where split-second decision-making has life-and-death consequences, any such doubts and hesitations can be lethal. From the negotiating end, the officer-HT probably is familiar with the protocols and routines, and may be less responsive than the civilian HT. Nevertheless, human nature is still human nature, and in the few cases that have been successfully resolved, much the same kind of rapport-building negotiation has worked for officer-HTs as with others. Indeed, especially in these cases, the empathy factor based on mutuality of experience ("I've been there too, pal") may actually work to the advantage of the law enforcement negotiator.

Yet, this very identification factor can serve as a powerful deterrent factor to the officer-HT surrendering. The average civilian can rationalize his HT action by saying that he just went crazy under pressure and didn't realize the full scope and consequences of his actions, but a police officer is supposed to know better. Added to whatever stress already impelled this action is the potential shame that the surrendering officer will endure among his colleagues and the police community. Even if no injuries have occurred, the officer knows he will face arrest and possibly prison. And even if he avoids jail time, his career is over. Added to shame within his police family is that within his home family and community, fueled by the media frenzy that invariably attends "psycho-cop" stories. It may thus be easy for such officers to assume that there is "no way out." Such crises will therefore require exquisite skill to resolve successfully.

HTBC: Negotiating Recommendations

Use the empathy factor to your advantage. As a fellow officer, you know the kinds of job-related and personal stresses that can cause cops to burn out (Chapters 13 and 14). Keep it real but supportive. Without trying to sugar-coat the nature and consequences of his actions, provide the officer-HT with realistic hope as an antidote to overwhelming shame and despair.

Negotiator. Look, Frank, we've all been strung out like this, and something extra must have driven you to this point. I'm not gonna lie to you, this ain't exactly the best thing you could've done. The guys are gonna talk shit all over this, you know that, but deep down they understand what's going on' cause a lot of them have been close to falling in that hole themselves—maybe they just didn't have everything pile up all at once like you did. But let's just switch places for a minute—if you were us and, in spite of everything that's gone down, the guy inside decided to do the right thing and come out with everybody safe, wouldn't you have at least some respect for that guy? Knowing what he knows and still doing the right thing? Hey, no matter happens after you come out, I promise you won't go through this alone.

Finally, whatever happens in the aftermath, the best support for the officer will be from his close family members and from colleagues who really understand and want to help. Mental health clinicians who deal with such officers should make judicious use of these resources, when appropriate.

CONCLUSIONS

Few police operations combine the features of extreme danger to life, prolonged interpersonal dialogue under stressed conditions, fatigue, and emotional swings as do hostage negotiations. The good news is that the negotiation process is effective in preventing loss of life in 95 percent of cases—I wonder how many emergency medical procedures can boast a record like that. Indeed, the success of hostage negotiation strategies may be one of the best arguments for the inclusion of the principles of practical psychology as an essential component of law enforcement training.

Chapter 10

SUICIDE BY COP

As we saw in Chapter 7, an officer-involved shooting can be a stressful critical incident for many officers. More disturbing still is a special subset or kind of officer-involved shooting where the victim essentially "forces" the officer to be an unwilling instrument of his destruction.

The idea that a suspect would deliberately expose himself to police gunfire in order to effect his own death has probably long been familiar to officers, but the phenomenon was first formally articulated by Wolfgang in 1959, and the actual term *suicide by cop* was coined by police psychologist and sworn officer Karl Harris in 1983. Other terms for this phenomenon have been proposed, such as *officer-assisted suicide* (Homant et al., 2000), *law enforcement-assisted suicide* (Lord, 2000), and *suicide by victim-precipitated homicide* (Hillbrand, 2001). It's easy to see why–besides each being a mouthful–none of these latter terms ever caught on. The first two wordings place the officer in a Dr. Kevorkian-like role of willingly abetting the suspect's wish to die, which is hardly the case. And the last term sounds like it's all but calling the cop a murderer, although I'm sure that was not the intent of the term's author. Though still not the most graceful terminology, *suicide by cop* (SBC) is the descriptor that appears to have stuck, and is the term used by most law enforcement personnel, police psychologists, and media reporters when they talk about this phenomenon.

SUICIDE BY COP: FACTS AND STATS

It is estimated that approximately 10 percent of the approximately 600 police shootings a year in the U.S. are provoked SBC incidents. Most involve uniformed officers who are on duty at the time of the shooting, probably because such officers are easy to identify for suspects seeking to end their own lives. The greatest number of SBC incidents occur in the context of a police response to an armed robbery; the next most common situation is a domestic disturbance call. While some SBC incidents arise spontaneously out of the anger and panic of these situations, a good number of them appear to be planned, as shown by the fact that, in nearly a third of SBC cases, investigators find a suicide note which apologizes to the police for deliberately drawing their fire. Use of deadly force by police officers is correlated with the perceived danger of the immediate situation, not the actual danger, which is usually judged only in retrospect. For this and other reasons, officers involved in SBC incidents often feel a sense of powerlessness and manipulation, and this is typically reported to be an especially stressful and demoralizing form of shooting trauma (Feuer, 1998; Homant et al., 2000; Pinizzotto et al., 2005; Wilson, 1998).

SUICIDE BY COP: CHARACTERISTIC FEATURES

Although individual features of a SBC subject are determined by the subject's unique personality and life experiences, research has identified some common characteristics of these individuals and incidents (Feuer, 1998; Kennedy et al., 1998; Lord, 2000; Wilson, 1998).

The typical SBC subject is a white male in his mid-twenties with a history of drug and alcohol abuse. He has had prior contact with the law but usually for minor offenses, although this has probably given him some familiarity with how police operate and their responses to critical situations. Aside from substance abuse, he has probably had a history of other psychological disorders, the most common diagnosis being schizophrenia or bipolar disorder (Chapter 4), although there is at least one report of attempted SBC following a traumatic brain injury (Bresler et al., 2003). The subject is not necessarily a "loner" type, but the crisis episode is commonly precipitated by the rupture of some important relationship in connection with his self-esteem or social support, such as a family or job crisis, which leads to feelings of hopelessness, anger, and despair. Not surprisingly, a desperate reaction is most likely to be provoked where there is a confluence of such crises, such as getting fired and divorced at the same time.

In Wilson's (1998) study of SBC incidents, all SBC subjects resisted arrest or orders by police to surrender, and all possessed a firearm or other lethal weapon that they used to threaten others, which accounts for why such incidents were perceived as critical to officers, family, and any hostages that might have been involved. In fact, as noted in Chapter 9, SBC incidents and hostage crises may overlap, and fully two-thirds of SBC subjects in Wilson's (1998) study took hostages, which gave the crisis an added urgency.

Forty percent of SBC subjects in Wilson's (1998) study were intoxicated with alcohol, but, curiously, other drug use was rare. It may be that being strung out from lack of resources to obtain street drugs contributes to the crisis, and that alcohol is used as a second-choice drug, which then further disrupts judgment and self-control. Forty percent of SBC subjects had received a psychiatric diagnosis at one time or another, and 60 percent had histories suggesting a psychiatric disorder. The most common diagnoses were depression and substance abuse. Tellingly, 47 percent of this sample had attempted suicide previously. In Lord's (2000) study, many SBC attempts began as self suicide crises, but when law enforcement arrived on the scene, the subjects seemed to have chosen to delegate the lethal job to the officers.

MOTIVATIONS FOR SUICIDE BY COP

Why would someone choose to have themselves killed by a police officer? It must be noted that most of what we know about motivations for any kind of suicide, including SBC, comes from the study of people who have contemplated suicide and been talked out of it or changed their minds, or from people who have actually attempted suicide but survived. Aside from academic curiosity, achieving some insight into the SBC subject's behavior may be useful for counseling officers who are disturbed by their role in the subject's death (Homant et al., 2000). This will be further discussed later in this chapter.

Mohandie and Meloy (2000) have delineated a range of motivations for SBC, which in fact can be applied to any kind of suicide. Feelings of *hope-*

lessness, desperation, rage, and/or *revenge* usually occur in some combination in persons who attempt suicide. For such individuals, there appears "no way out," other than to die. What may be unique to SBC cases, however, is how these feelings are acted upon. Many suicidal persons are concerned about what others will think of them after their death. Indeed, many suicide attempters have reported elaborate fantasies about what others will feel, say, and do after the subject is gone, usually involving imagined scenes hand-wringing guilt and remorse on the survivors' parts for what "they've driven me to do." On rare occasions, suicidal police officers or ex-officers may stage SBC incidents precisely because they understand that once they fire their weapons at the responding officers, the latter will have no choice but to return fire (Hafenback & Nasiripour, 2005).

If the suicide attempter believes that taking one's own life bespeaks weakness or cowardice, what better face-saving way to *go out like a warrior* than in a hail of gunfire, brought down by overwhelming force of arms during his last act of heroic resistance? He didn't necessarily want to die, they'll all say; he was just killed while taking a stand, which further reinforces his status as the ultimate hero-victim, gratifying his need for validation, power, and importance. Often, this suicidal manipulation may not be conscious, the subject having truly convinced himself that he is just defending his integrity by resisting the police.

Another, related source of this clouding of motivations consists of *religious prohibitions against suicide*: the person may no longer want to dwell in this cold, cruel world, but he doesn't want to go to hell, either. With a SBC, he can essentially tell God that it's not his fault the police killed him. In many cases, the decision to have the police serve as executioners is made impulsively and, in some cases, the subject just as abruptly changes his mind and surrenders (Pinizzotto et al., 2005).

Practical considerations may underlie the wish to die but not to appear to have killed oneself, such as exclusion clauses for suicide on virtually all life insurance policies, or lessening the shame to one's family. Also, a person who wants to die may fear the physical pain and distress involved in actually taking his own life (cutting, suffocating), or he may be afraid of chickening out of the suicide at the last moment or doing a botched job which would only leave him a cripple or a vegetable. In this regard, SBC makes grim sense in terms of finality: being gunned down by multiple police bullets is an effectively lethal way to die.

SUICIDE BY COP: CUES AND SIGNS

Virtually any call with a distressed person can lead to a SBC incident, including domestic disturbance, robbery in progress, NWAG ("nut with a gun") calls, and so on. In fact, many encounters that might not have started with the subject being suicidal, may progress to that point as he feels his situation becoming increasingly desperate. As noted in Chapter 9, this is also the case with hostage crises. And, as with hostage crises, when it becomes clear that an encounter involves a threat to the subject's and/or others' lives, special caution must be taken in handling the incident. The following are some signs that a SBC incident may be brewing (Homant et al, 2000; Hutson, et al, 1998; Kennedy et al., 1998; Mohandie & Meloy, 2000).

Verbal Cues

Certain statements the subject makes during the incident may overtly or subtly indicate his or her desire to die by the hands of the police.

Explicit demands or challenges. "Come on, pigs, kill me! I don't give a shit. Come on—what are you waiting for?"

Giving up. "You want me so bad?—come arrest me. I got nowhere to go, so it might as well be to jail."

Setting deadlines. "I'm giving you till two o'clock to get out of here, then I'm coming out with my gun and I don't give a damn what happens."

Threats to others. "You guys clear out of here or the bitch gets it."

Blaze of glory. "No way I'm going back to jail. You ain't takin' me alive. This is the moment of truth!"

Noble loser. "You pigs knew it was just a matter of time till you got me. Well, here's your chance."

Verbal will; final plans. "Tell my daughter I'm sorry for everything. The keys to my safety deposit box are in the dresser drawer;" "I don't want no damn preacher at my funeral. Just have my brother say a few words;" "Tell everybody I just tried to do right in this world, okay?"

Religious references. "The final judgment will be in heaven;" "My pastor and I have an understanding;" "I'm right with God."

Behavioral Cues

Even without saying anything, a subject may indicate his or her desire to die by the hands of the police. Note that some of these cues are general cues to suicidal intent, while others may be more specific to SBC incidents.

The subject may *call in the crime report himself* to make sure there is a police presence and to prime them for danger when they arrive. As with many hostage crises (Chapter 9), the SBC subject may make *no substantive demands* or refuse to negotiate with police. *Drug or alcohol intoxication* is almost always a bad sign because it increases instability and impulsivity, but as is the case with hostage situations, sometimes this can cause the subject to fall asleep, permitting a safe resolution–however, don't count on it.

Certain actions by the subject may seem to clearly be goading the police into firing on him. He may advance on a police line, after being ordered to stop. The subject may brandish his weapon in a threatening way, point it at police, clear a threshold in a barricade situation, or actually begin firing; in fact, this is the decision point for officers' firing in 89 percent of SBC situations studied (Kennedy et al., 1998). Perhaps most distressing for officers who have killed a SBC subject, he may have been observed reaching for a supposed weapon that turned out to be a toy gun, other harmless object, or just a pantomine intended to manipulate the police into shooting him.

The SBC subject may point the weapon at himself or threaten another person. He may actually begin to harm himself or that person. Even when wounded, he may continue firing or attacking police or others, clearly signaling his intent to go out in a dramatic blaze of glory.

Contextual Cues

To the extent that law enforcement responders can obtain any information on the subject, certain situational, demographic, and historical details about the SBC subject may be useful for assessing risk.

Many of the *general risk factors for unstable, impulsive, violent behavior* discussed elsewhere in this book apply to the SBC subject. Such subjects typically have an extensive mental health history, including previous hospitalizations for being a danger to self or others. They may also have a criminal history, usually involving impulsive, spontaneous acts of violence. Many have had prior run-ins with police officers, and a few have had a family member or close associate killed in a police shootout. Some subjects identify with other SBC victims and some may fit the "blaze of glory" syndrome described earlier.

Subjects at high risk for SBC in standoff situations include those who have recently killed a significant other, killed a prized pet, destroyed or given away valued possessions, recently learned of a serious medical diagnosis, sustained a painful traumatic loss or bereavement, or may be facing a shameful life situation.

POLICE RESPONSE TO AN ONGOING SUICIDE-BY-COP CALL

The following are some basic guidelines for handling a potential SBC incident. As with all such recommendations, these should be tempered by training, experience, and common sense (Campbell, 2005; Homant et al., 2000; Hutson, 1998; Kennedy et al., 1998; Mohandie & Meloy, 2000). Readers will also note the similarity of many of these recommendations to those described for hostage crises in Chapter 9; again, these two types of incidents frequently overlap.

Assess the Situation

As with all potentially dangerous situations, *take every call seriously*, even if this is your umpteenth

"emergency" with one of the local regular 911-ers. You never know which crisis is going to be the fatal one.

As with all crisis situations, *secure the scene and assess the threat to safety* of the subject, any third parties, including hostages or innocent bystanders, and yourself and fellow officers.

Try to obtain as much *background information* as possible on the subject. This may actually be easier with SBC subjects, who tend to be familiar locals, than with hostage-takers, who may be outsiders who come into a neighborhood to commit a specific crime. With SBC subjects, sometimes the presence of a familiar, trusted officer is an asset;

other times, it may lead to more trouble, especially if the subject has had a beef with that officer in the past.

Evaluate Suicide Risk

The overall risk of suicide, which in turn may be an index of the likelihood of a SBC episode, can be evaluated in terms of three important factors, each with two dimensions (Clark, 1998; Gilliland & James, 1993; Greenstone & Leviton, 2001; Kleespies, 1998):

Suicidal intent can be either *remote:* "Times like these, you get to feeling life just ain't worth living. Or *immediate:* "I can't take another minute of this– I'm checkin' out."

Suicidal plan can be either *vague:* "I think I got some drain cleaner under the sink; I dunno, maybe I'll just turn on the gas, or turn on the car exhaust in the garage." Or *specific:* "I got the razor to my neck and I'm ready to go."

Suicidal means should be evaluated in terms of either *low availability:* "Dammit, I know my wife used to keep her pills around here somewhere." Or *high availability:* "Got my Smith in my hand, boys, so you do what you want."

Suicidal means should also be evaluated in terms of *low lethality:* "Don't think I can't do some damage with this hammer." Or *high lethality:* "I was an ordnance expert in the Navy, so when I tell you this baby's gonna take off the side of the house, you better get outa there."

Note that, whatever the immediate threat level of these various dimensions, officers should not relax their vigilance, because a seemingly low-risk situation can turn deadly in a flash.

Establish Contact

If you establish communication with the subject, *introduce yourself* and your organization by name and title. Try to *establish rapport* with the subject. Remember that, if there are no third parties in harm's way, the subject is primarily a danger to himself and possibly to officers responding to the scene. In most SBC situations, there may be more time and less of a sense of urgency than where hostages are involved. Unfortunately, this may also make the SBC scenario seem less important than a hostage crisis, and many officers may feel that it is a "waste of time" to spend hours talking down some nut who only wants to off himself.

So always remember a few things about *SBC versus hostage situations.* First, a life saved is a life saved, and it can be just as rewarding to rescue some poor dumb schmuck from himself as it is to talk down a cold-blooded hostage taker and keep him from harming innocent civilians. Second, you're a professional, and just as a paramedic doesn't get to decide who to resuscitate based on the subject's "worthiness quotient," it's not your call whose particular butt is worth expending your time and effort to save. Finally, as emphasized throughout this book, the types of crises encountered in law enforcement, and the methodologies used to handle them, have far more similarities than differences. So the active listening and negotiating skills you hone getting some disturbed street person to drop his tire iron may give you that lifesaving edge you'll need if you're ever first on the scene at a hostage standoff at the bank.

Determine the Main Problem

Again, as with hostage crises, sometimes in SBC cases there is no specific problem: "Politicians are all the same. You can't trust nobody. The world ain't never gonna change." And sometimes the issue is clearly defined: "I can't believe she's been banging my cousin. If she don't come back here right now and apologize, I'm gonna show her what she made me do."

Recalling the discussion in Chapter 9, it is sometimes helpful to ascertain if the subject's needs are *instrumental:* "They tell me they gotta repo my car 'cause I missed some payments. Without a car, I can't get to work. How'm I supposed to live?" Or *expressive:* "My ex-wife said it wasn't her business no more what happens to me. Well, we'll see how she feels about her 'business' when she's gotta clean my brains up off her new floor."

Talk the Subject Down

Use your toolkit of crisis intervention skills, guided by your knowledge, training, experience, judgment, and common sense, to bring the incident to a nonviolent resolution. Any combination of strategies may be employed, including the following.

Provide reassurance. "It sounds like you been through hell, man. But these cops out here want to help you, not hurt you. That's why we called in the paramedics, see?"

Comply with reasonable requests. "Well, I'm not allowed to bring your boss in here to talk to you, but I promise I'll give him that note you tossed us if you'll drop the gun and come out. In fact, so you know I'm not kidding, if you come out without a problem, I'll read the note right into my radio here, so you know everybody'll hear it."

If there are no demands, ask about immediate needs. As opposed to a hostage situation, there is less reason to make the SBC subject "bargain" for basic necessities. In fact, offering to make the subject more comfortable can be a humane, rapport-building gesture. However, you may want to suggest some kind of trade-off that will contribute to a non-lethal resolution: "Look, you've been in there for hours with no food, water, or AC. How about I send in some burgers and cold drinks if you'll at least put the rifle down, okay?"

Offer alternative, realistic optimism: "Hey, I can't just make them give you your back pay and benefits, you know that. But plenty of guys have gotten Workers Comp lawyers and filed claims, and eventually they got a fair deal. At least you'd be standing up for yourself and not just letting them win. I'll even ask my uncle who's a tax attorney for the names of some employment lawyers who can start you rolling, what do you say?"

Avoid being baited. One problem that may be unique to SBC incidents is that, if the subject is truly intent on dying, he may use the officer's rapport-building process against him. As communication develops, the officer feels more and more at ease, and approaches closer and closer to the

subject, whereupon the latter springs into an attack, leaving the officer no choice but to defend himself by lethal force. It is almost always these kind of manipulative *bait-and-rush* scenarios that officers find the most distressing and demoralizing aspect of SBC scenarios: "How could I have been such an idiot not to see that coming?" Therefore, as rapport and communication begin to develop, always maintain a safe physical position and keep one vigilant eye open for any sign of sudden threat.

Consider nonlethal containment. A variety of LTLs, or *less-than-lethal* weapons and containment technologies now exist, and more are coming on the market all the time. Sprays, gasses, gels, nets, tasers, and flash-bangs comprise only a partial list, and many officers have used their ingenuity to devise their own less-than-lethal measures to take down a subject, including pinning the subject with a ladder, throwing a blanket over him, or even squirting him with a restaurant mustard dispenser. Remember, of course, that officer safety is paramount, but if it is feasible to turn a suicide-by-cop incident into a tased-by-cop, sprayed-by-cop, laddered-by-cop, or garnished-by-cop incident, then a life has still been saved.

Employ appropriate follow-up. Again, as with hostage situations, don't neglect the subject after the crisis has been resolved. Remember of the principle of repeat customers cited throughout this book. Especially in smaller communities, and more so with SBC subjects who are likely to be treated and released—as opposed to hostage takers who almost always go to jail—you may well cross paths with the same character again, so you want his or her memory of you to be as positive as possible.

Therefore, following a successful resolution of the SBC crisis, spend a few moments with the subject, commend him for his courage in doing the right thing, repeat your reassurance and your confidence in his ability to get his life back in order, and even offer to provide whatever assistance you can realistically follow up on. In doing so, you reduce the likelihood of a repeat episode, and you contribute to the overall future safety of your fellow officers and the community as a whole.

AFTERMATH OF SUICIDE BY COP: POLICE OFFICERS' REACTIONS

As noted at the beginning of this chapter, if SBC is a special form of officer-involved shooting, then the psychological reactions of the involved officers can be expected to be as great or greater than with almost any other kind of shooting scenario. In my experience, these reactions also occur, perhaps to a lesser degree, with other types of suicides where the best efforts of the responding officers to talk the subject down fail to interdict his or her determination to take his or her own life.

The Psychodynamics of SBC

It must be remembered that SBC is not always a clear-cut situation (Homant et al., 2000, Praet, 2002). In the least ambiguous case, a disturbed citizen has a beef with police, so he purposefully calls them to the scene and then deliberately manipulates them into shooting him. Another relatively clear scenario involves a disturbed, suicidal subject who lacks the resolve to kill himself, so he baits the police into doing it for him.

But many situations begin with the subject threatening to kill himself, by himself, and then turn into a SBC incident only when the subject feels threatened or overwhelmed by the arriving police presence. In still other cases, the incident begins as an aggressive action by the subject, such as a robbery or domestic dispute, and only turns suicidal when the subject feels he is out of options; as noted earlier, many of these scenarios may overlap with hostage crises (Chapter 9). Officers involved in SBC shootings frequently second-guess themselves when they learn that the subject manipulated them into shooting him (Van Zandt, 1993). That aside, officers may reproach themselves for "unnecessarily" taking a subject's life (Clagett, 2004).

Still other cases, far more common in my experience, might be called *suicide in front of cop*. Here, the subject summons police to the scene, or they happen to arrive as part of a general call, and the subject makes a point of killing himself in full view of the officers (or within earshot, if by phone). This gesture may be performed out of sheer despair or capitulation, or the subject may want the officers–iconic symbols of societal authority–to "bear witness"

to his act of desperate martyrdom. Alternatively, he may be trying to exert a different form of manipulative control, not by actually inducing the cops to shoot him, but by forcing them to witness his death as a way of highlighting their failure to talk him down.

In my experience, it is this issue of *control* that seems to disturb officers the most. Police officers hate to feel that they've failed. In fact, paradoxically, many officers feel worse after failing to prevent a suicidal subject from taking his own life than they do after not being able to prevent a homicidal subject from killing another person. In turn, this reaction bothers them all the more because they believe they "should" feel worse about the homicide, since it involved the unwilling death of a helpless victim.

But, upon analysis and reflection, the psychological dynamic that emerges is this: The killer was either a cold-blooded scumbag who had no compunctions about taking another's life for his own gain, or else he was so whacked out from drugs or mental illness that he didn't know what he was doing or didn't care about the consequences. Either way, in a strange, evil, crazy sort of way, the killing was "bound" to happen. In the first case, the killer was determined to get what he wanted by using an innocent victim as a pawn. And in a way, the aggressively assertive, forthright cognitive style, temperament, and action-orientation of most cops allows them to unconsciously identify with the conviction to "do whatever it takes" to survive and overcome a situation, even if they consciously revile the actual criminal motives and agenda of the offender.

Not that cops are all secret felons by nature, but the force of character that enables them to barrel through tough situations in order to do good is similar in type–although opposite in goal–to the criminal's singleminded determination to do evil. And most cops have no trouble imagining themselves capable of "doing anything" in extreme circumstances, e.g., if their loved ones were in peril. Indeed, that is precisely the rationale of the extreme stress management and mental toughness training described in Chapter 5 of this book.

But giving up and taking one's own life is consciously far more distasteful and therefore repudiated in the thinking of most cops, perhaps because the idea of surrendering or being overwhelmed is indeed a secret fear of many officers (Chapter 11), which therefore must be forcefully banished from conscious consideration. Psychologically, then, failing to prevent a subject from killing himself may symbolically stand for the officer's unconscious fear that he may someday fail to prevent his own demons from wresting away his will to live. Worse still, where this officer becomes the actual instrument of death in a typical SBC case, the psychodynamically fearful introjection becomes all the more disturbing because it has been acted out in real life, albeit on the proxy of the dead subject. Here's someone who gave up, sold out, and had the cops write the check.

Psychotherapeutic Strategies with Officers Involved in a SBC Incident

In working with such officers, I recommend a flexible and graded approach. Begin with a standard *operational debriefing* much as would occur after an officer-involved shooting, hostage crisis, or other major critical incident. Guided by the 20/20 hindsight – 20/20 insight – 20/20 foresight principal, view the debrief as a learning tool, so that an unfortunately tragic outcome this time can lead to a potentially better outcome next time. If several officers were involved in the call, a formal *CISD debriefing* (Chapter 6) may be arranged to deal with shared reactions and to foster a sense of camaraderie and mutual support.

Notwithstanding the lesson in psychodynamics proferred above, individual psychotherapy with an officer involved in a SBC incident should not dive into a Freudian analysis, but rather should begin in a practical, educative format, employing reality-testing and cognitive techniques. If necessary, have the officer go through a frame-by-frame recollection (Chapters 6, 7) of the incident, clarifying in his own mind what he or she did, what the subject did, what the other officers did, and so on.

In this context, self-recriminations can be placed in the same kind of 20/20 "what-can-I-learn-from-

this?" framework. The counselor can encourage the perspective that a true professional doesn't unrealistically expect to get it perfect every time, but that the same true professional is responsible for learning from his or her mistakes. He or she *is* expected to extract the maximum amount of insight possible from the failures, in order to optimally hone his or her skills for next time: "If you're willing to assess your performance honestly, learn from your mistakes, practice and retrain for excellence, and give 110 percent on the next call, then you're doing your damn job, officer, and no one can ask for more."

Only if these practical measures prove insufficient to restore the officer's equanimity and confidence should the psychologist delve into the more individual, personal, psychodynamic reasons for the officer's difficulty in coping with the SBC aftermath. Even then, go slowly and cautiously, and only as deep as you need to.

Sometimes, it may be a contemporaneous stressor that is impacting on the officer's ability to cope with the SBC episode. Perhaps the call came around the same time as a family member was dealing with a serious illness. Maybe the incident itself was too close to home: it is not that rare for police officers to have at least one immediate or distant family member with a mental illness and one of these relatives may even have attempted or completed suicide.

The issue should never be forced, but sometimes it emerges that the officer has "been there," i.e., has him- or herself gotten fearfully close to considering the ultimate check-out (Chapter 11), and by dint of will-power, or not wanting to shame his family or colleagues, he was able to pull himself back from the brink. He may currently be going through a depressive crisis—and imagine the irony of a depressed officer trying to convince a suicidal subject to go on living and hoping. In a few rare cases, the experience may have a "scared-straight" effect on the officer: "Jeez, compared with what that poor bastard's going through, my problems don't seem so bad." But don't count on it, because everybody's pain is real to them, and persons in distress often lose the power of perspective. Acknowledge the distress, and keep the discussion focused on the positive, on the prospects for the officer's future competence and success.

CONCLUSIONS

Due to a combination of interpersonal manipulativeness, personal identification, and lack of heroic status, most officers find SBC calls to be among the most disturbing shooting incidents when they are forced to take the subject's life. By utilizing sensitive, supportive, yet pragmatic and confidence-building therapeutic approaches in an atmosphere of mutual trust and respect, the police psychologist can powerfully aid in restoring an officer's resilience and ability to bounce back from the stress of this special critical incident. By emphasizing that officers use intervention "failures" as tools for learning, purposeless remorse can be turned into very real life-saving skills for next time.

Chapter 11

POLICE OFFICER SUICIDE

One of my colleagues, Jim Cummings, a senior law enforcement official and continuing education instructor, starts out one of his police seminars by posing the following question: "Which individual is more likely to kill you during your service career than all other groups combined?" Responses tend to come in along the lines of "drug dealers," "crazy persons," "traffic stops," "gang members," and so on.

The correct answer always surprises the officers: *yourself.*

We understand that law enforcement is a profession that regularly places characteristically hard-driving, perfectionistic, and self-critical men and women into situations of tremendous interpersonal stress and human complexity. While an aggressively can-do attitude and success orientation may be a powerful motivator for professional excellence in policing, the down-side comes when this standard is applied too rigidly, creating the set-up for an emotional nose-dive when too many pressures mount up at once (Seligman et al., 1994; Solan & Casey, 2003; Violanti, 1996).

With all the focus on suicide-by-cop (Chapter 10), much less attention is devoted to what could

well be called "suicide *of* cop." This is a strange oversight, inasmuch as an officer who failed to provide cardiopulmonary resuscitation to a colleague struggling to breathe would no doubt be vilified by his peers and censured by his department. Shouldn't the same emphasis on *psychological* lifesaving techniques be part of the training of all officers (Quinnet, 1998)?

But denial of mortality is most entrenched when the potential source of that mortality is oneself. Of all the topics in my police academy classes, the subject of police officer suicide is the one that elicits the highest number of both winces and giggles. That's because this is an especially uncomfortable topic that hits close to home, that strikes at the heart of the vulnerability feelings that all officers secretly tote around, usually stuffed down at the bottom of their mental kit bag (Henry, 2004). The majority of officers in distress find various ways, healthy or unhealthly–but usually nonlethal–to deal with their problems and few opt to take the ultimate plunge into oblivion. But, as more than one officer has told me in a moment of candor, "Hey, we've all *thought* about it."

SUICIDE: "MYTHS" AND REALITIES

Many citizens, and even among a fair number of professionals, are misinformed about the nature of suicide. But even the blanket term "myths" may be misleading, which is why this section title has the word in quotes. That's because some common suppositions and misconceptions about suicide may indeed contain kernels of truth. Accordingly, this

section covers some facts and stats about suicide in general (Baechler, 1979; Baker & Baker, 1996; Bongar, 2002).

Those who threaten suicide don't really do it. The number of suicidal threats is far greater than the number of suicidal acts and most such threats are not followed by an actual suicide. But attempted or completed suicides are often preceded by one or more suicidal threats, so each threat has to be taken seriously. Most psychologists think of suicidal threats or gestures in clinically depressed subjects in much the same way as physicians consider chest pains in patients at risk for heart attack: most may be false alarms but, in both cases, if you miss the real one, the patient is dead. It is also true that many disturbed people use suicidal threats as an attention-seeking or manipulative ploy. But responding in a forthright way demonstrates both concern for the subject and the fact that there are real consequences (e.g., temporary involuntary commitment, a permanent mental health record) for "playing games." Therefore, all suicidal threats should be taken seriously.

Discussing suicide will impel the person to do it. Well-meaning friends, family members, first responders, and even some clinicians may avoid asking a subject about suicidal ideation for fear of "putting ideas in her head." In fact, just the opposite is almost always true. Most depressed persons have already thought of suicide, indeed, may be currently ruminating about it but reluctant to bring it up for fear of being seen as crazy or of having restrictive action taken. Yet most are actually relieved to have another person question them about their suicidal thoughts because it gives them the opportunity to discuss their fears and concerns. Many people express suicidal intentions or make suicidal gestures because they're really hoping to be rescued. If someone has actually not been considering suicide, usually the only consequence of your raising the issue will the person's disavowing it. But it is highly unlikely that an otherwise nonsuicidal person is going to abruptly sit bolt upright and say, "Gee, now that you mention it, maybe I *will* kill myself," just because you brought up the subject. Better to have as much information as possible, rather than too little.

Suicide is always an irrational act. Sometimes it is and sometimes it isn't. It is difficult for most people to relate to the excrutiating mental pain that would drive a person to end his or her life, especially if, to our eyes, the situation "isn't all *that* bad," or the person seems to "have everything to live for." But a clinically depressed person doesn't see things the way we do–or even the way he or she normally does when not overwhelmed by despair. In the depressed state, negatives are magnified and positives are discounted. In many such cases, a crushing pileup of adverse life events squeezes any hope for the future out of the person's life, making the rationale for suicide seem crystal clear: if everything in life is pain and nothing is pleasure, and it's never going to end, then what's the point of going on? Always remember that psychological pain cannot be measured by a standard barometer–everybody's pain is real to them.

Suicide is always an impulsive act. It sometimes is, in which case there is hardly sufficient time to intervene because the person completes the act with little or no warning. In many other cases, however, the individual will express his or her suicidal ideation to someone: family member, friend, clergy, clinician, or 911 operator. In such cases, the person is at least somewhat ambivalent about taking his or her own life and this leaves room for intervention.

Individuals who commit suicide are mentally ill. In most cases, suicide does not just occur in an emotional vacuum, but takes place in the context of a history of mood disturbances and erratic behavior. Indeed, a high proportion of suicide attempters have had at least some prior contact with the mental health and/or legal system. While there need not be a psychiatric diagnosis per se, most suicidal individuals are clinically depressed or struggling with some form of persecutory delusion, perhaps a combination of the two. Knowing the subject's history of mental illness is important mainly for predicting what kind of postcrisis life that person will be going back to, and thereby formulating an intervention strategy that realistically takes this variable into account.

Suicide runs in families. Mood disorders, such as depression and bipolar disorder, usually have a genetic-familial component and suicide is an additional risk factor in these syndromes so, in that sense, suicide can be said to run in families. This does not mean, however, that someone with a family history of depression and suicide is predestined to take their own life, only that the risk is somewhat greater than in others without such a legacy. Again, as with other family medical risks, proper treatment can help many individuals "beat the odds" of their family history. Of course, during an actual suicidal crisis, the primary priority is to keep the individual alive *right now* so that he or she can be provided access to appropriate therapeutic services later.

Once suicidal, always suicidal. Again, partly true. Since, as a general rule, the best predictor of future behavior is past behavior, a person who has attempted suicide once is at greater risk of attempting it again under conditions of stress that precipitate a depressive episode. The goal of any effective treatment is to give the person the coping skills necessary to reduce the frequency and intensity of these crises, and thereby make suicidality less of an automatic, reflexive choice for that individual.

Once the suicidal crisis has passed or the person's mood has improved, the danger is over. It may be over for that moment, but without follow-up treatment, there is increased risk of future crises, as noted above. This highlights the need for follow-up treatment after the immediate crisis has been resolved.

POLICE OFFICER SUICIDE: FACTS AND STATS

Police work is a dangerous business but, as noted in this chapter's introduction, not just for the reasons most people–even most cops–think (Baker & Baker, 1996; Cummings, 1996; Hamilton, 2003a; Hill & Clawson, 1988; Loo, 1999; Marzuk et al., 2002; Mohandie & Hatcher, 1999; Quinnet, 1998; Violanti, 1995, 1996). The suicide rate for law enforcement officers is two to three times the rate of the general population, and three times as many officers kill themselves–about 300 annually–as are killed by criminals in the line of duty. This makes officer suicide the single most lethal factor in police work. The true rate might even be higher, since many deaths of "undetermined cause" may in fact represent disguised suicides.

Suicide rates for U.S. police officers have been increasing since the 1920s, and are even higher in several other countries studied. Officer suicide rates tend to be higher in demographically diverse areas of the U.S. and other nations. Interestingly, the suicide rate among the Royal Canadian Mounted Police tends to be about half that of other agencies studied (Loo, 1986), perhaps because of a combination of demographic homogeneity of the force plus the high status and honor accorded this elite law enforcement agency in that country.

There is still some controversy as to whether suicide rates among police officers are higher than that of the general population, and much of this disparity may relate to regional and demographic differences (Marzuk et al., 2002). Overall, the suicide rate among police officers appears to be somewhat higher than that of the military and general civilian populations, respectively (Hamilton, 2003a).

Suicidal crises rarely occur in isolation, but are most commonly seen in officers with prior histories of depression or in those who have recently faced a combination of debilitating stressors, leading to feelings of hopelessness and helplessness. Often, there is a slow, smoldering build-up of tension and demoralization, which then abruptly accelerates, culminating in a suicidal crisis. It is not uncommon for there to be a pattern of such mood cycles over the course of the individual's lifetime. Nevertheless, suicidal crises in officers, as with most persons in acute distress, tend to be short. This means that timely intervention can literally make a life-or-death difference.

Like most people, officers typically commit suicide as a maladaptive response to intolerable personal, family, and/or work situations they feel they cannot resolve. Unlike many people, however, cops tend to be especially personally invested in their professional role as law enforcement officers, and thereby react very strongly when this status is threatened. Many cases of suicide reflect the cumulative impact of several stressors, often involving a combination of relationship and work problems–the two pillars of self-esteem that most officers rely on.

Alcohol complicates depression and suicidality for two reasons (Cross & Ashley, 2004). First, during a crisis, alcohol impairs judgment and increases the risk for impulsive behavior. Second, a history of alcohol abuse is often associated with a parallel history of mood disturbance and other impulsive, erratic, and even violent behaviors, such as stalking and intimidation, domestic violence, workplace aggression, or abuse of force on patrol (Chapter 13).

The good news is that, with appropriate treatment, about 70 percent of depressed, suicidal persons, including officers, improve considerably within a few weeks. This doesn't mean that depressed moods and suicidal thoughts won't ever crop up again, but a history of successful psychological treatment provides a support resource that the individual can rely on if and when the next crisis occurs. The most effective treatments for depression combine medication and psychotherapy, the former to stabilize the subject's emotional state, and the latter to explore reasons for the depression; to examine alternatives to suicide, substance abuse and other destructive behaviors; to reinforce coping skills and mobilize social support systems to forestall or mitigate future crises; and generally to provide the person with a sense of hope and positive self-regard.

PREDISPOSING FACTORS FOR POLICE SUICIDE: LAW ENFORCEMENT PERSONALITY AND THE "COP CULTURE"

Certain features of police work distinguish it from other occupations in terms of the intensity and personal identity-investment that characterize most officers. Accordingly, certain aspects of the so-called *"police personality"* and *"cop culture"* of most law enforcement agencies can, paradoxically, both buffer and exacerbate an officer's response to stress (Allen, 1986; Blau, 1994; Cummings, 1996; Henry, 2004; Miller, 2003; Mohandie & Hatcher, 1999).

The police culture reinforces a professional ethos that resonates with the personal philosophy many officers already bring to the job from their own family and cultural background. Notably, this includes a black-or-white, good-or-bad, *all-or-nothing, life-or-death perspective* on the world and the people in it. Shades of gray are often regarded as the bleeding colors of washed-out conviction and resolve, and this includes the officer's self-perception of his status as a law enforcement professional and as a human being. Not that all officers think like robots, but when it comes to matters of personal honor and peer prestige, two primary qualities that almost all officers adhere to are *self-reliance* and *infallibility*. Officers commonly believe that they should be able to handle most situations with a minimum of help and that "you're only as good as your last fuck-up."

At the same time, whether they admit it or not, most officers have an almost insatiable *craving for approval*. One of the gratifications of the police role is the respect it garners among civilians and the camaraderie it engenders among brother officers. In addition, many officers obtain great comfort and support from their families, which often is the one venue where they can both physically and emotionally hang up their cop uniform–"get out of the bag"–and relax with loved ones. Most of the time, this unstable alloy of self-reliance and need for social approval provides a thick but rigid shell of protection against assaults to the officer's self-esteem.

Unfortunately, this orientation leaves little room for acceptance of fallibility or error, and another phrase, "failure is not an option," is heard so often in police circles as to have become almost a cliché. An officer's brittle shell of self-esteem may shatter into a suicidal crisis if breached by a barrage of professional or family stresses, especially if they all come down at once. For such officers, shame is a far worse emotion than fear, and losing the respect of their peers or the support of their family is perceived as more critical than losing a limb or a lung to a suspect's bullet. Hence, life in the face of these kinds of crises may become literally intolerable.

To make matters worse, a distressed officer, wishing for some kind of human connection but reluctant to accept it for fear of appearing weak, may withdraw from or reject the well-meaning support offered by others. After several failed attempts to reach out, the sympathy of these persons may be exhausted, and they may then react with predictable counteravoidance. The officer, who probably is not even consciously aware of his role in pushing away the very human contact he craves, now sees the antipathy of others as "proof" that he has been abandoned and is all alone in the world, perpetuating the vicious cycle of *isolation-rejection.*

The rigidity that may characterize many officers' thinking, even in the best of circumstances, becomes even more stiff and inflexible during times of stress, leading to a variety of *cognitive distortions* that impair his ability to think himself out of the jam, chief among them a heightening of *dichotomous* thinking. The all-or-nothing value system then becomes further internalized ("If I can't get myself out of this, I must *really* be a fuck-up"), as well as projected onto others ("All those people I thought I could count on—when push came to shove, they bailed on me, too").

There is another feature of the police personality and cop culture that puts officers at risk for suicide. By virtue of temperament and training, most officers are *action-oriented* and accustomed to responding rapidly and decisively in critical situations. But what is certainly an asset in quickly controlling a dangerous suspect on patrol or making a snap judgment call in a hostage situation may prove a distinct disadvantage in situations that require more contemplation and introspective analysis. In such cases, action, in the absence of sufficient judgment or knowledge, degenerates into rudderless impulsivity, and the imperative to "do something" may propel the officer into self-destruction if this appears to be the only way out of a seemingly impossible jam.

Cop-culture and police-personality factors affect not just how an officer interprets his situation, but also how he is likely to react to it. Besides decisiveness, a feature of the typical law enforcement officer response style is *aggressiveness,* in the sense of a willingness and ability to forthrightly take command of a critical situation. This may include the use of deadly force if there is no other choice, and for a suicidal officer who feels personally threatened by a crisis state—as much as by any weapon-wielding suspect on the street—aggressive action against the self may represent the only choice he sees.

And then there's the gun. Obviously, immediate *access to a powerful firearm* characterizes the police profession and increases the danger of impulsively lethal responding. Even the ordinarily citizen who legally owns a firearm typically does not have this weapon at his side constantly. If the gun isn't right there, even the few seconds it takes to go to the closet, take down the lockbox, and punch in the combination or fumble with the key may interpose a sufficient interval for the person to think twice about actually blowing himself away. But for the average cop, the gun is literally attached to his hip, ready to be used at a moment's notice.

Yet, ready weapon notwithstanding, a good number of officers choose to take their own lives by other means, such as medication overdoses or car crashes. The rationale typically involves not wanting to dishonor their profession by using their service weapon, which is a more likely attitude in cases where the suicide has to do primarily with personal matters rather than job issues. However, in cases where the officer feels the department has betrayed or abused him, he may make a point of using his service weapon as a stark concrete symbol of how "this job has killed me." In still other cases, an officer may choose to use his gun precisely because, in his mind, this represents a "warrior's death," the modern equivalent of falling on one's sword (Hamilton, 2003c).

PREVENTING POLICE SUICIDE

Again invoking this book's theme that the best form of crisis intervention is crisis prevention, police departments can do much in the initial stages of selecting and acculturating the officers in their agencies in order to mitigate the predisposing factors to officer stress, depression, and suicide (Baker & Baker, 1996; Mohandie & Hatcher, 1999; Miller, 2005; Mohandie et al., 1996; Zelig, 1996).

As noted in Chapter 13, *psychological screening* is an important part of the selection process for new officers to ensure as much as possible that these recruits possess a reasonable degree of psychological stability and maturity. Periodic reassessments should also be part of the personnel SOP to assure that budding problems don't sprout unobserved into major crises. This presupposes an efficient, non-stigmatized referral system for dealing with officers in psychological distress, so that any problems detected can receive *appropriate treatment in a supportive atmosphere*. One way to reduce stigmatization and encourage troubled officers to come forward for help is via *education* about police stress, depression, and suicide, provided by means of inservice programs or outside continuing education.

Finally, as noted in Chapters 13 and 14, "healthy" law enforcement organizations contribute to the overall psychological health and resiliency of their officers by reinforcing *fair practices* and *open communication* among levels of the organization. This applies to virtually all public and private organizations, not just law enforcement agencies (Miller, in press).

POLICE SUICIDE: RISK FACTORS

A major part of prevention involves identifying and dealing with risk factors. Risks for suicide can be divided into general risks, and risks specifically related to police officers (Allen, 1986; Bongar, 2002; Cummings, 1996; Mohandie & Hatcher, 1999; Packman et al., 2004). With regard to general risks, there appear to be some demographic and clinical descriptors that put some individuals at special risk for suicide. Bear in mind, of course, that if someone threatens suicide, don't discount it just because he or she doesn't fit the right "profile."

Typically, caucasian males of middle or older age are at increased risk for suicide, largely because they are at increased risk for depression. A family history of suicide is a risk factor, as is a personal history of previous suicide attempts. A subject who is currently depressed, psychotic, or abusing substances, or who has a past history of these syndromes, is at increased risk. Recent significant changes in mood are also a danger sign. Subjects who live alone or are otherwise isolated may have no interpersonal resources to draw on when they become overwhelmed.

Subjects who have experienced a recent loss, either personal or job-related, are at risk, as are those struggling with a current medical crisis. The anniversary of a past loss or trauma may trigger a depressive and suicidal episode. Subjects who ruminate on past traumas or injustices may get themselves into an angry-depressed feedback loop that spurs impulsive violence, either outer- or inner-directed.

Some of the *specific risk factors for police suicide* overlap with general risk factors, while others are more unique to the police role. Officers who are under criminal or administrative investigation, especially if this represents the culmination of an otherwise shameful episode in the officer's career, may fear the loss of status and identity of the police role and, for some emotionally-invested officers, this may be too much to bear.

Officers may also become despondent because they feel they let their fellow officers down in a crisis situation, "froze" during a dangerous encounter, or failed to "pull their weight" on an assignment. The shame and despair is magnified exponentially if the presumed lapse of performance led to the injury or death of another officer.

For both police and the general population, *current intent and/or plan* are the two red flags that clinicians use to determine whether someone is an immediate suicide risk. Is the subject idly ruminating about what the world would be like without him, or is he intending to end his life right now? Has she been making final plans, such as giving away prized possessions or sending letters or e-mails apologizing to people for the wrongs she's done? Does he have vague ideas of how to die, or a well-thought out plan? Also important are *available means and methods:* if a subject talks about going out in a "blast," does he indeed have ready access to firearms or explosives? Has she recently been treated for chronic pain and have a collection of narcotic medications waiting to be swallowed?

POLICE SUICIDE: WARNING SIGNS

Beyond taking note of general risk factors, supervisors, fellow officers, family members, and friends can all be valuable resources in identifying officers in distress who may be at more immediate risk for suicide. Cues and clues may be verbal or behavioral, often admixed (Allen, 1986; Cummings,

1996; Miller, 2005; Mohandie & Hatcher, 1999; Quinnet, 1998). While not all suicidal officers will show all of these signs, even a few should raise sufficient concern for a supervisor to take action.

Verbal Cues

Threatening self. Verbal self-threats can be *direct:* "I'd be better off eating my gun." "That's it—I give up." Or they may be *indirect:* "It's a hell of a thing not to be needed in this world." "Enjoy the good times while you can—they never last."

Threatening others. Often, self-loathing is wholly or partially transmuted into hostility toward others, especially toward those believed to be responsible for the subject's plight. Verbal threats can be either *direct:* "I oughta cap that damn lieutenant for writing me up." Or *indirect:* "People with that kind of attitude deserve whatever's coming to them."

Surrendering control. As noted earlier, suicidal crises are rarely all-or-nothing, and a person in distress may be wrestling with the question of whether life is worth living, while at the same time being frightened of his or her own impulse to end it. In such cases, this individuals may "passively" resist the suicidal impulse by ceding some measure of control to others. For a chronically ill person in pain, this may mean handing over their narcotic medication to a spouse or friend to keep themselves from popping the whole bottle in a spasm of despair. For most police officers, it is their gun that is the constant lethal companion, so these officers, if the job allows it, may prefer to place some distance between themselves and their weapon: "As long as I'm on desk duty this week, can I keep my weapon in my locker? It's a pain in the ass to lug it around the station." Or the surrendering of control may be less specific and broader in scope: "Things are getting too hairy out here; I think I may need to check into the Bug Hilton to get my shit together."

Throwing it all away. A person who feels hopeless may lack the desire or resolve to actually take his or her own life, but may nevertheless feel he has nothing to lose, and so begins to talk about actions that are clearly out of bounds, a kind of "passive suicide" not dissimilar to the suicide by cop discussed in Chapter 10: "I'll drink or smoke what I want, on or off duty. So what if I piss positive? What are they gonna do—fire me? Arrest me? Shoot me?—ha-ha. Anyway, who gives a shit."

Out of control. This is probably the clearest and most unequivocal verbal clue to suicidality, next to directly threatening oneself: "If that Review Board burns me again, that's my last strike, and then I can't tell you what I'm gonna do."

Hostile, blaming, insubordinate. This can be subtle and sarcastic: "Yeah, right, Sarge, I'm really gonna make sure I dot all the I's and cross all the T's on that damn report—wouldn't want the department to get any grammar demerits." Or it can be spewingly overt: "Fuck you—this mess is all your fault and I'm not going down alone for this!"

Defeated. This may express itself as hopeless demoralization without necessarily being suicidal: "I've had it. I'm burnt. I'm ready for the Rubber Gun Squad." Or still subtle, but with more clear-cut harmful intent: "I've had it. I'm burnt. I'm ready for a permanent vacation." Or more overtly lethal: "I've had it. I'm burnt. I'm ready to go home and smoke out."

Morbid attraction to suicide or homicide. The officer may collect news stories about suicide or other violent deaths, talk about people who have killed themselves, and develop a morbid fascination with death and dying: "You know the story about that cop in Ohio who killed his family and himself? I know exactly how that poor bastard felt."

Overwhelmed. "My wife just left me, my checks are bouncing, I'm drinking again, and the IAD ferrets are gonna be crawling up my ass tommorow. I just can't take all this."

Out of options. "I did everything I could, and now I'm losing my house and my family, and I'm going to jail? No way that's happening, man, no fuckin' way."

Behavioral Cues

Gestures. These can be any kind of panotomined self-destructive or other-directed action, which for police officers most commonly consists of an inappropriate display of their gun or surrogate weapon. This can range from the officer just fooling around by putting his fingers in the shape of a gun to his head with a forced grin, to actually putting a cocked weapon to his head, chest, or throat with a serious-as-a-heart-attack expression on his face.

Weapon surrender. The officer gives his firearms to his partner or supervisor to hold for him, or locks them up somewhere.

Weapon overkill. This is the opposite pattern: The officer begins carrying more than one backup weapon, or begins to keep especially powerful weapons in his vehicle or on his person, ostensibly "for protection."

Excessive risk-taking. The officer enters into dangerous situations without his weapon, with an unloaded weapon, or without waiting for backup. Or, risk-taking may express itself more subtly as reckless driving or neglecting health issues.

Boundary violations. This involves flouting agency rules and generally stepping on the wrong departmental toes with a "so-sue-me" attitude. Examples include using departmental vehicles, office equipment, and computers for personal use. In some cases, this escalates to blatant insubordination.

Procedural violations. The officer puts his career in jeopardy by frank violations of departmental procedure, such as excessive force, drinking, sleeping or AWOL on duty, latenesses and absences, violations during training exercises, and an overall attitude of "just asking for trouble."

Final plans. The officer makes or changes a will, pays off debts, gives away possessions, especially prized police-related memorabilia, and makes excessive donations to charities, sometimes associated with a sudden increased interest in religion.

Surrendering control. The officer checks into a psychiatric or substance abuse facility, which may in fact be a healthy interim strategy.

INTERVENTION WITH THE POTENTIALLY SUICIDAL OFFICER

As a colleague, supervisor, or clinician, you may have identified an officer who is sufficiently depressed and demoralized to be considering taking his own life. He may not be actively suicidal at this point (the topic of the next section), but appropriate intervention at this stage might well forestall a more dangerous crisis to come (Allen, 1986; Miller, 2005; Mohandie & Hatcher, 1999; Quinnet, 1998).

Identify and Marshall "Natural Resources"

If the officer appears reluctant to discuss the issue with you, then you should make every possible effort to find friends, relatives and other people, e.g., clergy, that the officer trusts and has found a valuable source of support in the past. This is especially true for officers who fear the stigma of being shrunk by a mental health professional. This is also the rationale behind the Peer Counselor programs discussed in Chapters 6 and 7.

Officer: My life is getting more and more out of control. I don't know how much longer I can stand it.
Intervener: Have you talked to anyone about this?
O: Who the hell cares about my problems?
I: I seem to remember a couple of years ago you had something bugging you.
O: Yeah, that damn Review Board was breathing down my neck.
I: What did you do then? Did you talk to anybody about it?
O: Captain Smith was an okay guy. He helped me keep my head on straight, while they were dragging the thing out. Also, my cousin Eddie had just shipped in from Desert Storm, and we hit it off because he had been through some similar shit in the military.
I: What about ringing up these guys now?
O: Smitty retired last year and is off on some damn island somewhere.
I: What about your cousin?
O: Well, it's been a while. I guess I owe him call, anyway. But I don't want to just call him out of the blue bitching about my problems.

I: Just plain call him. If the current situation comes up in the conversation, deal with it. If not, just some friendly bullshitting with someone you trust can take the edge off, you know? Besides, you're doing him a favor, too, by calling him, right?

O: Yeah, okay, this might be a good time to reconnect anyway.

Clarify Internal State

A prominent emotion during states of depression is confusion. Potentially suicidal officers are probably already skewing their perceptions and interpretations in the direction of helplessness and hopelessness, while dismissing or discounting any positives. Interveners should try to create a more favorable balance by identifying and separating out areas of self-deprecation and despondency vs. self-worth and hope. The first step is to try to find out what the officer is thinking, which may be no small feat in officers who frequently "suffer in silence."

Intervener: You're not looking so great lately. What's going on?

Officer: Nothing I can't handle.

I: I realize that, but I've known you a long time so, just to humor me, give me a clue.

O: I don't even know, myself. Sometimes I think everything's under control, and then it all looks like shit.

I: Can you give me some examples of the "under control" parts and the "shit" parts?

O: I'm just getting everything going on the job, putting in extra time, getting my performance ratings up; then I get home and catch hell from the wife for never being around. And this is after she's complained that there's not enough money coming in to cover the bills. Like, is that a double message or what? But she doesn't see it that way and just blames me. So then I crash and feel like nothing I do ever works out.

I: But it sounds like you've been able to turn the work situation around, getting your ratings up, right? That shows that when you put your mind to something, you're able to get it done. Seems like you *can* handle things, but that doesn't mean that the shit never gets to you.

Reduce Sense of Isolation

As with most forms of crisis intervention, just helping the person feel like he or she is not all alone in the world can have a powerful effect. Reducing isolation can occur in two main, sometimes overlapping, ways: commiseration and support.

Commiseration relies on shared experience: "I've been there and I've gotten through it and so can you." *Support* lets the distressed person know that others are on his or her side and that, even if we haven't been through the same experience, we'll try to understand, empathize, and help in any reasonable way we can. While the unique life circumstances of individual traumatic crises may differ, the emotional responses to them and the coping strategies people use are near-universal (Regini, 2004), so there may well be something in the intervener's experience that may allow him or her to relate to the officer in distress. And even if not, just knowing that someone's got your back in a constructive way can be immensely reassuring in times of crisis, even if—God bless 'em—they've never had to deal personally with the kind of turmoil you're going through.

Intervener: Listen, I've had an easy run so far, no major critical incidents I've been involved in, no beefs with the brass or fights at home, so I'm not gonna give you a speech. But, hey, if you want to talk to me, I'm here. You don't have go through all this in a bubble, you know.

Officer: Okay, thanks.

I: Besides, you ought to talk to Raul in Automotive. He went through a similar thing about a year and a half ago, and he's a nice guy. In fact, he's helped a few guys out from time to time.

O: Yeah? I didn't know that. Okay, I'll think about it.

Encourage Active Problem-Solving and Realistic Alternatives

Sometimes, the best way for a person to break through a depressive, potentially suicidal, crisis is for them to take some corrective action, to achieve a measure of self-efficacy, competence, and confidence. But the depressed person may need some encouragement or concrete guidance to break the inertia of despair. On the other hand, be careful not to "push" the person to do more than he or she can realistically accomplish in his present state of diminished capacity, because you don't want to risk further demoralizing the officer if he feels that his inability to comply with what you're suggesting only proves how ineffectual he really has become.

Intervener: Well, have you tried sitting down with your wife and talking about this?

Officer: You kidding me? You know how many times I've tried that? She just gets mad or hysterical and storms off. It's hopeless!

I: Okay, so much for the direct approach. But you told me she overdramatizes the financial pressures and that, with your overtime, you're actually bringing in more than enough to cover the bills and then some. Why don't you write up a little budget statement that proves this and e-mail it to her? That way, there's no face-to-face blow-up and you get your point across because you know she's gonna read the e-mail, at least out of curiosity, right? And even if she doesn't buy it, at least you know you did everything possible to try to explain the situation.

O: Yeah, it's worth a shot. She spends all her time on the damn computer, anyway.

INTERVENTION WITH THE ACTIVELY SUICIDAL OFFICER

Sometimes the first chance you get to intervene with a depressed, suicidal officer is when a crisis has already developed. The officer is actively considering suicide and your task is to keep him or her alive long enough to get appropriate follow-up care. The intervention strategies discussed here derive from a set of basic established principles of crisis intervention (Berk et al., 2004; Campbell, 2005; Gilliland & James, 1993; Greenstone & Leviton, 2001; Kleespies, 1998; Miller, 1998, 2005; Reinecke, 2000), applied to the special needs of police officers in distress.

Define the Problem

As noted previously, some personal crises relate to a specific event, such as an officer who learns of a spouse's betrayal, or has suffered a severe career setback, or has been involved in a traumatic critical incident. Often, however, a crisis state will evolve cumulatively as the result of a number of overlapping stressors until it hits the proverbial breaking point. In such cases, the officer himself may be unclear as to what exactly led to the present crisis state. Furthermore, this confusion typically adds to anxiety and a sense of being overwhelmed, which is particularly destabilizing for officers who value control, especially over themselves. Feeling this sense of control slip away can escalate to panic and despondency in a rapidly-spiraling vicious cycle.

Thus, one immediate crisis-intervention goal is to help the subject clarify in his or her own mind

what exactly has led to the present crisis state. This often involves a set of *focusing and clarifying questions*, similar to the internal state clarification noted above for the potentially suicidal officer. But now, in the actively suicidal state, there is increased direction and urgency to the intervention.

Officer: I can't stand it anymore. My life is out of control. I don't see any way out.

Intervener: What's out of control?

O: Everything, man, everything. Nothing goes right, everything's turned to shit.

I: Can you give me an example?

O: Everything, the job, my wife–it's all going to hell.

I: [Focuses] What's going on with the job?

O: I work like a slave all year, put in for extra overtime, volunteer for the Chief's pet programs, and then they tell me the city says there's no more raises, overtime, or bonuses this year–and that's after we already put the down payment on the new house.

[In point of fact, the officer may have indeed impulsively and prematurely put the money down on the house without waiting to get confirmation about the raises, but this is not the time to bring that up. Ultimately, better planning and problem-solving to avoid similar traps in the future may become a goal of later therapy but, right now, you just want to keep the officer safe.]

I: Is that what's making you feel this way?

O: That's part of it, yeah. And then the wife, she's all over me because now she's scared we'll lose the house. So it's nonstop screaming and shit. And on top of that, IAD's now reopening my file because of some more bullshit complaints.

I: [Clarifies] So you got caught by surprise with the no-raise thing and the investigation, and now all the family plans are jacked up? And everybody's walking around like a raw nerve?

O: Right. Plus, I avoid going home to the fighting, so I'm spending more time at Paddy's, so I come home crocked, and that leads to more shit. And sooner or later, someone's gonna finger me for a drunk and that's gonna add to my jacket. I can't take this man, I'm getting ready to suit up.

Ensure Safety

As noted above, you're not going to solve all of the officer's problems in this one encounter. What you want to do is make sure he survives this crisis so he can avail himself of appropriate follow-up psychological services after the acute emergency has passed. For now, assume that if the officer contacted someone at all, or is even willing talk when you arrive, he has not made the irrevocable decision to end his life right here and now. Your job is to use this wiggle room productively by encouraging the officer to put even a few short steps between the thought of a self-destructive action and it's implementation.

Intervener: Is there anything in there with you that could hurt you?

Officer: I got my service Sig with a full mag. Yeah, that could hurt someone.

I: Any chance of you putting the gun away while we talk?

O: So what, so you can all bust in here and drag me away to the nut house?

I: Actually, I just want to make sure you're safe. If you're gonna do something, then you're gonna do it, but for right now, how's this? How about popping out the mag and the cap in the chamber, and putting everything on the table in front of you. That way, if you really want the gun, it's right there, but at least you'll give yourself a second to think about it.

O: Yeah, right, and the minute I take the mag out, you bust in and get me. Hey, I wasn't sleeping in that class, either, man.

I: Okay, I understand. Then how about at least putting the safety on? It takes, what, half a second to flip the switch back? Nobody's gonna do anything to you in half a second.

O: I'll think about it.

I: Thanks.

This approach can be applied to other potential methods of suicide; for example, the officer can be asked to put the knife on the table instead of holding it to his throat. He can be persuaded to keep the cap on the pill bottle while you're talking. If he's standing on a building ledge or on a curb beside heavy traffic, he can be encouraged to take just one pace backward.

Provide Support

This is just what it sounds like. As we've seen throughout this book, you don't necessarily have to categorically agree with any distressed subject's reasoning or point of view—and it's usually counterproductive to pretend you do when you don't—but a little empathy and commiseration can go a long way in establishing trust and encouraging a nonviolent resolution to the incident. It may also elicit some insight into issues that underlie the present predicament or that may have led up to it.

But remember, the goal of crisis intervention is not psychotherapy per se. You don't want to disregard a subject's important feelings and thoughts about his or her situation, but be careful to keep the conversation focused on resolving the present crisis, gently suggesting that the larger issues can be dealt with later—which of course implies that there *will* be a "later."

Intervener: Family and job stresses—they all just piled up, huh?

Officer: What a pile, yeah, that's a good way to put it. It seems my whole life, no matter what I do, nothing works out, everything turns to a pile of shit.

I: When a lot of shit happens at once, it can seem like that's all there ever was, even if there was some good stuff tucked away in there.

O: Good stuff, what good stuff? Good stuff is for other people. I get shit.

I: I hear you man. You sound like a guy who's tried to make it work, but sometimes too many damn things get in the way.

O: That's it–like there's fuckin' curse on me or something.

I: Hey, I'm not gonna give you any magical fairly dust speech, but sometimes curses can be broken.

O: Yeah, how?

I: I'm also not gonna pretend I have a precooked answer for you, but sometimes looking at things in a different way, trying things out you didn't do before, sometimes just staying away from certain toxic people or situations–things like that. At least it may be worth a shot. But right now, all I'm saying is I hear where you're coming from, I hear a world of hurt, and I'm hoping you can get things together for yourself.

O: I dunno, man, but hey, thanks anyway.

Examine Alternatives

Often, subjects in crisis are so fixated on their pain and hopelessness that their cognitive tunnel vision prevents them from seeing any way out. Your job is to gently expand the range of nonlethal options for resolving the crisis situation. Typically, this takes one of two forms: accessing practical supports and utilizing coping mechanisms.

Practical Supports. Are there any persons, institutions, or agencies that are immediately available to help the officer through the crisis until he or she can obtain follow-up care? Of course, you want to be reasonably sure that these support people will assuage, not inflame, the situation until professional help is obtained. Support systems or persons can consist of trusted relatives, friends, coworkers, supervisors, clinicians, clergy, and so on. Always be mindful of the risks and liabilities of relying on these support people instead of professional responders, and be prepared to make the call to commit the officer involuntarily if he truly represents a danger to himself.

Officer: I already told you, I'm not going to no damn hospital to be locked up and pumped full of drugs.

Intervener: Okay, let's leave the hospital out of it. I know you told me about your problems with the department and your wife, but is there anyone you know out there who's on your side, who could stand up for you and help you out?

O: I got a brother who's a good guy, but he lives across the country. Besides, I don't want my family involved in this.

I: Okay, anyone else, anyone more local, someone you trust?

O: I dunno, maybe my friend Mike. We were in the service together, and we got to be buddies. Then I didn't see him for about five years, until he moved to town about a year ago.

I: If Mike agreed to look after you for the rest of the weekend, till things cool off, would that be okay with you?

O: Yeah, we've been through some shit together, he'd understand.

I: Okay, then, if we call Mike?

O: Sure, go ahead.

Coping Mechanisms. These can consist of cognitive strategies, religious faith, distracting activities, accessing positive images and memories of family, and so on. You can appeal to both present and past coping mechanisms. For subjects who are feeling hopeless, it is often useful to recall past crises that were resolved without violence or self-harm. This shows that it's at least *possible* to get through the present crisis, and possibly come up with an even better solution this time than last time, so that the officer can prevent things from ever getting this bad again.

The caution here is that the subject may think that this present crisis is far worse than anything that's ever happened in the past–and sometimes this may be true–in which case, comparison with past, smaller crises may only serve to highlight the hopelessness of the present, bigger one. The intervener may therefore have to be creative in putting the present crisis in perspective.

Officer: I dunno, all these plans–what's the point? It's not like anything's gonna change in a couple of days. I'll still be under the same pile, no matter what.

Intervener: You said something earlier about how you've had bad shit happen many times before. Can you give me an example?

O: I dunno, lots of things.

I: Can you think of something specific?

O: What is this–a fucking test? Okay, about fifteen years ago, I got fired from a job for stealing tools. Only it wasn't me that stole them, it was another guy who hid the tools in my locker, but they found them on me before the other guy could get to them, so he just sat back and let me take the rap. They were ready to fire me and press charges. I could've gone to jail.

I: What'd you do?

O: I filed a grievance, and luckily we had a decent union on that job that backed me up with a lawyer. To make a long story short, they ended up finding that although the "evidence against me was compelling," quote unquote, the investigation technically didn't follow all their own rules and protocols, so they couldn't make it stick. So we worked out a deal where I'd resign without a severance package, but the charges wouldn't go on my record. Even though I wasn't guilty, I took the deal, since I needed to find another job. That's how I got my next security job, which led me to apply to the police academy and I wound up in this department.

I: So you went from almost being busted to becoming a cop. It sucked to be falsely accused, but you handled it, you used your brains and your willpower, and you made it come out the best way possible. When you put your mind to something, you're able to work it out.

O: Well, I had some help . . . .

I: Hey, everybody gets a little help, nobody does anything all by themselves. How'd you get your head through it all, knowing that the other guy did it?

O: That was probably the hardest part, knowing that the little shit was sitting there laughing. God, I wanted to fuck him up! But I knew if I did anything like that, they would see it as proof of my own guilt, plus I'd go to jail for sure. So I kept telling myself to be a stand-up guy, don't back down, see it through, and maybe someday what goes around comes around, but I don't think I really believed that.

I: You kind of talked yourself through it. And you kept yourself from doing something you knew would hurt you worse down the road.

O: Yeah, I guess so.

I: You think you could do something like that now, at least till we get a chance to figure out this whole deal? I mean just to get yourself and everyone safely through the next couple of days?

O: I dunno, maybe I could try.

Make a Plan

Again, this involves a combination of both practical supports and coping mechanisms. It also may involve making short-term and long-term plans.

Intervener: Okay, I want to make sure I have everything straight. I'm going to call Mike and see if you can stay with him till Monday morning. You're just going to kick back, watch the game, and avoid the bars, okay? You haven't done anything with the gun, it hasn't been fired, you didn't threaten anybody with it, so just holster it for the weekend or put it in a lockbox and everything should be cool with that. I suggest you tell your wife where you'll be so she doesn't worry, but tell her you need some time to chill and you'll contact her Monday. But first thing Monday morning, I want you to contact your EAP or go over to the County Clinic so you can get some help in dealing with this, all right?

Officer: Now I gotta see a shrink for the rest of my life.

I: Maybe not even for the rest of the month. But you may need a couple of sessions just to straighten things out. Besides, the department may require an FFD eval and maybe mandatory counseling, so you might as well score some points by taking the initiative on your own.

O: It's gonna be a long weekend, man.

I: Hey, I respect what you're doing, it's not easy. But, look, you already got yourself past having to go to the hospital and that's a matter of trust between us. Just tell yourself what you've told yourself in the past. You're a stand-up guy. You're not gonna give up till you work things out at work and at home, right?

O: I guess so.

I: Guessing will turn to knowing once you get the ball rolling.

Obtain Commitment

Finally, make sure the subject understands the plan and is reasonably committed to following it.

Intervener: We on the same page, man?

Officer: Yeah, okay.

I: All right, just so I'm clear, tell me what we agreed on.

O: What, you don't believe me?

I: Just so I'm clear in my own head, okay?

O: [Repeats the plan].

I: You're cool with this, you're gonna do it, right?

O: Yeah, yeah, I'll do it, I'll do it.

I: I'm proud of you, man. I'll call Mike and the Clinic, and then I'll check up with you on Monday, okay?

O: Yeah, yeah, whatever.

I: Okay??

O: Okay, okay [laughs]. Jeez, what a pain in the ass.

Of course, none of this is a foolproof formula, but applying the basic principles of crisis intervention in an atmosphere of sincere concern and respect can not only save a life in the short term, but perhaps even nudge that life in a more productive long-term direction.

POST-CRISIS MENTAL HEALTH INTERVENTION

Fitness for Duty and Return to Work

The general principles of psychotherapy with law enforcement officers have been covered in Chapter 6, and most of these can be applied to the treatment of officers following a suicidal crisis, with a few special considerations (Allen, 1986; Baker & Baker, 1996; Cummings, 1996; Miller, 2005; Mohandie & Hatcher, 1999; Quinnet, 1998; Violanti, 1996).

One obvious issue relates to *psychological fitness for duty* (FFD) of an officer whose emotional state has gotten sufficiently precarious to propel him to the brink of death. In many cases, such an evaluation will be a formal departmental requirement. But in some cases, officers may consult outside psychologists or other therapists privately, and the suicidal episode may have been quietly resolved without the department being aware of it. In other cases, the department does know about the episode but essentially trusts the psychologist to treat the officer any way he or she sees fit and to make the right call if there is any safety or job performance issue.

Some police psychologists have addressed the issue of a separation between the administrative evaluation and clinical treatment aspects of the psychologist's role (Blau, 1994; Flanagan, 1986; Mohandie et al., 1996; Scrivner, 2002; Sewell, 1986). After all, if an officer is eager to return to work, there may be an understandable motivation to "tell the shrink what he wants to hear" in order to get a clean bill of mental health. A preferable arrangement is to have one psychologist perform the initial FFD evaluation, turn the officer over for treatment to a clinical therapist, perhaps through the department EAP, and then have the officer re-evaluated

by the first psychologist after he or she has completed treatment with the clinician. An added benefit of this arrangement is that the two professionals can literally "compare notes," which reduces the chances of the officer running a deceptive game on either professional.

However, many departments don't have the luxury of this division of labor, so one police psychologist may have to do it all. In such cases, the psychologist should be sensitive to the clinical, administrative, confidentiality, and liability issues involved in treating distressed officers.

Special Psychotherapeutic Issues

Certain practical matters are especially important to address in treating an officer following a suicide attempt or gesture. Foremost are the twin issues of *safety* and *responsibility*. Inasmuch as the best prediction of future behavior is past behavior, it is likely that the officer will experience another emotional downturn some time in the future. And inasmuch as the best form of crisis intervention is crisis prevention, the therapy process should establish a system for identifying the triggers to a depressive episode and aborting the spiral of despair that may impel an officer to consider taking his or her own life.

For example, individuals in crisis may be encouraged to address the tailspinning cognitive distortions of the FIT model (Acosta & Prager, 2002), i.e., that the dire circumstances or problems of a person are (1) not necessarily *Forever:* they are not permanent conditions, but will pass or can be resolved; (2) not necessarily *Innate:* they may be influenced by changeable external factors, not just be the direct result of immutable inner faults; and (3) not necessarily *Total:* they comprise a subset of life, not the whole life itself.

This gives the subject realistic hope that the situation can be improved, and the process is best accomplished by delineating as concrete, practical, and cognitively-based a protocol for self-management as possible (Berk et al., 2004; Ellis & Newman, 1996). This can then be applied to any crises that begin to develop over time.

Therapist: The next time things get hairy for you, what are you going to do?

Officer: I think I'll be able to handle it a lot better.

T: You probably will, but to make sure that happens, give me a rundown of the plan we discussed.

O: Okay, if I start getting real depressed or angry, I'll call your office and make an appointment. If it's at night or the weekend, I'll call my friend Mike or, if it's real bad, I'll page you. In the meantime, I'll stay away from the booze—Jeez, doc, that's the hardest part.

T: Just for my own clarification, how will you know when you're getting "real depressed or angry"? And what kinds of things are likely to set you off? What'll you do when these things happen?

O: This *is* a tough test, isn't it? All right, if my asshole lieutenant starts riding me, I use the interpersonal coping skills we rehearsed to try and "de-escalate" the situation—I know you love that word, doc—and if things get out of hand, I take a few minutes to chill and get my bearings. I'll remember our discussions about what really makes a man a competent, responsible man, and I'll use all those coping skills we've talked about for the last couple of sessions. If my wife is supportive, I'll accept her help on its own terms, but if she's too ticked off or stressed out, or whatever, to be there for me and, especially if it looks like things are getting to the point of fighting at home, I'll de-escalate there, too. Oh yeah, and I'll remind myself that I've felt hopelessly out of luck before, but I was able to resolve it in the past and I can do the same thing now. Is that it?

T: That's about it. Now the key is to put it into practice.

POLICE SUICIDE SURVIVORS

Special considerations apply to the families of officers who have taken their own lives (Hamilton, 2003b). Whereas a line-of-duty death (Chapter 8) is viewed as a tragic but honorable demise, special shame may adhere to an officer's death by suicide, shame that affects the family in overt and subtle ways. In some departments, there may be debate over whether to grant the officer a full police funeral. More subtly, but just as painfully, the rush of support that greets families of slain officers may be choked to a trickle as fellow officers and their families overtly or subconsciously seek to avoid the "taint" of vulnerability that affixes to an officer suicide. Such families, denied the very support from their police community that they now most desperately need, may suffer excruciating trauma that complicates the sheer fact of their loved one's death. In such cases, the work of mental health professionals trained in the treatment of *stigmatized grief counseling* may be vital in helping such ostracized families to heal and move forward.

CONCLUSIONS

The general principles of crisis intervention can be productively adapted to the treatment of police officers in distress, as long as the clinician is willing to gain some familiarity with the police culture and the men and women of law enforcement who inhabit it. What may be unique about police psychology is the wide range of individuals that may be called upon to deal with any given crisis—mental health clinicians, police supervisors, peer counselors, fellow officers, and so on. Thus, this is one area where a cross-fertilization of ideas and expertise between psychology and law enforcement can be especially productive.

Chapter 12

SPECIAL UNITS:
UNDERCOVER AND SEX CRIMES INVESTIGATION

From *Miami Vice* to *Law & Order: SVU*, the public continues to display a fascination with special unit policing, partly due to the titillatingly lurid nature of the subject matter, and partly because such stories combine the features of vicarious danger and ultimate triumph (we hope) of good over evil. Of course, these portrayals typically overlook the plodding hard work that underlies most successful special unit operations, and obscures many of the psychological variables that can influence this kind of police work. As distinct from daily patrol, these special investigatory operations are typically carried out by trained detectives within a department or division of a law enforcement agency. This chapter will describe the role of psychological services in two specialized areas of policing: undercover operations and criminal investigations.

THE NATURE AND PURPOSES OF UNDERCOVER POLICING

An important part of gathering evidence to prosecute serious crimes involves the skillful infiltration of criminal groups by specially trained officers. While the targets of undercover operations carried out by law enforcement agencies may vary—narcotics, money laundering, illegal immigration, terrorism, and so on—the fundamental goal of all undercover operations is to develop prosecutable evidence by accessing subjects and their activities from the inside (Barefoot, 1975; Hibler, 1995).

In addition to types of targets, undercover assignments vary in terms of time frame, including everything from short-term, buy-bust scenarios to longer-term investigations lasting many months or years (Band & Sheehan, 1999). Undercover operations also differ in terms of methodology, each with its own particular set of stressors. At the most basic level is *plainclothes surveillance and enforcement*, conducted by nonuniformed officers either on foot or in a vehicle who, when necessary, will identify themselves as police officers. The second level of undercover work consists of *deep undercover*, where one's identity is changed by false documents, appearance is altered by hair grooming and costuming, and one's contact with family, friends, and other police officers is strictly limited. These kinds of investigations sometimes take several months or years to accomplish their aims. It is the deep *undercover officer* (UCO) who may be at greatest risk for the development of a stress disorder (Farkas, 1986).

As noted above, the goal of undercover operations is to develop prosecutable evidence that can hopefully lead to a larger-scale, system-wide shutdown of the criminal enterprise (Hibler, 1995). In the drug trade, for example, the primary focus of most law enforcement undercover activities is not to interrupt the short-term, street-level transactions between dealers and users, but is mainly directed at the primary cultivation, importation, manufacture, and other activities of the high level wholesaler (Girodo, 1985). Similarly, the purpose of infiltrating terrorist or extremist groups is not necessarily to stop individual acts of sabotage or destruction, but to get as close as possible to the organization's leadership to interdict the illegal activity at its source (Bolz et al., 1996; Smith, 1994). In the process, the UCO may have to knowingly stand by and observe the continuation of illegal and harmful activity, which itself can be a great source of stress and frustration.

Psychologically, the essence of all undercover operations is the same: *UCOs knowingly and purposefully develop relationships that they will eventually betray.* Officers working deep undercover hold the responsibility of infiltrating a target group by befriending its members, and then covertly collecting evidence of illegal activity. In this process, UCOs establish relationships with criminal suspects and law-abiding citizens alike, and both will help the officers establish identities and make the right connections without knowing the truth about them. Many undercover officers find this dual betrayal a difficult road to walk, adding to the stressors already inherent in undercover work (Band & Sheehan, 1999; Farkas, 1986).

Even in the age of terrorism, narcotics continues to be the largest area of focus for undercover law enforcement. Undercover narcotics work is one of the most hazardous and stressful jobs in policing. UC narcs must create and play a role that is not only dangerous but also puts them in daily intimate contact with the dregs of humanity. Police personnel working undercover assignments risk detection and violent retribution; for example, UC officers are ten times more likely than uniformed officers to be shot or shoot someone else (Geller, 1993). In addition to this ever-present danger, the work is physically, intellectually, and emotionally demanding (MacLeod, 1995).

It must be recognized that success or failure of an undercover operation is the consequence of many factors, some of which are beyond the control of the undercover team and the sponsoring law enforcement agency. A successful or unsuccessful undercover operation is a team effort, and although most UCOs pay lip service to the idea that the UCOs cannot be held individually accountable for the final outcome, no officer can avoid feeling the disappointment and anger of a blown operation (Hibler, 1995); indeed, the pain of such a failure is matched only by the recriminations observed after a failed hostage negotiation (see Chapter 9). The difference is, however, that while a hostage crisis typically evolves over hours or days, undercover operations may span years, heightening the sense of having "blown it big time" when something goes wrong. That's why, as we'll see presently, most successful undercover operations break the program into a series of stages, so that the whole operation does not stand or fall based on one or two unfortunate mishaps.

THE UNDERCOVER TEAM

As much as any operation in law enforcement, successful undercover work must be a model of planning, coordination, and timing. Probably in no other kind of operation are so many roles played by so many personnel over so long a period of time, under such sustained conditions of stress. Undercover police work is thus an area where police psychologists can make a vital contribution.

ROLE OF THE PSYCHOLOGIST IN UNDERCOVER OPERATIONS

As with all the areas of police psychology discussed in this book, the credibility of the psychologist rests on his or her ability to earn the trust of all involved. The role of the psychologist and psychological support in undercover operations is to function as an "honest broker" between all parties, to ensure that all of the personnel involved are heard and understood, and that their needs and risks are addressed to assure the success of the mission (Hibler, 1995).

For example, since 1972, the undercover program of the New Zealand Police Department has employed an external, independent mental health professional, as a member of the medical support team, to assist in the selection, training, health, welfare monitoring, and postdeployment rehabilitation of their undercover officers (MacLeod, 1995). Other departments around the world have similar programs.

Not surprisingly, views differ as to the nature of the fiduciary relationship between the psychologist and the undercover team members and police department. In one view, unlike the traditional clinical relationship between a patient and his or her psychologist, in undercover operations, the "patient" or client is the undercover program and the police agency itself. Consequently, there is no professional confidentiality, because to function as a team, members have to know each other's moves (Hibler, 1995). However, there is some room for discretion.

In the New Zealand program, strict medical privilege is enforced, personally sensitive material being protected from the police administration by doctor-patient confidentiality. The philosophy of that program is to give the highest priority to ensuring the health and welfare of the personnel involved; thus, the consultant psychiatrist possesses the authority (if required) to override police operational decisions (MacLeod, 1995). Few police departments in the United States would afford their mental health consultants such wide latitude of veto power, and law enforcement agencies must work out policies and protocols that are realistic for their own undercover teams.

PHASES OF AN UNDERCOVER OPERATION

For purposes of discussion, I have adopted Hibler's (1995) six-stage progression of an undercover operation, recognizing that these stages may overlap, blend into one another, and recycle with one another. The standard phases are (1) *selection* of personnel for the undercover team; (2) *training* of the team; (3) *planning* the operation; (4) *deployment*

of the team and carrying out of the operation; (5) *termination*, or closedown of the operation, either upon successful completion or because of unforeseen complications; and (6) *reintegration* of the undercover officer into normal work and life roles. Each of these phases has its own psychological implications, to be discussed below.

SELECTION

As with many police roles, those who seek involvement in undercover work are not always those who are the best qualified and, although in some departments, appointments to undercover teams may be based on little more than seniority, rank, or favoritism, most law enforcement executives understand the need to carefully screen and select officers who will make effective UCOs.

Screening and Selection of Undercover Officers

The screening and selection process will naturally include a variety of elements, such as the officer's knowledge of tactics, weapons, legal principles, undercover strategies, evidence collection and preservation, and so on. These elements may be assessed by means of performance record reviews, written tests, interviews, and role-play scenarios. The screening process may also include a

psychological component, which usually involves some combination of a structured clinical interview and psychological testing. These evaluations should be updated every six to twelve months and prior to every new major assignment, because while a person's basic personality structure doesn't change substantially over time, life circumstances and emotional states do (Band & Sheehan 1999; Hibler, 1995).

Chapter 13 discusses the concept of *screening-out* vs. *screening-in* as part of the selection process of police officers in general. For the specific purposes of UCO selection, Hibler (1995) suggests that the absolute screen-outs for undercover work are essentially the same as for police work in general. Nominees for undercover work should have a track record of competent performance in their present assignment, have effective interpersonal skills, and possess sufficient career experience to have crystallized and refined their basic law enforcement skills.

New trainees who have not learned how to perform their agency's routine duties will have no job to return to when their tour in undercover work is over. As we'll see later, it is important to have such a post-undercover role established, so that the officer does not flounder around the department following completion of his undercover assignment.

Screening-in involves at least two levels of consideration (Hibler, 1995). The first involves demonstrating general abilities that include a proven track record of being able to work both with others and alone; being able to work reliably without a great deal of direct supervision; being able to demonstrate good judgment, particularly under stress; and being able to handle boredom during periods of stagnation in progress.

The second screen-in level addresses readiness and suitability for a specific undercover operation. Qualifications here include two main elements: first, the absence of current conflicts at work or home that would interfere with commitment to the upcoming assignment; and second, task-relevant skills and personal attributes as defined by age, race, ethnic origin or gender, geographic, cultural, or experiential knowledge. Examples include being streetwise to a local inner city drug culture; being knowledgeable about banking and finances when infiltrating a white-collar money-laundering operation; being able to pilot a boat or plane in a narcotics trafficking case; or being fluent in the language and customs of a foreign-based political terrorist group.

Characteristics of Effective Undercover Officers

In a study of FBI agents, Hibler (1995) identified three basic groups of agents who volunteer for undercover assignments, and these findings can probably be extrapolated to most major police agencies. The largest group consists of agents who approach undercover work as a career move to stay competitive. The next largest group is composed of officers who view undercover work as a way of "doing their own thing" with minimal supervision. The third group are officers who are running away from their currently unpleasant working conditions and may not even be particularly attracted to undercover work, but will essentially "do anything" to escape their present circumstances; i.e., undercover is basically seen as the lesser of two evils.

In fact, Hibler (1995) notes that most special agents who are satisfied with their circumstances and their futures are hesitant to consider undercover work. Far from the glamour of TV shows and Hollywood, they see this work for what it is: long, thankless stretches of time and effort for which there is little chance to improve their circumstances and plenty of opportunity to stagnate. Altogether, most law enforcement personnel who are reasonably satisfied in their present jobs want nothing to do with undercover assignments. This may be one source of the Hollywood stereotype of UC agents that "you have to be at least a little crazy to do this kind of work."

But to be a truly effective UCO, you really can't be crazy—in fact, you have to be decidedly uncrazy and emotionally stable. As with any aspirational model, the following characteristics (Band & Sheehan, 1999; Hibler, 1995; MacLeod, 1995) comprise a *profile of the "ideal" UCO*. The closer real-life officers are to this model, the more effective the undercover team will be.

Ideally, UCOs should be experienced, seasoned investigators of reasonably mature age, with a secure police identity and prior experience in other areas of policing. They should have had some life experience outside the police force. They must be able and willing to accept training and supervision when necessary and to work hard at perfecting their craft. They should volunteer for undercover work because they believe in the goals and methodologies of undercover and have demonstrated appropriate moral and ethical values that correspond to their belief in the purposes of legitimate law enforcement activity in a free society. Their interest in undercover work should be motivated by a justifiable pride in their ability to excel in this type of endeavor. At the same time, this should not be pursued as a quest for glory or as an escape from less desirable work or an unpleasant personal life. That is, undercover work should be sought for its own sake, not as a "running-to" or "running-from" activity.

Undercover officers have to be able to show perseverance and resourcefulness in the face of complex, changing, ambiguous, and often dangerous circumstances, with very little external supervision or oversight. At the same time, they cannot become free agents or loose cannons, and must be comfortable taking direction and operating within their agency's policies, procedures, and guidelines. They must be highly proficient and flexible in their undercover role-plays, be proficient actors, and at the same time be able to maintain their core identities and commitment to the mission. They must be able and willing to spend long intervals away from family and friends.

UCOs must be self-confident without being egotistical; decisive without being rigid or stubborn; flexible without waffling; capable of independent action but able to quickly snap back as team players when necessary; focused and not prone to distraction from the main objective; stress-resilient and mentally tough without being overly cynical or aggressive; and generally psychologically stable and not prone to impulsivity, mood swings, or erratic behavior. Importantly, they must be able to purposefully and credibly establish, nurture, and maintain close, sometimes intimate, personal relationships with a variety of different types of people, knowing that these relationships will ultimately be betrayed as part of the larger mission and the overall goals of law enforcement.

TRAINING

As with any operation, the purpose of training is to develop and sharpen operational performance by acquiring knowledge and practicing skills necessary for functioning in the undercover arena. In fact, selection often overlaps with training as undercover candidates are further culled in the training process. Aside from any technical knowledge the undercover officer might need to fit into his or her role, the essential essence of undercover work involves *interpersonal skills*. These include the ability to deal convincingly with others, to be creative, flexible, and self-disciplined in carrying out the assignment, and to be able to exert good judgment and calm behavior under stress (Hibler, 1995; MacLeod, 1995).

Given the importance placed on training in most types of law enforcement operations, it is perhaps surprising how often this element of undercover work is overlooked. It's as if the Hollywood myth of the lone hero, winging it by wit, grit, spit and bullshit, comprises the guiding philosophy of many real-life teams. Indeed, many officers themselves seem to recognize this. More than a quarter of a group of Honolulu UCOs said they received no preparatory information about the nature of the undercover assignments they were sworn into. Over half of this subgroup felt such information would have been helpful in adjusting to their assignment. The need for more training was mentioned by almost half of this sample, as was more and better supervision and administrative support (Farkas, 1986).

The short shrift given to training of UCOs would be unthinkable in other areas of police work. For example, Band and Sheehan (1999) point out that SWAT teams have always had a history of being specially screened, tested, selected, trained, equipped, and rehearsed. Yet, UCOs often have not received the same attention, despite the fact that such officers frequently face levels of immediate or potential danger at least as great as any SWAT team member, and without the armed backup. Band and Sheehan (1999) propose a formal certification program for undercover officers that specifies the standards for testing, selection, training, and monitoring of undercover officers.

A good part of the impetus for comprehensive training may come from legal liability concerns (Girodo, 1985). One issue involves the concept of *negligent training* that applies to most public safety industries. If UCOs are shown to have been inadequately or improperly trained, and injuries or fatalities occur, these officers and their department—indeed, the whole municipality—may be held liable.

Insufficient training may also compromise the mission itself, in two ways. First, simply by being unprepared, mistakes may be made that lead to blown cover, botched arrests, or personal injury. Second, even if arrests are made, the perpetrators' defense counsel may later argue in court that the UCOs' improperly trained procedures or poorly monitored psychological status nullifies the legality of the bust.

The guiding principle for mental health professionals associated with undercover operations—indeed, in almost all team efforts—is that the client is the mission itself, and that all relevant components, including the officers' mental state and behavior, are subject to scrutiny and analysis at every phase of the operation, including training. Essentially, then, the message to undercover officers is: Your personality is the most important tool in this operation, and therefore will be subject to a "systems check" whenever it is deemed necessary. This also includes training officers to recognize symptoms of their own stress reactions that might compromise the operation.

PREPARATION

No operation of any kind can be successful without proper planning and preparation, and—continuing the cycle—the training phase of an undercover operation now transitions into the planning phase. Contrary to the previously mentioned lone-wolf, shoot-from-the-hip Hollywood stereotype, absence of a clearly articulated plan that is understood by all team members actually puts more of the stress and burden on the UCO, especially if the operation should fail or be aborted. Indeed, research has shown that most UCOs themselves would have preferred to have more, rather than less, information going into an operation, and most believe that had this information been available during prior missions, their subsequent postdeployment psychological adjustment would have been better (Farkas, 1986).

But this means the *right* information. To be effective, *planning must be based on credible intelligence.* The plan itself should be more than a rough outline; it should have a beginning, middle, and end, with contingency plans and provisions for foreseeable glitches and emergencies. The goals should be as specific as possible (simple intelligence-gathering vs. making street-level arrests vs. long-term infiltration and shutdown of a regional criminal operation), and the resources in manpower and material must be available to carry out the mission. Finally, for legal reasons, every aspect of the plan should be thought out as carefully as possible and documented in writing (Anderson et al., 1995; Hibler, 1995).

Another aspect of preparation involves *giving the undercover officers proper support.* Given the huge investment of manpower and the great risks involved, it may seem strange that many UCOs believe that managers and supervisors lack commitment, support, and sensitivity for the nature of undercover work. To combat this impression, Band and Sheehan (1999) recommend that managers include UCOs in decisions that affect the course and direction of the operation; provide *backstopping*, i.e., information accumulated to support the undercover role, as fully as possible; assign a *control officer* or contact agent who can keep the UCOs grounded in their law enforcement identities and purposes of the mission; and hold regular meetings with executive managers, who are guided by the principle that the first priority is the physical and emotional safety and well-being of the UCOs.

These planning efforts should also take into account the *personality and working style of the individual UCO.* Some officers may require more frequent contacts with their control officer, for both logistical feedback and moral support, whereas other officers may be more suited to working alone for longer periods. Even though screening and selection will hopefully have weeded out officers with serious psychological problems, UCOs will still have their individual personalities and operating styles, and the psychology of the officer is as important a factor in planning and carrying out the operation as any other aspect of the mission (Hibler, 1995).

The Cover Identity

The central feature of all undercover operations is creating a *cover identity* for the UCO. Obviously, this role must be as believable as possible. Movie portrayals depict chameleonic "masters of disguise" who can seamlessly slip in and out of any persona, from bespectacled professor to tattooed biker, but in reality, nobody is that good an actor. Even the most talented Hollywood stars are playing their prescribed roles for a brief period of time on an artificial set—they don't have to stay in character for days, weeks, or months at a time, continually improving behavior and dialogue along the way, with their lives and safety only one slip from disaster.

Accordingly, to assure maximum success, the undercover role should never be a total masquerade; in fact, the closer it is to the officer's real identity and persona, the better the chances of successfully pulling it off. Certainly, obvious features such as age, sex, ethnicity, and language fluency are important, but so are such factors as names; for example, cover names should closely resemble real names, so that the agent is not caught off guard if his cover name is suddenly called, or his real name is inadvertently mentioned (Buckwalter, 1983). Certainly, there will be some preparation and role development needed for any operation, but the guiding principle here is that the fewer features of the role that have to be artificially rehearsed, and the more similar the officer's true identity and life experience is to that of the cover, the less opportunity there will be for embarrassing and dangerous surprises (Anderson et al., 1995; Hibler, 1995). This doesn't mean that the UCO's lifestyle has to be an exact replica of the undercover role, just close enough to be comfortable.

An often overlooked feature of UCOs successfully maintaining their cover in the target criminal environment is that they are often conspicuous by their absence. As part of the role, such agents need not and should not be a constant presence in their targets' lives; in fact, the new player who is always hanging around might arouse the targets' suspicions. Remember, real criminals come and go, they disappear for periods of time, are shady about their doings and whereabouts, and seem to pop up only when they want something. Such realistic on-and-off behavior may well suit the UCO who needs time to decompress during the operation and to afford meetings with the control officer (Band & Sheehan, 1999; Hibler, 1995).

Target Profiling

Another aspect of the psychologist's involvement in mission planning and preparation deals more specifically with personality dynamics, behavioral profiles, and other knowledge points relevant to the infiltrated group's members. Such research may then lead to recommendations for how to interact and earn the trust of different targets of the operation. This degree of behavioral profiling may not be necessary for routine buy-and-bust drug cases which involve brief, uncomplicated undercover work. But when a large-scale operation that may involve long-term undercover interaction with high-level criminal personalities is being planned, some insight into the targets' inner workings is likely to prove useful. In addition, "internal profiling" involves determining which particular officers might be the best match for a particular target (Hibler, 1995).

DEPLOYMENT

As with all phases in the present model, the phase of preparation cycles over into the phase of deployment. Now the operation is set to go.

Predeployment Briefing

This is essentially a final briefing and "dress rehearsal" for the operation that unites the plan with the players (Hibler, 1995). At this point, everybody involved in the operation–UCO, control officer, support personnel, command, etc.–should understand their respective roles and how to interact with one another. Even though the burden of the operation is necessarily placed on the UCO, the operation itself should always be seen as a team effort.

Scheduling of contacts and ways of signaling trouble should be worked out in advance. Any last-minute questions or changes in plan based on new intelligence should be dealt with at this point.

Another consideration is planning for the UCO's family needs. Since he or she may be out of contact for some considerable period of time, a *family liaison* should be part of the undercover team. This person will serve as a confidential go-between to keep the family apprised, within the limits of the plan's confidentiality, of how the UC officer is doing.

A final, often overlooked, aspect of predeployment planning is what role the UCO will return to when the operation is completed. This will be discussed further below.

Stresses of Undercover Deployment

Serious stress reactions to undercover deployment are hardly inevitable, or no one could last very long in this kind of work. Indeed, the vast majority of problems encountered in one study of UCOs (MacLeod, 1995) consisted of technical and strategic matters, rather than health or psychological concerns. This was true despite the fact that all agents endured frequent threats of danger and some were subjected to physical assaults, although none were seriously injured. Minor escalations in anxiety following critical encounters, such as challenges to the undercover identity, were common, but no severe emotional disturbances, posttraumatic reactions, or psychotic episodes were noted during employment. Rarely did a UCO require pullout on mental health grounds and, in those few such cases, this was due primarily to mounting fear of danger and/or sagging motivation for the operation.

Still, the risk of stress reactions among UCOs is a great enough concern that several studies of undercover deployment stress have been undertaken. Farkas (1986) cites declassified FBI data indicating that the major sources of stress for agents under deep cover include the agent-supervisor relationship, maintaining the role requirements of the undercover operation, and strain on family and social relationships. Major psychological reactions noted in the FBI study include general paranoia and hypervigilance, as well as corruption of the agent's value system and commitment to the operation, including a growing sympathy for the targets.

Farkas's (1986) own study, which involved UCOs in the Honolulu Police Department, revealed that a variety of psychological symptoms may be associated with undercover police work and that these symptoms persist for a period of time after the operation ends. The most commonly reported symptoms included anxiety, heightened suspiciousness, loneliness, feelings of isolation, and relationship problems. Many officers were distressed at not being able to talk to anyone about the assignment and many suffered some deterioration in personal relationships as a result of their undercover deployment. All of the UCOs reported at least some psychological symptoms during their deployment, and about half identified themselves as having "psychological problems" that started an average of five months into the operation. A third of the officers felt that their problems were serious enough that they would have liked the opportunity to consult with a psychologist at some point during their undercover deployment.

The prime stressor inherent in any undercover deployment is the ever-present fear of discovery, which could endanger the UCOs as well as others. Other stresses are more technical in nature. When working wired or using surveillance equipment, hardware glitches can risk compromising the whole operation. Where the operation involves interagency collaboration, unresolved differences in objectives, procedures, or technical matters among the different agencies can prove disastrous for the assignment. Relatedly, mismatched personalities or selection of UCOs who are not familiar with the undercover environment and culture, or otherwise ill-suited for this particular deployment, can spell the downfall of the operation. Few UCOs can remain undercover for months at a time without a break. Lack of sufficient recovery time between deployment periods can thus prove stressful, and officers should be afforded the opportunity to "come in" when needed before continuing their operational roles. Indeed, with sufficient break time and other adequate support, some undercover operations can last for years, as in the case of "moles" and "sleepers" (Band & Sheehan, 1999).

Narcissistic Entitlement and the Thrill Factor

Psychological reactions to undercover deployment need not be stress-related per se. Recall the undercover personality profile discussed in the beginning of this chapter. Many of the reactions to deployment may represent exaggerations of these characteristics and behavioral styles, most commonly an exacerbation of narcissistic traits and attitudes during the thrill of deployment. MacLeod (1995) describes the emergence in some UCOs of a self-centered, pretentious, superior, and arrogant persona, a caricature of the hard-driving, competitive, and self-sufficient agent at the pinnacle of a complex, multilevel, operational police hierarchy.

In moderate doses, such tough-minded but flexible "healthy narcissism" (Millon & Davis, 1996, 2000) is actually an asset in dealing with the undercover role and is correlated with operational success. The problem arises at unhealthily escalating levels of egotistc self-absorption when the UCO begins to believe that he is a law unto himself, rather than a member—albeit a crucial member—of the undercover team. Remember, one of the reasons that undercover work is so attractive to some officers is that it permits a vicarious delving into the amoral power trip of the criminal: the same reason most of us like to watch *The Sopranos*, or read stories about famous serial killers. Abetted by a sensation-hungry and novelty-seeking temperamental style (Cloninger, 1987; Zuckerman, 1990), the officer may become increasingly susceptible to the seductions of power and pleasure afforded by the undercover role. The thrill of deception and manipulation has then become an end in itself, outweighing commitment to the law enforcement objectives.

At the same time, the UCO's inflated self-importance may lead him to expect greater and greater deference and consideration from the other members of his team, indeed, from his police peers generally. This may then breed resentment and alienation, as fellow officers come to shun the prima donna. The unfortunate result may be degenerating cooperation and a compromised mission.

Role Overidentification and the "Undercover Stockholm Syndrome"

Recall that successful undercover operations are all about forming and maintaining relationships. The targets are people, and even many career criminals have their "human" side. Many have families with children. Some may be quite likable and engaging, the kind of people the officer might enjoy having a beer or barbeque with—if only they weren't smuggling drugs, laundering currency, murdering rivals, or bombing buildings. One the greatest potential stresses of undercover work, then, is for an officer to form deceptive pseudofriendships with people he will ultimately have to betray, albeit in the cause of justice. Some UCOs are able to achieve the kind of mental dissociation necessary to accomplish this role, while others may be drawn into a questioning of their own loyalties and commitments, as their sympathy for the target grows—sometimes called the *undercover Stockholm syndrome* (Anderson et al., 1995; Band & Sheehan, 1999; Marx, 1988).

In fact, research shows that there is a direct relationship between a UCO's attachment to the targets and his or her perceived level of distress during and following the operation. In some cases, this has led to drug abuse, sexual indiscretions, and criminal activity on the part of the officers during their assignment. Officers have also reported negative effects on their subsequent careers following undercover assignments which involved betraying close attachments (Farkas, 1986).

Managing Deployment Stress

If we accept that the UCO's personality and behavior are the crucial tools in a successful undercover operation, then we can agree that proper attention to the agent's ongoing mental status is not just a psychologically cosmetic feel-good measure, but is as integral to the mission as maintaining the integrity of weapons or surveillance equipment. If the UCO's psyche breaks down, the mission breaks down. Conversely, effective, well-planned psychological monitoring and intervention services can assure that UCOs may work for long periods of time, even indefinitely as moles or sleepers (Band & Sheehan, 1999).

Although this chapter emphasizes the role of psychologists in assisting the undercover operation, as well as the idea that such an operation is a group effort, the sheer weight placed on the UCO to carry out the mission successfully implies that, to a large degree, these officers must be responsible for monitoring their own stress levels and knowing when to take appropriate steps to maintain their bodies and minds in optimal performance mode (Cheek & Lesce, 1988).

The next line of defense is the supervisor or *control officer*, who plays several roles. One is to keep the UCO informed of any strategic or logistical changes in the operation's goals or tactics. The other is to function as a "stress barometer" to assure that the UCO is dealing with the pressures of his role assignment in a reasonably healthy and adaptive way. This can only be accomplished by keeping in regular contact with the UCO. Ideally, the control officer should be someone in the department of equal or greater rank, who is experienced or familiar with undercover work, and who can serve as a mediator and buffer between the UCO and the undercover team, as well as with department and family liaisons (Anderson et al., 1995; Band & Sheehan, 1999; Marx, 1988).

One of the purposes of the UCO-control meetings is to reinforce the mission's purpose and the UCO's core identity as a law enforcement officer. This kind of reality check may be the only antidote to the Stockholm-like sympathy for the target described earlier. Hollywood portrayals depict the lone-wolf type of UCO officer as fiercely independent and resistant to meeting with his meddlesome control officer, who is usually portrayed as a rule-bound dork. The far more common reality is quite the opposite: when UCOs express any dissatisfaction with supervision, it is usually for *not enough* guidance and information, rather than too much, as well as poor overall communication of the team's expectations (Farkas, 1986). In fact, the single greatest factor in fomenting Stockholm-type affinities with criminal targets cited by UCOs themselves is perceived lack of administrative support: "They don't give a shit, so why should I?"

Finally, some departments build into the operation regular contact with a psychologist; in other departments, this is arranged on an as-needed basis, and in still other departments, there are simply no psychological services routinely available for undercover assignments (Anderson et al., 1995; MacCleod, 1995). Obviously, psychologists in this role must have some understanding of undercover work and police psychology in general. Again, for law enforcement officers who might have a general aversion to having their heads shrunk, the role of the psychologist on the undercover team must be conceptualized in the same way as other "maintenance" professionals: if your car breaks down, you bring it to the motor pool; if your wire or videocam malfunctions, you have the electronics tech look at it; if you bust your knee or get stabbed, the medic patches you up; and if you're getting fatigued, anxious, and forgetful, it's time to haul your brain into the psychologist for a tune-up.

The good news is that, while a significant number of UCOs suffer some form of psychological aftereffect as a result of their assignments, most of these remain in the mild to moderate range, most are resolved within a few weeks or months of the operation's close, and very few require that an UCO be pulled from a mission on psychological grounds alone (Farkas, 1996; McLeod, 1995). In fact, regular contact with the control officer and regular psychological monitoring are the best assurance that undercover stress or other psychological problems won't boil over to a degree that would compromise the mission and/or cause the UCO to be pulled. Here again, as in many areas covered by this book, the best form of crisis intervention is crisis prevention.

TERMINATION AND REINTEGRATION

Variously labeled *closedown* or *decompression,* the termination phase of an undercover operation is the formal end of the undercover part of the mission. Less glamorous, but equally important, is the phase that follows termination, in which the undercover team organizes their evidence and prepares for trial. Recognizing that most termination stress reactions, like most undercover role reactions in general, represent normal responses to highly unusual circumstances, the psychological strategies used to deal with these problems should reflect this wellness-based orientation of returning otherwise high-functioning personnel to their usual state of health and efficiency, as well as beginning the phase of reintegration into normal law-enforcement work—sometimes called "re-bluing" the officer (Hibler, 1995).

Some departments build a postassignment psychological assessment and psychological debriefing phase into their termination protocol, as a separate component from the more usual operational debriefing (MacLeod, 1995). As with psychological debriefings in general (Chapter 6), the purpose is to destigmatize the process, so that no UCO feels singled out for special treatment, and to make the process as palatable as possible.

Characteristics of Undercover Termination

There are three basic reasons why an undercover operation is terminated (Marx, 1988). First, the *mission has been successful,* the evidence needed has been gathered, arrests have been made or sufficient intelligence has been obtained for the next phase of law enforcement action. Second, after sufficient expenditure of time and resources, it becomes clear that the goals and purposes of the *operation cannot be accomplished* within the scope of the undercover plan, and the operation is unceremoniously terminated. Finally, in the worst case, the operation may have to be terminated because *cover is blown* or the security of the UCO or others is jeopardized.

Often, results are mixed: some useful evidence is gathered, some targets are apprehended, but all or most of the mission's objectives may not have materialized. Still, as in the case of "failed" hostage negotiations (Chapter 9) and other law enforcement actions, every effort should be made to learn something useful from even the most negative undercover outcome: 20/20 hindsight = 20/20 insight = 20/20 foresight.

Many undercover operations have no clear end point; the basic strategy is to keep the operation going as long as useful evidence and intelligence continue to be gathered. Here is where operational, psychological, and legal issues come together. Where a case is going well, the motivation may be to keep the UCO in the field as long as possible, despite signs of possible psychological deterioration which, paradoxically, might compromise the UCO's effectiveness in playing his role and in collecting further useful evidence and intelligence.

Certainly, from the perspective of the UCO's mental health, he should be called in periodically for a respite. But even from a practical and legal perspective, evidence gathered or arrest actions taken while an UCO is in an impaired mental state may later be challenged by the target's defense counsel. This may take the form of the UCO taking unnecessary risks, engaging in felonious behavior, using excessive force, and so on (Anderson et al., 1995). For example, recognizing that the UC agent's psychological health is the most important tool in an undercover mission, the FBI does not allow an agent to go under again for three years after coming out from a major operation (Marx, 1988). Whether a similar policy would be practicable in most regional and municipal law enforcement agencies is debatable, but the principle of keeping the UCO in tip-top mental shape certainly applies everywhere.

Psychological Reactions of UCOs to Undercover Termination

As noted earlier, the undercover role allows the UCO a certain degree of freedom and autonomy of action, and the return to routine police work can be quite a letdown, especially if the transition is abrupt. Former UCOs frequently complain of feeling micromanaged and "babied" by their current routine police duties and of not receiving proper respect and appreciation for their special role and efforts. A vicious cycle may ensue, as the entitled attitudes of these departmental prima donnas come to be resented by the rank and file, whose expressions of contempt or ridicule are taken by the former UCOs as even greater evidence of their own specialness which the other officers are seen as tacitly conceding by their expressions of petty jealousy (Hibler, 1995).

The freedom and independence of action afforded by the undercover role, combined with a narcissistically-tinged sense of personal mission, can in some cases lead to the development of a *savior complex* (Russell & Beigel, 1990), in which the UCO comes to see himself as the lone true bastion of justice battling the forces of lawlessness and corruption. Such officers may become cynical, angry, and resentful of authority. Some of this intense frustration may have a basis in reality if such agents have previously seen months of arduous and dangerous undercover work come to naught because of administrative screw-ups or unfair plea-bargains.

Rather than being able to invoke mature professional detachment and see such happenings as a necessary, if odious, part of their job ("you do the best you can, then you let the system work, and you win some and you lose some"), more narcissistically tunnel-visioned UCOs may take such events personally and come to believe that the directives and restrictions of their commanding officers unnecessarily impede them from their clear and noble pursuit of justice, an attitude approaching the Hollywood lone-hero model. In the real law enforcement world, signs of such iconoclastic UCO behavior have to be dealt with immediately and forthrightly.

Of course, the worst-case scenario from a mission point of view is where cover is blown, officers or innocent civilians are harmed, and targets get away (Russell & Beigel, 1990). Barring actual death or physical injury to an UCO, the psychological injury to the UCO's ego can be almost as painful, especially where the officer's own actions may have contributed to mission failure. When the fault lies with others, this reaction may be tinged with anger, as the officer sees "his" operation screwed up by incompetent others. Successful re-entry into normal life and work may be further impeded where betrayed criminals or their henchmen make persistent threats against the officer or his family. The continual vigilance required in such circumstances may mean that the officer can never really "come down" from the assignment. Even where physical danger is not a factor, the blown cover may mean that the officer's effectiveness as an UCO is over, at least for that locality.

Even with successful missions, following the euphoria and mutual congratulations of a job well done, there is likely to be a certain degree of emotional let-down, a kind of "postpartum depression" that follows the completion of an undercover assignment. Rarely, does this indicate clinical depression per se; in most cases, it can be attributed to a kind of rebound effect stemming from the abrupt release of high tension and vigilance that was required for the undercover role. In many operations, success may have been mixed, with some undercover objectives being accomplished, while others were not. In fact, many undercover operations have no real clear endpoint, but rather cycle into new phases as more information is gathered; in such cases, there may not be any distinct closure point. In most cases, officers whose identities are more strongly tied into the flash and glory of being an UCO, or who have had conflicts with other team members during the operation, are more likely to experience a letdown at the completion of the assignment (Russell & Beigel, 1990).

In Farkas's (1986) study, 42 percent of UCOs reported experiencing problems in their transition to another assignment. These problems commonly expressed themselves in the form of higher stress levels, impaired relationships with family, and greater concern for their safety following the assignment. In another group of UCOs, MacLeod (1995) found that relief, fatigue, and regret at betrayal of their criminal "friends" were universal components of the emotional let-down experienced

at the end of the undercover assignment. Most of the UCOs in that sample actually did fit the profile of the petulant, demanding, entitled departmental prima donna, superior and contemptuous of the petty inadequacies of their superiors and the system. Those who had experienced traumatic dreams during the assignment saw these diminish over time at mission's end, and about a quarter of the sample struggled briefly with posttraumatic stress reactions, but were able to re-establish psychological equilibrium relatively quickly. Whatever else undercover work may be, it apparently doesn't provide for much of a physical workout: on completion, all the agents embarked on exercise and dietary regimens, as most had gained weight during the sedentary activity necessitated by the undercover role.

Dealing with the Failed Mission

Failure may not be an option, but it has a nasty habit of happening anyway. As noted previously, operations rarely go exactly according to plan, and mission objectives, goals, and protocols may be changed midstream in response to new incoming intelligence and feasibility assessments. Indeed, as noted above, a certain flexibility should be built into the assignment to account for such potential turns in the road. However, when an unproductive operation is terminated or unforseen dangers crop up and fold the mission, there is a tendency to *seek someone to blame* for the failure, either others who have screwed up or, just as commonly, oneself for overlooking some sign or clue that could have staved off disaster.

Moreover, there may be anger and recrimination where personnel believe that others' screwups have marred their own good efforts. It is important for the police psychologist to be aware of an evolving vicious cycle, in which the self-flagellating officer, unable to bear his crippling guilt, projects it onto others who then understandably resent being labeled as the doofuses by the first officer: "Hey, don't put your shit on me, man. I'm not the one who knocked that door down before the signal." The more the psychologist, with departmental support, can help the agent come to grips with his own feelings and actions around the event, the less his guilt-turned-to-rage will have a chance to jeopardize his relationships with family, friends, and colleagues.

For such failed missions, Hibler (1995) recommends encouraging disappointed personnel to see their jobs as akin to firefighters who are paid to be ready and able to *do their best job* when called, but have *no guarantee that things will turn out* the way they expect. A floor may collapse, a cache of unknown stored chemicals may explode, someone may have negligently locked a fire escape door, and so on. Similarly, in MacLeod's (1995) program, all UCOs are considered successful at termination and officers are encouraged to reframe failure in terms of survival and sensible self-preservation by emphasizing that safety is priority one, and the success of the mission, while important, is secondary to the officers' well-being.

This is similar to the little speech I frequently encourage commanders to give to their police officers, firefighters, paramedics, and other critical service personnel who express self-recriminations following a failed mission: "You *are* 110 per cent refuckingsponsible for the efforts and actions which are under your control, but you are *not* necessarily responsible for the outcome, *if* that outcome could be influenced by any number of unforseen and uncontrollable factors. If you really did screw up in something you did, then go ahead and feel bad about it, let it burn and sting till you get it out of your system, but then pick your damn self back up and learn from the mistake, so next time you'll do it right–*that's* doing your job. And if the bad outcome was out of your control, don't waste this department's time and money beating yourself up about it, but learn what you can and realize that if this job were predictable and easy, then anyfuckingbody could do it, and we wouldn't need skilled and dedicated personnel who can act like *professionals* and be ready the next time."

While some version of this pep talk may sound logical and supportive, the reality is that it's rarely enough to mitigate the self-reproach these professionals feel when they believe or even suspect that they've let others down. Realistically, in my experience, some emergency service personnel will accept this view and others won't and, for adequate resolution of these issues, additional *administrative and/or psychological follow-up* may be necessary to examine any personal problems and reactions that might be complicating the officer's coping and adaptive processes.

Reintegration Syndromes

Several authors (Anderson et al., 1995; Girodo, 1991a, 1991b, 1991c; Russell & Beigel, 1990) have described a number of maladaptive responses by UCOs to the reintegration process.

Medalist syndrome. UCOs who have been the "stars" of important, high-level operations may go well beyond justifiable pride in a job well done and develop an attitude of inflated self-importance and entitlement that persists in their interactions with others in the department. Not surprisingly, this typically engenders a range of reactions in others, from bemusement to resentment.

Paranoia. Especially where the operation has had "loose ends," suspects have escaped, cover has been wholly or partially blown, or threats have been made against the UCO and his family, the officer may become hypervigilant and suspicious for quite some time following the undercover assignment. Depending on the nature and seriousness of the perceived danger, this continuing heightened state of alert may prove draining and debilitating to the officer's mental and physical health, and may affect his job functioning and family life.

Role generalization. This reaction occurs when the officer stays in character long after the undercover operation is over, and can include persistence of the undercover role's language, form of dress, general attitude, and so on. Of course, as noted above, to the extent that part of the selection process for UCOs may involve demographic similarities to the subculture they are to infiltrate, continuation of the undercover role may simply be a continuation of that officer's general lifestyle. However, it may be apparent to colleagues that the officer is taking things too far. Several subvarieties of role generalization are described below.

Rhetorical drama or "Miami Vice" syndrome. Coworkers may chuckle that the UCO still seems to be living in "TV-land." There may be a histrionic, attention-seeking quality to this officer's strutting and prancing around the department, unintentionally doing his best parody of the Hollywood secret agent–confusing the role with the actor and getting too into his character. Other than blowing one's own horn and being a royal pain in the ass, this type of harmless self-aggrandizement is usually tolerated with a large doses of either direct or behind-the-back derision.

Primate syndrome. This represents a more malignant character distortion, most commonly seen in UCOs who infiltrate motorcycle gangs, drug subcultures, or similarly scuzzy venues, in which officers may be forced or willing participants in some acts of violence or other sordid conduct. Immersion in this environment may then "rub off" on the officer and persist in the form of atypical dress and grooming, foul language, and thuggish behavior when the officer returns to the department, causing him to be generally regarded as an "ape" or a "dickhead" by his disenchanted peers. In other cases, the officer may hold it together while at work, only to persecute and alienate his family with his Neanderthal behavior.

Sympathy/identification with criminal target and subculture. In most cases, even the obnoxious "primate" recognizes the line between acting like a criminal lowlife and actually being one. Although rare, some UCOs–especially during prolonged assignments–may have developed close relationships with their targets. These relationships may be personal, i.e., actually coming to appreciate where the target "is coming from" and growing to like the target as a person. Or the relationship may be strictly utilitarian: it dawns on the officer that he can make a hell of lot more money switching sides or playing double agent than fulfilling his professional law enforcement oath of honor. Sometimes, the officer just gets used to the rush of excitement associated with living outside the rules of society. Often, there is a combination of motives.

Corrosion of law enforcement value system. As noted above, in the worst case, UCOs may be corrupted and turn, subtly or overtly, to criminal activity. More commonly, in less severe cases of immersion in and identification with the criminal subculture, the officer's previous notions of right and wrong, us

vs. them, may be muddied and make it hard to pursue his policing duties with full commitment and enthusiasm. This may make him more susceptible to corruption down the road, or it may impel him to leave his law enforcement career. In other cases, officers may use the defense mechanism of *reaction formation* to smother their doubts, and become superaggressive crusaders for justice, "cracking down" on criminals in their jurisdiction to prove to themselves that the law is always right. Paradoxically, these officers may violate their own codes when they feel compelled to go outside the law in order to uphold the law (also see Chapter 13).

Reintegrating the UCO to Regular Police Work

Even when the operation has been a success, a common problem is getting the UCO to stand down and start to resume other, nonundercover duties. Aristotle said that a virtue is the midpoint between two vices, and a few law enforcement supervisors have commented that you only find out about an UCO's true nature after the assignment ends. As noted above, the self-sufficient, tough-minded, sensation-seeking personality style of many UCOs is often the very asset that makes them so effective in this kind of work. However, such virtues may quickly sour into vices when the officer must return to ordinary police work which he may regard as boring and beneath him (Hibler, 1995; MacLeod, 1995).

At first, the returning UCO may be quite engaging and entertaining as he regales his colleagues with tales of danger and intrigue, because the cop was never born who didn't like a good story. But this soon wears thin, as his colleagues begin to wonder when he'll finally "get over himself." Anderson et al. (1995) go so far as to suggest that counseling professionals regard the emerging UCO as having a kind of multiple personality. While I wouldn't go to this diagnostic extreme, I do agree that part of the psychological decompression process must involve revalidating the officer's nonundercover personality by a gradual, not abrupt, transition into regular work and life roles. It would be just as big a mistake to take an UCO fresh from his assignment and plop him down at a desk or on a patrol beat, as it would to place him immediately into another undercover assignment without a break.

A certain period of *guided role-realignment* is therefore necessary to ensure both the stability of the officer's mental state and the success of future undercover missions. A crucial part of this involves allaying the UCO's fears that returning to a normal, "ordinary" identity will result in the collapse and disintegration of his tough-guy persona, with a resultant exposure of weakness (MacLeod, 1995). As in psychological counseling with officers in general (Chapter 6), the emphasis should always be on the process of building up, not breaking down. In this model, I offer the following recommendations for reintegrating the UCO's identity and activity back to regular police work.

First, as noted above, *make the transition gradual.* Remember that, even after the operation itself is long over, the UCO may still be involved in processing evidence, testifying at trial, and so on. During this follow-up period, time permitting, it may be useful to have him begin to perform some of his regular police duties. As the undercover case winds down, he will spend less and less time on it, and more and more time on his new roles and responsibilities.

Second, allow the returned UCO to keep his hand in his craft by encouraging him to *stay involved in training, supervising, and planning* for subsequent operations. This way, his healthy narcissism is channeled into work that is productive and directly related to his area of expertise: even if he's not out in the field, he is a vital part of the entire undercover law enforcement culture. It also provides a legitimate outlet for his war stories because, in the context of training, these now become case examples instead of self-centered windbagging.

Some officers are less ego-driven per se, but what they miss most about the operation is the sheer thrill of the experience. For such officers, the challenge is to find *other police roles that offer a commensurate amount of stimulation.* While, of course, not every law enforcement agency can accommodate every officer's wishes and temperaments, offering a returning UCO a spot on the SWAT, or hostage negotiation, or criminal investigation team—assuming they've otherwise earned it by their record and qualifications—can provide another

productive channel for their naturally high adrenalin and enthusiasm.

In all of these recommendations, the goal is to make the most of the positive energies of the returning UCO, while gradually transitioning him or her back into the more normal roles and responsibilities of law enforcement.

Dealing with the "Undercover Stockholm Syndrome"

Recall from Chapter 9 that hostages who spend long periods of time with their captors under conditions of life-threatening stress often form a seemingly paradoxical bond with, and allegiance to, their captors; this is especially likely where the hostage-takers and hostages come to be perceived as more human by one another. Indeed, it is typically the goal of hostage negotiators to foster this sort of "reverse Stockholm syndrome" in the hostage-takers in order to make it that much harder for them to inflict deliberate harm on their now-humanized hostages.

It is thus a natural human reaction that spending any considerable time with others under conditions of stressful challenge, and/or in collaboration on a common goal (including a criminal one) results in a Stockholm-type bond among those persons, even when the initial relationship may have been adversarial (Hibler, 1995). As noted earlier, then, it should not be surprising that UCOs often come to feel some empathy with, and sympathy for, their targets. Remember that the essence of an undercover operation necessarily involves betrayal in its starkest form—the UCO deliberately sets the target up for a bust—and all except the coldest psychopath will necessarily feel some remorse at turning on those who have sincerely trusted us, whatever the ultimate justification. Even though the best UCOs can compartmentalize these feelings for the sake of the greater good, it is only natural that they will have to deal with this human reaction.

To compound matters, especially in successful missions, the UCO's dealings with the targets are not likely to be over when the undercover part of the operation ends, because the officer may still have to face the target in court (Hibler, 1995). For the practical purposes of giving credible testimony, administrators and counselors must ensure that the

UCO is clear about the priorities and purposes of the mission, and that his testimony not be clouded by residual sympathies or hidden allegiances. This is not to encourage a callously hard-ass approach to the target (which many UCOs adopt anyway as a cover attitude or defense against letting themselves "go soft"), but to reorient the officer to his proper law enforcement role in the legal proceedings.

One way to do this is for the police psychologist to simply *encourage the officer to speak his mind* on how he feels about the targets and the work he has done. At first, expect minimization or denial: everything's cool, no problem. To get the officer talking, ask him what he thinks will happen to the targets; this often gets him to reveal some of the concerns he may have about burning someone who once trusted him. Follow this with a *reality check*. While no one can predict what the judge or jury will do, try to present a range of realistic options as to what might happen to the target and his family: jail time, witness protection program, and so on.

Emphasize that the feelings the officer may be having are not a sign of weakness or mental abnormality, but a *natural human response*. It may be useful to explicitly compare this to the Stockholm syndrome and reverse Stockholm syndrome that hostage negotiators experience after long hours speaking to a sympathetic hostage taker. Note that dealing with these human feelings productively is as much a part of professionalism as any other aspect of the operation—in fact the emotional side may be the toughest part of all. Emphasize that these remorseful feelings are what "good" people naturally experience when they have been called upon to do an ostensibly "bad" thing like betray confidences and friendships for the sake of a higher purpose. Remind the officer that, despite their circumstances, nobody forced these targets to become criminals, and remind the officer of the harm (drug addiction, violence) that their criminal activities have caused and that the undercover mission was intended to stop. If realistic, reassure the officers that the uninvolved, innocent families of the targets will not unnecessarily suffer for the actions of their parents or spouses.

Finally, in a number of cases, targets may be regarded not with sympathy, but quite the opposite, as miscreant scumbags with no redeeming human value. In such cases, *reorientation to professionalism* may have to take place in the other direction, encouraging the officers not to let their loathing for the subjects compromise their objectivity at trial or in subsequent investigations.

HOMICIDE AND SEX CRIMES INVESTIGATORS

Although typically occurring after the fact—the crime has already occurred—the work of criminal investigators is no less important if law enforcement efforts are to lead to arrest and conviction of the predators among us. Indeed, in the rare but important cases of serial crimes, prompt and knowledgeable investigation may well prevent uncounted future crimes from occurring.

Certain unique pressures are experienced by specially assigned officers, such as homicide detectives and sex crime investigators, who are involved in the investigation of particularly brutal crimes, including multiple murders, serial killings, or sexual abuse of a child. Stereotypes of the "hard-boiled" detective, both from within and outside the law enforcement profession, have contributed to the underrecognition and undertreatment of stress syndromes in this group. Interestingly, although I get very few clinical referrals of criminal investigators per se, presenting this topic in my police academy classes typically elicits a great deal of class participation, and it is my impression that these investigators are a very stressed bunch—so much so, that I can't resist coining a term for this phenomenon, *criminal investigator stress syndrome*, or CISS.

STRESSES OF CRIMINAL INVESTIGATION

There are several potential sources of stress for the homicide detective (Sewell, 1993, 1994). For one thing, the normally expected societal protective role of the police officer becomes heightened at the same time that his or her responsibility as a public servant who protects individual rights is compounded by the pressure to solve the crime. A multiple or serial murder investigation forces an officer to confront stressors directly related to his projected role and image of showing unflagging strength in the face of adversity and frustration, responding competently and dispassionately to crises, and placing the needs and demands of the public above his personal feelings. The sheer magnitude and shock effect of many mass murder scenes and the violence, mutilation, and sadistic brutality associated with many killings–especially those involving children–often exceed the defense mechanisms and coping abilities of even the most jaded investigator. Revulsion may be tinged with rage when innocent victims or fellow officers have been killed, and the murderer seems to be mocking law enforcement's attempts to catch him.

As the investigation drags on, the inability to solve the crime and close the case further frustrates and demoralizes the assigned officers and seems to jeeringly proclaim the hollowness of society's notions of fairness and justice. All the more vexsome are situations where the killer is known or suspected but the existing evidence is insufficient to support an arrest or conviction, leading the officers to fear that the perpetrator will remain free to kill again. Stress and self-recrimination are further magnified when the failure to apprehend the perpetrator is caused by human error, as when an officer's bungled actions or breach of protocol lead to loss

or exclusion of evidence or suppression of testimony, allowing the killer to walk.

All of these reactions are magnified by a cumulatively spiraling vicious cycle of fatigue and cognitive impairment, as the intense, sustained effort to solve the case results in sloppy errors, deteriorating work quality, and fraying of home and workplace relationships. Fatigue also exacerbates the wearing down of the investigator's normal psychological defenses, rendering him or her even more vulnerable to stress and failure (Sewell, 1993, 1994).

Especially in no-arrest cases, and particularly those involving children, some homicide detectives may become emotionally involved with the families and remain in contact with them for many years. Some detectives become obsessed with a particular case and continue to work on it at every available moment, sometimes to the point of compromising their work on other cases and leading to a deterioration of health and family life (Spungen, 1998).

Homicide and rape investigators typically deal with the "worst of the worst" of human behavior: molested and murdered children, preyed-upon elderly, torture, mutilation, and every kind of injury and death imaginable. These experiences can result in a pervasive, crushing sense of discouragement and despair, especially as officers see these kinds of crimes over and over again (Russell & Beigel, 1990; Henry, 2004). Investigating these crimes also brings detectives into regular close contact with distraught victims, either direct rape and assault victims or surviving family members of slain victims (Chapter 3).

SPECIAL STRESSES OF SEX CRIMES INVESTIGATORS

Adding to the stress is the unfortunate fact that, in many departments, there exists something of a rivalry among different units, especially between homicide and sex crimes units. Even in this day of TV glamorizations, like *Law and Order: SVU*, homicide is still regarded as the elite investigative unit in most departments (Henry, 2004; Peak, 2003), with the sex crimes unit a distant second. One way this manifests itself is in terms of allocation of departmental resources. For example, the case closure rate of homicides is almost always greater than that of sexual crimes (about 70% to 50%, respectively), despite the fact that homicide

victims are by definition deceased, while sexual assault victims are typically alive and able to recount their experiences to investigators (Lanning & Hazelwood, 1988).

Even more so than for other types of offenses, sex crimes–especially those against helpless victims like children or the elderly–evoke a certain special revulsion and corresponding denial in most of us. Thus, anyone who would actually choose to specialize in this type of crime may be imbued with a certain air of creepiness that serves to isolate and alienate them from the rest of their colleagues (Lanning & Hazelwood, 1988). After all, the thought of some people perpetrating violent, loathsome acts on others is so distasteful to the rest of us that anyone who would willingly immerse themselves in this kind of work must be two-thirds a weirdo him- or herself, right? This probably represents a reaction formation defense against the morbid voyeuristic streak we all harbor about lurid crimes of this type–hence, the wide television appeal. But when this reactive avoidance leads to alienation or ridicule of the sex crimes investigator within his or her own department, he or she is deprived of a valuable source of collegial support in the battle against stress and burnout.

Media portrayals can have another unintendedly negative effect as well. By giving the public the impression that most cases can be tidily solved in one episode, it may lead to unrealistic pressure on investigators to solve real-world cases that are typically more messy and ambiguous than the scripted scenarios on TV. This, of course, is just one example of the more general media-reality gap that characterizes most cop shows.

SELECTION AND TRAINING OF CRIMINAL INVESTIGATORS

In many departments, the appointment of officers to homicide or sex crime units is more a matter of seniority and promotion, and less a matter of specific selection criteria, as with hostage negotiators, undercover officers, or SWAT team members (Henry, 2004). Like members of these other specialized units, Lanning and Hazelwood (1988) recommend that sex crimes investigators should be self-selected volunteers who are then carefully screened and trained. Aside from *technical savvy*, investigators will spend a good deal of time speaking with victims, families, witnesses, suspects, and others who may be important to the case, so *good communications skills* are essential (Henry, 2004).

Screening also involves *weeding out unsuitable candidates*. These include officers who have an overly lurid or voyeuristic motive for doing this kind of work (beyond the natural sublimation mechanism noted above); those who may be going into it solely or mainly for personal issues, including a personal or family history of criminal victimization or sexual abuse; officers who have particular religious or political agendas; and those who see investigation as an easy career move, without the requisite commitment to the hard and dedicated work involved (Lanning & Hazelwood, 1988).

Characteristics of Successful Investigators

A number of traits and behaviors, as well as essential knowledge, skills, and abilities, appear to characterize the most successful criminal investigators (Sewell, 2003). First, they possess a basic *knowledge of the law* and the legal system to guide their efforts. They must have an extensive knowledge of investigative and forensic techniques and procedures; indeed, many of these professionals avail themselves of continued study and training, even on their own time and at their own expense (Henry, 2004).

These individuals are able to take a *broad and deep perspective* on their cases, to perceive complex patterns and connections within standard typologies of criminals and crime scenes, but also to be able to creatively "think outside the box" when necessary, to reel in elusive clues and flesh out skeletal inferences that may lead to valuable evidence.

Criminal investigation is hard work, it's long work, and it's often exhausting and ungratifying work. Successful investigators are able to marshal and *sustain motivation and persistence* to see the case through, from beginning to end–whatever the conclusion may be. This requires a certain level of tenacity and commitment that is beyond a nine-to-five mentality. It also requires the patience to deal with frustration and disappointments along the way, as well as the ability to be a self-starter and resist the boredom that can gradually gum up the engine of the investigator's drive to follow through on the case.

Certain cognitive and temperamental features characterize successful investigators. Naturally, a *curious and inquisitive mind* is an asset, characterized by the desire to go deeper into and know more about a phenonmenon. This is aided by a highly developed *attention to detail*, enabling the investigator to perceive minutiae that are overlooked by other observers, but may well prove crucial to solving the case.

Similar to crisis negotiators (Chapter 9), good investigators are people persons. They can read subtle interpersonal cues and can communicate effectively with suspects, witnesses, or civilians in ways that induce trust and the willingness to come forth with important information. They can also flexibly adapt their communication style to their audience, without appearing to be faking it.

Not faking it also applies to the investigators' professional and personal integrity. Successful investigators take justifiable pride in upholding the law through their daily dogged work in solving crimes. From a practical perspective, law enforcement agencies that are perceived as basically fair and honorable are far more likely to elicit cooperation from their citizenry when it comes to gathering vital information about crimes.

STRESS-COPING STRATEGIES OF CRIMINAL INVESTIGATORS

A variety of coping strategies used by criminal investigators have been described (Henry, 2004; Lanning & Hazelwood, 1988; Russell & Beigel, 1990). Some are used spontaneously by the officers themselves, some can be encouraged by departmental supervisors, and some can be taught by mental health professionals.

Defense Mechanisms and Mental Hardening

A number of authorities have commented on the general hardening that takes place in the mental life of criminal investigators. This is obviously the most convenient way of blocking out unpleasant material for guys and gals who are used to taking a tough, suck-it-up attitude towards unpleasant aspects of the job. Indeed, Chapter 5 presents some strategies for coping with critical incident stress that specifically incorporate a *mental toughening or hardening* approach. But these are for time-limited emergency situations; they are not designed to comprise the officer's full-time mindset.

When it persists, however, this psychological hardening reaction can take a number of forms, some of which may be conducive to productive coping, others less so. In many cases, this includes a *compartmentalization* or *isolation of affect*, in which the negative emotions are separated out and put in a "mental file cabinet" in order to allow the rest of the officer's cognitive faculties to keep functioning. Individuals differ in their ability to make this mental separation without undue emotional leakage into other areas of work and family life.

Intellectualization is the term used to describe the process of detoxifying an emotionally wrenching task or experience by adopting the stance of detached, objective, intellectual curiosity: for example, the emotional revulsion and horror of encountering the remains of a sexually mutilated corpse is diffused and diluted by immersion in the technical scientific minutiae of crime scene investigation and offender profiling (Holmes & Holmes, 1996; Miller, 2000; Ressler et al., 1988; Schlesinger & Miller, 2003; Turvey, 1999).

Sublimation refers to the process of turning a "bad" impulse into a socially acceptable, or even admirable, "good" activity or vocation. The classic example is the potential criminal slasher who becomes a skilled surgeon: he still gets to cut into people, but saves lives instead of taking them, and makes a good living in the process. In the law enforcement arena, this often manifests itself in taking the morbid curiosity and anxiety we all have about sex and murder, and channeling it into a productive career in forensic science. In this regard, sublimation is aided by intellectualization, which gives the immersion in the world of gore a scientific rationale. Again, as with the surgeon, this is not a form of psychopathology, but actually an adaptive defense mechanism.

Similarly, *humor* involves being able to take an ironic and therefore objectified perspective on things that make us uncomfortable—think for a moment about the subject matter of most stand-up routines and sit-coms, and you'll see why. Humor thus enables officers to deal with the grotesque by removing it by several stages in the form of a joke. As noted in Chapter 6, however, there is constructively healthy humor and destructively unhealthy humor. The former enables officers to defuse stress and anxiety, share an experience in a supportive atmosphere, and encourage a healthy bonding among members of an elite club. Unhealthy humor mocks the officers or victims themselves, distresses surviving family members, and sullies the department's honor. It may be as important for departmental leaders to model the appropriate expression of humor as it is to model appropriate grief (Chapters 6, 8, 15).

As just noted, one of the effects of healthy humor is to cement *peer support* among members of the investigative team and more widely among officers within the department. Typically, officers themselves report that recognition and support from their fellow officers constitute the most important stress-mitigating factor they can think of. Peer support can also be thought of more broadly in the form of collegial associations, such as memberships in professional societies, contribution to relevant publications and online databases, and so on—that is, building a nationwide and worldwide *community of support*, in addition to that within the department.

Professionalism

Implicit in what has just been said, the concept of *professionalism* subsumes all of the adaptive coping strategies noted above, as well as being a constructive principle of law enforcement generally. Lanning and Hazelwood (1988) have made some of these principles explicit for homicide and sex crimes investigators.

Professionalism begins with a certain *attitude* that says that the investigator will do his or her best job because of a general service orientation and specifically because the work provides professional satisfaction and a sense of accomplishment.

Professionalism encompasses the *physical space* in which the investigator works. There is no reason for the investigator's office to be unnecessarily grim, but bear in mind that this office will have a wide variety of individuals circulating through it—from liaison officers from other agencies in multijurisdictional investigations, to distraught family members of slain or assaulted victims—so officers should choose their decor accordingly. Certainly, explicit cartoons, crime scene souvenirs, or other malappropriate decorations or accouterments should not be in plain sight.

Confidentiality is part of professionalism. Victims and their families must be certain that their sensitive material—testimony transcripts, crime scene photographs, videotapes—will be seen only by those directly involved in solving the case. Aside from being the right and ethical thing to do, the assurance of reasonable privacy and dignity serves the practical function of encouraging better cooperation from victims and potential witnesses, which may yield information vital to solving the case.

Professionalism extends to the investigator's *language and behavior*. Again, this is not to encourage undertaker-like solemnity or schoolmarm correctness, but maintaining a certain decorum of speech and demeanor is important, not just for the public, but also for coworkers. Remember, sex crimes investigators must struggle with the "creep factor" even among their colleagues, so anything that contributes to the impression of serious professionalism—proper handling of gruesome or pornographic evidence, for example—will serve to heighten credibility. Again, without encouraging inappropriate overformality, the use of technical terms, not slang, should be encouraged. All professionals—doctors, lawyers, engineers—have their own distinctive terminology that serves to facilitate communication among them and highlights the fact that these are serious professions with knowledge and experience in what they do.

This is related to *expertise* as a key component of professionalism (Chapter 14). Henry (2004) notes how truly dedicated investigators spend much of their own time, and often at their own expense, reading books and journals, attending seminars and conferences, conferring with colleagues, and downloading software, all to increase their knowledge and expertise in forensic investigation. For such professionals, education does not end with the basic law enforcement curriculum; rather, it is a process that extends for, and suffuses into, all of one's professional career. Personally, I wish more psychologists had this attitude.

Professional Services

As in most areas covered by this book, the majority of homicide and sex crimes investigators will not require professional mental health intervention, even in the face of the most heinously traumatic investigations. However, where necessary, such services should be available in an easily accessible and nonstigmatized way, similar to the case for other special units discussed throughout this book. Mental health services may include several options, such as critical incident debriefing, individual stress-management counseling, or family therapy for emotional spill-over effects. As always, the department's true commitment to its personnel is shown by the quality of support services it chooses to provide.

Sewell (1993, 1994) has endeavored to adapt a CISD-like stress management model (Chapter 9) to the particular needs of special-assignment law enforcement officers, such as detectives who deal with the investigation of multiple murders and other violent crimes. The major objectives of this process are ventilation of intense emotions; exploration of symbolic meanings; group support under catastrophic conditions; initiation of the grief process within a supportive environment; reduction of the "fallacy of uniqueness;" reassurance that intense emotions under catastrophic conditions are normal;

preparation for the continuation of the grief and stress process over the ensuing weeks and months; preparing for the possible development of emotional, cognitive, and physical symptoms in the aftermath of a serious crisis; education regarding normal and abnormal stress response syndromes; and encouragement of continued group support and/or professional assistance.

Sewell (1994) regards such interventions as appropriate for two specific groups and at two specific times. First, the stress of first responders who have just dealt with the trauma of the original scene must be confronted quickly and decisively. Second, the stress of involved investigators must be handled regularly and as needed throughout the course of the crime's investigation and prosecution. In the regular debriefing sessions, whether for the first responders or case investigators, attendance should be mandatory and must be supported by the administration. Where an officer seeks additional debriefing assistance, the visits should be administratively encouraged and nonstigmatized.

CONCLUSIONS

Homicide and sex crimes investigators share with their undercover colleagues the stresses involved in maintaining careful attention and alertness over a span of time that may last from weeks to months to years. They also share tremendous responsibility for interdicting crime, either by preventive infiltration

of criminal organizations or by helping to apprehend and prosecute sexual and lethal predators before they can replicate their harm on innocent citizens. In this sense, these professionals represent separate but interlinked divisions in the battle against the corroding forces of civilized society.

PART IV

POLICE ADMINISTRATION AND FAMILY LIFE

Chapter 13

GOOD COP–BAD COP:
PRACTICAL MANAGEMENT OF PROBLEM OFFICERS

POLICING: RESPONSIBILITIES AND OPPORTUNITIES

Citizens who grew up in America a generation ago recall being taught, "the policeman is your friend," the one person you could go to if you were lost or in trouble. Most of us still take these expectations for granted because of the skill and dedication of the majority of law enforcement officers who perform their jobs competently and honorably. While there have always been corrupt, abusive, and incompetent cops, these were seen as the exception to the rule by most of the citizens who came in contact with them.

This perception began to change in the last 30 years as law enforcement officers increasingly found themselves on the wrong end of civil disturbances and investigations into violations of civil rights and police procedure. Especially in the last decade, we have seen an increasing number of news stories involving "rogue cops" involved in isolated or repeated acts of abuse and corruption at levels ranging from individual infractions to department-wide scandals. In a sense, police departments may be victims of their own success. In the 1990s, the Clinton administration launched an initiative to add 100,000 new cops to the streets of American cities. With federal money suddenly available, and municipalities uncertain of how long the largesse would last, many departments adopted the practice of hire first, ask questions later, and in many cases, quantity trumped quality as a hiring priority as standards were relaxed or overlooked to add new personnel as quickly as possible (Griffith, 2003b).

All this has led law enforcement psychologists and administrators to try to understand the individual and systemic factors that go into making good and bad cops. This is not just an academic exercise, as the success of efforts to adopt a truly effective community policing model in a growing number of jurisdictions will stand or fall based on whether citizens view their police forces as approachable protective resources or as hostile armies of occupation (Iannone & Iannone, 2001; Peak, 2003; Peak et al., 2004; Thibault et al., 2004).

Police and other law enforcement agents are unique among professionals in that the law and society give them the general right, and in many circumstances charge them with the obligation, to use *coercive physical force* to influence the behavior of citizens. Further, within the broad bounds of standard operating procedure, their decision to use such force is based largely on *their own judgment* as to what is appropriate in a given situation. No other professional that citizens deal with on a daily basis has that power (Bittner, 1970; Klockars, 1996). This engenders tremendous responsibility and, with it, the opportunity for abuse, corruption, and substandard performance.

TYPES OF OFFICER PROBLEMS

Admittedly, the term *problem officer* encompasses a wide range of behavior, from tardiness and failure to complete reports on time to brutality, extortion, and murder. While some extreme forms of behavior

221

automatically preclude retaining an officer on the force and may well incur criminal charges, many kinds of less serious infractions or patterns of substandard performance are amenable to change with the right approach. Accordingly, this section outlines some common forms of officer problems (Barker, 1978; Beigel & Beigel, 1977; Blau, 1986; Klockars, 1996; McCafferty & McCafferty, 1998; Peak, 2003; Sapp, 1997; Scrivner, 1999; Skolnick & Fyfe, 1993).

Excessive force is defined as the illegal or unreasonable use of force, with reasonableness determined by whether a prudent officer would have used the same amount of force in the same situation, based on information available to the officer at the time of the action. There is still a certain amount of subjectivity around the term and concept of "reasonableness," yet this standard is used successfully to decide a large number of civil, criminal, and internal investigation cases, and most officers explicitly or intuitively understand where to draw the line. Unfortunately, a small subset of officers seem to earn reputations, among citizens and peers alike, for resorting to strong-arm tactics on a consistent basis, and this may lead to charges of police brutality.

Police corruption typically involves using one's status as a police officer to obtain wrongful gains or benefits, and may involve any of the following.

Mooching: Receiving gratuities (such as free meals), sometimes in return for favors, which may be expressed or implied, present or future.

Chiseling: Demanding or accepting free or discounted admission to sports or other events not connected with police duties.

Favoritism: Granting immunity from police action to certain citizens or peers, such as fixing parking or traffic violations.

Prejudice: Treating certain groups differently, either better or worse.

Shopping: Stealing small items from an unsecured place of business on one's beat.

Heisting: Stealing expensive items from a crime scene, including appliances, electronics, jewelry, or vehicles, and attributing their loss to criminal activity.

Premeditated theft: Carrying out a planned burglary or other kind of larceny.

Extortion: Explicitly demanding a cash payment in return for protection against police action.

Bribes: Accepting an unsolicited cash payment from those who wish to avoid arrest.

Perjury: Lying to protect a fellow officer or oneself, in a court of law, during an Internal Affairs investigation, or for any other reason.

Carrying unauthorized weapons that have not been service-issued or approved, for personal use or to be used as illegal "throw-downs."

Keeping weapons or drugs that are confiscated from suspects.

Having sex with informants in vice and narcotics investigations.

Selling confidential information to lawyers, insurance companies, or criminals.

Loafing or *attending to personal business* while on duty.

Using abusive or deceptive means in interrogation of suspects.

Collecting kickbacks from lawyers for drunk driving arrests or auto accident investigations.

Physical assault and battery of suspects or citizens.

Anyone who has worked for any length of time with a major police department can no doubt add their own items to this list.

Marginal performance generally refers to "sins of omission," and includes such infractions as tardiness and absences; failure to complete paperwork; misuse of departmental equipment and property; insubordination and problems with chain of command; violation of rules, safety guidelines, and standard operating procedures (SOPs); failure to complete patrols adequately; corrupt or otherwise unprofessional behavior ("conduct unbecoming"); and special unit infractions. Again, any police manager could add items to this list.

In line with the *bad apple theory,* there is evidence that corruption and brutality are frequently linked. McCafferty and McCafferty (1998) cite a 1994 study in the New York City Police Department which found that corruption-prone officers were five times more likely than other officers to have had five or more complaints filed against them about the use of unnecessary force. Thus, many kinds of problem behavior tend to cluster in certain "bad cops."

TYPES OF PROBLEM OFFICERS

One approach to understanding problem officers is to view the individual personality and behavioral style of the officer as a primary factor in bad-cop policing. This has led to a number of typologies of police officers (Golembiewski & Kimm, 1990; McCafferty et al., 1998; Miller, 2003a, 2004; Muir, 1977; Robinette, 1987; Scrivner, 1994, 1999; Shev & Howard, 1977; Weitzel, 2004; White, 1972; Worden, 1996), several of which will be recognizable to most police managers.

The *tough cop* holds the cynical view that people are motivated mainly by selfish interests and believes that the citizenry are generally hostile toward police. He conceives of the role of police officers as "keeping the lid on" or "drawing the line," even if that involves the liberal dispensation of street justice when he feels the situation calls for it.

Clean-beat crime fighters also emphasize the law enforcement function of the police and justify hardline enforcement in terms of its deterrent effect on crime, but are somewhat less cynical in outlook, seeing crime control as just part of their job as good cops. While they are very energetic and proactive on patrol, they may lack the hard-boiled street sense of the tough cop, or they may be able to sublimate this tough-minded attitude into aggressive, but not abusive, policing.

Cowboys or *hot-dogs* are young, inexperienced, immature, highly impressionable and impulsive rookies, with a taste for action and a low tolerance for frustration. These officers may actually be quite effective in their police work if their gung-ho enthusiasm can be channeled productively, and they need not necessarily evolve into permanent tough cops if they receive responsible field training and supervision during the formative stages of their police careers.

At the other end of the career spectrum are the veteran *dinosaurs* or *burnout cases*, who are feeling the pressure from a variety of long-standing stressors, which may include past unresolved trauma from critical incidents, frustrated advancement opportunities within the department, overwork and overinvestment in the police profession, disillusionment with the criminal justice system, resentment toward an indifferent or hostile citizenry,

and looming retirement with threatened loss of status and work-identity. These officers may fall into a coasting pattern, where they do the minimum possible to get by, or they may grow increasingly demoralized and irritable to the point that their anger spills over onto coworkers and citizens alike. This downward slide is frequently lubricated by alcohol. Although less common, many departments have their share of older, veteran hot-doggers as well.

Another group of officers consists of those with *personal problems*, some of which may be related to the personality patterns described later in this chapter, but just as often may reflect a combination of poor choices and bad luck. Such officers may have financial stresses, relationship difficulties, parent-child issues, illness in the family, or other problems that weigh on their ability to do their daily jobs effectively. Sometimes, this sets up a vicious cycle in which the officer turns to alcohol or drugs or makes risky financial or legal decisions that cause even more trouble and accelerate the downward spiral, in some tragic cases lead to officer suicide (Chapter 11). This category frequently overlaps with the burned-out officer type. It is especially in these kinds of cases, that proper administrative and psychological intervention can be quite rewarding in salvaging an otherwise doomed career.

Problem-solvers are officers who tend to take a broad, existential view of human nature, recognizing that people's behavior is commonly influenced by complex sets of physical, economic, and social circumstances, a perspective that is often at odds with the black-and-white, us-versus-them, law-and-order approach to policing that characterizes many departments. Problem-solver officers conceive of the police role as offering assistance and fostering creative conflict resolution as an alternative to making busts and cracking heads. If anything, such officers may be prone to underutilizing their legitimate coercive authority where it would be otherwise appropriate and necessary. Their problem, then, is not knowing when to be tough when they need to be.

Less philosophical motives drive the *avoiders* who, unable or unwilling to cope with the daily demands of policing, prefer simply to do the absolute minimum amount of work necessary to meet their supervisors' expectations. Their basic approach is to lie low and not make waves. Often, however, this shades over into frank dereliction of duty, as these officers shirk more and more responsibility so long as they can get away with it. This type of behavior may occur at any stage of an officer's career, and if it occurs in the late career stages, it may overlap with the burnout type described above. It may also be related to an avoidant personality style (see below), but if this pattern appears abruptly after a preceding period of adequate performance, supervisors should try to determine if some new stressor is putting a strain on an otherwise good officer's job functioning.

Probably the healthiest balance is achieved by the *professionals*, or *natural cops*, who seem to intuitively know how to handle both work-related and personal pressures. These officers' own healthy personalities form the foundation of their confidence and good judgment on the job, and they are able to productively absorb and assimilate the lessons learned from formal training as well as continued experience in the field. Natural cops believe that law enforcement is fundamentally about helping people, but they understand that this sometimes requires the judicious use of legitimate coercive force and that being courteous and professional doesn't mean taking crap. As a result, these officers are neither overly aggressive nor passive, and they don't resent legitimate legal restrictions on their authority, because they are confident of their ability to handle most situations successfully. This is essentially the aspirational model of officer conduct that most departments would like their officers to emulate but which, as yet, is sufficiently infrequently to become "news" when it occurs, as the following local human interest story illustrates (Allen, 2001).

Officer Midian Diaz of the Boynton Beach Police Department "has had a hankering for law enforcement since he was a young boy playing ball in south New Jersey. He admired his cousin—a corrections officer—and friends who were on the police force. And everything about police work filled him with pride and excitement.

"But it took Diaz, 40, a patrolman recently named the Boynton Beach Police Department's 2000 Officer of the Year, a few years to return to his first love." In the meantime, notes the article, he accumulated a number of other life experiences, including joining the Marines and working in construction.

Unlike many recipients who receive the Officer of the Year honor because of a specific heroic deed or event, the article points out, Diaz was selected because of his overall performance. "It's his efforts for the entire year that stood out," Boynton Beach Police Chief Marshall Gage said. "This is a man that goes out and gives one hundred and ten percent every day. He does an exceptional job and not all his work is measured in number of arrests or number of tickets that he gives out."

According to the article, colleagues and supervisors say that Diaz leaves a positive impression on those who meet him. "He's very good when dealing with the public," his supervisor, Sgt. Eric Jenson, wrote in Diaz's last evaluation: "He shows compassion to victims and he has the skill to calm excited people with his verbal communication. Midian is an asset to the department."

There appears to be some influence of Diaz's age and life experience on his mature attitude and behavior in policing. "I've been around the block," Diaz notes. "When I fell into this business, I knew what it was like with the problems with the kids and domestic [incidents]. I think that helps me with police work, starting late in my career. I can walk into a lot of scenarios that happen and relate to that person or to that incident." He has had no reprimands.

The story also highlights that being a good cop does not necessarily mean being a perfect cop or a supercop. One of the recommendations for improvement listed in Diaz's latest evaluation was that superiors "would like to see him diversify and take classes in other areas of police work in preparation for a specialty unit when one comes available." Lt. Charles Kuss wrote that Diaz "has his weaknesses, he continues to work on his spelling and grammar." However, a key trait of success seems to be the ability to respond to constructive criticism not as a personal attack, but as a challenge to become better. Thus, the lieutenant adds that Diaz "takes direction well and continues to improve." Even Diaz's colleagues say "he has been working hard to hone his skills."

POLICE PERSONALITIES:
TRAITS, TYPES, DISORDERS, AND STRATEGIES FOR MANAGEMENT

As noted in Chapter 4, we all have *personality traits*. Some people are outgoing and gregarious; others keep to themselves. Some people are orderly and meticulous, while others enjoy life spontaneously but are never able to organize their lives. Some are open and trusting, while others are cynical and suspicious. Some people are egocentric and impulsive, only out for their own benefit or gratification, while others may be overly self-deprecating, never seeming to effectively assert themselves or stand up for their rights.

But when these personal quirks begin to grate harmfully on others or significantly derail the success of the persons themselves, the career consequences can be ruinous for a highly demanding profession such as policing. In extreme cases, psychologists speak of an individual having a *personality disorder*, which is defined as "an enduring pattern of inner experience and behavior that deviates markedly from the expectations of the individual's culture, is pervasive and inflexible, has an onset in adolescence or early adulthood, is stable over time, and leads to distress or impairment" (APA, 1994). Personality-disordered individuals typically have little insight into their own behavior and poor understanding of the adverse impact they have on themselves and others. They characteristically justify their self-defeating or offensive behavior as being due to uncontrollable fate or someone else's fault. It is the *extremes* of their self-perception and conduct toward others that distinguish personality disordered individuals from those with more moderate personality traits and styles (McCafferty & McCafferty, 1998; Miller, 2003a, 2003b; Millon & Davis, 2000; Sperry, 1995).

In some cases, symptoms of more severe personality disturbance or other mental disorder can lie dormant for some time until an overwhelming crisis or cumulative series of lower-level stresses overwhelms an officer's coping mechanisms. In these select cases, screening and early recognition of more serious personality disorders will enable supervisors to refer the officer to appropriate psychological services before the problem begins to wreak havoc on the department and the officer's career (see below).

In several places throughout this book, I've used the framework of personality types and disorders to explain the behavior of various groups of people; now we turn the clinical lens on the officers themselves. The purpose of the present section is to provide police supervisors and administrators with some insight into the minds of the people they work with, and to suggest some practical strategies for maximizing the working relationships among officers' personality styles in a departmental environment–before things get to the point of requiring formal disciplinary action. Personalities are not easy to change, but they often can be accommodated, and a seemingly obstreperous or hopeless officer may be salvageable if you know how to play to his strengths and minimize or overcome his interpersonal and job-related weaknesses. Also bear in mind that it is common for people to have partial syndromes and mixtures of different personality traits or styles.

Histrionic Personality

Behavioral description and work style. Histrionic personality is a pattern of excessive emotionality, attention-seeking, need for excitement, flamboyant theatricality in speech and behavior, an impressionistic and impulsive cognitive style, and use of exaggeration to maintain largely superficial relationships for the purpose of getting emotional needs met by being admired and cared for by others. These are the "showboats" of the police department. They love to be the focus of attention and will do anything to garner accolades from colleagues and citizens. They enjoy being in the news and will often work overtime and volunteer for extra assignments–as long as this keeps the spotlight on them. Fellow officers may tire of these officers' endless renditions of their own exploits.

Typically regarded as basically competent and enthusiastic officers, the danger arises when their craving for attention fails to be adequately met. Then histrionic officers tend to become depressed and angry, and are particularly prone to develop psychosomatic ailments and symptoms. Worse, if sufficient attention can't be gleaned by doing good works, they may resort to more aggressive policing, believing that this is what is required to gain further recognition and "earn their chops." This perhaps originally well-intentioned tactic of becoming more effective officers may quickly escalate to abuse of force, more as a result of poor judgment than inherent meanness.

Management strategies. Good humor is infectious, and your histrionic officer may provide a refreshing dose of levity in an otherwise somber departmental environment. However, sometimes real work requires people to cut the comedy and get down to business, and if a critical situation demands a more serious effort and workplace tone, the perennially breezy, upbeat demeanor of the histrionic employee may soon take on a queasy, saccharinny quality. However, if you let the histrionic officer play to his strengths—as a departmental spokesperson, front desk person, crisis hotline staffer, or community relations officer—he may quickly become a credit to your department because his friendly, helpful style will genuinely make people feel good about themselves and your law enforcement agency.

But almost any job in the real world of policing has aspects that involve dealing with dull, ordinary scutwork. Unfortunately, this is not the personality who takes well to poring over details; he will quickly get bored and his efficiency will lag. If your histrionic employee is chronically late or messy with his work, supervision will be necessary. Police supervisors and managers need to take a highly supportive approach in describing and reinforcing positive, work-relevant behavior, but be able to back off a few emotional steps when excessive praise and attention are sought for their own sake.

Gentle, reality-based guidance ("I really appreciate your effort and enthusiasm, but you need to work a little harder on your reports and documentation to make sure they're completed accurately and on time") may protect the officer's self-esteem while refocusing his efforts on work-related tasks. Try to provide as much detail as necessary, so that the histrionic employee understands clearly how to carry out the task, but not so much explicit direction that he becomes dependent on your spoon-feeding him every detail of the project. Overall, if you provide the proper level of instruction and

guidance, and generously lavish praise when it's genuinely due, you will have an unusually loyal and pleasant officer.

Borderline Personality

Behavioral description and work style. Borderline personality is a pattern of instability in interpersonal relationships, fragile self-image, and wild emotional swings. In this personality type, police officers may exhibit a pattern of erratic and intense relationships, alternating between overidealization and devaluation of colleagues, departmental brass, and citizens. They may show self-damaging impulsiveness in the form of car chases, citizen harassment, and other abuse of authority. Signs of emotional instability include inappropriately intense anger and/or depressive mood swings and possible suicidality (Chapter 11). Persistent identity disruption may manifest itself in disturbances of self-image, blurred interpersonal boundaries and relationships, confused professional goals and values, and a chronic feeling of emptiness that may impel the quest for stimulation via substance abuse or job-related provocation of incidents or other excessive actions.

Management strategies. Many of these officers have good intentions, but all too frequently, their emotions get away from them and they have no clue as to how to control their reactions. As much as possible, try to provide this officer with models of stability and reliability, such as consistent and fair departmental policies, strong and reliable leaders, or pairing him with a calm and steady partner or training officer. Reward accomplishments appropriately, but set limits firmly. Give constructive criticism in as positive a context as possible ("You're doing a great job on the youth project. Here are some ways to make even better use of your skills"). To borrow a concept from psychoanalytic theory, by providing the right kind of *holding environment*, your borderline employee will probably try to do his best job for you. Just be prepared to weather occasional storms along the way.

Narcissistic Personality

Behavioral description and work style. Narcissistic personality is a pattern of grandiosity, sense of entitlement, arrogance, need for admiration, and lack of empathy for others' feelings or opinions. Officers with this pattern believe that rules are for other cops and they are "above the law" because of their special powers of perception, insight, judgment, technical expertise, or physical prowess. They expect others to appreciate, admire, and defer to them, and will become prickly or outright rageful when they don't get the perks, promotions, benefits, and special consideration they feel they deserve.

Management strategies. If the narcissistic officer is doing an acceptable job, and there is genuinely room for improvement, then a collaborative, hand-on-the-shoulder, "we're in this together" type of coaching style from someone the officer respects may be effective. The narcissistic officer may welcome the attention from higher-ups, especially if the coaching session includes soliciting the employee's input and advice: "You see the problem, don't you? You've usually got some good ideas about these things—how do *you* think we can use your experience in firearms instruction to make our department more productive?" Remember, the narcissist may often have some legitimately useful skills and suggestions—the problem is rarely lack of brilliant ideas or ability; it's the characteristic lack of follow-through ("Why should I have to do all the grunt work?") that causes the project to crash prematurely or rot on the vine.

A more malignant kind of narcissistic officer is the one whose sense of entitlement encompasses the right to manipulate and exploit others for his own purposes: this type often has features of the antisocial and paranoid personality styles as well. Often these officers can be found at middle management levels in the department, where they have established their own little underground network of "doing things the right way," intimidating their subordinates and sweet-talking their superiors to keep the lid on. After a departmental shake-up, ensuing investigations may reveal all kinds of unfair, corrupt, and illegal practices having occurred for years on the watch of these officers.

But even if not actually dishonest, narcissists can develop intense personal investments in their job roles, and this is one type of personality that may likely to resort to aggressive litigation or even workplace violence when terminated ("Who does that captain think he is to dress me down like that? Nobody appreciates me here; this is a crapass department that coasts on mediocrity. I'm suing the city. These pencil-pushers have to be taught a lesson, one way or another"). Thus, disciplining and, if necessary, firing these officers must be done carefully and tactfully, and be well-documented.

Antisocial Personality

Behavioral description and work style. Antisocial personality is a pattern of consistent disregard for, and violation of, the rights of others. It is typically associated with impulsivity, criminal behavior, sexual promiscuity, substance abuse, and an exploitive parasitic, and/or predatory lifestyle. While possessed of similar qualities of entitlement and self-importance as the narcissist, the antisocial personality is distinquished by his complete lack of conscience that allows him to believe that other people exist simply as sources of his personal gratification. If the narcissist's need for admiration is gratified by his position, he may actually show a benevolent *noblesse oblige* graciousness and loyalty to the underlings who serve him faithfully. No such consideration applies to the antisocial personality, who views all subservience as a sign of weakness to be exploited, because the "suckers deserve it."

Antisocial personalities have a need for high stimulation and will quickly grow bored with most kinds of routine police work. Conversely, when something piques their predatory interest, they can show almost superhuman energy and determination to get the dastardly deed done. They are into power and don't like to be crossed, so revenge may be a strong motive for their actions. Their impulsivity and lack of planning and judgment virtually guarantee that they will end up in some kind of trouble sooner or later.

But some antisocial personalities can be quite shrewd in a cunning-conning type of way, and the more intelligent among these officers may accumulate considerable departmental and street-level fiefdoms of wealth and power, or even rise to positions of great authority within the department before their complex webs of deceit begin to unravel. There are many bright antisocial and narcissitic personalities occupying the ranks of politics, business, law enforcement, the military, the clergy, and the medical field. Scary, isn't it?

Management strategies. Your antisocial officer will do the absolute minimum amount of work he can get away with, apply for every benefit and privilege, antagonize your good officers, jeopardize departmental integrity, and finally sue you, badmouth you, or even try to physically harm you when you discipline or fire him.

The best measure is prevention. Take your hiring responsibilities seriously, screen carefully, and check all references. The best predictor of future behavior is past behavior, so study his past work record. If you're already stuck with an antisocial employee, try to make the most of his skills by providing clear directions and monitoring his work. He craves excitement, so for short, simple tasks that involve firm, aggressive policing—such as dangerous first-in warrant searches or SWAT assaults—his fearless and unhesitating physical prowess may allow him to do an adequate or even superior job. But keep the supervisory reins tight to prevent abuse of authority or overly impulsive actions, such as excessively beating a suspect who dissed him, planting weapons or other evidence, or looting drugs or cash at a crime scene. Also, don't expect long-term follow-through on complex projects, unless he's using the system for his own purposes. Finally, have a well thought-out and carefully documented system of discipline, so if you have to fire him, you minimize your risk of his fomenting a legal hassle for spite and profit.

Paranoid Personality

Behavioral description and work style. Paranoid personality is a pattern of pervasive distrust and suspiciousness, so that others' actions and motives are almost invariably interpreted as deceptive, persecutory, or malevolent. Actually, these perceptions may be quite accurate; it's their interpretations that are skewed. Paranoids often show keen insight into human motives and actions, but they typically have only one interpretation: people are fundamentally mean, selfish creatures who will screw you the first chance they get. Because they often have a knack for technical details and are able to channel considerable energy in the direction of

goal accomplishment—if only to counter the threats of perceived enemies—paranoids may actually achieve considerable success at work. Indeed, they may naturally gravitate toward the ranks of detectives and investigators, including Internal Affairs, where their talent and enthusiasm for ferreting out "dirt" is actually encouraged and rewarded by the law enforcement culture.

However, an unchecked, overly cynical, us-against-them stance can lead to hair-trigger reactivity resulting in street-level abuse of force confrontations, or to overzealously pursued and ruinous investigations of honest citizens or fellow officers. Moreover, it is often not long before their innate suspiciousness is turned against their own colleagues and supervisors as the web of conspiracy grows in their minds. Thus emerges a vicious cycle of mistrust and hostility as coworkers come to shun their persistently obnoxious paranoid associate, only confirming his suspicions of plots and intrigue. This then leads to more outright avoidance and hostility and perhaps even self-protective preemptive strikes on the part of others, further fueling the paranoid's perceived need for anticipatory retaliation. Hence the adage, "Just because you're paranoid, it doesn't mean they're *not* out to get you."

Management strategies. If you supervise a paranoid officer, watch your back. This is not to suggest that you become paranoid yourself, but like the antisocial employee, the paranoid will have no compunction about deceiving or harming you to get what he feels he deserves. The motivational difference is that the antisocial takes advantage of people for the sheer power trip of ripping them off; the narcissist takes what he wants because he believes he truly deserves it; whereas the paranoid feels morally justified in using any means necessary to protect himself from the omnipresent danger of being tricked and cheated by those around him. A practical difference is that the antisocial's impulsivity will often impel him to make rash power grabs that may backfire and spell his doom, while the more cunning paranoid can afford to wait and carefully spin his web.

In managing the paranoid personality, take care to keep assignments logical and straightforward. Expect suspicious questioning of your own and others' motives and of the reasons for assignments, and be prepared for "helpful information" about the incompetence and/or malfeasance of fellow officers. As much as possible, offer calm, rational explanations for policing tasks, and provide forthright but nonconfrontational reality checks for paranoid misperceptions or misinterpretations, especially under conditions of stress, when conspiratorial cognition is more prone to spin out of control.

In general, paranoid officers respond better to tight logic than loose assurances, and also tend to accede to legitimate authority, so don't be afraid to pull rank and make it clear that you expect policies to be followed. In addition, paranoid personalities seem to have an affinity for technical matters, so they may make the ideal persons for electronics, computers, crime lab, and other technically-oriented assignments. Overall, if you can convince your paranoid employee that there is a direct connection between him doing his job properly and his chances of realistic appreciation and advancement within the department, he may become one of your most assiduous workers—although always and forever looking for the angle behind the actions of others.

Avoidant Personality

Behavioral description and work style. Avoidant personality is a pattern of social inhibition, feelings of inadequacy, and hypersensitivity to negative evaluation or criticism. Even relatively neutral interpersonal interactions or confrontations are approached with trepidation. Although it is unlikely that many individuals with this pattern would choose an in-your-face type of career like law enforcement, some officers may have initially been attracted to the helping aspects of policing and may have pursued their role of "Officer Friendly" as a form of self-therapy to garner goodwill and admiration from citizens and camaraderie from fellow officers. Avoidant officers are particularly susceptible to burnout and depression when their kindly and noble efforts don't glean the expected gratitude from the citizenry and earn only snickers from their more aggressive colleagues who quickly size them up as exploitable patsies by the citizens on their beat—the "grass-eaters" as opposed to the more aggressive "meat-eaters."

Management strategies. Give him a specific task to do, keep the supervision brief and positive, let him stay out of the spotlight, and the avoidant officer may be a reliable and faithful worker. Obviously, few jobs in policing allow officers to be total hermits, but if the position calls for good technical, clerical, mechanical, or physical skills, without much need for regular, direct interpersonal confrontation, the avoidant officer will probably do a good job: consider assignment to records, payroll, radio dispatch, equipment maintenance, even K-9 units (individuals who are skittish around people may get along great with animals) and other low human-contact positions.

Most jobs, however, require some kind of periodic supervision. Remember, the avoidant personality is not antisocial, just intimidated by people, especially authority figures. So keep the supervision light, more in line with a coaching and counseling approach, rather than as criticism or discipline per se. Of course, if the avoidant officer consistently fails to perform up to par, and won't respond to direct instruction or gentle encouragement, you may have to be more forceful. If he can't tolerate appropriate constructive criticism, he will probably eventually just leave the department.

Dependent Personality

Behavioral description and work style. Dependent personality is a pattern of submissive and clinging behavior stemming from an excessive need for care and guidance. Whereas avoidants fear people and prefer to be away from them, dependents need people and dread only their rejection or lack of support. Dependent personalities look to others to provide guidance and direction, and officers with this pattern may actually be good, dedicated soldiers, as long as independent decision making is kept to a minimum. Interactions with colleagues, supervisors, or citizens are apt to be taken more personally than with other cops, as dependents are always looking for work-related validation of their essential worthiness and likeability. Thus, performance may suffer if they are denied these strokes and become depressed and demoralized by the stresses of policing.

Worse, such impaired performance may ultimately lead to a poor departmental evaluation, which can be a further devastating blow, because once in a relatively secure position, the threatened loss of a job may seem literally like the end of the world. This may actually precipitate a suicidal crisis or an increase in abuse of force incidents as these officers attempt to overcompensate to "prove themselves." On the other hand, such officers typically make dedicated and loyal departmental employees if a stable, safe, and secure position can be found for them in the department.

Management strategies. It might seem that his need for approval and eagerness to please would make the dependent officer the ideal assistant or subordinate, and for simple, directed tasks this may be true. Problems arise, however, when he has to take any kind of initiative or make an independent decision. At first gratified by the new rookie's eagerness to learn, trainers and supervisors may soon become weary and irritated by the dependent's seemingly endless quest for reassurance. Likewise, coaching and counseling such employees is initially rewarding, as they appear to eagerly soak up every lesson and recommendation. After a while, however, managers may feel, "Enough is enough–can't he do anything without me holding his hand?" Other employees may resent the extra attention the dependent officer gets, while at the same time growing tired of his constant queries for direction and reassurance.

However, if you are able to provide a low-stress, progressive type of corrective supervision that gradually helps the dependent officer master the tasks he needs–and if you can keep the emphasis on complimenting the good behavior, rather than criticizing the bad–the dependent employee may eventually feel secure enough in the work relationship to do a really great job. Remember: the dependent personality truly wants to do well; approval is his greatest reinforcer. If you can train him carefully and dose your approval accordingly, you may have a loyal, competent, and stable employee.

Obsessive-Compulsive Personality

Behavioral description and work style. The obsessive-compulsive personality is preoccupied with orderliness, perfection, and control. With a mind exquisitely attuned to detail, these individuals tend to excel in jobs that require exactitude and precision, even seeming to relish the kinds of repetitive tasks that would quickly numb the psyches of more action-oriented officers. Typically bright, obsessive-compulsives tend to gravitate toward jobs that make the best use of their high-level cognitive skills and devotion to detail–engineering, economics, computer science, and others. At the same time, they are much less likely to have the intuitive flashes of insight or to possess the glib social adroitness of the histrionic or narcissistic personality. Obsessive-compulsives are not necessarily shy, as are avoidants, but overall, they'd rather get back to the work on their desks than hang around the rec room.

The main psychological dynamic of this personality type consists of order and control. Obsessive-compulsives are extremely uncomfortable with imprecision, ambiguity, or lack of clarity. The more of an intellectual and physical grasp they have of a situation, the better. These are the classic by-the-book cops and, as long as they operate in situations covered by this literal or figurative "book," they perform exquisitely. In management positions, these individuals may keep their departments or divisions humming along but may be stubbornly resistant to changes in policies or organization.

Problems arise when this cognitive style intrudes into work situations where more spontaneity and sociability are required. If not sure what to do, these individuals may be paralyzed with indecisiveness. They will squirm uncomfortably at a difficult arrest procedure or witness interview that isn't carefully scripted, but they will then go back to the office and produce a meticulously polished, articulate, and professional-looking arrest and booking report. They will sign up for every special marksmanship, conflict resolution, advanced investigation, or other continuing education course, but seem clueless about how to apply these skills to the messy real world of the police beat. At best, they derive their satisfaction from a job well done; at worst, there is no such thing as good enough and they will make themselves sick–and drive everyone around them crazy–trying to be better than perfect.

Management strategies. This is the "detail man (or woman)" you want working on your special projects. In fact, histrionic or narcissistic managers often pick obsessive-compulsive assistants because they are able to translate the boss's scattered agendas into practicable, workable plans. A pair of obsessive-compulsive partners may initially work well together, each complementing the other's feverish pace; however, there is the danger of competition developing between them for the highest degree of perfection. More casual, laid-back officers will probably find the obsessive-compulsive partner irritating, with his constant nit-picking, useful though it may be to the overall quality of their mutual law enforcement work.

As a manager, recognize that the obsessive-compulsive employee is most probably doing his absolute best for you at all times. His errors are likely to be those of commission: too much attention to detail risks bogging down and suffocating the whole project. An appropriate strategy is to give the obsessive-compulsive officer some direction. Let him know in what areas he can ease up and streamline the project, and on what elements of the task you want him to focus his laser-beam concentration. The obsessive-compulsive officer also responds well to honest praise, so don't forget to thank him for a job well done.

Schizoid Personality

Behavioral description and work style. Schizoid personality is a pattern of aloof detachment from social interaction, with a restricted range of emotional expression. These are people who don't need people, and are perfectly happy being left by themselves. Consequently, they are not typically drawn to the people-oriented profession of policing. However, some schizoid types may function adequately in certain departmental settings. They will be the "oddballs" of the department who keep to themselves, never really causing any trouble, but never forming any kind of solid bond with their fellow cops. In interactions with citizens, they are generally low-key, but may have a tendency to explode in unfamiliar or threatening situations. Also, they may have a tendency to decompensate and become delusional under prolonged, intense stress, and are more likely to be the source of citizen complaints about "weird behavior" rather than abusive force per se.

Management strategies. Schizoid personalities may be well suited to isolated, low-level jobs of limited interpersonal complexity. In the briefing area, squad room, locker room, or cafeteria, they will probably keep to themselves, but may be among the most predictably reliable of workers, having few interpersonal entanglements to interfere with their schedules. They will come in on time, follow orders, accommodate shift changes, all without complaint, unless their job interferes with something more important, like a religious group meeting or idiosyncratic personal routine. Then they may abruptly quit the department, because the job no longer "fits" them. A fair number of schizoid personalities are actually quite intelligent and may possess superlative technical skills—the classic "computer geeks"—that may be an asset to any high-tech law enforcement administration.

Actually, the less you see your schizoid officer, the better, since he will typically work best under conditions of both interpersonal distance and quiet, nonthreatening support. Positions in which monitoring can be impersonal—for example, group supervision or the new "e-management"—may be especially suitable for this officer, as well as jobs in which there is some structure and pacing inherent in the work itself.

Just don't expect your schizoid employee to laugh at your jokes, commiserate with your personal troubles, or respond to standard carrot-and-stick approaches to motivation and discipline. Let him know what you want done, how you want him to do it, when it's expected to be completed, and then let him alone. To compensate for the schizoid tendency to occasionally get off track, conduct brief and focused periodic supportive supervision sessions to monitor and productively guide his progress.

POLICE-CITIZEN INTERACTIONS

Of course, personality traits don't exist in a vacuum and are usually most clearly expressed in interactions with other people. Unlike many other professions, patrol policing involves daily confrontations with citizens, a fair proportion of which are likely to be unpleasant or dangerous. Cultural norms have come to dictate a general expectation that citizens will respond a certain way when confronted by an authority figure such as a police officer. Conversely, citizens have come to expect a certain manner of behavior from the officers themselves. Thus, one of the situational factors that affect an officer's propensity toward abusive behavior or misconduct is the attitude and behavior of the citizens he or she encounters, especially when these deviate from the "unwritten rules" (Cancino, 2001; Cancino & Enriquez, 2004; Toch, 1996).

Given the challenging and dangerous job they do, most officers believe that the last thing they deserve is to be treated with disrespect by the citizens they're supposed to be trying to protect. Hence, *contempt of cop* may be seen as among the worst offenses a citizen can commit while interacting with police officers (Lardner & Reppeto, 2000) and may result in overly harsh treatment, especially if the citizen is a suspect in other crimes. An officer's justification for more forceful treatment often hinges on the idea that a citizen's hostile attitude signifies defiance of the larger social institutions the officer represents, and that these miscreants–affectionately known as "assholes"–therefore pose a greater danger to the officers and overall menace to society than more compliant suspects: "an asshole who disrespects a cop is capable of anything" (Toch, 1996).

These are situations ripe for *vicious cycles*. Conflicts and confrontations often stem from what citizens view as overly brusque street interrogations, capricious misdemeanor arrests, or gratuitous hassling by cops. The citizen's expressed resentment then leads to his or her failure of the *attitude test*, prompting further rough language and action by the officer. The citizen's resistance may then escalate to outright aggression, leading to his or her arrest on far more serious charges–assault of a police officer–than might have originally been under question.

While many of these situations unintentionally careen out of control, some officers are in fact quite adept at provoking such scenes for their own amusement or, worse, to provide grounds for *cover arrests* on charges related to the confrontation itself. That is, the officer ticks off the citizen, the citizen makes some threatening move or gesture, and now the cop has him on assault of an officer, resisting

arrest, and so on. This accomplishes the purposes of legitimizing the officer's use of force to control the situation, automatically converts the citizen into a criminal, thereby decreases the credibility of excessive force complaints and, as an added bonus, contributes to the officer's arrest record and productivity in cleaning up his beat (Toch, 1996).

Deliberate *officer malfeasance* may account for some instances of abusive street justice, but a far more frequent cause is probably *lack of communication skills, training, and experience* in handling interpersonal confrontations, forcing these officers to fall back on heavy-handed assertions of authority. This tendency is frequently associated with insecurity and a corresponding inability to professionally distance oneself from citizen expressions of resentment–most often, harmless verbal spewing–that don't necessarily rise to the level of an arrestable offense. Citizens are often ingenious in the ways they can instigate and provoke officers without strictly violating the law, and many officers habitually react angrily to these confrontations as personal insults and lash out in retaliation, which may further fuel community resentment toward police generally (Cancino, 2001; Geller & Toch, 1996; Toch & Grant, 2005).

A related dynamic involves *displacement*. This particular asshole, here and now, stands symbolically for all the citizen insults, departmental rebukes, miscarriages of justice, and even personal slights the officer has had to grudgingly tolerate throughout his career. Police officers are often cynical about the criminal justice system and are frequently tempted to dispense street justice themselves. To their credit, either out of conscience or fear of sanction, they usually suppress this urge to "thump the asshole," even those who may appear to be clearly "asking for it." However, if an officer is feeling particularly stressed out at the time a particular encounter occurs, the situation may quickly flash over into a violent confrontation as he takes his pent-up frustrations out on the hapless, if not entirely innocent, suspect (Grant & Grant, 1996; Toch, 1996). Importantly, to the extent that these unfortunate confrontations are due primarily to a lack of training and experience in communication skills, conflict resolution strategies, and stress management, they are potentially correctable.

LAW ENFORCEMENT ADMINISTRATION AND CULTURE

As noted above, the personal quirks, pathologies, and dysfunctional policing styles of problem officers do not operate in isolation, and understanding the behavior of "bad cops" is incomplete unless we also examine the cultures and philosophies of the organizations in which these officers are trained, socialized, and work on a daily basis. From a practical perspective, such a top-down approach holds great potential to effectively guide police reform, as organizational factors are sometimes more readily altered than are the attitudes and personalities of individual officers and the citizens they confront (Delattre, 1991; Worden, 1996).

As noted in several places in this book, a kind of generic *cop culture* exists in most departments, which emphasizes the danger and unpredictability of police work, the collegial loyalty and reliance of officers on each other for backup, a certain degree of discretionary autonomy in handling situations, and the need to assert and maintain one's authority and credibility. The police culture in many departments thus frequently sets up a conflict between giving officers a great deal of latitude in exercising their individual judgment and style of policing, and then seeming to come down hard with sanctions if certain, often unclear, protocols are breached (Armacost, 2004; Barker, 1983; Blau, 1986; Cancino & Enriquez, 2004; Delattre, 1991; Peak, 2003; Worden, 1996).

Some departments may be tempted to address excessive force and other disciplinary and performance problems by setting up rigid, bureaucratic systems of oversight and management which, paradoxically, then seem to worsen the problem. Other departments, usually by default, take the exact opposite route: departmental control is conspicuous by its absence, as supervisors tolerate police officer misbehavior because they lack the will or ability to detect, prevent, or constrain it (Fyfe, 1996; Worden, 1996; Iannone & Iannone, 2001). In either case, police administration mismanagement abets the tendency of some bad apples to sow the seeds of abuse and dereliction and eventually come to corrupt the whole departmental barrel.

The other systemic issue involves *training*, as problems with departmental philosophy and personal conduct often begin at the level of the police academy. Despite required courses and curricular lip-service about law enforcement ethics, legalities, and human relations, instructors in many training programs regale recruits with lurid, if unrepresentative, war stories that feature the use of marginally justifiable violence against dangerous evildoers. *Hot calls*–harrowing chases, dangerous apprehensions, first-in scenarios–are, after all, what "real" police work is about, the heroic activities that forge the crystallization of a cop's identity and public image as a courageous crime-fighter.

During the probationary and rookie phases of training, the greatest influence on recruits and new officers comes from their *field training officers* (FTOs), whose attitude and behavior can substantially shape the new recruit's conduct for years to come (Toch, 1996). All too often, FTOs inculcate trainees with cynical doubts about the relevance of academy classroom education to the hard-bitten realities of policing on the street. Their attitude seems to be that effective police work would be impossible if officers had to follow to the letter all those pesky rules and procedures dreamed up by clueless, desk-bound bureaucrats with too much free time. The challenge, then, is to integrate training and experience so that reality does not necessarily have to conflict with professionalism.

BAD COP TO GOOD COP: SOLUTIONS AND STRATEGIES

As preceding sections have illustrated, there are a number of contributors to the problem of police misconduct, and consequently, several solutions need to be coordinated in addressing these problems. Accordingly, efforts at correction and enhancement of police performance will require departmental commitment to adequate selection, training, and socialization of officers to create a force of competent and flexible law enforcement problem solvers (Toch & Grant, 2005). Indeed, research shows that police managers prefer to salvage officers whenever possible (Peak, 2003; Robinette, 1987).

Different officers are dysfunctional for different reasons, and police departments therefore need to develop an integrated system of interventions to target different groups of officers at different phases of their careers. Importantly, interventions must address not just officer personality characteristics, but organizational practices of the departments in which the officers work (Grant & Grant, 1996; Scrivner, 1999). Indeed, many recommendations offered in this section can be regarded as police psychology distillations of the general principles of personnel and management psychology that have been applied in a wide range of public and private organizations (Iannone & Iannone, 2001; Lowman, 1993; Sperry, 1996; Grote, 1995; Miller, in press; Peak et al., 2004; Stone, 1999; Thibault et al., 2004).

SELECTION AND SCREENING

The first step in preventing police misconduct logically entails not hiring misconduct-prone officers. If only it were that simple. Scrivner (1999) points out that much of the selection process for police candidates is actually deselection, or *screening out*, of potentially troublesome candidates based on a variety of practical and psychological criteria. An alternative approach to selecting candidates for police work is the *screening in* of those individuals who are suitable and desirable. It seems only reasonable that hiring only the "best and brightest" would provide superior personnel who would be least prone to abuse of force and other indiscretions of police behavior (Grant & Grant, 1996; Johnson, 1983).

Coming from the field of clinical psychology, which is diagnosis-oriented and psychopathology-modeled, most current screening protocols typically focus on identifying the characteristics of "bad" officers, the better to eliminate them from consideration. In the process, much potentially useful knowledge about what makes a "good" officer is overlooked, as well as insights about how career experiences mitigate or reinforce these characteristics. In general, psychologists have been better at screening out than screening in, although neither as yet has attained any great level of precision (Bartol, 1996). Moreover, even the best preemployment screening protocol cannot necessarily anticipate emotional and psychological problems that may develop after the selection process, during an officer's tenure on the force (Scrivner, 1999).

Nevertheless, certain index signs are useful. *Screening-out red flags* include drug or alcohol abuse; behavioral disorders due to brain injury or serious psychiatric disability; a history of serious juvenile delinquency; chronic conflicts with authority; misconduct or poor performance in former jobs; financial problems; or a criminal record. A particularly important feature of the evaluation is the candidate's style of handling anger and aggression, both in the past and presently (McCafferty & McCafferty, 1998). Indeed, these are basic criteria for almost all types of employee screening but especially for those positions that concern public safety. Personality testing per se typically screens out about 15 percent of police candidates (Bartol, 1991; 1996).

Screening-in protocols should assess not just behavioral styles and character traits, but the potential for both formal training and learning from experience. Especially, for modern professional police forces, there is growing recognition of the value of problem-oriented policing and the need for patrol officers who have good overall intelligence, especially abstract reasoning, mental flexibility, interpersonal creativity, and problem-solving skills (Grant & Grant, 1996; Hancock & McClung, 1984; Johnson, 1983). Other related positive traits and qualities include psychological maturity, common sense, reliability, conscientiousness, and the ability to apply discretion in an ethical and equitable manner (Sanders, 2003). Ideally, officers should be college graduates or be willing to attain degrees as part of their career advancement (Sanderson, 1977). Leaders, supervisors, and higher-ranking officers should be mature, seasoned individuals with a well-developed sense of integrity and professionalism (McCafferty & McCafferty, 1998; Peak, 2003). The challenge is to find or develop selection measures and protocols that can accurately identify and predict these positive traits.

Yet even the best screening protocol is really only a behavioral snapshot of the officer's psychological qualifications at the beginning of his or her career. Ideally, *evaluations and reassessments* should be a regular component of an officer's progress through his or her law enforcement career. Such reassess- ments should be balanced with *monitoring, training, and supervision safeguards* throughout the officer's tenure with the department (Scrivner, 1999).

EDUCATION AND TRAINING

Certain skills and qualities are largely innate: you either have them or you don't. Many skills, however, can be taught, albeit to varying degrees that depend on the individual involved. The general training models employed by most police psychologists are based on principles of adult learning that involve a combination of didactic classroom instruction, behavioral participation, simulated patrol scenarios, and role playing. The emphasis is on developing a range of both physical and psychosocial intervention skills that assume frequent, and often unpleasant, interactions between citizens and police. Such exercises are most productively focused on learning to anticipate problems before they arise and generating productive and flexible problem-solving strategies as an alternative to force (Cooper, 1999; Klockars, 1996; Scrivner, 1994, 1999).

Much training, experience, and socialization of new recruits occur on the street under the guidance and influence of their *field training officers* (FTOs). In the ideal case, the recruit is paired with a senior officer who is skilled in resolving problems on his or her beat. Analyzing and discussing the new officer's response to real-life incidents in an individualized and supportive way can powerfully contribute to the recruit's interpersonal skill-building and policing effectiveness (Grant & Grant, 1996; Griffith, 2003c). Police training also has an attitudinal component: it socializes officers into their respective departments and inculcates departmental philosophies, values, and expectations. These seeming "intangibles" in fact have great impact on officers' behavior on the street (Fyfe, 1996; Griffith, 2003b).

Conflict management training enhances officers' communication skills as the primary tools for controlling potentially violent people. Naturally, nonviolent tactics will not always work, and police must be competently trained in how and when to use appropriate physical force when necessary (Geller & Toch ,1996). A paradigm that may be productively applied to police work comes from the field of corporate conflict resolution and appeals to the martial arts concept of true strength emanating from inner confidence, peace, and wisdom; of power as a tool that is best used quietly; and of true respect inhering as much in force restrained as in force expressed. Such a model might be practically reinforced by training in communication skills that appeal to this kind of "verbal judo" approach (Cooper, 1999; Crawley, 1995; Potter-Efron, 1998; also see Chapters 2, 3, and 9).

Tactical conflict management or violence reduction exercises have been developed in police training programs in a number of major cities (Geller & Toch ,1996). Through instruction and role playing, officers learn how to control a potentially violent encounter and how to de-escalate rather than exacerbate tensions between themselves and citizens. Just as officers will vary in their proficiency at marksmanship, surveillance, and other law enforcement skills, not all officers will attain the same level of proficiency in verbal violence reduction strategies. However, given the opportunities to explore their strengths and weaknesses safely and nonpunitively, most officers can gain a working knowledge of their skill limitations and will learn to overcome some deficiencies and to compensate for those they cannot change (Fyfe, 1989, 1996; Geller & Toch, 1996).

Indeed, the most successful diplomats, combat soldiers, emergency medical personnel, trial lawyers, and others have developed the ability to maintain their professionalism under stressful and confrontational conditions and, to varying degrees, this is also a skill that can be learned. This type of professional approach is defined as a cognitively flexible, nonjudgmental attitude that says that most people's behavior, no matter how bizarre or provocative, may usually be explained by factors that go beyond the dichotomies of good and evil, "I'm-right-you're-wrong."

For police trainers, this translates into helping officers learn to depersonalize the unavoidable insults and verbal attacks by citizens that come with the job of community policing. This type of training often includes a heavy emphasis on cross-cultural sensitivity and response styles to acquaint officers with the demographic subpopulations of their beats, including different manners and styles citizens have of dealing with authority figures (Fyfe, 1996). As noted above, the "professionals" or "natural cops" seem to do this instinctively. And even if every officer cannot be expected to become an adept street-corner psychologist, cultural anthropologist, diplomat, or philosopher, most officers can at least be trained to view alternatives to force as a means of safe, effective policing.

Training may include citizens, too (Rahtz, 2005). Typically, citizens' impressions of police use of force consist of extreme stereotypes from Hollywood dramas or sensationalized news stories. Few members of the general public understand what goes into determining an officer's decision to use force and the risks and liabilities involved. In some municipalities, attempts are recently being made to correct this misinformation through the use of *Citizen Police Academies* (CPAs). Some CPAs are designed specifically to enhance the working relationship between the police and other groups that serve the public, such as mental health professionals, but the knowledge and perspective they offer can be invaluable in enlightening the everyday citizen about the way in which police officers carry out their duty to protect.

COACHING AND COUNSELING

Coaching and counseling may be considered a more focused, individualized application of education and training that directly addresses a particular officer's problematic behavior in the context of supervisory session. Coaching and counseling both require constructive confrontation of the problem officer's behavior, but it is important to realize that confrontation need not—indeed, should not—ever be gratuitously hostile, offensive, or demeaning. Professionalism and respect can characterize the interaction of a superior with a subordinate in any supervisory setting, including coaching, counseling, discipline, or even termination. The focus is on correcting the problem behavior, not bashing the officer. Supervisors should be firm but civil, preserving the dignity of all involved (Grote, 1995; Stone, 1999).

Coaching

The difference between coaching and counseling lies in their focus and emphasis. *Coaching* deals directly with identifying and correcting problematic behaviors. It is concerned with the operational reasons those behaviors occur and with developing specific task-related strategies for improving performance in those areas. Most of the direction and guidance in coaching comes from the supervisor, and the main task of the supervisee is to understand

and carry out the prescribed corrective actions. For example, an officer who fails to complete reports on time is given specific deadlines for such paperwork as well as guidance on how to word reports so that they don't become too overwhelming. An officer who behaves discourteously with citizens is provided with specific scenarios to role-play in order to develop a repertoire of responses for maintaining his authority without abusing the public.

One useful model of law enforcement coaching (Robinette, 1987) divides the process into four stages.

1. *Identify and define the problem.* "There have been five complaints filed against you for excessive force or abusive behavior in the past three months."

2. *State the effect of the problem.* "When citizens view an officer's behavior as unnecessarily harsh, it makes it harder and more dangerous for all of us to do our jobs. Each officer's actions have repercussions for every other officer and for the whole department."

3. *Describe the desired action.* "There seem to be some common threads in these complaints. Let's review some of these situations and see if we can come up with better responses. But

the bottom line is, your style of interaction with citizens has to change." [Supervisor and officer review scenarios and discuss alternative responses, using discussion and role-play as needed.]

4. *Make it attractive.* "We appreciate your efforts to be an enthusiastic, top-notch cop. These new ways of doing your job will help you to be even more effective on patrol."

5. *Document and summarize.* "Okay, I'm noting here that we reviewed this and that you agree to make these changes."

Counseling

Counseling differs from coaching in two main ways. First, it is less task-focused and more supportive, empathic, nondirective, and nonevaluative, and seeks to understand the broader reasons underlying the problematic behavior. This is especially appropriate when the difficulty lies less in a specific action or infraction and more in the area of attitudes and style of relating, where there may be a more general factor accounting for a range of problem behaviors. Second, counseling is less top-down directive than coaching, and puts more of the burden of change on the supervisee, encouraging the officer to creatively develop solutions to his or her difficulties. Much of the feedback to the supervisee is in the form of *reflective statements*, so that a kind of Socratic dialogue emerges, moving the supervisee increasingly in the direction of constructive problem solving.

Supervisor: Do you know why I asked to speak with you today?

Officer: Well, I guess there have been some complaints about me.

[Discussion continues about the nature of the complaints and their consequences]

S: I see you've been here seven years with a pretty good record. What's been going on lately?

O: I dunno, maybe the job's getting to me. Ever since the McGillicuddy shooting, it's like everything seems to drag. And the civilians seem more of a pain in the ass than ever–every little thing ticks me off. Oh yeah, and things at home haven't been going that great either.

[Some further discussion about job and personal problems]

S: Well, I'm glad you told me that, and I understand things have been rough the past couple of months, but I'm sure you understand that we need to maintain a certain standard of professionalism. I'm going to refer you to our EAP for some counseling to help you get your bearings. In the meantime, I'd like you to take the next few days to think of some ways you can improve how you're doing things out on patrol. Jot 'em down, in fact, and we'll meet next time to discuss this further. You do your part, and we'll help you get through this, agreed?

O: Okay, I'll try.

S: Well, I need you to do more than try, because the situation does have to change. So get back to me with some specifics next week and we'll take it from there, okay?

O: Okay, Sarge.

DISCIPLINE AND INTERNAL REVIEW

If accommodative educative, coaching, and counseling measures have been ineffective, some sort of departmental internal review and discipline, ranging from an official reprimand, to termination, to the actual filing of criminal charges against the officer, may be indicated.

Good discipline begins with *assessment and monitoring* of the officer's behavior to detect precursors and patterns of excessive force and other problems, so that interventions can be applied as early as possible. To this end, police managers should be attentive to signals of deterioration in officer behavior well before it reaches the point of formal excessive force or other complaints (Scrivner, 1999).

Another problem in many departments is an overly heavy-handed approach to discipline, once misconduct has been discovered. Discipline should be *consistent, impartial, immediate, and definitive.* Ideally, the goal should be to stop the misbehavior, while salvaging an otherwise effective officer. To this end, interventions should be *step-wise and targeted* to a specific problem. Using nonpunitive interventions, such as coaching, counseling, and re-training, is usually preferable to using punitive measures, at least at the initial stages (of course, depending on the seriousness of the offense). But such supportive approaches go only so far with some officers. Those cops who engage in overtly and repeatedly unacceptable conduct must be firmly sanctioned on the grounds that they present a threat both to the community's citizens and to the safety of their fellow officers (Toch, 1996).

One disciplinary protocol developed specifically for police sergeants in charge of patrol officers (Garner, 1995) specifies five basic principles of corrective action:

1. Have as much *background information* as possible and know the full story.

2. Have the required *administrative support* before taking corrective action.

3. *Know the officer* as well as possible.

4. Frame *constructive criticism in a supportive context*–remember to raise the good points, not just the bad.

5. Try to obtain *agreement, commitment, and buy-in* from the officer, so that the final solution feels like his or her decision, too.

Serpas et al. (2003) describe an innovative law enforcement disciplinary system that has been adopted by the Washington State Patrol. The system is designed to allow officers to sidestep a lengthy internal investigation either by admitting a mistake, accepting an appropriate sanction and moving on, or by volunteering information to exonerate themselves. Every effort is made to deal with minor misconduct at the lowest possible departmental level, and to ensure that any sanctions or punishments attached to a particular behavior are reliable, valid, and predictable. In essence, although the authors do not make this citation explicit, their approach is a police-specific application of Grote's (1995) *discipline without punishment* system designed for dealing with all kinds of employee misconduct.

Sadly, not every bad cop can be salvaged. Despite all reasonable efforts at training and counseling, officers who are persistently and irredeemably violent, corrupt, or incompetent must be dismissed from the force. In some cases, formal legal charges may have to be brought. If things have progressed to this point, discipline should be consistent, impartial, immediate, and definitive. It is the responsibility of the leaders of law enforcement agencies to find ways of overcoming the obstacles to discipline and dismissal, including the conspiracy of silence, peer pressure, and civil service issues (Griffith, 2003b; McCafferty & McCafferty, 1998; Peak, 2003; Perez & Muir, 1996; Thibault et al., 2004). The weeding out of the few truly bad cops is a fundamental prerequisite for the ability of the many good cops to serve their communities with skill and honor.

FITNESS FOR DUTY EVALUATIONS

In cases where it is suspected that personal traits, disorders, or stress reactions are causing or contributing to an officer's problem behavior, a formal *psychological fitness for duty* (FFD) evaluation may be ordered to: (1) determine if the officer is psychologically capable of remaining in his or her job and exercising the police role; (2) if not, then what measures, if any, are recommended to make him or her more effective and able to function up to the standards of the department; and (3) what kinds of reasonable accommodations, if any, must be in place to permit the officer to work in spite of the residual disabilities. The FFD evaluation thus combines elements of risk management, mental health intervention, labor law, and departmental discipline (Rostow & Davis, 2002, 2004; Stone, 1995, 2000).

In this respect, police managers who wish to refer their officer for an FFD evaluation may have to navigate some tricky terrain through legal and union territory. As a rule, under the Americans with Disabilities Act (ADA), for positions that involve public safety workers, such as police, firefighters, and emergency medical personnel, courts have generally tended to afford greater discretion to employers seeking to require a psychological FFD evaluation for a worker if there is great potential for that worker's impaired mental state to put the public at risk (Wolfkinson, 2003). This applies as well to physicians, transportation workers, and those who work with children–even to psychiatrists and psychologists (Anfang et al., 2005). One primary driver of such an evaluation is concern for liability, such as claims of negligent hiring, negligent retention, and so on; these issues are endemic in the public and private employee sector (Miller, 2001a, 2001b).

Fitness for Duty Evaluation Stages

One useful protocol for the Fitness for Duty Evaluation of police officers (Stone, 1995) will be summarized here. Bear in mind that these stages and components may be modified, depending on the needs of an individual department as well as the specific referral questions involved (e.g., a neuropsychological evaluation in cases of a suspected brain concussion, or a toxicology screen for suspected drug abuse).

Stage 1: Behaviors of concern. In this stage, a police officer has engaged in some behavior that calls into question his emotional stability, judgment, or self-control, and this sends up a signal to supervisory personnel.

Stage 2: Agency assessment. Someone within the agency becomes formally alerted to the officer's problem and the fact that the officer poses a threat or embarrassment to the department. This may occur through citizen complaints, direct observation of superiors, training reports by the FTO, or–far less commonly–reports by fellow officers.

Stage 3: Evaluation. An evaluator is enlisted to perform a FFD evaluation. Current guidelines by the International Association of Chiefs of Police (IACP) require the evaluator to be a licensed psychologist or board certified psychiatrist with law enforcement experience. The guidelines, however, do not specify how much experience is sufficient and there is as yet no generally accepted formal credentialing for police psychologists as a distinct professional specialty. Thus, the level of law enforcement experience of these clinicians is likely to vary con-

siderably and departments should use their best judgment in evaluating their evaluators. Bear in mind that the results of an FFD evaluation may be brought before a court or a governmental commission and that someone's entire career may hinge on the FFD's conclusions.

Stage 4: Treatment plan. In light of the Americans with Disabilities Act (ADA), the responses to law enforcement FFD referral questions may often have to go beyond simply an either-or answer about fitness for duty and may require the evaluator to state the specific measures that must be taken in order for this officer to be fit or to maintain fitness, analogous to the *reasonable accommodations* principle in general disability evaluations (Rostow & Davis, 2004; Stone, 2000). In addition, provisions may have to be made for less clear-cut cases in which officers may teeter on the border between fitness and nonfitness or alternate between fit at some times and not fit at others. This again raises the need for qualified examiners to work closely with departmental officials so that the most fair and accurate evaluation of the officer can be carried out.

The Psychological Fitness for Duty Evaluation Report

In their comprehensive volume on the subject, Rostow & Davis (2004) provide a useful and practical format for psychological FFD evaluation reports, which I outline here along with my own comments and suggestions. The exact style and content of the report may vary according to the needs and preferences of the individual psychologist and police agency, but should contain the following basic elements:

Identifying data. The officer's name, identifying demographics, departmental referral identification, name of the evaluator, and dates of the evaluation.

Reason for evaluation. Describe the main incidents, issues, and referral questions that have led the officer to the psychologist's office. Although a wide range of data may be relevant to the individual's overall psychological functioning, the focus of the evaluation itself should be relatively specific to the question at hand. Sometimes, officers are referred without clear indications for why an FFD evaluation is being ordered ("He's got an attitude problem"). In such cases, the psychologist may have to take responsibility for helping the referring agency refine its referral question ("What problematic behaviors is this officer showing that reflects his bad attitude?"). Also, somewhere in the beginning of the report should be a statement that clarifies issues of *informed consent* and the uses to which the evaluation findings may be put.

Background information. The information in this section can be narrow, i.e., what took place during or around the incidents in question; or broader, i.e., what has been the officer's general experience within the department that may shed light on the specific referral issues. Again, the scope and range of such background data are defined by their relevance to the referral questions. For example, conflicts with previous employers may be relevant; history of physical abuse as a child may not. Details of his dealings with drug suspects on duty may be pertinent if they affect his job performance; marital infidelities or weekend barhopping may not, if they have no impact on his job effectiveness.

Clinical interview and behavioral observations. Consistent with the present book's emphasis on speech content, voice tone, eye contact, body language, and general appearance, much useful information can be gleaned about a subject from a good clinical interview. How the subject answers questions is just as important as what he or she says. Clinical status– anxious, depressed, delusional, evasive, intoxicated, hung-over, angry, guilty, lackadaisical–can be determined most accurately only by an interpersonal interaction with the subject. Another important feature of this interaction is to develop a rapport with the subject sufficient to allow accuracy of responding and test-taking.

Review of records. Depending on the individual case, the volume of pertinent records can range from a few spare sheets to literally cartons of documents delivered by truck (this is an occupational hazard for any forensic psychologist). Not all of these records may be directly relevant to your case, but you won't know that until you've rolled up your sleeves and

sorted through them. For me, distilling this raw data down to a few paragraphs or pages that will summarize the main points useful for the reader, and then integrating this with the information gained from the clinical interview and test findings, is one of the most challenging and time-consuming aspects of report writing (Mark Twain once wrote, "If I'd had more time, I would have written you a shorter letter"). Be clear about the sources of the records you cite: you may be expected to justify every statement you make at a subsequent deposition or trial.

Psychological test findings. Again, there is no universal, "official" psychological test battery for FFD evaluations, and each psychologist has his or her preferences (some use no psychometric testing at all), but there are certain standards as to what kinds of diagnostic issues should be addressed by these instruments. Some psychological tests are specifically designed for law enforcement assessment, while others are general tests of psychological traits that can be adapted to the law enforcement FFD referral questions. The basic areas that should be covered by these measures include: general intelligence; cognitive functioning (attention, concentration, memory, reasoning); personality functioning; assessment of mood (anxiety, depression); and screening for psychotic symptoms (delusions or hallucinations). Some psychologists insert specific measures for *malingering* to gauge if the subject is being truthful in his reports and in his test responses. In this section, be sure to document both the actual test scores and their interpretation. For example:

"A Full-Scale IQ score of 98 on the WAIS-III places this officer's overall intelligence in the average range."

"A T-score of 86 on the Psychopathic Deviate scale of the MMPI-2 suggests high impulsivity and a characteristic disregard for rules and authority."

Conclusions and discussion. This is where you put it all together. This section should be a succinct summary of the main points relevant to the FFD questions, with documentation of your reasoning on each point. For example:

"Psychological test findings are essentially within normal limits, with the exception of a tendency to disregard rules and conventions and to respond impulsively under stress. This is supported by the officer's statement that 'If I know the SOP is wrong, it's my responsibility to do it the right way, isn't it? If I try to go through channels and make any recommendations to the brass, they just blow me off. That's why I went ballistic in the lieutenant's office when he told me I could be suspended.' This is further corroborated by records indicating three prior disciplinary actions in the officer's present department, and at least one prior suspension in his previous job.

"Overall findings are consistent with an officer of average intelligence, no major mental disorder, high ability and skill in certain job-related areas (firearms and vehicles), but with a long-standing tendency to disobey authority and respond impulsively, but not violently, under conditions of stress."

Recommendations. This is perhaps the most challenging section of the report, because here you have to boil down your findings to specific recommendations that will affect this officer's future life and career. Again, although there is no one standard model for expressing this, the protocol of alternatives preferred by Rostow & Davis (2004) is both psychologically valid and practical:

Unfit for duty. The officer is unfit for duty and is not likely to become fit in the foreseeable future, with or without psychological treatment. Examples include the effects of a traumatic brain injury, a long-standing severe personality disorder, or a substance abuse problem that continues to get worse.

Unfit but treatable. The officer is currently unfit, but appears to be amenable to treatment that will restore him to fitness in a reasonable amount of time. For example, a depressed, alcoholic officer agrees to enter a 12-step abstinence program, attend psychotherapy sessions, and take prescribed antidepressant medication as needed.

Following the recommended course of treatment, the officer will usually be referred for a *posttreatment evaluation.* The recommendations of that evaluation may include maintenance of abstinence and continuation of psychological treatment in some form.

No psychological diagnosis. There is nothing in the results of the psychological FFD evaluation to suggest that the officer's unfitness for duty is related to a mental disorder or mental heath diagnosis. In such cases, the officer will usually be referred back for administrative coaching or counseling, further education and training, or disciplinary action. We psychologists sometimes need to remind ourselves that people can exhibit rotten behavior for any number of self-serving reasons without having to peg it to a psychological "disorder." When that's the call, we need to make it.

Invalid evaluation. The officer has failed to cooperate with the evaluation, has not been truthful, and/or has shown malingering or other response manipulation on psychological tests. This can range from an officer sitting in stony silence, arms crossed, opening his mouth only to say, "I'm not saying nothing to no damn shrink without a lawyer;" to a subject waltzing into the exam all smiles, talking a blue streak, telling a long and involved tale of woe ("I was framed!"), and working just too damn hard to ingratiate himself with the evaluator. Alternatively, the subject can behave appropriately, but his account doesn't jive with the records. Or the test findings are inconsistent and invalid. Again, aside from a few psychometric indices on some tests, malingering or response manipulation is often not something that leaps off the page and identifies itself, but has to be carefully teased out, put together, and documented by the evaluating psychologist. This, too, is part and parcel of a competent clinical evaluation and good report-writing skills.

PSYCHOLOGICAL SERVICES

One of the functions of an FFD evaluation is to make recommendations for education, retraining, counseling, or treatment, and the latter are some of the ways that police psychologists become directly involved with officers and their lives. Unfortunately, within many departments, referral of officers for mental health services when their job performance has begun to deteriorate is viewed as punishment within a disciplinary context, rather than as a proactive human resource intervention that might forestall further problems and help contribute to that officer's better job performance and overall health (Scrivner, 1999).

In this regard, one national survey of police psychologists found that psychologist-assisted training and counseling, along with supervisory monitoring of officer behavior, were regarded as better management mechanisms for excessive force and other police behavioral problems than simply retesting officers periodically, a practice that often prompts opposition from many rank-and-file and union groups who may resist the idea of "having our heads examined" without due cause (Grant & Grant, 1996).

Psychotherapy and other psychological services for law enforcement officers are covered in Chapter 6. Briefly, the goal of departmentally referred psychological treatment is to use the *minimum depth and intensity of intervention necessary* to restore the officer to his adequate baseline functioning or to modify a preexisting pattern of problem behavior that interferes with the police role. In some cases, when a certain level of clinical trust and comfort has been established, officers may later opt for further, more extensive individual or family therapy to work on personal issues of special concern to them, once the original departmentally-referred issue has been resolved.

Another way to do it is to *recommend psychological counseling to troubled officers before the situation rises to the level of a disciplinary issue.* Many officers are actually glad to be afforded this option once they have been given "permission" by a commanding officer to see the psychologist without stigma. Or at the very least, they can use the brass's recommendation as a face-saving excuse to do what they might have been thinking about doing anyway: "Oh well, the captain said I gotta see the shrink, so I guess I better go ahead and have my head examined." As with most recommendations, the more buy-in obtained by the officer, the more likely the process is to be successful. In fact, in my own practice, I see far more voluntary (or quasi-voluntary) referrals of police officers for psychotherapy than mandated referrals. Again, this may partly be a matter of demographics, but a good proportion of this trend is almost certainly due to the mental health-supportive philosophies of most of the police agencies I work with.

In addition to individual approaches, police psychologists who work closely with a given department may be able to help their agency *collect valuable human resource data* that is relevant to policy. For example, by profiling officers who tend to become abuse-of-force violators, psychologists can help police administrators better understand the complex interaction of personal and systemic factors that contribute to such problems (Grant & Grant, 1996). Consistent with the overall theme of this book, such a system of research should also include "*positive profiling*" of officers who are likely to perform competently and even outstandingly on the job. The overall principle here is that by involving psychologists at the front end of policy and planning for personnel selection, training, and performance monitoring, the need may be lessened at the back end for more extensive counseling, psychotherapy, and disciplinary action later on.

ADMINISTRATIVE AND DEPARTMENTAL SOLUTIONS

As noted earlier, to fully address the problems of police misconduct and poor performance, these must be treated as system-wide problems that include departmental administrative policies as well as individual elements of the human resource system, such as selection, training, supervision, and counseling. These services would ideally be integrated into a structure that maximizes their impact on the individual officer and on the department overall (Scrivner, 1999).

Consistent with the leadership literature from management psychology, *integrity* begins at the top (IACP, 1990). In this view, the most important factor for prevention of corruption in a law enforcement agency is a *leader* who is mature, seasoned, stable, utilizes cognitively flexible thinking, and has personal integrity and a strong personal ethic (Geller & Toch, 1996; Griffith, 2003a; McCafferty & McCafferty, 1998; White, 1972). This will be further elaborated in Chapter 14. For now, understand that police leaders who set a strong, positive tone for their agencies and back it up with firm and fair action, should be able to expect a department they can be proud of.

CONCLUSIONS

Not every officer can be a Supercop, just as not every officer who is exposed to temptation will become a chronic goof-off or miscreant. But between these extremes, police managers can effectively influence the behavior of their marginal personnel in the direction of enhanced competence and performance by adopting the basic *best-practices model* described in this chapter. Considering the cost of replacing a lost officer, successful salvage efforts make sound fiscal, as well as psychological, sense.

Start with an administration that provides a model of ethical leadership. Establish clear policies with regard to standards and practices and utilize effective selection and hiring criteria that exemplify these standards. Assure that initial training and socialization of officers are guided by your departmental philosophy and employ individualized coaching and counseling modalities to deal with potentially solvable performance problems as they arise. Identify psychological problems as early as possible and refer officers for FFD evaluations and psychological services in the context of support, not punishment. If internal investigation, formal disciplinary action, or termination becomes necessary, carry it out with respect and dignity for all sides and provide ample documentation for all actions taken. Indeed, these are general principles that have been applied to a wide range of successful public agencies and private organizations. Police departments deserve no less.

Chapter 14

IN COMMAND: LAW ENFORCEMENT
ADMINISTRATION AND LEADERSHIP

As we saw in the last chapter, most police agencies—most organizations of any type, for that matter—are only as good as their leaders. No matter how democratized the decision-making process in an organization, someone still has to make the difficult command decisions, to sit at the desk on which the proverbial buck often drops with a thud. Especially in a hierarchically organized system such as law enforcement, the role of *competent leaders* is crucial. As we've seen, most operational teams—undercover, SWAT, hostage team—have a commander whose responsibility it is to make sure everything runs as smoothly as possible. This chapter will discuss two types of administrative and leadership stress: command decision making during critical incidents, and the daily stresses of managing a police organization.

COMMAND DECISION MAKING UNDER STRESS

Chapters 6 through 8 discussed the role of law enforcement leaders in critical incidents from the perspective of managing officer reactions and dealing with the aftereffects of those incidents. Here, we discuss what the *operational command leader* actually thinks, says, and does during a major critical incident, such as a hostage crisis, multivehicle accident, terrorist attack, civil disturbance, industrial accident, or natural disaster.

In my management seminars for emergency services administrators, after going through all the protocols and strategies for dealing with a critical incident, I'm almost always asked some version of the following question: Why are some leaders just better at it than others? That is, during critical incidents, what allows one commanding officer to remain calm and focused in the heat of battle, while another is more likely to fold under pressure? Are certain commanders just "born leaders" or is superior command leadership a quality that can be learned?

Actually, as with all human traits and skills, it's a little of both: a combination of innate talent,

bolstered and refined by hard work and proper training. Think of the professional athlete, artist, or musician. Certainly, without a natural gift for his or her sport or skill, all the training in the world won't take the individual past the B range. But raw talent alone is insufficient—the athlete or artisan has to work at developing that skill to its ultimate level in order to attain and stay in the A+ zone. In fact, research shows that those individuals at the top of their fields never coast; if anything, they put in many times more effort than those with less innate talent. That is, they take what's great and make it greater. This applies both to individuals (Briggs, 1988; Simonton, 1994) and to organizations (Collins, 2001; Le Storti, 2003).

It's the same with the kind of decision-making and people-influencing skills that comprise true leadership. By dint of intellect, temperament, and personality, some individuals may be "natural born leaders." But without honing those skills in the real world of managing people under stress, this will remain a largely undeveloped potential.

With that in mind, the following is a representative inventory of skills and traits that most psychologists and emergency service professionals would agree on as comprising the basis for *effective incident command leadership* during most kinds of critical incidents (Bartlett, 2004; Flin, 1996; Hodgkinson & Stewart, 1991; Weisaeth, 1989).

Communication. This involves both input and output. The effective leader quickly and accurately assimilates what others tell him from a morass of often rushed, confused, and conflicting information, and is able to translate complex plans and strategies into specific, focused directives to appropriate personnel.

Team management. The effective leader coordinates the efforts of individual team members into a united force. He or she is able to delegate responsibilities as needed, but can quickly jump in and take personal control where necessary.

Decision making under stress. It's not enough to keep from panicking under life-and-death conditions; the effective command leader must be able to think clearly and make critical split-second decisions under fire. This requires the ability to distinguish signal from noise, to take in and distill the relevant environmental data and come up with a useful response. The key is not to be "relaxed," but to maintain an *optimal arousal state* of focused concentration without distracting anxiety (Chapter 5).

Planning, implementing, and evaluating. This is related to the above point. Grace under pressure does little good if the leader lacks the cognitive skills to quickly and efficiently size up a situation, rule-in and rule-out the appropriate actions, implement those actions, and then accurately assess their effect on the overall crisis management situation. For skilled critical incident command leaders, this cyclical process seems to act in a seamless, coordinated flow—which is why skilled crisis commanders always seem to make their job of managing emergencies "look easy." It *isn't* easy, but skill, practice, and experience provide the level of expertise that almost always makes the commander's decisions the right ones.

Emotional stability. Undergirding the traits of superior command leadership lies a certain basic emotional ballast and stability of character. Often subsumed under the heading of "charisma" or "chops," this leadership quality is more than just the brashness, swagger, and popularity that these terms imply. Rather, it consists of a calm, purposeful, self-assured interpersonal style that inspires the troops with confidence and commands respect without having to fish for it. This kind of leadership loyalty can't be bought, coerced, or cajoled—the team members will go out on a limb for this commander because they absolutely trust his or her judgment and commitment to the job and to their own well-being.

Naturalistic Decision Making (NDM)

In the cool, logical world of the academic classroom or corporate boardroom, decisions are usually made by a dispassionate, algorithmic process: first access all the relevant information, then weigh the evidence carefully, and finally come up with a balanced spreadsheet of risks and benefits to guide the appropriate decision. But in the real world of emergency crisis management, cognitive psychology is increasingly recognizing the importance of understanding how effective decision makers operate under conditions of chaos and confusion, that is, how they employ *naturalistic decision making,* or NDM (Klein, 1989, 1993, 1998), sometimes referred to as *tacit knowledge* (Hedlund et al., 2003), which is uniquely concerned with rapid decision making in complex, naturalistic, messy, real-time settings. NDM has been studied for over decade in the field of military and civilian emergency response (Flin, 1996; Klein, 1998), but only recently has it begun to be applied specifically to day-to-day police work (Spaulding, 2005).

Decision making in such naturalistic settings is characterized by several important factors (Klein, 1993; Orasanu & Connolly, 1993). First, the *goals are typically ill-defined and the tasks poorly structured.* When arriving on the scene, it's rarely immediately clear what is the appropriate action to take. Instead, important chunks of information will be missing, and that which is available may be incomplete, ambiguous, or just plain wrong. Think of what transpires in the first few minutes of a major chemical spill, traffic pile-up, or hostage crisis. Further, the *conditions and requirements of the situation are usually not static*, but may shift from moment to moment, as the crisis continues to unfold and more data come in. This may necessitate the response team immediately implementing *action feedback loops*, which are real-time reactions to changed conditions.

Complicating the above factors are the *high stress levels* inherent in most emergency situations. The stakes are usually high, typically involving life and death, and the time pressure is intense, as decisions must be arrived at, implemented, and/or changed at a moment's notice. Further, these plans and directives must often be communicated to multiple members of the response team, many of whom may be in different locations and not immediately accessible. By the time an instruction reaches one team member, the plans may have already changed or new information may have just come in. Finally, on-scene commanders must be mindful of the broader implications of their actions for their agency and the community at large.

Recognition-Primed Decision Making (RPDM)

In both critical and nonemergency situations, effective command decision-makers seem to invoke a type of decision-making skill that doesn't require the kind of algorithmic, trial-and error deduction that is typical taught in formal courses on reasoning and decision making. Instead, by virtue of having accumulated a comprehensive storehouse of knowledge and experience, leaders who have become true experts in their fields rely on *recognition-primed decision making*, or RPDM (Bowers et al., 1996; Flin, 1996; Klein, 1989, 1993, 1996, 1998; Orasanu & Backer, 1996; Orasanu & Connolly, 1993). This is a kind of holographic, at-a-glance kind of command decision making that usually results in the right answer and the appropriate response to the challenge at hand. During crises, when there is a lot of activity and potential for confusion, RPDM is vital, and most effective commanders employ it intuitively.

That's because the commander's deep and broad knowledge and experience is marshaled by his or her brain instantaneously. The comparisons and weighing of factors that the current situation requires have all been done thousands of times in the past, in thousands of situations, either in real life, in training scenarios, or in independent study. So when the time comes for accurate knowledge to be applied to the present crisis, the commander's brain doesn't have to laboriously scroll down the list of options until the right one appears; instead, his brain quickly sizes up the situation and instantly "googles" the correct response, which is then communicated to the response team. It may look like the commander is operating on a hunch, but it is really an instantaneous distillation of a vast storehouse of operational wisdom applied to the current situation.

Hitting the Ground Running: NDM and RPDM in Action

In the thick of a crisis situation, experienced incident commanders seem to concentrate on assessing and classifying the situation that presents itself. They can quickly size up details that may escape the novice and integrate and make sense of the diverse data by a process called *pattern matching*. Once they recognize that they are dealing with a particular type of event, their knowledge-based intuitive RPDM springs into action and these commanders are able to immediately identify the appropriate response to handle it. They perform a rapid mental feasibility study of that course of action, imagining how they would implement it, as an internal check on whether anything important might go wrong. If they envisage any problems, then the plan might be modified, but only if the whole plan is rejected do they consider another strategy.

In carrying out this internal, mental evaluation, the command decision maker seems to combine all the relevant data to construct a plausible explanation for the situation. This is called *story building* (Klein, 1998; Pennington & Hastie, 1993), a concept adapted from legal research on juror psychology. In the present context of emergency decision making, this internal story building allows the commander to develop an almost instantaneous "theory of the case" to guide his or her subsequent actions. Before any such action is implemented there is a brief mental evaluation to check whether there are likely to be any problems and what they might consist of. This kind of mental simulation is called *preplaying*, kind of an action replay in reverse, that is, projecting the action forward in time.

Even though it is described here as a series of steps, to the actual on-scene decision maker, the RPDM process feels like an intuitive response rather than an analytic comparison or rational choice of alternative options. Key *recommendations from the RPDM model* are as follows (Klein, 1993, 1998).

First, focus on the *assessing the situation as soon as possible*, even before you arrive on the scene, as soon as you first get the call. Importantly, in any complex crisis situation, you may never have all the information or all the resources needed to make a decision that will ensure the absolutely best possible outcome; your job is not to optimize, but to *satisfice* (Flin, 1996; Klein, 1998), that is, to make the decision and implement the appropriate action that will control and stabilize the situation for right now—just enough for additional follow-up planning and implementation to take place. In other words, sometimes you may not be able to turn the heat off at its source, so you may have to settle for keeping the lid on so the whole pot doesn't blow in order to buy time to search for the pilot light or fuel line when you get the chance.

This kind of decision making may require you to employ the internal, mental serial generation and evaluation of options, and check them against their appropriate mental simulation—the story building, discussed above. Still, it is uncanny how, for knowledgeable, seasoned, and experienced expert decision makers, their first option usually proves to be the most workable one, that is, it satisfices. Use further incoming data to *revise the plan* as necessary, and focus on elaborating and improving options for a successful outcome.

The Role of Expertise

Again, the ability to employ RPDM depends on a track record of knowledge and experience—*expertise,* or what some might call *wisdom*—that guides the thinking of the true master of any domain, from emergency management, to medicine, to business, and so on (Flin, 1996; Klein, 1998; Leonard & Swap, 2005; Sternberg, 2002).

Expert command decision makers differ from novices in several fundamental ways. Their track record allows them to employ richer and more sophisticated mental models to guide their proactive data-seeking during critical incidents: they intuitively know what to look for and what to disregard or put on the back burner. Through experience that usually spans at least ten years or more, they have learned to seek both disconfirming and confirmatory evidence as a check against overconfident responding. As a result, their mental models are more intricate and allow them to perceive more complexity in the situation, to read the situation in finer-grained detail, to construct more comprehensive theories of the case, and thus better anticipate what could go wrong and what actions are likely to be right. Expert commanders tend to store their memories and knowledge of tactical situations in the form of complex dynamic physical images, or *war stories.*

Again, the ability to do all this effectively depends on having accumulated a long and valid track record of knowledge and experience, usually spanning decades. It's the same principle by which accomplished athletes, musicians, and other experts carry out their craft with an almost unnatural ease and skillfulness. And while, like any other human trait or talent, different individuals will show different levels of natural aptitude for a given skill, almost all practitioners can learn to be better than they are by continued learning, practice, and application. Remember the principle from Chapter 1: *It's the training, stupid.*

THE LAW ENFORCEMENT EXECUTIVE: ORGANIZATIONAL STRESS MANAGEMENT THROUGH PERSONAL INTEGRITY

But it is not merely major critical incidents that police administrators have to deal with. Successfully managing a small, medium, or large police agency involves all the stresses and challenges of running any private or public organization, with the added factor of having your department's "product or service" consist of frequent, often unpleasant, contact with citizens, sometimes in life-and-death circumstances. Indeed, expertise-guided naturalistic decision making doesn't just apply to emergencies, but informs most of the major and minor command decisions and judgment calls that the law enforcement supervisor makes every day.

ORGANIZATIONAL STRESSES IN LAW ENFORCEMENT

Police agencies have undergone important changes in recent decades, some in line with changes in the larger organizational world, others more specific to law enforcement agencies, and all a potential source of stress for today's police managers (Anderson et al., 1995; Griffith, 2003; Grinder, 2003; Margolis, 2004; Peak, 2003; Sewell, 1988, 1992, 2002).

Police managers have *many masters*, from senior-ranking departmental officials, to city and county leaders, to citizen and community groups, the media, employee union groups, and even their own families. As in any hierarchical organization, police middle managers are responsible *for* the people below them and responsible *to* the people above. This task is frequently complicated by *poor communication* through different levels of command and by an emphasis on exceptional failures rather than more common successes (the "you're-only-as-good-as-your-last-screw-up" principle).

Middle- or upper-level police managers (captains, assistant chiefs) may come to *feel isolated* from the daily street-level realities that patrol officers face, leading to friction: "Easy for the brass to tell us what to do; they're not out here every day." As public organizations across the country face tightening budgets, *opportunities for advancement* within departments tend to shrink, as do opportunities for transfer to other agencies, and police managers may feel stuck in a career rut, leading to frustration, demoralization and burnout.

Demands for greater technical proficiency and changes in police tactics, strategies, philosophies, and community relations require that police managers maintain adequate education and training of their personnel at the same time that *resources* for such activities are dwindling. There is rarely time to get everything accomplished, schedules are maxed out, and the manager always feels just one unscheduled emergency away from chaos. Seemingly *arbitrary directives* from courts or politicians may force police managers to change policies and routines, further destabilizing daily schedules and protocols and leading to resentment at all levels of the department.

Often, new programs are pushed through from above without appropriate planning, training or support, creating *unfunded mandates* in terms of both time and money. Even when middle managers try to institute productive programs, these may be swept away by political fiat if higher-ups decide that there are "more important" things for the department to do. Increased time away from family and frayed nerves upon return home further erode the *manager's support system.* And all the time, the street-level troops are scrutinizing their police commanders for signs of weakness or disingenuousness.

A vicious cycle may thus ensue, whereby deteriorating morale within the department leads to poor police performance, resulting in either lackadaisical supervision as a form of command capitulation or to overly draconian supervision to "keep the lid on," which further erodes troop morale. Resentful cops then continue to shirk duties and/or escalate abuse of force incidents which lead to more citizen complaints, censure by top brass and city officials, and finally, perhaps, to a complete overhaul of the department, often by a new administration that is sent in to "clean things up." Unfortunately, without addressing the core problems, the pattern soon begins again.

POLICE SUPERVISION STYLES

Hopefully, as this book has by now made clear, typologies are useful if they help us understand and more effectively deal with people and problems. But they can be counterproductive if they serve only to stifle creative thinking by pigeon-holing people into inflexible categories. In this spirit, Engel's (2001, 2004) research has yielded a classification of police supervisory styles that administrators may find helpful in their own self-examinations and efforts to improve their managerial skills.

Traditional Supervisors

These supervisors expect aggressive enforcement of the law and have high levels of traditional police task-orientation, with less interest in notions of community policing or of having their officers be local problem-solvers or "social workers." They are more directive in their decision-making and expect their subordinate officers to produce measurable outcomes, particularly arrests and citations, along with the necessary paperwork and documentation. Consistent with their emphasis on authority, discipline, control, and chain of command, these supervisors are more likely to give advice and instruction to subordinates but less likely to reward them. Not surprisingly, traditional supervisors spend significantly less time per shift engaging in encounters with citizens, and have little interest in participating in victims groups, community programs, and so on.

Active Supervisors

These supervisors prize their willingness and ability to go out in the field and do their own share of street-level police work. They are authoritative and directive, and tend to inspire loyalty and group cohesion among their subordinates for "walking the walk." However, their emphasis on a my-way-or-the-highway approach to supervision risks choking their troops with overcontrol and micromanagement. Generally, these seem to be the kind of cops who are promoted to management because they genuinely earned it, but are just not comfortable being "desk jockeys" and who have not mastered the skills of delegation and positive reinforcement as supervisory training tools.

Innovative Supervisors

These supervisors are generally more amenable to innovative changes in policing and supportive of community policing and problem solving efforts. They expect their subordinates to embrace these new initiatives and philosophies enthusiastically, which might not always be realistic. They are less concerned with rigidly enforcing rules and regulations, report writing, or other task-oriented activities, and favor a relations-oriented approach to supervision that relies more on coaching and mentoring than discipline and directing (see Chapter 13). Overall, they would prefer to delegate than micromanage. These supervisors also spend far more of their time directly interacting with citizens and community groups.

Supportive Supervisors

These supervisors typically get high marks with respect to supporting and protecting their troops from what they see as unfair actions on the part of both their own departmental higher-ups and antagonistic elements in the community. They are also likely to be cheerleaders and boosters for the men and women under their command. Like the innovative supervisor, they support individual initiative and creative approaches to law enforcement and community relations. However, they may have a tendency to permit their troops to slack off on certain necessary functions, such as writing reports or sticking to their shifts. In fact, these kinds of supervisors may be ripe for exploitation by less well-meaning subordinates and may unknowingly abet misconduct, abuse, or corruption by being "too nice" and shielding their officers from the consequences of their actions (Christopher Commission, 1991; Crank, 1998; Mollen Commission, 1994; Skolnick & Fyfe, 1993).

Engel (2000, 2001, 2002, 2004) emphasizes that no one single supervisory style should be considered the "ideal" standard for police supervision, as each style is associated with both benefits and problems. Indeed, it would be nice if we could blend the positive qualities of each style and winnow out the negatives. The policy implication is that police administrators should recognize the need for better training of first-line supervisors to achieve the organization's goals as exemplified by the leader of the police agency.

MANAGING POLICE ORGANIZATIONAL STRESS: THE LAW ENFORCEMENT EXECUTIVE

An excellent place to start the process of police organizational stress management is with Sewell's (1992, 2002) conceptualization of the police commander as a *law enforcement executive.* In this aspirational model, the police manager embodies the qualities and actions of a true organizational leader. Such a police leader has a vision or *internal mission statement* that guides his or her image of the goals and purposes of the department. He or she has the *energy and stamina* to stay the course and see projects through to completion, as well as to deal with the day-to-day challenges of running a department or section. The law enforcement executive has command of the *traditional management skills*–planning, organizing, staffing, training, communicating, reporting, and budgeting–yet possess the ability to *creatively improvise* in the service of his or her vision or mission.

Chief (no pun intended) among leadership qualities are *credibility* and *respect*, because without these, most other management skills will be ineffective. Credibility comes from within and is a product of communicating and acting consistently with the executive's values, beliefs, and principles, as embodied in his or her vision. Personnel in any type of organization may not always agree with the leader's opinions and directives, but they will respect them and follow them to the extent that they believe the leader to be a person of honor, who operates out of principle, and who is willing consider alternative viewpoints in an atmosphere of mutual respect (Bolino & Turnley, 2003).

Because the law enforcement executive straddles several worlds, he or she must possess comprehensive knowledge about how police organizations work, must keep current on the latest developments in policing, and be able to adapt to the stresses of organizational change. The executive must have as broad and detailed a *knowledge base* as possible about the community that the department serves (Peak et al., 2004; Thibault et al., 2004). While some of this data can be gleaned by intensive up-front *research*, much of it will necessarily be a function of *experience*, as the executive's knowledge base continues to unfold.

Stress management for the law enforcement executive has two main components: (1) managing his or her *own stress*, the better to be able to function as an efficient and productive commanding officer; and (2) helping *other personnel* in the department manage their own stresses. All too often, in police agencies as well as other organizations, the endemic stresses that build up cumulatively over time are a symptom of systemic problems within the department. Instead of taking the difficult but necessary steps of instituting deep organizational changes, departments often contract with outside mental health clinicians or agencies to conduct superficial "stress

management" courses (Sewell, 1986), as if a few classes on diaphragmatic breathing and anger management will make a dent in the problems that confront the department's personnel every day.

However, there are productive ways that police managers can address stress within their own departments and, although these don't necessarily require a psychologist to implement successfully, they are based on a few commonsense *psychological principles of leadership* (Ayres, 1990; Grinder, 2003; Jurkanin et al., 2001; Sewell, 2002).

To begin with, the law enforcement leader must be *visible and accessible*. He or she must be seen by the troops as being actively involved in the running of the department, receptive to constructive feedback, and sincerely concerned with both the welfare of his or her personnel and their excellence in performance of their duties. In the presence of organizational changes or departmental crises, the ideal leader should be a bedrock of *stability and consistency*; the troops should know that he or she can be counted on to do the right thing, to not confuse urgency with crisis, and to handle problems effectively. He should teach by example, "walking the walk" of integrity, not just preaching about it. This often involves putting in the extra time and effort it takes to be an effective manager, not just living by the clock.

To maintain morale, the police executive must treat all members of the department with *reasonable respect*. Even though individual management styles may vary–from formal and hierarchical to casual and egalitarian–it is intriguing how the basic common elements of respect and integrity suffuse through successful organizations of all different types. The troops know when their commanders are treating them right and will strive to reciprocate. Too many leaders confuse respect with fear, as in "I'm the boss, so you better respect me, or else." People will obey you and kowtow to you out of *fear*, but only as long as they have to, or until someone more fearful comes along to knock you out of first place. But people who *respect* you will remain loyal even when they don't have to, because true respect is built on consistency, trust, and integrity.

Effective police executives demand excellence, but they freely *acknowledge and reward* their troops' honest effort and hard work. They *delegate responsibly*, avoid micromanaging, but know when to step in and help out when appropriate. They make a good-faith effort to rehabilitate underperforming officers, but know when to cut their losses and won't let a truly bad apple continue to rot the departmental barrel. This means that true leaders are not afraid of *constructive feedback* from above and below, and are always ready and willing to learn and expand their knowledge base. In fact, as noted earlier, the more knowledge accumulated and integrated from as many diverse sources as possible, the greater the likelihood of being able to make quick and direct decisions in real-time: the recognition-primed decision making (RPDM) discussed above. *Learning* comes from a variety of sources, from formal textbooks and academic courses, to self-study, to practical field experience, to feedback and constructive criticism from the troops. A true leader never makes subordinates afraid to confront him or her with conflicting data if the goal is to improve the department's overall performance. True leaders are not afraid to be wrong if the correction will lead to being right in the future: remember this book's refrain about 20/20 hindsight, insight, and foresight.

Education and the incremental acquisition of knowledge also work in the other direction, too, and true leaders will make *continuing education and training* a priority of their troops' involvement in the organization. Many departments link continuing education credits to pay bonuses, but the police executive should set the example of making new learning a virtue in itself. Aside from the training necessary to do their jobs, nobody should be forced to cram extra information into their brain if they don't want to, because the last thing the police leaders wants to do is turn learning into a punishment. Much more effective is to create what I call a *culture of knowledge* (Miller, in press), where becoming smarter and smarter about an aspect of law enforcement or any other type of professional work is not something regarded as a nerdy indulgence, but seen as a admirable exercise in self-development as a true professional, on a par with intensive postgraduate firearms practice or advanced crisis negotiation training. Indeed,

many police professionals, such as crime scene investigators, behavioral profilers, and lab technicians, often acquire such knowledge on their own time and at their own expense (Henry, 2004).

As noted earlier, all too often, departments in trouble fail to recognize, or choose to ignore, the connection between their organizational culture and the current crisis, so instead of making the tough but necessary systemic changes needed to reform the department, they subcontract an outside consultant organization to come in and give a brief "stress management" or "ethics" or "diversity training" course, convincing themselves that this discharges their obligation to their personnel (Sewell, 1986). Having been both student and teacher of such courses, I can attest to the palpable cynicism that often seethes through the room as the classes typically become either droning monologues by the instructor with students sullenly refusing to participate, or deteriorate into angry bitch sessions which only serve to further entrench the departmental bitterness against an uncaring administration who are seen as trying to "shape us up by throwing a course at us."

True organizational reform is not easy, and it doesn't happen overnight (Toch et al., 1975; Toch & Grant, 2005). Even very committed law enforcement executives often bang their heads up against a recalcitrant municipal, state, or federal bureaucracy that is used to doing things the old way and expects the department leader to straighten out his or her own house—without, however, being given the latitude or resources to make the truly needed changes. But if the police executive is a person of integrity, the rank-and-file personnel will genuinely appreciate his or her efforts to improve conditions on their behalf and, even more importantly, will respect and comply with required changes on their part, if these are seen as being fair and equitably distributed throughout the department. In other words, it's not all or nothing: a police executive with a vision can almost always accomplish something valuable, even if external circumstances force the reality to fall far short of the goals.

ROLE OF THE POLICE PSYCHOLOGIST IN ORGANIZATIONAL STRESS MANAGEMENT

Police psychologists can play several roles in helping departments manage the stress of organizational change or just the stresses of daily departmental life (Blau, 1994; Sewell, 1986, 2002).

Direct Clinical Services

Police psychologists can see officers and in *individual and/or family therapy* to deal with personal or professional stresses that may affect their performance at work. Officers will avail themselves of this resource to the extent that its legitimacy and usefulness are supported and modeled by the departmental leadership.

This is not just a nice idea but a practical one that makes fiscal sense. DeAngelis (1993) reports a fairly extensive pilot study in England where a group of 250 public safety workers who received stress counseling were compared to a matched control group of 100 workers who did not. Four or five counseling sessions were initially provided, and referral was made to a mental health professional if more treatment was needed. The counseled group showed less depression, less anxiety, and less somatic concerns, and there was a 66 percent decline in sickness-related absences. As for cost-effectiveness, it was found that every 175 people who received the brief counseling represented a savings of about $200,000 in sickness absence. The most effective use for the individually oriented counseling approach seemed to be with marital difficulties and other personal problems; another large group of stress difficulties that were addressed in counseling had to do directly with work-related problems.

Education and Training

Psychologists can provide *training* in techniques of organizational stress management in the form of departmental workshops and seminars, formal academic courses at the local police academy or community college, roll-call minicourses or "brown bag" lunch meetings, or any other venue that will enhance learning and mastery of stress management skills. Again, support from the brass is crucial in implementing and sustaining these programs.

Management Coaching

Psychologists with expertise in industrial/organization and management psychology can provide *coaching and consultation services* to assist in organizational change, personnel management, executive coaching, and departmental crisis management. Many psychologists already do this in a variety of public agencies and private corporations, but its utilization within law enforcement agencies has been slower. Hopefully, this will continue to change.

ON THE SPOT: TESTIFYING IN COURT

Many police officers, from patrol grunts to top brass, cite testifying in court as one of the most stressful aspects of the job. Many cops rightfully perceive this as an adversarial system, where they can be skewered by clever defense attorneys during hostile and aggressive cross-examination. The criminal justice system is often perceived as a revolving door, where all of an officer's hard work at investigation, arrest, and testimony can be weaseled away on technicalities, putting bad guys back on the street and making the cop's job all the more dangerous and exhausting (Anderson et al., 1995; Mogil, 1989).

The testimony process may also be inherently uncomfortable for many officers. Many patrol officers will have to testify only a few times in their careers, while others, particularly detectives who investigate crimes, as well as traffic cops, may have court testimony as a regular part of their work schedule. Remember that your job as a police officer witness is to ensure that the facts you present tell the complete story and that your delivery of these facts makes your testimony clear, credible, and convincing. This section provides some recommendations for testifying in court based on the experiences of a number of my law enforcement colleagues and my own experience as an expert witness in psychology and neuropsychology (Miller, 1996, 1997).

Types of Witnesses and Types of Testimony

One area that forensic psychologists and law enforcement officers share in common is that their work often has them in court. There are some important differences, however. One involves a difference in the kinds of testimony given in a criminal trial. A *fact witness* is someone who has personal knowledge of events pertaining to the case. They may be *eyewitnesses* who actually observed the crime taking place, or they may be familiar with aspects of the defendant's background, behavior, or other factors that are pertinent to the case. It is usually up to the judge to decide what aspects of a witness's testimony are admissible in the trial. Fact witnesses may not testify as to *hearsay* evidence ("John told me that Fred committed the murder") and they usually may not offer an *opinion* ("Fred was always the quiet type, you know, the kind that's likely to snap under pressure").

Opinions are the province of the *expert witness*, who is either retained by the prosecution or defense or appointed by the court to make statements about aspects of the case that he or she has personally not observed. This is typically the domain of credentialed specialists in forensically-related fields, such as a medical examiner ("The wounds were consistent with forceful stabbing by a serrated blade and the cause of death was excessive bleeding, leading to cardiocirculatory collapse"); crime lab expert ("The fingerprints and DNA evidence on the kitchen knife are a statistical match to the defendant); psychologist ("The defendant's prior history of injury to the brain's frontal lobe, past record of impulsive violence upon provocation, and intoxication at the time of his arrest make it highly probable that he would have reacted violently to his wife's insulting remarks"); and a host of other experts in specialized fields.

Unlike fact witnesses, experts are there precisely to offer opinions that may assist the *triers of fact* (judge or jury) in understanding specialized technical knowledge that would otherwise be beyond their expertise. Expert witnesses also can rely on hearsay evidence, usually in the form of third-party records ("I reviewed Fred's school disciplinary records and the records of the hospital and brain injury rehab clinic where he was treated following his car accident"). Other hearsay evidence concerns interviews with collaterals ("I spoke with Fred's daughter, who was awakened during the attack on her mother"). Although experts are allowed more leeway in testimony than fact witnesses, the content of their testimony is also carefully vetted by the court for admissibility.

Police officers who are called to court may find that their testimony sometimes straddles the domains of fact and expert witness. For example, they may be queried about what they did and what the defendant did, like a fact witness, and then asked to state an opinion like an expert witness. Or they may state such an opinion, which the opposing attorney may challenge, and the judge must decide to admit it into the record or not.

Attorney: Officer Jackson, can you tell us how you first approached the defendant while undercover?

Officer: Well, actually, he first approached me.

A: What do you mean?

O: I was undercover as a street person, and the defendant came over and asked me if I "needed directions."

A: And what did you answer?

O: That I was "going uptown."

A: Can you explain to this court what that conversation means?

O: Well, in that neighborhood, "needing directions" means if you want to buy drugs, and "uptown" is coke or sometimes crystal meth—some kind of upper, you know, a stimulant.

A: But at no time did the defendant actually ask you if you, quote-unquote, "wanted to buy drugs," did he?

O: Not in those words.

A: So you don't know for sure if he really intended to sell you drugs or was just trying to help out.

O: Of course I knew. That's the language they use.

A: Officer Jackson, are you an expert in linguistics?

O: No, but I'm an expert on that neighborhood—I've worked undercover there for five years.

Remember, that judges have wide discretion as to what they will allow. Later, I'll discuss some protocols of testimony that will maximize the likelihood of getting your points across accurately and effectively.

Preparing for Testimony

Psychologists and other clinicians—medical, mental health, or otherwise—understand the importance of *proper record keeping*. Even if we don't specialize in forensics, it is only a matter of time until some attorney requests copies of our records for a civil case, criminal case, or even a charge of malpractice against us. The basic rule is: always take notes on the assumption that someday, somewhere, somehow, somebody is going to go over them with a fine-tooth comb and pick apart everything you wrote. And especially when doing evaluations and writing reports for the court, forensic psychologists are trained to carefully weigh every word, sentence, and idea so that they express as precisely and unambiguously as possible what it is we want to say.

The corollary for law enforcement officers is: be prepared. Develop a well-organized, standardized, and readable style for writing reports. From the very beginning of any case, pay close attention to *documentation*—not just because your reports will be read by critical eyes, but because writing out your thoughts in words is an excellent way of clarifying, organizing, and remembering the points you will want to get across, should this case come to trial. Draw pictures to help your description and to jog your memory. Of course, many reports use standardized forms, such as accident report forms with checklists and diagrams, but don't be afraid to add your own words and illustrations if it will help you explain a potentially confusing situation.

Another aspect of testimony preparation involves a principle that has run through this book with respect to dealing with people: *know your customers*. Find out something about the judge, the defense attorney, and the composition of the jury. You will probably have one or more meetings with the prosecutor to *go over your testimony*. Ideally, the goal is not for the attorney to spoon-feed your words to you, but for both of you to clarify the substance of your testimony, to agree on a terminology that will best express what you have to say, and to get a sense of what you will be asked by both sides.

Review your case. And review it again. In fact, there is no such thing as too much preparation. The more thoroughly you know your facts and theories about the case, the easier it will be to answer questions thrown at you from "left field" because you won't be relying on rote memorization of individual answers to different questions; your knowledge and recollection will be an organic, holistic, automatic process that is hard to trip up by clever cross-examination.

Rehearse. Most of this will be mental rehearsal,

going over the facts of the case and your testimony in your head. You might also rehearse out loud, while driving in your car or in front of a mirror at home. If trial testimony is unfamiliar to you, visit a courtroom and observe other trials in progress. Get a feel for the process and protocols of the courtroom. Of course, for officers who testify regularly, these processes will have become more and more automatic as time goes on and familiarity increases, but even for the most seasoned witness, there is still no substitute for adequate preparation, and many a veteran "expert" has let his or her overconfidence lead to loose ends which are then used by a clever attorney to hang them.

On the Stand

Again, certain aspects of courtroom demeanor cannot be programmed; every witness brings his or her own unique style to the stand. Nevertheless, there are a few principles of effective testimony that all witnesses can productively apply (Anderson et al., 1995; Mogil, 1989; Vinson & Davis, 1993). Many of these are reminiscent of the verbal and nonverbal communication styles discussed in other sections of this book.

Your *general attitude* should be one of confidence but not cockiness. To the average juror, a police officer conveys some air of authority and respect; use this to your advantage. Maintain composure and dignity at all times. Remember, no matter how nasty the cross-examination, you are not the one on trial here (when you *are* the defendant will be considered below). It is not you who is there to convict the defendant; your job is to present the facts and evidence that will hopefully lead to a conviction. As with all aspects of police work, always remember this: *you are a professional.*

Body language is important. Like your mother said, sit up straight and don't slouch. If there is a microphone in front of you, sit close enough so that you don't have to lean over every time you speak. Keep your presentation materials neatly organized in front of you, so you can find documents and exhibits when needed.

While testifying, look at the attorney while he or she is questioning you, then switch your eye contact to the jury while answering the question; it's them you have to establish a connection with, and jurors tend to find witnesses more credible when they "looked straight at us." Be neither overly aloof nor overly intense. *Open, friendly, and dignified* are the attitudinal words to remember. *Speak as clearly, slowly, and concisely* as possible to be understood. Keep sentences short and to the point. Keep your voice tone even and use a normal conversational tone. Don't mumble, shout, or waffle, but neither should you speak in a robotic monotone. Your general attitude toward the jury should convey a sense of collegial respect: you are there to present the facts as you know them to a group of mature adults who, you are confident, will make the right decision.

Listen carefully to each question before you respond. If you do not fully understand the question, ask the attorney to repeat it or rephrase it. Don't be baited into giving a quick answer; if you need a couple of seconds to compose your thoughts, take them. Speak as clearly and concisely as possible. *Answer the question* completely, but don't overelaborate or ramble. If you don't know the answer to the question, state plainly, "I don't know." Don't try to bluff your way out of a tricky question. The opposing attorney will manage to seize on the one piece of evidence you didn't present or the one inconsistency in your testimony and make a whole case out of it. Don't become defensive. Above all, be honest. If anyone in the courtroom detects even a whiff of deliberate untruth, especially from a police officer, it can stink up the rest of your entire testimony, and indeed, the whole case.

Attorneys will typically phrase questions in a way that constrains your answers in the direction they want you to go. If you feel you cannot honestly answer the question by a simple yes-or-no answer, say so: "Sir, if I limit my answer to yes or no, I will not be able to give factual testimony. Is that what you wish me to do?" Sometimes, the attorney will voluntarily reword the question. If he presses for a yes-or-no answer, at that point either your attorney will pop up to make an objection or the judge will intervene. The latter may instruct the cross-examining attorney to allow you more leeway in responding, or to rephrase his or her question, or the judge may simply order you to answer the question as it has been asked, in which case that's what you do, with a resigned expression on your face.

If you feel you must explain yourself, you may ask the judge, not the attorney, if you may *qualify your answer*, that is reply beyond the narrow scope of the question: "Your honor, may I qualify? I want to be as accurate as possible." Remember that the reason for all the courtroom rules and procedures is to standardize and systematize the trial process, so judges are ordinarily reluctant to make arbitrary changes. Sometimes, the judge will allow you to expand on your answer, cautioning you not to stray from the topic; other times, he or she will direct you to just answer the question as asked. But at least you tried to make yourself clear and this will not be lost on the jury.

Another attorney ploy is to phrase questions in such a way as to almost force you to respond in a wishy-washy manner, often prefacing your answer with such squish-factor phrases, as "I believe," "I estimate," "To the best of my knowledge/recollection," "As far as I know," "What I was able to piece together," "I'm pretty sure that," etc. If the facts warrant it, *be as definite about your answers as possible*; if they don't, honestly state that this particular piece of your testimony may not be a clear perception or recollection, but be firm about what you *are* sure about.

But, in general, try *not to answer beyond the question*. For example, if the attorney asks you to phrase your answers in precise measurements that are not relevant or that you can't accurately recall, don't speculate, unless you're actually asked to do so. For example,

Attorney: Officer Jackson, you say you saw the defendant take two drug vials out of his jacket pocket. How far away from the defendant were you when you made this observation?

Officer: About half a block away.

A: How many feet away would that be?

O: I don't know.

A: Surely, officer, you can estimate the distance. Was it a hundred feet? Two hundred? Fifty? Ten?

O: I really can't accurately estimate the number of feet. But on that block, between myself and the defendant, there was a liquor store, a dry cleaner, and the front steps of a post office. The defendant was standing right next to the first step, close enough to observe his hand movements clearly.

A related ploy is when the attorney asks you to estimate something reasonable, like the amount of time that has passed (which most people can roughly gauge in terms of minutes or hours), and then switches to other topics, while maneuvering you to preserve the estimative mindset. Now, suddenly, everything is an estimate: you're *estimating* what the suspect looked like, you're *supposing* where you were, you're *paraphrasing* what you said, you're describing what you did "to the best of my recollection," you're *theorizing* about what the suspect intended, and so on. Later, in your cross-examination, or in his or her summation, the defense attorney will state something like this: "And officer Jackson really hasn't described anything solid has he? Everything is an estimate, a guess, an inference. Ladies and gentlemen of the jury, is a loose collection of "maybe's" and "I-guess-so's" sufficient evidence to convict a man and deprive him of his freedom?

Again, this doesn't mean you should inject false surety into naturally iffy information, but try to emphasize that the ambiguity lies with the subject matter, not with your own perceptions and interpretations.

Attorney: Officer, could you see how much cocaine the defendant had in the plastic bag? Could you see exactly how many ounces it was?

Officer: Exactly how many ounces, no.

A: So you can only guess what the amount was, is that correct?

O: Obviously, I couldn't measure the cocaine in the suspect's hands. But I could clearly see that he was holding an 8-ounce ziploc bag and the amount of powder in the bag was almost enough to fill it. So that's got to be at least six or seven ounces, well above the two-ounce limit for felony possession and sale.

Again, if you don't know the answer to a question, just say you don't know. Jurors will respect and appreciate honest ignorance of a few details far more that your trying to fit every answer into the procrustean bed of your testimony.

Police Officer as Defendant

You hope it never happens to you, but it's always a possibility that hangs over every cop's head: you become the defendant in a criminal or civil case. Once again, you may be called upon to testify in court, and the general principles of testimony outlined above still apply. But this time, the stakes are higher and rules are a little different (Chambers, 1996; Griffith, 2005).

Now your role switches from dispassionate fact or expert witness to the person on trial. You may not be afforded the same deference and respect as you were in the official police officer witness role. Accordingly, your *demeanor*, while still professional, should shade slightly more to the deferential and humble side. This does not mean that you should bow and scrape to the jury, but your attitude should convey that you are confident in putting your fate in their hands and are trusting them to do the right thing.

Another issue relates to the *stress of litigation* and its management. It is not uncommon for officers who have been criminally charged or civilly sued to seek psychological counseling, stress debriefing, or other mental health services. This raises issues of confidentiality and admissibility of *psychological records*. As stated in Chapters 6 and 7, it is rare for courts to order the release of confidential mental health records, except under the most extreme circumstances. Still, this can never be entirely ruled out. Therefore the advice I give my patients who are undergoing any kind of legal charges is this: Tell me about your feelings, tell me about your symptoms, tell me about your coping efforts, but if there is a piece of factual case evidence that you're not sure you should tell me, *ask your lawyer* first. And if he or she advises you not to tell me, then don't. We can still do effective psychotherapy without my having to know every technical detail and, that way, neither of us are put in the position of having to worry about revealing a secret that has never been told—at least to me.

Psychologists should beware, however, that this is by no means a legal panacea, because the psychologist him- or herself may be subpoenaed to testify and the line of questioning by the prosecutor or plaintiff's attorney can be skillfully used to make it look like the shrink is hiding something, or at least that he or she is an incompetent dupe.

Attorney: Dr. Lopez, during the course of your psychological treatment of Officer Jackson, did he render to you a history of the event he is charged with and description of what took place?

Psychologist: He pretty much told me what's in the record regarding the charges against him.

A: Did he tell you how many times he struck Mr. Williams after he had been handcuffed and restrained?

P: No.

A: Isn't that something you would want to know when taking a clinical history from Officer Jackson?

P: The exact number of blows isn't really an important detail at that point.

A: Did he tell you how he felt during his altercation with Mr. Williams? Was he mad? Frightened? Enraged? Was he looking for revenge?

[At this point, the defendant's attorney will probably object.]

P: We really didn't discuss that in our first session. I was more concerned with how he was feeling at the moment.

A: And how *was* he feeling, doctor? Did he express remorse? Was he sorry for what he'd done? Or was he glad Mr. Williams got what he deserved?

[Probably another objection.]

P: He was generally upset about the injuries Mr. Williams received. As it has already been well-documented in the record, Officer Jackson maintains that the injuries were accidental, sustained while Mr. Jackson was violently resisting arrest in a state of extreme intoxication.

A: And that's it, doctor? That's all you got from Officer Jackson in that first session? You mean to say, you spent an hour with Officer Jackson, and all he told you was what was in his initial statement? What *do* you do discuss during those sessions—baseball scores?

P: I believe I just answered the questions you asked me.

The lesson here is that no party to the case is immune from manipulative, even abusive, cross-examination from lawyers who are hell-bent on proving their point and pressing their case. So, as much as possible, reassure yourself that—officer and doctor alike—you're probably going to get slapped around no matter what, that it's part of the process, and just try to maintain as much composure and dignity as possible. Remember, part of trial testimony is the impression you make on the jury by your demeanor, language, and grace under pressure, so, as much as possible, avoid being either cowed into submission or baited into an overreaction. I know, easier said than done. But that's one more reason to go over your testimony before the trial; to anticipate challenges and become comfortable with the substance of your case.

Psychological Support

While crime victims are often afforded access to mental health services before, after, and during the trial (Young, 1988, 1994), defendants and witnesses typically enjoy no such benefits—after all, only the victims are suffering, right? Indeed, it would seem almost unseemly to offer state-sanctioned psychological help to someone who is accused of perpetrating a crime. Ironically, convicted felons have access to mental health services while in prison, but usually not during the trial that put them there. Any such counseling usually consists of a jailhouse continuation of whatever private psychotherapeutic services were taking place prior to the arrest—and if the defendant hasn't made bail, this is dependent on the shrink's willingness to make house calls to the jail.

Especially for police officers who have been accused of a crime, psychological help should be available if he or she needs and requests it. All parties in the criminal justice system should remember that the more stressed out a defendant is, the less coherent and consistent is his testimony likely to be. Unless there is some specific judicial ruling against it, police departments owe their officers the basic courtesy of supporting them through the criminal or civil litigation process with access to psychological services as necessary.

DIVERSITY STRESS IN POLICE WORK

Law enforcement agencies are becoming more ethnically and gender-diverse, with more minorities and women rising to higher levels of authority in police organizations (Anderson et al., 1995; Bell,

1982; Blau, 1994; Tyre, 2004). However, few accessible systematic studies of race and gender factors in police work have existed until recently.

Stresses of Diversity in Policing

Toch (2002) has conducted an extensive, in-depth study of stress in policing, including diversity stress, and a few of his findings are summarized here.

Women choose police work for a variety of reasons, chief among them the autonomy and freedom they find on the job. Many contrast police work with their previous jobs in office work, sales, or industry, where their independence was constrained, not just by the routine ordinariness of the job, but by their subservient role as women. At least officially, as cops, these women are in positions of authority equal to their male counterparts. Women also like the pay and benefits of police work and many cite the hours as a plus: the typical ten-hour, four-day law enforcement work week actually gives them more time to take care of family and personal matters. Where they have a choice, most women prefer the day shift, even though this is perceived as slower in action than night patrol. Like their male counterparts, female officers complain about long stretches of boredom, punctuated by brief, intense episodes of adrenalin-pumping action.

On the negative side, more than half of *female officers* claim they have been discriminated against within their departments because of their sex, and two-thirds of the women contend that their advancement opportunities have been hindered. On the other hand, there seems to be something of a disconnect, or maybe a selection factor, with regard to female advancement within law enforcement. That is, rank-and-file women officers may experience residual discrimination and frustration of career goals, but those few who make it through the gauntlet may actually be rising to the top in increasingly higher numbers (Tyre, 2004).

But first they have to make it through patrol. If you think about it, partnered patrol policing is virtually unique among professions in the fact that two people are required to spend hour after hour in close proximity, often seated within inches of each other in a cramped vehicle. There are few things short of hell that are worse than being yoked to someone you don't get along with for an entire work shift, day after day after day. Not surprisingly, then, the single most important factor cited by female police officers as contributing to job quality is the personality of their partner. A "good partner" is one with whom the female officer can establish a basic rapport, can be trusted to back her up, not get her in trouble, and to have a policing style that is similar to her own. These are probably prerequisites for a good partner in general, no matter what the sex.

But gender is nevertheless important, because males and females do differ with regard to basic cognitive and temperamental style. Female officers cite "ego" as being the major impediment to working with male partners, as well as what they perceive as an overly aggressive style of handling problems on patrol, rather than utilizing negotiation and conflict resolution skills (Chapters 2 & 3). At the same time, some female officers feel pressure to be more aggressive themselves in order to prove themselves as "real cops" (Balkin, 1988). Consistency is also important: it can be frustrating, irritating, and disorienting to have become acclimated to one partner, only to have him or her changed to someone else, and start the "honeymoon" all over again.

Even in this day and age, many citizens are actually surprised when a female officer responds to a call. If male and female officers are present, the citizen will typically assume the male is in charge and direct conversation to him. Similarly, *black female officers* report that white citizens often prefer talking to a white officer—which should not be all that surprising, since it is basic human nature to feel most comfortable with people most like ourselves. On the other hand, many black female officers report that black citizens see them as cops first, and "sisters" second; i.e., black officers are identified primarily with the color of their uniform, not their race. This issue of divided loyalty is one that *black officers* of either sex have to face within their communities (Johnson, 2005). On a positive note, Toch's (2002) survey showed no reluctance among any of the respondents to work with an officer of a different race based on race alone. Again, what seems paramount in partner satisfaction is the personality compatibility of the two officers.

Diversity Stress: Recommendations

Accept reality. We live in a sexually and racially polarized society, and this is reflected both in the police population and in the population of the communities they serve. Ideally, all officers should be able to deal with all kinds of people in all kinds of situations. In reality, though, there is nothing inherently discriminatory about letting people play to their strengths: if a particular officer or officers seem to have a greater understanding of, rapport with, and credibility among the citizens of a particular neighborhood, why not let them be the emissaries of the police force within those communities? Whatever good will they establish will then hopefully generalize to good will among the citizens and local police force more generally, allowing better communication among all concerned and heightening the credibility of all officers.

Indeed, although common culture and ethnicity are factors to be considered in assigning officers to particular beats, often temperament, personality, and the level of basic courtesy and respect characterizing the interactions between cop and civilian are equally, if not more, important. People trust consistency of behavior far more than they do similarity of appearance or language: if a particular cop is known as a good guy who keeps his cool, hears citizens out, takes them seriously, and enforces the law assertively but fairly, he will be trusted far more than an officer of the same race, sex, or language who acts like a supercilious prick.

Partners: Pair personalities, not profiles. The same principle applies to selecting officers to patrol as partners. Where possible, officers who patrol together should be compatible in personality and temperament, no matter what their race or gender (Miller, 2003a, 2003b). This doesn't mean they have be cookie-cutter copies of each other. Indeed,

it is often helpful if each officer has a unique perspective or skill set he or she can bring to the team so that the two partners can complement each other. But, again, reality may dictate that in a multicultural patrol area, it might make sense to have an ethnically diverse team—for two reasons. First, on the basis of just plain human nature, people will feel most comfortable connecting with someone they feel similar to, so one officer may be able to calm down an agitated citizen or obtain necessary information about a crime simply because he or she is the same race or gender.

At the same time, it may be instructive for citizens to observe ethnically diverse police partners cooperating and collaborating for the overall safety of their patrol areas, as sort of a model for how people of different backgrounds can work together for a common cause. Of course, it would be naïve to assume that this kind of "rainbow coalition policing" will automatically undo a lifetime of hardbitten cynicism based on real-life discrimination and injustice, but what better place to start than with society's ultimate street-level symbols of law and order: patrol police officers? Naturally, this is predicated on the assumption that the officers in question are really ethical and dedicated to good police work, and are not collaborating in exploiting or abusing, rather than serving, the people in their communities (Chapter 13).

Be fair. Oh yeah, you're saying, that sounds real simple when we read it on a page, but in the real world, what's really "fair"? As a general guide, any decision that is made on the basis of identifiable criteria and can be documented and defended against criticism is fair if it applies to all personnel equally. Remember, in the domain of diversity, "fair" doesn't mean everyone has to like the decision; in fact, they may detest and loathe it—as long as what they detest and loathe applies to everyone equally.

SENIORITY AND RETIREMENT

Problems of Seniority

Having been there, done that, and seen it all, senior officers present a particular challenge to law enforcement administration (Johnson, 2004). In the

best case, such an officer will be a positive role model to younger cops, bestowing his or her accumulated wisdom and expertise on the comers-up, and helping them to be more effective in their work. Often, this is in their role as FTOs (field training officers), but even more commonly represents an informal influence. In the worst case, the old dinosaurs will infect the department with their burnt-out cynicism, prematurely souring the enthusiasm and motivation of the younger cops, leading to departmental insubordination, demoralization, and possibly misconduct and corruption (Golembiewski & Kim, 1990; also see Chapter 13).

Discipline, both positive and negative, may have little effect on recalcitrant veteran officers who have long ago come to understand that a supervisor's threats have little meaning, while at the same time, commendations and awards for good service represent little more than additional junk to clear off one's desk and wall at retirement: "Those plaques and a token will get me on the subway." Further, one possibly negative side-effect of police departments becoming democratized "flat organizations" and moving away from the hierarchical military model is a commensurate deterioration in respect for—or at least obedience to—authority in general.

The other thing that has been flattening out in law enforcement organizations around the country is the opportunity for promotions and pay raises, further contributing to the "so-what" attitude of many senior officers. If the intrinsic rewards of the job have long since faded away, and opportunity for advancement has plateaued, the general trend will be for a veteran officer to, at best, just spin his wheels and do the minimum till retirement or, at worst, to yield to the temptation to "get while the getting is good," and fall into the world of police corruption (Childers, 1991; Johnson, 2004).

Managing the Veteran Officer

Johnson (2004) offers some recommendations for managing senior officers, which largely concur with my own research and experience in senior employee management (Miller, in press).

Provide personal recognition. This is delicate, because while you may want to give the veteran a few (presumably deserved) motivating pats on the back, you don't want to be seen as playing favorites and end up alienating the younger officers ("What do you have to do to get some recognition around here—grow a beard?"). So be sure to base the extra attention on factors that have to do with the veteran's

unique experience. Remember the earlier discussion of naturalistic decision making and tacit knowledge: many veteran police officers may have indeed accumulated a valuable knowledge base that can benefit other officers. If so, this leads to the next recommendation.

Increase empowerment and responsibility. Again, without appearing to bestow special privileges, try to utilize the senior officer's experience and expertise in practical ways. One route is through the training mode: perhaps the veteran would make an ideal FTO or training officer. Indeed, Griffith (2003) explicitly compares FTOs to parents raising the next generation of cops and instilling both values and skills. Especially for younger chiefs and captains who have assumed command of a police agency, a way of defusing some of the natural suspicions and hostility that comes with such a new position is to proactively solicit the help and support of lower-ranking, but more experienced, officers. Empowerment also means letting the veteran officer do his or her job with a minimum of over-the-shoulder supervision; assume he or she has the responsibility to do the right thing with a minimum of prodding and then let him do it.

Vertical and lateral position change. If slots are open, and if the officer merits it, then a promotion may be one way of sustaining focus and motivation for the remainder of the veteran officer's tenure. In many departments, however, this may simply not be a realistic option, so some kind of lateral transfer to a new section or job role may be an alternative. Sometimes even this isn't possible because of departmental organization, city or county regulations, or union contracts, so the challenge then becomes how to make the officer's remaining time interesting enough to keep his or her remaining tenure from degenerating into burnout.

Listen. Corny as it sounds, sometimes just letting the veteran tell his stories can have a powerfully reinforcing effect on his self-identity as a cop and his motivation to finish his stretch with enthusiasm and honor. As a commanding officer, your genuine interest in what the veteran has to tell you will help him construct a *career narrative* that can solidify his feelings of self-efficacy. Things often become clearer in our own minds when we tell it to others (that's why people keep diaries and journals) and this kind of narrative sense-making helps us find the meaning and structure in what otherwise may look like a series of disjointed life events. So listen to the veteran officer as much as you can—besides, you might learn something.

Law Enforcement Retirement Stress

The very fraternal nature of policing makes retirement a particularly stressful challenge for many officers. In the new economy, public service jobs such as law enforcement are becoming the last bastions of stable employment, where a worker can spend most of his or her productive career in one organization, having built up the set of tribal loyalties and relationships endemic to any long-standing community. Even for officers retiring on the best of terms, the separation can be wrenching. Nevertheless, very few law enforcement agencies specifically provide retirement counseling or guidance to their departing officers.

Accordingly, the following recommendations (Rehm, 1996; Violanti, 1990) may help ease the transition of retiring officers:

Postcareer or "second career" planning. This should actually begin well before retirement and should help the officer focus on how his law enforcement career develops over time, and leads into his planning for an enjoyable and productive retirement.

Financial planning. This is the corollary to the above. It is surprising how many officers, who make decent money with their overtime and moonlighting jobs, nevertheless complain of being broke as the time of retirement nears. Some simple, common-sense financial planning can ameliorate the financial insecurity that may exacerbate the stress of separation.

Psychological support. This can range from informal encouragement by colleagues and the brass, to the establishment of *Retired Officers' Associations* (ROAs), to referral for psychological counseling in cases where the officer is having a particularly difficult time, especially if other family or personal issues are complicating the retirement process. This may also involve follow-up services for the officer and his family.

Honor and tradition. Some kind of formal ceremonial "passing-of-the-torch" ritual should be observed. Most departments give the retiring officer his badge and gun to keep as mementos of his dedicated service. It is always in the best interests of the department that retiring officers leave as satisfied and happy as possible.

CONCLUSIONS

Within law enforcement agencies, stress is multidirectional: from the top-down, from the bottom-up, and from side-to-side. Like all close-knit social groups, a police department is a tribal family unit, in which the cycles of work, love, hate, loyalty, jealousy, honor, betrayal, life, and death are played out. Aside from the military, few other organized service agencies have so intimate a stake in the health, fitness, and well-being of their members. To the extent that officers and their commanders and administrators respect and trust one another, those departments will run smoothly and serve their communities effectively and honorably.

Chapter 15

SIGNIFICANT OTHERS:
FAMILY STRESSES AND FAMILY SOLUTIONS

Here's the conventional wisdom: Because of the stressful nature of the work they do, police officers' families are riven with strife, and their divorce rates stratospherically surpass that of the general population. Right?

Wrong—it's about the same. In fact, research suggests that if police families can survive for the first three years, they have no greater risk of breaking up than other families. Furthermore, second police marriages tend to be even more stable and to endure as well or better than first or second marriages in the general population (Bibbins, 1986; Terry, 1981).

Actually, considering the stresses and challenges of law enforcement work, it may seem surprising that the marriages and family lives of these professionals do not seem to differ dramatically from those of workers in other fields—which may speak volumes about the overall state of marriage and family life in contemporary American and Western society. However, there are a number of unique pressures and problems that affect law enforcement families. In fact, most of the voluntary referrals I get from police agencies have to do with family and relationship problems.

FAMILY STRESSES AMONG LAW ENFORCEMENT PERSONNEL

While it need not involve the kinds of severe critical incident stress described in Chapters 6-8, over 75 percent of spouses of police officers report stress directly related to their mates' jobs, and a number of factors appear to contribute to this (Alexander & Walker, 1994; Anderson et al., 1995; Bibbins, 1986; Blau, 1994; Borum & Philpot, 1993; DeAngelis, 1991; DeAngelo, 1994; Kirschman, 1997; Means, 1986; Reese, 1987; Toch, 2002). The following sections describe some typical family problems and some creative clinical and commonsense solutions coming from both the professional literature and my own clinical experience.

Schedule and Shift Changes

Frequently, the demands of the job and loyalties to the department compete with the officer's marriage for time and commitment, as many officers keep unconventional schedules and often work overtime shifts. Many departments rely on four-day, 12-hour shifts, and few police officers work the traditional nine-to-five. Where available, many officers put in considerable overtime, either for the extra money, or because putting in as much time as possible is consistent with the department's macho culture, or because of bona fide dedication to their work, as in the case of criminal investigators and special unit officers (Chapter 12). With regard to the latter, such police operations as hostage negotiation, SWAT team mobilization, or undercover work are, by their very nature, outside the purview of clock or calendar.

Thus, families that cherish stability and predictability may find it hard to accommodate when their loved one has to suddenly change weekend plans, stay late on a job and miss dinner, or be called in for mandatory overtime to make up for a municipal budget crisis. Even if not doing departmental work, many of these high-energy, go-getting officers have extra jobs or business ventures that keep them super-busy even when off-duty from their police role. Many of these officers justify their workaholism on the basis of the need to provide their families with a good lifestyle and, while the families may certainly appreciate this, they'd also like to actually *see* their hard-working loved one at least once in a while.

Police psychologists, by the way, are not immune from this, either. You think my family likes it when I'm beeped in the middle of the night, or during a holiday dinner, to make an on-scene call to a critical incident? And even this is far less disruptive than a call that comes in the middle of a busy work day, requiring me to shuffle patient schedules to accommodate the emergency. In fact, many seasoned police psychologists warn their would-be protégés not to commit themselves to critical incident response or hostage negotiation teams if they can't be expected to drop what they're doing to respond to an emergency (Blau, 1994; Greenstone, 2005; McMains, 1988; Mc-Mains & Mullins, 1996). At least, most police officers can justify their wacky schedules by telling their families that it's just part of the job. Families of psychologists are not always so understanding, but most appreciate the value of what their loved one is doing. Also, emergency call-outs for psychologists are usually much however less frequent than the shift and schedule disruptions experienced by sworn officers.

The Law Enforcement Culture

Stereotypical "tough guy" macho values and attitudes–among both men and women cops–pervade the law enforcement culture. These include such characterological and behavioral traits as control, dominance, authority, and lack of sentimentality. These are precisely the traits that naturally conflict with the more cooperative, emotionally expressive, and relationship-oriented attitudes generally considered important in marriage and family life.

Divided Loyalties: Job Commitment vs. Family Commitment

Another aspect of law enforcement culture is the formation of powerful bonds of solidarity among fellow officers and boundaries around this tribal inner circle that exclude nonmembers. The officer's spouse may feel left out, often leading to jealousy, as the officer seems to be far more involved with his departmental clanmates than with his marital soulmate and their family. A vicious cycle may develop as the spouse's palpable resentment further alienates the officer, who then spends even more time on the job and away from home, creating a higher risk for the development of substance abuse or extramarital affairs.

Overprotectiveness

Many officers try to create a "protective bubble" (Reese, 1987) around their families to shield them from the unsavory and distressing aspects of their work, as well as to make the officer's home a separate haven from the pressures of the job. Thus, an officer may turn to his spouse for support during a particularly stressful time, then virtually the next moment clam up and refuse to discuss anything about the job. The resulting emotional seesaw takes its toll on the spouse and on the marriage.

A related problem concerns wider interpersonal isolation, as the officer's missed social engagements and immersion in the job drive friends away from the couple, making the spouse feel even more alone and abetting the temptation toward dalliances of desperation on the distaff side of the relationship.

Suspiciousness and the "Cop Channel"

On the job, law enforcement officers must maintain a keen sense of alertness, vigilance, and mental preparedness, which often includes an occupationally reinforced suspiciousness and general distrust of people's motives, statements, and actions. Carried over into the home, this back-to-the-wall, question-everything attitude often seems frankly paranoid. The occupational cynicism and distrust heightens the spouse's feeling of being a perennial suspect under investigation ("Don't you ever trust me?") and puts a general damper on feelings of intimacy, as the officer never seems to let down his guard. As more than one spouse has put it to me: "He's on the Cop Channel—all cop, all the time."

In extreme cases, pent-up anger and frustration from the job may spill over into verbal abuse or physical violence at home (see below). The spouse may be reluctant to report the violence because of feared termination or censure of the officer by the department or because she concludes that "they'll all be on his side anyway."

Being a "Cop's Kid"

Children, especially adolescents, are often caught between feelings of loyalty and pride in their parent's work and anxieties about peer rejection because of common pejorative peer attitudes toward authority figures such as police officers. Actually, this is a general problem for children of parents in any of the helping or service professions—the dilemma of the "cop's kid," "shrink's kid," or "preacher's kid."

Dual Law Enforcement Couples

Occasionally, both spouses work in law enforcement, sometimes in the same department—perhaps that's how they met. An advantage of this arrangement is that each partner is able to truly understand the problems, pressures, and perspectives of the other. Even where one spouse is a cop and the other is in a related public safety/emergency services field, such as a firefighter-paramedic, many of the stresses are similar. In such cases, the carryover of the us-versus-them mentality from the department to the marriage may have a positive effect on connubial cohesion.

The disadvantage is the potential blurring of personal and professional roles, especially where one spouse holds a different rank in the same department. A related problem occurs where the spouse's role as protector interferes with his or her objectivity in perceiving the spouse as a work partner. However, even the most obtuse commander will usually have sense enough not to pair spouses as partners or shiftmates. Finally, in the fishbowl atmosphere of most departments, a married couple's relationship may be subject to kidding and meddling—some good-natured, some not—by coworkers.

FAMILY THERAPY WITH LAW ENFORCEMENT COUPLES

Borum and Philpot (1993) have described a number of effective marital therapy strategies that clinicians can use with police couples where at least one member is an active officer; these are presented here, along with my own comments and suggestions (Miller, 1998, 2002, 2005). Therapeutic goals basically involve: (1) strengthening the marital boundary around the couple, relative to the departmental boundary; (2) reducing divided loyalties, triangulation, and jealousies between the job and the marriage; and (3) increasing intimacy and bonding between the couple. A number of practical and therapeutic strategies can contribute to this.

First, use the common us/them police mentality as a metaphor for the officer to begin to understand the need to create an equivalent *us/them atmosphere for the marital dyad*. The goal of this should be inclusion and solidarity, not paranoia and isolation.

Help the couple develop ways to *create more time for each other*. This may involve explicitly scheduling times for communication about nonjob-related or generally nonproblem matters. Assign "caring days" homework, i.e., lists of nice things to do for each other—if you don't like that syrupy terminology, call it something else. If practical, have the couple plan a "secret vacation" together, a romantic holiday that they keep from everyone except a few select people.

Help the spouses gain insight into divided loyalties and triangulation, and teach them to *deal effectively with one another*, instead of communicating with and through third parties. Teach them how to identify and appropriately express emotion to one another. Teach problem-solving, negotiation, and conflict-resolution skills. Help the spouses expand their social world beyond the department and immediate families. It may also be useful to teach them to cognitively and emotionally compartmenalize in an adaptive way, so that they can turn on their "feeling channel" at home and turn it off at work, as needed. Many officers do this naturally.

Identify, emphasize, and mobilize strengths that have thus far kept the marriage together. Have the spouses describe their early dating days, what attracted them to each other, old love letters, shared good times, private jokes, "our song," and so on. Ironically, the same characteristics that originally attracted the lovers to one another often become polarized and are now a source of friction. For example, the very logical, emotionally stilted police officer may have originally been attracted to his wife because of her open affection and warmth, which made it a little easier and safer for him to access and express his own feelings. In fact, several observers have pointed out that male police officers frequently pair up with females in a helping or people-related profession, like nursing, social work, teaching, sales, or human resources.

But when the spouse comes to look to her husband for additional emotional nurturance, perhaps related to some crisis, perhaps just expressing a heightened need for closeness, he becomes intimidated and freezes up, turning into a superrational computeroid to "balance out" his spouse's emotionality. The therapist may have to provide reframing-type reality checks to focus the behavior of both husband and wife in a more productive, intimacy-enhancing, but nonthreatening direction. This can be effectively accomplished as long as it takes place in the context of the therapist's thorough understanding of the couple's dynamics, within a trusting therapeutic relationship, and on the basis of a solid grounding in couples and family therapy strategies (Carlson & Sperry, 1998; Figley, 1998; Weeks & Treat, 1992) - not used as "therapy tricks" or cookbook-like quick-fix devices, which may serve only to further disenchant the couple with the therapy process and with their hopes of forging a more solid relationship.

SPECIFIC PROBLEMS AND SOLUTIONS FOR LAW ENFORCEMENT FAMILIES

Over the years, I've come across a variety of common and uncommon problems that affect police officers and their families, and these seem to fall into certain categories or clusters. This section will describe these common patterns of law enforcement family issues and the therapeutic and practical measures I've found useful in dealing with them (Miller, 2002, 2005). Hopefully, this insight and advice will add to the therapeutic toolbox of clinicians who work with cops and their loved ones; provide supervisors and administrators with some practical guidelines for counseling the men and women under their command; and provide a reality check for affected officers that, hey, your family's not the only one that's going through this, and just because other officers don't talk about it, it doesn't mean that all of their family lives are perfect and yours sucks.

Also note that these problems range in seriousness from moderately annoying to potentially fatal for the relationship, but in this section, I'll offer some practical strategies for couples to deal with these issues on their own. Of course, when necessary,

officers and their families are encouraged to get professional help, and administrators are encouraged to encourage them.

The "Cop Channel:" Overtime, Overwork, Overcommitment

Most police spouses recognize and appreciate that their officer is a dedicated cop and a hard worker. But often, the police role, police behavior, and police attitudes come to intrude upon family time and family relationships. Overzealousness may turn into compulsive overcommitment, as the officer seems to never pass up an overtime opportunity or turn down a special detail. He typically justifies this by emphasizing the sacrifices he's making for his family's financial well-being, all the while ignoring their pleas that they would gladly pass up the extra cash for a little more time with him.

Worse, he begins to neglect household chores and tasks, either because there is simply no time to pay the bills, mow the lawn, fix the sink, and take the kids to music lessons, or because he feels he is entitled to crash and recuperate when he does come home and shouldn't have to be bothered with the petty details of homemaking when he's been out there for umpteen hours doing "real work." In either case, more and more daily responsibilities fall on the spouse, fueling further resentment.

Basically, I've observed that there are three main reasons that some officers overcommit themselves. Two are related to the job itself, and the third has to do with life outside the job.

The first potential reason is *overidentification with the police role.* There are some guys (and a few gals) who really do feel they're supposed to take up permanent residence in the Cop Channel. Their enthusiasm for their work crowds out all other priorities because nothing consolidates their identity and gives them greater personal validation than being a cop. Actually, this gung-ho attitude may at first be viewed as a positive quality, as the officer's hard work comes to be admired and he is rewarded by promotions, pay raises, and access to plum assignments.

But this can go on only to a certain point. Nobody has inexhaustible energy or motivation and, pushed to the limit, such an officer is a prime candidate for burnout and job stress, which in turn can lead to family distress. The solution is balance: spouses should try to validate their officer's commitment to the job, but emphasize that "recharging the batteries" by taking some occasional time off will only enhance his law enforcement effectiveness. Ideally, police administrators should reinforce this balance concept, but often they themselves are torn between allocating well-deserved R&R and not wanting to interrupt the services of one of the department's star producers. The mixed messages this sends can be frustrating both the officer and his family.

The second reason for overcommitment, frequently related to the first, is *insecurity about their law officer status.* The high productivity of some officers may be driven by the need to constantly "prove themselves" to their coworkers and their department by taking on more and more work and bigger and bigger assignments. Again, in many cases, the departmental culture actually reinforces this: only a wuss or a slacker turns down a job. Here, the challenge is to help the officer develop a feeling of realistic confidence and accomplishment in the good

job that he's doing, so he can chill out a little and not feel constantly compelled to demonstrate his worth as a cop.

In the third situation, the *police job is a respite from the family.* In other words, the officer spends so much time away from home precisely because work is an escape from a distressing home life. Here, the task is to focus on healing the home front so that productive work is balanced by a supportive and fulfilling family life. In these cases, each family has to find the particular strategy that works for them, with the help of a mental health professional, if necessary.

Secrets, Suspicions, and Surveillance

Bad enough the officer is spending all his available free hours working his butt off overtime, but when he does finally come home and his spouse asks him about his day, he clams up or just spits out one-word answers, leaving the spouse feeling even more excluded and rejected from her mate's world. And then, when they do steal a few hours away together, he persists in "cop mode," remaining hypervigilant and suspicious of his surroundings, seeming to find it impossible to relax and just enjoy the outing.

Even worse, he begins to become more and more controlling and overprotective of family routines and activities, demanding to know where spouse and kids are going, when they'll be back, and what they'll be doing. This is typically rationalized as a concern for the family's safety. After all, who knows better than a cop about all the nasty things that can happen out in the cold, cruel world? This maddening combination of secrecy, suspicion, and overcontrol strains the goodwill of even the most understanding and supportive families.

Paradoxically, the common thread that ties these problems together is the very need to maintain the home as a sanctuary and refuge from the grim realities and pressures of the police job. One of the main reasons cops don't like to talk to their families about their work has to do with *protection* and *compartmentalization:* they don't want to expose their families to the putrid reality of what they experience on a given day, and they don't want to sully their own home environment with talk or reminiscences about the job. Another reason relates to *saturation:*

even if nothing dramatic has happened that day, after spending their shift patrolling their beat, surveilling potential felons, ticketing traffic violators, arresting petty crooks, and resolving mundane street squabbles, the last thing the officer wants to do upon returning home is to rehash it.

For some officers, especially detectives and investigators, this overprotective controlling style is reinforced by the natural inclination of their own personalities. Psychological research has shown that people's basic temperaments and cognitive styles influence major decisions in their lives, such as who they pick to marry and the types of jobs they choose (Gardner et al., 1959; Miller, 1990). So it may be no surprise that the kind of mind that feeds on data-gathering, likes to pick apart and analyze things, enjoys "putting two and two together," maintains a "healthy skepticism," questions everything, and is most in its element when ferreting out the facts about one thing or another, will naturally gravitate toward a field like investigative police work.

The problem is not being able to turn it off after work. Precisely because this "search mode" orientation is so much a part of the officer's personality, it naturally intrudes into recreational activities and personal relationships where it can be damaging. No spouse wants to feel like a perpetual suspect, and it can become irritating and draining if the ostensibly off-duty officer treats every family gathering and social situation as if he were casing the joint for clues. In the worst cases, under extreme stress, this natural suspiciousness can decompensate into outright paranoia, and the family can feel like they're being stalked. In a few extreme cases, they are.

Spouses may have to compromise in terms of how much feedback they're likely to get and how relaxed their mate will be during family activities. If the officer is amenable to discussing the issue, point out that you don't expect him to stop being a cop, but that his excessive secrecy and overprotectiveness are corroding your ability to be the supportive spouse you want to be. Sometimes, he may not be aware of the deleterious effects his attitudes and behavior are having on the family.

Alternatively, confronting the issue, however gently, will get you nowhere if the officer just rationalizes and justifies his behavior as "protecting my family." In such cases, you may even be regarded as ungrateful for questioning his actions and his

motives. If talking about it seems to get nowhere, try to teach by example. That is, do your best to actually make the home a separate safe haven from the rigors of police work. As long as it's sincere, show that you're on his side, and his defensiveness may relax somewhat and allow him to loosen up and enjoy family time. If the problem persists unabated, it may be time to get professional help.

Infidelity and Betrayal

Now, if someone's bound to cheat, they're going to cheat, and they hardly need a psychological explanation or any other excuse to do what they've already made up their mind to do. But in many cases, otherwise stable dyadic relationships begin to fray under the pressures of police work and the temptations of infidelity become harder and harder to resist.

I'm often asked by police wives what percentage of officers cheat on their mates, and if this rate is higher than that for the general population. Another question is, "Why do they do it?" Which is really a way of asking, "What can I do to prevent *my* mate from doing it?" Unfortunately, I haven't come across any hard statistics on this subject, but my overall impression is that the rate of law enforcement infidelity is not much different from that of other working male populations whose jobs combine the features of: (1) long shifts with considerable time away from home, and (2) daily exposure to a multitude of different kinds of people.

It's probably not that the police profession turns every cop into a philanderer, but rather that philanderers who are looking for ways to cheat will find ample opportunity in the hurly-burly environment of police work. No doubt, this applies to long-distance truckers, night shift nurses, traveling salesmen, military personnel, and others. The bottom line is that if someone steadfastly chooses to be faithful, no one job and no one temptation is automatically going to "make" them cheat. At the other end of the spectrum, if someone has no qualms about breaking their vows to sate their love jones, the police profession offers ample opportunities for dalliances of convenience. The gray area arises in the case of all those officers in between: neither saints nor sinners, but only too human. In these cases, the usual risk factors for infidelity–family conflict, career disappointments, low self-esteem—operate on the vulnerable officer, just as they would for anyone else.

Spouses also want to know how they can "tell" if their mate is having an affair—on or off the job. Unfortunately, there are no magic spells or talismans you can use to infallibly divine whether your mate is being true blue. You need to use your instincts and your basic knowledge of your spouse to come to a conclusion that makes sense. Beyond that, unless you have a specific reason to assume that your mate is cheating on you, don't walk around sweating that a law enforcement career will automatically turn your otherwise faithful partner into a booty-hound. If it seems like you've got a faithful, reliable spouse, relax and enjoy each other. If real problems are brewing, deal with them in a constructive way. Another way of saying this is, don't "profile" your mate as a cheater just because he's a cop. If there are specific indicators that make you suspicious, deal with them; otherwise, give yourself and him a break.

An interesting line of questioning I sometimes get on this subject comes from police officers themselves who want advice about how to resist temptation on the job, or what to do if they've already stepped over the line and now want to come clean and fix everything up. Maybe it's been too many late evenings chatting up the night shift nurse at local medical center. Or a female suspect is all too willing to trade favors for a break on an arrest, and it's late, and I'm tired. Or it's another cop in the same or different department, and we seem to have so much in common. The trouble is, these guys never seem to think ahead to the time when the affair may be coming to an end, and that's when the real problems often start, especially if the ending isn't something that's mutually agreed upon.

In Chapter 1, I talked about three levels of prevention. Recall that primary prevention is what you do to lower the chances of the bad event happening in the first place. All moralizing aside, a purely practical reason to resist sexual temptation on the job is the potential for severe career repercussions, and this involves the issue of *professional boundaries*. A seemingly harmless sexual dalliance with a citizen while on duty can come back to haunt the officer in the form of a harassment complaint or even criminal sexual assault charges. It might lead to criminal cases being thrown out because of contamination of evidence or testimony. That's definitely a nightmare the officer doesn't need.

So when faced with temptation, I ask officers to remind themselves that maintaining a certain degree of professional detachment and decorum is part of their "mental uniform." It doesn't mean being cold or aloof with citizens, just not becoming either inappropriately angry and hostile or overly charming and flirty with those citizens. Even if someone "throws herself" at the officer, either to curry favor or just because she flat-out likes him, he should be prepared to courteously but firmly decline the offer. A simple "No, ma'am" stated in his official cop voice will usually be enough to discourage such advances, without seeming like a stinging rejection.

But a lot of sexual affairs don't start that way. Often the temptation comes from someone the officer already knows, either from his patrol area, a local hospital or business, or even his own department (Anderson, 2004). He may even have had a friendship with this person for years and now one or both of them is considering taking it to the next level. The officer and that nurse may never have intended to one day find themselves doing the wild thing when they first started sharing stories about their kids and commiserating over the pressures of shift work and the loneliness of being on-call so late at night. Such harmless little intimacies have a way of swelling into sinister longings, however, and then it's sometimes devilishly difficult to maintain the boundary between the personal and the professional.

In these cases, only the officer can decide if he wants this to happen. If not, he should be up front and let the other person know that escalating to the horizontal bop would only jeopardize an otherwise good friendship. If the would-be paramour is persistent, the officer may have to make himself scarce until she gets the message.

But what if it's already happened? The million-dollar question is whether or not the officer should tell his mate, and my answer surprises many officers: *It depends.* That is, while honesty is almost always the best policy, it's not invariably so. Remember, we're dealing strictly with the practical here, and I will never presume to trump someone's religious or moral convictions.

But if the officer has truly resolved in his own conscience to forgo all others and work on his relationship, I tell him that the decision to tell or not to tell then depends on a few important "if's." *If* you truly believe the affair was a mistake, and *if* you are as close to 100 percent certain as anyone can ever be that you will never again let this kind of thing happen, and *if* there is no credible way your mate could ever find out about it unless you told her, and *if* it would cause immeasurable pain to your mate should she learn of it, then you may be justified in keeping the episode to yourself—*not* just to let your own sorry self off the hook, but to spare your spouse unnecessary agony and preserve an otherwise good relationship for both of you.

Before you take this route, however, ask yourself how you would feel if the situation were reversed, and realize that if your mate does discover the infidelity and your subsequent concealment, it will probably ruin any chance of trust between you ever again. Remember, the function of this "don't ask–don't tell" policy is to spare your mate unnecessary pain and preserve the relationship that you've recommitted yourself to in your own heart. But, again, if you have moral or religious beliefs that impel you in the direction of the truth at all costs, or if you truly believe that the highest form of respect for someone is to grant them honesty and allow them to deal with that truth, however unpalatable, then you must follow your conscience and, if this comes from a sincere place in your soul, then bless you for accepting the full consequences of your actions and your mate for seeing past the betrayal and accepting the sincerity of your recommitment.

In most cases, however, this will all be moot because your mate will, in all likelihood, have already discovered the affair, or at least strongly suspect it, and now she confronts you and wants answers and a pound of flesh. Even if the confession has come from you, and you express your sincere desire to get the relationship back on track, absolution will rarely come at so low a price as an apology and the promise not to do it anymore. In addition, both the offending officer and the spouse often ask me: what's a sure sign of proof that the erstwhile strayer has truly changed his ways and what is an appropriate period of time to wait before resuming normal relationships?

The answer here is another resounding, "It depends." Once again, I tell the officer that only if you yourself have truly resolved in your own heart of hearts that such infidelities are a thing of the past can you expect your mate to believe it, and to try to work her way back to trusting you. But be prepared for a probationary period, during which you may have to be extra-considerate of your mate's coldness, moodiness, and other hurt reactions as she works toward feeling secure with you again. At the same time, your probation shouldn't be endless, and by six months or so postpenance, if your spouse is still strongly ambivalent about accepting you back into her heart and you've both done everything you reasonably can to make it work, then it may be time to make a decision. Professional help may be useful, but don't rely on a counselor to fix what the two of you (or one of you) isn't willing to work on. In all honesty, not every story has a happy ending, but if the changes are sincere, then many couples do manage to move past the affair and rebuild their lives together.

Driven to Drink

At several places throughout this book, the specter of alcohol abuse has haunted officers' attempts to cope with the stresses of police work. In the most severe cases, the problem substantially affects the officer's job and some action is taken by the department. Far more commonly, however, problems with alcohol first arise in the family context, and in many cases, the impetus to get help for the problem comes from the officer's desire to keep his family intact, as much as, or even more than, his desire to keep his job.

Questions I get about alcohol use in police officers typically come either from the spouse and, somewhat more rarely, from the officer himself. From the spouse's side, the story is usually that her husband has always been a social drinker, but lately he's been drinking a lot more. He often complains about the department, local politics, family stresses and so on, and she thinks his drinking is turning into a problem. What should she do about this?

The short answer, I usually advise, is to confront the problem. Gently, supportively, but firmly, express your concern to your husband. If he concedes there's a problem, ask what he can do to get it under control. If he feels he wants to but can't, offer to get him professional help.

More likely, though, the officer will brush off the spouse with some version of "I can handle it," or "What am I supposed to do to relieve my stress from work?" The hard truth is that—like infidelity or any other bad habit—if someone wants to drink too much, there are always a million good excuses to do so. His work and personal stresses may be perfectly legitimate but he's found a dysfunctional way to deal with it.

But before you call the temperance league, ask yourself what you mean by "problem drinking." Not that I'm encouraging the regular liberal use of alcohol as a balm to life's ills, but common sense says that there's a difference between the hard-working cop who throws a few back with the boys on the weekend, and the officer who races to get blotto after every shift. Only you and your mate know what works for your relationship and your family.

If it's really a problem you can't deal with, and if your spouse rebuffs your attempts to intervene, get help for yourself from a professional specializing in addictions. Alternatively (or additionally), seek help from your departmental EAP for referral to specialized groups or programs. Sometimes, it's better to go this route yourself rather than to wait for the department to sanction the officer. On the other hand, be careful about being accused of "meddling" and "stirring up trouble" by your angry mate before you've given him a fair chance to deal with the problem himself. Use your judgment.

When the officer himself raises the problem, it usually goes something like this: "I've always been a social drinker, and it's never been a big deal. But lately, the pressures of the job and stresses at home have been getting to me, and I've been drinking a lot more. Nothing nasty, mind you—no blackouts, drunk driving charges, bar fights, or any of that stuff. I stay stone cold sober on my shift and I haven't missed a day of work because of alcohol, although once or twice I was a little late to roll call because of a bad headache. I've had all the classes and seen all the videos on cops and alcohol, and I've thought of seeing an EAP counselor, but I'm afraid of opening up that can of worms. What can I do?"

At this juncture, it's tempting to give the officer the party line, "If you think you have a drinking problem then you *do* have a drinking problem, so get help right away." But, again, living in the real world, the officer knows that even a well-meaning decision like this can have repercussions. Of course, if the problem has dangerously escalated, or if the officer himself feels he is losing control, then I recommend going into an abstinence-based program immediately. Otherwise, for lower-level problems that are just starting to develop, I usually like to keep intensive professional help or a 12-step program in reserve, knowing they're there if we need them, but start with some strategies that the officer can use to help himself.

Drinking is often a *vacuum activity*, that is, it expands to fill the empty time and space created by a lack of other activities. As with any bad habit, it's almost impossible to tell someone to "just don't do it." What's more effective is to encourage them to "do something else." So I tell the officer that if you've got another activity that's enjoyable, use that to replace drinking time. Go bowling. Go fishing. See a movie. Find a nondrinking crowd on your off-hours and hang out with them. Spend more time with your family. Or if family stresses are part of the problem, until things get sorted out, put in more constructive overtime at work—without overstressing yourself, that it, and as long as overwork is not part of the family stress itself.

Keeping busy should take care of a good portion of the drinking-alone problem. But we all know that alcohol is often part of the cop culture and that a good deal of "brotherhood of the badge"-type bonding takes place at the local tavern. Here's where only you know if you can tread the thin line between chugging a few with the brothers over laughs and getting shitfaced and stupid. If, understandably, you don't want to stigmatize yourself as the "dry cop" or "Officer AA" in the group, try limiting your time at the pub gatherings. Arrive late and leave early—use any excuse you like. Drink slowly to keep the blood alcohol concentration low. Sip a Bud instead of a Jack on ice. Alternate the Stoli and Coke with just a Coke. Keep food in your stomach. Once again, only you know if you can pull these stratagems off without losing control of your alcohol intake.

If you do really feel you're getting out of control, you may have to take firmer measures with yourself—and it still doesn't mean going to meetings yet.

First, try this: Stop drinking for one day. Just one day, so you know you can do it. If possible, expand the nondrinking time to more days of the week or later hours of some days. Doing this will give you a feeling of control over yourself which can be a powerful self-esteem builder and spur further control efforts. Of course, this is essentially the "one-day-at-a-time" philosophy of Alcoholics Anonymous, but without the meetings. If you're successful in abstaining for a while, see if you can ratchet back your alcohol consumption to the "social drinking" level you've always found comfortable.

If none of this works, then further measures are necessary. Now may be the time to see a mental health professional or a peer counselor, but not just to help you with the alcohol problem. If the stresses of life are running you down, the therapist or counselor may help you deal more effectively with these. Hopefully, then you'll feel more in control of your life, and you won't need to drown yourself. This goes for whether the problems involve the job, family, or both.

Finally, if you need to get out the big guns—AA or an inpatient treatment center—realize that saving your career and preserving your family are as good a set of reasons as any to get your life back on track. In most cases, however, with a little willpower and determination, you can use the self-help strategies outlined above to take back control of your life.

Cops and Kids

Guess what—it's not just the spouses who complain about their officer-mates; the kids complain about their officer-parents, too. Sometimes it seems a cop just can't cut a break from his own family, doesn't it?

In my experience, barring critical incidents and other extreme family stresses (Chapters 6–8, 11), there are two main areas where cop's kids have problems. One is *getting more time with the parent* and the other is the baggage that comes from *being a cop's kid* in the first place.

As for the time factor, sometimes the officer himself will raise the issue of insufficient time, and in many of these cases, the blame can be placed on crazy departmental schedules. But no such easy buck-passing applies where the officer-parent chooses to max out on overtime or deliberately chooses time-consuming special projects. In such cases, it's not uncommon to hear officers complain that they just can't find time to be with their kids and family.

Well, of course you can't. No one who does any kind of demanding work ever *finds* time for outside activities—they *make* time. Look, nobody's asking you to quit your job or become a short-shift slacker, but no cop works 24/7/365. Sometimes a little inventive schedule juggling on everyone's part can allow at least a little extra kid and family time. It really all depends on your priorities.

For example, how about junior getting up a half-hour earlier a few days a week to have breakfast with dad before he leaves for work (of course, junior goes to bed a little earlier the night before). Or if dad happens to have a weekday off, have him pick up his daughter from school and go out for a Coke and a little father-daughter time before starting homework.

When larger blocks of time do become available—a lucky weekend together, for example—make the most of it. Try not to schedule too many chores and responsibilities, leaving ample time for pure family fun. Even a day or afternoon at the beach or park can be refreshing if everyone makes a point of having a good time.

And even if your family understands that dad can't physically be around while he's working, there's nothing to prevent you calling the kids to say you miss them, leaving them little notes before you go off to work, and bringing home a little present after your shift. Remember, *parental presence* is more than a warm body—it's a feeling your child gets when he or she knows you care, even if you can't be there in person.

The other main category of problems involving children of police officers comes from that dubious status itself. Ministers have "preachers' kids," physicians have "docs' kids," psychologists and psychiatrists have "shrinks' kids," and police officers have "cops' kids." What all these offspring have in common is a parent whose profession is unusual, intimidating, authority-based, and frequently misunderstood.

One problem these kids often have is the expectation that they're supposed to be "extra good" because their parent represents some higher authority (God, the field of medicine, mental health, or the law). Peers may tease them and this may spur the kids to prove their bad boy chops in any number of situationally antisocial or illegal ways, ranging from silly pranks to serious crimes. Then, when they're caught, they expect their law enforcement parent to bail them out of trouble.

Sometimes, cops' kids get ragged on because of some report in the media. Reporters love stories about police scandals and "dirty cops," and your child may be assailed by jeering questions like, "Hey, where'd you get that cool bike—did your dad buy it with his drug money?"

Older children and teen friends may have had their own run-ins with the law, and may take out their resentment on the cop's kid in their group: "Hey, is your dad out there beating up some guy for running a red light?" In other cases, the classmates or their parents or friends may feel let down and disappointed by the perceived failure of law enforcement to adequately respond to a recent crisis: "Sure, your dad couldn't stop our house from being robbed because he was too busy writing parking tickets for little old ladies."

Sometimes, it's jealousy. Despite its foibles, the law enforcement profession is still looked up to by most people, and if your child's dad is a cop and his friend's dad is something else, or unemployed, or not there at all, he may well project his sour grapes onto you and your kid. Worse, your own child may then recyle this resentment and turn it around on you: "Nobody likes me and it's all your fault—why can't you have a regular job like everybody else's parents!"

What can you can do to help your child deal with his or her friends' antics?

First, remember that direct confrontation of schoolyard teasing is rarely an effective strategy because it just confirms the "gotcha reaction" and reinforces future baiting and harassment. What often works better is *deflection*. If your child is hit with a "who'd-your-dad-shoot-today?" crack, teach him to use Socratic dialogue queries. For example, he can reply with something like, "What's *your* dad do?" If the other kid answers this surprise question, your child can then say, "That's interesting, what kind of stuff does a [lawyer, store manager, truck driver, contractor, small business owner, cook, nurse, etc.] do during the day? Ditto for the other kids.

This creates a forum for your child to educate his or her peers about what his police officer parent does for a living. Now it's become a discussion, not a rank-out session. But remember—this only works if he actually knows what an officer's job is like, so discuss it with him and ensure that he has enough info-ammunition to handle the debates. Also, if the teasing continues unrelentingly, it may be time to take action through the school administration, although most kids, especially cop's kids, won't want to have their parents get involved because it makes them look like crybabies. In these cases, difficult parental judgment calls may have to be made.

Second, don't use your police authority in an inappropriate way. If your kid gets in trouble trying to out-bad his friends, stick up for him as would any *good parent*, but don't let your child—and the other children in his group—see that he's got a free pass to do whatever he wants, just because his parent is a police officer. All this does is erode your child's sense of responsibility and confirm the other kids'—and their parents'—impression of your child as a wimp who needs mommy or daddy to bail him out or as a special species of entitled brat. In addition, it affirms the noxious stereotype of police officers as a corrupt bunch of insiders who "just take care of their own."

Finally, if you're proud of what you do, so will be your child. Try to keep grousing about the job out of family discussions and take the time to point out many of the positive things cops do to help people and the community. That way, when all else fails, your kid can respond to his harassers with a shrug and a confident reply: "Hey, say whatever you want, but I'm proud of what my dad/mom does. Deal with it."

DOMESTIC VIOLENCE IN POLICE FAMILIES

At one time, this was law enforcement's dirty little secret, although it's not much of a secret anymore. The issue of domestic violence among police families overlaps with the discussion of administrative discipline (Chapter 13), insofar as the officer's department will eventually become involved, however unwillingly, when the problem is persistent.

Police Officer Domestic Violence: Facts and Stats

It is not known whether police officers have a higher or lower rate of domestic violence than the general public, primarily because potentially higher rates of abuse–if they exist–would probably be offset by lower levels of reporting by fellow officers. The repercussions of an arrest and conviction on a domestic battery charge are far greater for a police officer than for the average citizen, because it can mean surrender of his weapon and loss of his law enforcement career.

Thus, until recently, many departments have maintained a conspiracy of silence around such occurrences, often persuading the complaining spouse that loss of her husband's job would be potentially devastating to the family, and urging the couple to settle things "off the record." In other cases, especially where the call is to the home of a senior officer, patrol partner, or member of a special team like SWAT or undercover, there may be the palpable, if unstated, threat of ostracism, lack of backup, or general opprobrium for cops who rat out other cops, similar to what occurs with other abuse-of-authority cases (Gallo, 2005; Kruger & Valltos, 2002; Lott, 1999; Sanders, 1997).

However, like other unlawful behavior on the part of officers that is actively or passively abetted, undeterred domestic violence undermines the credibility and effectiveness of the department with both its own personnel and the general public, and sets the agency up for civil and criminal actions relating to negligence and malfeasance (Kruger & Valtos, 2002). And again, like other disciplinary protocols, a program of domestic violence response within police agencies need not be brutal or unfair; indeed, the more equitable and just it is perceived to be, the greater the likelihood it will be implemented and used as needed. Accordingly, the following is an outline of a protocol that addresses the key elements in police officer domestic violence intervention (Gallo, 2005; Kruger & Valltos, 2002; Lott, 1999; Sanders, 1997).

Police Officer Domestic Violence Intervention: Policies and Procedures

As with all of the departmental programs discussed in this book, success stands or falls with the level of commitment and buy-in by the upper administration. Police leaders need to demonstrate by both their words and deeds that unwarranted violence by police officers will not be tolerated in any venue. Many agencies endorse a *zero tolerance policy* with regard to violent behavior, but as with most such behavioral concepts, "zero" is not necessarily always an absolute quantity. Accordingly, departmental policy should spell out as clearly as possible what types of behaviors will not be tolerated. Two standards that most departments adhere to are *conduct unbecoming* and *failure to conform to law*. Most departments also require officers to make a report if a police call to their own residence has occurred, whether or not arrests were made.

As with most departmental policies and procedures, domestic violence protocols will have little real bite if they are not enthusiastically endorsed by the agency's leadership. Police leaders should have a good understanding of the dynamics of domestic violence and the magnitude of the problem, both within their own department and in their communities. A commitment to addressing the problem forthrightly in their own departments includes the creation of a culture of disapproval among department leaders, and the allocation of time and resources for adequate training and dealing with incidents.

Training

The key to any credible and permanent strategy for preventing domestic violence is adequate and appropriate training. Training for police officers should cover a comprehensive range of topics, including response, tactics, officer safety, and verbal crisis intervention and conflict-resolution skills. In particular, special training must be provided for officers on how to handle domestic violence calls involving other officers.

Problem Recognition

Astute police supervisors may be able to detect signs of impending or ongoing domestic violence in officers within their own department. The legitimate response to "What happens at home is my business" is, "No, it's not, because (a) if it escalates to an arrestable offense, we lose a good officer; (b) there are liability issues for the department of letting a potentially violent situation go unaddressed; and (c) any kind of family stress that affects our personnel concerns us."

Many of the *signals that a domestic violence problem may be brewing or ongoing* in a officer's family are generic stress-related symptoms, while others are more specific and may include increased isolativeness of the officer; signs of sleeplessness or alcohol abuse; emotional lability or Jekyll-and-Hyde personality; increased incidence of excessive force on the job; talking about the spouse in a particularly derogatory way; blaming the spouse for all the officer's problems; or signs of physical injury that are attributed to "accidents," but may represent wounds received in physical altercations with the spouse.

Investigation and Response to Incidents

Police departments should respond to domestic violence incidents with a comprehensive approach. Kruger and Valltos (2002) recommend that the Internal Affairs department immediately conduct an *initial preliminary inquiry* to determine the need for a formal internal investigation. The latter would follow the agency's established protocol for criminal misconduct cases, including suspension of the officer's police powers and reclamation of his weapon and police vehicle. The officers should be placed on *off-duty status*, pending administrative investigation and referral for a *psychological fitness-for-duty evaluation* (Chapter 13).

If the officer is found psychologically fit for duty, administrators might transfer the officer from off-duty to modified-duty status, such as noncontact status assignments (the dreaded "desk job"), until the investigation is complete. If the officer has sustained a *criminal conviction* related to the domestic battery charge, he will usually be terminated from the department. If *lesser or suspended charges* ensue, the department retains the right to keep the officer or let him go; if he stays, the officer will be expected to comply with any departmental follow-up measures, as well as with any court orders that arise from the case. Not to be neglected is the role of *counseling and family therapy* but, as noted several times throughout this book, this resource should be an option, not a requirement or punishment or, worse, a way of deflecting legitimate legal consequences for the officer's actions. Although I have experienced a few exceptions, for the most part, when people are "forced" to go to psychotherapy, true progress is rarely made.

CONCLUSIONS

Domestic violence usually represents the extreme end-point of an accumulation of family stresses, or it may simply be due to the personality and psychopathology of the perpetrator. However, even family crises that fall far short of violence can wrench the police family apart if not appropriately addressed. Even when family dissolution is not a threat, just living in "walking misery" at home can make performance on the job all the more problematic. Most cops cherish their families as havens away from the pressures of the job. Police psychologists should work with police administrators to devise ways of strengthening police families for the good of the officer, his or her spouse and kids, the department, and the community in general.

BIBLIOGRAPHY

CHAPTER 1: INTRODUCTION

Anderson, W., Swenson, D., & Clay, D. (1995). *Stress management for law enforcement officers.* Englewood Cliffs, NJ: Prentice-Hall.

Blau, T.H. (1994). *Psychological services for law enforcement.* New York: Wiley.

Briggs, J. (1988). *Fire in the crucible: The alchemy of creative genius.* New York: St. Martin's Press.

Dattilio, F.M., & Freeman, A. (Eds.) (2000). *Cognitive-behavioral strategies in crisis intervention* (2nd ed.). New York: Guilford.

Gilliland, B.E., & James, R.K. (1993). *Crisis intervention strategies* (2nd ed.). Pacific Grove, CA: Brooks/Cole.

Kleepsies, P.M. (Ed.) (1998). *Emergencies in mental health practice: Evaluation and management.* New York: Guilford.

Miller, L. (1994). Civilian posttraumatic stress disorder: Clinical syndromes and psychotherapeutic strategies. *Psychotherapy, 31,* 655–664.

Miller, L. (1998a). Our own medicine: Traumatized psychotherapists and the stresses of doing therapy. *Psychotherapy, 35,* 137–146.

Miller, L. (1998b). Psychotherapy of crime victims: Treating the aftermath of interpersonal violence. *Psychotherapy, 35,* 336–345.

Miller, L. (1998c). *Shocks to the system: Psychotherapy of traumatic disability syndromes.* New York: Norton.

Miller, L. (1999a). Treating posttraumatic stress disorder in children and families: Basic principles and clinical applications. *American Journal of Family Therapy, 27,* 21–34.

Miller, L. (1999). Workplace violence: Prevention, response, and recovery. *Psychotherapy, 36,* 160–169.

Miller, L. (1999). Atypical psychological responses to traumatic brain injury: PTSD and beyond. *Neurorehabilitation, 13,* 13–24.

Miller, L. (2000a). Law enforcement traumatic stress: Clinical syndromes and intervention strategies. *Trauma Response, 6*(1), 15–20.

Miller, L. (2000b). Traumatized psychotherapists. In F.M. Dattilio & A. Freeman (Eds.), *Cognitive-behavioral strategies in crisis intervention* (2nd ed., pp. 429–445). New York: Guilford.

Miller, L. (2002). Posttraumatic stress disorder in school violence: Risk management lessons from the workplace. *Neurolaw Letter, 11,* 33, 36–40.

Miller, L. (2003a). Law enforcement responses to violence against youth: Psychological dynamics and intervention strategies. In R.S. Moser & C.E. Franz (Eds.), *Shocking violence II: Violent disaster, war, and terrorism affecting our youth* (pp. 165–195). Springfield, IL: Charles C Thomas.

Miller, L. (2003b). Psychological interventions for terroristic trauma: Symptoms, syndromes, and treatment strategies. *Psychotherapy, 39,* 283–296.

Miller, L. (2005). Workplace violence and psychological trauma: Clinical disability, legal liability, and corporate policy. *The Doe Report,* www.doereport.com.

Peak, K.J. (2003). *Policing America: Methods, issues, challenges* (4th ed.). Upper Saddle River, NJ: Prentice-Hall.

Simonton, D.K. (1994). *Greatness: Who makes history and why.* New York: Guilford.

Toch, H. (2002). *Stress in policing.* Washington, DC: American Psychological Association.

Toch, H., & Grant, J.D. (2005). *Police as problem solvers: How frontline workers can promote organizational and community change* (2nd ed.). Washington, DC: American Psychological Association.

CHAPTER 2: STREET PSYCHOLOGY 101

Baehr, M.E., Furcon, J.E., & Froemel, E.C. (1968). *Psychological assessment of patrolmen: Qualifications in relation to field performance.* Washington, DC: Department of Justice.

Bradstreet, R. (1986). A training proposal: Developing silver-tongued officers. In J.T. Reese & H.A. Goldstein (Eds.), *Psychological services for law enforcement* (pp. 105–109). Washington, DC: Federal Bureau of Investigation.

Cooper, C. (1999). *Mediation and arbitration by patrol police officers.* New York: University Press of America.

Goldstein, H. (1990). *Problem-oriented policing.* New York: McGraw-Hill.

Goldstein, H. (1987). Toward community-oriented policing. *Crime and Delinquency, 33,* 6–30.

Herbert, S. (2001). Policing the contemporary city: Fixing broken windows or shoring up neo-liberalism? *Theoretical Criminality, 5,* 445–466.

Kassin, S. (2005). On the psychology of police confessions: Does innocence put innocents at risk? *American Psychologist, 60,* 215–228.

Kassin, S., & McNall, K. (1991). Police interrogations and confessions. *Law and Human Behavior, 15,* 233–251.

Peak, K.J. (2003). *Policing America: Methods, issues, challenges* (4th ed.). Upper Saddle River, NJ: Prentice-Hall.

Peak, K.J., & Glensor, R.W. (2002). *Community policing and problem solving: Strategies and practices* (3rd ed.). Upper Saddle River, NJ: Prentice-Hall.

Pritchett, G.L. (1993). Interpersonal communication: Improving law enforcement's image. *FBI Law Enforcement Bulletin,* July, pp. 22–26.

Shea, L., & Harpool, D. (1988). Tactical communications training for conflict diffusion. In J.T. Reese & R.M. Horn (Eds.), *Police psychology: Operational assistance* (pp.379–390). Washington, DC: Federal Bureau of Investigation.

Slaiku, K.A. (1996). *When push comes to shove: A practical guide to mediating disputes.* San Francisco: Jossey-Bass.

Thibault, E.A., Lynch, L.M., McBride, R.B., & McBride, B.R. (2004). *Proactive police management.* Upper Saddle River, NJ: Prentice-Hall.

Toch, H., & Grant, J.D. (2005). *Police as problem solvers: How frontline workers can promote organizational and community change* (2nd ed.). Washington, DC: American Psychological Association.

Wadman, R.C., & Ziman, S.M. (1993). Courtesy and police authority. *FBI Law Enforcement Bulletin,* February, pp. 23–26.

Zulawski, D.E., & Wicklander, D.E. (1993). *Practical aspects of interview and interrogation.* Boca Raton, FL: CRC Press.

CHAPTER 3: VIOLENCE ON PATROL

Binder, A., & Scharf, P. (1980). The violent police-citizen encounter. *Annals of the American Academy of Police Science, 452,* 111–121.

Broadfoot, P.A., Jones, J.W. (2005). Proactively addressing gangs effectively. *The Police Chief,* January, pp. 50–52.

Blau, T.H. (1994). *Psychological services for law enforcement.* New York: Wiley.

Clark, S. (1988). The violated victim: Prehospital psychological care for the crime victim. *Journal of Emergency Medical Services,* March, pp. 48–51.

Cooper, C. (1999). *Mediation and arbitration by patrol police officers.* New York: University Press of America.

Dewey-Kollen, J. (2005). Death notification training. *Law and Order,* May, pp. 12–14.

Everstine, D.S., & Everstine, L. (1993). *The trauma response: Treatment for emotional injury.* New York: Norton.

Frederick, C.J. (1986). Post-traumatic stress responses to victims of violent crime: Information for law enforcement officials. In J.T. Reese & H.A. Goldstein (Eds.), *Psychological services for law enforcement* (pp. 341–350). Washington, DC: USGPO.

Garner, G.W. (2005). Surviving domestic violence calls. *Police,* January, pp. 44–46.

Golden, J.S. (2004). De-escalating juvenile aggression. *The Police Chief,* May, pp. 30–34.

Goldstein, A.P. (1977). *Police crisis intervention.* Kalamazoo, MI: Behaviordelia.

Hendricks, J.E. (1984). Death notification: The theory and practice of informing survivors. *Journal of Police Science and Administration, 12,* 109–116.

Herman, S. (2002). Law enforcement and victim services: Rebuilding lives, together. *The Police Chief,* May, pp. 34–37.

Horstman, P.L. (1973). Assaults on police officers. *The Police Chief,* December, pp. 17–21.

Kennedy, D.B., & Homant, R.J. (1984). Battered women's evaluation of police response. *Victimology: An International Journal, 9,* 174–179.

Miller, L. (1998a). Psychotherapy of crime victims: Treating the aftermath of interpersonal violence. *Psychotherapy, 35,* 336–345.

Miller, L. (1998b). *Shocks to the system: Psychotherapy of traumatic disability syndromes.* New York: Norton.

Miller, L. (2001). Crime victim trauma and psychological injury: Clinical and forensic guidelines. In E. Pierson (Ed.), *2001 Wiley expert witness update: New developments in personal injury litigation* (pp. 171–205). New York: Aspen.

Reese, J.T. (1988). Psychological aspects of policing violence. In J.T. Reese & R.M. Horn (Eds.), *Police psychology: Operational assistance* (pp.347–361). Washington, DC: Federal Bureau of Investigation

Russell, H.E., & Beigel, A. (1990). *Understanding human behavior for effective police work* (3rd ed.). New York: Basic Books.

Rynearson, E.K. (1988). The homicide of a child. In F.M. Ochberg (Ed.), *Posttraumatic therapy and victims of violence* (pp. 213–224). New York: Brunner/Mazel.

Rynearson, E.K. (1994). Psychotherapy of bereavement after homicide. *Journal of Psychotherapy Practice and Research, 3*, 341–347.

Rynearson, E.K. (1996). Psychotherapy of bereavement after homicide: Be offensive. *In Session: Psychotherapy in Practice, 2*, 47–57.

Rynearson, E.K., & McCreery, J.M. (1993). Bereavement after homicide: A synergism of trauma and loss. *American Journal of Psychiatry, 150*, 258–261.

Sanders, D.L. (1997). Responding to domestic violence. *The Police Chief,* June, p. 6.

Silbert, M. (1976). *Crisis identification in management: A training manual.* Oakland, CA: California Planners.

Sprang, G., & McNeil, J. (1995). *The many faces of bereavement: The nature and treatment of natural, traumatic, and stigmatized grief.* New York: Brunner/Mazel.

Spungen, D. (1998). *Homicide: The hidden victims. A guide for professionals.* Thousand Oaks, CA: Sage.

Toch, H. (1977). *Police, prisons and the problem of violence.* Rockville, MD: National Institute of Mental Health.

Young, M.A. (1988). Support services for victims. In F.M. Ochberg (Ed.), *Posttraumatic therapy and victims of violence* (pp. 330–351). New York: Brunner/Mazel.

Young, M.A. (1994). *Responding to communities in crisis: The training manual of the crisis response team.* Washington, DC: National Organization for Victim Assistance.

CHAPTER 4: THE MENTALLY ILL

American Psychiatric Association (1994). *Diagnostic and statistical manual of mental disorders* (4th ed.). Washington, DC: American Psychiatric Association.

Bonta, J., Law, M., & Hanson, R.K. (1998). The prediction of criminal and violent recidivism among mentally disordered offenders: A meta-analysis. *Psychological Bulletin, 123*, 123–142.

Borum, R., Deane, M.W., Steadman, H.J., & Morrissey, J. (1998). Police perspectives on responding to mentally ill people in crisis: Perspectives of program effectiveness. *Behavioral Sciences and the Law, 16*, 393 405.

Borum, R., Swanson, J., Swartz, M., & Hiday, V. (1997). Substance abuse, violent behavior, and police encounters among persons with severe mental disorder. *Journal of Contemporary Criminal Justice, 13*, 236–250.

Bowker, A.L. (1994). Handle with care: Dealing with offenders who are mentally retarded. *FBI Law Enforcement Bulletin,* July, pp. 12–16.

Carter, D.L. (1993). Police response to street people: A survey of perspectives and practices. *FBI Law Enforcement Bulletin,* March, pp. 5–10.

Cordner, G.W. (2000). A community policing approach to persons with mental illness. *Journal of the American Academy of Psychiatry and the Law, 28*, 326–331.

Dupont, R., & Cochran, S. (2000). Police response to mental health emergencies: Barriers to change. *Journal of the American Academy of Psychiatry and the Law, 28*, 338–344.

Eccleston, L., Brown, M., & Ward, T. (2005). The assessment of dangerous behavior. In P. Fitzkirk & S.P. Shohov (Eds.), *Focus on behavioral psychology* (pp. 85–125). Melbourne: Nova Science.

Elliott, F.A. (1982). Neurological findings in adult minimal brain dysfunction and the dyscontrol syndrome. *Journal of Nervous and Mental Disease*, 680–687.

Elliott, F.A. (1984). The episodic dyscontrol syndrome and aggression. *Neurologic Clinics of North America, 2*, 113–125.

Elliott, F.A. (1992). Violence: The neurologic contribution. An overview. *Archives of Neurology, 49*, 595–603.

Finn, M.A., & Stalans, L.J. (2002). Police handling of the mentally ill in domestic violence situations. *Criminal Justice and Behavior, 29*, 278–307.

Fyfe, J.J. (2000). Policing the emotionally disturbed. *Journal of the American Academy of Psychiatry and the Law, 28*, 345–347.

Garner, G.W. (1995). Street smarts: Safely handling intoxicated persons. *FBI Law Enforcement Bulletin,* December, pp. 10–13.

Goldstein, S. (1997). Attention-deficit/hyperactivity disorder: Implications for the criminal justice system. *FBI Law Enforcement Bulletin,* June, pp. 11–16.

Hill, R., Quill, G., & Ellis, K. (2004). The Montgomery County CIT model: Interacting with people with mental illness. *FBI Law Enforcement Bulletin,* July, pp. 18–25.

Janik, J. (1992). Dealing with mentally ill offenders. *FBI Law Enforcement Bulletin,* July, pp. 22–28.

Lubit, R.H. (2003). *Coping with toxic managers, subordinates, and other difficult people.* Upper Saddle River, NJ: Prentice-Hall.

Mark, V.H., & Ervin, F.R. (1970). *Violence and the brain.* New York: Harper & Row.

Miller, L. (1993). *Psychotherapy of the brain-injured patient: Reclaiming the shattered self.* New York: Norton.

Miller, L. (1994a). The epilepsy patient: Personality, psychodynamics, and psychotherapy. *Psychotherapy, 31,* 735–743.

Miller, L. (1994b). Traumatic brain injury and aggression. In M. Hillbrand & N.J. Pallone, (Eds.), *The psychobiology of aggression: Engines, measurement, control* (pp. 91–103). New York: Haworth.

Miller, L. (1998). Brain injury and violent crime: Clinical, neuropsychological, and forensic considerations. *Journal of Cognitive Rehabilitation, 16*(6), 2–17.

Miller, L. (2000). The predator's brain: Neuropsychodynamics of serial killers. In L.B. Schlesinger (Ed.), *Serial offenders: Current thought, recent findings, unusual syndromes* (pp. 135–166). Boca Raton, FL: CRC Press.

Miller, L. (2003). Personalities at work: Understanding and managing human nature on the job. *Public Personnel Management, 32,* 419–433.

Miller, L. (2004). Personality-based interviews and interrogations. *International Association of Chiefs of Police Training Key #565.*

Millon, T., & Davis, R. (2000). *Personality disorders in modern life.* New York: Wiley.

Mohandie, K., & Duffy, J.E. (1999). Understanding subjects with paranoid schizophrenia. *FBI Law Enforcement Bulletin,* December, pp. 8–16.

Monahan, J. (1996). Violence prediction: The last twenty years and the next twenty years. *Criminal Justice and Behavior, 23,* 107–120.

Monroe, R.R. (1982). Limbic ictus and atypical psychoses. *Journal of Nervous and Mental Disease, 170,* 711–716.

Parker, R.S. (2001). *Concussive brain trauma: Neurobehavioral impairment and maladaptation.* Boca Raton, FL: CRC Press.

Pincus, J.H., & Tucker, G.J. (1978). *Behavioral neurology* (2nd ed.). New York: Oxford University Press.

Pinizzotto, A.J., & Deshazor, G.D. (1997). Interviewing erratic subjects. *FBI Law Enforcement Bulletin,* November, pp. 1–5.

Raine, A. (1993). *The psychopathology of crime: Criminal behavior as a clinical disorder.* San Diego, CA: Academic Press.

Reuland, M., & Margolis, G.J. (2003). Police approaches that improve the response to people with mental illness: A focus on victims. *The Police Chief,* November, pp. 35–39.

Riccio, C.A., Wolfe, M., Davis, B., Romine, C., George, C., & Lee, D. (2005). Attention deficit hyperactivity disorder: Manifestation in adulthood. *Archives of Clinical Neuropsychology, 20,* 249–269.

Russell, H.E., & Beigel, A. (1990). *Understanding human behavior for effective police work* (3rd ed.). New York: Basic Books.

Sperry, L. (1995). *Handbook of diagnosis and treatment of the DSM-IV personality disorders.* New York: Brunner/Mazel.

Vermette, H.S., Pinals, D.A., & Appelbaum, P.S. (2005). Mental health training for law enforcement professionals. *Journal of the American Academy of Psychiatry and the Law, 33,* 42–46.

Wilens, T.E., & Dodson, W. (2004). A clinical perspective of attention deficit hyperactivity disorder into adulthood. *Journal of Clinical Psychiatry, 65,* 1301–1313.

Wiley, K. (2005). Crisis intervention team: It's more than just training. *Training Wheel: The Training Journal of the Las Vegas Metropolitan Police Department,* April–June, pp. 10–15.

Will, M.A., & Peters, J.F. (2004). Law enforcement response to persons with aphasia. *The Police Chief,* Decmber, p. 24.

Williams, D. (1969). Neural factors related to habitual aggression: Consideration of difference between those habitually aggressive and others who have committed crimes of violence. *Brain, 92,* 503–520.

Wood, R.L. (1987). *Brain injury rehabilitation: A neurobehavioral approach.* Rockville, MD: Aspen.

CHAPTER 5: EXTREME STRESS MANAGEMENT

Asken, M.J. (1993). *PsycheResponse: Psychological skills for optimal performance by emergency responders.* Englewood Cliffs, NJ: Regents/Prentice Hall.

Band, S.R., & Vasquez, I.J. (1999). The will to survive. In L. Territo & J.D. Sewell (Eds.), *Stress management in law enforcement* (pp. 297–302). Durham, NC: Carolina Academic Press.

Blum, L.N. (2000). *Force under pressure: How cops live and why they die.* New York: Lantern Books.

Csikszentmihalyi, M. (1990). *Flow: The psychology of optimal experience.* New York: Harper & Row.

Flin, R. (1996). *Sitting on the hot seat: Leaders and teams for effective critical incident management.* New York: Wiley.

Gardner, R.W., Holzman, P.S., Klein, G.S., Linton, H.B., & Spence, D.P. (1959). Cognitive control: A study of individual consistencies in cognitive behavior. *Psychological Issues, 1,* 1–185.

Hanin, Y. (2000). Individual zones of optimal functioning (IZOF) model: Emotion-performance relationships in sport. In Y. Hanin (Ed.), *Emotions in sport* (pp. 65–89). Champaign, IL: Human Kinetics.

Hardy, L., Jones, G., & Gould, D. (1996). *Understanding psychological preparation for sport: Theory and practice of elite performers.* New York: Wiley.

Hays, K.F., & Brown, C.H. (2004). *You're on! Consulting for peak performance.* Washington, DC: American Psychological Association.

Henry, V.E. (2004). *Death work: Police, trauma, and the psychology of survival.* New York: Oxford University Press.

Honig, A.L., & Sultan, E. (2004). Reactions and resilience under fire: What an officer can expect. *The Police Chief,* December, pp. 54–60.

Huppert, J.D., & Baker-Morissette, S.L. (2003). Beyond the manual: The insider's guide to panic control treatment. *Cognitive and Behavioral Practice, 10,* 2–13.

Kabat-Zinn, J. (1994). *Wherever you go, There you are: Mindfulness meditation in everyday life.* New York: Hyperion.

Kabat-Zinn, J. (2003). Mindfulness-based interventions in context: Past, present and future. *Clinical Psychology: Science and Practice, 10,* 144–156.

Klein, G. (1996). The effect of acute stressors on decision making. In J. Driskell & E. Salas (Eds.), *Stress and human performance* (pp. 49–88). Hillsdale, NJ: Erlbaum.

Klein, G.S. (1954). Need and regulation. In M.R. Jones (Ed.), *Nebraska symposium on motivation.* Lincoln, NE: University of Nebraska Press.

Marra, T. (2005). *Dialectical behavior therapy in private practice: A practical and comprehensive guide.* Oakland, CA: New Harbinger.

Maynard, P.E., & Mary, E. (1982). Stress in police families: Some policy implications. *Journal of Police Science and Administration, 10,* 422–439.

Miller, L. (1990). *Inner natures: Brain, self and personality.* New York: St. Martin's Press.

Miller, L. (1994). Biofeedback and behavioral medicine: Treating the symptom, the syndrome, or the person? *Psychotherapy, 31,* 161–169.

Nideffer, R., & Sharpe, R. (1978). *Attention control training: How to get control of your mind through total concentration.* New York: Wideview Books.

Norcross, R.H. (2003). The "modern warrior." A study in survival. *FBI Law Enforcement Bulletin,* October, pp. 20–26.

Olson, D.T. (1998) Improving deadly decision force making. *FBI Law Enforcement Bulletin,* February, pp. 1–9.

Pinizzotto, A.J., Davis, E.F., & Miller, C.E. (2004). Intuitive policing: Emotional/rational decision making in law enforcement. *FBI Law Enforcement Bulletin,* February, pp. 1–6.

Privette, G., & Bundrick, C.M. (1991). Peak experience, peak performance, and flow: Personal descriptions and theoretical constructs. *Journal of Social Behavior and Personality, 6,* 169–188.

Scanff, C.L., & Taugis, J. (2002). Stress management for police special forces. *Journal of Applied Sport Psychology, 14,* 330–343.

Shale, J.H., Shale, C.M., & Shale, J.D. (2003). Denial often key in psychological adaptation to combat situations. *Psychiatric Annals, 33,* 725–729.

Shapiro, D. (1965). *Neurotic styles.* New York: Basic Books.

Shipley, P., & Baranski, J.V. (2002). Police officer performance under stress: A pilot study on the effects of visuomotor behavior rehearsal. *International Journal of Stress Management, 9,* 71–80.

Suinn, R. (1972). Removing emotional obstacles to learning and performance by visuo-motor behavior rehearsal. *Behavioral Therapy, 31,* 308–310.

Suinn, R. (1984). Visual motor behavior rehearsal: The basic technique. Scandinavian *Journal of Behavior Therapy, 13,* 131–142.

Suinn, R. (1985). Imagery rehearsal applications to performance enhancement. *The Behavior Therapist, 8,* 155–159.

Thelwell, R.R., & Greenlees, I. A. (2001). The effects of mental skills training package on gymnasium triathlon performance. *The Sport Psychologist, 15,* 127–141.

Thelwell, R.R., & Greenlees, I. A. (2003). Developing competitive endurance performance using mental skills training. *The Sport Psychologist, 17,* 318–337.

Thelwell, R.R., & Maynard, I. W. (2003). The effects of a mental skills package on repeatable good performance in cricketers. *Psychology of Sport and Exercise, 4,* 377–396.

Van Blaricum, M.A.L. (2005), Faceless cop killers. *Police,* February, pp. 54–56.

Violanti, J.M. (1999). Death on duty: Police survivor trauma. In J.M. Violanti & D. Paton (Eds.), *Police trauma: Psychological aftermath of civilian combat* (pp. 139–158). Springfield, IL: Charles C Thomas.

Williams, J., & Krane, V. (1997). Psychological characteristics of peak performance. In J. Williams (Ed.), *Applied sport psychology: Personal growth to peak performance* (pp. 137–147). Mountain View: Mayfield.

CHAPTER 6: CRITICAL INCIDENT STRESS

Alarcon, R.D. (1999). The cascade model: An alternative to comorbidity in the pathogenesis of posttraumatic stress disorder. *Psychiatry, 62,* 114–124.

Alexander, D.A. (1993). Stress among body handlers A long-term follow-up. *British Journal of Psychiatry, 163,* 806–808.

Alexander, D.A., & Walker, L.G. (1994). A study of methods used by Scottish police officers to cope with work-related stress. *Stress Medicine, 10,* 131–138.

Alexander, D.A., & Wells, A. (1991). Reactions of police officers to body-handling after a major disaster: A before-and-after comparison. *British Journal of Psychiatry, 159,* 547–555.

Allen, J.G., & Lewis, L. (1996). A conceptual framework for treating traumatic memories and its application to EMDR. *Bulletin of the Menninger Clinic, 60,* 238–263.

Almedom, A.M. (2005). Resilience, hardiness, sense of coherence, and posttraumatic growth: All paths leading to "light at the end of the tunnel"? *Journal of Loss and Trauma, 10,* 253–265.

American Psychiatric Association (1994). *Diagnostic and statistical manual of mental disorders* (4th ed.). Washington, DC: American Psychiatric Association.

Anderson, W., Swenson, D., & Clay, D. (1995). *Stress management for law enforcement officers.* Englewood Cliffs, NJ: Prentice-Hall.

Antonovsky, A. (1987). *Unraveling the mystery of health: How people manage stress and stay well.* San Francisco: Jossey-Bass.

Arendt, M., & Elklit, A. (2001). Effectiveness of psychological debriefing. *Acta Psychiatrica Scandinavica, 104,* 423–437.

Belles, D., & Norvell, N. (1990). *Stress management workbook for law enforcement officers.* Sarasota, FL: Professional Resource Exchange.

Bisson, J.I., & Deahl, M.P. (1994). Psychological debriefing and prevention of post-traumatic stress: More research is needed. *British Journal of Psychiatry, 165,* 717–720.

Blau, T.H. (1994). *Psychological services for law enforcement.* New York: Wiley.

Bohl, N.K. (1991). The effectiveness of brief psychological interventions in police officers after critical incidents. In J.T. Reese, J.M. Horn & C. Dunning (Eds.), *Critical incidents in policing* (pp. 31–38). Washington, DC: US Department of Justice.

Bohl, N. (1995). Professionally administered critical incident debriefing for police officers. In M.I. Kunke & E.M. Scrivner (Eds.), *Police psychology into the 21st century* (pp. 169–188). Hillsdale, NJ: Erlbaum.

Bordow, S., & Porritt, D. (1979). An experimental evaluation of crisis intervention. *Psychological Bulletin, 84,* 1189–1217.

Bowman, M. (1997). *Individual differences in posttraumatic response: Problems with the adversity-distress connection.* Mahwah, NJ: Erlbaum.

Britt, J.M. (1991). U.S. Secret Service critical incident peer support team. In J. Reese, J. Horn & C. Dunning (Eds.), *Critical incidents in policing* (pp. 55–61). Washington, DC: US Government Printing Office.

Brooks, G. (1998). *A new psychotherapy for traditional men.* San-Francisco: Jossey-Bass.

Carlier, I.V.E. (1999). Finding meaning in police traumas. In J.M. Violanti & D. Paton (Eds.), *Police trauma: psychological aftermath of civilian combat* (pp. 227–240). Springfield, IL: Charles C Thomas.

Carlier, I.V.E., & Gersons, B.P.R. (1995). Partial PTSD: The issue of psychological scars and the occurrence of PTSD symptoms. *Journal of Nervous and Mental Disease, 183,* 107–109.

Carlier, I.V.E., Lamberts, R.D., & Gersons, B.P.R. (1997). Risk factors for posttraumatic stress symptomatology in police officers: A prospective analysis. *Journal of Nervous and Mental Disease, 185,* 498–506.

Carlier, I.V.E., Lamberts, R.D., Van Uchelen, A.J., & Gersons, B.P.R. (1998). Disaster-related post-traumatic stress in police officers: A field study of the impact of debriefing. *Stress Medicine, 14,* 143–148.

Clary, M. (2005). War vets besieged by stress. *South Florida Sun-Sentinel,* March 28, pp. 1–2.

Corbett, S. (2004). The permanent scars of Iraq. *New York Times Magazine,* February 15, pp. 34–41, 56–61.

Creamer, M., & Forbes, D. (2004). Treatment of post-traumatic stress disorder in military and veteran populations. *Psychotherapy: Theory, Research, Practice, 41,* 388–398.

Cummings, J.P. (1996). Police stress and the suicide link. *The Police Chief,* October, pp. 85–96.

Davis, G.C., & Breslau, N. (1994). Posttraumatic stress disorder in victims of civilian and criminal violence. *Psychiatric Clinics of North America, 17,* 289–299.

DeAngelis, T. (1995). Firefighters's PTSD at dangerous levels. *APA Monitor,* February, pp. 36–37.

Dunning, C. (1999). Postintervention strategies to reduce police trauma: A paradigm shift. In J.M. Violanti & D. Paton (Eds.), *Police trauma: Psychological aftermath of civilian combat* (pp. 269–289). Springfield, IL: Charles C Thomas.

Durham, T.W., McCammon, S.L., & Allison, E.J. (1985). The psychological impact of disaster on rescue personnel. *Annals of Emergency Medicine, 14,* 664–668.

Dyregrov, A. (1989). Caring for helpers in disaster situations: Psychological debriefing. *Disaster Management, 2*, 25–30.

Evans, B.J., Coman, G.J., Stanley, R.O., & Burrows, G.D. (1993). Police officers' coping strategies: An Australian police survey. *Stress Medicine, 9*, 237–246.

Everly, G.S., & Boyle, S. (1999). Critical incident stress debriefing (CISD): A meta-analysis. *International Journal of Emergency Mental Health, 1*, 165–168.

Everly, G.S., Flannery, R.B., & Mitchell, J.T. (2000). Critical incident stress management: A review of the literature. *Aggression and Violent Behavior, 5*, 23–40.

Everly, G.S., & Mitchell, J.T. (1997). *Critical incident stress management (CISM): A new era and standard of care in crisis intervention.* Ellicott City, TX: Chevron.

Finn, P & Tomz, J.E. (1999) Using peer supporters to help address law enforcement stress. In L. Territo & J.D. Sewell (Eds.), *Stress Management in law enforcement* (pp. CHAPTER 15: law enforcement families 273-285). Durham: Carolina Academic Press.

Flannery, R.B., Fulton, P., & Tausch, J. (1991). A program to help staff cope with psychological sequelae of assaults by patients. *Hospital and Community Psychiatry, 42*, 935–938.

Fry, W.F. & Salameh, W.A. (Eds.). *Handbook of humor and psychotherapy.* Sarasota, FL: Professional Resource Exchange.

Fullerton, C.S., McCarroll, J.E., Ursano, R.J., & Wright, K.M. (1992). Psychological responses of rescue workers: Firefighters and trauma. *American Journal of Orthopsychiatry, 62*, 371–378.

Galovski, T., & Lyons, J.A. (2004). Psychological sequelae of combat violence: A review of the impact of PTSD on the veteran's family, and possible interventions. *Aggression and Violent Behavior, 9*, 477–501.

Gentz, D. (1991). The psychological impact of critical incidents on police officers. In J. Reese, J. Horn & C. Dunning (Eds.), *Critical incidents in policing* (pp. 119–121). Washington, DC: US Government Printing Office.

Green, B.L. (1993). Identifying survivors at risk. In J.P. Wilson & H. Raphael (Eds.), *International handbook of traumatic stress syndromes* (pp. 135–144). New York: Plenum.

Griffith, J., & Watts, R. (1992). *The Kensey and Grafton bus crashes: The aftermath.* East Linsmore: Instructional Design Solutions.

Hall, K.M., & Cope, D.N. (1995). The benefit of rehabilitation in traumatic brain injury: A literature review. *Journal of Head Trauma Rehabilitation, 10*, 1–13.

Hartsough, D.M. (1991). Stress, spouses, and law enforcement: A step beyond. In J. Reese, J. Horn & C. Dunning (Eds.), *Critical incidents in policing* (pp. 131–137). Washington, DC: US Government Printing Office.

Hays, T. (1994). Daily horrors take heavy toll on New York City police officers. *Boca Raton News*, September 28, pp. 2A–3A.

Henry, V.E. (2004). *Death work: Police, trauma, and the psychology of survival.* New York: Oxford University Press.

Higgins, G.O. (1994). *Resilient adults: overcoming a cruel past.* San Francisco: Jossey-Bass.

Holt, F.X. (1989). Dispatchers' hidden critical incidents. *Fire Engineering*, November, pp. 53–55.

Horn, J.M. (1991). Critical incidents for law enforcement officers. In J.T. Reese, J.M. Horn & C. Dunning (Eds.), *Critical incidents in policing* (rev. ed., pp. 143–148). Washington, DC: Federal Bureau of Investigation.

Janik, J. (1991). What value are cognitive defenses in critical incident stress? In J. Reese, J. Horn & C. Dunning (Eds.), *Critical incidents in policing* (pp. 149–158). Washington, DC: US Government Printing Office.

June, D.L. (1999). *Introduction to executive protection.* Boca Raton, FL: CRC Press.

Karlsson, I., & Christianson, S.A. (2003). The phenomenology of traumatic experiences in police work. *Policing: An International Journal of Police Strategies and Management, 26*, 419–438.

Kenardy, J.A., Webster, R.A., Lewin, T.J., Carr, V.J., Hazell, P.L., & Carter, G.L. (1996). Stress debriefing and patterns of recovery following a natural disaster. *Journal of Traumatic Stress, 9*, 37–50.

Kirschman, E.F. (1997). *I love a cop: What police families need to know.* New York: Guilford.

Kirschman, E.F. (2004). *I love a firefighter: What firefighter families need to know.* New York: Guilford.

Kobasa, S.C.O., Maddi, S., & Cahn, S. (1982). Hardiness and health: A prospective study. *Journal of Personality and Social Psychology, 42*, 168–177.

Kobasa, S.C.O., & Puccetti, M.C. (1983). Personality and social resources in stress resistance. *Journal of Personality and Social Psychology, 45*, 839–850.

Lazarus, A.A., & Mayne, T.J. (1990). Relaxation: Some limitations, side effects, and proposed solutions. *Psychotherapy, ,27*, 261–266.

Linden, J.I., & Klein, R. (1986). Critical issues in police peer counseling. In J.T. Reese & H.A. Goldstein (Eds.), *Psychological services for law enforcement* (pp. 137–139). Washington, DC: Federal Bureau of Investigation.

MacLeod, A.D. (1995). Undercover policing: A psychiatrist's perspective. *International Journal of Law and Psychiatry, 18*, 239–247.

Max, D.J. (2000). The cop and the therapist. *New York Times Magazine*, December 3, pp. 94–98.

McCafferty, F.L., McCafferty, E., & McCafferty, M.A. (1992). Stress and suicide in police officers: Paradigms of occupational stress. *Southern Medical Journal, 85*, 233–243.

McCarroll, J.E., Ursano, R.J., & Fullerton, C.S. (1993). Traumatic responses to the recovery of war dead in Operation Desert Storm. *American Journal of Psychiatry, 150*, 1875–1877.

McCarroll, J.E., Ursano, R.J., & Fullerton, C.S. (1995). Symptoms of PTSD following recovery of war dead: 13–15 month follow-up. *American Journal of Psychiatry, 152*, 939–941.

McFarlane, A.C. (1988). The aetiology of post-traumatic stress disorders following a natural disaster. *British Journal of Psychiatry, 152*, 116–121.

McMains, M.J. (1991). The management and treatment of postshooting trauma. In J.T. Horn & C. Dunning (Eds.), *Critical incidents in policing* (rev ed., pp. 191–198). Washington, DC: Federal Bureau of Investigation.

McNally, R.J., Bryant, R.A., & Ehlers, A. (2003). Does early psychological intervention promote recovery from posttraumatic stress? *Psychological Science in the Public Interest, 4*, 45–79.

McNally, V.J., & Solomon, R.M. (1999). The FBI's critical incident stress management program. *FBI Law Enforcement Bulletin*, February, pp. 20–26.

Meek, C.L. (1990). Evaluation and assessment of post-traumatic and other stress-related disorders. In C.L. Meek (Ed.), *Post-traumatic stress disorder: Assessment, differential diagnosis, and forensic evaluation* (pp. 9–61). Sarasota, FL: Professional Resource Exchange.

Merskey, H. (1992). Psychiatric aspects of the neurology of trauma. *Neurologic Clinics, 10*, 895–905.

Miller, L. (1991). Psychotherapy of the brain-injured patient: Principles and practices. *Journal of Cognitive Rehabilitation, 9*(2), 24–30.

Miller, L. (1992). Cognitive rehabilitation, cognitive therapy, and cognitive style: Toward an integrative model of personality and psychotherapy. *Journal of Cognitive Rehabilitation, 10*(1), 18–29.

Miller, L. (1993a). Psychotherapeutic approaches to chronic pain. *Psychotherapy, 30*, 115–124.

Miller, L. (1993b). Toxic torts: Clinical, neuropsychological, and forensic aspects of chemical and electrical injuries. *Journal of Cognitive Rehabilitation, 11*(1), 6–20.

Miller, L. (1993c). *Psychotherapy of the brain-injured patient: Reclaiming the shattered self.* New York: Norton.

Miller, L. (1994a). Civilian posttraumatic stress disorder: Clinical syndromes and psychotherapeutic strategies. *Psychotherapy, 31*, 655–664.

Miller, L. (1994b). Biofeedback and behavioral medicine: Treating the symptom, the syndrome, or the person? *Psychotherapy, 31*, 161–169.

Miller, L. (1995a). Tough guys: Psychotherapeutic strategies with law enforcement and emergency services personnel. *Psychotherapy, 32*, 592–600.

Miller, L. (1995b). Toxic trauma and chemical sensitivity: Clinical syndromes and psychotherapeutic strategies. *Psychotherapy, 32*, 648–656.

Miller, L. (1997a). Workplace violence in the rehabilitation setting: How to prepare, respond, and survive. *Florida State Association of Rehabilitation Nurses Newsletter, 7*, 4–8.

Miller, L. (1997b). Neurosensitization: A pathophysiological model for traumatic disability syndromes. *Journal of Cognitive Rehabilitation, 15*(6), 12–23.

Miller, L. (1998a). Our own medicine: Traumatized psychotherapists and the stresses of doing therapy. *Psychotherapy, 35*, 137–146.

Miller, L. (1998b). *Shocks to the system: Psychotherapy of traumatic disability syndromes.* New York: Norton.

Miller, L. (1998c). Ego autonomy and the healthy personality: Psychodynamics, cognitive style, and clinical applications. *Psychoanalytic Review, 85*, 423–448.

Miller, L. (1999a). Workplace violence: Prevention, response, and recovery. *Psychotherapy, 36*, 160–169.

Miller, L. (1999b). Critical incident stress debriefing: Clinical applications and new directions. *International Journal of Emergency Mental Health, 1*, 253–265.

Miller, L. (1999c). Tough guys: Psychotherapeutic strategies with law enforcement and emergency services personnel. In L. Territo & J.D. Sewell (Eds.), *Stress management in law enforcement* (pp. 317–332). Durham, NC: Carolina Academic Press.

Miller, L. (1999d). Psychological syndromes in personal injury litigation. In E. Pierson (Ed.), *1999 Wiley expert witness update: New developments in personal injury litigation* (pp. 263–308). New York: Aspen.

Miller, L. (2000a). Law enforcement traumatic stress: Clinical syndromes and intervention strategies. *Trauma Response, 6*(1), 15–20.

Miller, L. (2000b). Traumatized psychotherapists. In F.M. Dattilio & A. Freeman (Eds.), *Cognitive behavioral strategies in crisis intervention* (2nd ed., pp. 429–445). New York: Guilford.

Miller, L. (2002a). Posttraumatic stress disorder in school violence: Risk management lessons from the workplace. *Neurolaw Letter, 11*, 33, 36–40.

Miller, L. (2002b). What is the true spectrum of functional disorders in rehabilitation? *Physical Medicine and Rehabilitation: State of the Art Reviews, 16*, 1–20.

Miller, L. (2003a). Psychological interventions for terroristic trauma: Symptoms, syndromes, and treatment strategies. *Psychotherapy, 39*, 283–296.

Miller, L. (2003b). Family therapy of terroristic trauma: Psychological syndromes and treatment strategies. *American Journal of Family Therapy, 31*, 257–280.

Miller, L. (2004). Psychotherapeutic interventions for survivors of terrorism. *American Journal of Psychotherapy, 58*, 1–16.

Miller, L. (2005). Psychotherapy for terrorism survivors: New directions in evaluation and treatment. *Directions in Clinical and Counseling Psychology, 17*, 59–74.

Miller, L., & Schlesinger, L.B. (2000). Survivors, families, and co-victims of serial offenders. In L.B. Schlesinger (Ed.), *Serial offenders: Current thought, recent findings, unusual syndromes* (pp. 309–334). Boca Ratonm FL: CRC Press.

Mitchell, J.T. (1983). When disaster strikes . . . The critical incident stress process. *Journal of the Emergency Medical Services, 8*, 36–39.

Mitchell, J.T. (1988). The history, status, and future of critical incident stress debriefings. *Journal of the Emergency Medical Services, 13*, 47–52.

Mitchell, J.T. (1991). Law enforcement applications for critical incident stress teams. In J.T. Reese, J.M. Horn & C. Dunning (Eds.), *Critical incidents in policing* (rev. ed., pp. 201–212). Washington, DC: US Government Printing Office.

Mitchell, J.T., & Bray, G.P. (1990). *Emergency services stress: Guidelines for preserving the health and careers of emergency services personnel.* Englewood Cliffs, NJ: Prentice-Hall.

Mitchell, J.T., & Everly, G.S. (1996). *Critical incident stress debriefing: operations manual.* (rev. ed.). Ellicott City, TX: Chevron.

Mitchell, J.T., & Everly, G.S. (1997). Scientific evidence for CISM. *Journal of Emergency Medical Services, 22*, 87–93.

Mitchell, J.T., & Everly, G.S. (2003). *Critical incident stress management (CISM): Basic group crisis intervention* (3rd ed.). Ellicott City, TX: ICISF.

Modlin, H.C. (1983). Traumatic neurosis and other injuries. *Psychiatric Clinics of North America, 6*, 661–682.

Modlin, H.C. (1990). Post-traumatic stress disorder: Differential diagnosis. In C.L. Meek (Ed.), *Post-traumatic stress disorder: Assessment, differential diagnosis, and forensic evaluation* (pp. 63–89). Sarasota, FL: Professional Resource Exchange.

Nielsen, E. (1991). Traumatic incident corps: Lessons learned. In J. Reese, J. Horn & C. Dunning (Eds.), *Critical incidents in policing* (pp. 221–226). Washington, DC: US Government Printing Office.

Nordland, R., & Gegax, T.T. (2004). Stress at the front. *Newsweek,* January 12, pp. 34–37.

Ostrov, E. (1991). Critical incident psychological casualties among police officers: A clinical review. In J. Reese, J. Horn & C. Dunning (Eds.), *Critical incidents in policing* (pp. 251–256). Washington, DC: US Government Printing Office.

Palmer, C.E. (1983). A note about paramedics' strategies for dealing with death and dying. *Journal of Occupational Psychology, 56*, 83–86.

Parker, R. S. (2001). Concussive brain trauma: *Neuro behavioral impairment and maladaption.* Boca Raton, FL: CRC Press.

Paton, D., & Smith, L. (1999). Assessment, conceptual and methodological issues in researching traumatic stress in police officers. In J.M. Violanti & D. Paton (Eds.), *Police trauma: Psychological aftermath of civilian combat* (pp. 13-24). Springfield, IL: Charles C Thomas.

Paton, D., Smith, L., Violanti, J.M., & Eranen, L. (2000). Work-related traumatic stress: Risk, vulnerability, and resilience. In J. Violanti, D. Paton & C. Dunning (Eds.), *Posttraumatic stress intervention: Challenges, issues, and perspectives* (pp. 187–203). Springfield, IL: Charles C Thomas.

Raphael, B. (1986). *When disaster strikes: How individuals and communities cope with catastrophe.* New York: Basic Books.

Reed, B.T. (1986). Post-concussional syndrome: A disability factor in law enforcement personnel. In J.T. Reese & H. Goldstein (Eds.), *Psychological services for law enforcement* (pp. 375–381). Washington, DC: US Government Printing Office.

Reese, J.T. (1987). Coping with stress: It's your job. In J.T. Reese (Ed.), *Behavioral science in law enforcement* (pp. 75-79). Washington, DC: FBI.

Reese, J.T. (1991). Justifications for mandating critical incident aftercare. In J.T. Reese, J.M. Horn & C. Dunning (Eds.), *Critical incidents in policing* (rev. ed., pp. 213-220). Washington, DC: USGPO.

Robinson, R.C., & Mitchell, J.T. (1993). Evaluation of psychological debriefings. *Journal of Traumatic Stress, 6*, 367–382.

Seligmann, J., Holt, D., Chinni, D., & Roberts, E. (1994). Cops who kill–themselves. *Newsweek,* September 26, p. 58.

Sewell, J.D. (1986). Administrative concerns in law enforcement stress management. In J.T. Reese & H.A. Goldstein (Eds.), *Psychological services for law enforcement* (pp. 189–193). Washington, DC: FBI.

Sewell, J.D. (1993). Traumatic stress of multiple murder investigations. *Journal of Traumatic Stress, 6*, 103–118.

Sewell, J.D. (1994) The stress of homicide investigations, *Death Studies, 18*, 565-582.

Sewell, J.D., & Crew, L. (1984). The forgotten victim: Stress and the police dispatcher. *FBI Law Enforcement Bulletin,* March, pp. 7–11.

Sewell, J.D., Ellison, K.W., & Hurrell, J.J. (1988). Stress management in law enforcement: Where do we go from here? *The Police Chief,* October, pp. 94–98.

Sheehan, D.C., Everly, G.S., & Langlieb, A. (2004). Current best practices: Coping with major critical incidents. *FBI Law Enforcement Bulletin,* September, pp.

1–13.

Sheehan, P.L. (1991). Critical incident trauma and intimacy. In J.T. Reese, J.M. Horn & C. Dunning (Eds.), *Critical incidents in policing* (pp. 331–334). Washington, DC: Federal Bureau of Investigation.

Silva, M.N. (1991). The delivery of mental health services to law enforcement officers. In J.T. Reese, J.M. Horn & C. Dunning (Eds.), *Critical incidents in policing* (rev ed., pp. 335–341).

Silver, B.V., & Blanchard, E.B. (1978). Biofeedback and relaxation training in the treatment of psychophysiological disorders: Or, are the machines really necessary? *Journal of Behavioral Medicine, 1*, 217–239.

Simons, Y., & Barone, D.F. (1994). The relationship of work stressors and emotional support to strain in police officers. *International Journal of Stress Management, 1*, 223–234.

Solomon, R.M. (1988). Mental conditioning: The utilization of fear. In J.T. Reese & J.M. Horn (Eds.), *Police psychology: operational assistance* (pp. 391–407). Washington, DC: US Government Printing Office.

Solomon, R.M. (1990). Administrative guidelines for dealing with officers involved in on-duty shooting situations. *The Police Chief*, February, p. 40.

Solomon, R.M. (1991). The dynamics of fear in critical incidents: Implications for training and treatment. In J.T. Reese, J.M. Horn & C. Dunning (Eds.), *Critical incidents in policing* (pp. 347–358). Washington, DC: Federal Bureau of Investigation.

Solomon, R.M. (1995). Critical incident stress management in law enforcement. In G.S. Everly (Ed.), *Innovations in disaster and trauma psychology: Applications in emergency services and disaster response* (pp. 123–157). Ellicott City, TX: Chevron.

Solomon, R.M. & Horn, (1986). Post-shooting traumatic reactions: A pilot study. In J.T. Reese & H. Goldstein (Eds.), *Psychological services for law enforcement* (pp. 383–393). Washington, DC: US Government Printing Office.

Solomon, Z., & Benbenishty, R. (1988). The role of proximity, immediacy, and expectance in frontline treatment of combat stress reactions among Israelis in the Lebanon war. *American Journal of Psychiatry, 143*, 613–617.

Spungen, D. (1998). *Homicide: The hidden victims. A guide for professionals.* Thousand Oaks, CA: Sage.

Stein, M.B., Walker, J.R., Hazen, A.L. & Forde, D.R. (1997). Full and partial posttraumatic stress disorder:

Findings from a community survey. *American Journal of Psychiatry, 154*, 1114-1119.

Stuhlmiller, C., & Dunning, C. (2000). Challenging the mainstream: From pathogenic to salutogenic models of posttrauma intervention. In J. Violanti, D. Paton & C. Dunning (Eds.), *Posttraumatic stress intervention: Challenges, issues, and perspectives* (pp. 10–42). Springfield, IL: Charles C Thomas.

Sugimoto, J.D., & Oltjenbruns, K.A. (2001). The environment of death and its influence on police officers in the United States. *Omega, 43*, 145–155.

Taylor, S.E., Wood, J.V. & Lechtman, R.R. (1983). It could be worse: Selective evaluation as a response to victimization. *Journal of Social Issues, 39*, 19–40.

Tedeschi, R., & Calhoun, L. (1996). Posttraumatic growth inventory: Measuring the positive legacy of trauma. *Journal of Traumatic Stress, 9*, 455–471.

Tedeschi, R., Park, C., & Calhoun, L. (Eds.) (1998). *Posttraumatic growth: Positive change in the aftermath of crisis.* New York: Erlbaum.

Toch, H. (2002). *Stress in policing.* Washington, DC: American Psychological Association.

Trimble, M.R. (1981). *Post-traumatic neurosis: From railway spine to whiplash.* New York: Wiley.

Tyre, P. (2004). Battling the effects of war. *Newsweek*, December 6, pp. 68–70.

Ursano, R.J., & McCarroll, J.E. (1990). The nature of the traumatic stressor: Handling dead bodies. *Journal of Nervous and Mental Disease, 178*, 396-398.

Violanti, J.M. (1999). Death on duty: Police survivor trauma. In J.M. Violanti & D. Paton (Eds.), *Police trauma: Psychological aftermath of civilian combat* (pp. 139–158). Springfield, IL: Charles C Thomas.

Violanti, J.M. (2000). Scripting trauma: The impact of pathogenic intervention. In J. Violanti, D. Paton & C. Dunning (Eds.), *Posttraumatic stress intervention: Challenges, issues, and perspectives* (pp. 153–165). Springfield, IL: Charles C Thomas.

Weiner, H. (1992). *Perturbing the organism: The biology of stressful experience.* Chicago: University of Chicago Press.

Williams, T. (1991). Counseling disabled law enforcement officers. In J.T. Reese, J.M. Horn & C. Dunning (Eds.), *Critical incidents in policing* (pp. 377–386). Washington, DC: Federal Bureau of Investigation.

Wilson, J.P. (1994). The historical evolution of PTSD diagnostic criteria: From Freud to the DSM-IV. *Journal of Traumatic Stress, 7*, 681–698.

CHAPTER 7: OFFICIER-INVOLVED SHOOTING

Anderson, W., Swenson, D., & Clay, D. (1995). *Stress management for law enforcement officers.* Englewood Cliffs, NJ: Prentice Hall.

Antonovsky, A., & Bernstein, J. (1986). Pathogenesis and

salutogenesis in war and other crises: Who studies the successful coper? In N. Milgram (Ed.), *Stress and coping in times of war* (pp. 89–121). New York: Brunner/Mazel.

Artwohl, A. (2002). Perceptual and memory distortion during officer-involved shootings. *FBI Law Enforcement Bulletin*, October, pp. 18–24.

Ayoob, M. (1981). The killing experience. *Police Product News.*

Baruth, C. (1986). Pre-critical incident involvement by psychologists. In J.T. Reese & H.A. Goldstein (Eds.), *Psychological services for law enforcement* (pp. 413–417). Washington, DC: USGPO.

Blau, T.H. (1986). Deadly force: Psychological factors and objective evaluation–A preliminary effort. In J.T. Reese & H.A. Goldstein (Eds.), *Psychological services for law enforcement* (pp. 315–334). Washington, DC: US Government Printing Office.

Blau, T.H. (1994). *Psychological services for law enforcement.* New York: Wiley.

Blum, L.N. (2000). *Force under pressure: How cops live and why they die.* New York: Lantern Books.

Bowman, M. (1997). *Individual differences in posttraumatic response: Problems with the adversity-distress connection.* Mahwah, NJ: Erlbaum.

Cohen, A. (1980). "I've killed that man 10,000 times." *Police, 3*, 4.

Geller, W.A. (1982). Deadly force: What we know. *Journal of Police Science and Administration, 10*, 151–177.

Henry, V.E. (2004) *Death Work: Police, trauma, and the psychology of survival.* New York: Oxford University Press.

Honig, A.L., & Roland, J.E. (1998). Shots fired: Officer involved. *The Police Chief*, October, pp. 65–70.

Honig, A.L. & Sultan, E. (2004). Reactions and resilience under fire: What an officer can expect. *The Police Chief*, December, pp. 54–60.

Horn, J.M. (1991). Critical incidents for law enforcement officers. In J.T. Reese, J.M. Horn & C. Dunning (Eds.), *Critical incidents in policing* (rev. ed., pp. 143–148). Washington, DC: Federal Bureau of Investigation.

International Association of Chiefs of Police (2004). *Officer-involved shooting guidelines.* Los Angeles: IACP.

Klein, R. (1991). The utilization of police peer counselors in critical incidents. In J.T. Reese, J.M. Horn & C. Dunning (Eds.), *Critical incidents in policing* (pp. 159–168). Washington, DC: Federal Bureau of Investigation.

Loftus, E.F., Greene, E.L. & Doyle, J.M. (1989). The psychology of eyewitness testimony. In D.C. Raskin (Ed.). *Psychological methods in criminal investigation and evidence* (pp. 3-46). New York: Springer.

McMains. M.J. (1986a). Post-shooting trauma: Demographics of professional support. In J.T. Reese & H. Goldstein (Eds.), *Psychological services for law enforcement* (pp. 361–364). Washington, DC: USGPO.

McMains. M.J. (1986b). Post-shooting trauma: Principles from combat. In J.T. Reese & H. Goldstein (Eds.), *Psychological services for law enforcement* (pp. 365–368). Washington, DC: US Government Printing Office.

McMains, M.J. (1991). The management and treatment of postshooting trauma. In J.T. Horn & C. Dunning (Eds.), *Critical incidents in policing* (rev ed., pp. 191–198). Washington, DC: Federal Bureau of Investigation.

Milgram, N., & Hobfoll, S. (1986). Generalizations from theory and practice in war-related stress. In N. Milgram (Ed.), *Stress and coping in times of war* (pp. 22–41). New York: Brunner/Mazel.

Miller, L. (1990). *Inner Natures: Brain, Self and Personality.* New York: St. Martins Press.

Miller, L. (1998). Shocks to the system: *Psychotherapy of Traumatic Disability Syndromes.* New York: Norton.

Nielsen, E. (1991). Traumatic incident corps: Lessons learned. In J. Reese, J. Horn & C. Dunning (Eds.), *Critical incidents in policing* (pp. 221–226). Washington, DC: US Government Printing Office.

Rostow, C.D., & Davis, R.D. (2004). *A handbook for psychological fitness-for-duty evaluations in law enforcement.* New York: Haworth.

Russell, H.E., & Beigel, A. (1990). *Understanding human behavior for effective police work* (3rd ed.). New York: Basic Books.

Rynearson, E.K. (1988). The homicide of a child. In F.M. Ochberg (Ed.), *Posttraumatic therapy and victims of violence* (pp. 213–224). New York: Brunner/Mazel.

Rynearson, E.K. (1994). Psychotherapy of bereavement after homicide. *Journal of Psychotherapy Practice and Research, 3*, 341–347.

Rynearson, E.K. (1996). Psychotherapy of bereavement after homicide: Be offensive. *In Session: Psychotherapy in Practice, 2*, 47–57.

Rynearson, E.K., & McCreery, J.M. (1993). Bereavement after homicide: A synergism of trauma and loss. *American Journal of Psychiatry, 150*, 258–261.

Sheehan, P.L. (1991). Critical incident trauma and intimacy. In J.T. Reese, J.M. Horn & C. Dunning (Eds.). *Critical incidents in policing* (pp. 331-334) Washington DC: Federal Bureau of Investigation.

Solomon, R.M., & Horn, (1986). Post-shooting traumatic reactions: A pilot study. In J.T. Reese & H. Goldstein (Eds.), *Psychological services for law enforcement* (pp. 383–393). Washington, DC: USGPO.

Solomon, R.M., & Mastin, P. (1999). The emotional aftermath of the Waco raid: Five years revisited. In J.M. Violanti & D. Paton (Eds.), *Police trauma: Psychological aftermath of civilian combat* (pp. 113–123). Springfield, IL: Charles C Thomas.

Somodevilla, S.A. (1986). Post-shooting trauma: Reactive and proactive treatment. In J.T. Reese & H.

Goldstein (Eds.), *Psychological services for law enforcement* (pp. 395–398). Washington, DC: USGPO.

Sprang, G., & McNeil, J. (1995). *The many faces of bereavement: The nature and treatment of natural, traumatic, and stigmatized grief.* New York: Brunner/Mazel.

Williams, T. (1991). Counseling disabled law enforcement officers. In J.T. Reese, J.M. Horn & C. Dunning (Eds.), *Critical incidents in policing* (pp. 377–386). Washington, DC: Federal Bureau of Investigation.

Wittrup, R.G. (1986). Police shooting–An opportunity for growth or loss of self. In J.T. Reese & H. Goldstein (Eds.), *Psychological services for law enforcement* (pp. 405–408). Washington, DC: US Government Printing Office.

Zeling, M. (1986). Research needs in the study of post-shooting trauma. In J.T. Reese & H.A. Goldstein (Eds.), *Psychological services for law enforcement* (pp. 409–410). Washington, DC: USGPO.

CHAPTER 8: LINE-OF-DUTY DEATH

Aldwin, C.M. (1994). *Stress, coping, and development.* New York: Guilford.

Anderson, C. (2002). Report: Police slayings increase. *South Florida Sun-Sentinel,* December 3, p. 3A.

Bear, T.M., & Barnes, L.L.B. (2005). Postttraumatic growth in survivors of law enforcement officers killed in the line of duty. *Study conducted with the membership of Concerns of Police Survivors (COPS).*

Blum, L.N. (2000). *Force under pressure: How cops live and why they die.* New York: Lantern Books.

Bowman, M. (1997). *Individual differences in posttraumatic response: Problems with the adversity-distress connection.* Mahwah, NJ: Erlbaum.

Carson, L., & MacLeod, M.D. (1997). Explanations about crime and psychological distress in ethnic minority and white victims of crime: A qualitative explanation. *Journal of Community and Applied Social Psychology, 7,* 361–375.

Danto, B.L. (1975). Bereavement and the widows of slain police officers. In E. Schoenberg (Ed.), *Bereavement: Its psychological aspects* (pp. 150–163). New York: Columbia University Press.

Geller, W.A. (1993). Put friendly-fire shooting in perspective. *Law Enforcement News, 18,* 9.

Getzel, G.S. & Masters, R. (1984). Serving families who survive homicide victims. *Social Casework, 65,* 138-144.

Green, B.L. (1993). Identifying survivors at risk. In J.P. Wilson & H. Raphael (Eds.), *International handbook of traumatic stress syndromes* (pp. 135–144). New York: Plenum.

Haddix, R.C. (1999). Responding to line-of-duty deaths. In L. Territo & J.D. Sewell (Eds.), *Stress management in law enforcement* (pp. 287–296). Durham, NC: Carolina Academic Press.

Henry, V.E. (2004). *Death work: Police, trauma, and the psychology of survival.* New York: Oxford University Press.

Kaltman, S., & Bonanno, G.A. (2003). Trauma and bereavement: Examining the impact of sudden and violent deaths. *Journal of Anxiety Disorders, 17,* 131–147.

Kirschman, E.F. (1997). *I love a cop: What police families need to know.* New York: Guilford.

Lindy, J.D., Grace, M.C., & Green, B.L. (1981). Survivors: Outreach to a recalcitrant population. *American Journal of Orthopsychiatry, 51,* 468–479.

MacLeod, M.D. (1999). Why did it happen to me? Social cognition processes in adjustment and recovery from criminal victimization and illness. *Current Psychology, 18,* 18–31.

Miller, L. (1998a). Ego autonomy and the healthy personality: Psychodynamics, cognitive style, and clinical applications. *Psychoanalytic Review, 85,* 423–448.

Miller, L. (1998b). *Shocks to the system: Psychotherapy of traumatic disability syndromes.* New York: Norton.

Miller, L. (1999a). Treating posttraumatic stress disorder in children and families: Basic principles and clinical applications. *American Journal of Family Therapy, 27,* 21–34.

Miller, L. (1999b). Posttraumatic stress disorder in child victims of violent crime: Making the case for psychological injury. *Victim Advocate, 1*(1), 6–10.

Miller, L. (2003). Family therapy of terroristic trauma: Psychological syndromes and treatment strategies. *American Journal of Family Therapy, 31,* 257–280.

Niederhoffer, A., & Niederhoffer, E. (1978). *The police family: From station house to ranch house.* Lexington, KY: Heath.

Parkes, C.M. (1975). Determinants of outcome following bereavements. *Omega, 6,* 303-323.

Parkes, C.M., & Brown, R. (1972). Health after bereavement: A controlled study of young Boston widows and widowers. *Psychosomatic Medicine, 34,* 449–461.

Rynearson, E.K. (1988). The homicide of a child. In F.M. Ochberg (Ed.), *Posttraumatic therapy and victims of violence* (pp. 213–224). New York: Brunner/Mazel.

Rynearson, E.K. (1994). Psychotherapy of bereavement after homicide. *Journal of Psychotherapy Practice and Research, 3,* 341–347.

Rynearson, E.K. (1996). Psychotherapy of bereavement after homicide: Be offensive. *In Session: Psychotherapy in Practice, 2,* 47–57.

Rynearson, E.K., & McCreery, J.M. (1993). Bereavement after homicide: A synergism of trauma and loss. *American Journal of Psychiatry, 150,* 258–261.

Sawyer, S. (1988). *Support services to surviving families of line-of-duty death.* Maryland: COPS, Inc.

Sheehan, P.L. (1991). Critical incident trauma and intimacy. In J.T. Reese, J.M. Horn & C. Dunning (Eds.),

Critical incidents in policing (pp. 331–334). Washington, DC: Federal Bureau of Investigation.

Silver, R., & Wortman, C. (1980). Coping with undesirable life events. In J. Garber & M. Seligman (Eds.), *Human helplessness* (pp. 279–340). New York: Academic Press.

Sprang, G., & McNeil, J. (1995). *The many faces of bereavement: The nature and treatment of natural, traumatic, and stigmatized grief.* New York: Brunner/Mazel.

Spungen, D. (1998). *Homicide: The hidden victims. A guide for professionals.* Thousand Oaks, CA: Sage.

Stillman, F.A. (1987). *Line-of-duty deaths: Survivor and departmental responses.* Washington, DC: National Institute of Justice.

United States Department of Justice, Federal Bureau of Investigation (2003). *Uniform crime report: Law enforcement officers killed and assaulted, 1990–1993.* Washington, DC: U.S. Government Printing Office.

Violanti, J.M. (1996). The impact of cohesive groups in the trauma recovery context: Police spouse survivors and duty-related death. *Journal of Traumatic Stress, 9,* 379–386.

Violanti, J.M. (1999). Death on duty: Police survivor trauma. In J.M. Violanti & D. Paton (Eds.), *Police trauma: Psychological aftermath of civilian combat* (pp. 139–158). Springfield, IL: Charles C Thomas.

Violanti, J.M., & Aron, F. (1994). Ranking police stressors. *Psychological Reports, 75,* 824–826.

Williams. M.B. (1994a). Intervention with child victims of trauma in the school setting. In M.B. Williams & J.F. Sommer (Eds.), *Handbook of posttraumatic therapy* (pp. 203–220). Westport, CT: Greenwood Press.

Williams. M.B. (1994b). Impact of duty-related death on officers' children: Concepts of death, trauma reactions, and treatment. In J.T. Reese & E. Scrivner (Eds.), *Law enforcement families: Issues and answers* (pp. 111–119). Washington, DC: U.S. Printing Office.

Williams. M.B. (1999). Impact of duty-related death on officers' children: Concepts of death, trauma reactions, and treatment. In J.M. Violanti & D. Paton (Eds.), *Police trauma: Psychological aftermath of civilian combat* (pp. 159–174). Springfield, IL: Charles C Thomas.

Yalom, I. (1980). *Existential psychotherapy.* New York: Basic Books.

CHAPTER 9: HOSTAGE CRISES

Allen, S.W., Fraser, S.L., & Inwald, R. (1991). Assessment of personality characteristics related to successful hostage negotiators and their resistance to post traumatic stress. In J. Reese, J. Horn & C. Dunning (Eds.), *Critical Incidents in policing* (pp. 1–15). Washington, DC: US Government Printing Office.

Baruth, C.L. (1988). Routine mental health checkups and activities for law enforcement personnel involved in dealing with hostage and terrorist incidents by psychologist trainer/consultant. In J.T. Reese & J.M. Horn (Eds.), *Police psychology: Operational assistance* (pp. 9–20). Washington, DC: Federal Bureau of Investigation.

Blythe, B.T. (2002). *Blindsided: A manager's guide to catastrophic incidents in the workplace.* New York: Portfolio.

Bohl, N.K. (1997). Postincident crisis counseling for hostage negotiators. In R.G. Rogan, M.R. Hammer & C.R. Van Zandt (Eds.), *Dynamic processes of crisis negotiation* (pp. 46–56). Westport, CT: Praeger.

Bolz, F., Dudonis, K.J., & Schultz, D.P. (1996). *The counterterrorism handbook.* Boca Raton, FL: CRC Press.

Borum, R. (1988). A comparative study of negotiator effectiveness with "mentally disturbed hostage taker" scenarios. *Journal of Police and Criminal Psychology, 4,* 17–20.

Borum, R., & Strentz, T. (1992). The borderline personality: Negotiation strategies. *FBI Law Enforcement Bulletin, 61,* August, pp. 6–10.

Call, J.A. (2003). Negotiating crises: The evolution of hostage/barricade crisis negotiation. *Journal of Threat Assessment, 2,* 69–94.

Corcoran, M.H., & Cawood, J.S. (2003). *Violence assessment and intervention: A practitioner's handbook.* Boca Raton, FL: CRC Press.

Dattilio, F.M., & Freeman, A. (Eds.) (2000). *Cognitive-behavioral strategies in crisis intervention* (2nd ed.). New York: Guilford.

Flin, R. (1996). *Sitting on the hot seat: Leaders and teams for effective critical incident management.* New York: Wiley.

Fuselier, G.D. (1981a). A practical overview of hostage negotiations (Part I). *FBI Law Enforcement Bulletin, 50,* 2–6.

Fuselier, G.D. (1981b). A practical overview of hostage negotiations (Part II). *FBI Law Enforcement Bulletin, 50,* 10–15.

Fuselier, G.D. (1986). What every negotiator would like his chief to know. *FBI Law Enforcement Bulletin, 55,* 1–11.

Fuselier, G.D. (1988). Hostage negotiation mental health consultant: Emerging role for the clinical psychologist. *Professional Psychology: Research and Practice, 19,* 175–179.

Fuselier, G.D. (1999). Placing the Stockholm Syndrome in perpective. *FBI Law Enforcement Bulletin,* July, pp. 22–25.

Fuselier, G.D., & Noeser, G.W. (1990). Confronting the terrorist hostage taker. *FBI Law Enforcement Bulletin,* July, pp. 6–11.

Fuselier, G.D., Van Zandt, C.R., & Lanceley, F.J. (1991). Hostage/barricade incidents: High-risk factors and the action criteria. *FBI Law Enforcement Bulletin, 60,* January, pp. 6–12.

Getty, V., & Elam, J. (1988). Identifying characteristics of hostage negotiators and using personality data to develop a selection model. In J.T. Reese & J.M. Horn (Eds.), *Police psychology: Operational assistance* (pp. 159–171). Washington, DC: US Department of Justice.

Giebels, E, Noelanders, S., & Vervaeke, G. (2005). The hostage experience: Implications for negotiation strategies. *Clinical Psychology and Psychotherapy, 12,* 241–253.

Gilliland, B.E., & James, R.K. (1993). *Crisis intervention strategies* (2nd ed.). Pacific Grove, CA: Brooks/Cole.

Greenstone, J.L. (1995). Tactics and negotiating techniques (TNT): The way of the past and the way of the future. In M.I. Kurke & E.M. Scrivner (Eds.), *Police psychology into the 21st century* (pp. 357–371). Hillsdale, NJ: Erlbaum.

Greenstone, J.L. (2005). *The elements of police hostage and crisis negotiations: Critical incidents and how to respond to them.* New York: Haworth Press.

Greenstone, J.L., & Leviton, S.C. (2001). *Elements of crisis intervention: Crises and how to respond to them.* New York: Wadsworth.

Hammer, M.R., & Rogan, R.G. (1997). Negotiation models in crisis situations: The value of a communication-based approach. In R.G. Rogan, M.R. Hammer & C.R. Van Zandt (Eds.), *Dynamic processes of crisis negotiation* (pp. 9–23). Westport, CT: Praeger.

Hammer, M.R., Van Zandt, C.R., & Rogan, R.G. (1994). Crisis/hostage negotiation team: Profile of demographic and functional characteristics. *FBI Law Enforcement Bulletin, 63,* 8–11.

Hare, A. (1997). Training crisis negotiators: Updating negotiation techniques and training. In R.G. Rogan, M.R. Hammer & C.R. Van Zandt (Eds.), *Dynamic processes of crisis negotiation* (pp. 151–160.). Westport, CT: Praeger.

Hatcher, C., Mohandie, K., Turner, J., & Gelles, M.G. (1998). The role of the psychologist in crisis/hostage negotiations. *Behavioral Sciences and the Law, 16,* 455–472.

Hillbrand, M. (2001). Homicide-suicide and other forms of co-occurring aggression against self and against

others. *Professional Psychology: Research and Practice, 32,* 626–635.

June, D.L. (1999). *Introduction to executive protection.* Boca Raton, FL: CRC Press.

June, D.L. (Ed.) (2000). *Protection, security, and safeguards: Practical approaches and perspectives.* Boca Raton, FL: CRC Press.

Katz, D.S., & Caspi, I. (2003). *Executive's guide to personal security.* Hoboken, NJ: Wiley.

Kleepsies, P.M. (Ed.) (1998). *Emergencies in mental health practice: Evaluation and management.* New York: Guilford.

Klein, G. (1998). *Sources of power: How people make decisions.* Cambridge, MA: MIT Press.

Lanceley, F.J. (1999). *On-scene guide for crisis negotiators.* Boca Raton, FL: CRC Press.

Lazarus, A.A. (1993). Tailoring the therapeutic relationship, or being an authentic chameleon. *Psychotherapy, 30,* 404-407.

McMains, M.J. (1988a). Expanding the psychologist's role in hostage negotiations. *Journal of Police and Criminal Psychology, 4,* 1–8.

McMains, M.J. (1988b). Psychologists' roles in hostage negotiations. In J.T. Reese & J.M. Horn (Eds.), *Police psychology: Operational assistance* (pp. 281–318). Washington, DC: US Government Printing Office.

McMains, M.J. (2002). Active listening: The aspirin of negotiations. *Journal of Police Crisis Negotiations, 2,* 69–74.

McMains, M.J., & Mullins, W.C. (1996). *Crisis negotiations: Managing critical incidents and situations in law enforcement and corrections.* Cincinnati, OH: Anderson.

Miller, L. (1997). *Workplace violence and domestic violence: Prevention, response, and recovery.* Program presented at Domestic Violence Awareness Month Seminar, Palm Beach County Victim Services, West Palm Beach, Florida, October 17, 1997.

Miller, L. (1998). *Shocks to the system: Psychotherapy of traumatic disability syndromes.* New York: Norton.

Miller, L. (1999). Workplace violence: Prevention, response, and recovery. *Psychotherapy, 36,* 160–169.

Miller, L. (2000). *Crime victimization and workplace violence: A critical incident stress management approach.* Program presented to Center for Family Services, West Palm Beach, Florida, December 1, 2000.

Miller, L. (2001a). Workplace violence and psychological trauma: Clinical disability, legal liability, and corporate policy. Part I. *Neurolaw Letter, 11,* 1–5.

Miller, L. (2001b). Workplace violence and psychological trauma: Clinical disability, legal liability, and corporate policy. Part II. *Neurolaw Letter, 11,* 7–13.

Miller, L. (2001c). *Workplace violence and domestic violence: Strategies for prevention, response, and recovery.* Training program presented to Parkland Public Safety Department, Parkland, Florida, April 18, 2001.

Miller, L. (2002). How safe is your job? The threat of workplace violence. *USA Today Magazine*, March, pp. 52–54.

Miller, L. (2005). Workplace violence and psychological trauma: Clinical disability, legal liability, and corporate policy. *The Doe Report*, www.doereport.com.

Miller, L. (in press-a). Hostage negotiation: Psychological principles and practices. *International Journal of Emergency Mental Health*.

Miller, L. (in press-b). The terrorist mind: A psychological and political analysis. *International Journal of Offender Rehabilitation and Comparative Criminology*.

Misino, D.J. (2002). Negotiating without a net. *Harvard Business Review*, October, pp. 49–54.

Noesner, G.W. (1999). Negotiation concepts for commanders. *FBI Law Enforcement Bulletin*, January, pp. 6–14.

Noesner, G.W., & Dolan, J. (1992). First responder negotiator training. *FBI Law Enforcement Bulletin*, August, pp. 1 4.

Noesner, G.W., & Webster, M. (1997). Crisis intervention: Using active listening skills in negotiations. *FBI Law Enforcement Bulletin*, August, pp. 13–19.

Regini, C. (2002). Crisis negotiation teams: Selection and training. *FBI Law Enforcement Bulletin*, November, pp. 1–5.

Regini, C. (2004). Crisis intervention for law enforcement officers. *FBI Law Enforcement Bulletin*, October, pp. 1–6.

Rodriguez, G.J., & Franklin, D. (1986). Training hostage negotiatiors with psychiatric patients: A "hands-on" approach. In J.T. Reese & H.A. Goldstein (Eds.), *Psychological services for law enforcement* (pp. 497–500). Washington, DC: Federal Bureau of Investigation.

Rogan, R.G. (1997). Emotion and emotional expression in crisis negotiation. In R.G. Rogan, M.R. Hammer & C.R. Van Zandt (Eds.), *Dynamic processes of crisis negotiation* (pp. 26–43). Westport, CT: Praeger.

Rogan, R.G., Donohoe, W.A., & Lyles, J. (1990). Gaining and exercising control in hostage taking negotiations using empathic perspective-taking. *International Journal of Group Tension, 20*, 77–90.

Rogan, R.G. & Hammer, M.R. (1995). Assessing message affect in crisis negotiations: An exploratory study. *Human Communication Research, 21*, 553–574.

Rogan, R.G., Hammer, M.R., & Van Zandt (1994). Profiling crisis negotiation teams. *The Police Chief, 61*, 14–18.

Russell, H.E., & Beigel, A. (1990). *Understanding human behavior for effective police work* (3rd ed.). New York: Basic Books.

Russell, H.E., & Zuniga, R. (1986). Special stress factors in hostage/barricade situations when the perpetrator is a police officer. In J.T. Reese & H.A. Goldstein (Eds.), *Psychological services for law enforcement* (pp. 515–520). Washington, DC: Federal Bureau of Investigation.

Slatkin, A.A. (1996). Enhancing negotiator training: Therapeutic communication. *FBI Law Enforcement Bulletin*, May, pp. 1–6.

Slatkin, A.A. (2003). Suicide risk and hostage/barricade situations involving older persons. *FBI Law Enforcement Bulletin*, April, pp. 26–32.

Slatkin, A.A. (2005). *Communication in crisis and hostage negotiations*. Springfield, IL: Charles C Thomas.

Terestre, D.J. (2004). Talking him down. *Police*, March, pp. 26–32.

Terhune-Bickler, S.D. (2004). Too close for comfort: Negotiating with fellow officers. *FBI Law Enforcement Bulletin*, April, pp. 1–5.

Van Hasselt, V.B. & Romano, S.J. (2004). Role-playing: A vital tool in crisis negotiation skills training. *FBI Law Enforcement Bulletin*, February, pp. 12–17.

Wind, B.A. (1995). A guide to crisis negotiations. *FBI Law Enforcement Bulletin*, October, pp. 7–11.

CHAPTER 10: SUICIDE BY COP

Bresler, S., Scalora, M.J., Elbogen, E.B., & Moore, Y.S. (2003). Attempted suicide by cop: A case study of traumatic brain injury and the insanity defense. *Journal of Forensic Science, 48*, 190–194.

Campbell, R.K. (2005). Don't go with them: Suicidal subjects are a great danger to your physical and mental health. *Police*, May, pp. 60–63.

Clagett, R. (2004). After the echo. *Police*, March, pp. 42–49.

Clark, D.C. (1998). The evaluation and management of the suicidal patient. In P.M. Kleespies (Ed.), *Emergencies in mental health practice: Evaluation and management* (pp. 75–94). New York: Guilford.

Feuer, A. (1998). Drawing a bead on a baffling end game: Suicide by cop. *New York Times*, June 21, p. wk-3.

Gilliland, B.E., & James, R.K. (1993). *Crisis intervention strategies* (2nd ed.). Pacific Grove, CA: Brooks/Cole.

Greenstone, J.L., & Leviton, S.C. (2001). *Elements of crisis intervention: Crises and how to respond to them*. New York: Wadsworth.

Hafenback, J., & Nasiripour, S. (2005). Ex-NYPD officer killed in standoff. *South Florida Sun-Sentinel*, May 28, pp. 1A, 6A.

Hillbrand, M. (2001). Homicide-suicide and other forms of co-occurring aggression against self and against others. *Professional Psychology: Research and Practice, 32,* 626–635.

Homant, R.J., Kennedy, D.B., & Hupp, R.T. (2000). Real and perceived danger in police officer assisted suicide. *Journal of Criminal Justice, 28,* 43–52.

Hutson, H.R., Anglin, D., Yarbrough, J., Hardaway, K., Russell, M., Strote, J., Canter, M., & Blum, B. (1998). Suicide by cop. *Annals of Emergency Medicine, 32,* 665–669.

Kennedy, D.B., Homant, R.J., & Hupp, R.T. (1998). Suicide by cop. *FBI Law Enforcement Bulletin,* August, pp. 21–27.

Kleepsies, P.M. (Ed.) (1998). *Emergencies in mental health practice: Evaluation and management.* New York: Guilford.

Lord, V.B. (2000). Law enforcement-assisted suicide. *Criminal Justice and Behavior, 27,* 401–419.

Mohandie, K., & Meloy, J.R. (2000). Clinical and forensic indicators of "suicide by cop." *Journal of Forensic Science, 45,* 384–389.

Pinizzotto, A.J., Davis, E.F., & Miller, C.E. (2005). Suicide by cop: Defining a devastating dilemma. *FBI Law Enforcement Bulletin,* February, pp. 8–20.

Praet, B.D. (2002). Suicide by cop or death by indifference? *The Police Chief,* July, p. 14.

Van Zandt, C.R. (1993). Suicide by cop. *The Police Chief, 60,* 24–30.

Wilson, E.F., Davis, J.H., Bloom, J.D., Batten, P.J., & Kamara, S.G. (1998). Homicide or suicide: The killing of suicidal persons by law enforcement officers. *Journal of Forensic Science, 43,* 46–52.

CHAPTER 11: POLICE OFFICER SUICIDE

Acosta, J., & Prager, J.S. (2002). *The worst is over: What to say when every moment counts.* San Diego, CA: Jodere.

Allen, S.W. (1986). Suicide and indirect self-destructive behavior among police. In J.T. Reese & H.A. Goldstein (Eds.), *Psychological services for law enforcement* (pp. 413–417). Washington, DC: USGPO.

Baechler, J. (1979). *Suicides.* New York: Basic Books.

Baker, T.E., & Baker, J.P. (1996). Preventing police suicide. *FBI Law Enforcement Bulletin,* October, pp. 24–27.

Berk, M.S., Henriques, G.R., Warman, D.M., Brown, G.K., & Beck, A.T. (2004). A cognitive therapy intervention for suicide attempters: An overview of the treatment and case examples. *Cognitive and Behavioral Practice, 11,* 265–277.

Blau, T.H. (1994). *Psychological services for law enforcement.* New York: Wiley.

Bongar, B. (2002). *The suicidal patient: Clinical and legal standards of care.* Washington, DC: American Psychological Association.

Campbell, R.K. (2005). Don't go with them: Suicidal subjects are a great danger to your physical and mental health. *Police,* May, pp. 60–63.

Cross, C.L., & Ashley, L. (2004). Police trauma and addiction: Coping with the dangers of the job. *FBI Law Enforcement Bulletin,* October, pp. 24–32.

Cummings, J.P. (1996). Police stress and the suicide link. *The Police Chief,* October, pp. 85–96.

Ellis, T.E., & Newman, C.F. (1996). *Choosing to live: How to defeat suicide through cognitive therapy.* Oakland, CA: New Harbinger.

Flanagan, C.L. (1986). A comparison of the roles of police psychologist and the psychological consultant to law enforcement. In J.T. Reese & H.A. Goldstein

(Eds.), *Psychological services for law enforcement* (pp. 253–255). Washington, DC: Federal Bureau of Investigation.

Gilliland, B.E. & James, R.K. (1993). *Crisis intervention strategies* (2nd ed.). Pacific Grove, CA: Brooks/Cole.

Greenstone, J.L., & Leviton, S.C. (2001). *Elements of crisis intervention: Crises and how to respond to them.* New York: Wadsworth.

Hamilton, M. (2003a). Cop killer. *Police,* May, pp. 18–21.

Hamilton, M. (2003b). Survivor stories. *Police,* May, pp. 22–23.

Hamilton, M. (2003c). Eating a gun. *Police,* May, p. 24.

Henry, V.E. (2004). *Death work: Police, trauma, and the psychology of survival.* New York: Oxford University Press.

Hill, K.O., & Clawson, M. (1988). The health hazards of street level bureaucracy: Mortality among the police. *Journal of Police Science, 16,* 243–248.

Kleespies, P.M. (Ed.) (1998). *Emergencies in mental health practice: Evaluation and management,* New York: Guilford.

Loo, R. (1986). Suicide among police in a federal force. *Suicide and Life Threatening Behavior, 16,* 379–388.

Loo, R. (1999). Police suicide: The ultimate stress reaction. In J.M. Violanti & D. Paton (Eds.), *Police trauma: Psychological aftermath of civilian combat* (pp. 241–254). Springfield, IL: Charles C Thomas.

Marzuk, P.M., Nock, M.K., Leon, A.C., Portera, L., & Tardiff, K. (2002). Suicide among New York City police officers, 1977–1996. *American Journal of Psychiatry, 159,* 2069–2071.

Miller, L. (1998). *Shocks to the system: Psychotherapy of traumatic disability syndromes.* New York: Norton.

Miller, L. (2003). Police personalities: Understanding and

managing the problem officer. *The Police Chief,* May, pp. 53–60.

Miller, L. (2005). Police officer suicide: Causes, prevention, and practical intervention strategies. *International Journal of Emergency Mental Health, 7,* 101-114.

Miller, L. (in press). *Practical Psychology at work: Behavioral science for superior management.* Binghamton: Haworth.

Mohandie, K., & Hatcher, C. (1999). Suicide and violence risk in law enforcement: Practical guidelines for risk assessment, prevention, and intervention. *Behavioral Sciences and the Law, 17,* 357–376.

Mohandie, K., Piersol, F. & Klyver, N. (1996). Law enforcement turmoil and transitions and the evolving role of the police psychologist. In J.T. Reese & R. Solomon (Eds.), *Organizational issues in law enforcement* (pp. 383–396). Washington, DC: Federal Bureau of Investigation.

Packman, W.L., Marlitt, R.E., Bongar, B., & Pennuto, T.O. (2004). A comprehensive and concise assessment of suicide risk. *Behavioral Sciences and the Law, 22,* 667–680.

Quinnet, P. (1998). QPR: Police suicide prevention. *FBI Law Enforcement Bulletin,* July, pp. 19–24.

Regini, C. (2004). Crisis intervention for law enforcement officers. *FBI Law Enforcement Bulletin,* October, pp. 1–6.

Reinecke, M.A. (2000). Suicide and depression. In F.M. Dattilio & A. Freeman (Eds.), *Cognitive-behavioral strategies in crisis intervention* (2nd ed., pp. 84–125). New York: Guilford.

Scrivner, E.M. (2002). Psychology and policing: A dynamic partnership. *Monitor on Psychology,* June, p. 66.

Seligmann, J., Holt, D., Chinni, D., & Roberts, E. (1994). Cops who kill–themselves. *Newsweek,* September 26, p. 58.

Sewell, J.D. (1986). Administrative concerns in law enforcement stress management. In J.T. Reese & H.A. Goldstein (Eds.), *Psychological services for law enforcement* (pp. 189–193). Washington, DC: FBI.

Solan, G.J., & Casey, J.M. (2003). Police work addiction: A cautionary tale. *FBI Law Enforcement Bulletin,* June, pp. 13–17.

Violanti, J.M. (1995). The mystery within: understanding police suicide. *FBI Law Enforcement Bulletin,* July, pp. 19–23.

Violanti, J.M. (1996). *Police suicide: Epidemic in blue.* Springfield, IL: Thomas C Thomas.

Zelig, M. (1996). Workplace violence: The law enforcement setting. In J.T. Reese & R. Solomon (Eds.), *Organizational issues in law enforcement* (pp. 309–316). Washington, DC: Federal Bureau of Investigation.

CHAPTER 12: SPECIAL UNITS

Anderson, W., Swenson, D., & Clay, D. (1995). *Stress management for law enforcement officers.* Englewood Cliffs, NJ: Prentice-Hall.

Band, S.R., & Sheehan, D.C. (1999). Managing undercover stress: The supervisor's role. *FBI Law Enforcement Bulletin,* February, p. 1–6.

Barefoot, J. (1975). *Undercover investigation.* Springfield, IL: Charles C Thomas.

Bolz, F., Dudonis, K.J., & Schultz, D.P. (1996). *The counterterrorism handbook.* Boca Raton, FL: CRC Press.

Buckwalter, A. (1983). *Surveillance and undercover investigation.* Boston: Butterworth.

Cheek, J.C., & Lesce, T. (1988). *Plainclothes and off-duty officer survival.* Springfield, IL: Charles C Thomas.

Cloninger, R. (1987). A systematic method for clinical description and classification of personality variants. *Archives of General Psychiatry, 44,* 573–588.

Farkas, G.M. (1986). Stress in undecover policing. In J.T. Reese & H. Goldstein (Eds.), *Psychological services for law enforcement* (pp. 433–440). Washington, DC: US Government Printing Office.

Geller, W.A. (1993). Put friendly-fire shooting in perspective. *Law Enforcement News, 18,* 9.

Girodo, M. (1985). Health and legal issues in undercover narcotics investigations: Misrepresented evidence. *Behavioral Sciences and the Law, 3,* 299–308.

Girodo, M. (1991a). Symptomatic reactions to undercover work. *Journal of Nervous and Mental Disease, 179,* 626–630.

Girodo, M. (1991b). Personality, job stress, and mental health in undercover agents. *Journal of Social Behavior and Personality, 6,* 375–390.

Girodo, M. (1991c). Drug corruption in undercover agents: Measuring the risk. *Behavioral Sciences and the Law, 9,* 361–370.

Henry, V.E. (2004). *Death work: Police, trauma, and the psychology of survival.* New York: Oxford University Press.

Hibler, N.S. (1995). The care and feeding of undercover agents. In M.L. Kurke & E.M. Scrivner (Eds.), *Police psychology into the 21st century* (pp. 299–317). Hillsdale, NJ: Erlbaum.

Holmes, R.M., & Holmes, S.T. (1996). *Profiling violent crimes: An investigative tool* (2nd ed.). Thousand Oaks, CA: Sage.

Lanning, K.V., & Hazelwood, R.R. (1988). The maligned investigator of criminal sexuality. *FBI Law Enforcement Bulletin,* September, pp. 1–10.

MacLeod, A.D. (1995). Undercover policing: A psychiatrist's perspective. *International Journal of Law and Psychiatry, 18,* 239–247.

Marx, G.T. (1988). *Undercover: Police surveillance in America.* Berkeley, CA: University of California Press.

Miller, L. (2000). The predator's brain: Neuropsychodynamics of serial killers. In L.B. Schlesinger (Ed.), *Serial offenders: Current thought, recent findings, unusual syndromes* (pp. 135–166). Boca Raton, FL: CRC Press.

Millon, T., & Davis, R. (1996). *Disorders of personality: DSM-IV and beyond.* New York: Wiley.

Millon, T., & Davis, R. (2000). *Personality disorders in modern life.* New York: Wiley.

Peak, K.J. (2003). *Policing America: Methods, issues, challenges* (4th ed.). Upper Saddle River, NJ: Prentice-Hall.

Ressler, R.K., Burgess, A.W., & Douglas, J.E. (1988). *Sexual homicide: Patterns and motives.* New York: Free Press.

Russell, H.E., & Beigel, A. (1990). *Understanding human behavior for effective police work* (3rd ed.). New York: Basic Books.

Schlesinger, L.B., & Miller, L. (2003). Learning to kill: serial, contract, and terrorist murderers. In R.S.

Moser & C.E. Franz (Ed.), *Shocking violence II: Violent disaster, war, and terrorism affecting our youth* (pp. 145–164). Springfield, IL: Charles C Thomas.

Sewell, J.D. (1993). Traumatic stress of multiple murder investigations. *Journal of Traumatic Stress, 6,* 103–118.

Sewell, J.D. (1994). The stress of homicide investigations. *Death Studies, 18,* 565–582.

Sewell, J.D. (2003). Training strategies and techniques for criminal investigators. In M.J. Palmiotto (Ed.), *Policing and training issues* (pp. 235–258). Upper Saddle River, NJ: Prentice-Hall.

Smith, B.L. (1994). *Terrorism in America: Pipe bombs and pipe dreams.* Albany, NY: State University of New York Press.

Spungen, D. (1998). *Homicide: The hidden victims. A guide for professionals.* Thousand Oaks, CA: Sage.

Turvey, B. (1999). *Criminal profiling: An introduction to behavioral evidence analysis.* New York: Academic Press.

Zuckerman, M. (1991). *Psychobiology of personality.* New York: Cambridge University Press.

CHAPTER 13: PROBLEM OFFICERS

Allen, C.R. (2001). Worth his wait: He's Boynton's best. *South Forida Sun Sentinel,* May 23, p. 3B.

American Psychiatric Association (1994). *Diagnostic and statistical Manual of Mental Disorders* (4th ed) Washington, DC: American Psychiatric Association.

Anfang, S.A., Faulkner, L.R., Fromson, J.A., & Gendel, M.H. (2005). The American Psychiatric Association's resource document on guidelines for psychiatric fitness-for-duty evaluations of physicians. *Journal of the American Academy of Psychiatry and the Law, 33,* 85–88.

Armacost, B.E. (2004). Organizational culture and police misconduct. *George Washington Law Review, 72,* 453–546.

Barker, T. (1978). An empirical study of police deviance other than corruption. *Journal of Police Science and Administration, 6,* 264–272.

Barker, T. (1983). Rookie police officers' perceptions of police occupational deviance. *Police Studies, 6,* 30–38.

Bartol, C.R. (1991). Predictive validation of the MMPI for small-town police officers who fail. *Professional Psychology: Research and Practice, 22,* 127–132.

Bartol, C.R. (1996). Police psychology: Then, now, and beyond. *Criminal Justice and Behavior, 23,* 70–89.

Beigel, H., & Beigel, A. (1977). *Beneath the badge: A study of police corruption.* New York: Harper & Row.

Bittner, E. (1970). *The function of the police in modern society.* Rockville, MD: National Institute of Mental Health.

Blau, T.H. (1986). Deadly force: Psychological factors and objective evaluation–A preliminary effort. In J.T. Reese & H.A. Goldstein (Eds.), *Psychological services for*

law enforcement (pp. 315–334). Washington, DC: US Government Printing Office.

Cancino, J.M. (2001). Walking among giants 50 years later: An exploratory analysis of patrol officer use of violence. *Policing: An International Journal of Police Strategies and Management, 24,* 144–161.

Cancino, J.M., & Enriquez, R. (2004). A qualitative analysis of officer peer retaliation. *Policing: An International Journal of Police Strategies and Management, 27,* 320–340.

Cooper, C. (1999). *Mediation and arbitration by patrol police officers.* New York: University Press of America.

Crawley, J. (1995). *Constructive conflict management: Managing to make a difference.* London: Nicholas Brealy.

Delattre, E.J. (1991). *Against brutality and corruption: Integrity, wisdom, and professionalism.* Tallahassee, FL: Florida Criminal Justice Executive Institute.

Fyfe, J.J. (1989). Police/citizen violence reduction project. *FBI Law Enforcement Bulletin, 58,* 18–25.

Fyfe, J.J. (1996). Training to reduce police-civilian violence. In W.A. Geller & H. Toch (Eds.), *Police violence: Understanding and controlling police abuse of force* (pp. 165–179). New Haven, CT: Yale University Press.

Garner, G.W. (1995). *Common sense police supervision: A how-to manual for the first-line supervisor* (2nd ed.). Springfield, IL: Charles C Thomas.

Geller, W.A., & Toch, H. (1996). Understanding and controlling police abuse of force. In W.A. Geller & H. Toch (Eds.), *Police violence: Understanding and controlling police abuse of force* (pp. 292–328). New Haven, CT: Yale University Press.

Golembiewski, R.T., & Kim, B. (1990). Burnout in police

work: Stressors, strain, and the phase model. *Police Studies, 13*, 74–80.

Grant, J.D., & Grant, J. (1996). Officer selection and the prevention of abuse of force. In W.A. Geller & H. Toch (Eds.), *Police violence: Understanding and controlling police abuse of force* (pp. 150–164). New Haven, CT: Yale University Press.

Griffith, D. (2003a). What characteristics make a good chief? *Police,* June, p. 14.

Griffith, D. (2003b). Cracking down on bad cops. *Police,* October, pp. 68–74.

Griffith, D. (2003c). Policing the police. *Police,* October, pp. 76–79.

Grote, D. (1995). *Discipline without punishment: The proven strategy that turns problem employees into superior performers.* New York: Amacom.

Hancock, B.W., & McClung, C. (1984). Abstract-cognitive abilities in police selection and organization. *Journal of Police Science and Administration, 12,* 99–108.

Iannone, N.F., & Iannone, M.P. (2001). *Supervision of police personnel* (6th ed.). Upper Saddle River, NJ: Prentice-Hall.

International Association of Chiefs of Police (1990). The Law Enforcement Code of Ethics. *The Police Chief, 57,* 10.

Johnson, K. (1983). Law enforcement selection practices: The United States and Canada. In I.L. Barak-Glantz & E.H. Johnson (Eds.), *Comparative criminology* (pp. 103–119). Newbury Park, CA: Sage.

Klockars, C.B. (1996). A theory of excessive force and its control. In W.A. Geller & H. Toch (Eds.), *Police violence: Understanding and controlling police abuse of force* (pp. 1–22). New Haven, CT: Yale University Press.

Lardner, J., & Reppeto, T. (2000). *NYPD: A city and its police.* New York: Henry Holt.

Lowman, R.L. (1993). *Counseling and psychotherapy of work dysfunctions.* Washington, DC: American Psychological Association.

McCafferty, F.L., & McCafferty, M.A. (1998). Corruption in law enforcement: A paradigm of occupational stress and deviancy. *Journal of the American Academy of Psychiatry and Law, 26,* 57–65.

McCafferty, F.L., Souryal, S. & McCafferty, M.A. (1998). The corruption of a law enforcement officer: A paradigm of occupational stress and deviancy. *Journal of the American Academy of Psychiatry and Law, 26,* 433–458.

Miller, L. (2001a). Workplace violence and psychological trauma: Clinical disability, legal liability, and corporate policy. Part I. *Neurolaw Letter, 11,* 1–5.

Miller, L. (2001b). Workplace violence and psychological trauma: Clinical disability, legal liability, and corporate policy. Part II. *Neurolaw Letter, 11,* 7–13.

Miller, L. (2003a). Police personalities: Understanding and managing the problem officer. *The Police Chief,* May, pp. 53–60.

Miller, L. (2003b). Personalities at work: Understanding and managing human nature on the job. *Public Personnel Management, 32,* 419–433.

Miller, L. (2004). Good cop–bad cop: Problem officers, law enforcement culture, and strategies for success. *Journal of Police and Criminal Psychology, 19,* 1–20.

Miller, L. (in press). *Practical psychology at work: Behavioral science for superior management.* Binghamton: Haworth.

Millon, T., & Davis, R. (2000). *Personality disorders in modern life.* New York: Wiley.

Muir, W.K. (1977). *Police: Street corner politicians.* Chicago: University of Chicago Press.

Peak, K.J. (2003). *Policing America: Methods, issues, challenges* (4th ed.). Upper Saddle River, NJ: Prentice-Hall.

Peak, K.J., Gaines, L.K., & Glensor, R.W. (2004). *Police supervision and management in the era of community policing* (2nd ed.). Upper Saddle River, NJ: Prentice-Hall.

Perez, D.W., & Muir, W.K. (1996). Administrative review of alleged police brutality. In W.A. Geller & H. Toch (Eds.), *Police violence: Understanding and controlling police abuse of force* (pp. 213–233). New Haven, CT: Yale University Press.

Potter-Efron, R.T. (1998). *Work rage: Preventing anger and resolving conflict on the job.* New York: Barnes & Noble.

Rahtz, H. (2005). Citizen Police Academy: Teaching the public about use of force. *Law and Order,* April, pp. 47–51.

Robinette, H.M. (1987). *Burnout in blue: Managing the police marginal performer.* New York: Praeger.

Rostow, C.D., & Davis, R.D. (2002). Psychological fitness for duty evaluations in law enforcement. *The Police Chief,* September, pp. 58–66.

Rostow, C.D., & Davis, R.D. (2004). *A handbook for psychological fitness-for-duty evaluations in law enforcement.* New York: Haworth.

Sapp, A.D. (1997). Police officer sexual misconduct: A field research study. In P.F. Cromwell & R.G. Dunham (Eds.), *Crime and justice in America: Present realities and future prospects* (pp. 139–151). Upper Saddle River, NJ: Prentice Hall.

Sanders, B.A. (2003). Maybe there's no such thing as a "good cop." Organizational challenges in selecting quality officers. *Policing: An International Journal of Police Strategies and Management, 26,* 313–328.

Sanderson, B.E. (1977). Police officers: The relationship of college education to job performance. *The Police Chief,* August, pp. 62–63.

Scrivner, E.M. (1994). *The role of police psychology in controlling excessive force.* Washington, DC: National Institute of Justice.

Scrivner, E.M. (1999). Controlling police use of excessive

...orce: The role of the police psychologist. In L. Territo & J.D. Sewell (Eds.), *Stress management in law enforcement* (pp. 383–391). Durham, NC: Carolina Academic Press.

Serpas, R.W., Olson, J.W., & Jones, B.D. (2003). An employee disciplinary system that makes sense. *The Police Chief*, September, pp. 22–28.

Shev, E.E., & Howard, J.J. (1977). *Good cops, bad cops*. San Francisco: San Francisco Book Co.

Sanderson, B.E. (1977). Police officers: The relationship of college education to job performance. *The Police Chief*, August, pp. 62–63.

Skolnick, J.H., & Fyfe, J.J. (1993). *Above the law: Police and the excessive use of force*. New York: Free Press.

Sperry, L. (1995). *Handbook of diagnosis and treatment of the DSM-IV personality disorders*. New York: Brunner/Mazel.

Sperry, L. (1996). *Corporate therapy and consulting*. New York: Brunner/Mazel.

Stone, A.V. (1995). Law enforcement psychological fitness for duty: Clinical issues. In M.I. Kurke & E.M. Scrivner (Eds.), *Police psychology into the 21st century* (pp. 109-131). Hillsdale, NJ: Erlbaum.

Stone, A.V. (2000). *Fitness for duty: Principles, methods, and legal issues*. Boca Raton, FL: CRC Press.

Stone, F.M. (1999). *Coaching, counseling, and mentoring: How to choose and use the right technique to boost employee performance*. New York: Amacom.

Thibault, E.A., Lynch, L.M., McBride, R.B., & McBride, B.R. (2004). *Proactive police management*. Upper Saddle River, NJ: Prentice-Hall.

Toch, H. (1996). The violence-prone police officer. In W.A. Geller & H. Toch (Eds.), *Police violence: Understanding and controlling police abuse of force* (pp. 94–112). New Haven, CT: Yale University Press.

Toch, H. & Grant, J.D. (2005). *Police as problem solvers: How frontline workers can promote organizational and community change* (2nd ed.) Washington, DC: American Psychological Association.

Weitzel, T.Q. (2004). Managing the problem employee: A road map for success. *FBI Law Enforcement Bulletin*, November, pp. 25–32.

White, S.O. (1972). A perspective on police professionalization. *Law and Society Review, 7*, 61–85.

Wolkinson, B. (2003). Mental fitness for duty examinations under the ADA. *Employee Relations Law Journal, 29*, 38–54.

Worden, R.E. (1996). The causes of police brutality: Theory and evidence on police use of force. In W.A. Geller & H. Toch (Eds.), *Police violence: Understanding and controlling police abuse of force* (pp. 23–51). New Haven, CT: Yale University Press.

CHAPTER 14: ADMINISTRATION AND LEADERSHIP

Anderson, W., Swenson, D., & Clay, D. (1995). *Stress management for law enforcement officers*. Englewood Cliffs, NJ: Prentice-Hall.

Ayres, R. (1990). *Preventing law enforcement stress: The organization's role*. Alexandria, VA: National Sheriff's Association.

Balkin, J. (1988). Why policemen don't like policewomen. *Journal of Police Science and Administration, 16*, 329–387.

Bartlett, D.D. (2004). How to select and train SWAT snipers. *Police*, August, pp. 25–31.

Bell, D.J. (1982). Policewomen: Myth and reality. *Journal of Police Science and Administration, 10*, 112–120.

Blau, T.H. (1994). *Psychological services for law enforcement*. New York: Wiley.

Bolino, M.C., & Turnley, W.H. (2003). Going the extra mile: Cultivating and managing employee citizenship behavior. *Academy of Management Executive, 17*, 60–73.

Bowers, C.A., Weaver, J.L., & Morgan, B.B. (1996). Moderating the performance effects of stressors. In J. Driskell & E. Salas (Eds.), *Stress and human performance* (pp. 163–192). Hillsdale, NJ: Erlbaum.

Briggs, J. (1988). *Fire in the crucible: The alchemy of creative genius*. New York: St. Martin's Press.

Chambers, D. (1996). Police-defendants: Surviving a civil suit. *FBI Law Enforcement Bulletin*, March, pp. 34–39.

Childers, J. (1991). Plateauing in law enforcement. *FBI Law Enforcement Bulletin, 60*(6), 16–18.

Christopher Commission (1991). *Report of the Independent Commission on the Los Angeles Police Department*. Los Angeles: Christopher Commission.

Collins, J. (2001). *Good to great: Why some companies make the leap . . . and others don't*. New York: Harper Business.

Crank, J.P. (1998). *Understanding police culture*. Cincinnati, OH: Anderson.

DeAngelis, T. (1993). Workplace stress battles fought all over the world. *APA Monitor*, January, p. 22.

Engel, R.S. (2000). The effects of supervisory styles on patrol officer behavior. *Police Quarterly, 3*, 262–293.

Engel, R.S. (2001). Supervisory styles of patrol sergeants and lieutenants. *Journal of Criminal Justice, 29*, 341–355.

Engel, R.S. (2002). Patrol officer supervision in the community policing era. *Journal of Criminal Justice, 30*, 51–64.

Engel, R.S. (2004). How police supervisory styles influence patrol officer behavior. *Training Wheel: The Training Journal of the Las Vegas Metropolitan Police Department,* January-March, pp. 46–49.

Flin, R. (1996). *Sitting on the hot seat: Leaders and teams for effective critical incident management.* New York: Wiley.

Golembiewski, R.T., & Kim, B. (1990). Burnout in police work: Stressors, strain, and the phase model. *Police Studies, 13,* 74–80.

Griffith, D. (2003). What characteristics make a good chief? *Police,* June, p. 14.

Griffith, D. (2005). On the hook. *Police,* September, pp. 42-51.

Grinder, D. (2003). People-oriented leadership. *The Police Chief,* October, pp. 30–34.

Hedlund, J., Forsythe, G.B., Horvath, J.A., Williams, W.M., Snook, S., & Sternberg, R.J. (2003). Identifying and assessing tacit knowledge: Understanding the practical intelligence of military leaders. *Leadership Quarterly, 14,* 117–140.

Henry, V.E. (2004). *Death work: Police, trauma, and the psychology of survival.* New York: Oxford University Press.

Hodgkinson, P., & Stewart, M. (1991). *Coping With catastrophe.* London: Routledge.

Johnson, A. (2005). No shield for blacks with badge. *South Florida Sun-Sentinel,* April 18, pp. 1B, 2B.

Johnson, R.R. (2004). Motivating senior officers. *Law and Order,* July, 134–138.

Jurkanin, T.J., Hoover, L.T., Dowling, J.L., & Ahmad, J. (2001). *Enduring, surviving, and thriving as a law enforcement executive.* Springfield, IL: Charles C Thomas.

Klein, G. (1989). Recognition-primed decisions. *Advances in Man-Machine Systems Research, 5,* 47-92.

Klein, G. (1993). A recognition-primed decision (RPD) model of rapid decision making. In G. Klein, J. Orasanu, R. Calderwood & C. Zsambok (Eds.), *Decision making in action* (pp. 79–103). New York: Ablex.

Klein, G. (1996). The effect of acute stressors on decision making. In J. Driskell & E. Salas (Eds.), *Stress and human performance* (pp. 49–88). Hillsdale, NJ: Erlbaum.

Klein, G. (1998). *Sources of power: How people make decisions.* Cambridge, MA: MIT Press.

Leonard, D., & Swap, W. (2005). *Deep smarts: How to cultivate and transfer enduring business wisdom.* Boston: Harvard Business School Press.

Le Storti, A.J. (2003). *When you're asked to do the impossible: Principles of business teamwork and leadership from the U.S. Army's Elite Rangers.* Guilford: Lyons Press.

Margolis, G.J., & March, N.C. (2004). Creating the police department's image. *The Police Chief,* April, pp. 25–34.

Miller, L. (1996). Making the best use of your neuropsychology expert: What every neurolawyer should know. *Neurolaw Letter, 6,* 93–99.

Miller, L. (1997). The neuropsychology expert witness: An attorney's guide to productive case collaboration. *Journal of Cognitive Rehabilitation, 15*(5), 12–17.

Miller, L. (2003a) Police personalities: Understanding and managing the problem officer. *The Police Chief,* May, pp. 53-60.

Miller, L. (2003b). Personalities at work: Understanding and managing human nature on the job. *Public Personnel Management, 32,* 419–433.

Miller, L. (in press). *Practical psychology at work: Behavioral science for superior management.* Binghamton: Haworth.

Mogil, M. (1989) Maximizing your courtroom testimony. *FBI Law Enforcement Bulletin,* May, pp. 7-9.

Mollen Commission (1994). *Report of the Commission to Investigate Allegations of Police Corruption.* New York: Mollen Commission.

Orasanu, J., & Backer, P. (1996). Stress and military performance. In J. Driskell & E. Salas (Eds.), *Stress and human performance* (pp. 89–125). Hillsdale, NJ: Erlbaum.

Orasanu, J. and Connolly, T. (1993). The reinvention of decision making. In G. Klein, J. Orasanu, R. Calderwood & C. Zsambok (Eds.), *Decision making in action* (pp. 127-166). New York: Ablex.

Peak, K.J. (2003). *Policing America: Methods, issues, challenges* (4th ed.). Upper Saddle River: Prentice-Hall.

Peak, K.J., Gaines, L.K & Glensor, R.W. (2004). *Police supervision and management in an era of community policing* (2nd ed.). Upper Saddle River, NJ: Prentice-Hall.

Pennington, N. & Hastie, R. (1993). A theory of explanation-based decision making. In G. Klein, J. Orasanu, R. Calderwood & C.E. Zsambok (Eds.), *Decision making in action: Models and methods* (pp. 188-201). Norwood: Ablex.

Rehm, B. (1999). Retirement: A new chapter, not the end of the story. In L. Territo & J.D. Sewell (Eds.), *Stress management in law enforcement* (pp. 393-400). Durham: Carolina Academic Press.

Sewell, J.D. (1986). Administrative concerns in law enforcement stress management. In J.T. Reese & H.A. Goldstein (Eds.), *Psychological services for law enforcement* (pp. 189-193). Washington DC: FBI.

Sewell, J.D. (1988). The boss as victim: Stress and the police manager. *FBI Law Enforcement Bulletin,* February, pp. 15-19.

Sewell, J.D. (1992). The law enforcement executive: A formula for success. *FBI Law Enforcement Bulletin,* April, pp. 22-26.

Sewell, J.D. (2002). Managing the stress of organizational change. *FBI Law Enforcement Bulletin,* March, pp. 14-20.

Simonton, D.K. (1994). *Greatness: who makes history and why.* New York: Guilford.

Skolnick, J.H. & Fyfe, J.J. (1993). *Above the law: police and the excessive use of force*. New York: Free Press.

Spaulding, D. (2005). Intuitive decision making. *Police*, March, pp. 62-64.

Sternberg, R.J. (Ed.) (2002). *Why smart people can be so stupid*. New Haven: Yale University Press.

Thibault, E.A., Lynch, L.M., McBride, R.B. & McBride, B.R. (2004). *Proactive police management*. Upper Saddle River: Prentice-Hall.

Toch, H. (2002). *Stress in policing*. Washington DC: American Psychological Association.

Toch, H., Grant, D. & Galvin, R. (1975). *Agents of change: A study of police reform*. Cambridge: Schenkman.

Toch, H. & Grant, J.D. (2005). *Police as problem solvers: How frontline Workers can promote organizational and community change* (2nd ed.). Washington DC: American Psychological Association.

Tyre, P. (2004). Ms. Top Cop. *Newsweek*, April 12, pp. 48-49.

Vinson, D.E. & Davis, D.S. (1993). *Jury persuasion: Psychological strategies and trial techniques*. Little Falls, NJ: Glasser Legalworks.

Violanti, J.M. (1990). Police retirement: The impact of change. *FBI Law Enforcement Bulletin, 59*(3), 12-15.

Weisaeth, L. (1989). A study of behavioral responses to an industrial disaster. *Acta Psychiatrica Scandinavica, 85*, 13-24.

Young, M.A. (1988). Support services for victims. In F.M. Ochberg (Ed.), *Posttraumatic therapy and victims of violence* pp. 330-351. New York: Brunner/Mazel.

Young, M.A. (1994). *Responding to communities in crisis: The training manual of the crisis response team*. Washington DC: National Organization for Victim Assistance.

CHAPTER 15: LAW ENFORCEMENT FAMILIES

Alexander, D.A., & Walker, L.G. (1994). A study of methods used by Scottish police officers to cope with work-related stress. *Stress Medicine, 10*, 131–138.

Anderson, J.L. (2004). Managing professional relationships: Considerations for the FTO and probationary officer. *Law and Order*, June, pp. 56–58.

Anderson, W., Swenson, D. & Clay, D. (1995). *Stress management for law enforcement officers*. Englewood Cliffs, NJ: Prentice-Hall.

Bibbins, V.E. (1986). The quality of family and marital life of police personnel. .In J.T. Reese & H.A. Goldstein (Eds.), *Psychological services for law enforcement* (pp. 423–427). Washington, DC: USGPO.

Blau, T.H. (1994). *Psychological services for law enforcement*. New York: Wiley.

Borum, R., & Philpot, C. (1993). Therapy with law enforcement couples: Clinical management of the "high-risk lifestyle." *American Journal of Family Therapy, 21*, 122–135.

Carlson, J., & Sperry, L. (Eds.) (1998). *The disordered couple*. New York: Brunner/Mazel.

DeAngelis, T. (1991). Police stress takes its toll on family life. *APA Monitor, 22*(7), 38.

DeAngelo, J.J. (1994). Alcoholism and chemical dependency in law enforcement: Its effects on the officer and the family members. In J.T. Reese & E. Scrivner (Eds.), *Law enforcement families: Issues and answers* (pp. 57–66). Washington, DC: U.S. Department of Justice.

Figley, C.R. (Ed.) (1998). *Burnout in families: The systematic costs of caring*. Boca Raton, FL: CRC Press.

Gallo, G. (2005). A family affair: Domestic violence in police families. *Police*, February, pp. 36–40.

Gardner, R.W., Holzman, P.S., Klein, G.S., Linton, H.B., & Spence, D.P. (1959). Cognitive control: A study of individual consistencies in cognitive behavior. *Psychological Issues, 1*, 1–185.

Greenstone, J.L. (2005). *The elements of police hostage and crisis negotiations: Critical incidents and how to respond to them*. New York: Haworth Press.

Kirschman, E.F. (1997). *I love a cop: What police families need to know*. New York: Guilford.

Kleespies, P.M. (Ed.) (1998). *Emergencies in mental health practice: Evaluation and management*. New York: Guilford.

Kruger, K.J., & Valltos, N.G. (2002). Dealing with domestic violence in law enforcement relationships. *FBI Law Enforcement Bulletin*, July, pp. 1–7.

Lott, L.D. (1999). Deadly secrets: Violence in the police family. In L. Territo & J.D. Sewell (Eds.), *Stress management in law enforcement* (pp. 149–155). Durham, NC: Carolina Academic Press.

McMains, M.J. (1988). Psychologists' roles in hostage negotiations. In J.T. Reese & J.M. Horn (Eds.), *Police psychology: Operational assistance* (pp. 281–318). Washington, DC: US Government Printing Office.

McMains, M.J., & Mullins, W.C. (1996). *Crisis negotiations: Managing critical incidents and situations in law enforcement and corrections*. Cincinnati, OH: Anderson.

Means, M.S. (1986). Family therapy issues in law enforcement families. . In J.T. Reese & H.A. Goldstein (Eds.), *Psychological services for law enforcement* (pp. 140–142). Washington, DC: Federal Bureau of Investigation.

Miller, L. (1990). *Inner natures: Brain, self and personality*. New York: St. Martin's Press.

Miller, L. (1998). *Shocks to the system: Psychotherapy of traumatic disability syndromes*. New York: Norton.

Miller, L. (2002). "Ask the Police Psychologist" (weekly online column). *Handcuffed Hearts: A Website for Law Enforcement Families*, handcuffedhearts.com.

Miller, L. (2005). "Police Psychology 101" (monthly column). *Law & Order Magazine.*

Reese, J.T. (1987). Coping with stress: It's your job. In J.T. Reese (Ed.), *Behavioral science in law enforcement* (pp. 75–79). Washington, DC: FBI.

Sanders, D.L. (1997). Responding to domestic violence. *The Police Chief,* June, p. 6.

Terry, W.C. (1981). Police stress: The empirical evidence. *Journal of Police Science and Administration, 9,* 61–75.

Toch, H. (2002). *Stress in policing.* Washington, DC: American Psychological Association.

Weeks, G.R., & Treat, S. (1992). *Couples in treatment: Techniques and approaches for effective practice.* New York: Brunner/Mazel.

INDEX

A

Abnormal behavior, signs and symptoms of, 48–49
Accident victims, 44–45
Active listening techniques
    in hostage crises, 156–159
    on patrol, 21
    specific techniques (*see* Hostage crises)
Administration, law enforcement, 244–261
    command decision making, 244
        naturalistic decision making (NDM), 245–247
        recognition-primed decision making (RPDM),
        246–247
Affirmations in stress management, 80–81
Agnosia, 62
Alcohol abuse
    among police officers, 269–272
    role in officer suicide, 185–186
Alcohol intoxication in mentally disturbed citizens,
    58–59
Alcoholic dementia, 58
Alzheimer's disease, 62
Amnesia, 65
Antisocial personality disorder
    in citizens, 57–58
    in hostage-takers, 166
    in police officers, 227–228
Aphasia, 48
Apraxia, 62
Aprosodia, 48–49
Arbitration for citizen disputes, 26–27
Arousal, control of in stress management, 71–72
Attention, control of in stress management, 75–78
Attention deficit hyperactivity disorder (ADHD), 61
"Authentic chameleon" as communication style, 155, 156
Authoritativeness vs. authoritarianism, 31
Avoidant personality
    in citizens, 56
    in hostage-takers, 165–166
    in police officers, 229

B

Bipolar disorder, 52
Body identification of crime victims, 43–44
Borderline personality
    in citizens, 55–56
    in hostage-takers, 166–167
    in police officers, 226

C

Calm show of force, in defusing potential violence, 49
Children of law enforcement officers, 271–272
    critical incidents and, 114–115
    line-of-duty death and, 139–140
Citizens, responses of to police discourtesy, 16–17
Coaching of police officers, 236–237
Cognitive restructuring in stress management, 82–83
Cognitive style, 76
Command decision making by law enforcement leaders,
    244–247
Communication skills
    for patrol officers, 19–22, 28
    in policing, 19
Community-Oriented Policing (COP), 17
Community-Oriented Policing and Problem Solving
(COPPS), 18–19
Community policing, vii, 17, 18–19
Conduct disorder, 57
Conflict resolution
    on patrol, 22–23
    skills for patrol officers, 27–28
Coprolalia, 65
"Cop's kids," 271–272
Counseling of police officers, 237
Couples, law enforcement (*see* Families, law enforcement)
Court testimony (*see* Testifying in court)
Crime victims, 37–38
    body identification of, 43–44
    citizen observers, 45–46
    crisis intervention with, 39–42

death notification of survivors, 42–43
effects of and psychology of victimization, 37–38
law enforcement on-scene response to, 38–42
victim advocacy for, 44
Criminal investigators, 213–218
sex crimes investigators, 214–215
stresses of, 213–215
stress-coping strategies of, 216–218
successful investigators, characteristics of, 215–216
Criminal investigator stress syndrome (CISS), 213
Crises, types of, 5–6
Crisis intervention and stress management, 9–11
Crisis intervention model, 7–9
Crisis intervention, principles of, 9–10
Crisis prevention, 6–7
Critical incident stress, 88–115
and children, 114–115
and families, 112–115
and posttraumatic stress disorder (PTSD), 93–96
critical incident peer support programs, 101–104
critical incident stress debriefing (CISD), 97–99
critiques of, 104–106
indications for, 97
in law enforcement, 88–89
special law enforcement applications of, 99–101
structure and phases of, 97–99
organizational and departmental responses to, 111–112
psychological interventions for, 96–111
psychotherapy for, 106–111

D

Death notification of homicide victim survivors, 42–43
Delirium tremens (DTs) in alcohol withdrawal, 58
Delusions, 49
Delusional disorders, 53
Dementia, 61–62
Dependent personality
in citizens, 56
in hostage-takers, 165–166
in police officers, 229–230
Depressant narcotics, 59
Depression
in hostage-takers, 164–165
in mentally disordered citizens, 51
in suicidal police officers, 186–187
Dispatcher stress, 92–93
Diversity in police work, 257–259
recommendations for, 259

stresses of, 258
Domestic disputes, 33–37
characteristics of, 33–34
citizen reactions to police response to, 34–35
police officer handling of, 35–37
Domestic violence in police families, 272–274
characteristics of, 273
repercussions of, 273
intervention strategies, 273–274
investigation and departmental action, 273
training in, 273
Drug intoxication in mentally disturbed citizens, 58–59
Dysthymic disorder, 51

E

Epidemiology of crises, 6–7
Epilepsy, 62–64
temporal lobe epilepsy, violence in, 63–64
Excessive force, 222
Expertise in law enforcement, 247
Executive, law enforcement (*see* Law enforcement executive)

F

Families, law enforcement, 262–274
children of police officers, 271–272
couples therapy for, 264–265
critical incidents and, 112–115
domestic violence, in 272–274
line-of-duty death and, 135–139
special problems of
alcohol abuse, 269–271
infidelity, 267–269
overwork, 265–266
suspiciousness, 266–267
stresses of, 262–264
Fitness-for-duty (FFD) evaluation of law enforcement officers, 238–241
Flight of ideas, 49
"Flow" in peak performance, 70–71

G

Gangs, juvenile, dealing with, 31–33
Generalized anxiety disorder, 51
Grief leadership, 112
Gun, significance of for police officers, 116

H

Hallucinations, 49
Hallucinogenic drugs, 59
"Herding" technique
    for domestic disputes, 36
    for mentally disturbed citizens, 64
Histrionic personality
    in citizens, 55
    in police officers, 225–226
Homicide investigators, 90–92, 213–214
Hostage crises, 143–173
    high-risk factors in, 151–152
    hostage crisis response team, 145–146
        role of police psychologist on, 146–149
    hostage negotiations, 152–169
        active listening techniques for, 156–159
            emotion labeling, 157
            "I" statements, 158–159
            minimal encouragers, 158
            open-ended questions, 159
            paraphrasing, 157
            reflecting/mirroring, 157–158
            silence and pauses, 158
        basic protocol for, 152–153
        communication strategies for, 153–156
        demands and deadlines in, 159–162
        signs of progress in, 162
        surrender ritual in, 167–169
        with mentally disordered hostage-takers, 162–167
            antisocial-psychopathic hostage-takers, 166
            avoidant-dependent hostage-takers, 165–166
            borderline hostage takers, 166–167
            depressed hostage-takers, 164–165
            paranoid hostage-takers, 164
            schizophrenic hostage-takers, 163–164
    hostage negotiators, 145
        characteristics of successful negotiators, 149–151
    hostages, 169–171
        debriefing of, 171
        reactions of, 169–170
        recommendations for, 170–171
        survival predictors of, 169–170
    types of, 144–145
        domestic crisis, 144
        foiled robbery scenario, 144
        ideological motivation or terrorism, 145
        mentally disordered hostage-taker, 144
        planned criminal hostage-taking, 144

prisoner riot or escape attempt, 145
workplace violence crisis, 144
Hostage-taking-by-cop (HTBC), 171–173
    effects on other officers, 172
    negotiating recommendations, 172–173
    officer profile, 172

I

Imagery in stress management, 78–79
Interpersonal communiciation processes, 21–22
Intoxication, signs and symptoms of, 58–59

J

Juvenile subjects
    dealing with potential violence, 31–33

K

Killed on duty, risk factors for, 69–70
Kinesics, 21

L

"Law and Order: SVU" television series, 214
Law enforcement executive, 247–252
    law enforcement executive stress management, 249–252
        role of police psychologist in, 251–252
    law enforcement organizational stress, 248
    supervision styles, 248–249
Leadership, law enforcement, 244–261
    command decision making under stress, 244–247
        naturalistic decision making (NDM), 244–247
        recognition-primed decision making (RPDM), 246–247
    expertise in leadership, 247
Line-of-duty death (LODD), 133–140
    administrative and departmental response, 140
    children and, 139–140
    family survivors of, 135–139
        interventions for family survivors of LODD, 137–139
    reaction of peer officers, 133–135

M

Major depressive disorder, 51

Mediation for citizen disputes, 23–26
Mentally ill citizens, 47–66
    law enforcement response to, 47–48
    patrol officer strategies for, 49–66
        alcohol and drug intoxication, 58–59
        anxiety and mood disorders, 50–52
        attention deficit hyperactivity disorder (ADHD),
          61
        dementia, 61–62
        epilepsy, 62–64
        mental retardation, 59–61
        narcolepsy, 64–65
        personality disorders, 55–58
        paranoid disorders, 54–55
        schizophrenia, 52–54
        Tourette's syndrome, 65
        Traumatic brain injury, 65
    Signs and symptoms of, 48–49
Mentally retarded citizens, 59–61

N

Narcissistic personality
    in citizens, 56
    in police officers, 226–227
Narcolepsy, 64–65
Naturalistic decision making, 245–247
The Negotiator movie, 171

O

Obsessive-compulsive personality in police officers,
    230–231
Operational assistance, viii
Officer-involved shooting (OIS), 116–132
    law enforcement programs for, 128–132
officer reactions during incident, 117–118
    memory and behavioral disturbances, 117–88
    sensory-perceptual distortions, 117–118
officer reactions following incident, 118–121
    factors affecting officer reaction, 120–121
    reaction phases, 118–119
    reaction signs and symptoms, 119–120
    reaction typologies, 118
    on-scene departmental response to, 121–122
    on-scene psychological response to, 122–124
    peer-support programs for, 126–128
    psychological follow-up intervention for, 124–126
Officer survival training, 87

Optimum arousal level (OAL), 72
Organizational stress, 248–252
    role of police psychologist in coping with, 251–252
Orientation, for time, place, and person, 48

P

Panic disorder, 51
Paranoid disorders, 54–55
    in hostage-takers, 164
Paranoid personality, in police officers, 228–229
Pathological intoxication, 58
Patrol policing, 15–29
Peak performance under pressure, 70–71
    "flow" experience in, 70–71
    psychological skills for, 71
Peer support
    for critical incident stress, 101–104
    for officer-involved shootings, 126–128
Personality disorders
    in citizens, 55–58
    in police officers, 225–231
Phobias, 51
Police officers, why men and women become, 4–5
Police psychology, vi
Posttraumatic stress disorder (PTSD)
    in law enforcement critical incident stress, 93–96
    in mentally disturbed citizens, 51
Practical psychologists, police officers as, 3
Practical psychology, 3–11
Prevention, in epidemiology, 6–7
Problem officers, 221–243
    law enforcement culture and, 233
    officer problem types, 221–222
    personalities, police, 225–231
    police-citizen interaction, 231–232
    problem officer types, 223–225
    solutions for, 233–243
        coaching and counseling, 236–237
        education and training, 235–236
        departmental strategies, 242–243
        discipline and internal review, 237–238
        fitness-for-duty evaluation, 238–241
        psychological services for, 241–242
        selection and screening, 234–235
Problem-Oriented Policing (POP), 17–18
Professionalism in police work, viii
Proxemics, 21
Psychological services, viii

Psychological survival training, 84–87
Psychopaths, 57 (*see also* Antisocial personality disorder)
Psychotherapy for law enforcement officers, 106–111
Psychotic disorders, 52–54

R

Recognition-primed decision making (RPDM)
    in command leadership, 246–247
    in patrol policing, 14
Relaxation techniques, 74–75
Rescue and recovery teams, 91–92
Resiliency to critical incident stress, 96

S

Scanning, Analysis, Response, Assessment (SARA)
    model, 18
Schizoid personality disorder
    in citizens, 56–57
    in police officers, 231
Schizophrenia, 52–53
    in hostage-takers, 163
Sex crimes investigators, 214–215
Special units, 198–218
    criminal investigation, 213–218
    undercover operations, 198–213
Speech disorders, 48–49
Stimulant narcotics, 59
Stress
    in policing, 3–11
    organizational, in law enforcement, 248
Stress management, 9–11
    principles of, 9–10
    strategies for law enforcement officers, 69–87
Suicide-by-cop (SBC), 174–182
    characteristics of, 175
    motivations for, 175–176
    police officer reactions to aftermath of, 180–181
    police officer response to, 177–179
    psychodynamics of officer reaction, 180–181
    psychological intervention strategies for, 181
    signs of, 176–177
Suicide of police officer, 183–197
    intervention with,
        actively suicidal officer, 192–196
        post-crisis mental health intervention, 196–197
            fitness-for-duty evaluation in, 196
        potentially suicidal officer, 190–192

predisposing factors for, 186–187
prevention of, 187–188
risk factors for, 188
suicidal officer, characteristics of, 185–187
suicide myths and realities, 183–185
survivors of, 197
warning signs of, 188–190
Survival response training, 111

T

Task-relevant instructional self-talk (TRIST), in stress
    management, 83
Teenage crowds, dealing with, 32–33
Testifying in court, 252–257
    on the stand, 254–256
    police officer as defendant, 256–257
    preparing for, 253–254
    testimony, types of, 253–254
    witnesses, types of, 252–253
Thought-stopping, in stress management, 81–82
Tourette's syndrome, 65
    coprolalia in, 65
Traumatic brain injury, 65
Twenty/twenty hindsight=insight=foresight principle, 10

U

Undercover policing, 91, 198–213
    characteristics of, 198–213
    undercover operation
        deployment, 204–207
            psychological reactions to, 205–206
            stresses of, 205
            "undercover Stockholm syndrome" in, 212–213
            failed mission and, 209–210
            problems of reintegration, 211–212
            psychological reaction of officers to, 208–209
            reintegration syndromes, 210–211
        phases of, 200–213
        preparation, 203–204
        selection, 200–202
            characteristics of successful undercover officers,
                201–202
        termination and reintegration, 207–213
        training, 202–203
        types of, 198–199
    undercover team, 199
        role of police psychologist on, 199–200

V

Violence
    between citizens and officers, causes of, 30
    strategies for, 30–46
Visual-motor behavioral rehearsal (VMBR), in stress
            management, 79–80
Veteran officer, 259–261
    management strategies for, 260–261
    retirement stresses, 261
    seniority, 259–260